Alienation and the Social System

WITHDRAWN

ALIENATION
and the
SOCIAL SYSTEM

EDITED WITH INTRODUCTORY ESSAYS BY
Ada W. Finifter

JOHN WILEY & SONS, INC.
New York • London • Sydney • Toronto

Cover: Detail from the sculpture "Spelrum Futurum"
by Walter Bengtsson. Original in Kaknas
Radio-TV Tower, Stockholm, Sweden. Reproduced
with permission of Walter Bengtsson.

Library of Congress Cataloging in Publication Data
Finifter, Ada W.   1938-   comp.
Alienation and the social system.

Bibliography: p.
1. Alienation (Social Psychology)—Addresses,
essays, lectures. 2. Anomy—Addresses, essays,
lectures. I. Title.

HM291.F48   301.6'2'08   70-180242
ISBN 0-471-25887-3
ISBN 0-471-25889-X (pbk)

Printed in the United States of America.

10 9 8 7 6 5 4 3 2 1

to my parents

Preface

Interest in alienation has blossomed in recent years not only among intellectuals but also in the general public. The communications media comment frequently on the alienation of the student, the intellectual, the black, the poor white, and other minorities. But even the "silent majority" has been described as alienated. President Nixon, in his 1971 State of the Union address, commented, "Let's face it. Most Americans today are simply fed up with government at all levels." Popular disaffection and feelings of powerlessness were given as one reason for proposing an extensive reorganization of the executive branch of government. Official recognition of the importance of alienation was also demonstrated in the recent government report on the quality of social life in the United States, *Toward a Social Report* (1969), in the chapter entitled "Participation and Alienation."

A great deal of scholarly attention has also been devoted to alienation. Researchers have been concerned with clarification of the meaning of "alienation," with its social and psychological causes, and with its implications for processes of change and stability in social systems.

One goal of this book is to organize some of the scholarly literature on alienation in a way that emphasizes its relationship to broad social concerns. I hope this volume also will contribute to a clarification of future research needs through the juxtaposition of diverse approaches and contexts for studying alienation and through the attention thereby invited to points of strength and weakness and of similarity and divergence in the research literature. Finally, the grouping of these studies into a single book, organized in a way that emphasizes their relevance to a variety of social science concerns, may encourage the growing attention that the concept of alienation has been receiving in college classrooms in recent years.

In addition to the contributors I would like to thank several other people. My husband, Bernard M. Finifter, provides a constant source of encouragement and intellectual challenge and stimulation. The appreciation he has given me of the social-psychological perspective has been especially useful. Very thoughtful comments and suggestions were also made by Melvin Seeman, James Q. Wilson, Jack Citrin, and Edgar Litt. Patricia Conlin was especially helpful in the proofreading and indexing. Students in my seminars on alienation have been a source of new and stimulating ideas. Finally, I am grateful to the Department of Political Science, Michigan State University, which made available assistance, secretarial help, and time for me to work on this project.

East Lansing, Michigan   ADA W. FINIFTER
December 28, 1971

Contents

Introductory Notes   1

PART I. CONCEPTS OF ALIENATION

Introduction   3

KARL MARX   Alienated Labour   12

EMILE DURKHEIM   Anomy   18

STEVEN LUKES   Alienation and Anomie   24

✓KENNETH KENISTON   The Varieties of Alienation: An Attempt
at Definition   32

✓MELVIN SEEMAN   On the Meaning of Alienation   45

PART II. DIFFUSE ALIENATION: ANOMIA, POWERLESSNESS,
AND MISANTHROPY

Introduction   55

LEO SROLE   Social Integration and Certain Corollaries   60

BONNIE BULLOUGH   Alienation in the Ghetto   66

MORRIS ROSENBERG   Misanthropy and Political Ideology   76

PART III. ALIENATION IN ACADEMIA

Introduction   85

ARTHUR L. STINCHCHOMBE   Rebellion in a High School   88

PART IV. ALIENATION FROM WORK:
THE MARXIAN HERITAGE

Introduction   103

ROBERT BLAUNER   Alienation and Modern Industry   110

LEONARD I. PEARLIN   Alienation from Work: A Study of
Nursing Personnel   138

LOUIS A. ZURCHER, JR., ARNOLD MEADOW, AND SUSAN LEE ZURCHER
✓ Value Orientation, Role Conflict and Alienation from Work:
A Cross-Cultural Study   153

GEORGE A. MILLER   Professionals in Bureaucracy: Alienation
Among Industrial Scientists and Engineers   164

PART V.   ALIENATION FROM THE POLITICAL SYSTEM

Introduction   181

✓ ADA W. FINIFTER   Dimensions of Political Alienation   189

SAMUEL C. PATTERSON, G. R. BOYNTON, AND RONALD D. HEDLUND
Perceptions and Expectations of the Legislature and Support for It   213

JOEL ABERBACH AND JACK WALKER   Political Trust and
Racial Ideology   226

DEAN JAROS, HERBERT HIRSCH, AND FREDERIC J. FLERON, JR.
The Malevolent Leader: Political Socialization in an
American Sub-Culture   253

PART VI.   ALIENATION AND THE SOCIAL SYSTEM:
STABILITY AND CHANGE

Introduction   269

✓ MAURICE ZEITLIN   Alienation and Revolution   275

✓ ERIK ALLARDT   Types of Protests and Alienation   289

✓ WILLIAM GAMSON   Means of Influence, Political Trust,
and Social Control   305

✓ DAVID EASTON   Responses of Political Systems to Stress on Support 319

Selected Bibliography   347

Index   357

Alienation and the Social System

INTRODUCTORY NOTES

When people reflect on the problems of contemporary society, one of the ideas that comes up most frequently is "alienation." Yet in many discussions "alienation" is used primarily as a vague image to suggest a great variety of attitudes, values and behaviors, instead of in clear and specific ways that would increase meaningful communication. The resulting confusion about its meaning has been so great that several writers have suggested that the concept be abandoned altogether. But the peculiar attraction it exerts for intellectuals, students, social critics, and social scientists indicates that the idea of alienation will not easily or quickly yield its prominent position in contemporary thought. To diminish some of the ambiguity surrounding it, a number of recent scholarly efforts have been directed to clarifying and specifying the use of the term.

These efforts suggest two separate axes for analysis of an attitude of alienation. One focuses on the *referent* or object of alienation: From *what* is the individual alienated? Objects or referents may include, for example, interpersonal relations, the political system, the job or workplace, the university, or other social institutions or organizations.

Second, we may ask what is intended to be communicated when we say that an individual is "alienated." The focus here is on the *meaning* of alienation. What, spe-

cifically, is the nature of the relationship between the individual and the object or referent of the alienated attitude? The quality of this relationship defines the sense in which the individual feels alienated. For example, an individual may feel that he cannot affect important decisions (at his job or in politics, for example), that officials or authorities are corrupt, that he is alone and friendless, or that particular activities in which he is required to engage do not reflect his true needs and potential. To be more concise, these attitudes might be described as a sense of powerlessness, cynicism or normlessness, anomia, and self-estrangement. All of these are important dimensions of the general concept of alienation. Yet, since any given individual described as "alienated" may not be so in all of these different ways, it is important to specify the aspect of alienation which is meant. Thus, we can imagine a variety of *dimensions* of alienation as well as a variety of *referents* of alienation. Both of these specifications need to be made in order to describe adequately an attitude of alienation.

The organization of this collection of studies emphasizes both of these principal concerns. To begin with the second, the initial section of the book presents readings that explore various meanings that have been given to the concept of alienation. We shall examine closely what different writers have meant when they used

1

this term, in the hope that a clearer understanding may emerge as we detect points of convergence and divergence.

Following the first section, the focus shifts to the object or referent of attitudes of alienation. We begin with studies which emphasize the somewhat diffuse attitudes of alienation from interpersonal relations and society in general, and then move to an examination of alienation from three specific social referents—academic institutions, work, and the political system. Hopefully, this organization will contribute to an identification of some common structural causes of alienation, regardless of the social institution in which they are present. At the same time, it emphasizes the unique ways in which alienation is expressed in a variety of social milieux. The final section of the book presents several discussions of ways in which alienation may affect or be affected by social system change and stability.

The introductory essays preceding each section have several goals. I have tried to indicate the dominant problems and concerns in each area and to suggest how each selection relates to these concerns. The introductions also consider particular research problems and prospects. Different issues are raised in each section because the literature has developed from a variety of concerns and perspectives. The discussions also refer to other relevant studies which are not included in this collection; these are indicated by references to publication dates. Citations for these works and many others not mentioned specifically, but germane to the concerns of this book, will be found in the bibliography. As the book itself does, the bibliography emphasizes recent empirically oriented studies.

The fact that a particular framework is used to organize the literature means that some approaches are not as well represented as others. In particular, there is relatively little attention to psychological analyses which are concerned mainly with an amplification of the concept of alienation as *a personality syndrome*. Because this collection emphasizes the social structural context of attitudes of alienation, the psychological approach is somewhat tangential to its perspective. Future research developments may make it possible to integrate these two branches of analysis into an overarching theory capable of accounting for variation in individual responses to alienating social situations partially on the basis of personality variables. Several of the articles included in this book represent significant beginnings in this direction.

I have also deemphasized broad-ranging discussions of the alienating effects of various global conditions of modern life such as industrialism, mass society, urbanization, and so on. There is little doubt, however, that some of these highly insightful general discussions stimulated the interest of many of the authors whose works are represented here and served as sources for some of the hypotheses which they test.

The concept of alienation has a long history in theology, philosophy, and social criticism, and a much shorter one in contemporary social science. It is the very diversity of this legacy which has contributed to both the richness of the intellectual tradition of the concept and the ambiguity that currently surrounds it. This book represents only one part of this intellectual effort, focusing on some dominant themes in research on alienation in the contemporary behavioral sciences.

PART I

CONCEPTS OF ALIENATION

Introduction

The purpose of this section is to clarify what contemporary social scientists mean when they talk about "alienation." So many meanings have been attributed to this concept, many of them vague and mystical, that it verges on losing much of its scientific utility. Even in empirical research alone, the term "alienation" has been used to refer to powerlessness, estrangement, self-estrangement, anomie, discontent, hostility, isolation, meaninglessness, frustration, and a host of other cognate and occasionally peripheral concepts. Some of these differences in usage may be relatively unimportant in that the same basic meaning is intended (although differences in terminology can obscure this intention). When the same meaning is not intended, however, the use of words which are not clearly defined and distinguished may mask important differences in the phenomena being discussed.

Although the concept of alienation was used before Marx, it is in his writings that it first became an empirical and sociological, rather than a metaphysical or theological, concept. The inspiration for much of the contemporary literature on alienation is frequently traced back to Marx's early analyses of alienated labor. The selection reprinted here is from the *Economic and Philosophical Manuscripts,* written in 1844 when Marx was only twenty-six. It is in these early writings that his interest in alienation is most clearly developed as a humanistic philosophy.

In this selection, Marx distinguishes among four aspects of alienation. Although he discusses *alienation from the objects produced* first, he sees this aspect of alienation as a result of the fact that *man is alienated from the work process itself.* "How could the worker stand in an alien relationship to the product of his activity if he did not alienate himself in the act of production itself? The product is indeed only the résumé of activity, of production." Since, for Marx, man is alienated from his daily work activities, *he also becomes alienated from himself,* from his own creative potential and the social bonds that define him as human (his "species-being"). Finally, as a result of being alienated from his own humanity, *he also becomes alienated from his fellow workers, and from other men in general.* Thus, the four aspects of alienation described by Marx are not

3

separable and independent dimensions of alienation but are seen as links in a complex chain of development. The original alienation from the *work process* is hypothesized to reverberate far beyond the work setting to lead to alienation in all other areas.

There is sharp disagreement among scholars as to whether Marx's later work continues the development of the same basic theme of alienation in different terms, or whether he, in fact, rejected these earlier analyses as the product of a youthful romanticism. The conflicting analyses of Erich Fromm (1961) and Daniel Bell (1959), for example, provide an introduction to this controversy. Whether Marx moved to another type of analysis in a later period, however, does not affect the quality or validity of the early work itself nor its subsequent impact on contemporary thought.

The selection by Emile Durkheim is from his study, *Suicide,* in which he develops a theory of human needs and aspirations to explain variations in suicide rates among different social groups and at different times. One of the "types" of suicide which Durkheim posits in this theory is "anomic" suicide. Durkheim defines a breakdown of norms as a state of social "anomie"[1] (from the Greek *anomia,* lawlessness). This *social* condition becomes manifest at the *individual* level as uncertainty as to proper action and belief. If an individual is not able to cope with the anxiety produced by this uncertainty and insecurity, he may be driven to take his life. Thus, Durkheim uses this theory to explain the higher rates of suicide observed in times of both sudden economic depression and sudden prosperity, following the death of a spouse, and among divorced rather than married or single people. In each of these cases, there is a relatively abrupt loss of effective normative regulation. In the selection reprinted here, Durkheim spells out his reasons for believing that man needs normative guidance and regulation.

Durkheim's concept of anomie has been extended to the political realm by de Grazia (1948). In this analysis, de Grazia argues that political associations, mass movements, and even war itself are responses by which men seek to achieve political community and to overcome the sense of disintegration that is anomie.

The lack of social integration of an individual in a state of anomie, focusing as it does on the isolation of the individual and his separation from society, is frequently considered as a variant of alienation. But because anomie represents a diffuse and unwanted separation between an individual and social norms, rather than an active rejection of society, there are important differences between it and many other variants of alienation. Steven Lukes examines the differences between Durkheim's concept of anomie and Marx's concept of alienation. He argues that these concepts assume basically different, and in some ways, diametrically opposed, views of human nature. While Durkheim assumes that man needs social regula-

---

[1] When Durkheim's work was translated into English, the French word "anomie" was translated as "anomy", as in the selection reprinted here. Nevertheless, almost all scholars continue to spell this concept in the original French way and I shall follow this usage here.

tion and control for happiness, Lukes suggests that Marx's vision is that the basic nature of man requires freedom from social restraint in order to achieve the complete development of human potential. These divergent conceptions of human nature would therefore lead to quite different designs of ideal societies to eliminate alienation. The analysis concludes with a discussion of the possibilities of empirical evaluation of these opposing views of man.

While Lukes emphasizes the distinctions between Marx's concept of alienation and Durkheim's concept of anomie, there are also points of convergence between them. It is true that, in Marx's view, the worker yearns for freedom from the oppression of the mode of production in which he is engaged. But this is only one aspect of alienation for Marx. The worker also yearns for a more intimate relationship between his inner needs and potentials and his work activities. He desires an *integration* between himself and the products and process of his labor, such that both might be an expression of his needs and potential rather than merely of his physical skill. Similarly, man's nature being social (his "species-life"), the ideal state for Marx's man is in cooperation with other men. This need for integration is, of course, at the heart of the problem of anomie. The similarity between the concepts may become clearer if we distinguish between the *integration of* an individual into the social structure, accomplished by fulfillment of individual needs in social processes, and the *imposition on* the individual of arbitrary demands and restrictions and alien social values. Durkheim, perhaps, did not consider the extent to which integration can become imposition when social norms become rigidified. Nevertheless, he viewed integration as necessary not to establish authoritarian control *over* men but to respond to a basic human need. Similarly, Marx too thought that the social structure, through a reformed work process, could contribute to the fulfillment of human needs. Although the case that Lukes makes for the basic differences between the values underlying the concepts of alienation and anomie is persuasive, perhaps it is this need for integration in both cases which has led researchers and others frequently to use these terms interchangeably.

Durkheim's focus on "anomie" as a *social* condition points to another axis in the multifaceted concepts of alienation and anomie. This is that each can be viewed either as a description of a society from the "objective" perspective of an outside observer or as the perspective of an individual *in* a given situation who reports certain "subjective" feelings. In Durkheim's analysis, for example, anomie refers to a *societal* condition of normative breakdown. Durkheim makes an outsider's "objective" evaluation that the strength of normative regulation is disturbed under certain conditions. One can either accept Durkheim's evaluation of the existence of anomie or establish some other "objective" criterion in order to determine the relative degree of anomie existing in different groups or at different times. In either case, the judgment does not depend on the subjective evaluations of individuals concerning their own feeling-states, although the existence of social anomie *is* expected to result in a counterpart *subjective* feeling among members of the affected group. As we shall see in the section on "diffuse alienation," one attempt to measure the individual level, subjective counterpart of social anomie is the attitude scale of "anomia."

Marx also uses the concept of alienation both at the social level, from an "objective" perspective, and at the individual level, in a "subjective" sense. The description of the worker as alienated from the objects and process of work, for example, is not based only on subjective, *expressed* dissatisfactions of workers; presumably, many had been socialized to expect no more than they actually received, therefore felt content, and did not subjectively experience dissatisfaction or alienation. For Marx, however, contentment under the conditions he described is an example of "false consciousness," for his judgment of the existence of alienation is based not only on subjective feelings and recognition of alienation but also on an external, "objective," and humanistic criterion derived from *his own* standards as to the appropriate relationship between a man and his work.

The distinction between the "objective" and "subjective" approaches to alienation tends to parallel the distinction between philosophical and empirical analyses of this concept. The philosophical approach is frequently based in the writer's judgments as to alienating *social* conditions and processes, while the empirical approach relies almost entirely on subjective evaluations of attitudinal alienation. Paradoxically, the empiricist's approach allows him to define alienation objectively, as it were, relying on the attitudes of his respondents rather than on his own value judgments, while the "objective" approach is usually based on the subjective value judgments of the analyst as to the existence of alienation in different societies or at different historical periods. The reliance of empirical analysis on individual level attitudinal or subjective measures, however, is not a necessary one. Angell (1951), for example, suggests empirical measures of the "moral integration" of cities which to some extent indicate the opposite of social anomie. The interest of government officials and behavioral scientists in establishing "social indicators" to measure the social quality of life, as indicators such as gross national product and unemployment rates do in the economic realm, should increase future efforts in this direction. What indicators to use in measuring alienation and anomie is a fascinating question that will be with us for many years.

With the selection by Kenneth Keniston, we return to the consideration of "subjective" alienation, for Keniston is interested in alienation as an attitudinal stance. The four aspects of alienation he discusses can be interpreted as stages in the development of an alienated individual's attitudes. Keniston first asks *from what* the individual is alienated, focusing, as this book does, on the referent of alienation. The importance of specifying the object of alienation is also emphasized by Clark (1959) and by Horton (1964). This focus on the object of alienation alerts us to the possibility that individuals may be alienated from one or more social institutions without necessarily being alienated from others. Alienation *may* be generalized from one social sector to another, but this is an empirical, and not a definitional, problem. In order to explore this problem, the possibility of independence of attitudes toward several social institutions should not be precluded by a definition of alienation which *presumes* a generalized attitude.

The second question on which Keniston focuses suggests clearly the developmental nature of his analysis, for he asks about the nature of the alienated relationship which has *replaced* the original and presumably positive one. In other words, in what does alienation consist? Keniston's discussion of this question suggests that there are at least two aspects to it, one concerning the *nature* of the alienation and a second concerning its *intensity*. Later in this section, we will see that Seeman's analysis is directed toward the identification of the basic nature of different types of alienation and thus may be considered an extended examination of Keniston's second question. Intensity, of course, is a formal property which can be applied to any dimension of alienation. One can feel more or less powerless, more or less isolated, and so on.

Third, Keniston asks how the individual *expresses* his alienation. What does he *do* about it? With this question, Keniston explores possible *consequences* that alienation can have. And, finally, the last question really returns to the beginning by asking about the *source* of the individual's attitude of alienation. Does he actively choose this stance or is it imposed on him by others? Keniston argues that only freely chosen attitudes of rejection should be classified as "alienations." Combining the various possible answers to the remaining three questions creates a large number of different types of attitudes. At the conclusion of his analysis, Keniston builds a typology of alienations based on these different combinations. Because Keniston's discussion of the concept of alienation actually includes variables occurring at different points in time (both causes and consequences of alienation), it is more than a "definitional" essay; it is actually a beginning of an entire theory of alienation. The "explicit rejection of traditional American culture" defined by Keniston as the prototypical form of alienation is very similar to a type of alienation studied by Nettler (1957) and discussed in Seeman's analysis as "isolation."

This section concludes with an article which in an important sense serves as a bridge between philosophical and critical writings on alienation and contemporary empirical work. This is Melvin Seeman's analysis of the meaning of alienation. In this article, Seeman discusses five separate usages and meanings of the concept of alienation which can be extracted from the wide variety of writings on this subject. He also lends cohesion to his synthesis by interpreting each variety of alienation in terms of the expectations that individuals have for social processes and values or the satisfactions and rewards they receive from them. For example, powerlessness, the most commonly used variety of alienation, is defined as "the expectancy or probability held by the individual that his own behavior cannot determine the occurrence of the outcomes, or reinforcements, he seeks." Other kinds of alienation Seeman distinguishes are meaninglessness, normlessness, isolation, and self-estrangement.

Seeman does not argue that this list of varieties of alienation is a logically exhaustive typology. Rather, he has synthesized from past literature the major ways in which others have actually used this term. Alternative forms of alienation have been suggested, for example, by Dean (1961) and by Dowdy (1966), among others, and alternative ways of conceptualizing and organizing the components of alienation have also been put forward (Scott, 1963; Browning, 1961). While these analyses suggest ways in which the concept of alienation may be further developed, none to date has had the impact or inspired the number of empirical studies that Seeman's has. Among studies presented in this volume, those by Blauner, Finifter, and Bullough make explicit use of one or more concepts of alienation discussed by Seeman. In addition, his typology is used by Abcarian (1965), Dean (1961), and Middleton (1963), among others. Seeman's own research has focused mainly on the concept of powerlessness.

A number of studies have been carried out expressly to investigate whether the various dimensions of alienation, and related concepts such as anomia, are separable empirically, as well as analytically (Dean, 1961; Neal and Rettig, 1963, 1967; Struening and Richardson, 1965; Finifter, 1970). The results of these studies generally lend support to an approach to the study of alienation which emphasizes the various dimensions of this concept, in that measurements of the separate dimensions tend to be only weakly correlated with each other. At the same time, the correlations are not so low as to indicate that the various types are totally unrelated. The dimensional approach therefore seems particularly useful in recognizing the theoretical and empirical meaningfulness of several variants of alienation, which, at a broader level of abstraction, may all be viewed as part of one general domain of feeling. We are thus alerted to look for differences as well as similarities in the causes and consequences of the various component attitudes. It is on the empirical establishment of such differences that the validity of the dimensional approach ultimately depends.

The variety of meanings attached to the concept of alienation will become increasingly clear in the empirical studies which follow this section, for a number of different measures of alienation are utilized. In view of the extraordinarily complex history and usage of this concept, it is difficult to abstract from these many definitions one basic meaning which would unify them without at the same time glossing over subtle, but significant, nuances of meaning. However, there does appear to be a convergence around the idea of a *discrepancy between a set of values and the socially structured opportunities for achievement of these values*. Marx's concept of alienation and Durkheim's concept of anomie are each rooted in certain assumptions about the nature of human needs and the capacities of social systems to satisfy them. Thus, for Marx, men become alienated because their needs for self-expression are frustrated in the work situation; for Durkheim, needs for social integration and clear social goals are not achievable under conditions of normative uncertainty. Similarly, several of the types of alienation described by Keniston exhibit discrepancies between desired integration states and actual life situations. Although Seeman, at one point in his discussion of powerlessness, rejects the notion of discrepancy, he appears to use this concept in his focus on individuals' goals, values, and standards.

Additional examples of discrepancy definitions of alienation appear in many selections throughout the book. Most measures of personal and political powerlessness may be viewed in terms of the rift between an individual's role expectations and his realistic judgment of his ability to influence events. The measure used by Patterson and his colleagues of the difference between expectations and perceptions of a political institution is a very explicit statement of the discrepancy theme. Stinchcombe's complex concept of "expressive alienation" from high school includes a component emphasizing students' perceptions of inconsistencies between norms and their application by school authorities. Stinchcombe is also very much concerned with the fact that alienation from the high school is produced when the goals and aspirations students set for themselves find little expression in their high school curricula.

Thus, there seems to be a convergence in both theoretical and empirical writings around the idea that alienation is produced by a discrepancy between strongly internalized aspirations, norms and values, on the one hand, and the opportunities perceived by the individual for fulfilling them, on the other. People may be said to be alienated *from* the object, social institution, or opposing values perceived to be responsible for the existence of the discrepancy. Which of the *dimensions* of alienation is produced depends on the particular values or norms which are involved. For example, an individual with a strong desire to determine his own work pace or the type of work he does but who perceives that he is unable to exercise control over these may be described as alienated from work along the powerlessness dimension. A person who thinks that politicians do not observe the rules or norms defined as part of *their* roles (for example, honesty or responsiveness) may be said to be alienated from the political system on the normlessness dimension. A student who perceives no relationship between academic requirements and his own career or personal goals is alienated from school; in this case, the alienation involves a sense of meaninglessness. An advocate of women's liberation may feel isolated from prevailing norms and values defining the role of women in society. In each of these cases, the referents and dimensions of alienation differ. The *referents* are work, politics, school, and a set of social values. The *dimensions* of alienation are *powerlessness* based in a value for *control, normlessness* based in an expectation of *adherence to social norms by others, meaninglessness* based in a need for *rationality and comprehensibility,* and *isolation* based on *competing value systems.*

There are a number of important implications in this approach to defining alienation which should be spelled out. First, the discrepancy notion implies that individuals may be *more or less* alienated, since discrepancies may vary in size. At one extreme, the policies or values of a particular social institution may be viewed not only as irrelevant but as antithetical to a given person's values. At this point, a great separation or estrangement exists for the individual. At the other extreme, a set of values may be so completely embodied in another or so consistent with social practice that a state of perfect integration exists. Between these outer limits are found all the more common discontinuities between sets of values and between values and social conditions.

Second, the discrepancy notion does not necessarily assume one fixed value standard with varying perceptions of congruence between it and actual practices. Since this definition of alienation is "subjective," it is based on the aspirations, norms, and values held by individuals. Differences can exist among individuals in the extent of alienation because of varying perceptions of social conditions *or* because of varying commitments to particular values. Two individuals with similar value positions may differ in their degree of alienation because of differences in the way they perceive social reality, but they might also differ in alienation levels on the basis of similar perceptions of social reality viewed from very different value positions. It is clear, for example, that many people who share the value of political democracy differ in their feelings about a given political system because they disagree about the extent to which political democracy actually exists in that system. Conversely, people's descriptions of political reality may agree quite closely, but they may not be equally alienated because their values are divergent or because the same value is held with a different degree of intensity.

Finally, it should be noted that increases or decreases in alienation may result from changes on *either* side of this alienation "equation." That is, values, social practices, and evaluations of them are all subject to change. Alienation may therefore increase as a result of change in values unaccompanied by corresponding changes in social practice or as a result of changes in social policy which are not supported by congruent value development. Contemporary alienations reflect both of these processes. Many current statements of political alienation in the United States, for example, expressly invoke *traditional* American values and point to discrepancies between these values and contemporary political or social policy. On the other hand, many expressions of alienation from high school and college are based in *changing* values regarding the role of students in school decision making. Here, academic practices are changing more slowly than students' aspirations for participation.

As we have seen, the discrepancy notion is firmly rooted in the alienation-anomie tradition. One additional major usage is in Merton's (1957) theory of deviant behavior, in which he considers that a disjunction between cultural values and socially approved means for achieving these values leads to a state of anomie (Durkheim's weakening of social norms). Deviant behavior results as people attempt to adapt to this disjunction by using illegitimate means to achieve the culturally sanctioned goals. There are at least two major differences between Merton's conceptualization and the definition of alienation developed here. First, Merton's theory refers to an actual *social* condition of discrepancy between cultural values and the socially structured opportunities for achievement of these values. The definition of alienation suggested here is intended to refer to a *perceived* disjuncture from any set of values held by an *individual*. Thus, the one is an "objective" theory of anomie and the other is a "subjective" conception of alienation. How subjective alienation develops under conditions of objective anomie is one of the questions to which research needs to be directed. Second, Merton emphasizes cultural goals which are very widely shared in the society and receive great social emphasis (for example, his stress on the American goal of "success"). In contrast, the definition offered here is based on the particular goals held by individuals, be these unique or widely shared. This definition permits us to consider that individuals may also be alienated *from* widely shared goals or the institutions which perpetuate these goals because they subscribe to a competing value framework (as in Seeman's "isolation," for example).

The general definition of alienation suggested above can be viewed as a partial response to the need for a unifying framework for understanding many of the current diverse meanings and dimensions of alienation. The specification of these empirical types and their referents in finer detail is the task of the remaining sections of this book.

ALIENATED LABOUR

Karl Marx

. . . Thus we have now to grasp the real connexion between this whole system of alienation—private property, acquisitiveness, the separation of labour, capital and land, exchange and competition, value and the devaluation of man, monopoly and competition—and the system of *money*.

Let us not begin our explanation, as does the economist, from a legendary primordial condition. Such a primordial condition does not explain anything; it merely removes the question into a grey and nebulous distance. It asserts as a fact or event what it should deduce, namely, the necessary relation between two things; for example, between the division of labour and exchange. In the same way theology explains the origin of evil by the fall of man; that is, it asserts as a historical fact what it should explain.

We shall begin from a *contemporary* economic fact. The worker becomes poorer the more wealth he produces and the more his production increases in power and extent. The worker becomes an ever cheaper commodity the more goods he creates. The *devaluation* of the human world increases in direct relation with the *increase in value* of the world of things. Labour does not only create goods; it also produces itself and the worker as a

SOURCE: Reprinted from *Karl Marx: Early Writings,* translated and edited by T. B. Bottomore, 121–133, copyright T. B. Bottomore, 1963, by permission of C. A. Watts & Co., Ltd., London.

commodity, and indeed in the same proportion as it produces goods.

This fact simply implies that the object produced by labour, its product, now stands opposed to it as an *alien being,* as a *power independent* of the producer. The product of labour is labour which has been embodied in an object and turned into a physical thing; this product is an *objectification* of labour. The performance of work is at the same time its objectification. The performance of work appears in the sphere of political economy as a *vitiation* of the worker, objectification as a *loss* and as *servitude to the object,* and appropriation as *alienation.*

So much does the performance of work appear as vitiation that the worker is vitiated to the point of starvation. So much does objectification appear as loss of the object that the worker is deprived of the most essential things not only of life but also of work. Labour itself becomes an object which he can acquire only by the greatest effort and with unpredictable interruptions. So much does the appropriation of the object appear as alienation that the more objects the worker produces the fewer he can possess and the more he falls under the domination of his product, of capital.

All these consequences follow from the fact that the worker is related to the *product of his labour* as to an *alien* object. For it is clear on this presupposition that the more the worker expends himself in work the more powerful becomes the world of objects which he creates in face of himself, the poorer he becomes in his inner life, and the less he belongs to himself. It is just the same as in religion. The more of himself man attributes to God the less he has left in himself. The worker puts his life into the object, and his life then belongs no longer to himself but to the object. The greater his activity, therefore, the less he possesses. What is embodied in the product of his labour is no longer his own. The greater this product is, therefore, the more he is diminished. The *alienation* of the worker in his product means not only that his labour becomes an object, assumes an *external* existence, but that it exists independently, *outside himself,* and alien to him, and that it stands opposed to him as an autonomous power. The life which he has given to the object sets itself against him as an alien and hostile force.

Let us now examine more closely the phenomenon of *objectification;* the worker's production and the *alienation* and *loss* of the object it produces, which is involved in it. The worker can create nothing without *nature,* without the *sensuous external world.* The latter is the material in which his labour is realized, in which it is active, out of which and through which it produces things.

But just as nature affords the *means of existence* of labour, in the sense that labour cannot *live* without objects upon which it can be exercised, so also it provides the *means of existence* in a narrower sense; namely the means of physical existence for the *worker* himself. Thus, the more the worker *appropriates* the external world of sensuous nature by his labour the more he deprives himself of *means of existence,* in two respects: first, that the sensuous external world becomes progressively less an object belonging to his labour or a means of existence of his labour, and secondly, that it becomes progressively less a means of existence

in the direct sense, a means for the physical subsistence of the worker.

In both respects, therefore, the worker becomes a slave of the object; first, in that he receives an *object of work,* i.e. receives *work,* and secondly, in that he receives *means of subsistence.* Thus the object enables him to exist, first as a *worker* and secondly, as a *physical subject.* The culmination of this enslavement is that he can only maintain himself as a *physical subject* so far as he is a *worker,* and that it is only as a *physical subject* that he is a worker.

(The alienation of the worker in his object is expressed as follows in the laws of political economy: the more the worker produces the less he has to consume; the more value he creates the more worthless he becomes; the more refined his product the more crude and misshapen the worker; the more civilized the product the more barbarous the worker; the more powerful the work the more feeble the worker; the more the work manifests intelligence the more the worker declines in intelligence and becomes a slave of nature.)

Political economy conceals the alienation in the nature of labour in so far as it does not examine the direct relationship between the worker (work) and production. Labour certainly produces marvels for the rich but it produces privation for the worker. It produces palaces, but hovels for the worker. It produces beauty, but deformity for the worker. It replaces labour by machinery, but it casts some of the workers back into a barbarous kind of work and turns the others into machines. It produces intelligence, but also stupidity and cretinism for the workers.

The direct relationship of labour to its products is the relationship of the worker to the objects of his production. The relationship of property owners to the objects of production and to production itself is merely a *consequence* of this first relationship and confirms it. We shall consider this second aspect later.

Thus, when we ask what is the important relationship of labour, we are concerned with the relationship of the *worker* to production.

So far we have considered the alienation of the worker only from one aspect; namely, *his relationship with the products of his labour.* However, alienation appears not merely in the result but also in the *process* of *production,* within *productive activity* itself. How could the worker stand in an alien relationship to the product of his activity if he did not alienate himself in the act of production itself? The product is indeed only the *résumé* of activity, of production. Consequently, if the product of labour is alienation, production itself must be active alienation—the alienation of activity and the activity of alienation. The alienation of the object of labour merely summarizes the alienation in the work activity itself.

What constitutes the alienation of labour? First, that the work is *external* to the worker, that it is not part of his nature; and that, consequently, he does not fulfill himself in his work but denies himself, has a feeling of misery rather than well-being, does not develop freely his mental and physical energies but is physically exhausted and mentally debased. The worker, therefore, feels himself at home only during his leisure time, whereas at work he feels homeless. His work is not voluntary but imposed, *forced labour.* It is not the satisfaction of a need, but only a *means* for satisfying other needs. Its alien character is clearly shown by the fact that as soon as there is no physical or other compulsion it is avoided like the plague. External labour, labour in which man alienates himself, is a labour of self-sacrifice, of mortification. Finally, the external character of work for the worker is shown by the fact that it is not his own work but work for someone else, that in work he does not belong to himself but to another person.

Just as in religion the spontaneous activity of human fantasy, of the human brain and heart, reacts independently as an alien activity of gods or devils upon the individual, so the activity of the worker is not his own spontaneous activity. It is another's activity and a loss of his own spontaneity.

We arrive at the result that man (the worker) feels himself to be freely active only in his animal functions—eating, drinking and procreating, or at most also in his dwelling and in personal adornment—while in his human functions he is reduced to an animal. The animal becomes human and the human becomes animal.

Eating, drinking and procreating are of course also genuine human functions. But abstractly considered, apart from the environment of human activities, and turned into final and sole ends, they are animal functions.

We have now considered the act of alienation of practical human activity, labour, from two aspects: (1) the relationship of the worker to the *product of labour* as an alien object which dominates him. This relationship is at the same time the relationship to the sensuous external world, to natural objects, as an alien and hostile world; (2) the relationship of labour to the *act of production* within *labour.* This is the relationship of the worker to his own activity as something alien and not belonging to him, activity as suffering (passivity), strength as powerlessness, creation as emasculation, the *personal* physical and mental energy of the worker, his personal life (for what is life but activity?), as an activity which is directed against himself, independent of him and not belonging to him. This is *self-alienation* as against the above-mentioned alienation of the *thing.*

We have now to infer a third characteristic of *alienated labour* from the two we have considered.

Man is a species-being not only in the sense that he makes the community (his own as well as those of other things) his object both practically and theoretically, but also (and this is simply another expression for the same thing) in the sense that he treats himself as the present, living species, as a *universal* and consequently free being.

Species-life, for man as for animals, has its physical basis in the fact that man (like animals) lives from inorganic nature, and since man is more universal than an animal so the range of inorganic nature from which he lives is more universal. Plants, animals, minerals, air, light, etc. constitute, from the theoretical aspect, a part of human consciousness as objects of natural science and art; they are man's spiritual inorganic nature, his intellectual means of life, which he must first prepare for enjoyment and perpetuation. So also, from the practical aspect, they form a part of human life and activity. In practice man lives only from these natural products, whether in the form of food, heating, clothing, housing, etc. The universality of man appears in practice in the universality which makes the whole of nature into his inorganic body: (1) as a direct means of life; and equally (2) as the material object and instrument of his life activity. Nature is the inorganic body of man; that is to say nature, excluding the human body itself. To say that man *lives* from nature means that nature is his *body* with which he must remain in a continuous interchange in order not to die. The statement that the physical and mental life of man, and nature, are interdependent means simply that nature is interdependent with itself, for man is a part of nature.

Since alienated labour: (1) alienates nature from man; and (2) alienates man from himself, from his own active function, his life activity; so it alienates him from the species. It makes *species-life* into a means of individual life. In the first place it alienates species-life and individual life, and secondly, it turns the latter, as an abstraction, into the purpose of the former, also in its abstract and alienated form.

For labour, *life activity, productive life,* now appear to man only as *means* for the satisfaction of a need, the need to maintain his physical existence. Productive life is, however, species-life. It is life creating life. In the type of life activity resides the whole character of a species, its species-character; and free, conscious activity is the species-character of human beings. Life itself appears only as a *means of life.*

The animal is one with its life activity. It does not distinguish the activity from itself. It is *its activity.* But man makes his life activity itself an object of his will and consciousness. He has a conscious life activity. It is not a determination with which he is completely identified. Conscious life activity distinguishes man from the life activity of animals. Only for this reason is he a species-being. Or rather, he is only a self-conscious being, i.e. his own life is an object for him, because he is a species-being. Only for this reason is his activity free activity. Alienated labour reverses the relationship, in that man because he is a self-conscious being makes his life activity, his *being,* only a means for his *existence.*

The practical construction of an *objective world,* the *manipulation* of inorganic nature, is the confirmation of man as a conscious species-being, i.e. a being who treats the species as his own being or himself as a species-being. Of course, animals also produce. They construct nests, dwellings, as in the case of bees, beavers, ants, etc. But they only produce what is strictly necessary for themselves or their young. They produce only in a single direction, while man produces universally. They produce only under the compulsion of direct physical needs, while man produces when he is free from physical need and only truly produces in freedom from such need. Animals produce only themselves, while man reproduces the whole of nature. The products of animal production belong directly to their physical bodies, while man is free in face of his product. Animals construct only in accordance with the standards and needs of the species to which they belong, while man knows how to produce in accordance with the standards of every species and knows how to apply the appropriate standard to the object. Thus man constructs also in accordance with the laws of beauty.

It is just in his work upon the objective world that man really proves himself as a *species-being*. This production is his active species-life. By means of it nature appears as *his* work and his reality. The object of labour is, therefore, the *objectification of man's species-life;* for he no longer reproduces himself merely intellectually, as in consciousness, but actively and in a real sense, and he sees his own reflection in a world which he has constructed. While, therefore, alienated labour takes away the object of production from man, it also takes away his *species-life,* his real objectivity as a species-being, and changes his advantage over animals into a disadvantage in so far as his inorganic body, nature, is taken from him.

Just as alienated labour transforms free and self-directed activity into a means, so it transforms the species-life of man into a means of physical existence.

Consciousness, which man has from his species, is transformed through alienation so that species-life becomes only a means for him. (3) Thus alienated labour turns the *species-life of man,* and also nature as his mental species-property, into an *alien* being and into a *means* for his *individual existence.* It alienates from man his own body, external nature, his mental life and his *human life.* (4) A direct consequence of the alienation of man from the product of his labour, from his life activity and from his species-life, is that *man is alienated* from other *men.* When man confronts himself he also confronts *other* men. What is true of man's relationship to his work, to the product of his work and to himself, is also true of his relationship

to other men, to their labour and to the objects of their labour.

In general, the statement that man is alienated from his species-life means that each man is alienated from others, and that each of the others is likewise alienated from human life.

Human alienation, and above all the relation of man to himself, is first realized and expressed in the relationship between each man and other men. Thus in the relationship of alienated labour every man regards other men according to the standards and relationships in which he finds himself placed as a worker.

We began with an economic fact, the alienation of the worker and his production. We have expressed this fact in conceptual terms as *alienated labour,* and in analysing the concept we have merely analysed an economic fact.

Let us now examine further how this concept of alienated labour must express and reveal itself in reality. If the product of labour is alien to me and confronts me as an alien power, to whom does it belong? If my own activity does not belong to me but is an alien, forced activity, to whom does it belong? To a being *other* than myself. And who is this being? The *gods?* It is apparent in the earliest stages of advanced production, e.g. temple building, etc. in Egypt, India, Mexico, and in the service rendered to gods, that the product belonged to the gods. But the gods alone were never the lords of labour. And no more was *nature.* What a contradiction it would be if the more man subjugates nature by his labour, and the more the marvels of the gods are rendered superfluous by the marvels of industry, the more he should abstain from his joy in producing and his enjoyment of the product for love of these powers.

The *alien* being to whom labour and the product of labour belong, to whose service labour is devoted, and to whose enjoyment the product of labour goes, can only be *man* himself. If the product of labour does not belong to the worker, but confronts him as an alien power, this can only be because it belongs to *a man other than the worker.* If his activity is a torment to him it must be a source of *enjoyment* and pleasure to another. Not the gods, nor nature, but only man himself can be this alien power over men.

Consider the earlier statement that the relation of man to himself is first *realized, objectified,* through his relation to other men. If he is related to the product of his labour, his objectified labour, as to an *alien,* hostile, powerful and independent object, he is related in such a way that another alien, hostile, powerful and independent man is the lord of this object. If he is related to his own activity as to unfree activity, then he is related to it as activity in the service, and under the domination, coercion and yoke, of another man.

Every self-alienation of man, from himself and from nature, appears in the relation which he postulates between other men and himself and nature. Thus religious self-alienation is necessarily exemplified in the relation between laity and priest, or, since it is here a question of the spiritual world, between the laity and a mediator. In the real world of practice this self-alienation can only be expressed in the real, practical relation of man to his fellow men. The medium through which alienation occurs is itself a *practical* one. Through alienated labour, therefore, man not only produces his relation to the object and to the process of production as to alien and hostile men; he also produces the relation of other men to his production and his product, and the relation between himself and other men. Just as he creates his own production as a vitiation, a punishment, and his own product as a loss, as a product which does not belong to him, so he creates the domination of the non-producer over production and its product. As he alienates his own activity, so he bestows upon the stranger an activity which is not his own.

We have so far considered this relation only from the side of the worker, and later on we shall consider it also from the side of the non-worker.

Thus, through alienated labour the worker creates the relation of another man, who does not work and is outside the work process, to this labour. The relation of the worker to work also produces the relation of the capitalist (or whatever one likes to call the lord of labour) to work. *Private property* is, therefore, the product, the necessary result, of *alienated labour,* of the external relation of the worker to nature and to himself.

Private property is thus derived from the analysis of the concept of *alienated labour;* that is, alienated man, alienated labour, alienated life, and estranged man.

We have, of course, derived the concept of *alienated labour (alienated life)* from political economy, from an analysis of the *movement of private property.* But the analysis of this concept shows that although private property appears to be the basis and cause of alienated labour, it is rather a consequence of the latter, just as the gods are *fundamentally* not the cause but the product of confusions of human reason. At a later stage, however, there is a reciprocal influence.

Only in the final stage of the development of private property is its secret revealed, namely, that it is on one hand the *product* of alienated labour, and on the other hand the *means* by which labour is alienated, *the realization of this alienation.*

This elucidation throws light upon several unresolved controversies—

1. Political economy begins with labour as the real soul of production and then goes on to attribute nothing to labour and everything to private property. Proudhon, faced by this contradiction, has decided in

favour of labour against private property. We perceive, however, that this apparent contradiction is the contradiction of *alienated labour* with itself and that political economy has merely formulated the laws of alienated labour.

We also observe, therefore, that *wages* and *private property* are identical, for wages, like the product or object of labour, labour itself remunerated, are only a necessary consequence of the alienation of labour. In the wage system labour appears not as an end in itself but as the servant of wages. We shall develop this point later on and here only bring out some of the consequences.

An enforced *increase in wages* (disregarding the other difficulties, and especially that such an anomaly could only be maintained by force) would be nothing more than a *better remuneration of slaves,* and would not restore, either to the work-er or to the work, their human significance and worth.

Even the *equality of incomes* which Proudhon demands would only change the relation of the present-day worker to his work into a relation of all men to work. Society would then be conceived as an abstract capitalist.

2. From the relation of alienated labour to private property it also follows that the emancipation of society from private property, from servitude, takes the political form of the *emancipation of the workers;* not in the sense that only the latter's emancipation is involved, but because this emancipation includes the emancipation of humanity as a whole. For all human servitude is involved in the relation of the worker to production, and all the types of servitude are only modifications or consequences of this relation.

ANOMY

Emile Durkheim

No living being can be happy or even exist unless his needs are sufficiently proportioned to his means. In other words, if his needs require more than can be granted, or even merely something of a different sort, they will be under continual friction and can only function painfully. Movements incapable of production without pain tend not to be reproduced. Unsatisfied tendencies atrophy, and as the impulse to live is merely the result of all the rest, it is bound to weaken as the others relax.

SOURCE: Reprinted with permission of The Macmillan Company and Routledge and Kegan Paul, Ltd., from *Suicide* by Emile Durkheim, 246–254. Copyright 1952 by the Free Press, a Corporation.

In the animal, at least in a normal condition, this equilibrium is established with automatic spontaneity because the animal depends on purely material conditions. All the organism needs is that the supplies of substance and energy constantly employed in the vital process should be periodically renewed by equivalent quantities; that replacement be equivalent to use. When the void created by existence in its own resources is filled the animal, satisfied, asks nothing further. Its power of reflection is not sufficiently developed to imagine other ends than those implicit in its physical nature. On the other hand, as the work demanded of each organ itself depends on the general state of vital energy and the needs of organic equilibrium, use is regulated in turn by replacement and the balance is automatic. The limits of one are those of the other; both are fundamental to the constitution of the existence in question, which cannot exceed them.

This is not the case with man, because most of his needs are not dependent on his body or not to the same degree. Strictly speaking, we may consider that the quantity of material supplies necessary to the physical maintenance of a human life is subject to computation, though this be less exact than in the preceding case and a wider margin left for the free combinations of the will; for beyond the indispensable minimum which satisfies nature when instinctive, a more awakened reflection suggests better conditions, seemingly desirable ends craving fulfillment. Such appetites, however, admittedly sooner or later reach a limit which they cannot pass. But how determine the quantity of well-being, comfort or luxury legitimately to be craved by a human being? Nothing appears in man's organic nor in his psychological constitution which sets a limit to such tendencies. The functioning of individual life does not require them to cease at one point rather than at another; the proof being that they have constantly increased since the beginnings of history, receiving more and more complete satisfaction, yet with no weakening of average health. Above all, how establish their proper variation with different conditions of life, occupations, relative importance of services, etc.? In no society are they equally satisfied in the different stages of the social hierarchy. Yet human nature is substantially the same among all men, in its essential qualities. It is not human nature which can assign the variable limits necessary to our needs. They are thus unlimited so far as they depend on the individual alone. Irrespective of any external regulatory force, our capacity for feeling is in itself an insatiable and bottomless abyss.

But if nothing external can restrain this capacity, it can only be a source of torment to itself. Unlimited desires are insatiable by definition and insatiability is rightly considered a sign of morbidity. Being unlimited, they constantly and infinitely surpass the means at their command; they cannot be quenched. Inextinguishable thirst is constantly renewed torture. It has been claimed, indeed, that human activity naturally aspires beyond assignable limits and sets itself unattainable goals. But how can such an undetermined state be any more reconciled with the conditions of mental life than with the demands of physical life? All man's pleasure in acting, moving and exerting himself implies the sense that his efforts are not in vain and that by walking he has advanced. However, one does not advance when one walks toward no goal, or—which is the same thing—when his goal is infinity. Since the distance between us and it is always the same, whatever road we take, we might as well have made the motions without progress from the spot. Even our glances behind and our feeling of pride at the distance covered can cause only deceptive satisfaction, since the remaining distance is not proportionately reduced. To pursue a goal which is by definition unattainable is to condemn oneself to a state of perpetual unhappiness. Of course, man may hope contrary to all reason, and hope has its pleasures even when unreasonable. It may sustain him for a time; but it cannot survive the repeated disappointments of experience indefinitely. What more can the future offer him than the past, since he can never reach a tenable condition nor even approach the glimpsed ideal? Thus, the more one has, the more one wants, since satisfactions received only stimulate instead of filling needs. Shall action as such be considered agreeable? First, only on condition of blindness to its uselessness. Secondly, for this pleasure to be felt and to temper and half veil the accompanying painful unrest, such unending motion must at least always be easy and unhampered. If it is interfered with only restlessness is left, with the lack of ease which it, itself, entails. But it would be a miracle if no insurmountable obstacle were never encountered. Our thread of life on these conditions is pretty thin, breakable at any instant.

To achieve any other result, the passions first must be limited. Only then can they be harmonized with the faculties and satisfied. But since the individual has no way of limiting them, this must be done by some force exterior to him. A regulative force must play the same role for moral needs which the organism plays for physical needs. This means that the force can only be moral. The awakening of conscience interrupted the state of equilibrium of the animal's dormant existence; only conscience, therefore, can furnish the means to re-establish it. Physical restraint would be ineffective; hearts cannot be touched by physio-chemical forces. So far as the appetites are not automatically restrained by physiological mechanisms, they can be halted only by a limit that they recognize as just. Men would never consent to restrict their desires if they felt justified in passing the assigned limit. But, for reasons given above, they cannot assign themselves this law of justice. So they must receive it from an authority which they respect, to which they yield spontaneously. Either directly and as a whole, or through the agency of one of its organs, society alone can play this moderating role; for it is the only moral power superior to the individual, the authority of which he accepts. It alone has the power necessary to stipulate law and to set the point beyond which the passions must not go. Finally, it alone can estimate the reward to be prospectively offered to every class of human functionary, in the name of the common interest.

As a matter of fact, at every moment of history there is a dim perception, in the moral consciousness of societies, of the respective value of different social services, the relative reward due to each, and

the consequent degree of comfort appropriate on the average to workers in each occupation. The different functions are graded in public opinion and a certain coefficient of well-being assigned to each, according to its place in the hierarchy. According to accepted ideas, for example, a certain way of living is considered the upper limit to which a workman may aspire in his efforts to improve his existence, and there is another limit below which he is not willingly permitted to fall unless he has seriously bemeaned himself. Both differ for city and country workers, for the domestic servant and the day-laborer, for the business clerk and the official, etc. Likewise the man of wealth is reproved if he lives the life of a poor man, but also if he seeks the refinements of luxury overmuch. Economists may protest in vain; public feeling will always be scandalized if an individual spends too much wealth for wholly superfluous use, and it even seems that this severity relaxes only in times of moral disturbance. A genuine regimen exists, therefore, although not always legally formulated, which fixes with relative precision the maximum degree of ease of living to which each social class may legitimately aspire. However, there is nothing immutable about such a scale. It changes with the increase or decrease of collective revenue and the changes occurring in the moral ideas of society. Thus what appears luxury to one period no longer does so to another; and the well-being which for long periods was granted to a class only by exception and supererogation, finally appears strictly necessary and equitable.

Under this pressure, each in his sphere vaguely realizes the extreme limit set to his ambitions and aspires to nothing beyond. At least if he respects regulations and is docile to collective authority, that is, has a wholesome moral constitution, he feels that it is not well to ask more. Thus, an end and goal are set to the passions. Truly, there is nothing rigid nor absolute about such determination. The economic ideal assigned each class of citizens is itself confined to certain limits, within which the desires have free range. But it is not infinite. This relative limitation and the moderation it involves, make men contented with their lot while stimulating them moderately to improve it; and this average contentment causes the feeling of calm, active happiness, the pleasure in existing and living which characterizes health for societies as well as for individuals. Each person is then at least, generally speaking, in harmony with his condition, and desires only what he may legitimately hope for as the normal reward of his activity. Besides, this does not condemn man to a sort of immobility. He may seek to give beauty to his life; but his attempts in this direction may fail without causing him to despair. For, loving what he has and not fixing his desire solely on what he lacks, his wishes and hopes may fail of what he has happened to aspire to, without his being wholly destitute. He has the essentials. The equilibrium of his happiness is secure because it is defined, and a few mishaps cannot disconcert him.

But it would be of little use for everyone to recognize the justice of the hierarchy of functions established by public opinion, if he did not also consider the distribution of these functions just. The workman is not in harmony with his social position if he is not convinced that he has his desserts. If he feels justified in occupying another, what he has would not satisfy him. So it is not enough for the average level of needs for each social condition to be regulated by public opinion, but another, more precise rule, must fix the way in which these conditions are open to individuals. There is no society in which such regulation does not exist. It varies with times and places. Once it regarded birth as the almost exclusive principle of social classification; today it recognizes no other inherent inequality than hereditary fortune and merit. But in all these various

forms its object is unchanged. It is also only possible, everywhere, as a restriction upon individuals imposed by superior authority, that is, by collective authority. For it can be established only by requiring of one or another group of men, usually of all, sacrifices and concessions in the name of the public interest.

Some, to be sure, have thought that this moral pressure would become unnecessary if men's economic circumstances were only no longer determined by heredity. If inheritance were abolished, the argument runs, if everyone began life with equal resources and if the competitive struggle were fought out on a basis of perfect equality, no one could think its results unjust. Each would instinctively feel that things are as they should be.

— Truly, the nearer this ideal equality were approached, the less social restraint will be necessary. But it is only a matter of degree. One sort of heredity will always exist, that of natural talent. Intelligence, taste, scientific, artistic, literary or industrial ability, courage and manual dexterity are gifts received by each of us at birth, as the heir to wealth receives his capital or as the nobleman formerly received his title and function. A moral discipline will therefore still be required to make those less favored by nature accept the lesser advantages which they owe to the chance of birth. Shall it be demanded that all have an equal share and that no advantage be given those more useful and deserving? But then there would have to be a discipline far stronger to make these accept a treatment merely equal to that of the mediocre and incapable.

But like the one first mentioned, this discipline can be useful only if considered just by the peoples subject to it. When it is maintained only by custom and force, peace and harmony are illusory; the spirit of unrest and discontent are latent; appetites superficially restrained are ready to revolt. This happened in Rome and Greece when the faiths underlying the old organization of the patricians and plebeians were shaken, and in our modern societies when aristocratic prejudices began to lose their old ascendancy. But this state of upheaval is exceptional; it occurs only when society is passing through some abnormal crisis. In normal conditions the collective order is regarded as just by the great majority of persons. Therefore, when we say that an authority is necessary to impose this order on individuals, we certainly do not mean that violence is the only means of establishing it. Since this regulation is meant to restrain individual passions, it must come from a power which dominates individuals; but this power must also be obeyed through respect, not fear.

It is not true, then, that human activity can be released from all restraint. Nothing in the world can enjoy such a privilege. All existence being a part of the universe is relative to the remainder; its nature and method of manifestation accordingly depend not only on itself but on other beings, who consequently restrain and regulate it, Here there are only differences of degree and form between the mineral realm and the thinking person. Man's characteristic privilege is that the bond he accepts is not physical but moral; that is, social. He is governed not by a material environment brutally imposed on him, but by a conscience superior to his own, the superiority of which he feels. Because the greater, better part of his existence transcends the body, he escapes the body's yoke, but is subject to that of society.

But when society is disturbed by some painful crisis or by beneficent but abrupt transitions, it is momentarily incapable of exercising this influence; thence come the sudden rises in the curve of suicides. . . .

In the case of economic disasters, indeed, something like a declassification occurs which suddenly casts certain individuals into a lower state than their previous one. Then they must reduce their requirements, restrain their needs, learn greater self-control. All the advantages of social influence are lost so far as they are concerned; their moral education has to be recommenced. But society cannot adjust them instantaneously to this new life and teach them to practice the increased self-repression to which they are unaccustomed. So they are not adjusted to the condition forced on them, and its very prospect is intolerable; hence the suffering which detaches them from a reduced existence even before they have made trial of it.

It is the same if the source of the crisis is an abrupt growth of power and wealth. Then, truly, as the conditions of life are changed, the standard according to which needs were regulated can no longer remain the same; for it varies with social resources, since it largely determines the share of each class of producers. The scale is upset; but a new scale cannot be immediately improvised. Time is required for the public conscience to reclassify men and things. So long as the social forces thus freed have not regained equilibrium, their respective values are unknown and so all regulation is lacking for a time. The limits are unknown between the possible and the impossible, what is just and what is unjust, legitimate claims and hopes and those which are immoderate. Consequently, there is no restraint upon aspirations. If the disturbance is profound, it affects even the principles controlling the distribution of men among various occupations. Since the relations between various parts of society are necessarily modified, the ideas expressing these relations must change. Some particular class especially favored by the crisis is no longer resigned to its former lot, and, on the other hand, the example of its greater good fortune arouses all sorts of jealousy below and about it. Appetites, not being controlled by a public opinion become disoriented, no longer recognize the limits proper to them. Besides, they are at the same time seized by a sort of natural erethism simply by the greater intensity of public life. With increased prosperity desires increase. At the very moment when traditional rules have lost their authority, the richer prize offered these appetites stimulates them and makes them more exigent and impatient of control. The state of de-regulation or anomy is thus further heightened by passions being less disciplined, precisely when they need more disciplining.

But then their very demands make fulfillment impossible. Overweening ambition always exceeds the results obtained, great as they may be, since there is no warning to pause here. Nothing gives satisfaction and all this agitation is uninterruptedly maintained without appeasement. Above all, since this race for an unattainable goal can give no other pleasure but that of the race itself, if it is one, once it is interrupted the participants are left empty-handed. At the same time the struggle grows more violent and painful, both from being less controlled and because competition is greater. All classes contend among themselves because no established classification any longer exists. Effort grows, just when it becomes less productive. How could the desire to live not be weakened under such conditions?

This explanation is confirmed by the remarkable immunity of poor countries. Poverty protects against suicide because it is a restraint in itself. No matter how one acts, desires have to depend upon resources to some extent; actual possessions are partly the criterion of those aspired to. So the less one has the less he is tempted to extend the range of his needs indefinitely. Lack of power, compelling moderation, accustoms men to it, while nothing excites envy if no one has superfluity. Wealth, on the other hand, by the power it bestows, deceives us into believing that we depend on ourselves only. Reducing the resistance we encounter from objects, it suggests the possibility of unlimited success against them. The less limited one feels, the more intolerable all limitation appears. Not without reason, therefore, have so many religions dwelt on the advantages and moral value of poverty. It is actually the best school for teaching self-restraint. Forcing us to constant self-discipline, it prepares us to accept collective discipline with equanimity, while wealth, exalting the individual, may always arouse the spirit of rebellion which is the very source of immorality. This, of course, is no reason why humanity should not improve its material condition. But though the moral danger involved in every growth of prosperity is not irremediable, it should not be forgotten.

ALIENATION AND ANOMIE[1]

Steven Lukes

Both Marx and Durkheim were profound critics of industrial society in nineteenth-century Europe. What is striking is the markedly different bases of their criticisms of the ills of their societies, which can best be brought out by a careful consideration of the different assumptions and implications that belong to the two concepts of alienation and anomie, which they respectively employed.[2] These concepts were elaborated by the two thinkers in their earliest writings and remain implicit as basic and integral elements in their developed social theories. Thus a study of the differing perspectives which they manifest should be fruitful. . . .

Alienation and anomie have in common the formal characteristic that they each have a multiple reference to: (1) social phenomena (states of society, its institutions, rules and norms); (2) individual

SOURCE: Reprinted from Peter Laslett and W. Runciman, *Philosophy, Politics, and Society,* 3rd Series (Oxford: Basil Blackwell, 1967), 134, 140–144, 149–156, by permission of the author.

[1] My thanks are especially due to Dr. S. Avineri, Professor Sir I. Berlin and Mr. J. P. Plamenatz for their kind and helpful comments on an earlier draft of this article.

[2] For other discussions of these concepts, treating them together but in ways rather different both from one another and from that adopted here, see J. Horton, "The Dehumanisation of Anomie and Alienation", *British Journal of Sociology,* XV, 4, December 1964, and E. H. Mizruchi, "Alienation and Anomie", in I. L. Horowizt (ed.), *The New Sociology: Essays in Social Science and Social Theory* (New York, 1964).

states of mind (beliefs, desires, attitudes, etc.); (3) a hypothesized empirical relationship between (1) and (2); and (4) a presupposed picture of the "natural" relationship between (1) and (2). Thus, whereas Marx sees capitalism as a compulsive social system, which narrows men's thoughts, places obstacles in the way of their desires and denies the realization of "a world of productive impulses and faculties," Durkheim sees it as a state of moral anarchy in the economic sphere, where men's thoughts and desires are insufficiently controlled and where the individual is not "in harmony with his condition." We will later notice the extent to which (3) is related to (4) in the two cases. Let us here concentrate on (3), and in particular on the difference between the hypotheses in question.

Compare what the two thinkers have to say about the division of labour. For Marx it is *in itself* the major contributing factor in alienation, in all its forms, and not just for the worker but for all men. All men are alienated under the division of labour (for, as he says, "capital and labour are two sides of one and the same relation" and "all human servitude is involved in the relation of the worker to production, and all the types of servitude are only modifications or consequences of this relation"). Men have to enter into "definite relations that are indispensable and independent of their wills," they are forced to play determined roles within the economic system, and, in society as a whole, they are dehumanized by social relations which take on "an independent existence" and which determine not only what they do, but the very structure of their thought, their images of themselves, their products, their activities and other men. Alienated man is dehumanized by being conditioned and constrained to see himself, his products, his activities and other men in economic, political, religious and other categories—in terms which deny his and their human possibilities.

Durkheim sees the division of labour as being (when properly regulated) the source of solidarity in modern industrial society: the prevalence of anomie is due to a lag in the growth of the relevant rules and institutions. Interdependence of functions (plus occupational groups) should lead to growing solidarity and a sense of community, although the division of labour in advanced societies is also (ideally) accompanied by the growth of the importance of the individual personality and the development of values such as justice and equality. For Durkheim the economic functions of the division of labour are "trivial in comparison with the moral effect it produces." By means of it "the individual becomes aware of his dependence upon society; from it come the forces which keep him in check and restrain him." When educating a child, it is "necessary to get him to like the idea of circumscribed tasks and limited horizons," for in modern society "man is destined to fulfill a special function in the social organism, and, consequently, he must learn in advance how to play this role." The division of labour does not normally degrade the individual "by making him into a machine": it merely requires that in performing his special function "he feels he is serving something." Moreover, "if a person has grown accustomed to vast horizons, total views, broad generalities, he cannot be confined, without impatience, within the strict limits of a special task."

By now it should be apparent that alienation, in Marx's thinking, is, *in part,* what characterizes precisely those states of the individual and conditions of society which Durkheim sees as the solution to anomie: namely, where men are socially determined and constrained, when they must conform to social rules which are independent of their wills and are conditioned to think and act within the confines of specialized roles. Whereas anomic man is, for Durkheim, the unregulated man who needs rules to live by, limits to his desires, "circumscribed tasks" to perform and "limited horizons" for his thoughts, alienated man is, for Marx, a man in the grip of a system, who "cannot escape" from a "particular, exclusive sphere of activity which is forced upon him."[3]

Whence does this difference derive? In part, obviously, from the fact that Marx and Durkheim wrote at different periods about different stages of industrial society. Also it is clear that Marx was concerned chiefly to describe the alienated worker, while Durkheim saw economic anomie as primarily characterizing employers. But there is also a theoretical difference that is striking and important: these concepts offer opposite and incompatible analyses of the relation of the individual to society.

Compare Marx's statements that "it is above all necessary to avoid postulating 'society' once again as an abstraction confronting the individual" and that communism creates the basis for "rendering it impossible that anything should exist independently of individuals" with Durkheim's that society is "a reality from which everything that matters to us flows," that it "transcends the individual's consciousness" and that it "has all the characteristics

[3] But Durkheim obviously did not want to see men treated as commodities or as appendages to machines. (See *Division of Labour,* ed. G. Simpson, Glencoe, 1933, pp. 371–3), and Marx had much to say, especially in Vol. III of *Capital,* about avarice and unregulated desires prevalent under capitalism (see also his account of "raw communism" in the 1844 manuscripts).

of a moral authority that imposes respect." Marx begins from the position that the independent or "reified" and determining character of social relationships and norms is precisely what characterizes human "pre-history" and will be abolished by the revolutionary transition to a "truly-human" society, whereas Durkheim assumes the "normality" of social regulation, the lack of which leads to the morbid, self-destructive state of "non-social" or Hobbesian anarchy evident in unregulated capitalism. Social constraint is for Marx a denial and for Durkheim a condition of human freedom and self-realization.

It is my contention that one can only make sense of the empirical relationships postulated between social conditions and individual mental states which are held to constitute alienation and anomie by taking into account what Marx and Durkheim see as the "natural" (or "human" or "normal" or "healthy") condition of the individual in society. Alienation and anomie do not identify themselves, as it were, independently of the theories from which they derive: witness the diversity of contemporary uses of the terms. They are, in fact, only identifiable if one knows what it would be *not* to be alienated or anomic, that is, if one applies a standard specifying "natural" states of institutions, rules and norms and individual mental states. Moreover, this standard must be external. That is, neither the individual mental states nor the social conditions studied can provide that standard, for they themselves are to be evaluated for their degree of alienation and anomie.

Thus despite recent attempts to divest these concepts of their nonempirical presuppositions,[4] they are in their original form an inextricable fusion of fact and value, so that one cannot eliminate the latter while remaining faithful to the original concepts.

[4] See e.g. B. F. Dohrenwend, "Egoism, Altruism, Anomie and Fatalism: A Conceptual Analysis of Durkheim's Types," *American Sociological Review,* 24, 1959, p. 467, where anomie is

The standard specifying the "natural" condition of the individual in society involves, in each case, a theory of human nature. Marx's view of man is of a being with a wide range of creative potentialities, or "species powers" whose "self-realization exists as an inner necessity, a need." In the truly human society there will be "a new manifestation of *human* powers and a new enrichment of the human being," when "man appropriates his manifold being in an all-inclusive way, and thus is a whole man." Man needs to develop all his faculties in a context where neither the natural nor the social environment are constraining: "objects then confirm his individuality . . . the wealth of subjective human sensibility . . . is cultivated or created" and "the practical relations of everyday life offer to man none but perfectly intelligible and reasonable relations wih regard to his fellow men and to nature." With the end of the division of labour, there will be an end to "the exclusive concentration of artistic talent in particular individuals and its suppression in the broad mass." The "detail worker of today," with nothing more to perform than a partial social function," will be superseded by "an individual with an all-round development, one for whom various social functions are alternative modes of activity."[5] Furthermore, with the end of the social determination of "abstract"

described as "ambiguous . . . indistinct . . . and infused with value judgments about what is 'good' and 'bad' ", and e.g., M. Seeman, "On the Meaning of Alienation," *American Sociological Review,* 24, 1959.

[5] Cf. the famous passage from the *German Ideology* in which Marx writes of "communist society, where no one has one exclusive sphere of activity but each can become accomplished in any branch he wishes" and where it is "possible for me to hunt in the morning, fish in the afternoon, rear cattle in the evening, criticize after dinner, just as I have a mind, without ever becoming hunter, fisherman, shepherd or critic." See also *Capital* (Moscow, 1959), I, pp. 483–4 and Engels, *Anti-Dühring* (Moscow, 1959), pp. 403 and 409. On the other hand, Marx seems to have changed his attitude at the end of his life to a concern with leisure in the "realm of freedom."

individual roles, man's relationship with man and with woman will become fully human, that is, fully reciprocal and imbued with respect for the uniqueness of the individual. As Marx says, "the relation of man to woman is the most *natural* relation of human being to human being. . . . It also shows how far man's needs have become human needs, and consequently how far the other person, as a person, has become one of his needs, and to what extent he is in his individual existence at the same time a social being." Thus Marx assumes that the full realization of human powers and "the return of man himself as a *social,* i.e. really human, being" can only take place in a world in which man is free to apply himself to whatever activity he chooses and where his activities and his way of seeing himself and other men are not dictated by a system within which he and they play specified roles.

Durkheim saw human nature as essentially in need of limits and discipline. His view of man is of a being with potentially limitless and insatiable desires, who needs to be controlled by society. He writes:

To limit man, to place obstacles in the path of his free development, is this not to prevent him from fulfilling himself? But . . . this limitation is a condition of our happiness and moral health. Man, in fact, is made for life in a determinate, limited environment. . . .

"Health" for man in society is a state where "a regulative force" plays "the same role for moral needs which the organism plays for physical needs," which makes men "contented with their lot, while stimulating them moderately to improve it" and results in that "calm, active happiness . . . which characterizes health for societies as well as for individuals." Durkheim's picture of a healthy society in modern Europe is of a society that is organized and meritocratic, with equality of opportunity and personal liberty, where men are attached to intermediary groups by stable loyalties rather than being atomized units caught in an endemic conflict, and where they fulfil determinate functions in an organized system of work, where they conform in their mental horizons, their desires and ambitions to what their role in society demands and where there are clear-cut rules defining limits to desire and ambition in all spheres of life. There should be "rules telling each of the workers his rights and duties, not vaguely in general terms but in precise detail" and "each in his sphere vaguely realizes the extreme limit set to his ambitions and aspires to nothing beyond . . . he respects regulations and is docile to collective authority, that is, has a wholesome moral constitution." Man must be governed by "a conscience superior to his own, the superiority of which he feels": men cannot assign themselves the "law of justice" but "must receive it from an authority which they respect and to which they yield spontaneously." Society alone "as a whole or through the agency of one of its organs, can play this moderating role." It alone can "stipulate law" and "set the point beyond which the passions must not go"; and it alone "can estimate the reward to be prospectively offered to every class of human functionary, in the name of the common interest". . . .

What is the relevance of these concepts today? This question needs to be subdivided into three more specific questions, which follow the lines of the preceding argument. First, how valid is the empirical hypothesis which each embodies? To what extent do they succeed in identifying and adequately explaining phenomena in modern industrial societies? Second, how plausible is the theory of human nature which each presupposes? What does the evidence from past and present societies, from sociology and psychology, suggest about the plausibility of their respective hypothetical predictions, and about the nature of the changes which men and institutions would have to undergo to attain the conditions they predict and advocate? And third, how desirable is the ideal, how attractive is the vision to which each ultimately appeals? How today is one to evaluate these ideals: what degree of approximation to either, or both (or neither), are we to think desirable?

These questions are challenging and far-reaching. Here I shall raise them and offer tentative suggestions as to how one might begin to answer them.

I   One problem in answering the first question is to know at what level of generality it is being posed. How *specifically* is one to read Marx's account of alienation and Durkheim's of anomie? Marx and Durkheim identified certain features of their own societies and offered explanations of them. But they may also be seen to have identified features characteristic of a number of societies including their own; indeed, one may even see them, to some extent, as having identified features which may be said to characterize any conceivable society. Is it a specific type of technology, or form of organization, or structure of the economy, or is it the existence of classes or of private property, or the accumulation of capital, or the division of labour, or industrial society, or the human condition which is the crucial determinant of alienation? Is it the lack of a specific type of industrial organization (technical or administrative?), or the absence of appropriate occupational groups, or an economy geared to the pursuit of profit, or the cultural imperatives of a "success ethic," or the fact of social mobility, or the erosion of a traditionally stable framework of authority, or social change, or industrial society, or the human condition, that is the major factor leading to anomie? Alienation and anomie are phenomena which have particular aspects, unique to particular forms of society or institution, other aspects which are more general and still others which are universal. We may attempt to identify new forms of these phenomena, using these concepts and the hypotheses they embody

in the attempt to describe and explain them. They are in this sense concepts of "the middle range." They allow for specific new hypotheses to account for particular new forms, or they may account for them by means of the existing, more general hypotheses. In general, the contemporary forms of alienation and anomie are best approached on the understanding that their causes are multiple and to be sought at different levels of abstraction. A systematic investigation of alienation and anomie would range from the most particular to the most universal in the search for causes.

Marx and Durkheim attributed, as we have seen, certain types of mental condition (specified positively, in terms of what occurs, and negatively, in terms of what is precluded) to certain types of social condition. Marx pointed to meaninglessness of work and a sense of powerlessness to affect the conditions of one's life, dissociation from the products of one's labour, the sense of playing a role in an impersonal system which one does not understand or control, the seeing of oneself and others within socially-imposed and artificial categories, the denial of human possibilities for a fully creative, spontaneous, egalitarian and reciprocal communal life. He attributed these, in particular, to the form taken by the division of labour under capitalism and, more generally, to the fact of class society. Durkheim pointed to greed, competitiveness, status-seeking, the sense of having rights without duties, the concentration on consumption and pleasure, the lack of a sense of community with others, of a feeling of limits to one's desires and aspirations, and of the experience of fulfilling a useful function and serving a purpose higher than one's own self-interest, and the denial of human possibilities for an ordered and balanced life, where everyone knows his station and its duties. He attributed these, in particular, to the industrial revolution and the failure of society to provide appropriate groups to adjust to it, and, more generally, to social disorganization.

We are familiar with countless examples of these phenomena, though in many cases not all the features isolated by the concepts are necessarily present. Let me give just two examples.

Alienation is found today in perhaps its most acute form among workers in assembly-line industries, such as the motor-car industry, where, as Blauner writes in his sensitive study of workers' alienation, "the combination of technological, organizational and economic factors has resulted in the simultaneous intensification of all the dimensions of alienation." Here, in the extreme situation, "a depersonalized worker, estranged from himself and larger collectives, goes through the motions of work in the regimented milieu of the conveyor-belt for the sole purpose of earning his bread," "his work has become almost completely compartmentalized from other areas of his life, so that there is little meaning left in it beyond the instrumental purpose," and it is "unfree and unfulfilling and exemplifies the bureaucratic combination of the highly rational organization and the restricted specialist. In relation to the two giant bureaucracies which dominate his life, he is relatively powerless, atomized, depersonalized, and anonymous."[6]

Likewise, anomie is noticeably evident and acute among "the Unattached," well described by Mary Morse, especially those in "Seagate"—the drifting, purposeless and unstable teenagers, who felt no connection with or obligation to family, work, school or youth organization, the children of *nouveau riche* parents, suffering from "a sense of boredom, failure and restlessness" and refusing "to accept limitations, whether their own or external." Often there was "a failure to achieve unrealistic or unattainable goals they had set

for themselves or had had set for them"; also there was "a general inability to postpone immediate pleasure for the sake of future gain," there was "a craving for adventure," and "leisure-time interests were short-spanned, constantly changing and interspersed liberally with periods of boredom and apathy." Finally, they showed "pronounced hostility towards adults," adult discipline was quite ineffective and, in general, "all adults in authority were classed as 'them'—those who were opposed to and against 'us'."[7]

These are merely two instances, but they illustrate the general point made above. The causes of alienation and anomie must be sought at different levels of abstraction. At the most specific level, all sorts of special factors may be of primary importance. In a case of alienation, it may be the technical or organizational character of an industry or the structure of a bureaucracy; in a case of anomie, it may be a combination of personal affluence and a breakdown, rejection or conflict of norms of authority at home, at school and at work. But clearly, too, the nature of the wider society is of crucial importance. The extent and nature of social stratification, the structure of the economy, the character of the political system, the pace of industrialization, the degree of pluralism, the nature of the predominant social values—all these will affect the nature and distribution of alienation and anomie. Again, one can plausibly argue that *some* degree of alienation and of anomie is inseparable from life in an industrial society, characterized as it is, on the one hand, by the ramifying growth of organization and bureaucracy in all spheres of life, by economic centralization and by the increasing remoteness and technical character of politics; and, on the other, by built-in and permanent social changes, by the impermanence of existing status hierarchies

[6] R. Blauner, *Alienation and Freedom: The Factory Worker and his Industry* (Chicago and London, 1964), pp. 182 and 122.

[7] M. Morse, *The Unattached* (Penguin Books, London, 1965), pp. 75–6 and 28–9.

and the increasing role given to personal ambition and career mobility. And at the most general level, they may each be seen to relate to the most universal features of social structure and social change. In this sense, some alienation must exist wherever there are reified social relations, socially-given roles and norms; while some anomie must exist wherever hierarchies disintegrate and social control is weakened.

II What about the plausibility of Marx's and Durkheim's theories of human nature? They each had definite views about men's needs, which they believed to be historically generated and empirically ascertainable. How plausible today is the picture of mutually co-operative individuals, each realizing a wide range of creative potentialities, in the absence of specific role-expectations, lasting distinctions between whole categories of men and externally imposed discipline, in conditions of inner and social harmony, where all participate in planning and controlling their environment? What, on the other hand, is the plausibility of the view of human happiness, in which men are socialized into specific roles, regulated, and to some extent repressed, by systems of rules and group norms (albeit based on justice, equality of opportunity and respect for the individual), serving the purposes of society by fulfilling organized functions—all of which they accept and respect as constituting a stable framework for their lives?

These questions confront all those who hold versions of these ideals today. One cannot begin to appraise either, or compare them with one another, until one has come to some view about the likelihood of either being realized. What evidence is there that if the social conditions are constituted in the way Marx and Durkheim wanted, men would experience and would value highly the satisfactions of which they speak? Here one would, for example, need to examine all the ac-

cumulated evidence throughout history of experiments in community-living and in workers' control, of communes, collective farms and kibbutzim, on the one hand; and of experience in "human relations" and personnel management, of professionalism and of life in organizations, on the other. There is a vast amount of such evidence available, but it has never been systematically reviewed in this light.

Let us look at two examples in this connection. In the opinion of Friedmann the Israeli kibbutz represents "an original and successful application, on a limited scale, of communist principles," nearer to "the ethical ideal defined by the philosophy of Marx and Engels (for instance, with regard to the role of money, the distinction between manual and intellectual labour, family life)" than life in Moscow or on a kolkhoz. "The kibbutz movement," he writes, "despite its limitations and its difficulties, constitutes the fullest and most successful 'utopian' revolutionary experiment, the one which approximates most closely to the forms of life which communism has assigned itself as an aim. It is in the kibbutzim that I have met men of ample culture, and even creators, artists, writers, technicians, among whom the contradiction between intellectual and manual work, denounced by Marx, is truly eliminated in their daily life." Friedmann goes on, of course, to qualify and elaborate this: in particular, he outlines the perpetual confrontation between the kibbutzim and the wider society, devoted to economic growth and "imbued with models of abundance, where, with the development of the private sector, there is proclaimed a sort of material and moral New Economic Plan."[8] He examines the attempts of the kibbutzim to reduce to a minimum the tensions and frustrations of community life and asks the crucial questions:

[8] G. Friedmann, *Fin du Peuple Juif?* (Paris, Gallimard, 1965), pp. 95, 99, 96.

whether the kibbutz will be able to adapt to the economic and technical demands of an industrial society, while retaining its essential values; and whether the wider society will evolve in a direction that is compatible or incompatible with these values.

Let us take a second example, which relates to the plausibility of Durkheim's ideal, the overcoming of anomie. Perhaps the best instance is the evidence accumulated and interpreted by the theorists of modern managerialism, concerned to remedy "the acquisitiveness of a sick society"[9] and treating the factory, the corporation and the large organization as "a social system." Particularly relevant are the writings of the "organicists," whose aim is to promote "the values of social stability, cohesion and integration"[10] and to achieve, within the "formal organization" (the "explicitly stated system of control introduced by the company") the "creation and distribution of satisfactions" among the members of the system.[11] Selznick, who typifies the attempt to explore communal values within large corporations and administrative organizations, argues that the organization requires "stability" in its lines of authority, subtle patterns of informal relationships, "continuity" in its policies and "homogeneity" in its outlook.[12] Another writer describes its reification and normative significance for those who participate in it in the following terms—terms of which Durkheim might well have approved: "One might almost say that the organization has a character, an individuality, which makes the name real. The

scientist will not accept any such reification or personalizing of an organization. But participants in these organizations are subject to no such scientific scruples, and generations of men have felt and thought about the organizations they belonged to as something real in themselves."[13] For Selznick, social order and individual satisfaction are reconciled when "the aspirations of individuals are so stimulated and controlled, and so ordered in their mutual relations, as to produce the desired balance of forces."[14]

I have merely suggested two areas in which one might look for evidence that is relevant to the plausibility of the hypothetical predictions which partially constitute Marx's and Durkheim's theories of human nature. Clearly there is much else that is relevant in, for instance, the work of industrial sociologists, social psychologists, in community studies and the writings of organization theorists. It is also important to look at what evidence there is about the prevalence of existing tendencies in modern societies which favour or hinder the sorts of changes which would be necessary in order to approach these ideals. Here it would be necessary to look, for example, at the changes in the nature of occupations brought about by automation—the replacement of the detail worker by the more educated and responsible technician; at the effects of economic planning on small-scale decision-making; at the effects of the growth of organizations on status aspirations; at contemporary trends in consumption patterns. All this, and much else, is relevant to an assessment of the costs of approaching either ideal in our societies. Without these detailed inquiries, it is hardly possible to state firm conclusions, but it would appear that Durkheim's ideal is much nearer to and easier of realization in the industrial

[9] E. Mayo, *The Human Problems of an Industrial Civilisation* (New York, Macmillan, 1933), pp. 152–3.

[10] I am particularly indebted in the discussion of this example to the pages on this subject in S. S. Wolin, *Politics and Vision* (London, Allen and Unwin, 1961), pp. 407–14.

[11] F. J. Roethlisberger and W. J. Dickson, *Management and the Worker* (Cambridge, Mass., Harvard University Press, 1939), p. 551.

[12] Wolin, *op. cit.,* p. 412.

[13] E. W. Bakke, *Bonds of Organization,* quoted in Wolin, *op. cit.,* p. 506.

[14] P. Selznick, *Leadership in Administration,* quoted in Wolin, p. 413.

societies of both West and East than is that of Marx.

III Finally, how is one to evaluate these ideals? To do so involves a commitment to values and an assessment of costs. Either may be seen to conflict with other values or may not be considered to be worth the cost of its realization. Both sociological evidence and conceptual inquiry are relevant in the attempt to decide these matters, but in the end what is required is an ultimate and personal commitment (for which good, or bad, reasons may, none the less, be advanced). One may, of course, hold, as both Marx and Durkheim in different ways did, that one's values are, as it were, embedded in the facts, but this is itself a committed position (for which, again, good, or bad, reasons may be advanced).

This is no place to argue about these matters at the length they require. Let it be sufficient to say that these two quite opposite and incompatible ideals represent in a clear-cut form two major currents of critical and normative thinking about society, to be found throughout the whole tradition of political and social theory in the West and still very much in evidence. It is becoming increasingly common for

that tradition to be attacked, by the advocates of a "scientific" social and political theory, as being rudimentary and speculative, and lacking in scientific detachment. It is all rather like Sir James Frazer's view of primitive religion as "bastard science." What is required, it is argued, is the abandonment of concepts which are internally related to theories of the good life and the good society. Evaluation of this sort should be kept strictly apart from the process of scientific inquiry.

Yet the desire for scientific rigour is not in itself incompatible with the sort of inquiry which is concerned precisely to put to the task of empirical analysis concepts which have the type of relation I have outlined to theories of human nature and thereby to prior evaluative perspectives. This type of inquiry is exactly what has primarily characterized social and political theory in the past (under which heading I include the writings of the classical and many modern sociologists). The case for eliminating it necessarily involves advocating the abandonment of the application of models of alternative and preferred forms of life to the critical analysis of actual forms. That case has yet to be made convincing.

THE VARIETIES OF ALIENATION: AN ATTEMPT AT DEFINITION

Kenneth Keniston

Although formal discussions of alienation itself are largely limited to the last 150 years, the theme of alienation—of estrangement, outcastness, and loss—is an archetypal theme in human life and his-

SOURCE: From *The Uncommitted*, 451, 453–458, 460–474, copyright, 1962, 1965, by Kenneth Keniston. Reprinted by permission of Harcourt Brace Jovanovich, Inc. and the author.

tory. Adam and Eve were estranged from God and outcast from Eden; and since then in every tradition known, themes of irrevocable loss of former closeness abound in myth, literature, history, and life. The myth of the hero is typically a tale of the alienation and exile which precede his heroic return to his native home.

The history of nations is in part a history of wandering, exile, outcastness, and the search for a homeland. The chronicle of innovation, too, involves the repudiation of established patterns and values in order to create new ones. Revolutionaries from Christ to Castro have been separated from their homes by emigration, exile, and ostracism, and have returned from their alienation in the desert or the mountains only when they could bring new doctrines by persuasion and force. In all religions, the possibility of man's estrangement from the Divine Order is fundamental; indeed, perhaps the central function of religion is to prevent this estrangement of man from God and God from man. The possibility of "alienation" is predicated on the nature of human development, of social organization, of religious thought, and of history. . . .

Four Questions About Alienation

Although in ordinary speech we often speak of someone simply as "alienated," in fact we always imply he is alienated *from* something or someone. Husbands become alienated from their wives, peasants from their land, workers from their labor, men from their gods, societies from their traditional virtues. Alienation always has an object or a *focus*. For example, "self-alienation" as discussed by Fromm, Horney, and others, implies a lack of connection between an individual and some deep, vital, and valuable part of himself. Or the "alienation of the intellectual" implies his lack of commitment to the values of his society. Or the "alienation of the modern worker" points to his lack of relationship to the work process or to his own labor. And although a lack of connection in one area *may* generalize to other areas, it need not always. The alienated intellectual may be unalienated from his inner "productivity" or "real self"; the alienated worker may be at least superficially unalienated from the values of the industrial society that is purportedly alienating him.

Thus, the first question to ask of alienation is, "Alienated from what?"

Secondly, the concept of alienation does not specify what alienation consists of. The rhetoric of the concept implies that something desirable, natural, or normal has been lost—that is, that a positive relationship has ceased to exist. But we need to specify what replaces the lost relationship. If a Communist becomes alienated from the Party, we do not know whether he is merely disenchanted, whether he now vehemently rejects Communism, whether he no longer cares about politics at all, or whether he blames himself for his loss of his old faith. In many cases, alienation merely implies lack of any relationship at all—detachment and indifference; but in other cases, it implies active rejection, vehement opposition, open hostility. A second question to ask of alienations, then, is "What relationship if any, has replaced the lost one?"

Thirdly, alienation can be expressed in a variety of ways. In one sense the revolutionary and the psychotic are both highly alienated from the norms and values of their society—both reject these norms and values. Yet there is a vast difference in the way their rejection is expressed: the revolutionary actively attempts to transform his society; the psychotic has undergone a regressive self-transformation that leaves his society relatively unaffected. One major way of classifying alienation is therefore according to their *mode:* e.g., whether they are alloplastic (i.e., they involve an attempt to transform the world) or autoplastic (they involve self-transformation). Finally, alienations have different agents or sources: some are imposed while others are chosen. Merely to note that an individual is "alienated from society" does not tell us whether he deliberately rejects his society or whether it excludes him. Most of the sociological discussions of alienation that derive from Marx's work deal with imposed alienations (of which the alienated individual remains largely unaware). For Fromm or Kahler the alienated man is rarely aware that he is alienated from his work or himself. Indeed, paradoxically, the dawning of awareness of such imposed alienation usually entails the growth of a new chosen alienation from capitalist-industrialist society, and thus marks the end of self-alienation and alienation from work. To be sure, imposed and chosen alienations may be intimately connected: the rejected man may reject those who have rejected him. But often, these two forms of alienation are unrelated, as with the Black Bourgeoisie which accepts the values and norms of the white society from which it is excluded, or as with the successful alienated artist who is accepted and embraced by the very bourgeois society he repudiates. Thus, a further question relevant to a definition of alienations is "Who (or what) is the agent of the alienation?"

In brief, then, while the concept of alienation in every variation suggests the loss or absence of a previous or desirable relationship, it requires further specification in at least four respects:

1. *Focus:* Alienated from what?
2. *Replacement:* What replaces the old relationship?
3. *Mode:* How is the alienation manifest?
4. *Agent:* What is the agent of the alienation?

These four questions provide a basis for a virtually limitless number of varieties of alienation. One can be alienated from almost anything; an enormous number of new kinds of relationships may replace the lost one; alienation may be expressed in a great variety of modes, and have a great number of agents. In fact, however, most discussions of alienation concentrate on a relatively limited number of possibilities, some of which I will discuss below. For purposes of clarity, I will reserve the term "alienation" for only one of these possibilities—for an explicit rejection, "freely"

chosen by the individual, of what he perceives as the dominant values or norms of his society—and will use other terms to characterize other types of alienation.

Some Types of "Alienation"
COSMIC OUTCASTNESS

For Inburn*, it will be recalled, human existence was "a short time spent in a physical world with inscrutable void on the other side," a time without inherent meaning or purpose, a time unconsciously felt to involve a "Fall," an exile from purpose, warmth, and meaning. Central to this outlook (which is common to many alienated young men) is a sense of existential outcastness, of "thrownness" into a world not made for man and indifferent to his fate. In previous centuries in Western society, this same sense of cosmic outcastness was usually expressed as a sense of religious outcastness, as a fall from grace, as loss of faith, or as an estrangement from God. In the twentieth century, however, this sense is probably best expressed in existentialism, with its denial that the world has essential meaning. Human life is in this context "absurd," lacking inherent purpose: "meaning" must be artificially manufactured by men in the process of existence. And since any one man's answers to the riddles of life are individual and private, they will often be irrelevant and meaningless to other men. Truth is subjective and solipsistic. . . .

Psychologically, it is not easy to accept the death of God (and of all the structures premised on His existence) without a feeling of deprivation and rage. Most modern accounts of man's existential outcastness —of his "thrownness" into the world, of the inherent absurdity of existence, of the difficulty in communion between men— though they are presented as "factual," also convey a resentment, anger, bitterness, and disillusion that we have seen in

* Ed. note: Inburn is the name Keniston gave to a prototypical alienated student discussed in *The Uncommitted.*

the philosophies of alienated students. Men never feel bitter about "facts" unless the "facts" are felt to be disappointingly different from some unstated alternative. Here the alternative is clear—a lost world view in which the universe was made for Man by a caring God, truth was objective, and men could communicate by referring to a shared objective reality. Inevitably, then, disappointment and bitterness have accompanied the progressive erosion of faith that God made the universe as the arena for man's salvation. Those who feel most outcast from the cosmos are of course those whose individual lives sensitize them to these themes: their feelings of cosmic outcastness usually parallel more personal themes of alienation. But at the same time, what they experience acutely is a problem that inevitably and increasingly affects modern men.

DEVELOPMENTAL ESTRANGEMENTS

Behind the sense of existential outcastness in alienated students we have seen another kind of "alienation"—a sense of the loss in individual life of ties and relationships that can never be re-created. These "alienations," which I will call "developmental estrangements," are crucial and salient in the lives of alienated students; but comparable if milder estrangements exist in the lives of us all. . . . For in all human development, forward growth and development means the abandonment, loss, or renunciation of what went before. . . .

The first expulsion is from the womb. Especially in times of illness, stress, and fatigue, we all still long, if not for the prenatal state itself, then for those of its qualities which an adult can allow himself to desire—security, warmth, protection, even oblivion. The fantasies and sometimes the expressed wishes of small children clearly express their desire to be inside, protected, surrounded, and forever united with their mothers; and though adults consider such desires "regressive,"

we often forget that untroubled sleep gives us all much the same security, warmth, and sanctuary.

Yet the "trauma" of birth is not only a trauma but an event vitally necessary for both mother and neonate, without which neither can survive; and if all goes well the mother experiences not so much a loss as a joyous gain. For the infant, too, timely birth enables him (who would otherwise begin to waste in the womb) to enter the world and the long course of human development. For most of us birth symbolizes not so much expulsion from a desirable oblivion as the opening of a new world; and the meanings of birth are universally joyous and glad. Occasionally, to be sure, the losses outweigh the gains, as when the mother cannot bear to exchange the fetus within for the infant without, or when the newborn arrives ill-equipped to cope with the world. But what usually prevail, psychologically and physically, are the forces of forward movement. . . .

The later estrangements of development follow much the same pattern. Psychologically, perhaps the most fundamental of these estrangements is the loss of the early mother-child relationship. The mere fact of physiological maturation forces a child to move from unthinking dependence on a mother not yet differentiated from the rest of the world to a more and more qualified and realistic awareness of what his mother can and will do for him, and when. This loss of symbiotic dependency comes at the same time as, and partly because of, his enormously increased powers of observation, discrimination, and conceptualization. As is usually true, the satisfactions of one period promote the very qualities that will lead to the later abandonment of these satisfactions: if all goes well, the infant abandons his infancy eagerly.

The estrangements from the womb and from infantile dependency are followed by a gradual move away from total control by parents to more and more self-control. We ordinarily think of the birth of will as an emancipation, not a loss; yet in adulthood many men and women secretly long to abandon their free will, and they often manage to bequeath its effective exercise to others—spouses, employers, and political leaders. Even in early childhood the first beginnings of will and self-control entail new responsibilities for one's deeds and misdeeds; and as all parents know, some children find it easier for a time to relinquish autonomy and responsibility to Mother. And other children, though they insist on autonomy, are for a time unwilling to pay its price of growing responsibility. These related events—the gradual development of will and autonomy, the concurrent advent of responsibility, blame, and guilt, the loss of moral innocence—constitute another universal theme in myth and literature: many religions, for example, promise relief from responsibilities and blame if one will only will the will of God. . . .

The estrangements of adulthood are usually less obvious to us, for most current psychologies overemphasize the visible dramas of early years and neglect the more gradual changes of adulthood. But every stage in development involves the same dialectic of estrangement and growth. Marriage entails an enormous gain in intimacy and sharing at the same time that it means a loss of freedom and irresponsibility. So, too, the birth of children requires from parents an enormous curtailment of personal self-seeking and egocentricity while it also gives them a sense of tangible connection with the future and an unprecedented expansion of themselves into their children. Especially for a man, adult work can mean tangible accomplishments, useful achievements, and even creativity; but it also involves a further increase in social responsibilities and involvedness. For men and women alike, the maturation of their children means a loss of the mutual dependence between parents and children, though at the

same time it is the much desired fruition of years of effort in rearing these children. The advent of old age, with its steady physical decline and progressive loss of strength, also means gaining a new freedom from the cares and responsibilities of the rest of life. And the contemplation of proximate death can mean both the despair of life's inevitably unfulfilled potentials and the satisfactions of recalling what one has done and been.

Every stage of human development, then, necessarily involves a dialectic between estrangement from the past and growth into a future where past needs must be modified, and new needs, requirements, and satisfactions must be accepted. Most men and women find the future powerful enough not only to pull them into it but to erase any conscious nostalgia for the past. Nonetheless this nostalgia persists in some corner of all our psyches, making us unconsciously responsive to (and sometimes angrily repudiative of) the complaints of those who wish aloud to go home again. . . .

HISTORICAL LOSS

Like individual life, historical development invariably entails a dialectic between gain and loss. Most social innovations replace customs, outlooks, or technologies that are in that measure left behind; and those who are most firmly attached to what has been replaced inevitably mourn their loss. In a time like our own, when social change is rapid, worldwide, and chronic, one of the most keenly felt "alienations" is the acute sense of historical loss. . . .

In retrospect, such historical losses as these now seem to us more than outweighed by the social and human gains they brought: few men now mourn the nomadic life. But as we approach the present, the balance of historical loss and historical gain is harder to strike. Partly, no doubt, this is because we find it most difficult to judge what we are closest to. But lack of historical distance alone will not adequately explain the deep ambivalence with which many men of the twentieth century view the gains of our own era. For, while in every society some few men have always regretted the passing of older ways, it is indicative of our modern collective ambivalence to historical change that systematic discussions of alienations, estrangement, and historical loss have been largely confined to the past century. Many such discussions have been indirectly or directly inspired by Marx, who in his early writings made "alienation" a central concept in his diagnosis of the evils of capitalist society. For Marx, "alienation" means above all the worker's loss of control over his own labor in a capitalist economy: in factory labor, what the worker makes is no longer his own—as it was for the craftsman or the free farmer. This alienation from his labor has far-reaching consequences: the very act of working, which should be a man's fundamental mode of relationship to the world, increasingly becomes merely a way of earning his economic subsistence. Thus, the worker becomes profoundly alienated from a central part of himself: he comes to see himself as a mere commodity to be sold on the marketplace, devoid of inherent human dignity. And finally, the worker extends his view of himself to others, and all human relationships degenerate into encounters between commodities, each of which has a price but none of which has dignity.

Although the young Marx's analysis of alienation also points to man's secondary estrangement from himself and from his fellows as a consequence of his primary loss of relationship to his work, the central meaning of "alienation" for Marx comes closest to the concept for historical loss. What is lost is a "natural," "integral" connection between men and their own work —a connection seen in the peasant, the artisan, the independent craftsman. Other "alienations" follow from this first and primary estrangement. Furthermore, for Marx, alienation was imposed and not chosen; its victims were usually unaware of the extent of their separation from their work, themselves, or their fellow men. Those most profoundly affected by the historical loss of an integral connection with work were the proletariat. Paradoxically, for Marx as for most modern neo-Marxists, alienation begins to end with the awareness of alienation: only by the awareness of alienation can a worker gain the "class-consciousness" which will enable him to struggle to create a classless society where men will no longer be alienated from their labor.

SELF-ESTRANGEMENT

For Marx, alienation from one's labor leads indirectly to alienation from one's self. For other writers, most notably Karen Horney, alienation from self—or what I will call "self-estrangement"—is primary and not derivative. Self-estrangement (or self-alienation) entails for Horney and her followers a lack of contact between the individual's "conscious self" and his "real self," manifest in a sense of unreality, emptiness, flatness, and boredom. The immediate origins of this condition are psychological, not social, although Horney allows that modern society may in turn encourage the psychological factors that promote self-estrangement. The individual is separated from that part of himself which is most "real," vital, and important. He is separated from his own deepest feelings, needs, and fantasies. As a result, his entire existence and his every act assume a quality of unreality: to observers, therapists, and even to himself, he seems not quite "there."

Other writers, most notably Fromm, Pappenheim, and Kahler, also use extensively a similar concept—although all agree with Marx in tracing its origins to the social conditions of modern capitalist (or industrial) society. For Fromm, for example, "self-alienation" involves a lack of contact between the individual's conscious self and his "productive" potential —the individual sees himself as a mere object among objects, and treats himself and others as commodities on the market. Self-alienation is therefore a primary characteristic of the "marketing personality;" absence of self-alienation becomes virtually synonymous with "productivity" and psychological soundness.

Despite its extensive use, the concept of self-estrangement often remains nebulous and difficult to define, partly because it presupposes a "real self" or a "capacity for productive living" which remains invisible though potential. In practice, then, self-estrangement is a term with more extensive normative connotations than empirical denotations; furthermore, one of the primary characteristics of the individual who is self-estranged is that he does not realize the extent of his separation from what is best within him. His alienation from himself is seen as largely imposed from without, either by malign psychological influences, or by the corrupting effects of capitalist society.

Individual Alienation

All of the aforementioned varieties of alienation, like most others which have been or could be distinguished, involve a loss of relationship whose agent is not the self. Furthermore, in each of these "alienations" the broken or absent relationship is replaced by no relationship at all. However, I have been concerned with another variety of alienation — with alienation whose immediate agent is the self (which is "freely" chosen rather than imposed) and with alienation that involves an active rejection of the focus of alienation (rather than merely the absence of relationship with it). In particular, I have started from a study of a group of youths who articulately and deliberately reject what they see as the dominant values of American society. And although I have argued that the sources of this alienation are complex—involving psychological, social, cultural,

and historical forces—the defining criterion of alienation in the sense I have used this term is the *explicit rejection of traditional American culture.* At the same time, however, I have argued that the deliberate and conscious rejection of our dominant cultural values among these students is not the only form of individual alienation. It may prove helpful, therefore, to distinguish more systematically some of the varieties of individual alienation, and to examine their relationship to each other.

A Classification of Alienations and Conformisms

I earlier noted four questions that must be answered in any attempt to define the meanings of "alienation." Two of these questions have already been answered with regard to what I am calling "individual alienation." First, the alienated individual is the agent of his own alienation; he chooses to be alienated; his alienation is conscious and largely egosyntonic. Second, what replaces the original or "natural" relationship is a stance of manifest rejection. Defined as a general psychological attitude, individual alienation can therefore be seen as one end of a continuum that runs from alienation (rejection) through commitment to conformism (compulsive acceptance) at the other end. Any specific attitude toward a set of behavioral norms or cultural values can, in principle, be placed somewhere along this continuum. And since we are dealing with a continuum, rather than with a dichotomy, it becomes important in each case to specify the *degree of alienation/conformism* involved. At the extreme of alienation, we would place acute psychoses, total cultural refusals, subversive and revolutionary activities, sociopathic criminality, etc. Less alienated, but still involving a rejection of central behavioral norms and/or values would be such common phenomena as non-conformity, neurosis, detachment, and social reform. And at the far extreme of conformism, we would include repressive policing activities, slavish social acquiescence, compulsive psychological conformity, Babbittry, the politics of reaction, and extreme cultural traditionalism. Closer to the center of the continuum, but still toward the conformism end, we would locate asceticism, accommodation, compliance, traditionalism, and conservatism.

These examples indicate that a classification of individual alienations merely in terms of degree of alienation/conformism is not enough. For a more adequate classification, we must return to the two remaining questions introduced in earlier pages: What is the *focus* of alienation? In what *mode* is the alienation expressed?

Although I have earlier suggested that alienation may have many foci, two of them are particularly relevant to this discussion. These are a focus on *behavioral norms* as contrasted with a focus on *cultural values*. Behavioral norms are the common social expectations about the kind of behavior that is proper, appropriate, and legal in any society. Sometimes such expectations are sanctioned by law and coercive police power: their rejection therefore involves criminality and delinquency; in other cases, social norms are sanctioned merely by social approval and disapproval, and those who violate these norms will merely be considered non-conformists. "Cultural values," on the other hand, refer not to specific expectations about behavior but to general conceptions of the desirable. Normally, the precise behavioral implications of any general cultural value require considerable specification: e.g., it is not immediately obvious what behavior should follow from accepting a value like "progress," "achievement," or "democracy."

Turning to the second question, the mode of alienation/conformism, we can usefully classify the way in which alienation is expressed according to whether it is primarily *alloplastic* or *autoplastic*. Alloplastic alienations are those expressed primarily as attempts to change the world; autoplastic alienations are expressed through the mode of self-transformation.

It now becomes possible to classify individual alienations along three distinct dimensions: *attitude* (alienation vs. conformism), *focus* (behavioral norms vs. cultural values), and *mode* (alloplastic vs. autoplastic). Figures 1, 2, and 3 indicate the possibilities created by superimposing each of these continua upon the other. Figure 1 illustrates the cross-classification of attitude and focus: a rejection of behavioral norms is termed *violation,* to distinguish it from a rejection of cultural values, or *repudiation.* Acceptance of behavioral norms is termed [*obedience*] whereas acceptance of cultural values is called *confirmation.*

Figure 2 shows the cross-classification of attitude and mode. Alloplastic alienation involves *change,* whereas autoplastic alienation involves *maladaptation.* Conformism, when alloplastic, can be termed *conservation,* whereas autoplastic conformism involves *submission.*

Figure 3 shows the cross-classification of focus and mode. Combining alloplasticity with behavioral norms gives us the area of *activity,* whereas combining it with cultural values involves the issue of *ideology.* The autoplastic mode with regard to behavioral norms involves the question of *adjustment,* whereas the autoplastic mode and the matter of cultural values gives us the area of *internalization.*

In each of the first three figures, the terms in parentheses indicate the alternatives in the third dimension not included in each two-dimensional cross-classification. Thus, for example, in Figure 3, each of the eight major issues suggested by the cross-classification of focus and mode has both an alienated and a conformist end. Figure 3, with alienation/conformism added as a third dimension, can thus be visualized as a three-dimensional space, with the first, alienated, concepts above the surface of the page and the second,

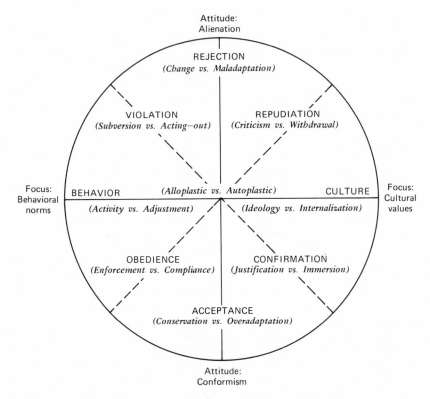

Figure 1. Attitude and focus.

conformist, concepts below the surface of the page. Figure 4 is a representation of the alienated plane of Figure 3, and gives us a classification of varieties of aliena-tion in eight major areas: these are sum-marized in the table below. Similarly, Fig-ure 5 shows us the non-alienated, con-formism, plane of Figure 3. Here, the same eight areas are involved in a classifi-cation of the varieties of conformism.

FOCUS/MODE	AREA	ALIENATION	CONFORMISM
1. norms	behavior	violation	obedience
2. norms/autoplastic	adjustment	"acting-out"	compliance
3. autoplastic	personality	maladaptation	over-adaptation
4. values/autoplastic	internalization	withdrawal	immersion
5. values	culture	repudiation	confirmation
6. values/alloplastic	ideology	criticism	justification
7. alloplastic	politics	change	conservation
8. norms/alloplastic	activity	subversion	enforcement

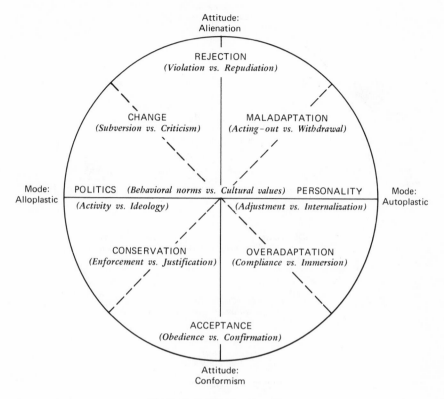

Figure 2. Attitude and mode.

Figures 4 and 5 now permit us to classify specific forms of alienation and conformism according to their approximate location along the two continua of focus and mode. Thus, for example, alienation expressed in the area of behavior may involve revolution, terrorism, criminality, delinquency, non-conformity, sociopathy; whereas conformism expressed in the same area will involve such attitudes as counterinsurgency, vigilantism, submission, compliance, and accommodation. Or, to take another example, alienation that is primarily focused on cultural values may take the form of artistic creativity, "inner emigration," cultural refusal, cultural innovation, etc.; whereas conformism in the area of values will be expressed in Babbittry, faithfulness, apologetics, custody of culture, or ideological conservatism.

The classification proposed and illustrated in Figures 4 and 5 is only one of the many classifications which might be or have been suggested. For example, Talcott Parsons in *The Social System* suggests a usage of "alienation" and "conformity" that broadly parallels that proposed here, and a different way of classifying alienations. Robert Merton's widely used classification of forms of deviance and conformity provides still another way of classifying the behavioral sequelae of alienations and conformisms. Both Parsons' and Merton's classifications differ from that

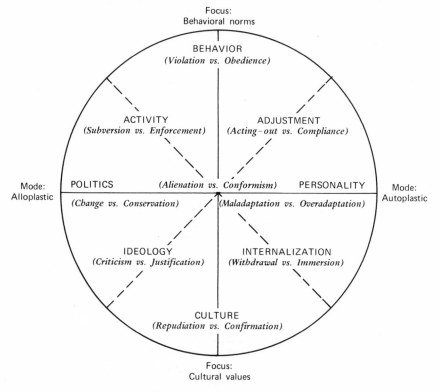

Figure 3. Focus and mode.

proposed here in that they are primarily sociological, emphasizing overt behavior, whereas this classification is psychological, a classification of attitudes. A sociological and psychological classification of alienation may not overlap perfectly: two individuals with identical attitudes may behave very differently, depending upon the situation in which they find themselves.

Furthermore, this classification of alienations is a classification of attitudes and not of individuals. The same individual can, and usually does, exhibit more than one form of alienation and/or conformism; indeed, an individual may be highly alienated in one area and conformist in another. For example, although most of the alienated students exhibited attitudes in the areas of repudation and withdrawal,

at least some combined extreme cultural refusal with marked neurotic trends, while others combined misanthropy and a mild tendency toward delinquency. Furthermore, any given individual may be markedly alienated in one area and markedly conformist in another: for example, the criminals studied in *The Authoritarian Personality* were markedly alienated in their norm-violating behavior; but at the same time, many were conformist in their political attitudes.

The ultimate usefulness of any effort at classification rests on its capacity to arrange observable phenomena in a way that is not only theoretically but empirically meaningful. The usefulness of this classification might be explored by attempting to answer some of the following questions.

Figure 4. Varieties of alienation.

1. Do extremely alienated individuals have common psychological characteristics regardless of the area in which their alienation is expressed? For example, rejection of paternal exemplars might be a factor of considerable etiological importance in *all* alienated attitudes among males.

2. Do individuals whose attitudes fall largely within one quadrant of Figure 4 exhibit other specific communalities: e.g., in family background, life style, life adjustment, fantasy, and ideology? For example, there is a striking similarity between the reported backgrounds of male homosexuals and male schizophrenics. Preliminary research on the common characteristics of students active in the civil rights movement suggests a different pattern of family constellation and filial attitude.

3. When an individual whose alienation is initially expressed largely in one area of Figure 4 changes, does he tend to move to a contiguous area? For example, observers have noted the tendency of political movements to change from initial social reformism to ever more radical and active efforts to change the status quo, which may end in revolution and even in terrorism (moving, as it were, around the edge of the diagram in Figure 4). Or, to take another example, the alienated students seemed to have two major alterna-

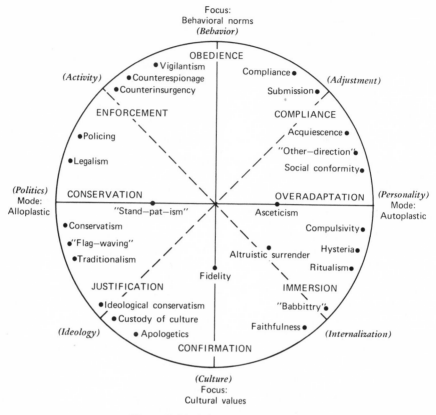

Figure 5. Variities of conformism.

tives—to move toward greater maladaptation or to move toward greater involvement in society; both moves would be to contiguous areas in Figure 4. Such students seem unlikely to become terrorists, criminals, or delinquents (a move which would involve a drastic "jump" across Figure 4).

4. When an individual becomes "converted" from extreme alienation to extreme conformism (or vice versa) does the *area* of his alienation/conformism remain the same? For example, revolutionaries and terrorists who suddenly switch to a conformist position by virtue of the success of their revolution probably tend to become policemen, vigilantes, and counterrevolutionaries rather than ritualists, "Babbitts," or apologists for the new regime. Similarly, "converted" social reformers and radicals often tend to become ideological defenders of the status quo or ideological authoritarians, rather than, for example, ascetics or social conformists. It would also seem reasonable to assume that "reformed" misanthropes tend toward "Babbittry" after their reform.

5. This classification would seem to suggest that common patterns may characterize individuals in any given quadrant of Figures 4 and 5, and that these patterns may contrast sharply with those found in polar opposites on these diagrams. For example, the common characteristics of homosexuals, addicts, schizophrenics and anomic individuals should contrast in

some ways with the patterns found among radicals, the civil-disobedient, the non-violent resisters, and social reformers. Or again, Figure 4 would suggest that the etiology of "acting-out" delinquency (so-ciopathy, juvenile delinquents, criminality) should be different in some ways from the etiology of cultural innovation, cultural refusal, social criticism and inner emigration.

ON THE MEANING OF ALIENATION*

Melvin Seeman

At the present time, in all the social sciences, the various synonyms of alienation have a foremost place in studies of human relations. Investigations of the "unattached," the "marginal," the "obsessive," the "normless," and the "isolated" individual all testify to the central place occupied by the hypothesis of alienation in contemporary social science.

So writes Robert Nisbet in *The Quest for Community*,[1] and there would seem to be little doubt that his estimate is correct. In one form or another, the concept of alienation dominates both the contemporary literature and the history of sociological thought. It is a central theme in the classics of Marx, Weber, and Durkheim; and in contemporary work, the consequences that have been said to flow from the fact of alienation have been diverse, indeed.

Ethnic prejudice, for example, has been described as a response to alienation—as an ideology which makes an incomprehensible world intelligible by imposing upon that world a simplified and categorical "answer system" (for example, the Jews cause international war).[2] In his examination of the persuasion process in the Kate Smith bond drive, Merton emphasizes the significance of pervasive distrust: "The very same society that produces this sense of alienation and estrangement generates in many a craving for reassurance, an acute need to believe, a flight into faith"[3] —in this case, faith in the sincerity of the persuader. In short, the idea of alienation is a popular vehicle for virtually every kind of analysis, from the prediction of voting behavior to the search for *The Sane Society*.[4] This inclusiveness, in both its historical and its contemporary import, is expressed in Erich Kahler's remark: "The history of man could very well be written as a history of the alienation of man."[5]

SOURCE: Reprinted from the *American Sociological Review*, 24, 6 (December 1959), 783–791, by permission of the author and publisher.

*This paper is based in part on work done while the author was in attendance at the Behavorial Sciences Conference at the University of New Mexico, in the summer of 1958. The conference was supported by the Behavioral Sciences Division, Air Force Office of Scientific Research, under contract AF 49(638)-33. The work on alienation was carried out in close conjunction with Julian B. Rotter and Shephard Liverant of The Ohio State University. I gratefully acknowledge their very considerable help, while absolving them of any commitment to the viewpoints herein expressed.

[2] T. W. Adorno *et al.*, *The Authoritarian Personality*, New York: Harper, 1950, pp. 617 ff.

[3] R. K. Merton, *Mass Persuasion*, New York: Harper, 1946, p. 143.

[4] Erich Fromm, *The Sane Society*, New York: Rinehart, 1955.

[5] *The Tower and the Abyss*, New York: Braziller, 1957, p. 43.

[1] New York: Oxford, 1953, p. 15.

A concept that is so central in socio-logical work, and so clearly laden with value implications, demands special clarity. There are, it seems to me, five basic ways in which the concept of alienation has been used. The purpose of this paper is to examine these logically distinguishable usages, and to propose what seems a workable view of these five meanings of alienation. Thus, the task is a dual one: to make more organized sense of one of the great traditions in sociological thought; and to make the traditional interest in alienation more amenable to sharp empirical statement.

I propose, in what follows, to treat alienation from the personal standpoint of the actor—that is, alienation is here taken from the social-psychological point of view. Presumably, a task for subsequent experimental or analytical research is to determine (a) the social conditions that produce these five variants of alienation, or (b) their behavioral consequences. In each of the five instances, I begin with a review of where and how that usage is found in traditional sociological thought; subsequently, in each case, I seek a more researchable statement of meaning. In these latter statements, I focus chiefly upon the ideas of expectation and value.[6]

Powerlessness

The first of these uses refers to alienation in the sense of *powerlessness*. This is the notion of alienation as it originated in the Marxian view of the worker's condition in capitalist society: the worker is alienated to the extent that the prerogative and means of decision are expropriated by the ruling entrepreneurs. Marx, to be sure, was interested in other alienative aspects

of the industrial system; indeed, one might say that his interest in the powerlessness of the worker flowed from his interest in the consequences of such alienation in the work place—for example, the alienation of man from man, and the degradation of men into commodities.

In Weber's work, we find an extension beyond the industrial sphere of the Marxian notion of powerlessness. Of this extension, Gerth and Mills remark:

> Marx's emphasis upon the wage worker as being "separated" from the means of production becomes, in Weber's perspective, merely one special case of a universal trend. The modern soldier is equally "separated" from the means of violence; the scientist from the means of enquiry, and the civil servant from the means of administration.[7]

The idea of alienation as powerlessness is, perhaps, the most frequent usage in current literature. The contributors to Gouldner's volume on leadership, for example, make heavy use of this idea; as does the work of C. Wright Mills—and, I suppose, any analysis of the human condition that takes the Marxist tradition with any seriousness. This variant of alienation can be conceived as *the expectancy or probability held by the individual that his own behavior cannot determine the occurrence of the outcomes, or reinforcements, he seeks.*

Let us be clear about what this conception does and does not imply. First, it is a distinctly social-psychological view. It does not treat powerlessness from the standpoint of the objective conditions in society; but this does not mean that these conditions need be ignored in research dealing with this variety of alienation. These objective conditions are relevant, for example, in determining the degree of realism involved in the individual's re-

---

[6] The concepts of expectancy and reward, or reinforcement value, are the central elements in J. B. Rotter's "social learning theory"; see *Social Learning and Clinical Psychology*, New York: Prentice Hall, 1954. My discussion seeks to cast the various meanings of alienation in a form that is roughly consistent with this theory, though not formally expressed in terms of it.

[7] H. H. Gerth and C. W. Mills, *From Max Weber: Essays in Sociology*, New York: Oxford, 1946, p. 50.

sponse to his situation. The objective features of the situations are to be handled like any other situational aspect of behavior—to be analyzed, measured, ignored, experimentally controlled or varied, as the research question demands.

Second, this construction of "powerlessness" clearly departs from the Marxian tradition by removing the critical, polemic element in the idea of alienation. Likewise, this version of powerlessness does not take into account, as a definitional matter, the frustration an individual may feel as a consequence of the discrepancy between the control he may expect and the degree of control that he desires—that is, it takes no direct account of the value of control to the person.

In this version of alienation, then, the individual's expectancy for control of events is clearly distinguished from (a) the *objective* situation of powerlessness as some observer sees it, (b) the observer's *judgment* of that situation against some ethical standard, and (c) the individual's sense of a *discrepancy* between his expectations for control and his desire for control.

The issues in the philosophy of science, or in the history of science, on which these distinctions and decisions touch can not be debated here. Two remarks must suffice: (1) In any given research, any or all of the elements discussed above—expectancies, objective conditions, deviation from a moral standard, deviation from the actor's standards—may well be involved, and I see little profit in arguing about which is "really" alienation so long as what is going on at each point in the effort is clear. I have chosen to focus on expectancies since I believe that this is consistent with what follows, while it avoids building ethical or adjustmental features into the concept. (2) I do not think that the expectancy usage is as radical a departure from the Marxian legacy as it may appear. No one would deny the editorial character of the Marxian judgment, but it was a judgment about a state of affairs—the elimination of individual freedom and control. My version of alienation refers to the counterpart, in the individual's expectations, of that state of affairs.

Finally, the use of powerlessness as an expectancy means that this version of alienation is very closely related to the notion (developed by Rotter) of "internal *versus* external control of reinforcements." The latter construct refers to the individual's sense of personal control over the reinforcement situation, as contrasted with his view that the occurrence of reinforcements is dependent upon external conditions, such as chance, luck, or the manipulation of others. The congruence in these formulations leaves the way open for the development of a closer bond between two languages of analysis—that of learning theory and that of alienation—that have long histories in psychology and sociology. But the congruence also poses a problem —the problem of recognizing that these two constructs, though intimately related, are not generally used to understand the same things.[8]

In the case of alienation, I would limit the applicability of the concept to expectancies that have to do with the individual's

[8] Cf. W. H. James and J. B. Rotter, "Partial and One Hundred Percent Reinforcement under Chance and Skill Conditions," *Journal of Experimental Psychology,* 55 (May, 1958), pp. 397–403. Rotter and his students have shown that the distinction between internal and external control (a distinction which is also cast in expectancy terms) has an important bearing on learning theory. The propositions in that theory, they argue, are based too exclusively on experimental studies which simulate conditions of "external control," where the subject "is likely to perceive reinforcements as being beyond his control and primarily contingent upon external conditions" (p. 397). Compare this use of what is essentially a notion of powerlessness with, for example, Norman Podheretz's discussion of the "Beat Generation": "Being apathetic about the Cold War is to admit that you have a sense of utter helplessness in the face of forces apparently beyond the control of man." "Where is the Beat Generation Going?" *Esquire,* 50 (December, 1958), p. 148.

sense of influence over socio-political events (control over the political system, the industrial economy, international affairs, and the like). Accordingly, I would initially limit the applicability of this first meaning of alienation to the arena for which the concept was originally intended, namely, the depiction of man's relation to the larger social order. Whether or not such an operational concept of alienation is related to expectancies for control in more intimate need areas (for example, love and affection; status-recognition) is a matter for empirical determination. The need for the restriction lies in the following convictions: First, the concept of alienation, initially, should not be so global as to make the *generality* of powerlessness a matter of fiat rather than fact. Second, the concept should not be dangerously close to merely an index of personality *adjustment*—equivalent, that is, to a statement that the individual is maladjusted in the sense that he has a generally low expectation that he can, through his own behavior, achieve any of the personal rewards he seeks.[9]

[9] It seems best, in regard to the adjustment question, to follow Gwynn Nettler's view. He points out that the concepts of alienation and anomie should not "be equated, as they so often are, with personal disorganization defined as intrapersonal goallessness, or lack of 'internal coherence' . . . [their] bearing on emotional sickness must be independently investigated." "A Measure of Alienation," *American Sociological Review,* 22 (December, 1957), p. 672. For a contrasting view, see Nathan Glazer's "The Alienation of Modern Man," *Commentary,* 3 (April, 1947), p. 380, in which he comments: "If we approach alienation in this way, it becomes less a description of a single specific symptom than an omnibus of psychological disturbances having a similar root cause—in this case, modern social organization."

With regard to the question of the generality of powerlessness, I assume that high or low expectancies for the control of outcomes through one's own behavior will (a) vary with the behavior involved—e.g., control over academic achievement or grades, as against control over unemployment; and (b) will be differentially realistic in different areas (it is one thing to feel powerless

Meaninglessness

A second major usage of the alienation concept may be summarized under the idea of *meaninglessness*. The clearest contemporary examples of this usage are found in Adorno's treatment of prejudice; in Cantril's *The Psychology of Social Movements,* in which the "search for meaning" is used as part of the interpretive scheme in analyzing such diverse phenomena as lynchings, the Father Divine movement, and German fascism; and in Hoffer's portrait of the "true believer" as one who finds, and needs to find, in the doctrines of a mass movement "a master key to all the world's problems."[10]

This variant of alienation is involved in Mannheim's description of the increase of "functional rationality" and the concomitant decline of "substantial rationality." Mannheim argues that as society increasingly organizes its members with reference to the most efficient realization of ends (that is, as functional rationality increases), there is a parallel decline in the "capacity to act intelligently in a given situation on the basis of one's own insight into the interrelations of events."[11]

This second type of alienation, then, refers to the individual's sense of understanding the events in which he is engaged. We may speak of high alienation, in the meaninglessness usage, when *the individual is unclear as to what he ought to believe—when the individual's minimal*

with regard to war and quite another, presumably, to feel powerless in making friends). My chief point is that these are matters that can be empirically rather than conceptually solved; we should not, therefore, build either "generality" or "adjustment" into our concept of alienation. This same view is applied in the discussion of the other four types of alienation.

[10] See, respectively, Adorno *et al., op. cit.;* Hadley Cantril, *The Psychology of Social Movements,* New York: Wiley, 1941; and Eric Hoffer, *The True Believer,* New York: Harper, 1950, p. 90.

[11] Karl Mannheim, *Man and Society in an Age of Reconstruction,* New York: Harcourt, Brace, 1940, p. 59.

standards for clarity in decision-making are not met. Thus, the post-war German situation described by Adorno was "meaningless" in the sense that the individual could not choose with confidence among alternative explanations of the inflationary disasters of the time (and, it is argued, substituted the "Jews" as a simplified solution for this unclarity). In Mannheim's depiction, the individual cannot choose appropriately among alternative interpretations (cannot "act intelligently" or "with insight") because the increase in functional rationality, with its emphasis on specialization and production, makes such choice impossible.

It would seem, for the present at least, a matter of no consequence what the beliefs in question are. They may, as in the above instance, be simply descriptive beliefs (interpretations); or they may be beliefs involving moral standards (norms for behavior). In either case, the individual's choice among alternative beliefs has low "confidence limits": he cannot predict with confidence the consequences of acting on a given belief. One might operationalize this aspect of alienation by focusing upon the fact that it is characterized by a *low expectancy that satisfactory predictions about future outcomes of behavior can be made.* Put more simply, where the first meaning of alienation refers to the sensed ability to control outcomes, this second meaning refers essentially to the sensed ability to predict behavioral outcomes.

This second version of alienation is logically independent of the first, for, under some circumstances, expectancies for personal control of events may not coincide with the understanding of these events, as in the popular depiction of the alienation of the intellectual.[12] Still, there are obvious connections between these two forms of alienation: in some important degree, the view that one lives in an intelligible world may be a prerequisite to expectancies for control; and the unintelligi-

bility of complex affairs is presumably conducive to the development of high expectancies for external control (that is, high powerlessness).[13]

Normlessness

The third variant of the alienation theme is derived from Durkheim's description of "anomie," and refers to a condition of *normlessness*. In the traditional usage, anomie denotes a situation in which social norms regulating individual conduct have broken down or are no longer effective as rules for behavior. As noted above, Merton emphasizes this kind of rulelessness in his interpretation of the importance of the "sincerity" theme in Kate Smith's war bond drive:

> The emphasis on this theme reflects a social disorder—"anomie" is the sociological term—in which common values have been submerged in the welter of private interests seeking satisfaction by virtually any means which are effective. Drawn from a highly competitive, segmented urban society, our informants live in a climate of reciprocal

[12] C. Wright Mills' description reflects this view: "The intellectual who remains free may continue to learn more and more about modern society, but he finds the centers of political initiative less and less accessible. . . . He comes to feel helpless in the fundamental sense that he cannot control what he is able to foresee." *White Collar,* New York: Oxford, 1951, p. 157. The same distinction is found in F. L. Strodtbeck's empirical comparison of Italian and Jewish values affecting mobility: "For the Jew, there was always the expectation that everything could be understood, if perhaps not controlled." "Family Interaction, Values and Achievement," in D. C. McClelland *et al., Talent and Society,* New York: Van Nostrand, 1958, p. 155.

[13] Thorstein Veblen argues the same point, in his own inimitable style, in a discussion of "The Belief in Luck": ". . . the extra-causal propensity or agent has a very high utility as a recourse in perplexity" [providing the individual] "a means of escape from the difficulty of accounting for phenomena in terms of causal sequences." *The Theory of the Leisure Class,* New York: Macmillan, 1899; Modern Library Edition, 1934, p. 386.

distrust which, to say the least, is not conducive to stable human relationships. . . . The very same society that produces this sense of alienation and estrangement generates in many a craving for reassurance. . . .[14]

Elsewhere, in his well-known paper "Social Structure and Anomie," Merton describes the "adaptations" (the kinds of conformity and deviance) that may occur where the disciplining effect of collective standards has been weakened. He takes as his case in point the situation in which culturally prescribed goals (in America, the emphasis upon success goals) are not congruent with the available means for their attainment. In such a situation, he argues, anomie or normlessness will develop to the extent that "the technically most effective procedure, whether culturally legitimate or not, becomes typically preferred to institutionally prescribed conduct."[15]

Merton's comments on this kind of anomic situation serve to renew the discussion of the expectancy constructs developed above—the idea of meaninglessness, and the idea of powerlessness or internal-external control. For Merton notes, first, that the anomic situation leads to low predictability in behavior, and second, that the anomic situation may well lead to the belief in luck:

> Whatever the sentiments of the reader concerning the moral desirability of coordinating the goals-and-means phases of the social structure, it is clear that imperfect coordination of the two leads to anomie. Insofar as one of the most general functions of the social structure is to provide a basis for predictability and regularity of social behavior, it becomes increasingly limited in effectiveness as these elements of the social structure become dissociated. . . .
> The victims of this contradiction be-

tween the cultural emphasis on pecuniary ambition and the social bars to full opportunity are not always aware of the structural sources of their thwarted aspirations. To be sure, they are typically aware of a discrepancy between individual worth and social rewards. But they do not necessarily see how this comes about. Those who do find its source in the social structure may become alienated from that structure and become ready candidates for Adaptation V [rebellion]. But others, and this appears to include the great majority, may attribute their difficulties to more mystical and less sociological sources. . . . in such a society [a society suffering from anomie] people tend to put stress on mysticism: the workings of Fortune, Chance, Luck.[16]

It is clear that the general idea of anomie is both an integral part of the alienation literature, and that it bears upon our expectancy notions. What is not so clear is the matter of how precisely to conceptualize the events to which "anomie" is intended to point. Unfortunately, the idea of normlessness has been over-extended to include a wide variety of both social conditions and psychic states: personal disorganization, cultural breakdown, reciprocal distrust, and so on.

Those who employ the anomie version of alienation are chiefly concerned with the elaboration of the "means" emphasis in society—for example, the loss of commonly held standards and consequent individualism, or the development of instrumental, manipulative attitudes. This interest represents our third variant of alienation, the key idea of which, again, may be cast in terms of expectancies. Following Merton's lead, the anomic situation, from the individual point of view, may be defined as one in which there is a *high expectancy that socially unapproved behaviors are required to achieve given goals.*

[14] Merton, *op. cit.*, p. 143.
[15] R. K. Merton, *Social Theory and Social Structure*, Glencoe, Ill.: Free Press, 1949, p. 128.

[16] *Ibid.*, pp. 148–149, 138.

This third meaning of alienation is logically independent of the two versions discussed above. Expectancies concerning unapproved means, presumably, can vary independently of the individual's expectancy that his own behavior will determine his success in reaching a goal (what I have called "powerlessness") or his belief that he operates in an intellectually comprehensible world ("meaninglessness"). Such a view of anomie, to be sure, narrows the evocative character of the concept, but it provides a more likely way of developing its research potential. This view, I believe, makes possible the discovery of the extent to which such expectancies are held, the conditions for their development, and their consequences either for the individual or for a given social system (for example, the generation of wide-spread distrust).

The foregoing discussion implies that the means and goals in question have to do with such relatively broad social demands as the demand for success or for political ends. However, in his interesting essay, "Alienation from Interaction," Erving Goffman presents a more or less parallel illustration in which the focus is on the smallest of social systems, the simple conversation:

> If we take conjoint spontaneous involvement in a topic of conversation as a point of reference, we shall find that alienation from it is common indeed. Conjoint involvement appears to be a fragile thing, with standard points of weakness and decay, a precarious unsteady state that is likely at any time to lead the individual into some form of alienation. Since we are dealing with obligatory involvement, forms of alienation will constitute *misbehavior of a kind that can be called mis-involvement.*[17]

[17] *Human Relations,* 10 (February, 1957), p. 49 (italics added).

Goffman describes four such "mis-involvements" (for example, being too self-conscious in interaction), and concludes: "By looking at the ways in which individuals can be thrown out of step with the sociable moment, perhaps we can learn something about the way in which he can become alienated from things that take much more of his time."[18] In speaking of "misbehavior" or "mis-involvement," Goffman is treating the problem of alienation in terms not far removed from the anomic feature I have described, that is, the expectancy for socially unapproved behavior. His analysis of the social microcosm in these terms calls attention once more to the fact that the five variants of alienation discussed here can be applied to as broad or as narrow a range of social behavior as seems useful.

Isolation

The fourth type of alienation refers to *isolation.* This usage is most common in descriptions of the intellectual role, where writers refer to the detachment of the intellectual from popular cultural standards —one who, in Nettler's language, has be-

[18] *Ibid.,* p. 59. Obviously, the distinction (discussed above under "powerlessness") between objective condition and individual expectancy applies in the case of anomie. For a recent treatment of this point, see R. K. Merton, *Social Theory and Social Structure,* Glencoe, Ill.: Free Press, 1957 (revised edition), pp. 161–194. It is clear that Srole's well-known anomie scale refers to individual experience (and that it embodies a heavy adjustment component). It is not so clear how the metaphorical language of "normative breakdown" and "structural strain" associated with the conception of anomie as a social condition is to be made empirically useful. It may be further noted that the idea of rulelessness has often been used to refer to situations in which norms are unclear as well as to those in which norms lose their regulative force. I focused on the latter case in this section; but the former aspect of anomie is contained in the idea of "meaninglessness." The idea of meaninglessness, as defined above, surely includes situations involving uncertainty resulting from obscurity of rules, the absence of clear criteria for resolving ambiguities, and the like.

come estranged from his society and the culture it carries.[19] Clearly, this usage does not refer to isolation as a lack of "social adjustment"—of the warmth, security, or intensity of an individual's social contacts.

In the present context, in which we seek to maintain a consistent focus on the individual's expectations or values, this brand of alienation may be usefully defined in terms of reward values: The alienated in the isolation sense are those who, like the intellectual, *assign low reward value to goals or beliefs that are typically highly valued in the given society.* This, in effect, is the definition of alienation in Nettler's scale, for as a measure of "apartness from society" the scale consists (largely though not exclusively) of items that reflect the individual's degree of commitment to popular culture. Included, for example, is the question "Do you read Reader's Digest?", a magazine that was selected "as a symbol of popular magazine appeal and folkish thoughtways."[20]

The "isolation" version of alienation

[19] Nettler, *op. cit.*, p. 672.

[20] *Ibid.*, p. 675. A scale to measure social isolation (as well as powerlessness and meaninglessness) has been developed by Dean, but the meanings are not the same as those given here; the "social isolation" measure, for example, deals with the individual's friendship status. (See Dwight Dean, "Alienation and Political Apathy," Ph.D. thesis, Ohio State University, 1956.) It seems to me now, however, that this is not a very useful meaning, for two reasons. First, it comes very close to being a statement of either social adjustment or of simple differences in associational styles (i.e., some people are sociable and some are not), and as such seems irrelevant to the root historical notion of alienation. Second, the crucial part of this "social isolation" component in alienation—what Nisbet, for example, calls the "unattached" or the "isolated"—is better captured for analytical purposes, I believe, in the ideas of meaninglessness, normlessness, or isolation, as defined in expectancy or reward terms. That is to say, what remains, after sheer sociability is removed, is the kind of tenuousness of social ties that may be described as value uniqueness (isolation), deviation from approved means (normlessness), or the like.

clearly carries a meaning different from the three versions discussed above. Still, these alternative meanings can be profitably applied in conjunction with one another in the analysis of a given state of affairs. Thus, Merton's paper on social structure and anomie makes use of both "normlessness" and "isolation" in depicting the adaptations that individuals may make to the situation in which goals and means are not well coordinated. One of these adaptations—that of the "innovator" —is the prototype of alienation in the sense of normlessness, in which the individual innovates culturally disapproved means to achieve the goals in question. But another adjustment pattern—that of "rebellion"—more closely approximates what I have called "isolation." "This adaptation [rebellion] leads men outside the environing social structure to envisage and seek to bring into being a new, that is to say, a greatly modified, social structure. It presupposes alienation from reigning goals and standards."[21]

Self-Estrangement

The final variant distinguishable in the literature is alienation in the sense of *self-estrangement*. The most extended treatment of this version of alienation is found in *The Sane Society,* where Fromm writes:

In the following analysis I have chosen the concept of alienation as the central point from which I am going to

[21] Merton, "Social Structure and Anomie," *op. cit.,* pp. 144–145. Merton is describing a radical estrangement from societal values (often typified in the case of the intellectual)—i.e., the alienation is from reigning *central* features of the society, and what is sought is a "greatly" modified society. Presumably, the "isolation" mode of alienation, like the other versions, can be applied on the intimate or the grand scale, as noted above in the discussion of Goffman's analysis. Clearly, the person who rejects certain commonly held values in a given society, but who values the society's tolerance for such differences, is expressing a fundamental commitment to societal values and in this degree he is not alienated in the isolation sense.

develop the analysis of the contemporary social character. . . . By alienation is meant a mode of experience in which the person experiences himself as an alien. He has become, one might say, estranged from himself.[22] In much the same way, C. Wright Mills comments: "In the normal course of her work, because her personality becomes the instrument of an alien purpose, the salesgirl becomes self-alienated;" and, later, "Men are estranged from one another as each secretly tries to make an instrument of the other, and in time a full circle is made: One makes an instrument of himself and is estranged from It also."[23]

There are two interesting features of this popular doctrine of alienation as self-estrangement. The first of these is the fact that where the usage does not overlap with the other four meanings (and it often does), it is difficult to specify what the alienation is *from*. To speak of "alienation from the self" is after all simply a metaphor, in a way that "alienation from popular culture," for example, need not be. The latter can be reasonably specified, as I have tried to do above; but what is intended when Fromm, Mills, Hoffer, and the others speak of self-estrangement?

Apparently, what is being postulated here is some ideal human condition from which the individual is estranged. This is, perhaps, clearest in Fromm's treatment, for example, in his description of production and consumption excesses in capitalist society: "The *human* way of acquiring would be to make an effort qualitatively commensurate with what I acquire. . . . But our craving for consumption has lost all connection with the real needs of man."[24] To be self-alienated, in the final analysis, means to be something less than one might ideally be if the circumstances in society were otherwise—to be insecure,

given to appearances, conformist. Riesman's discussion of other-direction falls within this meaning of alienation; for what is at stake is that the child learns "that nothing in his character, no possession he owns, no inheritance of name or talent, no work he has done, is valued for itself, but only for its effect on others. . . ."[25]

Riesman's comment brings us to the second feature of special interest in the idea of self-alienation. I have noted that this idea invokes some explicit or implicit human ideal. And I have implied that such comparisons of modern man with some idealized human condition should be viewed simply as rhetorical appeals to nature—an important rhetoric for some purposes, though not very useful in the nonanalytical form it generally takes. But Riesman's assertion contains, it seems to me, one of the key elements of this rhetoric—one, indeed, that not only reflects the original interest of Marx in alienation but also one that may be specifiable in a language consistent with our other uses of alienation.

I refer to that aspect of self-alienation which is generally characterized as the loss of intrinsic meaning or pride in work, a loss which Marx and others have held to be an essential feature of modern alienation. This notion of the loss of intrinsically meaningful satisfactions is embodied in a number of ways in current discussions of alienation. Glazer, for example, contrasts the alienated society with simpler societies characterized by "spontaneous acts of work and play which were their own reward."[26]

---

[22] Fromm, *op. cit.*, pp. 110, 120.

[23] Mills, *op. cit.*, pp. 184, 188.

[24] Fromm, *op. cit.*, pp. 131, 134 (italics in original).

[25] David Riesman, *The Lonely Crowd*, New Haven: Yale University Press, 1950, p. 49. Although the idea of self-estrangement, when used in the alienation literature, usually carries the notion of a generally applicable human standard, it is sometimes the individual's standard that is at issue: to be alienated in this sense is to be aware of a discrepancy between one's ideal self and one's actual self-image.

[26] Glazer, *op. cit.*, p. 379.

Although this meaning of alienation is difficult to specify, the basic idea contained in the rhetoric of self-estrangement —the idea of intrinsically meaningful activity—can, perhaps, be recast into more manageable social learning terms. One way to state such a meaning is to see alienation as *the degree of dependence of the given behavior upon anticipated future rewards,* that is, upon rewards that lie outside the activity itself. In these terms, the worker who works merely for his salary, the housewife who cooks simply to get it over with, or the other-directed type who acts "only for its effect on others"—all these (at different levels, again) are instances of self-estrangement. In this view, what has been called self-estrangement refers essentially to the inability of the individual to find self-rewarding—or in Dewey's phrase, self-consummatory—activities that engage him.[27]

[27] The difficulty of providing intrinsically satisfying work in industrial society, of course, has been the subject of extensive comment; see, for example, Daniel Bell, *Work and Its Discontents,* Boston: Beacon Press, 1956. A similar idea has been applied by Tumin to the definition of creativity: "I would follow Dewey's lead and view 'creativity' as the esthetic experience, which is distinguished from other experiences by the fact that it is self-consummatory in nature. This is to say, the esthetic experience is enjoyed for the actions which define and constitute the experience, whatever it may be, rather than for its instrumental results or social accompaniments in the form of social relations with others." Melvin M. Tumin, "Obstacles to Creativity," *Etc.: A Review of General Semantics,* 11 (Summer, 1954), p. 261. For a more psychological view of the problem of "intrinsically" governed behavior, see S. Koch, "Behavior as 'Intrinsically' Regu-

Conclusion

I am aware that there are unclarities and difficulties of considerable importance in these five varieties of alienation (especially, I believe, in the attempted solution of "self-estrangement" and the idea of "meaninglessness"). But I have attempted, first, to distinguish the meanings that have been given to alienation, and second, to work toward a more useful conception of each of these meanings.

It may seem, at first reading, that the language employed—the language of expectations and rewards—is somewhat strange, if not misguided. But I would urge that the language is more traditional than it may seem. Nathan Glazer certainly is well within that tradition when, in a summary essay on alienation, he speaks of our modern ". . . sense of the splitting asunder of what was once together, the breaking of the seamless mold in which *values, behavior,* and *expectations* were once cast into interlocking forms."[28] These same three concepts—reward value, behavior, and expectancy—are key elements in the theory that underlies the present characterization of alienation. Perhaps, on closer inspection, the reader will find only that initial strangeness which is often experienced when we translate what was sentimentally understood into a secular question.

lated: Work Notes Toward a Pre-Theory of Phenomena Called 'Motivational,' " in M. R. Jones, editor, *Nebraska Symposium on Motivation,* Lincoln: University of Nebraska Press, 1956, pp. 42–87.

[28] Glazer, *op. cit.,* p. 378 (italics added).

PART II

DIFFUSE ALIENATION:

ANOMIA, POWERLESSNESS,

AND MISANTHROPY

Introduction

In contrast with attitudes of alienation that are directed at particular social institutions, each of the concepts discussed in this section refers to a feeling of estrangement from other people in general or society at large. In this introductory section, we shall focus particularly on some of the similarities among the concepts of anomia, powerlessness, and misanthropy and how they are related to other types of alienation.

As part of a study of ethnic prejudice in a city in Massachusetts, Leo Srole devised a scale of anomia, which he intended as a measure of "self-to-others alienation." This scale has become one of the most widely used attitude measures in social research. Srole begins with an interest in applying Durkheim's concept of "anomie" to individuals. When Durkheim used this term, he referred to a social condition of "deregulation" or breakdown in the norms guiding behavior. Although Durkheim was obviously interested in individual reactions to this state (as demonstrated in his study of suicide), he regarded anomie itself as a *social* rather than individual property. Srole applies the basic notion of lack of normative integration to the *individual* level by defining *anomia* in terms of the social malintegration of individuals.[1] In the selection reprinted here, Srole describes how the anomia scale was constructed and specifies the particular aspect of anomia that each question was designed to measure. It is important to note that agreement with these items does not necessarily imply an active hostility toward, or rejection of, society as do some other measures of alienation (for example, compare Stinchcombe's measure in the next section). Rather, Srole's scale reflects Durkheim's stress on the positive values to be derived

---

[1] Among users of these terms, the convention has developed to use anomi*e* to refer to the social condition and anomi*a* to refer to the individual attitude.

from individual dependence on social ties and measures the individual's sense of isolation from any such network. A high score on the Srole scale therefore indicates a feeling of aloneness and helplessness in the face of a lack of social structure and regulation.

What is the relationship of the Srole anomia scale to other concepts of alienation? It is included in the section on "diffuse alienation" because of its *referent,* "self-to-others" as Srole describes it. Thus, it is designed not to measure attitudes toward a *particular* social institution but rather to tap a pervasive attitude toward society at large. But can we also view the Srole scale as measuring a particular *dimension* of alienation? A review of Srole's reasons for including each of the questions suggests some clear conceptual parallels between the anomia scale and several other types of alienation. For example, "the individual's sense that community leaders are detached from and indifferent to his needs" is related to both powerlessness as discussed by Seeman and political powerlessness and perceived political normlessness as discussed by Finifter in the section on political alienation. Also, Srole's idea of "the individual's perception of the social order as essentially fickle and unpredictable, i.e., orderless" seems clearly similar to Seeman's "meaninglessness." In spite of these and other conceptual similarities, however, Neal and Rettig (1963), using the statistical technique of factor analysis, found that Srole's questions emerge as a dimension separate from items devised to measure *economic* and *political* normlessness and powerlessness. It is possible that the anomia scale is separable precisely because it does have a diffuse rather than a specific referent. Since the Srole scale places relatively heavy emphasis on personal life situations, it is also possible that it may measure personal disorganization or maladjustment to a greater extent than active alienation from society. Although many writers have used the Srole scale as a *de facto* measure of "alienation," it should be noted that its relationship to other commonly used measures of alienation is an important question that remains to be definitively answered.

One of Srole's purposes in his study was to determine which of two scales—the anomia scale or one measuring authoritarianism—was more strongly related to ethnic prejudice. On the basis of his data Srole concluded that anomia was more important. A scholarly debate ensued as to the relative power of anomia and authoritarianism in causing discriminatory attitudes. Lutterman and Middleton (1970) present a useful summary of this controversy. One of the difficulties is that the particular questions in commonly used versions of both of these scales are so worded that "agree" responses always indicate either authoritarianism or anomia, as the case may be. Because of this, the scale scores for these variables may become correlated through the phenomenon of "acquiescence response set"—the tendency of some people to agree with *whatever* statement is presented to them. If the two scales are related through their common relationship to acquiescence response set, it is then virtually impossible to sort out their independent effects on other variables. This problem in the anomia scale is discussed by Lenski and Leggett (1960) and some negatively worded items are presented in Robinson and Shaver's (1969) discussion of the scale. Another methodological evaluation of the Srole scale is undertaken by Miller and Butler (1966).

The volume edited by Clinard (1964) reviews some studies that relate the Srole anomia scale to delinquency and other criminal and deviant behavior. These studies are inspired by a theory developed by Robert Merton (1957), which elaborates on Durkheim's analysis of anomie. Merton stipulates that a disjuncture (or lack of integration) between cultural goals and the means available to individuals to achieve these goals leads to a state of anomie in a society. Merton posits that one of the ways individuals react to this lack of congruence is to develop illegitimate means to achieve the goals in place of the legitimate means that are not available to them. As a case in point, Merton considers the American value of "success." Since the means to achieve success (for example, a good education and job opportunities) are not equally available to all, one possible result is that members of groups who do not have access to the necessary means resort to crime to achieve the goals. In testing this theory, the Srole anomia scale is frequently used as an indicator of the degree to which the individual perceives the society as "deregulated" or anomic; this perception, according to Merton's theory, is a variable that intervenes between disadvantaged social status and deviant behavior.

A number of other areas have also been studied using the Srole anomia scale. McDill and Ridley (1962) and Rose (1962), for example, find that anomia is negatively related to political participation, and Olsen (1961) and Templeton (1966) investigate its relationship to various political attitudes. An alternative conception and measure of anomia is presented by McClosky and Schaar (1965).

Although the research literature on anomia establishes its relationship to prejudice against minority groups, the selection by Bonnie Bullough examines the consequences of anomia for minority group members themselves. Since anomia partially measures lack of confidence in others and also contains an element of hopelessness, it seems logical that it should affect the zeal with which people living in ghetto areas search for higher quality housing. Bullough also uses a second measure of diffuse alienation, a scale of powerlessness based on the work of Rotter and Liverant (1962). In addition to examining the relationships between both anomia and powerlessness and residence in ghetto versus integrated areas, she discusses how experiences with racial integration affect the development of these attitudes of alienation.

The powerlessness scale used by Bullough, also called the "internal-external control" scale, is designed to measure the extent to which the individual feels that it is possible for him to control events rather than that control is imposed on him by external sources. This scale clearly operationalizes the dimension of alienation referred to by Seeman as powerlessness, although it is a diffuse and generalized kind of powerlessness. Rather than focusing on expectancy for control in any one specific area, the scale includes items which range over a variety of life experiences and situations. (Several recent studies explore the role of similar measures of powerlessness in participation in ghetto riots and other manifestations of alienation among blacks. These relationships are discussed in the section on political alienation.)

Another kind of diffuse alienation is conceptualized by Morris Rosenberg as "misanthropy," more commonly and positively known as "faith in people." Rosenberg views this concept as a basic "attitude toward human nature." An examination of the particular items Rosenberg uses to measure this attitude reveals some similarity with those used in the Srole scale; both contain items about the untrustworthiness and selfishness of other people. One advantage of Rosenberg's measure is that it is less subject than the Srole scale to the problems of acquiescence response set, since the five-item misanthropy scale includes one negatively worded item and two items which present substantive alternatives rather than agree-disagree choices.

Rosenberg's reasons for expecting a relationship between misanthopy and *political* attitudes include the hypothesis that this basic attitude toward human nature is applied to particular situations—in this case, to include actors in the political realm and also aspects of political ideology that incorporate basic views of human nature. Thus, the suggestion here is that attitudes toward society *in general* influence attitudes toward specific social referents. In the section on political alienation, some further confirmation of this idea is provided in Finifter's finding that faith in people is negatively related to two different dimensions of political alienation.

A number of interesting questions are raised by these findings and the possibility that other types of diffuse alienation may also be related empirically to attitudes directed against specific social institutions. Such relationships suggest that individuals who are diffusely alienated may resist changing their attitudes toward specific social institutions because these attitudes are rooted in a fundamental conception of human nature rather than, or in addition to, shortcomings of the institution itself. Change in any given social sector, even in a direction presumably desirable to the individual, may therefore not be perceived or, if perceived, may merely lead to a new emphasis on the estranging qualities of *other* institutions. The existence of diffuse alienation may then severely limit the possibilities of decreasing levels of more specific types of alienation through programs of institutional change, unless the more basic attitudes toward human nature can be affected also.

On the other hand, specific alienations do not necessarily have to be rooted in a diffuse alienation like misanthropy. For example, statements of alienation from contemporary political institutions are sometimes linked explicitly to a basic trust in people coupled with a sense that impersonal institutional processes are somehow eluding the control of essentially cooperative and trustworthy human beings. Political alienation based on a misanthropic view of human nature might lead to political apathy, while political alienation coupled with a basically trusting view of human nature might be more typical of an idealistic believer in "participatory democracy." Thus, to what extent attitudes of diffuse alienation are, in fact, related to more specific types of alienation, whether there are feedback processes, and how these work are crucial questions for future research. The behavioral consequences of specific alienations are likely to depend at least partially on the basic view of human nature or individual potential with which they are coupled.

If more specific alienations are at least sometimes outgrowths of diffuse alienation, then changing either of these types of attitudes depends on knowing the sources of attitudes of diffuse alienation. Research suggests that anomia, powerlessness, and misanthropy are frequently products of disadvantaged social backgrounds and the culture of poverty in which individuals consistently face situations of disappointment and discouragement. But social status is by no means a sufficient explanation for diffuse alienation. A recent study found that among college students, at least, trust in other people consistently declined over the last half of the decade of the sixties (Hochreich and Rotter, 1970). The opening of college campuses to disadvantaged youth has not proceeded fast enough to explain this persistent decline. These findings suggest that diffuse alienation itself may be dependent on how people view particular social institutions, for the faith of these students in *political* institutions was decreasing at the same time. Thus, a vicious feedback cycle may be entered where increasing political alienation tends to increase diffuse alienation toward society at large, and these negative attitudes may in turn be projected on still other institutional sectors. On the other hand, if diffuse alienation is responsive to attitudes toward specific institutions, then *increasing* faith in those institutions may decrease diffuse alienation. Thus, positive changes in one area can also have repercussions in many others. In this sense, diffuse alienation may be an important key to change in all other areas.

In addition to the work reported here, Rosenberg (1957) has studied the relationship between misanthropy and attitudes toward occupational success. His scale is also widely used by others, such as Almond and Verba (1963) in their study of political attitudes. The concept of powerlessness is used extensively in Seeman's research, in which he focuses mainly on the role of organizational memberships in decreasing feelings of powerlessness (1966; Neal and Seeman, 1964) and on the relationship between powerlessness and decreased motivation for learning information which would be useful in the particular life situations of individuals (1963, 1967; Seeman and Evans, 1962).

SOCIAL INTEGRATION AND CERTAIN COROLLARIES: AN EXPLORATORY STUDY

Leo Srole

This article has evolved from a preliminary report of a study conducted in Springfield, Massachusetts, in 1950. Although the study was originally conceived as applied rather than pure research, the attitude-type scale devised afforded an operational formulation of the anomie concept. This formulation was broader, however, than that specified by Durkheim. . . .

Concepts, Hypotheses and Research Design

The objective of the Springfield study was the measurement and assessment of the impact of a series of ADL* card advertisements (anti-discrimination and American Creed messages) that were posted under controlled conditions in vehicles of the public transit system. . . .

The "target" audience studied was the Springfield transit riding population, defined arbitrarily as individuals of age 16 and over who paid four or more fares in the average week. Because available resources limited us to a relatively small sample, heterogeneity in the sample was reduced by excluding those minority groups in the target audience which, for obvious reasons, could be expected to be

especially receptive to the test cards' thematic contents, i.e., Negroes, Jews, and the foreign-born. The sample was, therefore, delimited to white, Christian, native-born transit riders. By means of a "hybrid" sampling design combining randomized selection of blocks (within walking distance of transit lines) and age-sex quota selection of individuals within these blocks, 401 individuals between the ages of 16-69 (mean 40.3 years, SD 14.5 years) were interviewed in their homes.

Differential audience "penetration" effects of the test transit cards were expected to be mediated by a number of intervening variables, e.g., prior attitudinal set toward minority groups. Accordingly, respondents were classified by degree of attitudinal acceptance or rejection of minority groups in general, on the basis of two different kinds of data in combination:

1. Responses to five structured social distance questionnaire items referring by indirection to Negroes, Jews, foreigners, etc.[1]

[1] The five agree-disagree items were:

(1) It is better for a child if he keeps to playmates of the same religious background as his own.

(2) There are a good many people in the U. S. who ought to go back to the countries they came from.

(3) It would be better all around if white children had swimming pools for themselves.

(4) Refugees from Nazi Germany should be kept out of the United States and sent to Palestine instead.

SOURCE: Reprinted in slightly abridged form from the *American Sociological Review*, 21, 6 (December 1956), 709–716, by permission of the author and publisher. Leo Srole is Professor of Social Sciences, Department of Psychiatry, College of Physicians & Surgeons, Columbia University, and Chief of Psychiatric Research, New York State Psychiatric Institute.
*Anti-Defamation League of B'nai B'rith

60

2. Spontaneous comments revealing underlying attitudes toward minority groups. These were unexpectedly elicited in many cases by the projective nature of the special versions of the posted car cards (text converted into hieroglyphics) used in the interview to test message recall.

It seems likely that unguarded, spontaneous comments elicited by projective-type pictorial stimuli, in combination with structured questionnaire items that avoided direct reference to minority groups, provide a relatively sensitive (i.e., valid) and reliable measure of attitudes toward such groups.[2]

Considerations of questionnaire design compelled placement of our structured attitudes-to-minorities items early in the instrument. Moreover, in order to divert respondent attention from their common, underlying element, these items were scattered among questions of quite different content. These diversionary items afforded a "hitch hike" opportunity to test

[*footnote 1 continued*
(5) In the South they have pretty much the right slant about having separate colleges for white students.
[2] It should be noted how this combination was effected. Sorted first were the respondents who in their spontaneous comments revealed their underlying attitudes toward minority groups. Among such: (a) those who spoke only favorably of minority groups and who similarly gave favorable replies to at least four of the five structured items were placed in the Positive or "Tolerant" attitude category; (b) those who spoke only unfavorably of minority groups and who similarly gave unfavorable replies to at least four of the five structured items were placed in the Negative or "Prejudiced" attitude category; (c) all others spontaneously commenting favorably or unfavorably or both and giving "mixed replies" (two favorable and three unfavorable, or vice versa) to the five structured items were placed in the intermediate "Ambivalent" category.

Respondents who did not spontaneously reveal their attitudes toward minority groups could be classified only on their replies to the structured items, as follows: (a) four or five favorable replies—Positive; (b) two or three unfavorable replies—Ambivalent; (c) four or five unfavorable replies—Negative.

hypotheses centering on Durkheim's concept of anomie. These hypotheses center on a pair of antinomic Greek terms, "eunomia" and "anomia." The former originally denoted a well ordered condition in a society or state, the latter its opposite. The two terms can be adapted with some license to refer to the continuum of variations in the "integratedness" of different social systems or sub-systems, viewed as molar wholes. They can also be applied to the parallel continuum of variations seen from the "microscopic" or molecular view of individuals as they are integrated in the total action fields of their interpersonal relationships and reference groups.

Although research employing the macroscopic approach to the phenomena of integration in large social systems has appeared in recent years, it still presents formidable operational problems. On the other hand, the molecular approach has the advantage of being readily fitted to the established operational apparatus of the sample survey. With the molecular approach, the immediate analytical objective would be to place individuals on a eunomia-anomia continuum representing variations in interpersonal integration with their particular social fields as "global" entities. More concretely, this variable is conceived as referring to the individual's generalized, pervasive sense of "self-to-others belongingness" at one extreme compared with "self-to-others distance" and "self-to-others alienation" at the other pole of the continuum. For semantic neatness the terms eunomia-anomia are here used to refer specifically to this sociopsychological continuum.

It may clarify this conception of the eunomia-anomia dimension on the molecular level to note the likelihood that in the individual adult it covers more than the cumulative consequences of his particular integrations in his current social roles and groups. Specifically, three more inclusive sets of forces are also seen as operating in his contemporary situation.

1. Reference groups beyond his immediate field of action, within which acceptance and ultimate integration are sought.

2. Generalized qualities of the molar society penetrating his contemporary action field, as these affect (a) his life-goal choices, (b) his selection of means toward these goals, and (c) his success or failure in achieving these goals.

3. The socialization processes of his interpersonal relationships during childhood and adolescence, as these have conditioned the interpersonal expectations, value orientations, and behavioral tendencies of his current personality structure.

Accordingly, individual eunomia-anomia is viewed as a variable contemporary condition having its origin in the complex interaction of social[3] and personality factors, present and past. In short, the condition is regarded as a variable dependent on both sociological and psychological processes. As such, it warrants direct attack in the wideranging strategy of research.[4] . . .

In the writer's view "self-to-others alienation" may be regarded as the common element[5] in Durkheim's conceptualization of *anomie, egoisme, altruisme,* and *fatalisme* as different but often overlapping forms of suicide. Second, there has been reflected among some social scientists a sense of the limited utility of Durkheim's specification of anomie as referring to the breakdown of those moral norms that limit desires and aspirations (a breakdown which he tended to associate with rather special "change of role" circumstances). This development has been accompanied by diversification in the usage of the term, in one direction toward convergence with the broader concepts of dysfunction and malintegration in molar social systems.[6] The convergence most closely approximating the definition proposed here is to be seen in (1) MacIver's definition of anomie as "the breakdown of the individual's sense of attachment to society"[7] and (2) Lasswell's reading of the concept as refer-

[3] Under the influence of the Cornell mental health investigation, the notion of the sociogenesis of individual anomia was refined to include the self-generated or psychogenic type of alienation from others. This, of course, extends the sociogenic time perspective to earlier stages of the life history when more narrowly localized social processes of a malintegrating kind set in motion psychopathological processes of alienation from self and others. Remaining of central interest, however, are the individuals entering adulthood as "normal" personalities but in whom anomia develops in response to objective conditions of stressful malintegration in their social worlds.

[4] Operationally speaking, (Robin Williams, *American Society,* New York: A. A. Knopf, 1951, p. 537) appears to take a dissenting position: "Anomie as a social condition has to be defined independently of the psychological states thought to accompany normlessness and normative conflict. . . . The basic model for explanatory purposes is: normative situation $\longrightarrow$ psychological state $\longrightarrow$ behavioral item or sequence." But in an interesting footnote he adds: "Strictly speaking, of course, the arows should be written $\longleftarrow \longrightarrow$: the relations are reciprocal." If the relations are reciprocal, as we concur, then the explanatory model is significantly altered. With

such alteration, considerations of operational efficiency, rather than of a unidirectional causal theory, may dictate to the investigator at what point his research should break into the chain. Clearly, verbalizable psychological states of individuals and their situational concomitants are more readily accessible to the instruments of the researcher than is the operationally complicated cultural abstraction that Williams calls the "normative structure" and seems to predicate as the researcher's *necessary* point of first attack.

[5] This general point of view has been expressed by Ivan Belknap and Hiram J. Friedsam, "Age and Sex Categories as Sociological Variables in the Mental Disorders of Later Maturity," *American Sociological Review,* 14 (June, 1949), p. 369: "Ultimately, *suicide altruiste* may also be an anomic phenomenon, since the group actually extrudes the particular individual, providing no further 'place' for him. *Egoisme,* another of Durkheim's type of suicide is also perhaps significant only as a cause of *anomie.*"

[6] An outstanding example is provided in Robert K. Merton's "Social Structure and Anomie: Revisions and Extensions" in his *Social Theory and Social Structure,* Glencoe, Illinois: The Free Press, 1949.

[7] Robert M. MacIver, *The Ramparts We Guard,* New York: The Macmillan Co., 1950, pp. 84–92.

ring to the "lack of identification on the part of the primary ego of the individual with a 'self' that includes others. In a word, modern man appeared to be suffering from psychic isolation. He felt alone, cut off, unwanted, unloved, unvalued."[8]

The hypothesis within our framework that lent itself to testing in the Springfield study was this: social malintegration, or anomia, in individuals is associated with a rejective orientation toward out-groups in general and toward minority groups in particular.[9] To test this hypothesis it was necessary to devise a measure of interpersonal alienation or "anomia." This, we reasoned, could be constructed in opinion-poll format to represent, directly or indirectly, the respondent's definition or perception of his own interpersonal situation. To this end, we set down the ideational states or components that on theoretical grounds would represent internalized counterparts or reflections, in the individual's life situation, of conditions of social dysfunction. Five components from the larger series were selected for inclusion in the study. For each, "opinion" type statements of the simple agree-disagree type were framed and pretested (for verbal clarity and response distributions) in fifty interviews. From the pretest experience we selected one item which, with subsequent revisions, finally represented each anomia component in the Springfield questionnaire.[10]

The first of these postulated components was the individual's sense that community leaders are detached from and indifferent to his needs, reflecting severance of the interdependent bond within the social system between leaders and those they should represent and serve. The item selected to represent this component was the agree-disagree statement, "There's little use writing to public officials because often they aren't really interested in the problems of the average man."

The second hypothesized element of anomia was the individual's perception of the social order as essentially fickle and unpredictable, i.e., orderless, inducing the sense that under such conditions he can accomplish little toward realizing future life goals. The item that seemed to come closest to this facet of anomia was the Epicurean statement, "Nowadays a person has to live pretty much for today and let tomorrow take care of itself."

Closely related to this aspect of anomia was a third element: the individual's view, beyond abdication of future life goals, that he and people like him are retrogressing from the goals they have already reached. The item chosen to represent this component was the statement rejecting the American Creed doctrine of progress: "In spite of what some people say, the lot of the average man is getting worse, not better."

The fourth component postulated, and the one perhaps most closely approximating Durkheim's particular definition of anomie, was the deflation or loss of internalized social norms and values, reflected in extreme form in the individual's sense of the meaninglessness of life itself. Standing for this element was the item proposition: "It's hardly fair to bring children

---

[8] Harold Lasswell, "The Threat to Privacy" in Robert M. MacIver (editor), *Conflict of Loyalties,* New York: Harper and Bros., 1952.

[9] Williams (*op. cit.,* p. 536) independently arrived at substantially the same hypothesis: "It is enough to note here one possible connection between anomic conditions and problems of intergroup, or intercategory, relations. . . . [Anomie] is a context highly favorable to rigidly categorical definition of out-groups."

[10] John Harding has called our attention to the work of Rundquist and Sletto with a series of questionnaire items devised to measure generalized "morale." Examination of these items revealed their affinity with some of our anomia questions. There was, however, considerable di-

vergence in the two theoretical frameworks. Cf. Edward A. Rundquist and Raymond F. Sletto, *Personality in the Depression,* Minneapolis: University of Minnesota Press, 1936. Consideration of anomia in relation to cognate concepts like "morale" is being reserved for a later publication.

into the world with the way things look for the future."

The final anomia component was hypothesized as the individual's perception that his framework of immediate personal relationships, the very rock of his social existence, was no longer predictive or supportive, and was expressed by the item worded: "These days a person doesn't really know whom he can count on." . . .

After deciding on the inclusion of the five anomia items in the Springfield questionnaire, it became clear to us that we would also have to control analytically for the authoritarian personality factor, as measured in the California Study,[11] if we were to test adequately the hypothesis that orientation toward minority groups is related to the factor assumed to be reflected in our measure of anomia. For this specific purpose we incorporated into the questionnaire a shortened five-item version of the California F scale of authoritarianism.[12] . . .

Findings. The hypothesis motivating the construction and inclusion of the A [Anomia] scale in the Springfield study was that anomia is a factor related to the formation of negative, rejective attitudes toward minority groups. The Pearson correlation actually found in the Springfield data between A scores and M [Minority attitudes] was + .43, supporting the hypothesis.

The F scale was introduced into the study design to control for the factor of

authoritarian personality trends, known previously to be associated with attitudes to minorities. In Springfield, we found a Pearson correlation of + .29 between F scores and M.[13] . . .

Although lacking any basis for hypothesizing about the expected relationship of anomia scores and M when F scores are controlled, we were interested in the direction of this relationship. By the method of partial correlation, we have found that the correlation of .43 between A and M is negligibly reduced to .35 when F scores are partialled out. Thus, we can conclude that in our sample population anomia scores are related to attitudes toward minorities *independently* of the personality trends measured by the authoritarianism scale.

We next faced the question of the relationship of F scores and M when A scores are held constant. Again by the method of partial correlation, we find that when A scores are partialled out, the correlation of .29 between F and M is reduced to .12. We could conclude, therefore, that in our sample the correlation between authoritarian personality trends and attitudes toward minorities is partially accounted for by the anomia factor, i.e., F scores do *not* stand in a close relationship to M *independently* of the anomia factor.

We had originally hypothesized that the anomia factor would be significantly related in an inverse direction to socioeconomic status. In the Springfield interview, we accordingly asked for respondent's education and occupation of head of household, in order to combine them, equally weighted, into a composite status score. On the basis of the score distribution the sample was classified into three SES strata. Applying this measure of socioeconomic status, we find a Pearson correlation between A scores and SES of − .30, supporting the hypothesis. The corresponding correlation of F scores and SES is − .22; and

[11] T. W. Adorno, E. Frenkel-Brunswik, Daniel J. Levinson and R. Nevitt Sanford, *The Authoritarian Personality*, New York: Harper and Bros., 1950.

[12] The items are as follows:

(1) The most important thing to teach children is absolute obedience to their parents.

(2) Any good leader should be strict with people under him in order to gain their respect.

(3) There are two kinds of people in the world: the weak and the strong.

(4) Prison is too good for sex criminals. They should be publicly whipped or worse.

(5) No decent man can respect a woman who has had sex relations before marriage.

[13] For a sample of 401, the .01 level of confidence is achieved with an r of .13 or more.

of M and SES, $-.14$. Apparently then, in our sample population attitudes toward minority groups are to only a small degree a function of the status variable, whereas anomia is to a moderate degree, and authoritarian personality tendencies to an extent intermediate between A and M.

Discussion

. . . Recent unpublished research by others, and by the writer and his Cornell associates, in applying the A scale or adaptations of it have established significant connections between this measure of individual anomia and such diverse phenomena as social isolation among the aged, certain specific forms of psychopathology among metropolitan adults, the life threat represented by the exogenous condition of rheumatic heart disease, adolescents living in areas marked by different rates of drug addiction, etc.

These studies, by their cumulative weight, support the general hypothesis of an interactive process linking the individual state of anomia and interpersonal dysfunction in the social realm.

Of special interest in the Springfield data is the isolation of anomic states and authoritarian personality trends as relatively discrete dimensions that are closely related to each other, a finding corroborated by our current New York City study. It could be predicted of course that a personality with authoritarian tendencies bred in the family of origin would tend to be a "misfit" in a democratic social system, thereby generating the conditions both in itself and in the interpersonal milieu, that give rise to one type of self-to-others alienation.

On the other hand, we would follow Fromm and Merton[14] in hypothesizing a second kind of developmental sequence. To Fromm, among personalities basically "fitted" for a democratic society, escape reactions from socially generated "aloneness" and "helplessness" (i.e. individual anomia) may issue either in authoritarianism or "compulsive conformity." For Merton, individual "modes of adaptation" to dysfunctional "contradictions in the cultural and social structure" are differentiated on the basis of a more systematic and comprehensive typology of deviancy, including "ritualism" hypothesized as a dominant type. To freely paraphrase both writers, social dysfunction is the independent variable, the individual's state of self-to-group alienation is the intervening variable, and change in personality (Fromm) or adaptive modes (Merton) is the dependent variable.

As a closing note, there appears to be a trend among social scientists toward convergence of interest in the phenomena of social integration. Equipped with the advances of the past decade in theory and research technology, this trend gives promise of accelerating the scientific attack, powerfully and single-handedly launched by Emile Durkheim more than a half-century ago, on one of the most pervasive and potentially dangerous aspects of Western society, namely, the deterioration in the social and moral ties that bind, sustain and free us.

[14] *Escape from Freedom*, New York: Rinehart and Co., 1941, pp. 136–206; Merton, *op. cit.*

ALIENATION IN THE GHETTO[1]

Bonnie Bullough

Thirty years ago Chicago sociologists described the pattern of the urban Negro ghetto. The center of the "black belt" was occupied by the new arrivals to the city who were often unskilled and unemployed. The more successful and better-educated residents tended to move further out toward the periphery of the area; occasionally they even moved a short distance beyond the concentrated Negro area, so that there were neighborhoods which were temporarily integrated as the ghetto expanded.[2] In spite of the current revolutionary drive for integration, this over-all pattern has not changed much in the large cities of the North and West. Even in the sixteen states that have laws making dis-

SOURCE: Reprinted from *The American Journal of Sociology*, 72, 5 (March 1967), 469–478, by permission of the author and The University of Chicago Press. Copyright 1967 by The University of Chicago.

[1] I am indebted to Melvin Seeman for advice and help in all stages of the research and in preparation of this manuscript. Computing assistance was obtained from the Health Sciences Computing facility of the University of California, Los Angeles, sponsored by National Institutes of Health grant FR-3. I am supported by a U.S. Public Health special-nurse fellowship.

[2] E. Franklin Frazier, "The Negro Family in Chicago," in Ernest Burgess and Donald Bogue (eds.), *Contributions to Urban Sociology* (Chicago: University of Chicago Press, 1964), pp. 404–18. A similar pattern was described by St. Clair Drake and H. R. Cayton in *Black Metropolis* (New York: Harcourt, Brace & Co., 1945), pp. 174–213.

crimination in housing illegal there has been no massive movement toward residential desegregation.[3]

Recently, however, it has been reported that in Boston, Seattle, and Philadelphia there are isolated Negro families who have moved completely away from the old ghettos and have settled in previously all white areas.[4] In Los Angeles, where a similar movement has taken place, a small but growing number of Negro families have moved into the previously all white areas of the San Fernando Valley. Although actually a part of the sprawling city of Los Angeles, "the Valley" is separated from the older, central portion of the city by the Santa Monica mountain range. It is one of the fastest growing areas in the country, having developed in the last twenty years from a few scattered communities to one large solidly settled area with almost a million inhabitants. Even before the postwar building boom it contained one predominantly Negro community called Pacoima, which reported a Negro population

[3] "How the Fair Housing Laws are Working," *Trends in Housing*, IX (November-December, 1965), 3–4, 7–10.

[4] Helen MacGill Hughes and Lewis G. Watts, "Portrait of the Self Integrator," *Journal of Social Issues*, XX (April, 1964), 103–15; L. D. Northwood and Ernest A. T. Barth, *Urban Desegregation: Negro Pioneers and Their White Neighbors* (Seattle: University of Washington Press, 1965); and Commission on Human Relations, *Some Factors Affecting Housing Desegregation* (Philadelphia, 1962).

of 9,000 in 1960,[5] but the remaining large expanse of the Valley was until recently almost "lily white." It is too soon to say whether the movement of these scattered Negro families in Los Angeles or elsewhere portends future urban integration, but such a possibility cannot be discounted. In any case these first families, which I have called "barrier breakers," seemed like an interesting group of people to study.

Preliminary investigation of the families in Los Angeles who had made this move indicated that they tended to be well educated and occupationally successful, which is consistent with the findings reported in the other cities mentioned. Since portions of the Los Angeles ghetto also contain areas in which there are many well educated and successful Negroes, it was reasoned that socioeconomic status was not the only factor that determined who would be able to break through the barriers of housing discrimination. The problem for research, then, was to determine some of the social-psychological characteristics that distinguish the barrier breakers from other middle-class Negroes.

The main theoretical framework used to investigate the social psychological barriers to integration was an alienation one. Alienation would seem to be particularly important since it has been mentioned as an aspect of ghetto life by many writers, both popular and scholarly.[6] The aliena-

tion of many Negro residents of Los Angeles was dramatically demonstrated in smoke and flames across the skies of Watts during the riots. The rioters, however, were drawn primarily from the poorly educated, unemployed youth,[7] and the focus of this research, which was actually completed before the riots, was on the consequences of alienation for the well-educated, employed middle-class ghetto dwellers.

Previous studies have suggested that those who are less alienated are more likely to seek integration. Researchers in a southern Negro college found that students who felt that they themselves could control their own fate were more willing to participate in a civil rights demonstration.[8] In a study done in Nashville the Srole anomia scale was used to predict which families would seek an integrated school for their children.[9] Based on the conceptualization developed by Melvin Seeman, alienation in this research was viewed as not just a single attitude but as a group of attitudinal variables, which under certain conditions can be related, but which for conceptual clarity should not be confused with each other.[10] Three aspects of the alienation complex were investigated: (1) powerlessness; (2) anomia, which in Seeman's scheme is called normlessness; and (3) an orientation toward or away from the ghetto, which in his scheme would be called a type of value isolation.

---

[5] Marchia Meeker and Joan Harris, *Background for Planning* (Los Angeles: Research Department, Welfare Planning Council, Report #17, 1964), pp. 55–60. A Negro population of 334,916 was reported in 1960 in the city of Los Angeles; see Los Angeles County Commission on Human Relations, *Population and Housing in Los Angeles County: A Study in the Growth of Residential Segregation* (Los Angeles, 1963), p. 1.

[6] See, e.g., James Baldwin, *The Fire Next Time* (New York: Dial Press, 1963); Charles Silberman, *Crisis in Black and White* (New York: Random House, 1964), pp. 189–223; James Coleman, "Implications of the Findings on Alienation," *American Journal of Sociology*, LXX (July, 1964), 76–78; and Russel Middleton,

"Alienation, Race and Education," *American Sociological Review*, XXVIII (December, 1963), 793–97.

[7] John A. McCone (chairman), *Violence in the City—An End or a Beginning? A Report by the Governor's Commission on the Los Angeles Riots* (Los Angeles: State of California, 1965).

[8] Pearl Mayo Gore and Julian B. Rotter, "A Personality Correlate of Social Action," *Journal of Personality*, XXXI (March, 1963), 58–64.

[9] Eugene Weinstein and Paul Gusel, "Family Decision Making over Desegregation," *Sociometry*, XXV (March, 1963), 58–64.

[10] Melvin Seeman, "On the Meaning of Alienation," *American Sociological Review*, XXIV (December, 1959), 783–91.

In conceptualizing the direction of orientation as a type of alienation it should be noted that the alienation can be from the values and institutions of the Negro subculture or from the dominant society. It was hypothesized not only that powerlessness and anomia would be associated with ghetto life but that they played a key role in holding people within the old residential patterns. It was also hypothesized that the subjects would turn their attention away from the strictly segregated institutions of the ghetto as they moved out into integrated neighborhoods.

Sixty-one Negro families, scattered throughout the predominantly white section of the Valley, were located and interviewed during the winter and spring of 1964-65. All available Negro adult members of the household were included in the sample (three non-Negro spouses were excluded).[11] This yielded a sample of 104 persons, 54 men and 50 women. The names and addresses of these subjects were obtained through the efforts of members of the Valley Fair Housing Council, a local civil rights group. Members of the council used a wide variety of contacts to locate the subjects, including other organizations, work contacts, schools, and so on. The subjects themselves were able to furnish the names of some other Valley Negro families known to them. A control group of 106 persons, 48 men and 58 women from sixty-five families, was obtained by randomly sampling two middle-class neighborhoods with Negro populations of over 90 per cent. One of these areas was in the Pacoima section of the Valley, and the other was in central Los Angeles, several miles to the north of the now famous Watts area. Actually, the phy-

sical characteristics of all the sampled areas, integrated and ghetto, were somewhat similar. Most of the dwellings were single family with just an occasional apartment building; the neighborhoods were attractive and the yards well kept. Sixty-three persons from Pacoima and forty-three from the central Los Angeles area were interviewed; two white spouses were excluded from the sample. There seemed to be little difference between the two ghetto areas; the educational, occupational, and income levels were similar, as well as the findings on the alienation scales, so the two areas were combined for the final analysis.

The powerlessness scale that was used measures the extent to which the subject feels that he himself can control the outcomes of events that concern him.[12] The conceptualization of powerlessness is based on the social-learning theory of Julian B. Rotter, which, stated in a simplified way, holds that behavior is a function of values and expectations.[13] It has been argued that people tend to develop generalized expectancies, including those for control or lack of it. Since integration seems to be a commonly held value among Negroes, at least on the surface, it would seem that the expectation for successful integration would play an important role in determining who would make the effort to move into the integrated or predominantly white neighborhood. The powerlessness scale uses a forced-choice format so that subjects chose between pairs of items such as the following: (1) I have usually found that what is going to happen will happen, no matter what I do. (2) Trusting to fate has never turned out as

[11] Both spouses were included in the sample because there was some question ahead of time as to which one would be the most significant in deciding about moving and in carrying through the decision. As it turned out, there was agreement in most families, although in some one partner was a stronger force in the decision, but it could be either the husband or the wife.

[12] The powerlessness scale was developed by Shephard Liverant, Julian B. Rotter, and others. For a discussion of its use and development see Melvin Seeman, "Alienation and Social Learning in a Reformatory," *American Journal of Sociology*, LXIV (November, 1963), 270–84.

[13] Julian B. Rotter, *Social Learning and Clinical Psychology* (Englewood Cliffs, N.J.: Prentice-Hall, Inc., 1954).

well for me as making a definite decision.

The Srole anomia scale was selected as a second alienation measurement because it seems to be a more global type of measurement of the subject's lack of integration into the ongoing society. The Srole scale also captured the feelings of hopelessness and despair expressed by some of the subjects. It is a five-item Likert-type scale made up of statements such as the following:[14] In spite of what some people say, the lot of the average man is getting worse. A ten-item factual test was constructed to assess the amount of information subjects had about housing integration and the legal rights of minority people in the housing market. It included items such as: Restrictive housing covenants are still legal in California (false) and real-estate offices were defined as places of public accommodation so they are not supposed to discriminate (true).

A fourth scale, which measures the orientation toward or away from the ghetto, was built from information obtained in the interview schedule. It actually measures reported behavior rather than an attitude, but the behavior suggests an underlying orientation toward the Negro subculture of the ghetto or away from it. Subjects indicated what organizations they belonged to, their church affiliations, their chief leisure-time activities, the newspapers and magazines they read regularly, the schools they sent their children to, the racial identities of their close friends, and the degree of integration in their work situations. Each of these items was rated as to whether it was exclusively Negro or was reflective of an integrated situation.[15] It was expected that there would be some drifting away from a strictly segregated

life as a part of the process of moving out of the ghetto. Obviously, some of the items in this scale, such as the school, the church, and even the friendship choices, are affected by place of residence, so the fact that the ghetto dwellers and the outsiders would differ was to be expected. It nevertheless proved to be a useful device for looking at what happens to people when they move out.

A special methodological problem in a study such as this one is the possible biasing effect of the race of the interviewer. Approximately half of the interviews were done by white and half by Negro interviewers. The data were therefore analyzed controlling for this factor. Slight differences (not statistically significant) were found in the answers about the racial characteristics of friends; more people indicated that they had non-Negro friends when the interviewer was white. There did not seem to be other differences in responses that could be related to the race of the interviewer.

FINDINGS

As had been anticipated, the educational and income levels of the barrier breakers were high. Their median income was approximately $11,000 a year, which is well over the average Valley income.[16] The hope was that the ghetto samples would be of the same socioeconomic level as the people in the integrated sample, but due to the rather wide variety of income levels found in segregated neighborhoods the median income for the ghetto samples was lower, being approximately $9,700. There were, however, only six persons in the ghetto and two persons in the Valley-wide sample who reported family incomes

[14] Leo Srole, "Social Integration and Certain Corollaries: An Exploratory Study," *American Sociological Review*, XXI (December, 1956), 709–16.
[15] The items in this scale of ghetto (versus outside) orientation were scored in the following way: 0 if the activity was ghetto and only that, 1 if no direction could be determined, and 2 or 3

if the activity was clearly integrated or pointed to an outside interest. Eight items were included in the scale, and a range of scores from 0 to 19 was possible, with the low scores pointing toward the ghetto and the high scores indicating an outside interest.
[16] Meeker and Harris, *op. cit.*, p. 53.

of less than $5,000, so that poverty was not a factor in either area. Part of the difficulty in matching socioeconomic levels was due to the decision to avoid the mixed neighborhoods on the edge of the ghetto where the incomes might well have been more uniformly high but where some of the impact of segregated life would have been lost.

There were some factors that were similar in and out of the ghetto. The majority of people in both samples said they saw some value in living in an integrated or predominantly white neighborhood; 87 per cent of the Valley-wide group and 80 per cent of the ghetto dwellers indorsed such a statement, although the Valley residents could think of more concrete reasons why they felt that way. Both groups seemed to be made up of occupationally mobile people. The Bogue scale was used to assign numerical ratings to occupations, and about half of the people in each sample had moved up forty or more points beyond the level of their parents' occupations.[17] It was, for example, not at all unusual to find people with technical or professional jobs whose fathers had been laborers or their mothers domestic workers. This finding supports observations made by such writers as the late Franklin Frazier that there is a new and rapidly growing Negro middle class.[18] Possibly also related to the recent development of this middle class was the scarcity of older people in both groups. The median age in both samples was thirty-nine, but there was just one person over sixty in the Valley group, and in the ghetto sample there were just four.

When the powerlessness scores of the two groups were compared, significant differences were found; the people in the ghetto sample have a mean powerlessness

score of 3.01, while the outsiders' mean score is 2.48 ($t = 2.07$; $P < .05$). The people who have moved out thus indicate that they feel that they have more control over their own lives. Table 1 shows these scores with education, income, and sex controlled. As can be noted in the table, the greatest differences in powerlessness between the in- and out-of-the-ghetto samples show up in the high income and educational levels. This suggests that when the objective criteria for overcoming the barriers of housing discrimination are most favorable, the expectation for control of one's life helps predict who will actually make the move.

The anomia scores follow a similar pattern. In the ghetto the mean score on the anomia scale is 12.9; in the integrated community the mean score is 10.6; these differences are also significant ($t = 4.24$; $P < .001$). The controls for income and education indicate that, although the anomia scores vary more in relation to these factors, the area of residence still makes a difference at each level. There is a correlation between anomia and powerlessness; inside the ghetto it was $r = .43$ and outside it was $r = .37$. This suggests that there is indeed a relationship between these two kinds of alienation in this situation, although the two scales are not measuring the same thing.[19]

Most of the people now living in the Valley spent their childhoods in the ghetto or on its edge (only twelve people reported having grown up in predominantly white neighborhoods). Some explanation should be given as to why the two groups of people scored differently on the alienation

[17] Donald Bogue, *Skid Row in American Cities* (Chicago: University of Chicago Press, 1963), Appendix.

[18] E. Franklin Frazier, *Black Bourgeoisie* (Glencoe, Ill.: Free Press, 1957).

[19] The relationship of powerlessness and anomia is discussed by Arthur Neal and Melvin Seeman, "Organization and Powerlessness: A Test of the Mediation Hypothesis," *American Sociological Review*, XXIX (April, 1964), p. 222 n.; see also Arthur G. Neal and Salomon Rettig, "Dimensions of Alienation among Manual and Non-Manual Workers," *American Sociological Review*, XXVIII (August, 1963), 599–602.

Table 1. *Mean Powerlessness and Anomia Scores in the Valley-Wide and Ghetto Areas When Education, Income, and Sex Are Controlled*

	POWERLESSNESS		ANOMIA	
CONTROL	*Valley Wide* (N=101)	*Ghetto* (N=105)	*Valley Wide* (N=103)	*Ghetto* (N=105)
Education:				
College graduate ...	2.14 (N=43)	2.88 (N=32)	9.67 (N=43)	11.72 (N=32)
Some college or technical education ..	2.73 (N=42)	3.15 (N=39)	10.90 (N=42)	12.54 (N=39)
High School or less..	2.75 (N=16)	2.97 (N=34)	12.17 (N=18)	14.38 (N=43)
Income:				
$15,000 and over ...	2.05 (N=34)	3.05 (N=22)	9.91 (N=34)	12.60 (N=22)
$7,800-$15,000	2.59 (N=49)	2.80 (N=56)	10.26 (N=50)	11.77 (N=56)
Below $7,800	3.00 (N=18)	3.27 (N=26)	12.79 (N=19)	15.19 (N=26)
Sex:				
Male	2.55 (N=53)	2.77 (N=48)	10.77 (N=54)	12.65 (N=48)
Female	2.42 (N=48)	3.21 (N=57)	10.42 (N=49)	13.08 (N=57)

scales. This paper cannot, of course, supply all of the answers to that question, but if we look at some of the other factors associated with anomia and powerlessness some clues are offered. Anomia seems to correlate negatively with almost any of life's advantages,[20] so it would seem that the people with lower scores on the Srole scale, including those who moved out of the ghetto, somehow escaped some of the worst disadvantages. Table 2 shows the small but consistently negative correlations with several of these factors. Since powerlessness is a less global sort of attitude it does not correlate highly with as many variables; in this study the development of a high expectation for control

[20] Dorothy L. Meier and Wendell Bell, "Anomia and Differential Access to the Achievement of Life Goals," *American Sociological Review*, XXIV (April, 1959), 189–202.

seems most related to past and present experiences with integration, not only in housing but also in other aspects of life. Segregation and all that is associated with it emerges as such a crucial problem for Negroes that successful experiences with integration seem to raise the general level of expectation for control. Notice that the childhood experiences most related to lower powerlessness scores are those of integrated school experience and living in a racially mixed neighborhood while growing up.

It was expected from the beginning of the study that the Valley-wide residents would have lost some of their ties with the strictly segregated institutions within the ghetto. In fact, giving up some of the old customs and ties seems to be the price paid by any minority group that is assimilated. It was therefore not surprising that

Table 2. *Correlations (Pearson's r) of Powerlessness and Anomia*[a] *with Selected Factors*

	VALLEY WIDE	GHETTO
	Powerlessness	
Father's occupational level	−.04	−.004
Employed subject's occupational level	−.31**	−.05
Present income	−.18*	−.03
Educational attainment	−.17*	−.07
Amount of integrated schooling	−.22**	−.10
Neighborhood of childhood (segregated to integrated)	−.30**	−.24**
	Anomia	
Father's occupational level	−.04	−.20*
Employed subject's occupational level	−.22**	−.22**
Present income	−.23**	−.28**
Educational attainment	−.28**	−.31**
Amount of integrated schooling	−.13	−.19*
Neighborhood of childhood (segregated to integrated)	−.12	−.27**

[a] The numbers varied in these correlations from 79 to 105.
* Significant ($P < .05$).
** Significant ($P < .01$).

the Valley group had a mean score of 13.0 on the "ghetto-orientation" scale, while the mean of the ghetto sample was 9.7 ($t = 7.99$; $P < .001$). This wide difference on the ghetto-orientation scale indicates that the various aspects of integration tend to be related to each other; moving out of the ghetto is one part of a total life pattern. That this change in pattern is a long-term process is suggested by the fact that the last residence of 61 per cent of the Valley group was described as predominantly white or mixed, while only 23 per cent of the ghetto sample reported that the place they lived in last had even token integration.

It was of interest to find out that within each sample the drift away from a ghetto orientation was related to a greater expectation for control and to lower anomia scores. Table 3 shows the differences in powerlessness and anomia when the two samples are split at the median on orienta-

tion. As an alienation measurement the orientation scale is two sided. It indicates the degree to which the customs and associations of the subculture are selected over those of the mainstream of the society; movement away from one pole implies a movement toward the other. This type of value isolation is alienation of a different dimension than that assessed by the Srole scale in which movement away from the mainstream could mean a withdrawal into apathy. The concept of value isolation has been used to describe the alienation felt by intellectuals, although presumably members of any subculture that holds values that deviate from the commonly held societal values would be alienated in this sense.[21] Of course it is also possible to be alienated from the subculture. Since the ghetto orientation was related to both powerlessness and anomia, regardless of place of residence, it would seem that the

[21] Seeman, "On the Meaning of Alienation."

Table 3. Mean Powerlessness and Anomia Scores in the Valley-wide and Ghetto Areas When the Samples Are Divided at the Median[a] on Orientation

ORIENTATION	VALLEY WIDE	GHETTO
Powerlessness:		
Integrated orientation	2.38	2.63
	($N=49$)	($N=57$)
Ghetto orientation	2.75	3.45*
	($N=52$)	($N=48$)
Anomia:		
Integrated orientation	10.00	11.86
	($N=49$)	($N=57$)
Ghetto orientation	11.19*	14.10**
	($N=54$)	($N=48$)

[a] The median scores on the orientation scale were 13 in the valley-wide area and 9 in the ghetto.

* Differences between the mean scores of those with integrated or ghetto orientations were significant ($P < .05$).

** Significant ($P < .01$).

securely "locked-in" position within the Negro ghetto was not a particularly desirable state. The "marginal" or moving-out position may not be as undesirable as it is sometimes considered. Of course it can be argued that, since Negroes are already familiar with American culture, and yet not completely accepted by it, their position in the ghetto is already a marginal one.

One of the items used to make up the orientation scale was the racial makeup of the subject's church congregation. In addition to the racial characteristics of the individual congregation, the denominational identification also turned out to have predictive value. As can be noted in Table 4, not only were members of Baptist and Holiness churches more powerless than others, they were seldom found outside the ghetto. Methodists, whose churches also have been segregated historically, did not score so high on the powerlessness scale, and they were well represented in the Valley-wide area. Members of other Protestant churches, Catholics, and non-church members were the best represented in the Valley. The church is the focus of much of the social life within the ghetto, so that it may sometimes act

as a positive tie to hold people within the segregated areas.[22] These differences by denomination were not adequately anticipated in the planning of the study, so that data were not obtained about past religious identification. It is therefore not known whether certain church affiliations are associated with staying in the ghetto or whether people change their religious identifications when they move out.

Having found that Negroes who live outside the ghetto feel less powerless and less of the hopeless detachment measured by the anomia scale still leaves an unanswered question; are the feelings of alienation a selective factor that keeps some people from moving out, or does the experience of having successfully moved lessen the feelings of alienation? Probably both happen, but the evidence for alienation as a negative selective factor is strongest. Some of the correlations associated with childhood conditions suggest that feelings of alienation are fairly stable attitudes, developing sometimes over a life-

[22] E. Franklin Frazier, *The Negro Church in America* (New York: Schocken Books, 1964); Joseph R. Washington, Jr., *Black Religion* (Boston: Beacon Press, 1964).

Table 4. Mean Powerlessness Scores and Religious Identification*

RELIGION	VALLEY WIDE (N=101)	GHETTO (N=105)
Baptist	3.29 (N=7)	3.62 (N=29)
Methodist	2.17 (N=23)	2.95 (N=19)
Holiness	3.00 (N=3)	3.63 (N=8)
Other Protestant	2.10 (N=28)	2.27 (N=22)
Catholic	1.96 (N=24)	2.28 (N=17)
None	3.45 (N=16)	2.70 (N=10)

* Differences in religious affiliation in the two areas: $x^2 = 19.4$ ($P < .01$).

time. When the powerlessness scores of the Valley residents who have lived outside of the ghetto for more than five years were compared with the newcomers, the older residents did have lower scores, but even the newcomers were lower in alienation than the average for the ghetto.

As suggested by other research on alienation, one of the mechanisms by which higher expectation for control fosters integration is probably through its relationship with more effective social learning.[23]

[23] Seeman, "Alienation and Social Learning in a Reformatory"; see also Melvin Seeman and J. W. Evans, "Alienation and Learning in a Hospital Setting," *American Sociological Review,* XXVII (December, 1962), 772–82.

People who feel less powerless would thus be expected to have learned more about their rights in the housing market and how they might be able to secure a house or an apartment in an integrated area. Table 5 shows the differences in scores on the housing-facts test with the subjects divided at the median on their powerlessness scores; the low powerlessness group does tend to have learned more of these facts.

Both powerlessness and anomia seem to act as psychological deterrents to people making the kind of sustained effort that is necessary to be successful in overcoming the barriers to integration. Subjects in the ghetto were asked if they had ever looked for housing in an integrated or predomi-

Table 5. Mean Scores on the Housing-Facts Test When Divided at the Median in Each Area on the Powerlessness Scale[a]

POWERLESSNESS	VALLEY WIDE	GHETTO
Above median or at the median	7.10 (N=47)	6.27 (N=61)
Below median	7.37 (N=54)	7.02 (N=44)

[a] Both samples were split at 2.
* The differences in the ghetto sample were significant ($P < .05$).

nantly white neighborhood. Fifty-six of the people in that sample said they had done so at some time in their lives. However, when the ghetto sample was divided by this factor, the anomia scores were the same for the two groups (12.9), and the powerlessness scores were actually higher for the group that said they had looked (3.20 mean score as compared with 2.80). Just looking at these scores it would seem that alienation was not a selective factor. However, when these people were asked to elaborate on their experiences in looking, they characteristically told of a single experience in which they looked and were rebuffed. When the Valley residents told of their experiences they sometimes described years of searching until they were finally successful. Occasionally these accounts included reports of open refusals, but more often they were faced with a long series of evasions and trickery including realty salesmen who were "out" or ran to hide from them in the other room, managers who had no authority to rent the apartments, owners who could not be located, forms that could not be processed, returned deposits, and so on. The persistence shown by some of these people in the face of one disappointment after another is worthy of note. It would seem, then, that alienation as a selective factor may function more in fixing the amount of determination and effectiveness that the subjects bring to the task, rather than merely selecting who will make a single attempt. The people who were successful in moving out, despite the present barriers of discrimination, were unwilling to accept one act of prejudice as their final answer, and here an ultimate belief in a manageable world undoubtedly helped them.

SUMMARY AND CONCLUSIONS

When a group of integrated middle-class Negro subjects was compared with another group of middle-class subjects

who remained within the traditional Negro ghettos, significant differences in alienation were found. The integrated subjects had greater expectations for control of events that concerned them and less of a feeling of anomia. They also tended to orient themselves toward the mainstream of society rather than toward the segregated institutions of the Negro subculture. Alienation within the ghetto takes on a circular characteristic; not only is it a product of segregated living, it also acts to keep people locked in the traditional residential patterns.

The fact that alienation is such a circular process does not mean that nothing can be done to deal with the problems of segregation. It does mean that antidiscriminatory legislation alone cannot bring about instant integration. Instead such legislation would be more effective if accompanied by other efforts to overcome the psychological barriers to integration. The fact that anomia correlates with almost any kind of deprivation suggests the need for effective programs to combat poverty, unemployment, and lack of educational opportunity in the ghetto; these programs are needed not only for their own intrinsic worth but also to combat the feelings of hopelessness and despair that are a part of the ghetto attitude. The fact that choosing the integrated way of life in one sphere is related to choosing it in others suggests that any sort of program aimed at decreasing segregation is worth trying. A fair-employment-practices act can even help bring about more housing integration by giving the workers the experience of working together. Integrated school or church experiences give children the opportunity to set up patterns of mixed associations. However, the solution to the problems of segregation are not easy; the old patterns, supported by the psychological barriers of alienation, do not change rapidly.

MISANTHROPY AND POLITICAL IDEOLOGY*

Morris Rosenberg

Political research has shown that the individual's political ideology may be influenced by a number of different factors—his interpersonal relationships, group affiliations, "conditions of existence," personality characteristics, etc. There has been a tendency, however, to overlook the fact that *attitudes toward human nature* may also have some bearing on political attitudes and acts.

There are several reasons for expecting misanthropism to be implicated in political attitudes. First, political ideologies often contain implicit assumptions about human nature (e.g., the democratic doctrine assumes that most citizens are sufficiently rational to govern themselves). Secondly, since a political system basically involves people in action, the individual's view of human nature is likely to be linked to his evaluation of how well the system actually works (e.g., the belief that political dishonesty is rife in a democracy may be based less upon actual knowledge of political corruption than upon the general conviction that nearly everyone is dishonest). Thirdly, the individual's stand on certain specific political questions may be in-

fluenced by his assumptions about the nature of man (e.g., the belief that men are fundamentally lazy and will not work without the prod of necessity may induce the individual to oppose a public relief program). In other words, faith in people may be related to attitudes toward the *principles, practices,* and *policies* of a political system.

In the course of a study of college students' values conducted at Cornell University in 1952, an attempt was made to investigate the relationship between misanthropy and political ideology. In order to range the respondents along the "faith in people" dimension, we constructed a Guttman scale[1] consisting of the following five items:

1. Some people say that most people can be trusted. Others say you can't be too careful in your dealings with people. How do you feel about it?

2. Would you say that most people are more inclined to help others or more inclined to look out for themselves?

3. If you don't watch yourself, people will take advantage of you.

4. No one is going to care much what happens to you, when you get right down to it.

5. Human nature is fundamentally cooperative.

SOURCE: Reprinted from the *American Sociological Review,* 21, 6 (December 1956), 690–695, by permission of the author and publisher.

* The present report is part of a broader study of college students' values conducted at Cornell University under the direction of Edward A. Suchman, Robin M. Williams, Jr., Rose K. Goldsen and Morris Rosenberg.

[1] For a discussion of the logic of the Guttman méthods, see S. A. Stouffer, *et al., Measurement and Prediction,* Princeton: Princeton University Press, 1950, Chs. 3 and 6.

The coefficient of reproducibility of the "faith in people" scale was 92 per cent. In constructing this scale, a deliberate attempt was made to exclude items which could be construed as political in nature. The emphasis was on the respondent's feelings about people in general.

In order to investigate the relationship between the individual's global attitude toward human nature and his political ideology, three aspects of political ideology were considered: the image of the public and the legislator, attitudes toward freedom of speech, and the view of the state as an instrument of suppression.

Image of the Public and the Legislator

The institution of representative government is designed to enable the public, through its elected representatives, to translate its will into law. The individual would be unlikely to have confidence in this principle if he did not make at least the following assumptions:

1. That the great majority of citizens in a democracy are sufficiently rational and informed to make sound political decisions.

2. That the elected representatives are sincerely concerned with the wills and needs of their constituents, not exclusively interested in personal power and gain.

3. That most political representatives are men of integrity, and are not "bossed" by self-seeking minorities.

Let us first examine the assumption that men are sufficiently rational and informed to make sound political decisions. Students were asked to agree or disagree with the following statement: "The general public is not qualified to vote on today's complex issues." Table 1 indicates that 68 per cent of those with low faith in people agreed with this statement, compared with 32 per cent of the respondents with the highest faith in people.

Consider next the question of the responsiveness of public officials to the will of the people. Relatively speaking, those with low faith in people tend to deny that elected or appointed officials are concerned with the interests of most of the people. The misanthropes were nearly four times as likely as the philanthropists[2] to agree that "There's little use writing to public officials because often they aren't really interested in the problems of the average man."

Finally, there is evidence to indicate that the misanthrope is more likely than the philanthropist to believe that political representatives are not men of integrity, but are, rather, pawns in the hands of special interests. As Table 1 indicates, the lower one's faith in people, the more likely one is to believe that "Political candidates are usually run by political machines."

These three items were found to scale according to the Guttman method. Those who tended to agree with these statements were classified as "dubious" about the operation of representative government and those who tended to disagree were classified as "sanguine." As Table 1 shows, 76 per cent of those with the lowest faith in people were found in the "dubious" category, compared with 32 per cent of the respondents with the highest faith in people, a difference of 44 per cent. The misanthrope, it would appear, is more likely than others to feel that certain practices of democracy fall short of the avowed principles.

In considering these data, one may get the feeling that these results are simply tautological—that all we have demonstrated is that those with general low faith in people also have little respect for people involved in politics. This is quite true, but it is a fruitful tautology. We would not expect a misanthrope to build a bridge or shift the gears of an auto differently from a philanthropist. But we would expect him

[2] The term "philanthropist" is used in its literal meaning of "lover of mankind," rather than in the more popular sense of a benefactor to humanity or contributor to worthy causes.

Table 1. Faith in People and Image of the Public and Legislator

| | FAITH IN PEOPLE (IN PERCENTAGES) | | | | | |
	HIGH 1	2	3	4	5	LOW 6

"The general public is not qualified to vote on today's complex issues."*

	HIGH 1	2	3	4	5	LOW 6
Agree	32	46	45	54	55	68
Disagree	53	44	44	40	38	29
Undecided	15	10	11	6	7	3
Number of cases	(232)	(430)	(376)	(262)	(174)	(76)

"There's little use writing to public officials because often they aren't really interested in the problems of the average man."*

	HIGH 1	2	3	4	5	LOW 6
Agree	12	16	26	27	36	45
Disagree	68	65	55	53	47	39
Undecided	20	19	19	20	17	17
Number of cases	(236)	(445)	(376)	(262)	(176)	(76)

"Political candidates are usually run by political machines."*

	HIGH 1	2	3	4	5	LOW 6
Agree	66	69	76	78	83	92
Disagree	19	18	12	11	11	4
Undecided	15	13	12	11	6	4
Number of cases	(236)	(445)	(376)	(262)	(176)	(76)

Belief in the feasibility of democracy.*

	HIGH 1	2	3	4	5	LOW 6
Dubious (Score 2-3)	32	42	49	56	61	76
Sanguine (Score 0-1)	68	58	51	44	39	24
Number of cases	(236)	(445)	(376)	(262)	(176)	(76)

* $P(x^2) < .001$.

to be skeptical about the operation of democracy, because certain of the principles of democracy are founded upon certain assumptions about human nature. The way one looks at democracy depends in part upon the way one looks at humanity.

Freedom of Speech

The democratic concept of freedom of speech—the free market place of ideas—implies that most men are capable of arriving at sound judgments when exposed to different ideas. It assumes that they are capable of separating the wheat from the chaff, the true from the false, and arriving at sound conclusions. The advocate of freedom of speech is likely to believe that most men are not easily deceived, are not swayed by uncontrolled emotions, and are capable of sound judgment. The special virtue of freedom of speech, it is often assumed, lies in the fact that exposure to diverse points of view will give the people the soundest basis for arriving at the best decision.

In order to examine this question, we asked our respondents to agree or disagree with the following statements:

1. "People who talk politics without knowing what they are talking about should be kept quiet."

2. "Unrestricted freedom of speech leads to mass hysteria."

3. "People should be kept from spreading dangerous ideas because they might influence others to adopt them."

The relationships of faith in people to these items appear in Tables 2 and 3. In each case, it will be noted, the misanthropic respondents were more likely than others to be dubious about freedom of speech or to advocate its restriction. Since one can no more imagine a democracy without freedom of speech than without representative government or other civil rights, it appears that faith in people is clearly related to belief in the feasibility of the democratic form of government.

The State as an Instrument of Suppression

It is not unusual these days to hear people saying that the government should "do something" about certain deviant or unpopular groups. The public's reactions to such statements are usually comprehensible in terms of their liberalism or conservatism, isolationism or internationalism, etc. However, what often escapes the analyst's attention is the fact that one's position on the issue may be determined by one's attitude to the notion of "law" itself. In other words, the question of whether the government should suppress certain groups is not only dependent upon one's ideological sympathy with, or tolerance toward, the groups under consideration, but also upon whether one characteristically views the state as an instrument of suppression. We would expect those with low faith in people, *irrespective of their own ideological positions*, to tend to say that there ought to be a law against some deviant group.

For example, Cornell students were asked to agree or disagree with the statement: "The laws governing labor unions today are not strict enough." Responses to this statement were expected to reflect the more generalized attitude of "political liberalism." And this expectation is supported by the data. Fifty-two per cent of the Republicans, compared with 29 per cent of the Independents, and 21 per cent of the Democrats, agreed with the statement.

Nevertheless, Table 4 indicates that, irrespective of political liberalism (as measured by party affiliation), those with low faith in people tend to be more likely than those with high faith to advocate stricter government control of labor.

This point is illustrated again in responses to the statement: "Steps should be taken right away to outlaw the Commu-

Table 2. Faith in People and Restriction of Political Expression

	FAITH IN PEOPLE (IN PERCENTAGES)					
	HIGH 1	2	3	4	5	LOW 6

"People who talk politics without knowing what they are talking about should be kept quiet."*

	HIGH 1	2	3	4	5	LOW 6
Agree	21	20	28	30	37	40
Disagree	69	67	63	61	54	55
Undecided	10	13	9	9	9	5
Number of cases	(232)	(430)	(366)	(260)	(176)	(76)

* $P(x^2) < .001$.

Table 3. Faith in People and Attitudes Toward Freedom of Speech†

	HIGH 1	2	3	4	LOW 5,6
		FAITH IN PEOPLE (IN PERCENTAGES)			

"Unrestricted freedom of speech leads to mass hysteria."*

	HIGH 1	2	3	4	LOW 5,6
Agree or undecided	16	21	21	27	32
Disagree	84	79	79	73	68
Number of cases	(149)	(261)	(232)	(143)	(159)

"People should be kept from spreading dangerous ideas because they
might influence others to adopt them."*

	HIGH 1	2	3	4	LOW 5,6
Agree or undecided	32	38	37	40	51
Disagree	68	62	63	60	49
Number of cases	(149)	(261)	(229)	(142)	(158)

* $P(x^2) < .01$.

† The questions in Table 3 were asked in a study of values conducted at Cornell in 1950, whereas the "faith in people" scale was developed in 1952. On these questions, therefore, we are relating the same respondent's faith in people in 1952 to his attitude toward freedom of speech in 1950. One consequence of this procedure is to shrink the number of cases. Hence, the two lowest categories of faith in people (5 and 6) have been combined. Secondly, it is expected that some changes in faith in people and in political attitudes would have occurred during the two-year span. The error introduced by this procedure would almost certainly be in the direction of weakening, rather than strengthening, the statistical relationship. In order to show the relationships more clearly in these two questions, we have combined the agree and undecided categories. The results, it will be seen, are in the anticipated direction.

nist Party!" We find that 32 per cent of the Republicans, 21 per cent of the Independents, and 18 per cent of the Democrats agreed with the statement. Political liberalism is clearly a factor of significance with regard to this issue. However, the statement also reflects the notion that the state is an instrument of power designed to suppress a deviant group. Table 4 shows that, within each political group, those with low faith in people are more likely to advocate suppression of political deviants than are those with high faith in people. It is interesting to observe that the philanthropists show a slight tendency to take refuge in the "undecided" response. The reason, probably, is that those with high faith in people feel the same way about the Communist Party as the mis-

anthropes of the same political affiliation, but that they are reluctant to go so far as to advocate suppression.

These findings are particularly interesting because they refer to relatively concrete issues, rather than to some of the more abstract statements concerning civil liberties. The individual with low faith in people tends to believe in suppression of weak, deviant, or dangerous groups, irrespective of his political affiliation. But the misanthrope's tendency to suppress deviant groups is also reflected in his responses to certain more general questions. For example, the members of our sample were asked to agree or disagree with the following statement: "Religions which preach unwholesome ideas should be suppressed." Table 5 indicates that the most

Table 4. Faith in People and View of the State as an Instrument of Suppression

	Republicans FAITH IN PEOPLE (IN PERCENTAGES)			Democrats FAITH IN PEOPLE (IN PERCENTAGES)			Independents FAITH IN PEOPLE (IN PERCENTAGES)		
	HIGH	MED.	LOW	HIGH	MED.	LOW	HIGH	MED.	LOW
"The laws governing labor today are not strict enough."*									
Agree	44	55	70	14	21	37	24	30	43
Disagree ..	30	24	13	60	64	43	42	43	35
Undecided .	26	21	17	26	15	20	34	27	22
Number of cases ...	(276)	(281)	(104)	(96)	(87)	(49)	(276)	(249)	(87)
"Steps should be taken right away to outlaw the Communist Party."*									
Agree	28	29	50	15	17	27	14	22	37
Disagree ..	50	53	36	68	65	57	63	63	50
Undecided .	22	18	14	17	18	16	23	15	13
Number of cases ...	(276)	(281)	(104)	(96)	(87)	(49)	(276)	(249)	(87)

* $P(x^2) < .001$ for combined groups.

misanthropic people were twice as likely as the least misanthropic to agree with this view.

Finally, there appears to be a somewhat greater tendency among the more misanthropic respondents to advocate restrictions on the right to run for public office. Forty-six per cent of them felt that it was "unwise to give people with dangerous social and economic viewpoints a chance to be elected," whereas only 25 per cent of the least misanthropic respondents held this view (Table 5). With regard to these last two questions, once again, the philanthropists appear to be somewhat more likely than others to take refuge in the "undecided" category, whereas the misanthrope is relatively likely to take an unequivocal stand in favor of suppression.

On a variety of issues, then—freedom of speech, freedom of religion, the right to run for public office, etc.—the misanthrope has a greater tendency to advocate the suppression of deviant people or groups. The individual's view of human nature would appear to have significant implications for the doctrine of political liberty.

In sum, these data suggest that the way a man looks at people has a bearing upon the way he looks at certain political matters. There are many political matters, of course, which are unrelated to the individual's view of humanity. For example, faith in people has little to do with being a Democrat or a Republican, a liberal or a conservative (in the formal sense). But low faith in people is related to a distrust of the public, a conviction of public officials' unresponsiveness to the people, a belief that political machines run the candidates, a skepticism about freedom of speech, and a willingness to suppress certain political and religious liberties.

It is characteristic of sociological studies of political behavior to investigate the relationship between social position and political attitudes and acts. We are suggesting here, however, that it may also be fruitful to examine the problem of political behavior on a different level—the level of generalized attitudes. If we can discover

Table 5. Faith in People and Religious and Political Freedom

	FAITH IN PEOPLE (IN PERCENTAGES)					
	HIGH 1	2	3	4	5	LOW 6
"Religions which preach unwholesome ideas should be suppressed."*						
Agree	16	17	18	20	27	32
Disagree	66	62	63	64	52	56
Undecided	18	21	19	16	21	12
Number of cases	(232)	(440)	(372)	(261)	(174)	(75)
"It's unwise to give people with dangerous social and economic viewpoints a chance to be elected."†						
Agree	25	33	33	39	50	46
Disagree	56	54	50	49	40	46
Undecided	19	13	17	12	10	8
Number of cases	(232)	(430)	(366)	(260)	(174)	(76)

* $P(x^2) < .02$.
† $P(x^2) < .001$.

certain generalized attitudes, such as the attitude toward human nature, which spread out to influence people's reactions to a wide range of specific issues, then our ability to predict specific political reactions would be enhanced.

But the faith in people variable may also be relevant to non-political attitudes and behavior; there is reason to believe, in fact, that the individual's view of humanity may influence his reactions to a wide range of social phenomena. In the first place, faith in people is likely to affect his interpersonal relationships, both on a primary and secondary level. On the primary level, the misanthrope may experience difficulty in establishing close, warm bonds of friendship because of his basic distrust of, and contempt for, other people. On the secondary level, a misanthropic businessman may watch his employees and business associates "like a hawk," may be abnormally wary about granting others credit, may interpret signs of friendliness as devices of manipulation, etc. There is thus reason to expect the individual's degree of

misanthropy to influence his perception of others and his behavior toward them.

The individual's view of humanity may also influence his attitudes toward various institutional structures, social practices, and ideological principles. The misanthrope, for example, may oppose progressive education on the ground that children are innately evil and must therefore be kept under restraint. Or he may interpret acts of charity to be motivated chiefly by the desire to avoid the payment of taxes. Again, he may favor building up national military power on the ground that men are by nature bellicose and that war is therefore inevitable. There thus appears to be a wide range of attitudes and acts which may be influenced by the individual's view of humanity. If research confirms this impression, faith in people could prove to be a variable of importance to the social psychologist.

In this paper faith in people is treated as a generalized attitude. At present it is not entirely clear how this attitude is linked to the broader personality configuration of authoritarianism. There is evidence to suggest, for example, that the authoritarian personality type tends to have relatively low faith in human nature.[3] We

[3] See T. Adorno, *et al., The Authoritarian Personality,* New York: Harpers, 1950, pp. 148 and 154 for a discussion of the ethnocentric's negative evaluation of human nature. It is also relevant to note that Item 6 of the F-scale, Forms 45 and 40, p. 256, reads: "Human nature being what it is, there will always be war and conflict."

do not know, however, whether misanthropy is a central or peripheral part of the authoritarian personality structure. Further study would be required to determine the degree to which misanthropy is a reflection of authoritarianism and, conversely, the degree to which the predictive power of the scales of authoritarianism are attributable to the presence of the faith in people component.

PART III

ALIENATION IN ACADEMIA

Introduction

A great deal of research on student attitudes and behavior has been carried out in recent years, much of it inspired by the tremendously increased activism of American college students during the sixties. Student activism in this decade, however, was focused very heavily on problems originating outside of the universities. The Vietnam War, environmental pollution, and problems of poverty, for example, were dominant themes that motivated many of the most active students. To be sure, there were concerns voiced about the role of students in the decision making processes of the university and the role of the university in the community in which it was located, but these were of minor importance compared to the much more dominant issues of governmental policies.

It is understandable, therefore, that very little of the research on students focused on their alienation from their own academic institutions or on the role of the academic environment in producing feelings of alienation. Yet it is clear that the school as an institution is as likely a cause of alienation for students as the work environment is for workers or the political system for citizens. Indeed, there are growing indications that student concerns are becoming increasingly focused on the role of students in the management and goal determination of their own schools. The cry of "student power" and lamentations of student powerlessness make it clear that this dimension of alienation has been implicated as an important vector in the student-academic institution relationship. Students have even formed trade unions at a number of universities to achieve better wages and working conditions for teaching assistants. Some of these unions have utilized many of the traditional weapons of workers' unions, including the strike.

The extent to which academic curricula are geared to the needs, interests, and values of students—in a word, are "relevant"—is another prime concern of many students who wish to reorient activities and policies of high schools and colleges. Arthur Stinchcombe's study of the relationship between students and their high school revolves around the issue of curriculum as an important factor in determining whether students feel alienated from school. Stinchcombe's definition of alienation is particularly interesting in that it is related very closely to the situation of the high school and the particular and unique ways in which alienation may be expressed toward that institution. Stinchcombe views "expressive alienation" from high school as a set of attitudes and behaviors which express rejection of the values for which the high school stands. The alienated attitudes become manifest in behavior which is socially defined as objectionable within the school environment. The first part of Stinchcombe's argument establishes the interrelatedness of these alienated attitudes and rebellious behaviors in a syndrome which defines the concept of "expressive alienation."

Stinchcombe's major hypothesis is that expressive alienation results when students are involved in a program of study that is not related to their own goals and aspirations for the future. Their school activities then tend to have little meaning for them, and they begin to reject the values of the school and to engage in behavior which defies the norms of school authorities. The role of personal goals and aspirations in the development of attitudes of alienation is therefore a critical one. Stinchcombe does not view the school structure *per se* as necessarily alienating. Rather, this structure interacts with the goals and values of the individuals operating within it. If an individual views the social structure as consistent with, and supportive of, his goals, he is unlikely to feel alienated from it. On the other hand, if he perceives the activities in which he is required to engage as irrelevant to his own aspirations, he is more likely to feel alienated from, and rebel against, the confining environment.

Stinchcombe's theory of articulation between future goal aspirations and present academic work provides some interesting clues to help explain why, at the college level, students of the social sciences and humanities tend to be more active in political protests than students in the natural sciences and professionally-oriented fields such as engineering and business. Although many reasons have been put forward for this relationship, the articulation theory may advance explanation still further. Students of the professions and natural sciences have much broader job opportunities in nonacademic sectors of the society. They may perceive a fairly natural and easily travelled channel between their academic pursuits and a stable job opportunity structure outside. For students of the social sciences and humanities, the articulation between academic work and future job status is much less certain. For those who do not go on for advanced degrees, there are few job opportunities in their areas of interest. Even for those who complete graduate work, academic positions may not be available, and relatively few opportunities in these careers exist in private business and government. Given these relationships with the nonacademic world, feelings of isolation and estrangement from nonacademic sectors are much less likely to develop among students of the natural sciences and professions. In fact, Hajda (1961) has shown that social science and humanities graduate students are more likely to consider themselves as members of an intellectual minority than graduate students in the natural sciences and that this self-imposed minority group status is closely associated with a feeling of alienation and isolation from nonacademic people. Poor articulation between current activities and future aspirations may therefore lead to alienation from other sectors of the society as well as from the academic institution. Students who feel alienated from nonacademic social sectors might consequently be more sympathetic to protest activities defined as antibusiness and antigovernment.

While the reasoning behind this proposition seems logical, it has not yet been demonstrated that student activists are indeed more alienated than their more apathetic fellows either from their academic institutions or from other sectors of the society. Indeed, Keniston (1967) has recently suggested that it is, in fact, the most apathetic students who are culturally alienated and that a belief in the society and its basic values is actually a necessary motivation for student activism. Yet if student activists perceive great discrepancies between social norms and social policy, this would define a state of alienation for them too, although in a way different from that understood by many observers. That is, rejection of social policy coupled with an *affirmation* of basic social norms might be responsible for the alienation of many activists. More research is needed on the relationship between alienation and activism rather than continued reliance on the *a priori* assumption that student activists are more politically or academically alienated than others. There is a particular need for more attention to the basic value commitments of activists and nonactivists so as to further explore the discrepancy theme of alienation.

How can academic institutions be restructured to reduce the discrepancies between student aspirations and academic programs? In his discussion of reducing alienation in the high school, Stinchcombe is concerned with the relationship between the high school curriculum and the manpower needs of the labor market. As the demand for a college education becomes more widespread and the student population more heterogeneous, this becomes an important problem for colleges as well. What kind of articulation exists among the goals and aspirations of college students, the programs available to them, and the manpower needs of the society? To what extent should college programs be changed to increase this articulation? To what extent should the focus be on changing the goals and aspirations of college students themselves? What ought to be the social function of the educational institution? If the programs of high schools and colleges are designed to perpetuate the values of their students, can they be viable forces for creativity and social change? These questions suggest the range of empirical and normative concerns raised in considering the problem of alienation from academic institutions.

Another approach to student alienation is represented in Keniston's work (1965, 1968). Keniston is concerned mainly with the *psychological* origins and nature of a broad cultural alienation. For further analyses of alienation from the school *per se,* see the work of Epperson (1963), Rhea (1966, 1968), Watts and Whittaker (1968), and Wittes (1970).

REBELLION IN A HIGH SCHOOL

Arthur L. Stinchcombe

Delinquency and High School Rebellion

The student-teacher relation in high school is one of the few authority relations in modern society whose maintenance is consistently problematic. Though authority everywhere frequently meets with lack of enthusiasm by subordinates, it is not often openly flouted and insulted. Though authorities everywhere have difficulty persuading subordinates to be devoted to the goals of organizations, they only rarely have difficulty carrying on orderly social intercourse. It is consistently problematic whether orderly social intercourse will take place in classrooms. . . .

High school rebellion involves expression of alienation from socially present authorities; it may thus be called "expressive alienation." The contention here is that "rebellion" is a manifestation of "expressive alienation," and that high school rebellion has an emotional quality of hatred or sullenness.[1] Other deviant behavior may have the emotional quality of cynicism, or indifference to rules, or ignorance of correct behavior. Cynicism, indifference, indignation, or ideological disagreement with norms are other forms of alienation, different in emotional tone. The

adjective "expressive" should connote some of the special quality of alienation from high school authority, especially its responsive, non-ideological, unorganized, and impulsive character.

Two recent descriptions of the psychological quality of delinquents[2] may be abstracted to give an ideal-typical description of "expressive alienation."

1. It is non-utilitarian. No long-run goals, accomplishments, or rewards are necessary to motivate such deviance. Long-run goals may, of course, be supplied by institutionalization of juvenile delinquency, which links rebelliousness to adult criminal organizations and provides careers for delinquent leadership. But *as classroom rebellion* it does not require such institutionalization.[3]

2. It is malicious and negativistic, involving hatred of "nice" people and a negative attitude toward conformity in general.

SOURCE: Reprinted from Arthur L. Stinchcombe, *Rebellion in a High School* (Chicago: Quadrangle Books, 1964), copyright © 1964 by Arthur L. Stinchcombe, by permission of the author and publisher. Selection reprinted is condensed from pages 1–29, 40–47, 69–80, and 178–184. Footnotes and tables have been renumbered.

[1] Cf. Fritz Redl and David Wineman, *Children Who Hate* (Glencoe: The Free Press, 1951).

[2] *Ibid.*, pp. 240–242 (section entitled "Beyond the Reach of Education"), and Albert K. Cohen, *Delinquent Boys* (Glencoe: The Free Press, 1955), pp. 25–31.

[3] Though long-run goals can be added to the delinquent subculture, this is irrelevant to recruitment to these cultures. It is especially irrelevant to classroom rebellion, which cannot "earn its way." For a different view, see John I. Kitsuse and David C. Dietricke, "Delinquent Boys: A Critique," *American Sociological Review*, Vol. 24 (April 1959), pp. 208–215. "The delinquents whose activities are organized by a delinquent subculture are attending to more serious enterprises. There is no absence of rational, calculated, utilitarian behavior among delinquent gangs, as they exist today." (p. 213.)

3. It involves short-run hedonism. Specifically:

(a) Activities are rejected when frustration must be borne for the sake of achieving some goal.

(b) Activities whose motivation involves an image of a personal future tend not to be undertaken.

(c) Activities which sublimate impulses into "respectable" and disciplined behavior are rejected in favor of immediate gratifications.

(d) Fear of failure leads to rejection of activity involving the risk of failure.

(e) Interference with current "fun" by an authoritative adult (enforcing rules or setting goals) is interpreted as a hostile move, even if the rules and goals in themselves are considered legitimate by the delinquents.

4. It emphasizes group autonomy from adult interference on principle. As in other deviant social movements, connection with or loyalty to any section of the legitimate (in this case, adult) order is viewed with suspicion.

The first major hypothesis, then, is that students who are rebellious in high school are likely to have a psychological set with the above characteristics: *high school rebellion is part of a complex of attitudes toward psychologically present authority, characterized by non-utilitarianism, negativism, short-run hedonism, and emphasis on group autonomy.* But this specific kind of alienation from norms is itself traceable to the social structure of the school.

Explanations of Obedience and Rebellion

It has often been noted that the explanation of deviance has to be an explanation of conformity. For instance, Albert K. Cohen says:

A theory of deviant behavior not only must account for the occurrence of deviant behavior; it must also account for its failure to occur, or conformity. In fact, the explanation of one necessarily implies the explanation of the other. Therefore 'the sociology of deviant behavior' is elliptical for 'the sociology of deviant behavior and conformity'; it includes the explanation of the prevention, reduction and elimination of deviant behavior.[4]

This study attempts to explain disobedience (and consequently obedience) among high school students. Since the theory of obedience to authority has developed separately from the theory of adolescent rebellion, we must first discuss the relation between these theories.

The theory of obedience is most fully developed by Max Weber in his treatment of the forms of authority.[5] Each of Weber's three types of authority (bureaucratic, charismatic, and traditional) is described by specifying two main variables: (a) the type of control by authorities over the future status of subordinates, and (b) the type of commitment to symbols of legitimacy common among subordinates.

For instance, bureaucratic authority involves career commitment by the official, control of promotion by superiors on the basis of qualifications, and salary in keeping with the status of the office rather than need or family status. Further, the basis of legitimacy of bureaucratic authority is the loyalty of subordinates to a codified and rationalized body of rules and laws.[6]

[4] *Sociology Today,* edited by R. K. Merton, *et al.* (New York: Basic Books, 1959), pp. 463–64.

[5] Max Weber, *The Theory of Social and Economic Organization* (Glencoe: The Free Press, 1947), pp. 324–363.

[6] *Ibid.* Charismatic authority awards status to subordinates by arbitrary (inspired) decision by the leader. The symbol to which subordinates are loyal is the charismatic leader himself, a man especially chosen by the arbitrary will of God or History and endowed by this special choice with supernatural abilities. Traditional authority involves allocation on the basis of traditional rules (rather than either the whim of the leader or
[*footnote 6 continued on p. 90*

We are not here concerned with the classification of types of authority, nor with judging which type would be more effective for student-teacher relations. But Weber's emphasis on control of future status suggests the second basic hypothesis of this study. *We hold that high school rebellion,* and expressive alienation, *occurs when future status is not clearly related to present performance.* When a student realizes that he does not achieve status increment from improved current performance, current performance loses meaning. The student becomes hedonistic because he does not visualize achievement of long-run goals through current self-restraint. He reacts negatively to a conformity that offers nothing concrete. He claims autonomy from adults because their authority does not promise him a satisfactory future.

The future, not the past, explains adolescent rebellion, contrary to the hypothesis that deviant attitudes are the result of distinctively rebel biographies. Thus Sutherland holds that deviant attitudes are learned through association with others who hold such attitudes, that biographies of deviants are characterized by wider past association with other deviants.[7] Redl and Wineman trace the set of deviant attitudes to experiences, especially lack of love, which cripple the development of the ego.[8] We hold that deviant values or crippling of the ego are traceable to differences in the futures of adolescents. . . .

The social structure either provides or fails to provide a sensible and appealing career pattern to the student. Whenever present activity fails to make sense by being clearly connected to future increments of status, the student tends to be-

come expressively alienated and rebellious. The student who grasps a clear connection between current activity and future status tends to regard school authority as legitimate, and to obey. The problem of order, then, is created by the inability of the school to realistically offer any desirable status beyond high school to some of its students. . . .

The Study

The hypotheses above were developed during the course of about six months of anthropological observation and exploratory survey research in a California high school. The evidence for them was collected by survey techniques from the student body of the same school. . . .

Briefly, pencil and paper precoded schedules were administered by teachers in required social science classes. . . . Students absent on the day schedules were administered were not reached; otherwise a complete enumeration of the school was obtained. . . .

In this argument we will use an index of rebellion composed of three self-reported rebellious acts: skipping school with a gang of kids, receiving a flunk notice in a non-college-preparatory class, and being sent out of class by a teacher. . . .

The Psychological Quality of Adolescent Rebellion

[One] task of this chapter is to demonstrate that high school rebellion is part of a complex of attitudes toward the school environment, including short-run hedonism, negativism, alienation from school authority, and emphasis on autonomy. . . .

There is, first of all, a strong relation between rebellion and short-run hedonism. Next, rebellious students are negativistic, in that they evaluate conformity and conformists negatively. Rebellious students are alienated from school authorities, believing that teachers, principals, and the leaders among students conspire among themselves to do injustice. Finally, rebels are much more likely than well-be-

[*footnote 6 continued*
qualifications), with reward coming from the prerogatives of ascribed status (e.g., in feudalism, claims to the yield of a parcel of land). The basis of legitimacy is belief in the sacredness of traditional obligations of ascribed status.
[7] See Edwin H. Sutherland and D. R. Cressey, *Principles of Criminology* (5th ed.) (Philadelphia: Lippincott, 1955), pp. 77–80.
[8] *Op. cit.*

haved students to claim rights, for them selves and for their peers, that the school is unwilling to grant.

When all of these attitudes have been shown to be related to rebellion, we will have established that "expressive alienation" is an empirical entity. That is, we will have established that high school rebellion is ordinarily a symptom of an underlying psychological state that involves hedonism, negativism, alienation from authority, and claims to autonomy. This transforms the dependent variable of the study from rebellion *per se* to expressive alienation, one of whose *symptoms,* is rebellion. . . .

Short-run Hedonism

Short-run hedonism has several aspects, any of which could serve as measures of hedonistic attitudes toward school. The short-run hedonistic attitude involves an emotional aspect: hedonistic people are bored when the meaning of the activity is expressed in long-run goals. Hedonism involves a cognitive aspect: the world is interpreted as a place in which it does not pay to sacrifice existing pleasures for uncertain future goals. Hedonism involves a failure of the imagination: future goals do not seem as real or worthwhile as current gratification.

The meaning of classroom activity is given by long-run goals. Most classes require continuous orientation to longer-run pleasures in accomplishment. Only participation classes (such as music or physical education) are consistently immediately gratifying. Consequently, boredom in classes is an index of short-run hedonism. In Table 1, the proportion of students who consider half or more of their classes "pretty boring" is tabulated against rebellion. It is immediately clear that rebels are

Table 1. Rebels are more likely to find half or more of their classes "pretty boring," among both girls and boys. Data for upper classmen.

GIRLS			
Receipt of Non-College Flunk Notice		Have **Not** Been Sent Out	Have Been Sent Out
		Per Cent Finding Classes Boring	
Have **Not**	No	14% (293)	* (4)
Skipped	Yes	36% (42)	* (3)
Have	No	32% (81)	* (7)
Skipped	Yes	39% (31)	* (6)
All who have been Sent Out			25% (20)

* Too few cases for meaningful percentages.

BOYS			
Receipt of Non-College Flunk Notice		Have **Not** Been Sent Out	Have Been Sent Out
		Per Cent Finding Classes Boring	
Have **Not**	No	14% (207)	25% (44)
Skipped	Yes	17% (60)	39% (29)
Have	No	32% (66)	28% (46)
Skipped	Yes	28% (42)	59% (56)

more likely to be bored than are well-be-haved students, but among rebels the type and amount of misbehavior makes little difference. There are no strong and con-sistent differences among sub-groups of rebels. Only the extreme rebels among boys, those who have received flunk no-tices, *and* skipped with a gang, *and* been sent out of class, show much greater tend-ency to boredom. About three-fifths (59 per cent) report that half or more of their classes are pretty boring.

More boys than girls report boredom: about a fifth (21 per cent) of the girls, but 27 per cent of the boys, report extensive boredom,[9] but it is only rebellious boys who are more bored than girls. About one out of seven (14 per cent) of both boys and girls who have so far been well-be-haved are bored by most of their classes. But rebellious boys are both more numer-ous, and more likely to report boredom, than rebellious girls. . . .

Negativism

"Negativism" describes the attitude that rejects all conforming behavior, all moral attachment to legitimate institutions. The people, in particular, who have such moral attachments to the respectable world are disrespected. Not only are the rules worth-less, but only a person with no backbone would follow them.

This aspect of the negativistic attitude provides an indicator of negativism. Stu-dents were asked to mark as True or False a statement that one thing wrong with the school was the number of "squares" among the students, who would rather fol-low all the rules than have any fun. The statement of the question unfortunately connects the attitude with short-run he-donism, but clearly the predominant ele-ment is the rejection of conformists. The distribution of answers by sex and by be-

[9] The direct relation between sex and expressive alienation will not be tabulated separately in the tables of this chapter. The percentage alienated for boys and girls will be presented in the text.

havioral rebellion is reported in Table 2.

First, it is clear that negative attitudes toward conformity-in-general are more common among boys than among girls. Not only is the sex-difference substantial (32 per cent of boys and 17 per cent of girls agreeing), but well-behaved boys are considerably more likely than well-be-haved girls to evaluate conformity nega-tively. Second, a combination of offenses (skipping *and* flunking, being sent out *and* skipping, etc.) is most closely related to this attitude, which is to be expected. An atti-tude of rejection of conformity-in-general should result in the student getting into trouble in a number of different ways. . . .

Alienation from the Status System

In formal organizations, such as high schools, one of the central functions of authorities is to establish the status sys-tem of the organization. A status system is a socially established pattern of *judg-ment of persons,* with respect to their rela-tive worth. This may be worth for doing a particular job in the organization, or may be generalized to a judgment of worth "as persons." The connection between author-ity and the status system means that atti-tudes toward the status system itself partly determine attitudes toward authorities. . . .

Alienation from the status system can have several aspects. The judges may be held to be not applying the standards fair-ly; the standards may be considered ille-gitimate; it may be held that accidental factors prevent people from coming to the notice of the judges; it may be held that the type of information gathering used does not reveal the true worth of the per-son judged; or it may merely be held, without intellectual rationale, that rewards are unfairly distributed.

Table 3 reports the proportion of stu-dents holding that *teachers* did not allo-cate status according to intellectual merit, that "you have to get in good with the teachers in order to get a fair grade." The data in Table 3 again show a sharp sex-

Table 2. Rebellious students, especially those with multiple offenses, find "too many squares in this school." Data for upper classmen.

GIRLS		Have **Not** Been Sent Out	Have Been Sent Out
Receipt of Non-College Flunk Notice		Per Cent Seeing Too Many Squares	
Have **Not**	No	9% (293)	* (4)
Skipped	Yes	24% (42)	* (3)
Have	No	31% (81)	* (7)
Skipped	Yes	31% (31)	* (6)
All who have been Sent Out			50% (20)

* Too few cases for meaningful percentages.

BOYS		Have **Not** Been Sent Out	Have Been Sent Out
Receipt of Non-College Flunk Notice		Per Cent Seeing Too Many Squares	
Have **Not**	No	22% (207)	25% (44)
Skipped	Yes	20% (60)	66% (29)
Have	No	30% (66)	43% (46)
Skipped	Yes	48% (42)	52% (56)

difference, with boys again more alienated. A little over a quarter (26 per cent) of girls think teachers unfair, while 37 per cent of boys think so. Among the well behaved, however, the classroom status system administered by the teachers appears equally legitimate to boys and girls. The sex-difference is explained both by the greater number of rebels among boys, and by their greater alienation from the classroom status system.

Among girls rebellious classroom attitudes are apparently caused by flunking, but do not lead to rebellious behavior. The main relations in Table 3 are found between alienation from the classroom status system and classroom rebellion. Either flunking or being sent out of class is associated with high alienation, but skipping school is unrelated to thinking teachers

unfair. Among those whose classroom behavior is rebellious, no further differences are associated with either receipt of flunk notices or skipping with a gang. Rebels, particularly classroom rebels, see their teachers as unfair. . . .

Autonomy, Personal and Social

But expressively alienated students not only deny the morality of the school; they also hold a positive morality of their own. The authoritative demands of the school are not only greeted with cynicism—they are greeted with moral indignation. The demand for autonomy from illegitimate adult interference is a positive moral claim against the school.

The autonomy of a clique or subculture in an organization does not become a salient problem, either to the institution or to

Table 3. Rebels perceive teachers as unfair, among both girls and boys. Data for upper classmen.

		GIRLS	
	Receipt of Non-College Flunk Notice	*Have **Not** Been Sent Out*	*Have Been Sent Out*
		Per Cent Seeing Teachers Unfair	
Have **Not** Skipped	No	21% (293)	* (4)
	Yes	43% (42)	* (3)
Have Skipped	No	20% (81)	* (7)
	Yes	34% (31)	* (6)
		All who have been Sent Out	35% (20)

* Too few cases for meaningful percentages.

		BOYS	
	Receipt of Non-College Flunk Notice	*Have **Not** Been Sent Out*	*Have Been Sent Out*
		Per Cent Seeing Teachers Unfair	
Have **Not** Skipped	No	23% (207)	57% (44)
	Yes	25% (60)	52% (29)
Have Skipped	No	36% (66)	65% (46)
	Yes	43% (42)	54% (56)

the subgroup, unless the subgroup has a positive morality against the institution. For instance, if the internal morality of an autonomous group of workers supports high productivity, the effects are the same as if they had a positive attitude toward authority. Similarly the solidarity and autonomy of delinquents are salient to social workers, police, *and* to delinquents, precisely because their behavior will be different if they are autonomous. A subgroup with positive attitudes toward school and toward the law can have a high degree of internal solidarity and autonomy in decision making, without having to defend it. We need not assume that delinquent gangs have a higher degree of solidarity and autonomy than other cliques, but only that the solidarity is used in support of a deviant morality.

The solidarity of the delinquent gang is used, not only to protect offenders and

ensure discipline in the commission of crimes, but also to claim certain rights vis-à-vis the adult community. That is, the rebellious peer group is oriented toward getting, from legitimate institutions, rights that the institutions are not enthusiastic about giving; the conforming peer group conversely helps the institutions enforce the obligations laid down by authoritative people. While the solidarity may be of equal quality, its structural implications are quite different.

The rights claimed by delinquent groups are suggested by an account of Hollingshead of an experiment with out-of-school youth. "If one tells him [a lower class boy] he is foolish to spend his money for old cars, flashy clothes, liquor, gambling, and sex one will be told forcibly— we experimented on this point with a few Class V's we knew well—'No one can tell me how I am going to spend my money.

Did you earn it?' This insistence upon freedom to do what he desires brings him into conflict with the law with significantly greater frequency than the other classes."[10]

The delinquent subculture, then, claims for adolescents the personal autonomy ordinarily associated with adulthood. Advice not to spend "his own money" on a car is as much an invasion of a boy's rights as such advice would be to adults. This claim of adult rights (and, less enthusiastically, adult duties) by people still subjected to the high school system of social control based on the doctrine of immaturity of adolescents creates severe conflicts. Even among teachers there is considerable disagreement about how far the school has the right to interfere with the

[10] A. B. Hollingshead, *Elmtown's Youth* (New York: John Wiley, 1949), p. 444.

non-academic life of students. But the school must assume, administratively, that its students are adolescents; some of the students, however, assume that they are adults. . . .

[W]e want to establish that such claims result in (or are caused by the same things that cause) rebellious behavior. For this purpose, we have asked students to agree or disagree with a claim of adult smoking and adult car-owning rights. The claim for rights to smoke is related to sex and rebellion in Table 4.

The strong and consistent relation (only one inversion; boys otherwise well behaved are not differentiated by having been kicked out of a class) supports the hypothesis strongly. Rebellious students object to the school's regulation of smoking, particularly off-campus. The claim to adult smoking rights characterizes rebels; the attribution of legitimacy to regulations

Table 4. Rebels claim the right to smoke and oppose the claims of the school to regulate, among both girls and boys. Data for upper classmen.

| | GIRLS | | |
	Receipt of Non-College Flunk Notice	*Have Not Been Sent Out*	*Have Been Sent Out*
		Per Cent Claiming Right to Smoke	
Have **Not**	No	6% (293)	* (4)
Skipped	Yes	26% (42)	* (3)
Have	No	17% (81)	* (7)
Skipped	Yes	45% (31)	* (6)
		All who have been Sent Out	30% (20)

* Too few cases for meaningful percentages.

| | BOYS | | |
	Receipt of Non-College Flunk Notice	*Have Not Been Sent Out*	*Have Been Sent Out*
		Per Cent Claiming Right to Smoke	
Have **Not**	No	13% (207)	11% (44)
Skipped	Yes	17% (60)	31% (29)
Have	No	32% (66)	52% (46)
Skipped	Yes	40% (42)	59% (56)

enforcing adolescent status characterizes well-behaved students.

A similar question claiming that, like adults, adolescents can't get along without a car, shows a similarly strong relation. . . .

We hold, then, that some students are characterized by a complex of attitudes and behavior toward the school environment named "expressive alienation." Such alienated students are more likely than others to be rebellious—given the same opportunities, they are more likely to get into trouble. By establishing the correlation of rebellion to a number of other attitudes, we tentatively establish the emotional concomitants of this underlying state of alienation. The psychological state of expressive alienation, having as one of its manifestations rebellious *behavior,* has the following *attitudinal* manifestations:

1. Short-run hedonism. Specifically, rebels tend to react by boredom in situations whose moral center is a long-run goal (classrooms), fail to see the connection between current deprivation (work) and long-run gratifications (grades), and give less importance to long-run gratifications.

2. Negativism. Specifically, rebels reject people who conform ("squares").

3. Alienation from the status systems either created by authorities or closely connected to legitimate institutions. . . .

4. A culture of personal autonomy, holding that students have the same sort of rights as do adults, and specifically claiming adult car-owning and smoking rights. . . .

The Hypothesis of Articulation Restated

We suggest that the key to high school rebellion is to be found in the status prospects of students, rather than in their status origins. Juvenile delinquency statistics can be organized by the idea that expressive alienation is concentrated in adolescent populations confronted with a future of manual labor in a universalistic labor market. This suggests that the key fact is the future of students, not their origins. Since we know that origins partly determine futures, social class will be an important variable, but in an unusual way.

In order to secure conformity from students, the high school must articulate academic work with careers of students, although the careers are in the labor market and in households, outside the school. Various subgroups of students, holding different positions with respect to these external structures, create problems of authority within the high school.

First, girls who think they are going into the labor market almost unanimously aim for positions in the upper middle class or the bureaucratic sector of the lower middle class. If they are not oriented to these labor market sectors, they are oriented to marriage. Boys, on the other hand, are trapped by the labor market. They cannot get out of it, even when they face an "unsuccessful" future in it; one indication of the dilemma is that boys are much more likely to aspire to jobs they do not expect to get than are girls.

This poorer articulation of academic work with imagined future careers is reflected in boys' ambiguous answers to the curriculum interest question. Curriculum choice is a behavioral index of perceived articulation, for it is the formal device of articulation. A question asking students directly how much academic success matters in the labor market supports this interpretation: boys, especially boys giving vocational and ambiguous answers on the curriculum question and aiming for lower labor market positions, are much less likely to say that grades are important in getting good jobs. Since curriculum interest functions well to measure perceived articulation, and since it is a behavioral variable with meaning in real life rather than merely an attitude question, we will use it as an indicator of articulation in the following argument. . . .

The task of the next [section] is to show that those groups of students with the poorest articulation between current academic activity and future status increment are most expressively alienated.

The chain of causes we propose to explain the distribution of expressive alienation, then, takes roughly the following form:

1. Students' chances of success in the post-high school job market are determined by origin, ability, school attended, sex, and so forth.

2. The perceived value of school depends on the school's perceived connection with success. This perceived connection varies among social classes, ability groups, sexes, races, and neighborhoods.

3. Perceived lack of connection of school work to occupational success produces rebellion.

4. Perception is roughly accurate on these questions, hence rebellion is concentrated in groups which actually have poor articulation of current work with future status. . . .

Rebellion and Orientation to the Future

Table 5 presents the proportion of students who have either skipped school or been sent out of class or both, according to orientation to the future, curriculum interest, and sex. These three variables combined produce an ordering of students according to articulation of the present with the future.

In any sex and orientation group, those giving ambiguous answers to the curriculum question can be assumed to have poorer articulation. In any one curriculum group, those aiming for and expecting to achieve higher statuses can be assumed to have better articulation, and to see current academic activity as meaningful. Since girls on vocational curricula are destined for the bureaucratic labor market, while boys on such curricula will join the working class labor market, girls on vocational curricula should have much better articulation than boys. Consequently we expect to find the largest sex-difference in rebellion among those with vocational curricu-

Table 5. Percentage who have skipped or been sent out, by sex, image of the future, and curriculum interest.

| | CURRICULUM INTEREST | | |
| | College | | |
Image of the Future and Sex	*Preparatory*	*Vocational*	*Ambiguous*
Labor Market Oriented			
Upper Middle, Girls	9% (100)	10% (10)	17% (12)
Upper Middle, Boys	29% (151)	41% (27)	30% (20)
Lower than Upper Middle, Girls ...	28% (25)	23% (108)	23% (30)
Lower than Upper Middle, Boys ...	32% (93)	47% (163)	55% (297)
Marriage Oriented			
Partly Committed to Marriage Market	17% (70)	27% (106)	30% (47)
Fully Committed to Marriage Market	25% (28)	26% (65)	39% (67)

lum interests. Girls fully committed to marriage . . . should be among the most rebellious girls, according to the theory.

On the basis of the analysis above, we expect the following patterns to appear in the table:

1. Among those oriented to a particular level in the labor market or to the marriage market, those giving ambiguous answers to the curriculum question should be more rebellious. In four of the six lines, the figure on the right is greater than others on the same line, which bears out the hypothesis. Of the two failures, one is not very serious. Those boys who aim for the upper middle class but who are *on curricula aimed for the working class* (answering "vocational") are more rebellious. Their career bewilderment is probably nearly as great as that of boys headed for the upper middle class who answer "Don't Know" to the curriculum question. Consequently this inversion is not too serious. The girls aiming for the lower labor market also fail to support this hypothesis; this failure is serious, and will receive special analysis later.

2. Those girls fully committed to marriage, without even a curriculum interest to tie current activity with a temporary future in the labor market, should be highly rebellious. And in fact the highest proportion of girls rebellious is in the lower right cell (39 per cent), in correspondence with the hypothesis.

3. Boys aiming for non-professional sectors of the labor market, and particularly those committed to working class or to no curricula, should be the most rebellious of boys. And they are more rebellious than any group in the table—rebellious students constitute about half of boys oriented toward the lower sectors of the labor market.

4. In contrast to boys, girls seeking lower labor market positions (mostly secretarial) who are interested in vocational curricula should have good articulation of present activity with future status. Conse-

quently they should be well behaved. Since the comparable subgroup of boys was predicted to be among the most rebellious, the sex-difference in rebellion should be greatest here. The sex-differences in the rate of rebellion are larger in the column of students on vocational curricula than in any other column,[11] in accordance with the hypothesis.

In every respect save one, the distribution of rebellion is as predicted from the theory. But girls oriented to the lower labor market, without curriculum interest, do not turn out to have behaved very rebelliously (only 23 per cent).

Presumably the situation in which these girls find themselves is relatively transitory, since most of them will probably reorient to marriage. . . . Perhaps they have not had time to get into trouble, and consequently the indicator used above does not reflect their alienation, for the indicator is a history of rebellion throughout high school, and varies with the amount of time alienated.

We can use reports of amount of homework done, which is a much more short-run behavioral indicator, as a substitute. This avoids the problem of an indicator using a history of rebellion. Since the pattern of boys created no serious problems, and since it remains approximately the same with all the indicators, we will omit boys from the present analysis. The proportion of girls who report doing less than an hour of homework a night is reported in Table 6.

Here the pattern is clearly as expected. The two highest figures in the table (i.e., the groups doing least homework) are those with low labor market images and no curriculum interest (53 per cent) and those fully committed to the marriage market without curriculum interest (49 per cent). When we remove the problem of the time-span of alienation, the two

[11] Except for the difference involving lower labor market oriented girls without curriculum interest, to be examined immediately.

Table 6. Percentage spending less than an hour a day on homework, by image of the future and curriculum interest, for girls.

	CURRICULUM INTEREST		
Image of Future	*College Preparatory*	*Vocational*	*Ambiguous*
Labor Market Oriented			
Upper Middle	13% (100)	20% (10)	17% (12)
Lower than Upper Middle	25% (25)	29% (108)	53% (30)
Marriage Oriented			
Partly Committed to Marriage Market	21% (70)	35% (106)	38% (47)
Fully Committed to Marriage Market	14% (28)	35% (65)	49% (67)

subgroups expected to be rebellious turn out to be so. Girls oriented to the professional or bureaucratic sectors of the labor market, having good articulation, do their homework. Also, girls partly oriented to the labor market, partly to the marriage market, do their homework. Only those groups of girls who resemble boys in the low amount of status increment they can expect from the school, also resemble boys in the low amount of homework done. . . .

By and large, then, the data support the main contentions outlined above. The most rebellious, among both girls and boys, tend to perceive a poor connection between current academic activity and future status. This is indicated by the fact that those who express no curriculum interest are most rebellious and alienated, with other factors constant. It is also indicated by the higher rebelliousness of students aiming for lower positions in the labor market. Further support comes from the fact that sex-differences in rebelliousness are greatest among students with vocational curriculum choices, where the sex-difference in articulation is greatest.

And, though not unambiguously supported, it appears that the subgroups of girls most similar to the larger subgroup

of less intelligent boys in articulation, are most similar to them in the degree of alienation. Girls giving ambiguous answers on the curriculum question who are oriented either to low positions in the labor market or to positions not allocated by the school, seem to be most alienated. . . .

What Is to Be Done?

This leaves us then with the question of what to do about it? In the first place, it is not clear that anything needs to be done, in a fundamental sense. The rebellion we. talk about is basically an inconvenience to teachers and school administrators. Reasonably competent teaching and administration can exercise situational control, so that education may proceed. This means that some teachers will need to be fired for not being able to maintain classroom control, but most such teachers seem to me to be also ineffective educators at the high school level, and their elimination may be a good thing.[12] The main reasons for

[12] The reason for the correlation between disciplinary capacity and educational effectiveness is that dramatic sense—a sense of timing and a capacity to gauge audience response—is a prime tool of classroom control, and also a prime tool for focusing attention for educational purposes.

worrying about what is to be done are the unhappiness of adolescents whose adolescence is meaningless, and the possibility that expressively alienated students will find themselves in more serious trouble and go to prison. . . .

The major practical conclusion of the analysis above is that rebellious behavior is largely a reaction to the school itself and to its promises, not a failure of the family or community. High school students can be motivated to conform by paying them in the realistic coin of future adult advantages. Except perhaps for pathological cases, any students can be motivated to conform if the school can realistically promise something valuable to them as a reward for working hard. But for a large part of the population, especially the adolescents who will enter the male working class or the female candidates for early marriage, the school has nothing to promise.

This means that the problem of order in schools, of juvenile delinquency and expressive alienation, is not easy to solve. *For the reason that the school cannot promise much is that the society cannot promise much.* Tinkering a bit with the curriculum to "make it more meaningful" for duller children will have little effect. Culture is "meaningful" for the average man as it relates to something he wants to do. A high school student wants to grow up into an adult who is successful by adult standards. Culture that is not relevant to the problem of growing up successful, however useful it may be for citizens or householders, will not make school meaningful.

What are the possible courses of action that might lead to a worthwhile adolescence for those who will fill the ranks of the working class? The first requisite is a far more definite arrangement between the people who will hire manual labor and the schools which train it. Any increased labor market rights—increased chances of jobs, increased pay, advanced standing in

apprenticeship programs, etc.—will tend to render vocational training meaningful. At present, except in a very few schools in large cities, vocational training is a farce. It serves the function of a "liberal arts" preparation for living in the working class, but not the function of providing saleable skills. In fact, the dollars-and-cents economic value of Latin to the student is probably higher than the value of any vocational courses, except secretarial courses for girls.

The great difficulty is that employers of manual labor do not know what they need —or perhaps do not need anything in particular. Is there anything that a high school can teach which employers of manual labor would be willing to pay for, if it were learned well? In general, the answer is no. Neither physical abilities nor reliability, the two main variables of interest to employers of manual labor, are much influenced by schooling. Employers concerned with securing reliable workers may require high school diplomas as evidence of good discipline. Otherwise they can train workers better and cheaper than a high school can, on the job.

Although this is the general situation, there are a few cases in which connections can be made between school and jobs. Each increase in such connections should increase the meaningfulness of school for future workers, who create most of the trouble.

A second requirement is to extend secretarial training to boys who will not go on to college. Manual jobs are becoming scarcer, while the bureaucratic sector of the labor market is still expanding almost as fast as the professional sector. Insofar as vocational training for boys now is not a farce, it is preparing them for jobs which will not exist in the near future.

More fundamental experiments with the structure of careers in the whole society, so that jobs could become part of a real life-plan for the majority of workers, are apparently beyond our knowledge and power at the present time. If exact knowledge of what each man had to do to better his condition were available to him, and if it were guaranteed to each that by doing it he would improve his situation, much of the meaninglessness of work, and of education for work, would disappear. But this would entail a different society from the one we have now, a society of secure employment, with a predictable future of labor market demand, with precise information on where each man stands now and what he is capable of, and mechanisms by which opportunities in the labor market are offered to those, and only those, whose abilities it will stretch to get them. We are now closer to being technically able to construct the world of work this way than we ever have been before. But a society not yet capable of eliminating gross and obvious racial employment discrimination ought to be cautious about adopting utopian schemes to give exactly the right job to the right man.

The second point at which attention might be directed is the doctrine of adolescent inferiority. The doctrine that teachers are superior to students, and that students ought to imitate them in certain respects (especially in knowledge and competence), is necessary for systematic education. It is the justification for the teacher telling the student what to study. But in practically all societies, the doctrine of the inferiority of students is closely intertwined with the doctrine of the inferiority of the young. As we have seen, when students do not consider that the young are and ought to be inferior, they encounter trouble with the authority system. Among boys, particularly, the degree of acceptance of the doctrine that adolescents ought not to have adult rights is very closely related to rebellion.

The Puritanism of the traditional "official" culture of the United States makes it difficult to discuss rationally exactly when and how adolescents should be introduced to the adult rights of sex, tobacco, alcohol, high powered cars, and spending their own money as they please. Though most adults treat these things as the good things in life, they do not allow official representatives of the culture to say that these are the good things. It is this official hypocrisy that is behind the famous definition of a teacher as a man hired to tell lies to little boys. Even in the most Puritan cultures, purity is confined to a select minority, while most adults happily live out their unrespectable lives. Somehow children must avoid becoming like they are told to become in school, in order to become like adults. Rebellion, particularly for boys, is a nearly inevitable result of the two-faced character of ideals of adulthood. And, as we saw, boys do in fact claim many more of the rights of men, while still boys, than girls do.

It is not the province of a sociologist to say whether it is better for adults to become Puritans, or for school officials to defend our ideals of adulthood as they actually exist—sex, high-powered cars, liquor, and all—or to continue the hypocrisy. It seems likely that for some time we will continue with hypocrisy, with the strain between official and unofficial versions of what it means to be an adult. But it seems likely that we will decrease the stridency in our official Puritanism. Our focus here is on the side effects of this cultural strain, as students' objection to the doctrine of adolescent inferiority creates problems of authority in the high school.

This challenge to the doctrine is partly motivated merely by rebellion against the career meaninglessness of the school, as we showed above. But it is also clear that lack of belief in the inferiority and lesser rights of youth has an independent effect on rebellion. One of the most interesting questions emerging from the results here is the problem of how people learn what is appropriate for adolescents and what it means to be an adult. People vary a great deal, apparently, in their beliefs about age and its proper relation to behavior, and these variations cause striking variations in rebellion, in whether students participate primarily in the asexual official teen culture or in the proto-sexual dating teen culture, in how they think about military life, in their ratings of the importance of parents as opposed to peers in their behavior, and many other important things. We are almost as ignorant of how people learn or fail to learn to act their age as we are of how they learn to be men or women. . . .

Thus it might be possible to control much of the rebellion of high school students if one could teach "boys" to be boys instead of men. They really are men, as strong and as intelligent as other men, by the end of high school. False doctrines of inferiority have worked before to shore up authority systems, however, and presumably this one can be made to work better. Again, the worth of it is not a scientific question.

The psychological strain which produces the reaction formation may also be capable of reduction. If it does, indeed, turn out that the upper-middle class family has techniques for keeping the anxiety level near the optimum, for adjusting the amount of pressure to succeed to the ability of the child, the techniques of this adjustment could be studied. Some of these techniques might be of the kind that can be applied directly by the school to reduce the bitterness of failing students. And part of the techniques might be capable of being transmitted to lower-middle class and working class mothers and fathers, both through the school and through popular magazines.

Before this can be done, it is necessary to know a great deal more about the exact conditions under which failure hurts most, and how to relieve the hurt. It is one of the costs of equality of opportunity that people have no one to blame for their failures, and it is one of the comforts of holding securely an inferior position, as a woman for instance, that one need never fail. But exactly how much the failure entailed in equality has to hurt, and what salves to wounded egos are effective in relieving the pain if not in curing the failure, are topics well worth investigating.

There are ideological problems in studying this objectively. Men of good will, especially if they are close to adolescents, prefer to pretend that the various paths merely lead to different—but equally valuable—forms of success. This means that they have humane objections to calling failure by its name, even for purposes of investigation. The refusal to call things by their names may be one of the salves that in fact reduces the pain. I doubt that it has much effect, for I think that most adolescents do find out what is valued by society and translate this into self-judgments and judgments of each other within the school. But this deserves special investigation.

If it turns out that "failure" from the point of view of the larger society can be redefined as another path to success, this will probably have some impact on the motivational effectiveness of the system. That is, the much-discussed "wastage of talent" may be partly due to the effects of not telling adolescents clearly what the society regards as success and failure. If truck driving is defined as another kind of success, some potential nuclear physicists will prefer that kind of success. Again the worth of preventing high school expressive alienation is not a scientific question.

PART IV

ALIENATION FROM WORK:
THE MARXIAN HERITAGE

Introduction

Scholars concerned with alienation from work frequently trace their interest in this subject to Marx's early writings on alienation. In his analysis of alienated labour, however, Marx does not consider the possibility that the extent or kind of alienation might vary as a result of differences among types of industry or factory organizations. He is concerned mainly with the particular aspects of factory work which appear to him to be generic, and therefore inevitable, under a capitalistic system of economic organization.

In fact, however, industrial production under capitalism, as under other economic systems, has evolved in a number of different ways, which appear to vary in the extent to which they induce alienation among workers. Forms of industrial production differ in many structural features including, for example, the proportion of the product a worker is responsible for and the amount of freedom he has to alter his work pace. A worker who performs one small operation on a complex product that comes to his work station on a moving assembly line stands at one extreme of these dimensions, while a skilled craftsman who makes an entire product from start to finish represents the other extreme. Both of these conditions, and a variety of intermediate ones, are found in the organization of contemporary factory work.

The selection by Robert Blauner analyzes the different effects on alienation from work of these various patterns of industrial organization. Blauner's analysis is clearly influenced by both the humanistic concerns expressed by Marx and the contemporary interest in clarification of the concept of alienation. Building on Seeman's distinctions among dimensions of alienation, Blauner describes several different types of alienation from work and the particular aspects of factory life that contribute to each.

In the book from which this selection is excerpted, Blauner uses this framework to give a detailed analysis of the work environments of four different industries: printing, automobile manufacturing, and textile and

103

chemical production. He discusses how the form of production utilized in each industry stimulates or averts each type of alienation. Here, in addition to his general discussion of types of alienation from work, Blauner's summary of this comparative industrial analysis is presented. This comparative orientation suggests not only differences among contemporary industrial forms but a comparative *time* perspective as well. Blauner argues that the different production patterns of the four industries studied represent different stages of industrial evolution. Based on his analysis of these forms of organization, he develops an historical perspective which suggests that work alienation may *decrease* as industries become automated. To what extent and under what conditions automation can provide a work environment that is nonalienating are important questions for future research. The comparative industrial perspective developed by Blauner is likely to be useful in future analyses of this type. Other historical views of alienation from work are developed by Daniel Bell (1960) and Wilensky (1964).

In addition to the kinds of structural factors considered by Blauner, work alienation can also be affected by certain *personal* characteristics of individual workers. These characteristics may interact with working conditions and thereby affect the relationship between working conditions and alienation. Because individuals have different values, needs, and goals, they tend to react differently to social situations. This has important implications for studying their attitudes toward any social structure. It means, for example, that in studies of alienation from work, one ought also to take into account other relevant personal characteristics. Thus, a very simple model of the relationship between work and alienation includes the work environment as an independent variable, alienation from work as a dependent variable, and individual characteristics as specifying conditions under which the relationship between these variables may differ in kind or degree.

Which individual characteristics ought to be taken into account in this kind of model? There is no simple *a priori* answer to this question. Potentially, all characteristics of individuals that affect their values and aspirations might also affect the relationship between work organization and work alienation. A simple trichotomy of individual level characteristics can be established: *psychological characteristics,* such as personality traits, and two types of *social characteristics, ascribed,* which are more or less permanent and immutable qualities, and *achieved,* which are acquired in the course of one's lifetime. Both ascribed and achieved characteristics influence individuals through their effects on socialization experiences, and, thereby, the kinds of values and aspirations individuals come to hold. The three remaining studies of alienation in this section each illustrate the influence of one of these three types of individual characteristics on the way in which people respond to their work situations.

Leonard Pearlin, for example, begins with an interest in the way in which authority relationships and other structural conditions of a large hospital are related to alienation from work among nursing personnel. He specifies his analysis, however, by investigating how the *personality* characteristic of obeisance (and several other individual characteristics) affects this relationship. Since obeisant individuals positively value deference to authority, it follows that they should not become alienated from their work when they are actually involved in work structures where authority is exercised over them in a nonparticipatory fashion. Pearlin demonstrates clearly that the psychological characteristics and aspirations of individuals must be taken into account in assessing the degree to which specific work conditions are alienating.

A further type of qualification to a simple causal relationship between work situation and alienation from work is suggested by Louis Zurcher, Arnold Meadow, and Susan Lee Zurcher. They reason that different cultural backgrounds (an example of an *ascribed* characteristic) lead people to have different value orientations. Some of these values and norms may be directly relevant to the question of whether particular work situations will be perceived as alienating. For example, one defining characteristic of bureaucracies is the norm of universalism, which means that all individuals are to be treated equally, regardless of whether they are personal friends or total strangers. This norm is widely accepted as appropriate and legitimate for business and government operations in American society. When exceptions are made, they are normally recognized as such and may even be considered as legal violations under certain circumstances. If one accepts the norm of universalism as legitimate, then being required to comply with this norm on one's job should not be defined as restrictive or oppressive. But what happens in the case of people who have not been socialized to accept as legitimate this equal treatment of friend and stranger alike?

The analysis by Zurcher and his colleagues attempts to answer this question. Since a major source of differences among people in basic value orientations is the cultural or ethnic group to which they belong, the analysis is approached as a cross-cultural comparison. The groups studied are Mexicans, Mexican-Americans, and Anglo-Americans. All of the individuals in the sample work in the same type of bureaucratic organization. Any differences in their acceptance of the norm of universalism should therefore lead to differences in level of work alienation. Individuals from ethnic groups that emphasize particularistic values should be more alienated from work than members of groups that hold universalistic orientations. This study alerts us to the conditioning effects which cultural groups and the values they inculcate may have on individuals' reactions to work situations.

In the next selection, George Miller considers how an *achieved* characteristic affects reactions to work environment. Miller hypothesizes that among scientists and engineers both length and type of professional training will affect the strength of relationship between characteristics of the work environment and work alienation. Just as personality and ethnic background may affect the way in which individuals react to structural conditions, so professional training may also lead the individual to internalize certain values and expectations regarding his relationship to his work. When these professional socialization experiences and their consequent value systems differ as a function of different types of professional training, reactions to specific work environments may be expected to vary also. In professions whose norms lead members to expect high degrees of work freedom and decision-making autonomy, the reaction to restraints on such freedom and power is likely to be more marked than in other professions in which these norms are weaker or absent.

Miller's measure of alienation from work emphasizes a different aspect of work relatedness than the scale developed by Pearlin and also used by Zurcher. This latter scale emphasizes feeling of *power and control* over the work situation and work tasks, while Miller's measure emphasizes the degree of *personal or ego involvement* the individual has in his work. As Miller points out, a person who works for financial incentives rather than personal meaning in the work activity may be considered alienated along the self-estrangement dimension described by Seeman.

Although the contexts of these three studies are a hospital, banks, and an aerospace manufacturing and research firm, the essential structures and conditions analyzed are found in all bureaucratic organizations. These analyses, therefore, have broad relevance for understanding the development of attitudes of alienation in bureaucracies in general. Further studies of how bureaucratic structures affect work alienation are provided by Aiken and Hage (1966), Bonjean and Grimes (1970), and Crozier (1964).

Studies of alienation from work have progressed far beyond Marx's original analysis which inspired so many of them. Marx was concerned with the effect of working conditions within the industrial system and, most specifically, the factory. The selections reprinted here go on to consider a number of quite different factory, industrial, service, financial, and bureaucratic occupations and consider also the interaction between these work settings and the personalities, backgrounds, and status characteristics of individuals in producing various types of alienation. All of these conditions qualify and specify the original Marxian hypothesis of alienated labor.

In one sense, however, there is great discontinuity between these studies and Marx's analysis. A major variable with which Marx was concerned is the ownership of the means of production; yet none of the studies reported in this section is set in socialist societies. (Zeitlin's study of work alienation in Cuba is included in the final section of the book.) Marx's analysis in "Alienated Labour" makes clear, however, that his basic concern was *the form of work organization* that had developed under the capitalistic system. It is doubtful that a socialistic or communistic economic arrangement that permitted this form of work organization to survive would have received his approval, because it is not merely the fact that workers do not share in the economic profits of their labor to which Marx objected. He believed, for example, that equality of incomes for all members of a society "would only change the relation of the present-day worker to his work into a relation of all men to work. Society would then be conceived as an abstract capitalist." His analysis also led him to conclude that "although private property appears to be the basis and cause of alienated labour, it is rather a consequence of the latter . . ." The root evils for Marx are the much more basic facts regarding the worker's relationship to the *process* of production. No form of pecuniary arrangements can compensate for the fact that *man is dehumanized in the work process itself by the nature of the work task.* Marx objects to the fact that work organization in capitalistic systems deprives the worker of a context in which to develop his human potential for creativity through labor. Marx sees the worker as performing rote tasks which provide little or no opportunity to engage his creative and intellectual powers—only his manual abilities are required in tasks envisioned and designed by others.

Unfortunately, Marx did not generalize his analysis to nonfactory work, for it seems clear that men can also perform trivial, ego-alien, and stultifying activities in environments other than the factory. The observation that alienation in factory production is merely one instance of a more general trend toward depersonalization through bureaucratization was made by the German sociologist, Max Weber. As Gerth and Mills point out (1946, p. 50), from Weber's perspective, "The modern soldier is equally 'separated' from the means of violence; the scientist from the means of enquiry, and the civil servant from the means of administration." As large bureaucratic organization and specialization of work skills has become typical of both socialistic and capitalistic economies, it seems likely that the types of analyses reported here are equally relevant for both forms of economic organization. Further consideration of the problem of alienation in socialist societies may be found in Israel (1971) and in the collection of essays edited by Fromm (1965).

Another very important distinction between Marx's analysis and many contemporary social science analyses of alienation from work is the distinction between "objective" and "subjective" alienation. As discussed in the introduction to Part I, Marx is concerned with how workers themselves "subjectively" feel about their work, but he also views their condition from an "objective" perspective based upon his own values as to what the relationship between a man and his work *should* be. Thus, Marx applies an *external* standard, whereas most contemporary social scientists base their studies of work alienation on the subjective evaluations provided by the worker himself. One of the goals of the latter type of analysis is to allow the worker to define his own situation and to make the analysis less dependent on the particular value assumptions of the investigator.

A concept related to work alienation, which has generated an extensive literature, is "job satisfaction." One might view these concepts as opposite ends of a continuum, in which case to say that an individual is alienated from his work but satisfied with his job would be a contradiction in terms. However, Marx's focus on the relation of a worker to the *process* of work suggests an important distinction between these concepts and implies that they should *not* be considered as simple opposites. Work is, after all, only one aspect of a job. Jobs also involve wage or salary payments for products or for services performed, social relationships with others who work with or near the worker, specific employers, life styles at least partially determined by characteristics of the job (such as shift and length of vacations), and a variety of other social and economic arrangements that may be wholly or partially independent of the work process itself. Thus, workers may derive satisfaction from many aspects of a job other than the work activities themselves. Good pay and companionable fellow-workers may be coupled with a repulsive work routine. Indeed, Goldthorpe (1966) argues that the role of money in *attracting* workers to boring and menial jobs has been grossly understated. Thus, one way in which these concepts differ is in the broader nature of the empirical referents of "job satisfaction." *In addition to* attitudes toward the work itself, job satisfaction includes attitudes toward pay, physical comforts and facilities, and even the extent to which the job *provides freedom from itself,* for example, by offering good vacation schedules, company social activities, and work assignments that are not so physically exhausting that the worker is unable to enjoy his leisure time. The concept of alienation from work, on the other hand, focuses on the individual's relation to the *work process* and on the satisfactions and dissatisfactions provided by *the work itself.*

A summary way of stating these differences is to say that the concept "alienation from work" is used primarily in reference to the *intrinsic* rewards of work, while the concept "job satisfaction" is frequently used to refer to *both* the *intrinsic* rewards and also the *extrinsic* benefits that are not integral parts of man's relationship to his work. Marx himself lays the groundwork for this distinction between intrinsic and extrinsic rewards by specifying, as mentioned above, that the amount of money a worker receives does not affect whether or not his labor is alienated. If the worker is dehumanized by the type of work he has to perform, no amount of wages or fringe benefits can reduce the separation between the man and his labor, and consequently his alienation from work. Thus, alienation from work may be considered as the opposite pole of that dimension of job satisfaction concerned with *intrinsic* involvement in work and as conceptually unrelated to *extrinsic* satisfaction. Theoretically at least, a worker may be both alienated and extrinsically satisfied or nonalienated but dissatisfied with the extrinsic benefits of his job.

Many important questions about work arrangements follow from the distinction between intrinsic and extrinsic involvement in work. For example: In their efforts to improve working conditions, what determines whether workers and employers will focus on factors increasing intrinsic satisfaction as opposed to those increasing extrinsic satisfaction? What kind of trade-offs exist among money, physical facilities and other factors that increase extrinsic satisfaction, and factors that could reduce work alienation? Under what circumstances, for example, would workers be willing to accept less money if that would enable work arrangements to be restructured to provide more control over the work process?

The research reported in this section indicates that there is a complex interaction between the individual's personal characteristics and his work environment in the equation leading to alienation from or satisfaction with work. This suggests that workers may have different rank orderings of factors contributing to extrinsic and intrinsic job satisfaction. How do such preference orders differ as a function of individual characteristics? How do people sort themselves out to find jobs that are consistent with their personal values so as to increase job satisfaction and decrease work alienation?

Discussions of work alienation frequently emphasize the social and technological requisites for eliminating this problem. Under the influence of the "job enlargement" theory of work organization, for example, many modern industrial concerns have instituted production patterns that enable workers to produce large parts of machines and other products and occasionally to produce such items in their entirety. Hulin and Blood (1968) provide a recent review of studies of the effectiveness of job enlargement in decreasing work alienation. Their general conclusion is consistent with a major theme developed in this section: there is no simple relationship between job "size" and job satisfaction. Instead, the reactions of individuals depend very much on their backgrounds and attitudes. But if the perception of work as alienating depends at least partly on personal characteristics and aspirations, does it make sense to attempt to eliminate work alienation by changing the work environment without also changing individual values and goals? This question brings us back to the difference between subjective and objective alienation. Given certain personal values, many people may be intrinsically satisfied with jobs which an outside observer, from a particular normative position, may judge to be "objectively alienating." People working at such jobs may not *feel* alienated because they have not been socialized to expect jobs which provide opportunities for responsible and creative work. Who should be concerned with this type of problem? Seen in this light, the problem of work alienation is not only an empirical question but one which requires the perspectives of philosophers, politicians, and social scientists alike.

ALIENATION AND MODERN INDUSTRY

Robert Blauner

No simple definition of alienation can do justice to the many intellectual traditions which have engaged this concept as a central explanatory idea. One basis of confusion is the fact that the idea of alienation has incorporated philosophical, psychological, sociological, and political orientations. In the literature on the theory of alienation, one finds statements of the desired state of human experience, assertions about the actual quality of personal experience, propositions which link attitudes and experience to social situations and social structures, and programs for the amelioration of the human condition. My own perspective in this investigation is chiefly sociological, or perhaps social-psychological, in that alienation is viewed as a quality of personal experience which results from specific kinds of social arrangements.[1]

SOURCE: Reprinted from Robert Blauner, *Alienation and Freedom: The Factory Worker and His Industry*, (Chicago: The University of Chicago Press, 1964), 15–34 and 166–182, by permission of the author and publisher. Copyright 1964 by The University of Chicago. Footnotes have been renumbered.

---

[1] Although my main approach is not philosophical, it will become clear that the problems which I analyze attain their relevancy from a personal value system. Along with Marx, Erich Fromm (*The Sane Society* [New York: Rinehart & Co., 1955]), and Chris Argyris (*Personality and Organization* [New York: Harper & Bros., 1957]), I assume that work which permits autonomy, responsibility, social connection, and self-actualization further the dignity of the human individual, whereas work without these characteristics limits the development of personal potential and is therefore to be negatively valued.

This study also employs a multidimensional, rather than a unitary, conception of alienation. Alienation is a general syndrome made up of a number of different objective conditions and subjective feeling-states which emerge from certain relationships between workers and the sociotechnical settings of employment. Alienation exists when workers are unable to control their immediate work processes, to develop a sense of purpose and function which connects their jobs to the over-all organization of production, to belong to integrated industrial communities, and when they fail to become involved in the activity of work as a mode of personal self-expression. In modern industrial employment, control, purpose, social integration, and self-involvement are all problematic. In this chapter we discuss how various aspects of the technology, work organization, and social structure of modern industry further the four types of alienation which correspond to these nonalienated states: powerlessness, meaninglessness, isolation, and self-estrangement.[2]

---

[2] For identifying these dimensions of alienation I am indebted to a recent article by Melvin Seeman, "On the Meaning of Alienation," *American Sociological Review*, XXIV (1959), 783–91. The author helps clarify this confused area by distinguishing five different ways in which the alienation concept has been utilized in sociological theory and social thought. He attempts to restate the concepts of powerlessness, meaninglessness, normlessness, isolation, and self-estrangement in terms of a modern vocabulary of expectations and rewards. I have made a rather free adaptation of his discussion, redefining a number of his categories so that they better fit

Powerlessness: Modes of Freedom and Control in Industry

A person is powerless when he is an object controlled and manipulated by other persons or by an impersonal system (such as technology), and when he cannot assert himself as a subject to change or modify this domination. Like an object, the powerless person reacts rather than acts. He is directed or dominated, rather than self-directing. The non-alienated pole of the powerlessness dimension is freedom and control. Freedom is the state which allows the person to remove himself from those dominating situations that make him simply a reacting object. Freedom may therefore involve the possibility of movement in a physical or social sense, the ability to walk away from a coercive machine process, or the opportunity of quitting a job because of the existence of alternative employment. Control is more positive than freedom, suggesting the assertion of the self-directing subject over such potentially dominating forces as employers or machine systems.

The degree of powerlessness a student imputes to manual workers in industry today depends not only on his sociological and political perspective but also on the

[*footnote 2 continued*
the industrial situation, an application Seeman does not himself make. I have not treated normlessness as a separate dimension but consider some of its implications in my discussion of isolation.

In the earliest discussion of alienated labor, Karl Marx also took a multidimensional approach and distinguished economic, psychological, sociological, and philosophical aspects of alienation. In the *Economic and Philosophical Manuscripts of 1844* (Moscow: Foreign Langauges Publishing House, n.d.), the youthful Marx analyzed how the institutions of capitalism, private property, market economy, and money alienated the worker from the product of his work, in the process or activity of work, from other human beings and from his own human nature.

Again, the connection between some of Marx's dimensions and those employed in the present chapter is clear.

aspects of freedom and control he selects as the most important. There are at least four modes of industrial powerlessness which have preoccupied writers on "the social question." These are (1) the separation from ownership of the means of production and the finished products, (2) the inability to influence general managerial policies, (3) the lack of control over the conditions of employment, and (4) the lack of control over the immediate work process. It is my contention that control over the conditions of employment and control over the immediate work process are most salient for manual workers, who are most likely to value control over those matters which affect their immediate jobs and work tasks and least likely to be concerned with the more general and abstract aspects of powerlessness.

The very nature of employment in a large-scale organization means that workers have forfeited their claims on the finished product and that they do not own the factory, machines, or often their own tools. Unlike the absence of control over the immediate work process, "ownership powerlessness" is a constant in modern industry, and employees, therefore, normally do not develop expectations for influence in this area. Today the average worker no more desires to own his machines than modern soldiers their howitzers or government clerks their file cabinets.[3] Automobile and chemical workers, by and large, do not feel deprived because they cannot take home the Corvairs or sulfuric acid they produce.

Orthodox Marxism saw the separation from the means of production as the cen-

[3] It was Max Weber in his classic analysis of bureaucracy who expanded Marx's concept of the industrial worker's separation from the means of production to all modern large-scale organizations. Civil servants are separated from the means of administration; soldiers from the means of violence; and scientists from the means of inquiry. Hans Gerth and C. W. Mills, *From Max Weber: Essays in Sociology* (New York: Oxford University Press, 1946), p. 50.

tral fact of capitalism, the inevitable consequence of which would be the worker's general alienation from society. This has not happened: manual workers have required only steady jobs, reasonable wages, and employee benefits to put down at least moderate stakes in society and industry. Yet, despite the lack of any conscious desire for control in this area, we cannot know for certain whether or not the worker's alienation from ownership unconsciously colors the whole quality of his experience in the factory, as Erich Fromm, for one, argues.[4] The appeal of small-business ownership, stronger among manual than white-collar employees, suggests that there may be many workers like the automobile worker Ely Chinoy quotes, for whom employment itself is inherently alienating:

> The main thing is to be independent and give your own orders and not have to take them from anybody else. That's the reason the fellows in the shop all want to start their own business. Then the profits are all for yourself. When you're in the shop, there's nothing for yourself in it. So you just do what you have to do in order to get along. A fellow would rather do it for himself. If you expend the energy, it's for your benefit then.[5]

Like the separation from ownership, another facet of industrial powerlessness, the lack of control over decision-making, is also common to the modern employment relationship. Large-scale organizations are hierarchical authority structures with power concentrated at the top, and manual workers have little opportunity to control the major decisions of the enterprise. And unlike the worker quoted above, most employees do not seem to resent this aspect of powerlessness, which they also tend to

accept as a "given" of industry. The average worker does not want the responsibility for such decisions as what, for whom, and how much to produce; how to design the product; what machinery to buy; how to distribute jobs; or how to organize the flow of work. It is only when these decisions directly affect his immediate job and work load that he expects his labor organization to influence policy in his behalf— as the recent labor-management conflicts over work rules indicate.

A number of industrial reform movements have attempted to counteract this aspect of powerlessness. Early in the twentieth century, the classical advocates of workers' control—the socialist followers of Rosa Luxembourg in Germany, the American IWW, the French syndicalists, and the British shop-stewards' movements —raised the slogan of industrial democracy. But as labor reform movements became more sophisticated, they realized that large-scale production organizations cannot be governed directly and en masse. The sponsors of direct democracy gave way to the advocates of representative democracy and participation in management. The most important recent examples of this trend are "joint consultation" in England, codetermination in Germany, and the workers' councils of eastern Europe.[6] Yet the experience of these representative systems suggests that it is only the delegate or the participator, not the average worker, who actually feels he is influencing major decisions. Even those progressive firms which have encouraged mass participation in shop councils find that the average employee confines his interest to his own job and work group and leaves participation in the over-all plan to a select few.[7]

A third aspect of industrial powerless-

[4] Fromm, *op. cit.*

[5] Ely Chinoy, *Automobile Workers and the American Dream* (New York: Doubleday & Co., 1955), pp. xvi–xvii.

[6] Hugh Clegg, *A New Approach to Industrial Democracy* (Oxford: Basil Blackwell, 1960), p. 5.

[7] E. Jaques, *The Changing Culture of the Factory* (London: Tavistock Publications, 1951), and F. Blum, *Toward a Democratic Work Proc-*

ness, the lack of control over conditions of employment, is considerably more meaningful to American workers. Selig Perlman's characterization of the American working class as more "job conscious" than "class conscious" suggests that control of the opportunity for work itself within the oligarchic industrial system has been historically more relevant than the two more "revolutionary" aspects of control discussed above.[8]

Under early capitalism, the worker could be hired and fired at will by impersonal forces of the market and personal whims of the employer. As a commodity subject to supply and demand factors, his employment depended on the extent of his skills and the phase of the business cycle. This is no longer the case. The most important innovations sponsored by American labor unions have been aimed at reducing the historic inequality of power in the contractual situation of employment. Collective bargaining, the contract, grievance procedures, arbitration, seniority provisions, hiring halls, and now "guaranteed annual wages" have all been partially successful attempts to increase the control of employees over their conditions of employment.

In addition, a number of economic changes have greatly reduced the worker's powerlessness in this area. The severity of periodic economic crises has diminished as industry and government have imposed major checks on the anarchy of a free competitive system. Technological re-

quirements have increased the need for more skilled and responsible workers. Thus, the large corporation has recognized the advantage of a more permanent work force to its pursuit of economic stability and higher productivity.

As a result of these changes in economic life, technology, corporation policy, and union power, the worker's control over his employment is increasing in what Ralf Dahrendorf calls "post-capitalist society." The *worker,* who in classical capitalism was considered virtually a commodity or a cost of production and treated as *a thing,* is giving way to the *employee,* a permanent worker who is viewed much more as *a human being.* Many employees have job security based on seniority provisions or a *de facto* "common law" right to their jobs. The employment relationship no longer reflects merely the balance of power; it is more and more determined by a system of institutional justice.[9]

Economic security is not distributed equally in the industrial structure, for the trends outlined above have not developed evenly. Some firms, industries, and specific occupations are extremely unstable in employment, whereas others provide virtual tenure in jobs. Empirical studies constantly emphasize the important part which regularity of employment plays in workers' evaluations of particular jobs and companies.[10] As an area of significant concern for manual workers, control over employment conditions will be analyzed in the four industrial comparisons, with the major emphasis on variations in control over the immediate work process.

[footnote 7 continued
ess (New York: Harper & Bros., 1953). A most notable exception to this generalization seems to be the Scanlon plan which encourages workers to make suggestions for increasing efficiency, cutting costs, and raising profits through a system of company-wide meetings and a group bonus plan. Probably best suited for small companies, it has been remarkably successful in a number of cases. See, for example, Frederick Lesieur (ed.), *The Scanlon Plan* (New York: John Wiley & Sons, 1958).

[8] S. Perlman, *A Theory of the Labor Movement* (New York: August M. Kelley, 1949).

[9] This guiding idea informs the work of Philip Selznick, *From Power to Justice in Industry* (forthcoming). See also Howard Vollmer, *Employee Rights and the Employment Relationship* (Berkeley: University of California Press, 1960).

[10] Combining data from sixteen studies of employee attitudes, Herzberg and his collaborators found that security was the most important factor of ten job factors. See F. Herzberg, *et al., Job Attitudes: Review of Research and Opinion* (Pittsburgh: Psychological Service of Pittsburgh, 1957), p. 44.

Both sociologists and socialists, in their emphasis on the assembly-line work situation, have provided much data on the powerlessness of the worker in the face of a dominating technological system. Despite the fact that the assembly line is not the representative work milieu, these scholars have rightly emphasized the central importance of the worker's relation to technology as a major condition of alienation. For when a worker is dominated and controlled by the machine system in the very process of his work, he, in effect, becomes reduced to a mechanical device. Reacting to the rhythms of technology rather than acting in some independent or autonomous manner, he approaches most completely the condition of *thingness,* the essence of alienation.

Studies of the assembly line show that workers greatly resent the dominance of technology and constantly try to devise ways to gain some measure of control over the machine system. The resentment against this kind of powerlessness may reflect an awareness of its special degrading and humiliating features, as well as the knowledge that there are many alternative kinds of work situations in factory employment.[11]

[11] The high degree of importance which workers place on control of their immediate job conditions is attested to by numerous investigations. The economists Joseph Shister and Lloyd Reynolds found that among two large samples of workers, "independence and control" were the most important elements among eleven job characteristics accounting for both satisfaction and dissatisfaction with their present jobs. *Job Horizons* (New York: Harper & Bros., 1949), p. 7. In his study of a gypsum plant Alvin Gouldner attributed the outbreak of a wildcat strike to the company's abrogation of an "indulgency pattern," an informal situation in which the workers had maintained a great deal of freedom and control in their immmediate job realm. *Wildcat Strike* (Yellow Springs, Ohio: Antioch Press, 1954). In a survey of the literature on occupational differences in job satisfaction, the present writer found that variations in the degree of control over the conditions of work was the most important single factor accounting for these differences. "Work Satisfaction and Industrial

The variations in control over the immediate activity of work are a principal focus of the present study. . . .

Whether a worker controls his sociotechnical environment depends on his freedom of movement, freedom to make choices, and freedom from oppressive constraints. It is necessary to specify this final aspect of industrial powerlessness more precisely by distinguishing those individual freedoms which are the components or elements of control over the immediate activity of work. Of these, the most important is control over the *pace* of work.

A basic distinction can be made between those jobs which are machine-paced, with the rhythms of work and the timing of the operator's action depending on the speed of the machine or machine process, and those which are man-paced, in which the worker himself can vary the rhythms of his actions.[12] This distinction can be seen in two occupations outside the factory. The man who takes money or issues tickets at the toll plaza of a bridge or highway has virtually no control over the pace of his work, since it is determined by the flow of traffic. He can only respond. An unskilled clerk in an office who adds columns of figures all day on an adding machine, however, has considerable control over his work pace. Often he can slow down, speed up, or take a break at his own discretion, although supervisors and other

Trends in Modern Society," in Walter Galenson and Seymour Martin Lipset (eds.), *Labor and Trade Unionism* (New York: John Wiley & Sons, 1960), pp. 345–49.

Among other studies of workers' attitudes which confirm the importance of control are Theodore Purcell, *The Worker Speaks His Mind on Company and Union* (Cambridge, Mass.: Harvard University Press, 1954), p. 103; Gladys Palmer, "Attitudes toward Work in an Industrial Community," *American Journal of Sociology,* LXIII (1957), 24; and Nancy C. Morse and Robert S. Weiss, "The Function and Meaning of Work and the Job," *American Sociological Review,* XX (1955), 191–98.

[12] John Dunlop, *Industrial Relations Systems* (New York: Henry Holt & Co., 1958), pp. 52–53.

clerks might have some influence over his work pace.

Control over the pace of work is critical because it sets a man apart from the machine system of modern technology. The pace of work is probably the most insistent, the most basic, aspect of a job and retaining control in this area is a kind of affirmation of human dignity. This freedom is also crucial because it influences other work freedoms.

For example, when a man can control his work rhythm, he can usually regulate the degree of *pressure* exerted on him. Some work environments, like automobile and textile factories, are characterized by considerable pressure, while others, like print shops and chemical plants, have a relaxed atmosphere. . . . In addition, *freedom of physical movement* is much more likely when a worker controls his own work rhythm and also when he is relatively free from pressure. In American industry today many jobs require the worker to stay close to his station for eight hours a day, while others permit a great deal of moving around the plant. The automobile assembly line is again an extreme example of restricted physical movement, whereas the work milieu of the print shop permits a high degree of this freedom. Many manual workers consider free movement quite important; the rather common preference of manual workers for truck-driving, railroad, and construction work rather than factory jobs often represents an aversion to physically confining "inside" work.

Control over work pace generally brings some *freedom to control the quantity of production*. Of course, workers cannot keep their jobs without a minimum production. But many are able to vary the hourly and daily output greatly,[13] while

[13] This has been a common research finding in industrial sociology since the Western Electric study dramatized the fact. See especially the studies of Donald Roy—for example, "Quota Restriction and Goldbricking in a Machine

others have no power at all to control this. Similar to this is the freedom to control the *quality* of one's work. When a man sets his own pace and is free from pressure, as are craft printers, he can take the pains to do a job up to his standards of workmanship; in machine-paced systems with high-speed production, a worker's desire to put out quality work is often frustrated, as is the case with many automobile assemblers.

A final component of control over the immediate work process refers to *techniques*. In mass production there is generally little opportunity to make choices as to how to do one's job, since these decisions have been already made by engineers, time-study men, and supervisors. In other industrial settings, however, jobs permit some selection of work methods. There, workers can solve problems and use their own ideas.

These individual task-related freedoms —control over pace, freedom from pressure, freedom of physical movement, and the ability to control the quantity and quality of production and to choose the techniques of work—together make up control over the immediate work process. When rationalized technology and work organization do not permit the active intervention of the worker at any of these points, the alienating tendencies of modern industry, which make the worker simply a responding object, an instrument of the productive process, are carried to their furthest extremes.

Meaninglessness: Purpose and Function in Manual Work

A second dimension of alienation in industrial employment is meaninglessness. Bureaucratic structures seem to encourage feelings of meaninglessness. As division of labor increases in complexity in large-scale organizations, individual roles may seem to lack organic connection with the

Shop," *American Journal of Sociology*, LVII (1952), 427–42.

whole structure of roles, and the result is that the employee may lack understanding of the co-ordinated activity and a sense of purpose in his work.

Karl Mannheim saw meaninglessness emerging in bureaucracies as a result of the tension between "functional rationalization" and "substantial rationality." Functional rationalization refers to the idea that in a modern organization everything is geared to the highest efficiency. The number of tasks and procedures required for a product or a service are analyzed, and the work is organized so that there is a smooth flow and a minimum of costs. The rationale of the technical and social organization is comprehended fully only by a few top managers (and engineers in the case of a factory), if indeed by anyone at all. But along with the greater efficiency and rationality of the whole, the substantial rationality of the individuals who make up the system declines. The man who has a highly subdivided job in a complex factory and the clerk working in a huge government bureau need only know very limited tasks. They need not know anyone else's job and may not even know what happens in the departments of the organization next to them. They need not know how their own small task fits into the entire operation. What results is a decline in the "capacity to act intelligently in a given situation on the basis of one's own insight into the interrelations of events."[14]

Meaning in work depends largely on three aspects of the worker's relationship to the product, process, and organization of work. The first factor is the character of the product itself. Working on a unique and individuated product is almost inherently meaningful. It is more difficult to develop and maintain a sense of purpose in contributing toward a standardized prod-

uct, since this inevitably involves repetitive work cycles. The second point is the scope of the product worked on. It is more meaningful to work on the whole, or a large part, of even a standardized product than to perform one's tasks on only a small part of the final product. Third, purpose and function increase when the employee's job makes him responsible for a large span of the production process, rather than a small restricted sphere.

Tendencies toward meaninglessness therefore stem from the nature of modern manufacturing, which is based on standardized production and a division of labor that reduces the size of the worker's contribution to the final product. Whereas many independent craftsmen of the preindustrial era made the entire product themselves, from the first step in the operations to the last, an automobile assembler may spend all his time putting on headlights and never have anything to do with any other operation. These alienating tendencies may be overcome when job design or technological developments result in a wide rather than a narrow scope of operations for the employee. Purpose may also be injected into relatively fractionized jobs when the worker develops an understanding of the organization's total function and of the relation of his own contribution to that larger whole. However, such understanding is less likely to lead toward a sense of purpose and function if the worker's responsibilities and scope of operations remain narrow.

Like powerlessness, meaninglessness is unequally distributed among manual workers in modern industry. The nature of an industry's technology and work organization affects the worker's ability to wrest a sense of purpose from his work task—substantial irrationality is not the fate of all modern factory employees. This mode of alienation is most intensified when production is carried out in large plants. In the small factory it is easier for the worker to see the relationship of his

[14] K. Mannheim, *Man and Society in an Age of Reconstruction* (New York: Harcourt, Brace & Co., 1940), p. 59, cited in Seeman, *op. cit.*, p. 786.

contribution to the enterprise as a whole. Team production also reduces meaninglessness. It is easier for factory workers to develop a sense of purpose when they are members of work crews which carry out the job jointly than for employees who do their work individually. Finally there is less alienation in process technology than in batch or assembly methods of production. In the former system, work is organized in terms of an integrated process rather than in terms of subdivided tasks, and the worker's span of responsibility and job assignment is enlarged. An increased sense of purpose and function in work for the blue-collar employee may be one of the most important by-products of automation, since this technical system brings about smaller factories, production by teams rather than individuals, and integrated process operations.

Social Alienation: Integration and Membership in Industrial Communities

In contrast to Marx, who emphasized the powerlessness of workers in modern industry and saw the solution to the modern social problem in "restoring" control to the workers over their conditions of work, the French sociologist Emile Durkheim saw *anomie* (normlessness) and the breakup of integrated communities as the distinguishing feature of modern society. The massive social processes of industrialization and urbanization had destroyed the normative structure of a more traditional society and uprooted people from the local groups and institutions which had provided stability and security.

The transition to industrialism brought about tendencies toward social alienation, not only in the larger society but also in the factories and mills. Although the use of physical force and the threat of starvation as "incentives" expressed the callousness of many industrialists, it also reflected the fact that there was as yet no basis for an industrial community. With normative integration absent, machine-breaking, sab-

otage, strikes, and revolutionary activity not only represented protest against unbearable conditions but expressed the fact that workers had not yet developed a sense of loyalty to industrial enterprise or commitment to the new social role of factory employee.

In advanced industrial societies like the United States, the social alienation in factory employment characteristic of the early period has been greatly reduced. Even workers who lack control over their immediate work task and experience difficulty in achieving meaning and self-expression in the job may be spared the alienation of isolation, which implies the absence of a sense of membership in an industrial community. Membership in an industrial community involves commitment to the work role and loyalty to one or more centers of the work community. Isolation, on the other hand, means that the worker feels no sense of belonging in the work situation and is unable to identify or uninterested in identifying with the organization and its goals.

An industrial community is made up of a network of social relationships which are derived from a work organization and which are valued by the members of the community. For many factory workers the plant as a whole is a community, a center of belongingness and identification, which mitigates feelings of isolation. It is quite common for workers to come to a factory thirty minutes early every day to relax in the company of their friends. It has been argued that the human contacts of the plant community are critical in making work which is in other ways alienating bearable for mass production workers.[15]

[15] "Only the human contacts bring a touch of variety into the monotony of the daily work. . . . If you speak to a worker who has been sick for some time, and could not go to work, and he asks about the 'fellows' in the gang—then you realize the secret attraction which the plant has for many workers . . . the shop community is a major factor making the experience of work more positive." Blum, *op.cit.*, p. 77.

Beginning with the work of Elton Mayo and his associates, much research in industrial sociology has documented the role of informal work groups in providing a sense of belonging within the impersonal atmosphere of modern industry.

An industrial community also has a structure of norms, informal and formal rules, which guide the behavior of its members. Industrial organizations differ in the extent of normative integration, and this is important in determining the employee's sense of belonging to a cohesive work community. Industrial organizations are normatively integrated when there is consensus between the work force and management on standards of behavior, expectations of rewards, and definitions of fair play and justice, and when there are agreed-upon "rules of the game" which govern the relations between employees and employers. The norms and practices through which workers are disciplined and laid off, assigned wage rates relative to the earnings of others, and awarded promotions, are especially critical. These matters affect the worker's sense of equity with respect to the allocation of rewards and the standards of distributive justice and therefore often determine his sense of alienation from, or integration in, the industrial enterprise.

Although the maturation of industrial society has generally reduced the worker's isolation, the implications of bureaucratic organization for social alienation are somewhat mixed. Bureaucracy's norm of impersonal administration emphasizes formal procedures, and in many cases this creates a feeling of distance between workers and management. And the bureaucratic principle of the rational utilization of all resources to maximize organizational goals furthers the tendency to view employees as *labor,* as means to the ends of profit and company growth. But bureaucratic administration also enhances normative consensus through its emphasis on universalistic standards of justice and

"fair treatment" and thus makes it possible for employees to acquire the status of industrial citizenship. It is probably the policy and practices of individual firms, unique historical and economic conditions, and particularly the technological setting,[16] that determines whether bureaucratization increases or decreases social integration in a specific situation.

Industries vary not only in the extent but also in the basis of normative integration and in the key institutions which are the center of the work community and the focus of worker loyalties. It is important to stress that the company need not be the major focus of the industrial community, as the advocates of what has been called "managerial sociology" tend to assume. In some cases, occupational groups and unions, in other situations, the local community as a whole, are more important presently and potentially. . . .

Self-Estrangement

Self-estrangement refers to the fact that the worker may become alienated from his inner self in the activity of work. Particularly when an individual lacks control over the work process and a sense of purposeful connection to the work enterprise, he may experience a kind of depersonalized detachment rather than an immediate involvement or engrossment in the job tasks. This lack of present-time involvement means that the work becomes primarily instrumental, a means toward future considerations rather than an end in itself. When work encourages self-estrangement, it does not express the unique abilities, potentialities, or personality of the worker. Further consequences of self-estranged work may be boredom and monotony, the

---

[16] Technology has an important impact on social alienation because it determines a number of aspects of industrial structure that affect cohesion and integration: the occupational distribution of the blue-collar labor force, the economic cost structure of the enterprise, the typical size of plant, and the existence and structure of work groups.

absence of personal growth, and a threat to a self-approved occupational identity.

Self-estrangement is absent in two main situations: when the work activity, satisfying such felt needs as those for control, meaning, and social connection, is inherently fulfilling in itself; or when the work activity is highly integrated into the totality of an individual's social commitments. Throughout most of history, the problem of work has been dealt with in the latter manner. Adriano Tilgher, a historian of work ideologies, finds that the idea that work should be a creative fulfilment is peculiarly modern, with origins in the Renaissance. In many previous civilizations work was viewed as some kind of unpleasant burden or punishment.[17] Our modern feeling that work should be a source of direct, immediate satisfaction and express the unique potential of the individual is probably a result of its compartmentalization in industrial society. In preindustrial societies "uninteresting" work was highly integrated with other aspects of the society—with ritual, religion, family, and community or tribal relationships, for example. Therefore it could not become simply a means to life, because it was an immediate part of life's main concerns.

A number of fateful social changes have contributed to the compartmentalization of work. Most basic was the market economy which, in severing the organic connection between production and consumption, between effort and gratification, set the stage for the instrumental attitude toward work.[18] Second, the physical separation of household and workplace—an essential condition for the development of capitalism and bureaucratic organization, as Weber stressed—produced a hiatus between work life and family life. Third, with the secularization of modern society, the importance of the religious sanction in work motivation has declined; work and religion are now separated. Fourth, with the specialization brought about by industrial organization and the anonymity which urbanization has furthered, the average man's occupational role is not well known or understood: work is now separated from the community, as well as from the family and religion. Finally, the decline of the hours of work and the increase in living standards mean that less of life is devoted simply to problems of material existence. Time, energy, and resources are now available for other aspects of life,[19] which compete with work for emotional loyalties and commitments.

Self-estrangement is experienced as a heightened awareness of time, as a split between present activity and future considerations. Non-alienated activity consists of immersion in the present; it is involvement. Alienated activity is not free, spontaneous activity but is compulsive and driven by necessity. In non-alienated activity the rewards are in the activity itself; in alienated states they are largely extrinsic to the activity, which has become primarily a means to an end. Marx expressed these notions in his early work on alienation, the *Economic and Philosophical Manuscripts:*

> In his work, therefore, [the worker] does not affirm himself but denies himself, does not feel content but unhappy, does not develop freely his physical and mental energy but mortifies his body and ruins his mind. The worker therefore only feels himself outside his work, and in his work feels outside himself.

[17] Adriano Tilgher, *Work: What It Has Meant to Men through the Ages* (New York: Harcourt, Brace & Co., 1930).

[18] Hannah Arendt emphasizes this factor as the basic precondition of alienation. See *The Human Condition* (Chicago: University of Chicago Press, 1958), especially pp. 79–174.

[19] It has been often pointed out that the reduction of hours of work is only relevant to the past century or two. In the Middle Ages as much or more leisure time existed as at the present. See Harold Wilensky, "The Uneven Distribution of Leisure: The Impact of Economic Growth on 'Free Time,'" *Social Problems,* IX (1961), 33–34

He is at home when he is not working, and when he is working he is not at home. His labor is therefore not voluntary, but coerced; it is *forced labor*. It is therefore not the satisfaction of a need; it is merely a *means* to satisfy needs external to it. Its alien character emerges clearly in the fact that as soon as no physical or other compulsion exists, labor is shunned like the plague. External labor, labor in which man alienates himself, is a labor of self-sacrifice, of mortification.[20]

Since self-estranged activity is a means to an end rather than an end in itself, the satisfaction is in the future rather than the present, and the tone of feeling approaches *detachment* rather than involvement. The man on the assembly line is thinking about that beer he will have when the whistle blows; the packing-house worker at Hormel goes home from work "so he can accomplish something for that day."[21] The meaning of the job for the automobile worker is not the intrinsic activity itself but that "new car" or "little modern house," which the pay check, itself a future reward, brings closer.[22]

Lack of involvement results in a heightened time-consciousness. If it were possible to measure "clock-watching," this would be one of the best objective indicators of this mode of alienation. The "over-concern" with time is central to Fred Blum's perceptive discussion of alienation in a meat-packing plant and suggests that self-alienation is widespread in this kind of work. When Blum asked these workers whether they get bored on the job, a common response was that boredom was not a serious problem because "the time passes."

How could the passage of time possibly neutralize the monotony of the job? Whatever the answer may be, there is no doubt but that the time does, as a rule, pass fast. A large majority of workers, when asked: "When you are at work does the time generally pass slow or fast?" indicated that it usually passes quickly. Only a small minority feels that the time goes slowly. Many workers, however, intimated that sometimes the passage of time is slow and sometimes fast.[23]

On the other hand, involvement in work may come from control, from association with others, and from a sense of its purpose. A man who is controlling his immediate work process—regulating the pace, the quantity of output, the quality of the product, choosing tools or work techniques—must be relatively immersed in the work activity. For most employees, when work is carried out by close-knit work groups, especially work teams, it will be more intrinsically involving and rewarding. And involvement and self-fulfilment is heightened when the purpose of the job can be clearly connected with the final end product or the over-all goals and organization of the enterprise. On the other hand, there is no necessary causal relation between social alienation and self-alienation. A worker may be integrated in the plant community and loyal to the company and still fail to achieve a sense of involvement and self-expression in his work activity itself.

When work is not inherently involving it will be felt as monotonous.[24] The extensive industrial research on monotony[25] suggests the high degree of self-estrangement in factory employment. Unfortunately, the studies are so scattered that they do not permit an over-all assessment of the amount of felt monotony in the labor force. But the concern of industrial psychologists in England, France, Ger-

---

[20] K. Marx, *op. cit.*, pp. 72–73.
[21] Blum, *op. cit.*
[22] Chinoy, *op. cit.*

[23] Blum, *op. cit.*, p. 82.
[24] Of course, many people do not find monotonous work objectionable.
[25] A brilliant discussion is found in Georges Friedmann, *Industrial Society* (Glencoe, Ill.: Free Press, 1955), pp. 129–55.

many, and America with this topic, stimulated by management anxieties over dips in output, indicates that present-time involvement is a precarious thing, especially in repetitive jobs.[26]

Many industrial commentators feel that most modern jobs cannot be intrinsically involving and the best solution would be to make them so completely automatic that a worker would be free to daydream and talk to his workmates. Evidently, we are still far from this outcome, since the Roper survey, based on a representative sample of 3,000 factory workers, found that only 43 per cent could do their work and keep their minds on other things most of the time.* The most unsatisfactory situation seems to be the job which is not intrinsically interesting and yet requires rather constant attention.

Still, such work does not necessarily result in intense or even mild dissatisfaction. The capacity of people to adapt to routine repetitive work is remarkable. It is quite likely that the majority of industrial workers are self-estranged in the sense that their work is not particularly involving and is seen chiefly as a means to livelihood. Yet research in job satisfaction suggests that the majority of workers, possibly from 75 to 90 per cent, are reasonably satisfied with such jobs.[27] Thus, the typical worker in modern industrial society is probably satisfied *and* self-estranged.

Self-estranged workers are dissatisfied only when they have developed *needs* for

control, initiative, and meaning in work. The average manual worker and many white-collar employees may be satisfied with fairly steady jobs which are largely instrumental and non-involving, because they have not the need for responsibility and self-expression in work. They are therefore relatively content with work which is simply a means to the larger end of providing the pay checks for lives organized around leisure, family, and consumption.

One factor which is most important in influencing a man's aspirations in the work process is education. The more education a person has received, the greater the need for control and creativity. For those with little education, the need for sheer activity (working to "keep occupied") and for association are more important than control, challenge, and creativity.[28]

Finally, self-estranging work threatens a positive sense of selfhood because it fosters a damaging rather than an affirmative occupational identity. In a traditional society with little individuation, identity, the answer to the question "Who am I?" was not a problem for the masses of people. Identity, to the extent that this concept[29]

---

[26] Monotony, of course, is quite relative in the sense that minor alterations in the work routine or general situation (a new tool or a superintendent passing by) may give interest to a workday which, from an intellectual's vantage point, would appear the height of tedium.

*Editor's note: Part of the data reported by Blauner are based on a secondary analysis of a study of job attitudes conducted by Elmo Roper in 1947. Published materials and field studies carried out during 1959–62 were also utilized. For a complete description of the various data bases, see Blauner, *Alienation and Freedom,* esp. pp. 11–13 and Appendices C and D.

[27] Blauner, in Galenson and Lipset, *op. cit.*

[28] Morse and Weiss, *op. cit.;* Eugene Friedmann and Robert Havighurst, *The Meaning of Work and Retirement* (Chicago: University of Chicago Press, 1954). Herzberg and his collaborators also report that those in non-manual occupations and the more educated are more concerned with intrinsic job features. (Herzberg, *et al., op. cit.,* p. 54.)

Besides education, other important factors are intelligence, personality, and occupation itself. For the most part, white-collar and professional work involves more variety, control, purpose, and responsibility than blue-collar work. It is to some degree the work itself which a person secures that instills him with specific kinds of needs to be satisfied or frustrated in the work situation. A manual worker whose work does not involve such qualities, whose education has not awakened such aspirations, and whose opportunities do not include realistic alternatives, will not develop the need for intrinsically fulfilling work.

[29] Erik Erikson, "The Problem of Ego Identity," *Journal of the American Psychoanalytic Association,* Vol. IV (1956).

was meaningful in such a society, was largely provided through the kinship system, which means that it was not a matter of choice. In a modern industrial society in which there is marked occupational, social, and geographical mobility and in which considerable freedom of choice exists among various conflicting value systems, the development of personal identity is an ongoing creative process.

An industrial society tends to break down many important past sources of loyalty, such as extended kinship, local, regional, and even ethnic attachments. In their place, occupation becomes a more important element of general social standing, since more than any other attribute it influences the income and style of life a person leads. While people construct a sense of identity by a synthesis of early childhood identifications with a large number of later commitments and loyalties,[30] occupational identity has probably become a much more significant component of total identity in modern society than in the past. In an industrial society, it is primarily occupational status which is ranked in superior and inferior grades by the spontaneous processes of stratification. The estimates of the community and other men about the jobs we hold therefore greatly affect our own estimates of self-worth.

In general, working-class jobs in the United States have lower status than white-collar and professional ones. For this reason many factory workers are ambivalent about their work and do not find that occupational identity contributes to feelings of self-esteem and self-approval. In such a situation, there is probably a tendency to de-emphasize occupation and work as important components of selfhood and to stress in their place other loyalties and statuses, such as ethnic identifications and family relations.[31] Perhaps an indica-

tion of this dissatisfaction with working-class status is the fact that 59 per cent of the factory workers in the Roper study said that they would choose *different* occupations if they were able to "start all over again at the age of 15." In contrast, 80 or 90 per cent of those in various professional occupations would re-enter the *same* line of work if given a free choice.[32]

Self-estranging work compounds and intensifies this problem of a negative occupational identity. When work provides opportunities for control, creativity, and challenge—when, in a word, it is self-expressive and enhances an individual's unique potentialities—then it contributes to the worker's sense of self-respect and dignity and at least partially overcomes the stigma of low status. Alienated work —without control, freedom, or responsibility—on the other hand simply confirms and deepens the feeling that societal estimates of low status and little worth are valid.

The theory of alienation has been and continues to be a fruitful perspective on the world of work, but it must be pointed out that it is a limited perspective. With all its social-psychological subtleties, it does not fully comprehend the complexities and ambiguities of the inner meaning of work to the individual. As a polemic, it therefore condemns too much, and as a vision, promises too much.

Because it ignores what might be called the bipolar or two-sided ambivalence of work, alienation theory cannot totally explain the relationship between work and human happiness. For even the most alienated work is never totally unpleasant, never completely rejected by the worker. Necessity and force is never the whole story. The very worst jobs are rarely only means to exist but often become ends in themselves in some regard. Marx's con-

---

[30] *Ibid.*

[31] In her study of unskilled workers in a shipyard, Katherine Archibald has vividly documented their obsession with ethnic categorization.

Wartime Shipyard (Berkeley: University of California Press, 1947), pp. 40–127. The importance of kinship relations to manual workers has been noted by many researchers.

[32] Blauner, in Galenson and Lipset, *op. cit.*, p. 343.

ception of the function of work for man was too narrow, or perhaps too philosophical: he did not accept as essential the myriad of functions that even alienated work plays in the life-organization of human beings. Observation and research have disproved his statement that "as soon as no physical or other compulsion exist, labor is shunned like the plague." The need for sheer activity, for social intercourse, and for some status and identity in the larger society keeps even unskilled workers on the job after they are economically free to retire.[33]

Work is inherently ambivalent also at the opposite pole of freedom and non-alienation. Even in the most unalienated conditions, work is never totally pleasurable: in fact, the freest work, that of the writer or artist, usually involves long periods of virtual self-torture. Such non-alienated work is never completely an end in itself; it is never totally without the element of necessity. As Henri DeMan wrote in a profound study of the meaning of work:

> Even the worker who is free in the social sense, the peasant or the handicraftsman, feels this compulsion, were it only because while he is at work, his activities are dominated and determined by the aim of his work, by the idea of a willed or necessary creation. Work inevitably signifies subordination of the worker to remoter aims, felt to be necessary, and therefore involving a renunciation of the freedoms and enjoyments of the present for the sake of a future advantage.[34]

[Four Types of Alienation]

We have discussed four types of alienation often experienced by manual workers in industry. What do these dimensions have in common on a more general level? Basic to each one is the notion of fragmentation in man's existence and consciousness which impedes the wholeness of experience and activity. What distinguishes the separate dimensions is that they are based on different principles of division or fragmentation. Each dimension has its unique opposite, or non-alienated state, which implies a kind of organic wholeness in the quality of experience. Finally, each alienated state makes it more probable that the person (or worker) can be "used as a thing."

The split in man's existence and consciousness into subject and object underlies the idea of *powerlessness*. A person is powerless when he is an object controlled and manipulated by other persons or by an impersonal system (such as technology) and when he cannot assert himself as a subject to change or modify this domination. The non-alienated pole of the powerlessness dimension is the state of freedom and control.

Meaninglessness alienation reflects a split between the part and the whole. A person experiences alienation of this type when his individual acts seem to have no relation to a broader life-program. Meaninglessness also occurs when individual roles are not seen as fitting into the total system of goals of the organization but have become severed from any organic connection with the whole. The non-alienated state is understanding of a life-plan or of an organization's total functioning and activity which is purposeful rather than meaningless.

Isolation results from a fragmentation of the individual and social components of human behavior and motivation. Isolation suggests the idea of general societal alienation, the feeling of being in, but not of, society, a sense of remoteness from the larger social order, an absence of loyalties to intermediate collectivities. The non-alienated opposite of isolation is a sense of belonging and membership in society or

---

[33] E. Friedmann and R. Havighurst, *op. cit.* Morse and Weiss found that 80 per cent of a national sample said they would keep working if they inherited enough money to live comfortably (*op. cit.*).

[34] H. DeMan, *Joy in Work* (London: George Allen & Unwin, 1929), p. 67.

in specific communities which are integrated through the sharing of a normative system.

Self-estrangement is based on a rupture in the temporal continuity of experience. When activity becomes a means to an end, rather than an end in itself, a heightened awareness of time results from a split between present engagements and future considerations. Activity which is not self-estranged, but self-expressive or self-actualizing, is characterized by involvement in the present-time context. Self-estrangement also entails a separation between work life and other concerns. When work is self-estranging, occupation does not contribute in an affirmative manner to personal identity and selfhood, but instead is damaging to self-esteem.

Thus the four modes of alienation reflect different "splits" in the organic relationship between man and his existential experience: the subject-object, the part-whole, the individual-social, and the present-future dichotomies. Each makes it more possible to use people as means rather than as ends. Since "things" rather than human beings are normally used as means, alienation tends to turn people into things: thus thingness, in addition to fragmentation, is another common denominator of the various meanings of alienation.

In sum, a person is more likely to be used as an object under these conditions: (1) when he is powerless and lacks control; (2) when his role is so specialized that he becomes a "cog" in an organization; and (3) when he is isolated from a community or network of personal relations which would inhibit impersonal treatment. The result of being a means for the ends of others is that for himself, his (own) activity becomes only a means rather than a fulfilling end.

These *fragmentations* in man's experience all seem to have resulted from basic changes in social organization brought about by the industrial revolution. That is

why the alienation concept has a peculiarly modern ring. Few people in preindustrial societies seem to be alienated (the powerlessness of the masses might be the exception); in a bureaucratic mass society we are likely to regard huge numbers of people as alienated. Thus, the breadth of the alienation concept is due to the fact that it reflects the social conditions and consequences of the transition to an industrial society.[35] And conversely, when one studies the stabilization and reintegration of industrial societies in their more mature, advanced phases (a common perspective today of students of social organization), one is studying the conditions through which alienation is either overcome or rendered bearable for individuals and relatively harmless for society.

Within the world of work, the relative stabilization of an advanced industrial society has diminished some of the more glaring instances of alienation characteristic of the period of early industrialization in which Marx wrote. Yet the tendency to use people as things still persists in modern industry. And perhaps this is inevitable, since the nature of industrial organization is such that workers are productive resources and, therefore, to some degree, means to organizational goals.

But despite the common features of modern employment relations, industrial environments vary markedly in their alienating tendencies. Whether a worker approaches the state of being merely a commodity, a resource, or an element of cost in the productive process depends on his concrete relation to technology, the social structure of his industry, and its economic fortunes. . . .

---

[35] Note the similarity between this statement of alienation theory and the standard sociological analyses of modern industrial society (from Toennies to Parsons) which stress the predominance of instrumental over expressive orientations, of means over ends, of technology and organization over family and community.

Alienation and Freedom in Historical Perspective

The industry a man works in is *fateful* because the conditions of work and existence in various industrial environments are quite different. The print shop, the textile mill, the automobile plant, the chemical continuous-process operation—all important factory milieux in the present-day situation—illustrate the far-reaching diversity and pluralistic quality of American industrial life. . . . An employee's industry decides the nature of the work he performs eight hours a day and affects the meaning which that work has for him. It greatly influences the extent to which he is free in his work life and the extent to which he is controlled by technology or supervision. It also influences his opportunity for personal growth and development—to learn, to advance, to take on responsibility. His industry even affects the kind of social personality he develops, since an industrial environment tends to breed a distinctive social type.[36]

. . . Each dimension of alienation—powerlessness, meaninglessness, isolation, and self-estrangement—varies in form and intensity according to the industrial setting. There is thus no simple answer to the question: Is the factory worker of today an alienated worker? Inherent in the tech-

[36] From this point of view there is something misleading in the spate of such generalized titles as *Industrial Man, Blue Collar Man*, etc. It seems more appropriate to speak of "industrial men" or "blue-collar men," phrasings that do not connote such a uniformity of condition. Theodore Purcell's *Blue Collar Man* (Cambridge, Mass.: Harvard University Press, 1960), for example, is based on a study of workers in only one industry, meat-packing. Compare also William L. Warner and Norman H. Martin, *Industrial Man* (New York: Harper & Bros., 1959); Clark Kerr, *et al., Industrialism and Industrial Man* (Cambridge, Mass.: Harvard University Press, 1960); and Alex Inkeles, "Industrial Man: The Relation of Status to Experience, Perception and Value," *American Journal of Sociology*, LXVI (1960) 1–31.

niques of modern manufacturing and the principles of bureaucratic industrial organization are general alienating tendencies. But in some cases the distinctive technology, division of labor, economic structure, and social organization—in other words, the factors that differentiate individual industries—intensify these general tendencies, producing a high degree of alienation; in other cases they minimize and counteract them, resulting instead in control, meaning, and integration.

The method of comparative industrial analysis therefore illustrates the diversity and pluralism within modern manufacturing, highlights the unequal distribution of alienation and freedom among the factory labor force, and exposes the causal factors underlying these variations. In addition, it permits a historical perspective on the long-run changes in the relation between the manual worker and his work. Because of the uneven movement of modernization trends, industries coexist today that in a sense "belong" to different periods in the history of manufacturing. The four industries compared in this study vary in the degree of mechanization of technology, rationalization of division of labor, concentration of economic structure, and bureaucratization of social organization. By comparing the consequences of these variations in the four contexts, one gets a sense of the historic implications of long-range developments for alienation and freedom in the factory. . . .

The Three Types of Blue-Collar Work

As technology has developed higher levels of mechanization, there has been a shift in the job requirements of the factory employee. In printing and other craft technologies, traditional manual skill, the manipulation of "hard" materials by hand and with simple tools, is the dominant type of work. In continuous-process technology (oil refineries and heavy chemical plants), the mechanization of production and materials flow has reached the point where process operators neither see the product nor work on it directly with their hands. Instead they monitor the automatic control dials, inspect machinery, adjust valves, and record the data that describe the operations of the automated system. The dominant job requirement is no longer manual skill but responsibility. In place of the *able workman*, required when the worker's role in the productive process is to provide skills, a *reliable employee*, capable of accepting a considerable load of responsibility, is now needed in the automated industries.

Traditional manual skill and "non manual" responsibility differ in their basic qualities,[37] but both require considerable discretion and initiative. They therefore contribute to the dignity and self-respect of the factory worker. Unfortunately, the transition from one to the other is neither direct nor immediate. Craft technology rarely "evolves" into automated technology. The industries most characteristic of the middle stages of manufacturing development utilize machine and assembly-line techniques. Both these intermediate tech-

[37] The difference between these two modes of work is implied in Elliott Jaques' distinction between skill and *nous,* a Greek word which means mind or reason. Skill, according to Jaques, "is the capacity of a person to exercise sensory and perceptual judgment in carrying out the discretionary aspects of work. . . . Skill is made up of the capacity to respond intuitively to the sense of touch, sight, hearing, taste, smell, or balance, and physically to guide and manipulate one's work according to the sense or feel of the job in the course of doing it." *Nous,* on the other hand, is the "capacity to exercise mental judgment" in carrying out the discretionary aspects of work. It "is made up of the capacity to weigh up available information, to sense what other information, if any, ought to be obtained, and mentally to proceed on the basis of what feels like the best course of action where many factors in the situation are only unconsciously assessed, and some of the factors—perhaps even the most important ones—are simply unknown." Elliott Jaques, *Equitable Payment* (New York: John Wiley & Sons, 1961), pp. 81–82.

nologies bring about jobs that generally demand little manual skill or responsibility and thus epitomize the historic process that has been called "deskillization."

The textile and automobile assembly industries illustrate two different ways by which this deskillization has taken place. In the machine industries, traditional skill is undermined by the development of technology; in assembly-line production it is eliminated by the rationalization of work organization, by an extremely elaborate subdivision of labor. Both the expansion of technology and the growing subdivision of labor ultimately depend on the replacement of the unique product characteristic of craft industries by the more standardized product of mass production.

The erosion of traditional skill has largely completed its course in American industry, and present trends now suggest that such skill will increase in importance in the shrinking blue-collar sector. Traditional craft industries still play an important role in the economy and may enhance their significance even in a future automated society. The building construction industry, based largely on a traditional craft technology and traditional manual skill, is the largest single employer of blue-collar workers in the United States today. And a more affluent and educated public, reacting against the standardization of values and products in a mass society, may increase its future demand for unique and individuated articles.

Furthermore, automated manufacturing paradoxically increases traditional craft skill, which is applied, however, to maintenance problems rather than production work. Since automation involves a considerable increase in intricate plant machinery and technical processes, considerably more repairmen in various trades are needed to maintain this equipment. In the largest oil refineries and heavy chemical plants, there are as many or more maintenance employees than production employees. Within automated factories, two radically different kinds of blue-collar work coexist, each with its competing claim to skill and status.

On the other hand, technological change at present is probably reducing the relative importance of low-skilled machine and assembly-line work in the labor force. Automation is eliminating unskilled factory jobs at a faster rate than they are being created through the further deskillization of craft work. Still, many industries with machine and assembly-line technologies will maintain them and not automate, for both technical and economic reasons. The product market in the shoe industry, for example, does not readily permit the standardization of styles, sizes, and shapes which makes automation economically feasible.[38] In other industries, including motor vehicles, the manner in which the product is constructed makes the automation of assembly operations extremely difficult technologically. Thus, there is no immediate prospect for the total elimination of unskilled manual operations in old industries. Furthermore, some new industries may begin manufacturing their products by means of the older technologies, since it can take considerable time to develop the standardized product and consumer volume that permit a higher level of mechanization.

In the complex and diversified manufacturing sector of an advanced industrial society, at least three major kinds of blue-collar factory work exist at the same time: the traditional manual skill associated with craft technology; the routine low-skilled manual operations associated with machine and assembly-line technologies; and the "non-manual" responsibility called forth by continuous-process technology.[39] Although craft skill will con-

tinue to play a significant role, the shift from skill to responsibility is the most important historical trend in the evolution of blue-collar work. The relative decline of unskilled, standardized jobs is, in the long run, a positive development; [40] however, a considerable amount of the routine work that negates the dignity of the worker will very likely persist in the foreseeable future.

Technology, Freedom, and the Worker's Soup

Of the several dimensions of alienation, the impact of technology is greatest with respect to powerlessness, since the character of the machine system largely determines the degree of control the factory employee exerts over his sociotechnical environment and the range and limitations of his freedom in the work situation. In general, the long-run developments in this area parallel the historical evolution in blue-collar work. The interconnection between traditional manual skill and control is so intimate that theoretical distinctions between the two concepts become blurred: the very definition of traditional skill implies control over tools, materials, and pace of work. It is therefore no surprise that printers and other workers in craft technologies command a variety and degree of freedom unrivaled in the blue-collar world.

Machine technology generally reduces the control of the employee over his work process. Workers are rarely able to choose their own methods of work, since these decisions have been incorporated into the

[38] James Bright, *Automation and Management* (Boston: Harvard University Graduate School of Business Administration, 1958), pp. 30–37.

[39] These types correspond exactly with the three

stages in the evolution of manual work that Alain Touraine has distinguished at the Paris Renault Automotive Works. *L'évolution du travail ouvrier aux usines Renault* (Paris: Centre National de la Recherche Scientifique, 1955).

[40] Only in terms of the nature of manual work, of course; the loss of jobs resulting from these technological changes is a more serious matter to the individual worker than any historical improvement in the dignity of labor.

machines' very design and functioning. In the textile industry, pace and output are determined by the machine system and the organization of tasks; for the most part, operatives simply respond to the rhythms and exigencies of the technical system instead of initiating activity and exerting control.[41] In the assembly-line technology of the automobile industry, the worker's control is reduced to a minimal level. The conveyor-belt apparatus dictates most movements of the operative and pre-empts many of his potential choices and decisions.

An apparently trivial situation, the homely "case of the worker's soup," strikingly illustrates how a continuous-process technology restores the personal freedoms of the employee. This incident also points out the disparity in atmosphere between assembly-line and automated work environments. When asked about the possibilities of setting his own work pace, a chemical operator mentioned that the men often warm up a can of soup on a hot plate within the automated control room where they are stationed. Suppose this soup is on the stove, ready to eat, just at the time that's officially scheduled for the operator's round of instrument readings, an activity that takes about thirty minutes. "You can eat the soup first and do the work later, or you can take the readings earlier than scheduled, in order to have the soup when it's hot," reported this operator. In other words, the nature of production work in an automated technology makes it possible for the employee to satisfy personal and social needs when he feels like it, because he can carry out his job tasks according to his own rhythm.

<hr/>

[41] On the whole, powerlessness increases with growing mechanization within this group of industries. In the less-developed shoe and apparel industries workers operate individual machines, and they usually are able, therefore, to control both the pace at which they work and the quantity of their output. Since they can stop and start their own machines, they are also relatively free to leave their work stations for brief periods.

The automobile assembly-line worker who gets a craving for a bowl of soup is in an entirely different situation. He must wait for his allotted relief time, when another worker takes his place on the line, and if he still wants soup at that time he will probably drink it hurriedly on his return from the lavatory. Ironically but fittingly, his will be the "automated" soup, purchased from a commercial vending machine, since there is no room and no time for hot plates and cans of soup on an automotive conveyer belt.

If we shift from this consideration of long-run historical developments to look at the broad range of industrial environments today, it appears that only a minority of blue-collar workers are as controlled and dominated by technology or supervision as are automobile and textile workers. It is likely that most workers have jobs that permit them to set their own work pace, at least within limits—although adequate evidence on this point is lacking, unfortunately. Because of enlightened personnel policies and because an affluent society can afford a relaxed atmosphere at the point of production, most workers are free from intensive pressures on the job. Among all the factory employees in the Roper study, only 24 per cent said they had to work too fast. And because of prosperity, a more employee-oriented management, and the policing function of labor unions, the great majority of workers today are free from close and arbitrary supervision, a means of control that was quite prevalent a generation or two ago.

On the other hand, one aspect of control over the immediate work process is generally lacking in factory work: the freedom to choose the techniques and methods of doing the job. Predetermination of these decisions by engineers, foremen, and time-study men is the norm in mass-production industry. Probably only craftsmen and the few blue-collar operators in the new automated industries have much opportunity to introduce their own ideas in the course of their work. This general absence of opportunities for initiative is suggested by the fact that 51 per cent of the Roper factory workers said they could not try out their own ideas on the job— this was the only question relating to the objective work situation on which more than half of the respondents were dissatisfied.

Inherent in the idea of responsibility as the worker's job requirement is a degree of control over that area of the work process that is his domain. A long-run decline in powerlessness is therefore to be expected because of the character of automated technology and the nature of manual work in highly mechanized systems. But the unusual degree of freedom in industrial chemical plants is not simply a consequence of these factors. The economic expansion and general prosperity of the industry contribute much to the relaxed atmosphere on the job. Therefore automated industrial technology will not automatically guarantee freedom and control, since some automated firms and industries will be under economic stress in that far distant future when automation will be the dominant technology. In addition, automated technologies will take many forms, and variations within automated industries will result in different modes and levels of freedom.

Division of Labor and Meaning in Work

Along with the progressive mechanization of technology, another important historical trend in industrial development has been the increasing subdivision of labor within more and more rationalized systems of work organization. This has intensified the alienation of meaninglessness, making it more difficult for manual workers to find purpose and function in their work. There are hopeful signs in continuous-process plants, however, that automation is reversing this long-run development also.

Meaninglessness is rare in craft industries, because the products are unique rather than standardized and because the division of labor remains on the elementary level of craft specialization. Even the unskilled laborer shoveling cement on a building site is making a contribution toward the construction of a particular and tangible structure. His work is organized by the building problems of the individual site, and therefore he develops a task-completion orientation rather than a cyclical-repetitive approach to the job. In addition, craftsmen tend to work on large parts of the product: linotype operators set the type for all the pages of a book or magazine; hand compositors work on the whole page.

The increasing division of labor characteristic of both machine and assembly-line industries tends to undermine the "substantive rationality" natural to the craft organization of work. Product standardization in the mass-production industries means that work involves a repetitive cycle rather than a succession of distinctive tasks. Work organization further limits the employee to one segment of the product and a small scope of the process involved in its manufacture. Textile operatives, for example, are confined to one room in the mill, which contains a department carrying out only one process of the dozens required for the completion of the product, and in that room they generally perform only one or two of the total number of productive tasks. In automobile assembly, the proportion of product worked upon and the scope of operations becomes even more minute. And the operative's sense of purpose and function is reduced to a minimum when he attaches steering columns all day long and has nothing to do with any part of the automobile besides his own restricted specialty. It is highly ironic, and also tragic, that workers are confined to the most limited task assignments in the very industry where they know the most about the product and the processes because of the *expertise* gained working on their own cars.

Fortunately, however, fractionization of work does not continue to increase in a "straight-line" fashion as technology develops higher and higher levels of mechanization. The most characteristic feature of automation is its transfer of focus from an individual job to the process of production. The perspective of the worker is shifted from his own individual tasks to a broader series of operations that includes the work of other employees. Since automated processes are integrated and continuous rather than divided in the way that labor is divided, the responsibility of one employee for his share of a plant's process is inevitably linked to the responsibility of other workers.

Since the decentralized subplants that make up a continuous-process factory manufacture different products and since automated technology has reduced the number of workers necessary for each process, each man's job assignments and responsibilities differ from those of his workmates. Therefore each operator senses that he is contributing a unique function to the processing of his department's product, even though the product is standardized and remains the same from day to day. The unique function of each operator is enmeshed in a network of interdependent relations with the functions of others. And responsiblity as a job requirement demands thinking in terms of the collective whole rather than the individual part. For all these reasons, automation results in a widening of the worker's scope of operations[42] and provides new avenues for meaning and purpose in work.

There is little meaninglessness in craft production because each craftsman makes a contribution to a unique *product*. In continuous-process production there is little alienation of this type because each operator contributes a unique *function* in the processing of a standardized product.

[42] Bright, *op. cit.,* pp. 183–84.

Meaninglessness is most intensified on the automobile assembly line because both the product and the function of the individual worker is so highly standardized. Whereas the conveyer belt represents an extreme in this situation, as well as many others, the alienation of meaninglessness is probably more widespread and serious than that of powerlessness among the general labor force today, since the elaborate division of labor within the typical factory makes it difficult for most employees to relate their jobs to the larger purposes and goals of the enterprise.

Technology, Time Perspective, and Involvement

In the course of industrial development, there has probably been a tendency for manual work to become inherently less engrossing and for instrumental, external considerations to gain in importance over intrinsic task satisfactions. It is difficult for the manual worker to identify with the standardized products of mass-production industries or to become deeply involved in their manufacture. Therefore, like meaninglessness, self-estrangement in the work process tends to be a more common state among factory workers today than the alienation of powerlessness. But it is a mistake to view self-alienation simply as a generalized predicament of the factory worker in modern society, since its intensity depends on the specific conditions of industrial technology and the division of labor.

The nature of an industry's technology and its division of labor determine the rhythm of the manual worker's job and the characteristic orientation toward time that he experiences in the course of his work. They thus influence the degree to which the worker can become involved and engrossed in work activity and the degree to which he is likely to be detached or alienated from his immediate tasks. Craft technology and traditional manual skill create an unique-task work rhythm in which there is involvement in the present situation on the basis of images of the future completion of the product or task. The skilled worker must be emotionally engaged in the immediate activity of molding raw materials and solving problems of construction; craft work does not permit the barter of present-time gratifications for future rewards. On the other hand, the unskilled routine jobs in the standardized machine and assembly-line industries foster a repetitive-cycle work rhythm, a detachment from present tasks, and a concern with the future cessation of the activity itself, rather than the completion of specific tasks.[43] Since the intrinsic activity of the work in these industries tends to result in monotony rather than any immediate gratifications, the meaning of the job is largely found in instrumental future-time rewards: wages, fringe benefits, and, when present, economic security.

Continuous-process technology and the work of monitoring automatic equipment results in still another rhythm, one that is new and unique in factory settings. It is the variety and unpredictability of the "calm-and-crisis" mode of time experience that is probably most liberating. There are periods of routine activity when such tasks as instrument-reading and patrolling are carried out, periods of waiting and relaxing when the routine work is done and operations are smooth, and also periods of intense activity when emergency breakdowns must be controlled. In the two calm situations there is probably much detachment and monotony, coupled with an habituated attention to the potential occurrence of something extraordinary; however, in the crisis periods, total involvement in the immediate present results.[44]

Continuous-process technology offers more scope for self-actualization than ma-

chine and assembly-line technologies. The nature of the work encourages a scientific, technical orientation and the changing character of the technology results in opportunities for learning and personal development for a considerable section of the blue-collar labor force. In contrast, work in machine and assembly-line industries is rarely complicated by problems and difficulties that might challenge the worker's capacities and shake him out of his routine and thus offers little potential for personal development.

The effect of these technological variations on involvement in work can be seen when employees in each of these industries are asked whether their jobs are interesting or monotonous. The great majority of all factory workers consider their jobs interesting; the significant point is the pattern that relative differences in monotony take. As we advance up the scale of industrial development, the proportion of workers who find their jobs dull increases from a scant 4 per cent in the printing industry, to 18 per cent in the textile industry, and to 34 per cent in the automobile industry (and to 61 per cent of those unskilled auto workers concentrated on the assembly line). But in the chemical industry, only 11 per cent complain of monotony, which suggests that automation may be checking the long-run trend toward detachment and self-alienation in factory work.

Industrial Structure, Social Alienation, and Personality

The historical development of mechanized technology and rationalized work organization has influenced social alienation as well as powerlessness, meaninglessness, and self-estrangement, because these trends have affected industrial social structure. Different technologies result in variations in the occupational distribution of the industrial labor force, in the economic cost structures of the company, and in the size and layout of the factory. These factors, in turn, affect the degree of integration and cohesion in an industry and the

---

[43] The difference in time orientation between craft and machine-assembly tasks corresponds closely to Hannah Arendt's distinction between work and labor. *The Human Condition* (Chicago: University of Chicago Press, 1958).

[44] The unpredictability of problems and emergencies prevents even the smooth periods from becoming totally routine.

extent to which factory workers feel a sense of belonging in an industrial community. Because of variations in industrial social structure, industries differ in their modes of social control and sources of worker discipline, and distinctive social types and personalities are produced that reflect the specific conditions of their industrial environment.

Craft industries are usually highly integrated on the basis of the traditions and norms of the various occupational specialties, and social alienation is low because of the skilled worker's loyalty to, and identification with, his particular craft and trade union. Skilled printers, like workers in the building trades and other craftsmen, are relatively independent of their companies, since the market demand for their skills gives them mobility in an industrial structure made up of large numbers of potential employers. The occupational structure and economic organization of craft industries thus make the work force autonomous from management, rather than integrated with it or alienated from it. This autonomy is expressed in the skilled craftsman's characteristic (and characterological) resentment of close supervision. Since the management control structure has little effective power and since craft technology is too undeveloped to be coercive, the locus of social control in these work settings is the journeyman's own internalization of occupational standards of work excellence and norms of "a fair day's work." Work discipline in craft industries is therefore essentially self-discipline. The industrial environment produces a social personality characterized by an orientation to craftsmanship and quality performance, a strong sense of individualism and autonomy, and a solid acceptance of citizenship in the larger society. Satisfied with his occupational function, the craftsman typically has a highly developed feeling of self-esteem and a sense of self-worth and is therefore ready to participate in the social and political institutions of the community as well as those of his craft.

Because machine industries have low-skilled labor forces, occupational groups have less identity and autonomy. Therefore they rarely provide a basis for social integration. The unskilled worker in these industries is more dependent on his employer, and the company thus tends to be the central institution in the industrial community. A characteristic of machine industries that usually contributes to social integration is the large number of female employees. Male workers feel that their status is higher and that they are recognized as more important than the women. They have somewhat increased chances for promotion into the minority of jobs with skill or responsibility. Women, who tend to be more satisfied than men with the prevailing unskilled routine jobs, "cushion" the occupational floor in machine industries, raising the ceiling slightly for the men who might otherwise be frustrated in low positions.

In southern textiles, unique historical and geographical factors have been critical in producing a social structure that is more cohesive and highly integrated than most machine industries. With the mills located principally in small towns and villages, the industrial community centered around the factory is almost identical with the local community itself. Southern textile towns are traditional societies that are highly integrated, and commitment to mill employment seems to follow naturally from the strong loyalties to family, church, and locality. Social control is thus centered in the folkways of the community and the paternalistic domination of management. Factory discipline is not based on the internalized motivation characteristic of printers but stems from a number of largely external sources. These include a mechanized technology and subdivided work organization that is more coercive than that of the craft industries and the rather close supervision of foremen and other management representatives. Of course social control is also rooted in the tendency of the tradition-oriented textile worker to accept management authority and the industrial status quo. The typical social personality produced by this industrial environment is almost diametrically opposed to that of the craftsman. In addition to submissive attitudes toward authority, the textile worker tends to have little autonomy or individuation and to have a low level of aspiration, which includes an indifferent attitude to the meaningfulness of his work. The low estimate of self-worth and the absorption in the relatively narrow confines of kinship and church counter any expression of citizenship and participation in larger social worlds.

Two consequences of assembly-line technology and work organization, the "massified" occupational distribution and extremely large factories, are the critical elements underlying the social structure of the automobile industry. The mass of workers are at a uniform level of low skill, and the majority of men in assembly plants are paid almost exactly the same rate. The relative lack of occupational differentiation by skill, status, or responsibility creates an industrial "mass society" in which there are almost no realistic possibilities of advancement. The industry therefore lacks a built-in reward system for reaffirming its norms and integrating the worker into a community based on loyalty to the company. Social alienation is further intensified because automobile workers are low skilled, without strong occupational identity, and loyalty to an independent craft is not possible for most employees.

In addition, the technology and elaborate division of labor require a large physical plant and a sizable work force. As a rule, the larger the factory, the more tenuous is the employee's sense of identification with the enterprise and the greater the social and sympathetic distance between him and management. The automobile assembly plant stands at the apex of the historical development toward larger and larger factories: the proportion of workers employed in plants with more than

1,000 persons is 21 per cent in printing, 25 per cent in textiles, and 82 per cent in the transportation equipment industries! Automobile production may be the ideal example of an industry where large plants and firms have most contributed to the extreme development of an impersonal work atmosphere and to the breakdown of sympathetic communication and identification between employees and management.

In these circumstances, social control rests less on consensus and more on the power of management to enforce compliance to the rule system of the factory, a power sometimes effectively countervailed by the strong labor union, which has a legitimate mandate to protect certain interests of the workers.[45] The compelling rhythms of the conveyer-belt technology and the worker's instrumental concern for his weekly pay check are more important to him than internalized standards of quality performance or an identification with organizational goals in providing the discipline that gets work done in an orderly fashion. The social personality of the auto worker, a product of metropolitan residence and exposure to large, impersonal bureaucracies, is expressed in a characteristic attitude of cynicism toward authority and institutional systems, and a volatility revealed in aggressive responses to infringements on personal rights and occasional militant collective action. Lacking meaningful work and occupational function, the automobile worker's dignity lies in his peculiarly individualistic freedom from organizational commitments.

[45] The above formulation somewhat exaggerates the power conflict in the industry; the union also participates in the setting of the rules and, in a sense, aids the company by helping to secure the worker's compliance to them. To some degree this creates a basis for consensus. A system of norms has emerged from the conflict between the two organizations. Their past and present confrontations over such issues as union recognition, working conditions, wages, disciplinary rules, and grievances has created a framework of reciprocal expectations and obligations, even within a general atmosphere of mutual distrust and hostility.

Automation and Social Integration

Social alienation is widespread in the automobile industry because of the marked anomic tendencies inherent in its technology and work organization. In the chemical industry, on the other hand, continuous-process technology and more favorable economic conditions result in a social structure with a high degree of consensus between workers and management and an integrated industrial community in which employees experience a sense of belonging and membership. Social alienation is absent because of the combined effect of a number of factors: of first importance are the balanced skill distribution and the differentiated occupational structure that markedly contrast with the non-stratified structure in automotive plants.

Continuous-process technology results in a wide variety of occupational categories, and it requires workers at all levels of skill and responsibility. Because oil refineries and chemical plants produce an assortment of products and by-products, there are many different processes taking place in individual plant buildings, each of which has a work crew composed of slightly different job positions. Unskilled laborers are needed, as are large numbers of process operators at moderate, as well as high, levels of responsibility, and skilled maintenance craftsmen are also in demand. Such a status system is a socially integrating force, since it provides many high positions to which employees may aspire, and the successful workers most exemplify the values and standards of the company. When possibilities for greater rewards of higher pay and status exist, workers are motivated to perform well and internalize the goals of the enterprise.

Secondly, automation reverses another long-run trend, that of increasing factory size, and results also in a distinctive change in plant layout in these industries. A reduction in the number of employees in a plant operation is due partly to automation itself and partly to the companies' conscious decentralization policies. (Chemi-

cal and oil firms seem to prefer many medium-sized plants rather than few giant operations.)[46] More importantly, the decentralization principle is applied to a single factory. In steel mills, automobile assembly plants, textile mills, and print shops, the departments that carry out the various stages of the production process all exist under the same roof—so that there is, in essence, only one plant. But though chemical plants and oil refineries are spread out over a large terrain, they are decentralized into a large number of individual buildings or subplants that are spatially separated from each other. In each of these a different product is made or a particular process is carried out by a crew of operators who have collective responsibility for the total operation, as well as individual responsibilities for certain parts of it. These "Balkanized" units and the work teams attached to them serve as centers of employee loyalty and identification and give work in the continuous-process industries a cohesive "small plant" atmosphere, even though the employer is actually a large national corporation. These small work teams are an effective source of work discipline. Men perform up to standard because they do not want to let down their workmates or their department. Collective control by the working crew will probably become more important in many industries besides continuous-process ones, since team responsibility is the natural outgrowth of the integrated process inherent in automated technology per se.

Informal work groups are even more important to the worker and more central a factor in over-all morale in machine and assembly-line technologies because the unskilled, repetitive jobs lack intrinsic gratifications and make social satisfactions more imperative. Unfortunately, cohesive work groups are a problematic outcome in these technologies, because, unlike process

[46] Only 40 per cent of the chemical workers and 53 per cent of the oil workers are employed in establishments with more than 1,000 persons, compared to 82 per cent of automobile workers.

production, they do not naturally result in team operations or collective responsibility. In many simple machine and light-assembly industries, individual employees work very close to others who do similar or identical jobs, and informal cliques are formed which maintain norms of production and provide a sense of belonging and cohesion. In the textile industry, however, workers with multimachine assignments are spread out at great distances in very large rooms, so that no working groups can be formed. Similarly, automobile assembly production, with its serial operations, places each worker next to a different set of workers, so that stable groups with clear and distinct identities do not easily form.

A third factor contributing to social integration in the continuous-process industries is the changed character of automated work. The difference in the nature of work performed by production workers and managers has been one of the most significant factors underlying class conflict within the factory.[47] But with automation, the work of the blue-collar process operators becomes very similar to that of the white-collar staff—it is clean, includes record-keeping and other clerical tasks, and involves responsibility.[48] Thus automation may eliminate the "innate"

[47] The traditional distrust and mutual feeling of distance between men who work with their hands and tools and those who work with their "brains" and paper is probably as old as the division between literate and non-literate strata that emerged with the invention of writing. The tendency for white-collar employees to identify with the management rather than with the factory workers is partly due to the feeling that their clean, nonmanual work gives them more in common with their employers.

[48] Of course, automated operators are responsible for machinery and technical processes, which is not true of the work of most white-collar people. The close relationship to, and deep interest in, machinery is part of the manual worker's "natural" mentality in an advanced industrial society. In time this aspect of the job will presumably serve to make the automated employee's outlook similar to that of the engineer rather than the clerk, supervisor, or salesman.

hostility of men who work with their hands toward "pencil-pushers" and administrators. And, conversely, white-collar employees will probably gain an enhanced understanding of, and respect for, the work of blue-collar men, since the office staff's contact with the plant and its production problems increases in automated firms, due to the greater need for checking and consultation.

The cohesive social structure in the continuous-process industries is further supported by the economic basis of automated production. As industrial technology becomes more mechanized, the cost structure of the enterprise changes. Since the investment in expensive machinery rises sharply in automated industries and the number of production workers declines, the proportion of total cost that is capital equipment increases and the proportion of labor cost decreases. A capital-intensive cost structure means that heightened efficiency, increased output, and higher profits can more easily be attained through exploitation of technology rather than the exploitation of the worker. The hard-pressed textile firms and to a lesser extent the automobile assembly plants, with their relatively low levels of mechanization and high labor costs, attempt to remain competitive by getting as much as possible out of each worker. The cost structure furthers the tendency to use the workers as "means," as commodities in the classic Marxist sense. The economic base of automated technology allows a more enlightened management to view the workers as human beings, as partners in a collective enterprise, who, because of their responsibility for expensive machinery and processes, must be considered in terms of their own needs and rights.

In addition to the structural economic relations that result from the nature of automated production, contingent economic conditions have also contributed greatly to social integration. Heavy chemicals has been a highly prosperous growth industry. Economic prosperity has permitted large chemical companies to provide their employees with a regularity of employment and long-range job security that is not possible in less stable industries. Since security of employment is the fundamental precondition of a worker's commitment to his company and industry, economics is therefore basic to the cohesion and consensus in chemicals. A second precondition of employee loyalty and identification is an opportunity to advance and improve one's status. The long-term growth in the industry has brought with it the expansion of plants and labor force, making advancement, as well as permanent employment, a meaningful reality. Economic prosperity has furthered social integration in still another way: it has permitted a relaxed atmosphere on the job and co-operative rather than strained and, conflict-laden relations between workers and supervisors. In direct contrast, the economic fluctuations in the automobile industry mean that irregular employment is common, a fact that profoundly militates against an atmosphere of consensus and good will.

Due to all these factors, the social personality of the chemical worker tends toward that of the new middle class, the white-collar employee in bureaucratic industry. As a new industry whose important growth has been in the period of the large-scale corporation, heavy chemicals has been able to provide its blue-collar workers with the career employment (permanency, regular promotions, company benefits) that has generally been the fate only of white-collar people. The automated operator's work—light, clean, involving the use of symbols, and resulting in regular contact with engineers, salesmen, and supervisors—is also somewhat similar to that of the office employee. And his mentality is not far different; he identifies with his company and orients himself toward security. Like the white-collar man, this security comes from his status as an employee, from his dependence on the benevolent and prosperous company, rather than his own independence. Generally lukewarm to unions and loyal to his employer, the blue-collar employee in the continuous-process industries may be a worker "organization-man" in the making.

Of course the high degree of consensus and cohesion in the chemical industry is not typical. Nor is the situation in automobile assembly, where social alienation is so extreme, characteristic of the average manufacturing establishment. On the whole, social alienation is not as widespread in American industry as meaninglessness and self-estrangement are. The majority of blue-collar workers are committed to their roles as producers, and are loyal (although within limits)[49] to their employers. This is supported by the findings in the Roper study that 73 per cent consider their company as good or better than any other place to work in their industry; only 17 per cent said other companies were better, and 10 per cent were undecided. Although the development of technology through the assembly line has reduced the cohesion of industrial social structure, other long-term trends have probably lessened the social alienation of factory workers that was so prevalent in the early period of industrialization. Modern bureaucratic organization is based on universalistic standards of justice and fair treatment, and its system of rules has enhanced the normative integration of industry. The long period of economic prosperity and its concomitants—steady employment, higher wages, better living standards, and promotion opportunities—have profoundly contributed to the secu-

[49] Loyalty to the company does not preclude persistent loyalty to labor unions and occasional opinions that the interests of these organizations may conflict, as the proponents of the "dual loyalty" thesis have pointed out. Compare Ross Stagner "Dual Allegiance as a Problem in Modern Society," *Personnel Psychology,* VII (1954); Lois Dean, "Union Activity and Dual Loyalty," *Industrial and Labor Relations Review,* VII (1954) and Purcell, *op. cit.,* pp. 248–62.

lar decline in the worker's class consciousness and militancy, a development that reflects the growing consensus between employees and employers and the increase in the worker's feeling that he has a stake in industry.

Alienation Trends: The Long View

The historical perspective on alienation and freedom in the factory reveals a clear and consistent pattern. Because secular developments in technology, division of labor, and industrial social structure have affected the various dimensions of alienation largely in the same direction, there is a convergence of long-range trends in the relation of the factory worker to his work process. Alienation has traveled a course that could be charted on a graph by means of an inverted U-curve.

In the early period, dominated by craft industry, alienation is at its lowest level and the worker's freedom at a maximum. Freedom declines and the curve of alienation (particularly in its powerlessness dimension) rises sharply in the period of machine industry. The alienation curve continues upward to its highest point in the assembly-line industries of the twentieth century. In automotive production, the combination of technological, organizational, and economic factors has resulted in the simultaneous intensification of all dimensions of alienation. Thus in this extreme situation, a depersonalized worker, estranged from himself and larger collectives, goes through the motions of work in the regimented milieu of the conveyor belt for the sole purpose of earning his bread. Assuming that the industries compared in this book are to some degree prototypes of the historical epochs of manufacturing, the dominant and most persistent long-range trend is an increase in alienation and a corresponding decline in freedom.

But with automated industry there is a countertrend, one that we can fortunately expect to become even more important in the future. The case of the continuous-process industries, particularly the chemical industry, shows that automation increases the worker's control over his work process and checks the further division of labor and growth of large factories. The result is meaningful work in a more cohesive, integrated industrial climate. The alienation curve begins to decline from its previous height as employees in automated industries gain a new dignity from responsibility and a sense of individual function —thus the inverted U.[50]

[50] This does not imply that future developments in automation will result simply in a continuation of the major trend toward less alienation. Automated technology will take many forms besides continuous-process production, and the diversified economic conditions of future automated industries will further complicate the situation.

ALIENATION FROM WORK: A STUDY OF NURSING PERSONNEL

Leonard I. Pearlin

This study examines some of the structural properties of a mental hospital relevant to the alienation of its nursing force from its work. Alienation is an interest of long standing to social scientists concerned with a broad spectrum of issues. Increased social differentiation, the disappearance of community, the breakdown of regulatory norms and the difficulty of realizing the total self in mass society are all problems that have drawn people to the concept.[1] Like other concepts, however, the diffusion of its meanings seems to be proportionate to the number of issues to which it is related. Thus, Seeman identifies no less than five major variants: powerlessness, normlessness, meaninglessness, isolation and self-estrangement.[2] As employed in

this paper, the principal theme of alienation is that of subjectively experienced powerlessness which, Seeman notes, is the most common usage among the five variants.

Regardless of how it is conceptualized, alienation is typically treated as occurring within the framework of the total society or its major social institutions.[3] One exception is John P. Clark, who stresses the importance of studying alienation in specified social situations.[4] There are, we believe, a number of advantages that can result from this. By taking a clearly delineated organization for study, it becomes more possible to pinpoint the particular

SOURCE: Reprinted from the *American Sociological Review*, 27, 3 (June 1962), 314–326, by permission of the author and publisher.

[1] According to Nisbet, alienation—as reflected in literature, social science and theology—represents the central concern of our age. The image of man presented by students of these areas is not of one who does things, but of one helplessly acted upon by alien forces. Robert A. Nisbet, *The Quest for Community*, New York: Oxford University Press, 1953, pp. 3–22.

[2] Melvin Seeman, "On the Meaning of Alienation," *American Sociological Review*, 24 (December, 1959), pp. 783–791. Another writer, Dean, attempts to circumvent the problem of conceptual diffusion by incorporating into a single measure of alienation feelings of powerlessness, normlessness, and isolation. Dwight G. Dean, "Alienation: Its Meaning and Measurement," *American Sociological Review*, 26 (October, 1961), pp. 753–758.

[3] Nettler conceives of alienation, for example, as disenchantment with some prevailing social values and non-participation in institutionalized political, religious and family activities. Gwynn Nettler, "A Measure of Alienation," *American Sociological Review*, 22 (December, 1957), pp. 670–677. Even where the conceptualization of alienation is in terms of powerlessness, the powerlessness refers to the shaping of general life chances rather than in dealing with specific social situations. See, for illustration, John W. Evans, "Stratification, Alienation, and the Hospital Setting," *Bulletin of the Engineering Experiment Station*, The Ohio State University, 29 (November, 1960), pp. 42–45. A third study, dealing with alienation among graduate students, also takes the larger society as the major contextual setting. Jan Hajda, "Alienation and Integration of Student Intellectuals," *American Sociological Review*, 26 (October, 1961), pp. 758–777.

[4] John P. Clark, "Measuring Alienation Within a Social System," *American Sociological Review*, 24 (December, 1959), pp. 849–852.

138

structures, role sets or processes that have alienative consequences. When looked at on a societal level, by contrast, these antecedents of alienation are more obscured and are difficult to study reliably. In the present case the organization under study is a bureaucracy. This provides the opportunity to examine alienation within an organizational form that pervades many areas of social life, thus yielding a degree of generality to our findings. It can also be noted that to study alienation within a work setting is particularly strategic, for the central importance of work means that occupational experiences have an impact on participation in other social institutions. Alienation from work, therefore, is an area of study that links a matter within the purview of industrial sociology to broadly patterned social problems.

Our measure of alienation is made up of a four-item Guttman scale, part of an extensive questionnaire constructed for this study. The scale has a coefficient of reproducibility of .91. It is presented here in scale order with the alienative responses italicized:

1. How often do you do things in your work that you wouldn't do if it were up to you? Never; Once in a while; Fairly often; *Very often.*

2. Around here it's not important how much you know; it's who you know that really counts. *Agree;* Disagree.

3. How much say or influence do people like you have on the way the hospital is run? A lot; Some; *Very little; None.*

4. How often do you tell [your superior] your own ideas about things you might do in your work? *Never; Once in a while;* Fairly often; Very often.

These items, it can be seen, involve more than the powerlessness that people experience; they also capture an overtone of resentment at being deprived by outside forces of greater control over one's own work. The scale approximates what Clark feels is the essence of alienation; namely,

". . . the discrepancy between the power man believes he has and what he believes he should have—his estrangement from his rightful role."[5]

Our attention in this paper will be on the way certain structures within the hospital bear on the intensity of alienation experienced by nursing personnel. We shall be particularly interested in the authority structure, opportunity structure and the composition of work groups. There is considerable evidence that, once established, alienation influences the way personnel go about their work, their treatment values and attitudes toward patients. In this paper, however, we shall limit ourselves to conditions producing alienation rather than its consequences.

Setting of the Study

The subjects of the study are members of the nursing service at Saint Elizabeths Hospital.[6] This is a large Federal mental hospital, drawing its patients mainly from the District of Columbia. There are approximately 7500 inpatients on the rolls; about half are white and half Negro. The hospital itself is divided into twelve services and 156 wards. Two data collection instruments were used: one is a self-administered questionnaire given to all nursing personnel below the position of nursing supervisor. The other is a form, filled out by individuals in charge of each of the 156 wards, that asks for demographic and psychiatric characteristics of patient ward populations, the employment of various ward programs and policies, and staffing practices. Of the 1315 nursing personnel who received questionnaires, 1138, or 86 per cent, returned completed and usable

[5] *Ibid.,* p. 849.

[6] The author is indebted to Saint Elizabeths Hospital, and particularly to Miss Lavonne Frey, Director of Nurses, and other members of the Nursing Service who gave wholehearted support to this study. Responsibility for the data and their interpretation, however, is solely the author's.

questionnaires. Of the 156 ward forms distributed 152 were filled out.

Three nursing ranks are represented in the group to whom the questionnaire was directed, each differing in formally prescribed responsibilities, authority and rewards. The lowest rank, comprising 70 per cent of the nursing force, is called nursing assistants. Above them in authority are charge attendants who have been given the charge of wards in the absence of a professional nurse; this group represents 16 per cent of the total. The remaining group, smallest in number, is composed of registered nurses who head the lower ranks. These three groups are collectively referred to as nursing personnel. Forty per cent of them are males and sixty per cent are females.

Alienation and the Structure of Authority

Alienation, as we define it, is a feeling of powerlessless over one's own affairs—a sense that the things that importantly affect one's activities and work are outside his control. By this definition, alienation is necessarily bound to the hierarchical organization of responsibility and authority. Indeed, one of the things that distinguishes an organization from other types of collectivities is the differential allocation to some members of authority over the activities of others. Thus, inherent in an hierarchical arrangement is the unequal distribution of opportunities to decide on and initiate actions, whether one's own or others. By its system of authority—that is, the distribution of rights to influence the actions of others—an organization separates its members to varying degrees from decisions regarding their activities. From these statements we may wonder how anyone can escape alienation. Even within the same hierarchical organization, however, some conditions serve to minimize these feelings while others intensify them.

One condition that arouses intense alienation is the inability of subordinates to act back upon their superordinates. We can begin to demonstrate this by first examining the positional relations between superordinates and subordinates on ward units. Although hospitals are typically characterized by a multiple authority system, it is possible in most cases to distinguish a single outstanding authority figure for an individual worker. This was accomplished by the question: "There are many people who have something to do or say about the way wards are run and the care of patients. Who has *most* say or influence in what you do in your daily work?" It was possible for a respondent to choose from the formally established line of authority one of these distinct figures: the doctor, the nursing supervisor of his service, the head nurse, or the charge attendant. Eighty-seven respondents were unable to designate a single most important authority, giving a variety of combinations; together with those not answering the question, they are excluded from the following discussion.

Knowing the position of the respondent, the discrepancy between his position and that of the person he indicated as most influential could then be observed. The widest positional discrepancy that can occur is in the situation where a nursing assistant designates a doctor as his most significant authority. This is called a four-step disparity, for on ward units the doctor organizationally is four positions above the nursing assistant, with charge attendant, head nurse, and nursing supervisor positions intervening. Following this scheme, a three-step disparity is represented in the designation of a supervisor by an assistant and of a doctor by a charge attendant. The two-step disparity is found in the designation of a head nurse by an assistant, the supervisor by a charge attendant and a doctor by a head nurse. Finally, the one-step disparities, occurring between adjacent positions, are: the designation of a charge attendant by an assistant, a head nurse by a change attendant, and a supervisor by a head nurse.[7]

It is clear from Table 1 that there is a tendency for alienation to be most intense under conditions of great disparity and to decrease with positional distance between superordinate and subordinate parties.[8] This relationship is best understood by pointing up the limitations that positional disparity imposes on interaction between an authority and his subject. Interaction, even between superordinates and subordinates, is typically characterized by reciprocal influence.[9] This means that a subject

[7] The question arises as to whether these designations reflect authority relations as they actually exist or if they are only projections of something within the subjects. There is reason to believe that generally those designated are, in fact, most influential. One reason is that the distribution of designations conforms to our observations in the hospital. It is known that some doctors take an active interest in the operational details of one or more of their wards and are likely, as a result, to assume responsibilities that otherwise would fall to other people. This is even more frequently the case among nursing supervisors. Thus, the designations of doctors and supervisors by personnel in low positions are not out of keeping with actual practice.

[8] Because the widest positional disparities necessarily involve those in the lowest positions, it might be wondered if this relationship is not accounted for by the position of the person making the designation rather than by the disparity. This does not appear to be the case, however. Looking at charge attendants alone, for example, we find that those designating head nurses as most influential express less intense alienation than those indicating supervisors or doctors. Head nurses alone display a similar pattern: those naming supervisors are less alienated than those designating doctors. These results indicate that the relationship between positional disparity and alienation is not determined solely by the lowest group.

[9] The reciprocal influence of subordinates is not necessarily contrary to the desires of their superiors. Indeed, such influence may be actively invited; for, as Simmel pointed out, where subordinates are completely passive and do not act back upon their superordinates, the latter are deprived of the signs of their dominance. Georg Simmel, *The Sociology of Georg Simmel* (translated by Kurt H. Wolf), Glencoe, Ill.: The Free Press, 1950, pp. 181–183.

ordinarily exercises some control over the actions of his superior and, indirectly, his own affairs. Wide positional disparity, however, restricts reciprocity by increasing restraint and inhibition and decreasing spontaneity between an authority and his subject. As a result, influence would flow more unilaterally along the lines of formal authority arrangements. Such restrictions on interaction limit the subordinate's ability to exercise influence on his superiors and, consequently, feelings of powerlessness are exacerbated. Interaction between authorities and subjects in adjacent positions, on the other hand, would be more free of these limitations and their alienative effects. Positional disparity, therefore, represents a condition that inhibits reciprocal influence by subordinates and it is for this reason that it is alienative.

In interpreting the findings in Table 1 we imply that the desire for influence over their own affairs is common among personnel and, when prevented from realizing what they feel is rightfully theirs, alienation results. It is obvious, however, that influence is not desired by all people nor are they equally alienated when found in the same situation of positional disparity. A characterstic of personnel that is relevant in this respect is status obeisance. By status obeisance we refer to the value placed on authority for its own sake and the deference shown those in positions higher than one's own. A highly obeisant individual, we expect, would not feel that it is part of his rightful role to share influence with his superior, even where his own affairs are involved. More likely, he regards influence as belonging exclusively to those in authority. Conversely, he would be most unwilling to share what authority he might possess with those he considers inferior to himself.[10]

[10] In an earlier paper it was shown that those most obeisant toward their superiors are also most likely to elevate themselves above patients of low social standing. Leonard I. Pearlin and Morris Rosenberg, "Nurse-Patient Social Distance and the Structural Context of a Mental

Table 1. Positional Disparity in Authority Relations and Alienation

SCORE OF ALIENATION	FOUR-STEP DISPARITY	THREE-STEP DISPARITY	TWO-STEP DISPARITY	ADJACENCY
0	2%	12%	15%	19%
1	25	31	25	29
2	34	23	34	23
3	29	18	14	18
4	11	16	12	11
Totals	56	238	358	314

$$x^2 = 30.5$$
$$12 \text{ df}$$
$$P < .01$$

Table 2. Status Obeisance, the Positional Disparity Between Superordinate and Subordinate and Alienation

	LOW AND MODERATE OBEISANCE				HIGH OBEISANCE			
Alienation Score	4-Step Disparity	3-Step Disparity	2-Step Disparity	Adjacency	4-Step Disparity	3-Step Disparity	2-Step Disparity	Adjacency
0	..%	12%	16%	22%	5%	13%	12%	12%
1	22	30	21	25	32	32	32	36
2	28	18	33	20	41	27	35	31
3	34	22	16	20	18	18	12	13
4	16	18	14	13	5	11	9	8
Totals	32	148	248	220	22	85	98	86

$$x^2 = 33.2 \qquad\qquad x^2 = 4.98$$
$$12 \text{ df} \qquad\qquad 12 \text{ df}$$
$$P < .001 \qquad\qquad P > .05$$

Given such status values, situations of great positional disparity do not result in feelings of deprivation, for one does not experience loss in not having something he does not expect or feel is rightfully his. This is generally confirmed in Table 2, where is it seen that those low or moderate in obeisance are most alienated when their significant superiors are remote from them.[11] The alienative impact of this con-

dition on the highly obeisant, by contrast, is quite insignificant. Evidently those who regard authority with deference and awe do not seek a voice in their own affairs;

(b) I figure my supervisor knows better than I what's good for my ward or else she (or he) wouldn't be a supervisor. Agree or disagree?

(c) The best way to get along on this job is to mind your own business and just do as you're told. Agree or disagree?

(d) I like the idea of nurses and nursing assistants standing up when the doctor comes into the nursing station. Agree or disagree?

Respondents scoring 0 or 1 are "low;" those scoring 2 are categorized as "moderate;" and those scoring 3 or 4 are "high."

Hospital," *American Sociological Review*, 27 (February, 1962), pp. 56–65.

[11] Obeisance, measured by a Guttman scale, is presented in scale order:

(a) Do you ever feel like disagreeing with *what* [your superior] wants you to do or *how* he (or she) wants you to do it?

they are willing to have their superordinates speak for them.

We noted earlier that disparities dis-
couraged unconstrained interaction, thus
removing subordinates from opportunities
for reciprocal influence. However, regardless of positional relations, alienation still
results if authority is exercised in such a
manner as to inhibit relatively free interaction. Included in the questionnaire is
an item that allows us to observe how this
quality of authority as it is exercised bears
on alienation. It asks: "When [your su-
perior] wants you to do something, how
does he (or she) usually let you know
what is wanted?" There are three major
response categories: (a) simply tells me;
(b) asks me if I will; (c) explains to me
why he wants it. To exercise authority by
telling the subordinate what to do effectively minimizes any exchange between
superordinate and subordinate; when he
is asked to do something, the situation becomes more transactional; and when it is
explained why something is required, the
subordinate tends to become more of a
partner to the action. The first allows
little or no reciprocal influence and the
last a maximum of reciprocity. In Table
3 we find that alienation is greatest among
subjects simply told what to do and least
among those to whom the required action
is explained.

Status obeisance is again an important
characteristic in connection with the communication of authority. Just as it tended
to soften the impact of positional disparity, status obeisance minimizes the alienation that otherwise results from being
told what to do with little or no opportunity for reciprocal influence. The highly
obeisant are more likely to react to such
an authority style with the feeling that it
is rightful and proper rather than with
feelings of deprivation. It can be seen in
Table 4 that feelings of alienation of those
low and moderate in obeisance very closely depend on the way authority is exercised while the highly obeisant are generally insensitive to this condition. Instead
of being alienated from something they
want, such individuals are likely to experience peremptory authority as part of a
natural and just order.

Both positional disparity and the peremptory exercise of authority lead to alienation as a result of the constraints they
place on interaction and reciprocal influence by subordinates. Another condition
that limits the reciprocity a subject can
exercise with his superordinate is the extent to which an authority is accessible—
in the sheer physical sense—to his subject.
The bearing of this on alienation needs
little elaboration, for if a significant authority physically absents himself, he in

Table 3. The Way Authority is Exercised and Alienation

ALIENATION SCORE	TOLD TO DO IT	ASKED TO DO IT	EXPLAINED WHY IT IS TO BE DONE
0	6%	16%	21%
1	24	25	29
2	29	29	27
3	21	18	13
4	20	12	10
Totals	217	462	329

$$x^2 = 34.8$$
$$8 \text{ df}$$
$$P < .001$$

Table 4. The Status Obeisance of Subjects, the Way in Which Authority is Communicated to Them and Alienation

ALIENATION SCORE	LOW AND MODERATELY OBEISANT SUBJECTS			HIGH OBEISANT SUBJECTS		
	Told	*Asked*	*Explained*	*Told*	*Asked*	*Explained*
0	6%	19%	22%	7%	10%	18%
1	18	22	28	36	30	30
2	27	28	25	36	30	33
3	26	19	13	10	19	12
4	22	13	12	11	11	7
Totals	148	305	222	61	145	98

$$x^2 = 35.6 \qquad\qquad x^2 = 10.2$$
$$8 \text{ df} \qquad\qquad\qquad 8 \text{ df}$$
$$P < .001 \qquad\qquad P > .05$$

Table 5. The Designation of a Doctor as the Outstanding Authority, Assignment to Services Differing in the Time Doctors Spend on Ward Units and the Alienation of Personnel

Alienation Score	PERSONNEL DESIGNATING DOCTOR AS THE OUTSTANDING AUTHORITY			PERSONNEL DESIGNATING OTHERS AS OUTSTANDING AUTHORITIES		
	Dr. Present 30 Minutes or Less per Day	*Dr. Present 30 Minutes to One Hour per Day*	*Dr. Present More Than One Hour per Day*	*Dr. Present 30 Minutes or Less per Day*	*Dr. Present 30 Minutes to One Hour per Day*	*Dr. Present More Than One Hour per Day*
0	2%	17%	26%	15%	24%	13%
1	37	25	13	27	30	25
2	28	31	42	29	20	29
3	26	14	10	17	15	17
4	7	14	9	12	11	16
Totals	43	36	31	561	155	258

$$x^2 = 16.8 \qquad\qquad x^2 = 12.5$$
$$8 \text{ df} \qquad\qquad\qquad 8 \text{ df}$$
$$P < .05 \qquad\qquad P > .05$$

effect cuts his subjects off from the opportunity to act back upon him.

Evidence concerning the relationship between physical accessibility and alienation is drawn from two sources, one concerning physicians and the other service nursing supervisors. With regard to the physicians, on each of the ward information forms an estimate was made of the daily time usually spent by a doctor on the ward. These data were then pooled to yield a median for each of the twelve services.[12] These medians range from less

[12] A large number of staff is not assigned to a particular ward in a service, and these staff would be excluded if accessibility were observed at the ward level. By taking a median measure for the entire service it is possible to include such individuals in examining the effects of accessibility.

than fifteen minutes a day to over three hours a day. Table 5, then, separates personnel designating a doctor as their significant authority from those making other designations; it further divides them according to the median time doctors spend on wards in the services to which they are assigned.

The results of the table show a significant, though somewhat irregular, increase in alienation with the decrease in time doctors are found on ward units. But this is only true among personnel for whom the doctor is the outstanding authority. Among staff designating other superordinates, the time that doctors are present or absent from the patient care units makes no significant difference.

The same findings emerge when we focus on those for whom the service supervisor is the dominant authority. Approximately one month after the present study was conducted, an independent study was made to learn how the super-

visors of seven of the twelve services spend their time.[13] Supervisors in all services by and large face the same demands. They differ sharply, however, in the tasks to which they give most emphasis and the ways in which they satisfy the multitude of requirements of a well run service. The case in point with which we shall deal is the time they spend in clerical duties. There is a great deal of office work to which some supervisors give as little attention as possible, while others devote considerable time to them at the expense of other duties.

We can assume that the more time a person spends performing these clerical duties, the less face-to-face contact he will have with his staff on the ward units. Table 6 distinguishes staff who designate the supervisor as the outstanding authority and also divides personnel who work

[13] We are indebted to Mrs. Helen K. Sainato, Hospital Nurse Consultant at Saint Elizabeths Hospital, for making these data available to us.

Table 6. The Designation of the Nursing Supervisor as the Outstanding Authority, Assignment to Services Differing in the Time the Supervisor Spends at Clerical Duties and the Alienation of Personnel

Alienation Score	PERSONNEL DESIGNATING THE SUPERVISOR AS THE OUTSTANDING AUTHORITY		PERSONNEL DESIGNATING OTHERS AS OUTSTANDING AUTHORITIES	
	Three Hours or More Spent at Clerical Tasks per Week	*Less than Three Hours Spent at Clerical Tasks per Week*	*Three Hours or More Spent at Clerical Tasks per Week*	*Less than Three Hours Spent at Clerical Tasks per Week*
0	7%	25%	11%	20%
1	24	25	33	28
2	24	25	27	34
3	31	10	16	10
4	14	15	13	8
Totals	59	40	99	100
	$x^2 = 10.7$ 4 df $P < .05$		$x^2 = 6.8$ 4 df $P > .05$	

on services where the supervisor spends three hours or more a week at clerical tasks from those where less time is spent at this work. Among staff for whom the supervisor is the most important authority, a marked tendency is seen for alienation to increase with the time the supervisor spends doing clerical work. Again, the way the supervisor spends her time is of no significant consequence to personnel for whom someone else is the outstanding authority. Where one is both a dominant authority and physically absent, his subordinates are likely to experience intense alienation. Alienation, in sum, grows out of authority situations that insulate superordinates from the influence of their subjects, whether by physical distance, positional distance or peremptory authority.

Alienation and the Opportunity Structure

A mental hospital is established to meet community needs and to alleviate human suffering. It recruits to it individuals who possess the talents and training thought to be instrumental to these ends. The individuals recruited necessarily bring with them various motivations, values, and aspirations. In order to retain its staff and to maintain itself as an ongoing institution, it must gear itself not only for the attainment of the ends for which it was established, but also for the satisfaction of the diverse aspirations and opportunities sought by its members. One very prominent aspiration among our nursing personnel is for social advancement and the enhancement of life chances. When asked how important it is for them to get ahead in life, only four per cent indicated that it was of little or no importance. This becomes much more impressive when it is realized that these individuals work within a pyramidal structure, where the higher positions are relatively few in number and most personnel occupy positions at the base of the organization. The opportunity structure of the hospital, there-

fore, imposes extreme limitations on advancement and where mobility is achieved, it comes slowly. Thus, pervading the nursing force are strong desires for advancement; but the structure in which they are located has far fewer positions than there are people who would like to attain them. Such a situation produces a continued frustration of aspirations that can lead individuals to feel that the important forces that affect them in their work are beyond their control.[14] Such enduring barriers to desired rewards of work can produce a sense of utter powerlessness over one's occupational affairs.

Consider first the actual achievement histories of personnel. Since the hospital under study is a Federal institution, its positions are part of the Civil Service classification system. There are four positions open to non-professional nursing personnel: General Schedule (GS) 2, 3, 4, and 5. All non-professionals, with the exception of a few certified practical nurses, enter service at the lowest level, and movement from one level to another is neither fast nor assured; and one cannot go beyond the top level without earning the credentials of a professional. While there are few rising stars among this group, and none for whom the sky's the limit, there are differences in the speed with which they move from one level to another. Since our group of professional nurses includes only those working on ward units, the range of GS levels they embody is quite narrow; for this reason they are omitted from the present discussion.

---

[14] This will be recognized as the kind of situation Merton describes as producing anomie and suggests a possible link between powerlessness and anomic behavior. It is our view that alienation is an intervening phenomenon between the desire for unobtainable ends and the breakdown of normative controls. Thus, while alienation and anomie might be part of the same process, they are not the same thing. See Robert K. Merton, *Social Theory and Social Structure* (Second edition), Glencoe, Ill.: The Free Press, 1957, chap. IV.

By juxtaposing the GS levels of personnel with the years of their hospital employment, it is possible to distinguish among personnel according to the pace and extent of their achievements. Thus we consider the *limited* achievers to be those at a GS-2 level with seven or more years experience together with those at GS-3 with nine or more years experience. The *moderate* achievers are personnel at GS-2 with between three and seven years tenure, at GS-3 with employment of nine years or less and at GS-4 with experience of twelve years or more. Finally, the *high* achievers are at GS-4 with experience of less than twelve years and all 35 personnel at GS-5, regardless of the length of their experience. Those at GS-2 but with less than three years experience are not included, since this is too short a time to make a judgment. This exhausts all GS levels open to non-professionals and yields a composite index of both the level and pace of achievement.

Table 7, then, represents actual achievement experiences as they emerge within a limited opportunity structure. It shows how intense feelings of powerlessness are created among those who do not have rewards of occupational advancement. The work setting does not accord to them something they value and they are faced with a situation that will not yield to their desires.

We assume that limited achievers are disposed to intense alienation because they are unable to gain the rewards of work they feel are rightfully theirs. But what of the limited achievers who are not discontented with their occupational rewards, or of the high achievers who, despite their attainments, are dissatisfied with theirs? In the questionnaire were items asking for the degree of satisfaction with three work rewards that are linked to achievement: the adequacy of pay, of promotional opportunities, and the chances hospital work affords for "getting ahead in life." We shall bring together the evaluations personnel make in each of these areas with their achievement histories in order to observe their consequences for alienation. Since the number of high achievers is small, it is necessary in the following tables to combine response categories.

Table 8 shows the achievement patterns in conjunction with feelings about pay. Respondents were asked: "How do you feel about the pay on your job? Would you rate it as very good, good, fair, poor, or very bad?" The result of most interest here is that regardless of an individual's actual attainments, if he evaluates his monetary rewards negatively his chances of being alienated are greater. This means that the alienative effects of limited achievement are to a considerable extent vitiated if one feels adequately remunerated for his work. Conversely, high

Table 7. The Pace and Level of Occupational Achievement and Alienation

ALIENATION SCORE	LIMITED ACHIEVERS	MODERATE ACHIEVERS	HIGH ACHIEVERS
0	10%	14%	34%
1	30	27	26
2	25	29	27
3	21	16	6
4	14	14	7
Totals	365	436	85

$$x^2 = 33.5$$
$$8 \text{ df}$$
$$P < .001$$

Table 8. Achievement Patterns, Feelings about Work Rewards, and Alienation

FEELINGS ABOUT WORK REWARDS	ALIENATION SCORE (%)									
	0	1	2	3	4	TOTAL	N	x^2	df	P
Pay:										
Limited Achievers—								17.1	4	$<.01$
Very good, good	14	40	18	16	12	100	146			
Fair, poor, very bad	7	23	30	22	18	100	131			
Moderate Achievers—								33.3	4	$<.001$
Very good, good	18	42	23	13	4	100	137			
Fair, poor, very bad	12	21	34	17	16	100	271			
High Achievers—								10.0	4	$<.05$
Very good, good	34	43	17	3	3	100	35			
Fair, poor, very bad	30	15	34	9	12	100	34			
Promotion:										
Limited Achievers—								29.0	4	$<.001$
Very good, good	13	53	17	7	10	100	89			
Fair, poor, very bad	9	22	27	25	17	100	188			
Moderate Achievers—								30.2	4	$<.001$
Very good, good	19	42	25	8	6	100	124			
Fair, poor, very bad	12	22	32	19	15	100	288			
High Achievers—								7.4	4	$<.20$
Very good, good	30	41	22	..	7	100	27			
Fair, poor, very bad	33	21	29	10	7	100	42			
Chances of Getting Ahead:										
Limited Achievers—								30.8	4	$<.001$
No or some	10	15	22	32	21	100	104			
Pretty good, very good	12	41	24	12	11	100	172			
Moderate Achievers—								52.6	4	$<.001$
No or some	10	18	30	25	17	100	211			
Pretty good, very good	17	38	31	7	7	100	197			
High Achievers—								5.6	4	$>.20$
No or some	31	19	36	8	6	100	36			
Pretty good, very good	30	40	18	3	9	100	33			

achievement is not absolute insurance against alienation if one is disaffected with his pay. Alienation results from impotence to gain what one feels is rightfully his; if one is satisfied that he is receiving his due, this cannot be a source of alienation.

Virtually identical patterns emerge when we examine evaluations made of other work rewards. Table 8 contains answers to the question: "What about chances for promotion? Would you say chances for grade increases are very good, good, fair, poor, or very bad?" Also recorded in this table are responses to the query: "Do you think your work in the hospital offers you enough chance to get ahead in life?"—Practically no chance, some but not enough, a pretty good chance, a very good chance. As with the evaluation of pay, we find in each of these areas that while sheer achievement has a good deal to do with alienation, satisfaction or dissatisfaction with the concomitants of job advancement are important conditions for the vitiation or intensification of the alienative impact of achievement experiences. It can be concluded that it is not simply one's actual career within the opportunity structure that is relevant to alienation, but also whether one experiences deprivation or gain from rewards of money, job mobility and social status.

The Work Group and Alienation

Human groups perform many functions for their members. Perhaps foremost among these in relevance to alienation is the adoption by individuals of the group's norms to define their own means and ends of action. While they originate with the group, behaviors that are influenced by group norms are not perceived by members as imposed from without or external to themselves. Typically, these norms are internalized by individuals so that they are experienced as "mine." Behavior that is normatively channeled is not felt to be in response to coercive dictates over which one has no control. Such behavior more often expresses wishes and desires that can be both one's own and yet be shared with others. In place of feelings of powerlessness in the face of unsympathetic outside forces, behavior based on group shared norms can create a sense of personal voluntarism. As a result, when an individual is supported by group norms in performance of his work tasks, he is relatively protected from alienation. The same behavior, when directed by individuals or pressures coming from outside the group, can have alienative consequences.

We shall consider first the extent to which individuals experience aloneness in their work. A shifting kaleidoscope of staffing practices makes it impossible to use ward assignment information to classify personnel according to the amount of time they work alone. We can get an approximation of this, however, by dealing with the shift to which people are assigned. Because of the larger number of patient activities, wards are most liberally staffed during the day shift, less so for the evening shift, and most sparsely staffed during the night shift. While most personnel are permanently assigned to one or another of these three shifts, a fourth group rotates between them on a regular basis. As the number of personnel decreases from the day to night shifts, there is a corresponding decrease in the chance that one will be assigned to a ward with another worker. The same number of wards are being serviced by fewer people, with a resultant increase in the number of wards having but a single staff member or, in a number of cases, where a single staff member is assigned the care of more than one ward. The shifts, then, embody different degrees of aloneness in work and it is this, we feel, that accounts for the fact that alienation tends to vary with shift. Thus in Table 9 we see a decrease in the low alienation scores in moving from one shift to another and a commensurate increase in the higher scores. It is interesting that the group that rotates between shifts is intermediate in this re-

Table 9. The Working Shift of Personnel and Alienation

ALIENATION SCORE	DAY	EVENING	ROTATING	NIGHT
0	22%	14%	14%	7%
1	28	30	21	26
2	27	28	27	31
3	13	19	18	19
4	10	9	20	17
Totals	394	279	230	201

$$x^2 = 46.6$$
$$12 \text{ df}$$
$$P < .001$$

spect. Unlike those permanently assigned to the night shift, these individuals at least have an occasionally greater opportunity to work with others.

The relative isolation of late shift personnel can be pointed up more directly. Those on the night shift are significantly more likely than either evening or day shift staff to report that "having someone to sit and talk with" is a problem in their work; similarly, proportionately more of the evening shift make this statement than day shift. This is not surprising, since the evening and night shift workers are increasingly cut off from opportunities to communicate and interact with other personnel. At the same time, we see in Table 10 that those who define as a problem in their work being cut off from others, are, regardless of their shift, considerably more prone to feelings of intense alienation. Aloneness and its attendant absence of opportunities to communicate with others can deprive one of very important group support; this is likely to lead one to feel that he is mastered by his environment instead of having mastery over it.

Even among those who are part of a work group, neither the group nor its norms will mean much if they have no

Table 10. The Salience of Having Someone to Talk With as a Work Problem and Alienation

	"HAVING SOMEONE TO SIT AND TALK WITH IS . . ."		
Alienation Score	*No Problem for Me*	*A Small Problem for Me*	*A Big Problem for Me*
0	19%	14%	10%
1	28	27	17
2	29	29	21
3	12	21	27
4	12	9	25
Totals	619	317	157

$$x^2 = 58.7$$
$$8 \text{ df}$$
$$P < .001$$

affective ties to the group. One indication of the strength of the bonds between an individual and his work group is the extension of the relationship beyond the occupational site. Respondents were presented with two questions that are relevant in this regard. The first asks if, among the employees with whom they work on the *same wards,* they have friends they see outside of work. The second question is in reference to friends who don't work on the same wards but are assigned to the *same service.* Some factors, of course, interfere with the realization of extramural friendships despite any proclivities that might exist. One would be the fact, already noted, that many personnel have only limited opportunity to work uninterruptedly with the same co-workers. Another would be the residential dispersion of the nursing force throughout a large urban area. Nevertheless, the elaboration of working relations to a social level can be observed in cases where it occurs. This is done in Table 11 in relation to alienation. Those reporting no outside friendships among either service or ward colleagues are seen to have the higher alienation scores. Between those having outside friends only at the service level and those having as friends workers

from the same wards, we find a tendency for friends working on the same wards to be less alienated than those sharing only the same service. The closer physical proximity of ward friends than of service friends results in more ready availability of ward friends as supportive resources in coping with alienative forces. Friendship and face-to-face contact together in the work situation are somewhat more effective than either of these alone. When individuals are a part of the informal social structure of the hospital, they are more able to gain a meaningful sense of importance to their environment. Those without group ties, on the other hand, are more exclusively caught up by the formal organization, on which they can exercise relatively little impact.

Summary and Discussion

Alienation is thought by a number of theorists to represent one of the most prominent and crucial conditions of modern societies. Despite the importance attached to it, relatively few empirical studies of alienation have been made. Part of the reason for this perhaps lies in the fact that it is often not clear what people are alienated from—themselves, community institutions, the total society, or all of

Table 11. Outside Friendships Among Fellow Workers, Their Proximity in the Work Situation, and Alienation

ALIENATION SCORE	NO OUTSIDE FRIENDSHIPS REPORTED	FRIENDSHIPS WITH THOSE ASSIGNED TO SAME SERVICE BUT DIFFERENT WARDS	FRIENDSHIPS WITH THOSE ASSIGNED TO SAME WARDS
0	11%	20%	16%
1	23	25	33
2	33	24	27
3	18	18	14
4	15	13	10
Totals	415	369	321

$$x^2 = 30.4$$
8 df
$$P < .001$$

these. By examining alienation within the context of specific structures it is more possible to locate the forces, processes or events from which people feel alienated and to trace out the roots of these feelings. The present study does this within the framework of a work setting. This is a most strategic place to observe alienation, for the occupational sphere is one that can have far-reaching consequences at every level of social life.

This study focuses on three aspects of the organization of a mental hospital: its authority structure, opportunity structure, and work groups. With regard to authority, alienation was found to be most exacerbated under conditions that minimize interaction between superordinates and subordinates and, consequently, that reduce opportunities for the latter to influence informally the former. This is reflected in the findings that intense alienation is most likely to occur (a) where authority figures and their subjects stand in relations of great positional disparity; (b) where authority is communicated in such a way as to prevent or discourage exchange; and (c) where the superordinate exercises his authority in relative *absentia*. It was further discovered that neither positional disparity nor the peremptory exercise of authority was alienative for workers who have an obeisant regard for the honorific aspects of status.

The over-all picture of the opportunity structure of the hospital is that there are far fewer relatively high positions than there are aspirants for them. In selecting personnel to elevate to the choicer positions, differences in the pace and level of achievement naturally occur. Correspondingly, alienation is most conspicuous among the limited achievers and is remarkably low among the high achievers. Even among the limited achievers, however, if there is satisfaction with the rewards of pay, promotion and social mobility, much of what would otherwise be alienative is dissipated. Conversely, dis-

satisfaction with these rewards will breed alienation, even if one is a high achiever.

Finally, certain features of the work group were found to be relevant to alienation. Because behavior supported by group norms can create a sense of personal commitment and voluntarism, it was thought that those who work alone are more subjected to feelings that their activities are ruled by outside forces. The available evidence, drawn from assignments to the various shifts and expressed loneliness, suggests that this is the case. Affective bonds between fellow workers were also examined in relation to alienation. Thus, alienation occurs less among those who have established extrawork friendship relations with fellow workers and this was found to be especially true when the friends are part of the same face-to-face work group.

There are undoubtedly individuals who, solely by virtue of their personalities, are incapable of effectively engaging their environment. Regardless of the circumstances surrounding them, they would probably be alienated. In this paper we have largely ignored personality factors that by themselves are alienative, not because such factors are unimportant, but in order to highlight features of the organization as they bear on alienation. The hospital under study, like most large institutions, has the general features of a bureaucratic organization. While the fact of bureaucracy itself might give rise to alienation, it is important to emphasize that subsumed under the same parent organization is a good deal of structural variation. Some structural arrangements, we have seen, can be quite alienative, while others act as a barrier against it. Even within the bounds of a given bureaucratized setting, therefore, conditions and mechanisms exist to prevent estrangement from work, as well as the purposelessness and despair which must be close companions of alienation.

VALUE ORIENTATION, ROLE CONFLICT, AND ALIENATION FROM WORK: A CROSS-CULTURAL STUDY*

Louis A. Zurcher, Jr., Arnold Meadow, and Susan Lee Zurcher

The classic Western Electric studies conducted by the Elton Mayo team in the 1930's established that the employee's attitude toward the work organization is relevant to his job satisfaction and his productivity.[1] As they began to be aware that the employee's personality may or may not articulate with the expectations of the formal work organization, interested behavioral scientists developed theories of personality-organization interaction.[2] Generally, these theories and the

SOURCE: Reprinted from the *American Sociological Review*, 30, 4 (August 1965), 539–548, by permission of the authors and publisher.

* This research was supported by the National Science Foundation (Louis A. Zurcher, Cooperative Graduate Fellow), the National Institute of Mental Health (Grant #5-R11-MH-544-2, Arnold Meadow, Director), and by the Bureau of Business and Public Research, University of Arizona (Susan L. Zurcher, Research Assistant). The paper is based on the senior author's unpublished doctoral dissertation, University of Arizona, 1965. Without the complete co-operation of the management and personnel of the Valley National Bank (Tucson and Nogales, Ariz. branches) and the Banco Nacional de Mexico (Nogales, Sonora branches) this study would not have been possible. The authors wish to make special acknowledgement to John R. Henderson, Vice-President of the Valley National Bank, for his sustained interest and sound advice throughout the study.

[1] Fritz Roethlisberger and William Dickson, *Management and the Worker,* Cambridge: Harvard University Press, 1959.

studies that have sprung from them have been concerned with the description and amelioration of conflicts between the expectations of work organizations in a given society and the expectations of employees recruited from that same society. Such research, though certainly fruitful, has been somewhat restricted in its ability to describe the social and psychological situation of employees whose cultural orientation is markedly at odds with that of the work organization.

The purpose of this study is to examine, by cross-cultural comparison, components of a work situation in which an organizational expectation, influenced by the culture of one society, is clearly in conflict with a modal employee value, influenced by the culture of another society. We use the term value to mean "a selective orientation toward experience, implying deep commitment or repudiation, which influences the ordering of choices between possible alternatives in action."[3] We assume that the individual learns values in

[2] See, for example, E. Wight Bakke, *The Fusion Process,* New Haven: Yale University Press, 1955; Chris Argyris, *Personality and Organization,* New York: Harper, 1957; Daniel J. Levinson, "Role, Personality, and Social Structure in the Organizational Setting," *Journal of Abnormal and Social Psychology,* 58 (March, 1959), pp. 170–180.

[3] Clyde Kluckhohn, "The Study of Values," in Donald N. Barrett (ed.), *Values in America,*

his parent culture; "culture" is "the distinctive way of life of a group of people, their complete design for living."[4]

"Universalism vs. particularism," one of the "pattern variables" postulated by Parsons and Shils in their general theory of action, is the specific value conflict we shall examine in this paper.[5] Universalism, as we shall use it here, is a value orientation toward institutionalized obligations to society, and particularism is a value orientation toward institutionalized obligations of friendship. Parsons and Shils explain that in any given social situation, the actor's cultural background will influence his choice between the horns of the dilemma presented by each pattern variable.[6] Thus, if an individual is placed in a situation in which he must choose between particularism (duty to a friend) and universalism (duty to an abstract "society"), his choice will reflect the impact of his parent culture.

To the degree, then, that an individual's personality is affected by the socio-cultural milieu in which it developed, it will encompass certain values, and the individual will expect certain role behavior in himself and in others to be shaped around these values. Such values will also play a

key part in his general orientation to specific situations.

Typically, the U.S. is described as a universalistically oriented society. Complex technology and the accompanying reverence for the "scientific" and the "abstract," emphasis on individual independence and mobility, and a value on competition and achieved status tend to isolate an American from his concrete relation to others. This isolation, and its effect on human personality, has been a favorite topic of contemporary social philosophers such as Fromm, Riesman, and Buber.[7] In a universalistic society, friendship, as Cohen points out, tends to be expedient and manipulative, and valued mainly in terms of material or status gain.[8]

The American work situation reflects the societal ethos. Parsons writes that "the American occupational system is universalistic and achievement oriented. . . . Compared with other possible ways of organizing the division of labor, the predominant norms which are institutionalized in the American society and which embody the predominant value orientation of the culture give rise to expectations that occupational roles will be treated by their incumbents and those who are associated with them universalistically. . . ."[9]

These universalistic expectations are strikingly manifested in that most representative of American work organizations, the bureaucracy. Weber characterizes the bureaucratic work setting as one in which a rational organization is ordered by rules, with a high degree of disciplined behav-

[footnote 3 continued
Notre Dame: University of Notre Dame Press, 1961, p. 18.

[4] Clyde Kluckhohn, "The Study of Culture," in Daniel Lerner and Harold D. Lasswell (eds.), *The Policy Sciences,* Stanford: Stanford University Press, 1951, p. 86.

[5] According to Parsons and Shils, the individual in a social situation "is confronted by a series of major dilemmas of orientation, a series of choices that the actor must make before the situation has a definite meaning for him. Specifically, the actor must make five dichotomous choices before any situation will have a determinate meaning. The five dichotomies which formulate these choice alternatives are called 'pattern variables,' because any specific orientation (and consequently any action) is characterized by a pattern of the five choices." See Talcott Parsons and Edward A. Shils (eds.), *Toward A General Theory of Action,* Cambridge: Harvard University Press, 1959, pp. 76–77.

[6] *Ibid,* p. 79.

[7] Eric Fromm, *Escape from Freedom,* New York: Farrar and Rinehart, 1940; David Riesman, *The Lonely Crowd,* New Haven: Yale University Press, 1950; and Martin Buber, *I and Thou,* New York: Scribner's, 1958.

[8] Yehudi A. Cohen, "Patterns of Friendship," in Yehudi A. Cohen (ed.), *Social Structure and Personality,* New York: Holt, Rinehart and Winston, 1961, pp. 353–354.

[9] Talcott Parsons, *Essays in Sociological Theory,* Glencoe, Ill.: Free Press, 1954, p. 79.

ior, an established office hierarchy and clearly defined areas for the power of each office, and appointed specialists to fill these offices.[10] Within such a work structure the employee is expected to be impersonal in his relations with other employees and with clients or customers, to put loyalty to the company ahead of other loyalties, and to value the external motivators of status and achievement above the rewards of interpersonal relations. Merton, Mills, Whyte, Blauner, and Zurcher have discussed in detail the fact that the employee's "success" depends on his living up to such organizational expectations.[11]

Mexico, compared with the U.S., is a less technical, less "scientific," less urban society, and cultural values are predominately particularistic. A central factor accounting for the Mexican value on friendship appears to be the Mexican's deep involvement in an extended kinship system.[12] Furthermore, Mexicans are reported generally to distrust and disregard the authority of government and laws,[13] and seldom to feel responsibility under these "societal" obligations. Thus, whereas an Anglo-American tends to evaluate other individuals in terms of their accomplishments or "worth" in the eyes of so-

ciety, a Mexican assesses others primarily in terms of his personal relations with them, and seems less inclined to abstract from the personal to the normative, to relate to others in an impersonal, objective manner. This mode of interpersonal association seems strongly to be influenced by a profound dependence on the family. As Lewis points out, "Without his family, the (Mexican) individual stands prey to every form of aggression, exploitation, and humiliation. . .".[14] This "family" goes far beyond the basic nuclear family. Not only does it extend through a web of uncles, aunts, in-laws, and distant cousins, but also through a large number of *compadres,* or god-parents. The latter are given all the respect and courtesy due blood relatives, and "are morally bound to stand by each other in time of need and danger."[15] This personal and intimate mode of association with both true and fictive kin is extended into the adult's entire social world. Redfield observes that the result of such a pattern "is a group of people among whom prevail the personal and categorized relationships that characterize the families as we know them, and in which the patterns of kinship tend to be extended outward from the group of genealogically connected individuals to the whole society."[16] The "world view" of individuals in this type of society defines human relations in terms of "propinquity, intimacy, and solidarity" and influences perception of social situations in terms of "close personal bonds."[17]

The impact of such a "world view" is manifest in the patterns of Mexican business. According to McClelland, Mexican businessmen demonstrate a significantly

[10] Hans Gerth and C. Wright Mills (eds.), *From Max Weber: Essays in Sociology,* New York: Oxford University Press, 1946, p. 50.

[11] Robert Merton, "Bureaucratic Structure and Personality," in Alvin Gouldner (ed.), *Studies in Leadership,* New York: Harper, 1956; C. Wright Mills, *White Collar,* New York: Oxford University Press, 1953; William H. Whyte, *The Organization Man,* New York: Harper, 1948; Robert Blauner, *Alienation and Freedom: The Factory Worker and His Industry,* Chicago: University of Chicago Press, 1964, p. 9; and Louis A. Zurcher, Jr., "The Naval Recruit Training Center: A Study of Role Assimilation in a Total Institution," *Sociological Inquiry,* in press.

[12] Parsons and Shils, *op. cit.,* pp. 76–77 and Oscar Lewis, *Tepoztlan: A Village in Mexico,* New York: Holt, 1960, p. 88.

[13] Louis A. Zurcher, Jr. and Arnold Meadow, "On Bullfights and Baseball: An Analysis of the Interaction of Social Institutions," unpublished paper, University of Arizona, 1964.

[14] Lewis, *op. cit.,* p. 54.

[15] Edward P. Dozier, "Folk Culture to Urbanity: The Case of Mexicans and Mexican-Americans in the Southwest," unpublished paper, University of Arizona, 1964, p. 34.

[16] Robert Redfield, "The Folk Society," *American Journal of Sociology,* 52 (January, 1947), pp. 293–308.

[17] Cohen, *op. cit.,* pp. 353–354.

higher need for affiliation and a significantly lower need for achievement than do the Anglo-American businessmen.[18] Fayerweather reports that the former seem to be considerably more concerned with adjusting relations among people than with solving a problem efficiently at the expense of such relations. He describes a Mexican purchasing agent, working for a U.S. subsidiary in Mexico, who was encouraged by his Anglo boss to crack down on a production manager for storing too many excess parts, and on a particular supplier who was delivering, consistently late, poorly manufactured parts. The Mexican purchasing agent, though he fully understood the efficiency problem, could not be punitive, because he "was more interested in the personal relations involved. . . . He felt that the American did not understand how loyal and helpful the supplier had been in the past and how much the production manager had just wanted a high inventory to feel better."[19] Fayerweather comments that "in Mexico, very few people are actively opposed to being on time, following plans, or obeying any of the other rules of industrial discipline. When they do not obey them, it is because some conflicting avenue of action appeared and they felt it was very important. One of the major conflicting avenues of action is seen to be the maintenance of personal alliances."[20]

We do not mean to imply, of course, that every Mexican is clearly particularistic and every Anglo-American is clearly universalistic. In rural areas in the U.S., where people are more closely involved in extended kinships systems, the particularist orientation is doubtless more prevalent, while, on the other hand, one would expect to find a trend toward universalism in the highly urbanized areas in Mexico. At present, however, universalism can be considered the modal orientation in the U.S., and particularism in Mexico, these orientations having a significant impact on the patterns of daily living.

To determine the feasibility of carrying out a cross-cultural study of universalism-particularism, and to appraise the degree of particularism in a group of Mexican-Americans relative to a comparable group of Anglo-Americans, we conducted a pilot study in which we administered the Stouffer-Toby Conflict Scale[21] to 40 Mexican-American high school students and to 40 Anglo-American high school students, having first matched for sex, grade level, and socioeconomic class. Analysis of the data revealed that the Mexican-Americans were significantly more particularistic than their Anglo counterparts.

A survey of the literature, observation in both Mexico and the U.S., and the encouraging results of the pilot study, led us to hypothesize that a cross-cultural comparison of like-situated groups of Mexicans, Mexican-Americans, and Anglo-Americans would reveal that Mexicans are significantly more particularistic than Mexican-Americans, and that Mexican-Americans, by virtue of their marginal position between the two cultures, are significantly more particularistic than the Anglo-Americans.

We first decided that the cross-cultural sample should be composed of employees from the same type of work organization, thus providing a built-in control; then we asked, what if this work organization were a bureaucracy? Since a bureaucracy is forcefully universalistic in nature, might not these universalistic expectations conflict with the expectations of employees

---

[18] David McClelland, *The Achieving Society,* Princeton, N.J.: Van Nostrand, 1961, p. 289.

[19] John Fayerweather, *The Executive Overseas,* New York: Syracuse Press, 1959, pp. 1–3.

[20] *Ibid.,* p. 54.

[21] This is a Guttman scale sounding the degree of particularism by presenting four situations involving conflicts between obligation to a friend and more general social obligations, and forcing the individual to choose one set of obligations or the other. Samuel A. Stouffer and Jackson Toby, "Role Conflict and Personality," *American Journal of Sociology,* 56 (March, 1951), pp. 395–406.

having a particularistic orientation? Might not this conflict be manifest in a measure of the degree of alienation from work? We hypothesized that in a universalistic work organization, there would be a significant positive correlation between employee particularism and alienation from work and that Mexicans would be significantly more alienated than Mexican-Americans, who in turn would be significantly more alienated than Anglo-Americans. As a measure of alienation, we selected the Alienation From Work scale developed by Leonard Pearlin.[22] Pearlin states that his scale approximates what Clark feels is the essence of alienation, namely, "the discrepancy between the power a man believes he has and what he believes he should have—his estrangement from his rightful role."[23]

Our major hypotheses suggested the corollary hypotheses that both particularism and alienation would be negatively correlated with 1) level of position in the bank, 2) satisfaction with work and intention to make bank employment a career, and 3) length of bank employment.

Procedure

As the work environment for this study we chose the bank, because it provides an accessible and cross-culturally comparable bureaucratic organization from which to draw subjects. Mexican and American banks are almost identical in formal organization and operating procedures, the former being based on the structure of the latter.

Three groups were studied, the number of subjects in all three groups totaling 230. The first group was composed of native born, Spanish speaking (unilingual) Mexican citizens employed by two bank branches in Nogales, Sonora. The second group was composed of bilingual (Spanish-English)[24] Mexican-Americans employed by two bank branches in Nogales, Ariz., and the third group was composed of English speaking (unilingual) Anglo-Americans employed by nine bank branches in Tucson, Ariz. All 11 U.S. banks are branches of the same parent organization. Both of the Mexican banks are branches of the same Mexican parent organization. All employees of the banks (up to the position of vice-president and including at least one vice-president for each cultural group) who were at work on that day were administered the questionnaire. The final sample included all of these employees, with the exception of one Anglo-American who was removed from the Mexican-American group, and 14 Mexican-Americans who were removed from the Anglo-American group. The employees of the Nogales, Sonora banks are all Mexicans. The three groups were matched for proportion of officers (one to every five line employees) and were comparable for employee longevity (median is two to four years in each group).

The employees were gathered together, either before or after customer hours, and told by the investigators that their anonymous responses were considered confidential, would not be seen by any other bank personnel, and would be used for research purposes only by the University of Arizona. The employees were then given copies of the mimeographed questionnaires and went to their own work spaces to fill them out. When finished with the forms, the employees returned them to the investigators. Members of management simultaneously filled out the forms

---

[22] This is a four-item Guttman scale developed for hospital personnel. For the present study the word "hospital" in one item was changed to "bank." Leonard I. Pearlin, "Alienation from Work: A Study of Nursing Personnel," *American Sociological Review*, 29 (June, 1962), pp. 314–326.

[23] John P. Clark, "Measuring Alienation Within a Social System," *American Sociological Review*, 24 (December, 1959), pp. 849–852.

[24] Bilingualism and U.S. citizenship are conditions for employment in the Nogales, Ariz., bank branches.

and did not influence the employees in any way. The same procedure was employed in every bank branch.

The questionnaire packet contained, in the following order: 1) Biographical and employment questions; 2) the Stouffer-Toby Role Conflict Scale; 3) the Pearlin Alienation from Work Scale; and 4) the questions "Do you expect to continue with the bank for the rest of your working career? . . . . . . yes . . . . . . no;" and "Is your satisfaction with the position you hold . . . . . . above average . . . . . . average . . . . . . below average?"[25]

Results

Table 1 presents the distributions of Mexican, Mexican-American, and Anglo-American subjects for the particularism scale. (Since the Stouffer-Toby Role Conflict Scale is a four-item Guttman Scale, the scores may range from zero to four, with a score of zero indicating a minimum

[25] Since the Stouffer-Toby and the Pearlin Scales had been developed with different subject groups, and since they had been translated into Spanish for the Mexican group, we subjected them to tests for Guttman scalability. The Guttman coefficient of reproducibility derived from the subjects' scores in this study was .924 for the Stouffer-Toby Role Conflict Scale and .928 for the Pearlin Alienation from Work Scale. The x^2 comparison of the frequency of perfect scale scores with non-perfect scale scores was significant beyond the .001 level for the Role Conflict Scale and beyond the .02 level for the Alienation from Work Scale. The two instruments thus maintained scalability and unidimensionality with cross-cultural subjects and after translation into Spanish.

and a score of four indicating a maximum orientation toward particularism.) Orientation toward particularism differs significantly among the Mexican, Mexican-American, and Anglo-American subject groups.[26] To test the hypothesis that the Mexican group is more particularistic than the Mexican-American group, which is in turn more particularistic than the Anglo-American group, we compared the pattern of scale scores in each of the three groups with the pattern of scale scores in the other two. The results of these comparisons are as predicted and are statistically significant beyond the .02 probability level.[27]

The alienation data were similarly analyzed. (The Pearlin Alienation from Work Scale is also a four item Guttman Scale, and the scores may range from zero, minimum alienation, to four, maximum alienation.) Table 2 presents the frequency of scale scores by groups. The degree of alienation from work is significantly different among the Mexican, Mexican-American, and Anglo-American subjects. The hypothesis that the Mexican group is more alienated from work than the Mexican-American group, which in turn is more

[26] To test for overall significance of differences among groups we used the Extended Median Test for k Groups described in Sidney Siegel, *Nonparametric Statistics for the Behavioral Sciences*, New York: McGraw-Hill, 1956, pp. 179–184.

[27] To test for the significance of differences between groups we used the Median Test for Two Independent Groups (One-Tailed) described in Siegel, *op. cit.*, pp. 111–116.

Table 1. Cultural Origin by Particularism Scale Score*

CULTURAL ORIGIN	SCALE SCORE					NUMBER IN GROUP
	0	1	2	3	4	
Mexican	4	7	9	8	10	38
Mexican-American	21	12	4	5	1	43
Anglo-American	102	26	11	8	2	149
Total	127	45	24	21	13	230

*Chi square for k groups = 41.95; with two degrees of freedom, p < .001 level.

Table 2. *Cultural Origin by Alienation Scale Score**

| | SCALE SCORE | | | | | |
CULTURAL ORIGIN	0	1	2	3	4	NUMBER IN GROUP
Mexican	8	7	4	17	2	38
Mexican-American	8	7	16	8	4	43
Anglo-American	36	25	50	30	8	149
Total	52	39	70	55	414	230

*Chi square for k groups = 8.759; with two degrees of freedom, $p < .02$ level.

alienated than the Anglo-American group, was partially supported: The Mexicans were significantly more alienated from work in the bank than the Mexican-Americans and the Anglo-Americans (beyond the .05 probability level), but the Mexican-Americans were not significantly more alienated than the Anglo-Americans.

Table 3 presents, for all three cultural groups combined, correlations among the variables alienation, particularism, longevity, position level, satisfaction with position, and plans to continue working in the bank. Alienation is significantly and positively correlated with particularism, and significantly and negatively correlated with longevity, position level, satisfaction with position, and plans to continue working in the bank. In addition to its relation with alienation, particularism is significantly and negatively correlated with position level, satisfaction with position, and plans to continue working in the bank. Inspection of Tables 4–6, which present the correlations among the same variables for each cultural group separately, reveals that the positive correlation between alienation and particularism is significant for the Anglo-Americans, but not for the Mexican-Americans or the Mexicans.

The correlations among the variables for all groups combined and within each of the three groups are generally low, and thus account for a relatively small propor-

Table 3. *Correlations among the Variables Alienation, Particularism, Longevity, Position Level, Satisfaction With Position, and Plans to Continue Working in the Bank for All three Groups Combined****

	Alienation	Particularism	Longevity	Position Level	Satisfaction with Position	Plans to Continue
Alienation	....	....	....	....	....	....
Particularism	.151*	....	....	....	....	....
Longevity	—.154*	—.101	....	....	....	....
Position Level	—.276**	—.170*	.307**	....	....	....
Satisfaction with Position	—.274**	—.141*	.074	.145*	....	....
Plans to Continue	—.237**	—.260**	.130*	.169*	.270**	....

*$p < .05$.
**$p < .01$.
***All correlations reported in the paper are Pearson Product-Moment Coefficients.
$N = 230$; $df = 228$.

Table 4. Correlations among the Variables Alienation, Particularism, Longevity, Position Level, Satisfaction with Position, and Plans to Continue Working in the Bank for the Mexican Subject Group

	Alienation	Particularism	Longevity	Position Level	Satisfaction with Position	Plans to Continue
Alienation	....	....	....	....	....	....
Particularism	.068	....	....	....	....	....
Longevity	—.130	—.242	....	....	....	....
Position Level	—.100	—.050	.063	....	....	....
Satisfaction with Position	—.270	—.159	.219	—.021	....	....
Plans to Continue	—.218	—.247	.237	—.023	.194	....

$*p < .05$.
$N = 38$; $df = 36$.

Table 5. Correlations among the Variables Alienation, Particularism, Longevity, Position Level, Satisfaction with Position, and Plans to Continue Working in the Bank for the Mexican-American Subject Group

	Alienation	Particularism	Longevity	Position Level	Satisfaction with Position	Plans to Continue
Alienation	....	....	....	....	....	....
Particularism	.023	....	....	....	....	....
Longevity	—.307*	—.026	....	....	....	....
Position Level	—.491**	—.242	.270	....	....	....
Satisfaction with Position	—.253	—.145	.176	.511**	....	....
Plans to Continue	—.075	—.151*	.021	.176*	.171*	....

$*p < .05$.
$**p < .01$.
$N = 43$; $df = 41$.

tion of the variance. Nevertheless, these correlations are all in the expected direction (many of them significantly so), and the resultant pattern supports the initial hypotheses.

Discussion

Though both the particularism scale and the alienation scale were scalable and unidimensional, the small number of items (four in each) may limit the generality of the results. Furthermore, neither the concept of particularism nor that of alienation, even as operationally defined, are unequivocal. Friendship obligations, in Parsons' terminology, are diffuse and affectively toned as well as particularistic. Pearlin's "alienation" focuses largely on the feeling of lack of control over the work situation, and thus may be insensitive to other important components of alienation in the present study. More ex-

Table 6. Correlations among the Variables Alienation, Particularism, Longevity, Position Level, Satisfaction with Position, and Plans to Continue Working in the Bank for the Anglo-American Subject Group

	Alienation	Particularism	Longevity	Position Level	Satisfaction with Position	Plans to Continue
Alienation	....	....	....	....	....	....
Particularism	.209*	....	....	....	....	....
Longevity	—.118	—.127	....	....	....	....
Position Level	—.282**	—.217**	.365**	....	....	....
Satisfaction with Position	—.314**	—.151	.104	.145	....	....
Plans to Continue	—.300**	—.243**	.344**	.180*	.420**	....

*p < .05.
**p < .01.
N = 149; df = 147.

haustive questionnaires sounding particularism and alienation from work, plus inspection of employee records for absenteeism, disciplinary actions, and other indicators of industrial pathology, might have yielded better insights into the relations among these variables. In spite of the limited data, however, the consistency of the results obtained suggests several conclusions.

The hypothesis that the Mexican bank employees would be more particularistic than the Mexican-Americans, and the latter more particularistic than the Anglo-Americans, is supported; we have demonstrated that specific cultural values have a measurable impact on behavioral intent. Keeping in mind that hypothetical scale items might encourage a respondent to adopt more stereotyped roles than he would in a real-life situation, it can be said that when presented with a choice between duty to a friend and duty to society, the Mexican employees, and to a lesser degree the marginal Mexican-American employees, tend to align themselves with the friend. Anglo-American employees confronted with the same choice, however, tend to choose the universalistic alternative.

Following administration of the questionnaire, the investigators informally asked many of the employees what they thought the questionnaire was testing. The alienation scale was interpreted by all interviewed as a means of "finding out how much we like our job." But the particularism scale was viewed by the Mexicans as a "test of our *friendship*," and by the Anglo-Americans as "questions to see how *honest* we are." The contrasting value orientations were apparent even in the subjects' informal interpretation of the purposes of the scales.

Also as hypothesized, the data indicate that the Mexican bank employees are more likely to be alienated from work than are the Mexican-American or Anglo-American employees. The Mexican-Americans, however, in spite of their relatively high degree of particularism, are not more alienated than the Anglo-Americans. Informal interviews indicated a feeling among the Mexican-American employees that they "are making it" in their reference group, the Anglo white-collar world. The Mexican-American respondents indicated that they received much higher pay than their Mexican counterparts across the border, a fact which certainly ought to mitigate alienation from work. The investigators also observed that the Mexican-Americans are extremely active in a social club sponsored by the bank, and that many of the club officers have been Mexican-Americans. This organization may itself provide an outlet for the employees' particularistic needs, as Officer found in his Tucson study: Mexican-Americans, as a way of re-establishing primary group dependencies lost in migration, tend to be "joiners" of social clubs.[28] Meadow and Bronson described similar manifestations of this phenomenon in their analysis of the emotional support gained by Mexican-Americans who participate in small Protestant religious sects.[29]

The results tend to support the hypothesis that particularism and alienation are positively correlated. That is, employees with particularistic orientations tend to be alienated from work in the universalistically oriented bank. The relatively small correlations between alienation and particularism, for all groups combined and within each group, may be at least partially attributed to measurement error, the complexity of the concepts involved, and the fact that employees can be alienated from work for reasons other than a high degree of particularism (e.g., differentials in pay, promotional opportunities, etc.).

Alienation is consistently related to the other variables under consideration, for all groups combined and within the groups. Employees are *less* alienated from work: 1) the longer they have been working in the bank, 2) the higher their position, 3) the more satisfied they are with their jobs, and 4) when they plan to make the bank a career. This pattern cannot be explained solely in terms of the gradual socialization of new employees, for a highly alienated employee may not stay long with the bank, either because he voluntarily resigns or because his alienation motivates behavior that leads to his dismissal. This same selective factor must be assumed when considering the lower degree of alienation among the higher ranking employees. The negative relation between satisfaction and alienation, and between plans to continue and alienation, support the validity of the alienation scale itself.

The very low negative correlation between alienation and plans to continue working, among the Mexican-Americans as compared with the other two groups, may indicate that a feeling of lack of control over the work situation, or of inability to enact a "rightful role" in the bank, may be less important to the Mexican-American employee than the relatively high pay and Anglo white-collar status. This is similarly reflected in the comparatively strong positive relation between level of position and satisfaction with position in this group.

Particularism, for all groups combined and within each group, is also consistently related to the other variables. Generally, particularism diminishes (and conversely, universalism increases) as: (1) length of employment increases, (2) level of position increases, (3) satisfaction with the job increases, and (4) plans to continue with the bank as a career increase.

As with the alienation data, the relations between particularism and the other variables can be considered a function not only of gradual adjustment to and internalization of the bank's expectations, but as a function of a selection process. The bank, as a universalistic formal organization, encourages, with continued employment, service awards, and promotions, the employees who meet its expectations for employee behavior and attitude. Predominant among these expectations are the impersonality, the unquestioning loyalty to the organization, and the respect for the chain of command that are associated with universalism. A universalistic-

---

[28] James E. Officer, "Sodalities and Systematic Linkage: The Joining Habits of Urban Mexican-Americans," unpublished doctoral dissertation, University of Arizona, 1964.

[29] Arnold Meadow and Louise Bronson, "Religious Affiliation and Psychopathology in a Mexican-American Population," unpublished paper, University of Arizona, 1964.

ally oriented individual is likely to be at home with these expectations, to be more satisfied with his job, to plan to make the bank a career, and to have the best chances for promotion, while a particularistic individual is more likely to feel uncomfortable in the universalistic components of the job environment, and to resign or be dismissed for cause after a short time.

If the data were to be interpreted as describing the influence of the social system's pressures for conformity, these results would be in line with Merton's analysis of the effect of the bureaucratic organization on personality. Value orientations are, of course, important components of personality structure. But such an interpretation must be cautiously offered, since the relations between longevity and particularism and position level and particularism may be influenced as much by a selection factor as they are by a socialization process.

The relatively low negative correlation between longevity and particularism in the Mexican-American group suggests that particularistic needs are being met, and maintained even through extended years of service, in the close interpersonal relations of the bank social club. The low negative correlation between position level and particularism among the Mexicans (again as compared with the other two groups) indicates that the Mexican management, at least in responses to questionnaires, can maintain their particularistic view even under the influence of the bureaucracy. This is supported by the very low correlations for the Mexican group between position level and satisfaction with position, position level and plans to make the bank a career, and position level and alienation. Perhaps the Mexican managers, though not comfortable with the dissonance between their particularistic orientation and the organization's expectations, still value their jobs which are, relative to other jobs in Mexico, well-paid and prestigeful.

In conclusion, then, the results of this study, especially the between-group comparisons of particularistic value orientation, support Parsons and Shils' assumption that particularism is influenced by culture. The universalistic expectations in American culture and the particularistic expectations of Mexican society are reflected in the measures of the behaviorial intent of otherwise comparable Anglo-American and Mexican subjects. The marginal Mexican-Americans, though still influenced by their parent culture, tend to favor the universalistic value orientation of the country in which they now work and live, and within whose status structure they now function.

The pattern of results also indicates that particularistic individuals tend to be alienated from work in the universalistically oriented formal organization of a bank. This suggests that the compatibility of the individual's value orientations with the expectations of the work organization is *one* determinant of alienation from work. In this study, however, a highly particularistic value orientation was not always associated with a high degree of alienation, and correlations between alienation and particularism, though in the expected direction, were very low for the Mexican and Mexican-American groups. The interaction between individual and organization is complex, and other job factors may compensate for or offset the impact of a specific value conflict.

The influence of value orientations, as components both of organization and personality, has largely been overlooked in considerations of the "fusion" between individual and organization. These value structures, their sources, points of conflict, and their effects on behaviorial expectations are an important part of the dynamic of organizational behavior. We have attempted to measure the impact of conflict concerning one value orientation, and to analyze its influence on organizational expectations and occupational success.

PROFESSIONALS IN BUREAUCRACY: ALIENATION AMONG INDUSTRIAL SCIENTISTS AND ENGINEERS*

George A. Miller

Etzioni has said that most of us are born in organizations, educated by organizations, work for organizations, and spend much of our leisure time paying, playing, and praying in organizations.[1]

The modern scientist and engineer represent dramatic examples of the incorporation of professionals into organizations. At present, nearly three-fourths of all scientists in the United States are employed by industry and government, with the greatest proportion of these in industry.[2] Previous research findings show that businessmen are increasingly dependent upon the scientist and engineer for ideas necessary for the accomplishment of their organizational goals[3] and that the amount

of research conducted by staff scientists in industrial organizations is an important factor differentiating the dynamic from the more stagnant industries.[4] The employment of scientists and engineers in industry is not increasing at the same rate in all types of industry—as evidenced by the increase in the numbers of these professionals who are employed in the aerospace industry.[5] Moreover, the aerospace industry itself has become more and more dependent upon the federal government as an increasing proportion of its research and development is supported directly by the National Aeronautics and Space Administration and the Department of Defense.[6]

This growing interdependence has created conflicts for both the professional and his employing organization. Blau and Scott have shown that, although professional and bureaucratic modes of organization share some principles in common,

SOURCE: Reprinted from the *American Sociological Review*, 32,5 (October 1967), 755–768, by permission of the author and publisher.

* This investigation was supported in part by a Public Health Service Fellowship from the National Institutes of Health. The author is greatly indebted to L. Wesley Wager, University of Washington, for aid and criticism in the formulation of this research and to Samuel J. Surace, Warren D. TenHouten, and Ralph H. Turner for their many helpful comments on an earlier draft of this paper.

[1] Amitai Etzioni, *Modern Organizations,* Englewood Cliffs: Prentice-Hall, 1964, p. 1.

[2] William Kornhauser, *Scientists in Industry: Conflict and Accommodation,* Berkeley: University of California Press, 1962, p. 10.

[3] Simon Marcson, *The Scientist in American*

Industry, New York: Harper and Brothers, 1960, p. 5.

[4] Arthur L. Stinchcombe, "The Sociology of Organization and the Theory of the Firm," *Pacific Sociological Review,* 13 (Fall, 1960), p. 80.

[5] National Science Foundation, *Scientific and Technical Personnel in Industry,* 1960, Washington, D.C.: Government Printing Office, 1961, p. 20.

[6] National Science Foundation, *Research and Development in Industry 1960,* Washington, D.C.: Government Printing Office, 1963, p. 64.

they rest upon fundamentally conflicting principles as well.[7] Kornhauser concludes that most conflicts between the scientist or engineer and his employing organization stem from the basic organizational dilemma of autonomy vs. integration. These professionals must be given enough autonomy to enable them to fulfill their professional needs, yet their activity must also contribute to the overall goals of the organization.[8]

The professional who experiences such conflicts in his work may become alienated from his work, the organization, or both. This research examines work alienation as one major consequence arising from the professional-bureaucratic dilemma for industrial scientists and engineers.

Although it is clear that conflicts exist between professionals and their employing organizations, it is also clear that organizational administrators are not unaware of the problems and conflicts inherent in the employment of professional personnel. The research to date suggests that these organizations are attempting to become more professional and flexible. One method for alleviating conflicts is to modify the organizational structure by providing more *professional incentives* and lessening the degree of *organizational control* for the professional employee.[9]

However, these changes in the organizational structure may not be made available to all professionals. This paper will suggest that structural modification in professional incentives and organizational control will vary by (1) the length and type of training received by the professional, and (2) the type of organizational unit in which the professional performs his work activity.

PROFESSIONAL TRAINING

Orth describes the importance of professional training for the scientist or engineer who enters a bureaucratic organization, as follows:

Professional training in itself, whether it be in medicine, chemistry, or engineering, appears to predispose those who go through it to unhappiness or rebellion when faced with the administrative process as it exists in most organizations. Scientists and engineers *cannot* or *will not* . . . operate at the peak of their creative potential in an atmosphere that puts pressure on them to conform to organizational requirements which they do not understand or believe necessary.[10]

Kornhauser contends that the strength of professional loyalty and identification can be expected to vary by the *type* of training received by the professional. He notes that professions differ in their selectivity of recruitment, intensity of training, and state of intellectual development and that all of these factors affect the nature of the person's orientation.[11] Becker and Carper in a study of three groups of students found differences between those majoring in engineering and those majoring in physiology and psychology. The engineers felt that their future lay somewhere in the industrial system. For many, a broad range of positions within an organization was thought acceptable, including such "unprofessional" positions as manager or research supervisor.[12] Similarly, Clovis Shepherd found differences between scientists and engineers concerning their goals, reference groups and su-

---

[7] Peter M. Blau and W. Richard Scott, *Formal Organizations,* San Francisco: Chandler Publishing Company, 1962, p. 60.

[8] Kornhauser, *op. cit.,* pp. 195–196.

[9] These are two of the four areas of conflict identified and discussed by William Kornhauser. See Kornhauser, *op. cit.,* p. 45.

[10] Charles D. Orth, "The Optimum Climate for Industrial Research," in Norman Kaplan, ed., *Science and Society,* Chicago: Rand McNally, 1965, p. 141.

[11] Kornhauser, *op. cit.,* p. 138.

[12] Howard S. Becker and James Carper, "The Elements of Identification with an Occupation," *American Sociological Review,* 21 (June, 1956), pp. 341–348.

pervisory experiences. Engineers were typically more "bureaucratic" in their orientation, whereas scientists were more "professional." Shepherd attributes this difference to the more intensive training received by the scientists.[13] Goldner and Ritti also contend that engineers are more concerned with entrance into positions of power and participation in the affairs of the organization than with professional values and goals. They argue that engineers recognize power as an "essential ingredient of success" for them.[14]

In addition to differences in type of professional training, differences in the *length* of training are important. Those professionals who receive the Ph.D. degree should develop stronger professional loyalties and identifications than those persons with M.A. or M.S. degrees. This greater length of training also represents a greater investment on the part of the professional. It is reasonable to assume that he will *expect* higher rewards from the organization in return for his services. Moreover, if these rewards are not forthcoming, professionals with advanced degrees are in a better position to market their skills and find employment in an organization that does offer such rewards.

Some evidence exists for these assumptions. For example, Wilensky found that top staff experts in labor unions who had received serious job offers since their employment had more influence on union decisions than did those without such offers.[15] Paula Brown found that "key" scientists and engineers in a governmental laboratory were given "special considerations" by their administrators, were highly respected by them, and were able to "control" the laboratory to a considerable extent. Brown argues that professionals with less national prestige would not have been given the same treatment nor have been able to control the organization as effectively.[16] Pelz's and Andrews' findings parallel those reported earlier in a study undertaken by the Princeton Opinion Research Corporation. In both studies, those professionals with the Ph.D. degree and those trained as scientists participated most often in decisions regarding their work, had more individual freedom, and enjoyed more professional incentives.[17]

However, the "match" between organizational structure and the professional's length and type of training is seldom perfect. As Etzioni notes:

If personalities could be shaped to fit specific organizational roles, or organizational roles to fit specific personalities, many of the pressures to displace goals, much of the need to control performance, and a good part of the alienation would disappear. Such matching is, of course, as likely as an economy without scarcity and hence without prices.[18]

The above line of reasoning serves as the basis for the following hypotheses to be explored in this paper: (1) degree of alienation from work should be positively associated with degree of organizational control and negatively associated with number of professional incentives for all professional personnel; (2) the above relationships should be stronger for those

[13] Clovis Shepherd, "Orientations of Scientists and Engineers," *Pacific Sociological Review*, 4 (Fall, 1961), pp. 79–83.

[14] Fred H. Goldner and R. R. Ritti, "Professionalization as Career Immobility," *The American Journal of Sociology*, 72 (March, 1967), pp. 491–494.

[15] Harold L. Wilensky, *Intellectuals in Labor Unions: Organizational Pressures on Professional Roles*, Glencoe: The Free Press, 1956.

[16] Paula Brown, "Bureaucracy in a Governmental Laboratory," *Social Forces*, 32 (March, 1954), pp. 259–268.

[17] Donald Pelz and Frank M. Andrews, "Organizational Atmosphere, Motivation and Research Contribution," *The American Behavioral Scientist*, 6 (December, 1962), pp. 43–47. See also, *The Conflict Between the Scientific and the Management Mind*, Princeton: Opinion Research Corporation, 1959.

[18] Etzioni, *op. cit.*, p. 75.

professionals with the Ph.D. degree and those professionals trained as scientists than for professionals with the M.A. or M.S. degree and professionals trained as engineers.

ORGANIZATIONAL UNIT

An equally important conditioning variable is the type of organization in which the professional performs his work. Comparative organizational research shows that the greater the organization's dependence upon research, the more the organization will manifest high professional incentives and low organizational control.[19]

Structural variations *within* an organization may also be apparent. One instance where structural variation might be expected in an organization employing scientists and engineers is between those areas where application and development are the primary goals and those areas where the primary goal is pure or basic research. Most aerospace companies are engaged in both types of activity, but the basic research aspect is usually carried out in a special laboratory that is separated from the larger organizational unit.

This research allows for a comparison of these two very different types of organizational units and thus permits a further evaluation of the hypothesized relationship between organizational structure and work alienation. Specifically, there should be less organizational control and more professional incentives in the laboratory than in the larger unit. Therefore, less alienation from work should be experienced by professionals employed in the laboratory than by professionals employed in the larger organizational unit.

Method

Data were gathered during the summer of 1965 from scientific and engineering personnel employed in two divisions of one of the largest aerospace companies in

the United States. The organization, at the time of the study, employed over 100,000 persons within its five operating divisions and had separate facilities in four states and subsidiaries in Canada. The company is engaged in the manufacture of military aircraft, commercial airliners, supersonic jet transports, helicopters, gas-turbine engines, rocket boosters for spacecraft, intercontinental ballistic missiles, and orbiting space vehicles.

The largest of the five divisions is the Aero-Space Group, containing a missile production center and a space center. Included within the Aero-Space Group are a variety of independent laboratories, testing facilities, manufacturing areas, and the world's largest privately-owned wind tunnel. Shortly after this study was undertaken, a large space-simulation laboratory was completed.

In 1958 the company established a Basic Science Research Laboratory which operates independently from all other laboratories and divisions of the company. The principal product of the Laboratory is the scientific and engineering information made known to other divisions of the company by means of consultation and publication programs. The laboratory has three major objectives: (1) to carry on research programs that will put the company into direct and effective communication with the larger scientific community; (2) to choose and maintain a staff of competent specialists who will provide consulting advice in their chosen fields of specialization; and (3) to engage in exploratory and basic research in fields where new discoveries will be of value to the company's overall operations.[20]

The two divisions thus represent a sharp contrast in the nature of the work situation for the professionals involved. Professionals in the Basic Science Laboratory

---

[19] Kornhauser, *op. cit.*, pp. 148–149.

[20] These objectives were emphasized by the director of the laboratory in conversations with the author and appear in various company documents.

share an environment more like that of the university, whereas professionals in the Aero-Space Group are more representative of persons engaged in traditional research and development work and function primarily as staff personnel within the division.

Subjects for this study are non-supervisory scientists and engineers selected from the Aero-Space Group and the Basic Science Laboratory. All subjects held the degree of M.A., M.S., or Ph.D. in science, engineering, or mathematics. A listing of all employees meeting the above criteria was provided by the company and the selection of respondents was made from this listing. Twenty different types of engineers were represented, ranging from aerospace to electrical to nuclear engineers. Scientists included astronomers, chemists, and physicists. General, applied and theoretical mathematicians were included. Respondents within the two divisions were selected by the following criteria:

1. All Basic Science Laboratory personnel (N=66),
2. All persons in the Aero-Space Group with the degree of Ph.D. (N=74),
3. All persons in the Aero-Space Group with the degree of M.A. or M.S. in science or mathematics (N=164),
4. A 50 percent random sample of all persons in the Aero-Space Group with the degree of M.A. or M.S. in engineering (N=236).

In the analysis to follow, those persons with degrees in mathematics are included with those having degrees in science and both are labeled "scientists." The engineering personnel are treated as a separate group of "engineers." Because of the sampling design, the engineering group is under-represented in terms of their actual proportion in the organization although their proportion in the sample is greater than for any other professional specialty.

Data were gathered by means of a mail-back questionnaire sent to the homes of the study participants. The questionnaire was anonymous and a postcard was included for the respondents to sign and return after they had returned their questionnaires. This procedure allowed for subsequent follow-ups in the case of non-respondents and two such follow-ups were undertaken.

Seventeen of the original 540 subjects had either moved from the area or the addresses provided by the company were incorrect, leaving 523 potential subjects. Of this total, 84 percent returned the questionnaires and 80 percent (N=419) were completed sufficiently to be used in this analysis.

Measures

WORK ALIENATION

The work of professionals, as contrasted with the work of nonprofessionals, is characterized by high intrinsic satisfaction, positive involvement, and commitment to a reference group composed of other professionals.[21] In addition, as Orzack has demonstrated, the work of professionals plays a much more important role in their life than it does for the nonprofessional worker.[22]

For a scientist, the importance of and devotion to a particular style of life and work was best described by Weber. In his essay concerning science as a vocation, he indicates the importance of "inward calling" for the scientist:

. . . whoever lacks the capacity to put on blinders, so to speak, and to come up to the idea that the fate of his soul depends upon whether or not he makes the correct conjecture at this passage of his manuscript may as well stay

[21] Amitai Etzioni, *A Comparative Analysis of Complex Organizations,* Glencoe: The Free Press, 1961, p. 53.
[22] L. H. Orzack, "Work as a Central Life Interest of Professionals," *Social Problems,* 7 (1959), pp. 125–132.

away from science. He will never have what one may call the 'personal experience' of science. Without this strange intoxication, ridiculed by every outsider; without this passion, this 'thousands of years must pass before you enter into life and thousands more wait in silence'—according to whether or not you succeed in making this conjecture; without this, you have *no* calling for science and you should do something else. For nothing is worthy of man as man unless he can pursue it with passionate devotion.[23]

The scientist who is unable to find "self-rewarding work activities to engage him," who does not experience an "intrinsic pride or meaning in his work," and who "works merely for his salary" or other remunerative incentives is experiencing the type of alienation described by Melvin Seeman as self-estrangement.[24] As defined, self-estrangement is *not* the same as dissatisfaction with one's job. As Mills and others have pointed out, a person may be alienated from his work yet still be satisfied with his job.[25]

[23] Hans H. Gerth and C. Wright Mills, eds., *From Max Weber: Essays in Sociology,* New York: Oxford University Press, 1946, p. 135.

[24] Melvin Seeman, "On the Meaning of Alienation," *American Sociological Review,* 24 (December, 1959), p. 790.

[25] Mills argues that to equate alienation with what is commonly measured as "job dissatisfaction" by psychologists and sociologists is to misunderstand Marx. See C. Wright Mills, *The Marxists,* New York: Dell Publishing Company, 1962, p. 86. Harold Wilensky makes the same point and has developed a measure specifically directed toward ascertaining the social-psychological aspects of alienation from work within a framework of role-self analysis. See Harold L. Wilensky, "Work as a Social Problem," in Howard S. Becker, editor, *Social Problems: A Modern Approach,* New York: John Wiley and Sons, 1966, pp. 138–142. However, there does not appear to be agreement concerning this point. Aiken and Hage, for example, have recently developed a measure of alienation from work based on a factor analysis of items concerned with the "degree of satisfaction with various aspects of the respondents' work situation." See Michael

The measure of work alienation employed is a five-item cumulative scale consisting of statements referring to the intrinsic pride or meaning of work. Three statements were developed by the author and two were selected from Morse's scale of "intrinsic pride in work."[26] The statements are:

1. I really don't feel a sense of pride or accomplishment as a result of the type of work that I do.
2. My work gives me a feeling of pride in having done the job well.
3. I very much like the type of work that I am doing.
4. My job gives me a chance to do the things that I do best.
5. My work is my most rewarding experience.

Response categories provided for each statement were: (1) Strongly Agree; (2) Agree; (3) Disagree; and (4) Strongly Disagree. The response distribution to each item was dichotomized between those agreeing and those disagreeing with the statement. This procedure yielded a Guttman scale with the following characteristics: Coefficient of Reproducibility (Goodenough technique) = 0.91; Minimum Marginal Reproducibility = 0.70; Coefficient of Scalability = 0.69; and Coefficient of Sharpness = 0.69.[27]

Aiken and Jerald Hage, "Organizational Alienation: A Comparative Analysis," *American Sociological Review,* 31 (August, 1966), p. 501.

[26] Nancy Morse, *Satisfactions in the White Collar Job,* Ann Arbor: University of Michigan Press, 1953.

[27] The best description of the Goodenough technique is Allen L. Edwards, *Techniques of Attitude Scale Construction,* New York: Appleton-Century-Crofts, 1957, pp. 184 ff. Edwards states that, unlike the C. R. produced by the Cornell technique, the C. R. produced by the Goodenough technique *accurately* represents the extent to which individual responses can be reproduced from scale scores. The Coefficient of Scalability is described in Herbert Menzel, "A New Coefficient for Scalogram Analysis," *Public Opinion Quarterly,* 17 (Summer, 1953), pp. 268–280. The Coefficient of Sharpness is described by James A.

The scale scores were trichotomized to obtain three levels of work alienation. Persons with a scale score of "0" (30 percent) were classified as low, those with scale scores of "1" or "2" (40 percent) were classified as medium, and those with scale scores of "3," "4," or "5" (30 percent) were classified as high in experiencing alienation from work.[28]

ORGANIZATIONAL CONTROL

Organization implies the coordination of diverse activities necessary for effective goal achievement. Such coordination requires some mode of control over these diverse activities. Traditional bureaucratic modes of control differ significantly from the mode of control deemed appropriate by professionals. Whereas organizations tend to be structured hierarchically, professions tend to be organized in terms of a "colleague group of equals" with ultimate control being exercised by the group itself.[29] Hence, bureaucratic control violates the profession's traditional mandate of freedom from control by outsiders.[30]

One specific area where the nature of the organizational control structure becomes manifest is in the type of supervisor-employee relationship. This is a major source of conflict for the professional as it is for other types of organizational participants. In this respect, Baumgartel suggests that three styles of supervision (or leadership) can be identified, based upon rates of interaction, degree of influence, and decision-making. The three styles of supervision are: *Directive* (low rate of interaction and unilateral decision-making by the supervisor); *Participatory* (high rate of interaction and joint decision-making by supervisor and researcher); and *Laissez-Faire* (low rate of interaction, with the researcher making most of the decisions).[31]

In his study of scientists and supervisors in the National Institutes of Health, Baumgartel found that research performance, job satisfaction, and positive attitudes toward the supervisor were highest for Participatory, lowest for Directive, and intermediate for Laissez-Faire supervisors. These findings differ sharply from those reported by Argyris. Eighty-seven percent of the foremen studied by Argyris report that in order to be effective, they must try to keep everyone busy with work that guarantees a fair take-home pay, to distribute the easy and tough jobs fairly, and *to leave the employees alone as much as possible.* Argyris concludes that a successful foreman, from the point of view of both foremen and employees, is neither directive nor is he an expert in human relations.[32]

To determine the types of supervision evident in the present organization, the following question was asked:

[footnote 27 continued
Davis, "On Criteria for Scale Relationships," *The American Journal of Sociology,* 63 (January, 1958), pp. 371–380.

[28] Response categories were reversed in the first item to make them consistent with the others. Persons disagreeing or strongly disagreeing with each item were coded as "1" and those agreeing or strongly agreeing were coded as "0." Thus, a scale score of 5 means that the person "disagreed" with all five items and a scale score of 0 means that he "agreed" with all five items.

[29] Etzioni, *Modern Organizations, op. cit.,* p. 80.

[30] See for example, Eliot Freidson and Buford Rhea, "Knowledge and Judgment in Professional Evaluations," *Administrative Science Quarterly,* 10 (June, 1965), pp. 107–108, Ernest Greenwood, "Attributes of a Profession," *Social Work,* (July, 1957), pp. 45–55, and Everett C. Hughes, *Men and Their Work,* Glencoe: The Free Press, 1958.

[31] Howard Baumgartel, "Leadership, Motivations, and Attitudes in Research Laboratories," *Journal of Social Issues,* 12 (1956), p. 30, and "Leadership Style as a Variable in Research Administration," *Administrative Science Quarterly,* 2 (December, 1957), pp. 344–360.

[32] Chris Argyris, *Understanding Organizational Behavior,* Homewood: The Dorsey Press, 1960, p. 94. Italics added. Aiken and Hage found that rule observation, which implies close supervision by superiors, was the single best predictor of alienation from expressive relations. See Aiken and Hage, *op. cit.,* p. 506.

Which of the following statements most nearly represents the type of work relationship that exists between you and your immediate supervisor?

1. We discuss things a great deal and come to a mutual decision regarding the task at hand.
2. We discuss things a great deal and his decision is usually adopted.
3. We discuss things a great deal and my decision is usually adopted.
4. We don't discuss things very much and his decision is usually adopted.
5. We don't discuss things very much and I make most of the decisions.

Persons responding with statement number 4 above were classified as working for a Directive type supervisor (16 percent), those responding with statement number 5 above were classified as working for a Laissez-Faire type (45 percent), and those responding with statements 1, 2, or 3 above were classified as working for a Participatory type supervisor (39 percent).

The second empirical indicator of organizational control concerns the professional's freedom to choose or select the types of research projects in which he is implicated. Leo Meltzer found that scientists in industrial organizations usually have ample funds and facilities for research but very little freedom in the selection of research projects. Conversely, scientists in universities are usually short on funds but have freedom to do what they wish. Both freedom and funds were found to be correlated with publication rate, but were negatively correlated with each other. Meltzer concludes that freedom to choose research projects is representative of other variables which facilitate the intrinsic satisfactions which scientists derive from the actual content of their work.[33]

To ascertain the degree of freedom accorded professionals in this study, the following question was asked:

In general, how much choice do you have concerning the types of research projects in which you are involved?
1 ... Almost no choice
2 ... Very little
3 ... Some
4 ... A great deal

Persons responding "Almost no choice" or "Very little" were classified as low (38 percent), those indicating they had "Some" choice were classified as medium (40 percent), and those indicating they had "A great deal" of choice were classified as high (22 percent) in freedom to choose research projects.

PROFESSIONAL INCENTIVES

Previous research findings describe the incentives most sought after by scientists and engineers as (1) freedom to publish the results of their research, (2) funds for attending professional meetings, (3) freedom and facilities to aid in their research, (4) promotion based upon technical competence, and (5) opportunities to improve their professional knowledge and skills.[34] It is more common, however, for industry to slight professional incentives in favor of organizational incentives, such as promotions in the line, increases in authority, and increases in salary. This is the case because organizational incentives have proved satisfactory for other employees in the past and differing incentive structures are viewed as competing sources of loyalty.[35]

[33] Leo Meltzer, "Scientific Productivity in Organizational Settings," *Journal of Social Issues,* 12 (1956), pp. 32–40.

[34] See, for example, John W. Riegal, *Intangible Rewards for Engineers and Scientists,* Ann Arbor: University of Michigan Press, 1958, pp. 12–13, and Todd LaPorte, "Conditions of Strain and Accommodation in Industrial Research Organizations," *Administrative Science Quarterly,* 10 (June, 1965), pp. 33–34.

[35] Kornhauser, *op. cit.,* p. 135. The dependence of staff on line is discussed in Melville Dalton, *Men Who Manage,* New York: John Wiley and Sons, 1959.

Two empirical indicators of the professional incentive structure are utilized in this research. The first, *Professional Climate,* is a general index of the professional incentives made available to the professional by the organization and is composed of two items:

1. (Company) provides us with many opportunities to obtain professional recognition outside the company.
1 . . . Strongly disagree
2 . . . Disagree
3 . . . Agree
4 . . . Strongly agree
2. In general, how much time are you provided to work on or pursue your own research interests?
1 . . . Almost none
2 . . . Very little
3 . . . Some
4 . . . A great deal

The response distribution for each item was dichotomized between responses 2 and 3. Persons agreeing with the first statement and persons responding "some" or "a great deal" to the second question were classified as high. These two dichotomies were then cross-classified to obtain three levels of perceived professional climate: those high on both dimensions (28 percent), those high on one dimension (34 percent), and those low on both dimensions (38 percent).

A second indicator, *Company Encouragement,* attempts to discern the organization's encouragement of specific professional incentives. Three items comprise this index:

1. (Company) encourages us to publish the results of our research.
2. (Company) encourages us to attend our professional meetings.
3. (Company) encourages us to further our professional training by attending special lectures and/or classes at academic institutions.

Response categories provided for each

question were Strongly Disagree, Disagree, Agree, and Strongly Agree. The response distribution for each item was dichotomized between those who agreed and those who disagreed with the statement. Those disagreeing with all or two of the statements were classified as low (35 percent), those agreeing with two of the statements were classified as medium (28 percent), and those agreeing with all three statements (37 percent) were classified as perceiving high encouragement from the company.

Results

The first hypothesis states that alienation from work will be positively associated with degree of organizational control and negatively associated with number of professional incentives. Table 1 shows support for this general hypothesis.

There are fairly large differences between those professionals working for Directive and Participatory supervisors in the proportions with differing degrees of alienation. However the proportions of those with differing degrees of work alienation who work for Participatory and Laissez-Faire supervisors are almost identical. Thus, the major difference in the degree of alienation experience by these professionals occurs between those who work for a Directive Supervisor and those working for *either* of the other types.

The relationship between company encouragement and work alienation is much the same. Differences exist between those professionals with low and high company encouragement who experience alienation; however, the proportions of those experiencing differing degrees of alienation with medium and low company encouragement are very similar.

LENGTH OF PROFESSIONAL TRAINING

The original relationships just examined are expected to be conditional relationships. It was hypothesized that the relationships should be stronger for those pro-

Table 1. Relationship Between Work Alienation and Four Indicators of Organizational Control and Professional Incentive Structures

CONTROL-INCENTIVE STRUCTURE	WORK ALIENATION LOW	MED.	HIGH	N
Supervisor Type				
Directive	.10	.33	.57	63
Participatory	.32	.42	.26	158
Laissez-Faire	.35	.42	.23	176
		Gamma = —.30		
Research Choice				
Low	.11	.34	.55	150
Med.	.32	.48	.20	158
High	.56	.40	.04	87
		Gamma = —.64		
Professional Climate				
Low	.15	.34	.51	155
Med.	.29	.45	.26	133
High	.51	.43	.06	106
		Gamma = —.55		
Company Encouragement				
Low	.20	.39	.41	142
Med.	.26	.38	.36	107
High	.42	.44	.14	144
		Gamma = —.35		

fessionals with advanced training. Table 2 shows strong support for this expectation.

The relationship obtained in each partial is consistent in direction with that expected and the degree of association is much stronger for those professionals with the Ph.D. degree. In addition, the form of the relationships involving type of supervisor and company encouragement differs in the two partials.

The importance of length of professional training on the relationship between type of supervisor and work alienation is clear. The relationship obtained for those with the M.A. degree is similar to the original relationship. For those with the Ph.D. degree, however, type of supervisor is important and is reflected in the differences in degree of work alienation evident among professionals working for the three types of supervisors. The propor-

tions with various degrees of alienation are about the same for both Ph.D.'s and M.A.'s who work for a Directive supervisor. However, the Ph.D.'s differ from the M.A.'s with respect to the importance of the other two supervisor types. While there is no difference among those M.A.'s who experience high alienation, there is a 17 percent difference among the Ph.D.'s. Conversely, for those experiencing low alienation there is a 10 percent difference between those working for the two supervisor types. In fact, 56 percent of those with the Ph.D. degree experience low alienation under a Laissez-Faire supervisor as compared with only 27 percent of those with the M.A. degree.

The relationships obtained between company encouragement and work alienation are similar. As with type of supervisor, the partial obtained for those with the M.A. degree is very similar to that

Table 2. Relationship Between Work Alienation and Four Indicators of
Organizational Control and Professional Incentive Structures: by Length of
Professional Training

CONTROL-INCENTIVE STRUCTURE	LENGTH OF PROFESSIONAL TRAINING							
	M.A. DEGREE				Ph.D. DEGREE			
	WORK ALIENATION				WORK ALIENATION			
	LOW	MED.	HIGH	N	LOW	MED.	HIGH	N
Supervisory Type								
Directive	.10	.30	.60	52	.11	.33	.56	9
Participatory	.28	.47	.25	124	.46	.24	.30	33
Laissez-Faire	.27	.47	.26	122	.56	.31	.13	52
	Gamma = —.25				Gamma = —.40			
Research Choice								
Low	.11	.36	.53	131	.17	.17	.66	18
Med.	.33	.50	.17	127	.33	.34	.33	27
High	.42	.53	.05	38	.67	.31	.02	49
	Gamma = —.59				Gamma = —.71			
Professional Climate								
Low	.17	.34	.49	132	.09	.32	.59	22
Med.	.26	.50	.24	107	.48	.22	.30	23
High	.38	.55	.07	58	.67	.29	.04	48
	Gamma = —.45				Gamma = —.68			
Company Encouragement								
Low	.18	.42	.40	117	.29	.29	.42	24
Med.	.21	.42	.37	79	.41	.22	.37	27
High	.34	.48	.18	100	.63	.32	.05	41
	Gamma = —.29				Gamma = —.48			

observed in the original relationship, with little difference in degree of alienation evident for those with low and medium company encouragement. However, for the Ph.D.'s, these differences are more apparent and the degree of association is very different in the two partials. For the Ph.D.'s, the difference between those perceiving low and high company encouragement who experience high work alienation is 37 percent as compared with only 12 percent for those with the M.A. degree. Conversely, the same difference for those experiencing low alienation is 34 percent for the Ph.D.'s and only 14 percent for the M.A.'s.

TYPE OF PROFESSIONAL TRAINING

The strength of the original relationships is also expected to vary with type of

professional training. Specifically, the relationships should be stronger for those trained as scientists than for those trained as engineers. Table 3 shows only partial support for this expectation.

The relationship between type of supervisor and work alienation again remains consistent in direction but differs greatly in magnitude between the two partials. In the partial obtained for the engineering personnel, the relationship is similar to that observed in the original relationship and among professionals with the M.A. degree. Working for a Directive supervisor is associated with high alienation but little difference is evident in the degree of alienation between those persons working for Participatory and Laissez-Faire supervisors. In the partial obtained for the scientific personnel, however, there

Table 3. Relationship Between Work Alienation and Four Indicators of Organizational Control and Professional Incentive Structures: by Type of Professional Training

CONTROL-INCENTIVE STRUCTURE	TYPE OF PROFESSIONAL TRAINING							
	ENGINEERS				SCIENTISTS			
	WORK ALIENATION				WORK ALIENATION			
	LOW	MED.	HIGH	N	LOW	MED.	HIGH	N
Supervisory Type								
Directive	.09	.35	.56	32	.10	.28	.62	29
Participatory	.30	.42	.28	90	.34	.42	.24	67
Laissez-Faire	.21	.47	.32	89	.51	.36	.13	85
	Gamma= —.12				Gamma= —.49			
Research Choice								
Low	.10	.38	.52	92	.14	.28	.58	57
Med.	.26	.52	.22	89	.43	.40	.17	65
High	.59	.37	.03	27	.55	.42	.03	60
	Gamma= —.61				Gamma= —.60			
Professional Climate								
Low	.16	.31	.53	89	.15	.37	.48	65
Med.	.20	.53	.27	74	.43	.34	.23	56
High	.41	.50	.09	46	.59	.38	.03	60
	Gamma= —.49				Gamma= —.58			
Company Encouragement								
Low	.21	.42	.37	87	.19	.35	.46	54
Med.	.23	.35	.42	60	.30	.40	.30	46
High	.24	.53	.23	62	.57	.45	.08	79
	Gamma= —.13				Gamma= —.55			

is clearly a difference in the degree of alienation experienced by professionals working for all three types of supervisors. Working for a Directive supervisor leads to high alienation, but 11 percent more scientists experience high alienation under Participatory supervisors than under Laissez-Faire supervisors (as compared with a difference of only 4 percent for the engineering group).

Thus, the relationship between type of supervisor and degree of work alienation is conditional with respect to type and length of professional training. For those professionals with M.A. degrees or who have been trained as engineers, the major differences in alienation appear between those working for a Directive as opposed to *either* a Participatory or Laissez-Faire supervisor. For those persons with the Ph.D. degree or who were trained as sci-

entists, however, the less the supervision (as all three types are differentiated), the less the degree of alienation from work.

The relationship between company encouragement and work alienation is consistent in direction with that obtained in the original relationship but is much stronger for scientists than for engineers. For the scientists, the difference between those who perceive high and low company encouragement who experience high alienation is 38 percent, as compared with a difference of only 14 percent for the engineers. Conversely, there is little difference in degree of alienation among engineers who perceive low as opposed to high company encouragement. For the scientists, however, there is a corresponding difference of 38 percent.

Thus, the relationship between company encouragement and alienation from work is consistent with the general hypotheses. The greater the company encouragement, the less the feelings of work alienation among professionals. This relationship is stronger for those with the Ph.D. degree and for those trained as scientists than for those with the M.A. degree and for those trained as engineers.

Type of professional training *does not* appear to be an important conditioning factor in the relationships involving freedom of research choice or professional climate. The relationships obtained are strong but similar in both partials. These two variables were most strongly associated with work alienation in the original relationships. The degree of association remained high in the partials when length of professional training was controlled (although the relationships were stronger for the Ph.D.'s than for the M.A.'s, as expected). Unlike the relationships obtained with type of supervisor or company encouragement, however, the relationship between these variables and work alienation remain very strong and about the same for both scientific and engineering personnel.

This unanticipated finding suggests that these two aspects of the organizational structure are important to *both* scientists and engineers. Moreover, since these relationships also remained strong when length of professional training was controlled, it may be concluded that having freedom to choose research projects and working in a professional atmosphere are more important than type of supervisor or amount of company encouragement as these aspects of the organizational structure are related to the experiencing of work alienation among professionals.

ORGANIZATIONAL UNIT

As previously described, the goals of the Laboratory are more concerned with pure or basic scientific research whereas the goals of the Aero-Space Group are more concerned with traditional research and development work. Therefore, the Laboratory should be characterized by less organizational control and more professional incentives than the Aero-Space Group. In addition, since alienation from work is related to differences in organizational structure, professionals working in the Laboratory should experience less alienation than professionals working in the Aero-Space Group.

Table 4 shows striking differences in the control and incentive structures of the two organizational units. In each of the four comparisons, there is less control and more incentives in the Laboratory than in the Aero-Space Group.

That these differences in organizational structure are reflected in differences in the degree of work alienation experienced by the professionals is shown in Table 5. In the Laboratory, only 4 percent experienced high work alienation as compared with 34 percent of those persons in the Aero-Space Group. Moreover, 63 percent of those in the Laboratory experienced low alienation as compared to only 25 percent of those in the Aero-Space Group. Thus, type of organizational unit is clearly related to degree of work alienation in the expected direction.

A question may arise concerning this interpretation. It is clear that the properties of the organizational structure dealt with here are defined empirically in terms of the professional's *perception* of the type of structure in which he is employed. Therefore, a question may arise as to whether the respondents are *accurately* perceiving the structure or merely perceiving it in such a manner as to be *consistent* with their previous training.

This question is a crucial one since all of the previous findings rely upon empirical indicators which ask the respondent to describe the structure as he perceives it. Thus, these relationships may reflect an association between the way these persons perceive the structure and work alienation rather than an association between organizational structure and work

*Table 4. Respondents' Perceptions of Organizational Control and
Professional Incentive Structures: By Organizational Unit*

| | ORGANIZATIONAL UNIT | | | |
| CONTROL-INCENTIVE STRUCTURE | AERO-SPACE GROUP | | BASIC LABORATORY | |
	PERCENT	NUMBER	PERCENT	NUMBER
Supervisor				
Directive	17	(64)	2	(1)
Participatory	43	(158)	20	(10)
Laissez-Faire	40	(145)	78	(38)
Research Choice				
Low	42	(151)	8	(4)
Med.	44	(162)	6	(3)
High	14	(51)	86	(43)
Professional Climate				
Low	44	(158)	0	(0)
Med.	38	(136)	10	(5)
High	18	(64)	90	(45)
Company Encouragement				
Low	40	(142)	4	(2)
Med.	28	(100)	20	(10)
High	32	(112)	76	(37)
Total	100	(369)	100	(50)

*Table 5. Degree of Work Alienation in Aero-Space and Basic Laboratory
Organizational Units*

| | | WORK ALIENATION | | |
ORGANIZATIONAL UNIT	LOW	MED.	HIGH	N
Aero-Space Group	.25	.41	.34	349
Basic Laboratory	.63	.33	.04	49
		Gamma = —.69		

alienation. Moreover, it is clear from inspection of the previous tables that there is a "hidden" association between length and type of professional training and work alienation. Therefore, it is possible that the differences in degree of work alienation observed between the two organizational units is simply a result of the differing *composition* of the members within each unit with respect to length and type of professional training. To answer this question, it is necessary to examine the relationship between organizational unit and degree of work alienation while controlling for length and type of professional training.[36]

[36] This type of analysis controls for the compositional effect in terms of the similarity in length and type of professional training of the professionals employed by each unit. It should be indicated that differences in recruitment procedures, in professional ability, and in type of work actually engaged in by the professionals may also yield differences in the kinds of professionals employed by each unit and thus affect the relationship between their perceptions of the organizational structure and degree of work alienation.

Tables 6 and 7 show the partials obtained when length and type of professional training are controlled. It will be noted that the direction of association remains consistent across the four partials. The difference between Aero-Space Group and Basic Laboratory personnel in experiencing low work alienation is over 30 percent in all four partials, with Laboratory personnel experiencing much less alienation than Aero-Space personnel. Moreover, the difference between personnel with high work alienation in the two units is also 30 percent in three of four partials. This finding, then, lends additional support to the findings concerning the effects of organizational structure on feelings of work alienation among professional personnel.

Summary and Conclusions

This study examined the relationship between the type of organizational structure in which the professional performs his work activity and his experiencing feelings of alienation from work. This re-

lationship was explored for each of four empirical indicators of organizational structure for all professionals, and separately for professionals differing in length and type of professional training and for professionals working in two very different organizational units.

In general, the findings of this research support the hypothesis that alienation from work is a consequence of the professional-bureaucratic dilemma for industrial scientists and engineers. Differences in type of supervision, freedom of research choice, professional climate, and company encouragement were associated with degree of work alienation in the expected manner.

The conditioning effects of length and type of professional training on the above relationships were only partially supported by these data. Alienation from work was more strongly associated with type of supervisor and degree of company encouragement among scientists and professionals with advanced training than for engineers and professionals with less ad-

Table 6. Degree of Work Alienation in Aero-Space and Basic Laboratory Organizational Units: By Length of Professional Training

	LENGTH OF PROFESSIONAL TRAINING							
	M.A. DEGREE				Ph.D. DEGREE			
	WORK ALIENATION				WORK ALIENATION			
ORGANIZATIONAL UNIT	LOW	MED.	HIGH	N	LOW	MED.	HIGH	N
Aero-Space Group	.23	.44	.33	288	.36	.29	.35	59
Basic Laboratory	.54	.46	.00	13	.67	.28	.05	36
	Gamma = —.48				Gamma = —.59			

Table 7. Degree of Work Alienation in Aero-Space and Basic Laboratory Organizational Units: By Type of Professional Training

	TYPE OF PROFESSIONAL TRAINING							
	ENGINEERS				SCIENTISTS			
	WORK ALIENATION				WORK ALIENATION			
ORGANIZATIONAL UNIT	LOW	MED.	HIGH	N	LOW	MED.	HIGH	N
Aero-Space Group	.21	.43	.36	199	.31	.38	.31	147
Basic Laboratory	.58	.42	.00	12	.65	.30	.05	37
	Gamma = —.75				Gamma = —.62			

vanced training. Freedom of research choice and professional climate were strongly associated with work alienation for all professionals. Moreover, these relationships remained strong when length and type of professional training were controlled.

This unanticipated finding is important when it is recalled that the largest group of professionals employed by the organization are engineers with M.A. or M.S. degrees. These data suggest, therefore, that research freedom and professional atmosphere are more important to the majority of professional personnel than are type of supervision and specific professional incentives (as these factors are related to the experiencing of work alienation).

Although the relationships involving research freedom and professional atmosphere are *similar* for both scientists and engineers, these professionals may be experiencing work alienation for *different* reasons. Freedom of research choice, "having time to pursue one's own research interests," and having "opportunities to obtain professional recognition outside the company" may be interpreted by these professionals in terms of different goals and reference groups. If scientists and engineers differ in their professional goals, then the alienation manifested by engineers may result from their lack of power and participation in organizational affairs whereas the alienation manifested by scientists may reflect their lack of autonomy to pursue their work with the passion Weber described. This interpretation is consistent with the findings obtained in the relationships involving company encouragement and type of supervisor. That these relationships were stronger for the scientists and for those with advanced training may reflect the facts that the specific incentives comprising the company encouragement index are more important for the attainment of scientific than organizational goals, and that working for Participatory supervisors reflects participation in the decision-making process for engineers and violation of professional freedom for scientists who prefer to be left alone as much as possible.

Striking differences were found in the organizational structures of the Aero-Space Group and the Basic Science Laboratory. In addition, degree of work alienation was found to be highly related to type of organizational unit, with Laboratory personnel experiencing a very low degree of alienation as compared with Aero-Space personnel. This relationship remained consistent with respect to direction and degree when length and type of professional training were controlled.

The very different organizational structures evident in the Laboratory and the Aero-Space Group, as well as the effect of such structures upon work alienation for different types of professionals within these units, raise questions concerning the empirical generality of many studies to date which have focused on the Laboratory rather than the larger unit in their analysis. This research suggests that caution should accompany attempts to generalize across units within an organization. Studies of Laboratory personnel may yield findings very different from those obtained from professionals working in the larger organization—where most professional scientists and engineers are in fact employed.

PART V

ALIENATION FROM THE

POLITICAL SYSTEM

Introduction

In terms of the magnitude and pervasiveness of its influence on all members of the society, the political sector is the most important of the social systems considered in this book. Political alienation, therefore, may have very far reaching implications. Riots, violent protests, emigration and expatriation, and other behaviors that appear to express rejection of the political system or its norms and values are strong testimony of the importance of political alienation as a force in contemporary political life.

   A basic question to which research in this area has been directed is the nature and meaning of the concept of political alienation. This is one of the major concerns of my study, which opens this section. In this article, I consider how several of the dimensions of alienation identified by Seeman are relevant and meaningful in analyzing *political* alienation. The broad concept of political alienation is broken down into feelings of political powerlessness, normlessness, meaninglessness, and isolation, and each of these subtypes is described. Then, working with a large number of questions that tap different aspects of political alienation, factor analysis is used to demonstrate that there are empirical, as well as theoretical, grounds for considering political alienation as a multidimensional concept. Since I was able to measure two of the different types of political alienation, I then asked whether they were related in the same way to a variety of social and social psychological conditions that may be causes of political alienation. I found that this was not always the case. For example, although blacks generally score much higher than whites on the dimension of alienation called "perceived political normlessness," they do not feel much more "powerless" than whites. The fact that the two types of political alienation have different correlates indicates that it is important to specify which kind of political alienation one has in mind in discussing this concept. Because of their differences, powerlessness and normlessness are likely to lead to different types of political behavior, and I conclude my analysis with a discussion of the relationship between the two types of political alienation and their implications for peaceful or revolutionary participation in political systems.

Both of the types of alienation discussed in my study involve discrepancies between some ideal state and actual social conditions as perceived by the respondent. Normlessness involves a comparison of the actions of political elites with norms for appropriate behavior; powerlessness implies a judgment of the congruence betwen democratic theories of citizen influence on political decision making and the actual extent of such influence. However, the respondent's commitment to the values represented by the ideal state implied in each dimension of alienation is *assumed* rather than explicitly measured, on the premise that the norms involved are so basic to the American political system that they are probably universally shared in this study population.

The analysis by Samuel Patterson, G. R. Boynton, and Ronald Hedlund illustrates a more direct measurement of the perceived discrepancy between an ideal state and actual social conditions, as related to a state legislature. In this study, each individual first sets up his own normative standards for the operation of the legislature and then describes his perceptions of reality. The difference between the normative standard and the reality description is an empirical measure of the discrepancy between the expectations each citizen has about a political institution and his perception of how that institution actually works. The authors then investigate the extent to which this discrepancy is related to a more general measure of support for the legislature as a political institution. In this way, they directly test the hypothesis that alienation is produced by a discrepancy between expectations and perceptions.

It is noteworthy that the object of alienation or support in the Patterson study is not the political system in general but one particular political institution—the legislature of the state of Iowa. Measures of alienation that are specific to smaller political units within the nation may eventually lead to an increased focus on, and better understanding of, the ways in which particular types of political structure may increase or decrease feelings of political alienation. Particularly as discussions of political change and alternate forms of political decision making gain ground, there is a greater need for research emphasizing attitudes toward *specific* political institutions and on the relationship between types of political structure and levels of political alienation. This problem will be discussed in greater detail below.

Other analyses of the concept of political alienation are reported by Aberbach (1969), Agger, Goldstein and Pearl (1961), Lane (1962), and Olsen (1969). The concept of political "powerlessness," or some variant of it such as "futility," appears in practically all discussions of political alienation. This core aspect of estrangement from the political system has been explored in voting studies for a number of years, particularly in the work of Campbell and his associates (1954, 1960). In these studies, the concept is viewed from the positive perspective and called "political efficacy."

The selection by Joel Aberbach and Jack Walker focuses specifically on racial differences in political alienation. They, too, are concerned with definition and measurement of this concept and concentrate on a type of alienation that they call political "trust." One of their concerns is the differing conditions which lead to political distrust among whites and blacks in the Detroit area. One explanation of distrust that is of particular interest involves a group of variables considered collectively as "political expectations." Many of the questions used to measure political expectations are similar to questions that are used in my study to measure "political powerlessness" and "political normlessness." That Aberbach and Walker interpret as measures of *denial of expectations* questions used elsewhere to measure *alienation* again suggests the root concern of the concept of alienation with the aspiration-reality discrepancy.

Aberbach and Walker are concerned with the relationship between political trust and the development of hostile racial ideologies among both whites and blacks. An important part of this concern is their analysis of the types of behavior which are likely to be associated with low levels of political trust. Among blacks, a very interesting relationship is found between experiences with discrimination, political trust, and the individual's willingness to participate in a riot. This aspect of the analysis is formally similar to the "structure-individual characteristic interaction" approach discussed in the introduction to Part IV. In this type of approach, the effects of a particular social structure are examined separately in groups which differ in some individual characteristic. For example, Pearlin studied the relationship between control structure in the hospital and work alienation, among both obeisant and nonobeisant individuals and found that the degree of bureaucratization is related to alienation only for individuals who tend *not* to be submissive to authority. Here Aberbach and Walker use an analogous explanatory model emphasizing the interaction of perceptions of social structure and political attitudes in leading to willingness to riot. The structure involved in this case is the extent of racial discrimination. Using reported instances of discrimination as a subjective reflection of this structure, they find that *only when political trust is low* is there a very strong positive relationship between experienced discrimination and willingness to riot. Thus, even when discrimination is severe, recourse to extreme behavior may be forestalled as long as political alienation has not yet developed. As Aberbach and Walker point out, a "reservoir of good will" (that is, high political trust) provides time for society to correct discriminatory conditions. This study concludes with a thoughtful essay on policy recommendations to decrease racial polarization.

The attention paid by Aberbach and Walker to the effect of trust levels on willingness to participate in a riot points to an important trend in research on political alienation. A number of studies carried out in the early sixties reported that political alienation was related to negative voting on community issues. Gamson (1961) argued that alienated voters perceived the fluoridation controversy as an opportunity to retaliate against disliked local authorities who favored fluoridation. They therefore voted more heavily against fluoridation proposals than nonalienated citizens. Similarly, Horton and Thompson (1962) found that political alienation led to voting against school bond proposals. By the middle sixties, however, more serious forms of social protest were emerging, and research on the consequences of alienation shifted from concern with voting patterns to an investigation of the importance of attitudes of alienation in other types of protest behavior.

For example, a study by Ransford (1968) carried out shortly after the Watts riot of 1965 investigated the conditions under which blacks living in that area would be willing to use violence to achieve racial goals. He considered the effects of political powerlessness and a structural variable, the degree of isolation from interpersonal contact with whites. Ransford found that isolation from whites is an important precondition for willingness to use violence *only when the individual also feels a high degree of powerlessness.* Ghetto-type isolation *alone* is shown to be insufficient to produce violent responses to social conditions. Note that the findings of Ransford and of Aberbach and Walker support each other in showing how racial discrimination is not a sufficient condition for extreme protest but that, if political alienation is *also* present, racial isolation and discrimination can trigger off violent protest behavior.

A further analysis of the relationship between powerlessness and black militancy was recently reported by Forward and Williams (1970), who suggest a possible contradiction among different theories which use powerlessness as an explanation of riot participation. Contrary to the hypothesis that high powerlessness tends to *increase* the propensity to participate in riots, an alternative theory is that those who feel powerless will be *less* willing to use violence to fight for their rights. One of the implications of the Forward and Williams study is that the concept of "powerlessness" must be further refined. They find, for example, that student riot supporters in Detroit feel *personally* very efficacious (that is, had *low* scores on a *personal* powerlessness measure), but do feel great external barriers in *the political and social system.* This finding demonstrates the need to specify the *referent* of an attitude of alienation. A sense of personal control in daily life activities is not necessarily highly correlated with control over social structure. In the particular case of a group which has experienced significant barriers to effective political participation over a long period of time, the discrepancy in the two areas may be great. A generalized, rather than structure-specific, measure of powerlessness may then be very misleading. The emphasis on these separate aspects of powerlessness and the evidence showing that riot supporters are higher than nonsupporters in *personal* control also lends credence to a hypothesis advanced in my typology of alienation and political engagement. I suggest there that revolutionary leaders may come from that small segment of the population that feels high political alienation, including political powerlessness, but also a strong sense of *personal* power or control. The reasoning here is that a sense of *personal* control would encourage people to do something about a feeling of *political powerlessness*. Since individuals who express political powerlessness feel that the system is not amenable to change through regularized procedures, they may resort to riots or other destructive types of protest. On the other hand, given high political powerlessness, *and high personal powerlessness also,* it seems more likely that the individual will tend to withdraw from any type of political activity. Socialization practices stressing the worthiness and pride of groups with little *political* power will undoubtedly increase the num- of people in disadvantaged social groups who express the somewhat anomalous combination of personal efficacy and political powerlessness.

Interest in the socialization of political attitudes has led to increasing attention to the attitudes of children. The bulk of this research concludes that children typically have quite favorable attitudes toward political objects. Greenstein's (1960) research on perceptions of "the benevolent leader" is a classic statement of this finding. However, the samples used by many investigators of political socialization have systematically omitted minority groups. Since we know from studies of adults that political alienation is generally more prevalent in minority and low socio-economic status groups, it is highly likely that the type of samples used seriously affects the conclusions reached in many of the studies of political attitudes among children.

To deal specifically with this problem, Dean Jaros, Herbert Hirsch, and Frederic Fleron partially replicate two previous studies of political attitudes among children and young adults, but they study a sample of students living in Appalachia. By almost any standards, these youths live in abject poverty. The average socio-economic level of their families is far below that of youngsters studied by most other investigators. Not surprisingly, attitudes toward the political system in this group differ markedly from the attitudes reported in many previous studies. Appalachian youth appear to be part of an alienated, rather than supportive, sub-culture. Findings consistent with these on the difference between political alienation levels of black and white youth have recently been reported by Greenberg (1970) and Lyons (1970).

The reader may have noted that the nature of the research on political alienation is generally quite unlike that devoted to alienation from work. It will be useful, in developing a perspective on the political alienation literature, to focus more specifically on some of these differences.

One very basic difference between studies of work alienation and studies of political alienation lies in the type of referent to which the attitudes in question are directed. The referent of political alienation is usually assumed to be the political system of an entire country, or occasionally of smaller though still sizable political units such as cities or states. Frequently the precise referent is unspecified, and questions used to measure alienation refer very generally to "politics" or "government." (The Patterson study is a partial exception to these generalizations.) This is quite a different approach from that used by researchers studying alienation from work, who generally do not attempt to measure alienation from *the economic system* in its totality. They instead adopt a more specific focus on working conditions at the individual's job and the particular tasks he performs. Thus, it is not capitalism or socialism, for example, that serve as referents of alienation in the studies included in Part IV but rather the work people do in particular firms and industries. This difference in the character of the referent of alienation has important implications for the type of research that is carried out and for the kinds of variables that are investigated as causes of alienation.

One implication is that, although structural variables of the work situation play a dominant role as independent variables in studies of alienation from work, the major independent variables in studies of political alienation are more frequently characteristics of individual persons. Thus, rather than focusing on variables such as access to political decision-making, for example, researchers study differences in alienation among social groups.

This difference in orientation is an outgrowth of the fact that political alienation is defined in terms of the political system of a large social unit. It would facilitate the study of the effect of political structure on attitudes of political alienation if political systems came in as small and researchable units as the firm or industry. But it is difficult to find such analogues in the political system. Significant political units tend to be much larger and more encompassing, and hence there is much less variance in the political structure relevant to a given group of people than there is in their work places. For example, if one were to carry out a survey of attitudes of alienation with a sample of several hundred people in a given city, it would normally yield a very large number of different work places and kinds of work situations but only one significant political unit would be implicated. Since the political structure is a constant in this situation (because all the people in the sample live in the same political unit), differences in their levels of political alienation would have to be explained by *other* variables, such as their individual characteristics or their differential *perceptions* of the constant political structure.

Because political decision-making systems tend to be made up of very complex patterns of interaction, it is also difficult to define valid operational measures of structural variables such as "access." For example, in his study of *work* alienation, Pearlin used, as a measure of control structure, the number of steps in the hierarchy between an individual and the supervisor who has most say over his work activities. Some individuals are supervised by a person immediately superior to them in the work hierarchy while others need to take direction from someone several steps removed. It is clear that the possibilities for access to decision-making authorities differ in these situations. The student of *political* alienation is also interested in access to decision-making authority, but he is not likely to have available such a convenient and direct measure of this concept. He may, however, give structural *interpretations* to the variables he does have available, most frequently individual characteristics. It may be assumed, for example, that socio-economic groups differ in the extent of their political influence. Membership in a particular income group may therefore be used as an indirect measure of access to political decision-makers. When race is used as a variable leading to political alienation, explanations of the relationship will generally be cast in terms of the social implications of being black. In such cases, race is being used as a proxy measure of probable experiences with political structure. Almost all demographic or sociological variables can be used in this way. When Litt (1963) found that political cynicism in Boston increased with length of time individuals had lived in that city, he attributed this to the greater opportunities longer term residents had had *to become familiar with corrupt politics in that city* and thus focused on the social structural reasons for increased alienation. It is not that people get bored with, and therefore alienated from, city government as they live in Boston longer but rather that they probably come to know more about the actual structure of Boston politics.

Another way to approach the analysis of structural causes of political alienation is to use individuals' *perceptions* of the structure rather than direct measures of the structure itself. To the extent that perceptions have a reality base, they should reflect the ways in which structures have impinged on individuals. For example, Aberbach and Walker use a measure of reported experiences of racial discrimination. Although there may be some individuals who are insensitive to discriminatory treatment and others who perceive discriminatory behavior in cases where more objective evaluation would not support this judgment, by and large perceptions of social structure reflect more than idiosyncratic and subjective assessments. To the extent that these perceptions are based on actual experiences, they may be even more useful than measures based on other types of data that do not reflect the unique experiences of given individuals.

Although a research design is made much more complex when one desires to study actual political structure as a variable in the process leading to political alienation, it is, of course, possible to do so. In order to use political structure as a *variable,* however, at least two or more significant political units must be included in the research design. It is usually not possible to accomplish this after the fact in a national sample, for example, because the number of people studied who live in any given subunits, like particular cities, will generally not be sufficient to carry out an analysis of city-to-city differences. The research design must therefore anticipate the use of political structure as a variable from the beginning. Studies which explicitly aim at replication by using questions from previous research in other locales also increase the possibilities for these types of comparisons to be made. The Jaros study is a good example of this research strategy, which enabled a direct comparison of attitudes of alienation in Appalachia with those in Chicago and the United States as a whole, even though the Chicago and national studies had been carried out by other investigators.

It seems clear that differences in political structure significant enough to affect the degree of political alienation, even among individuals of similar socio-economic status, can exist at a sub-national level. Aberbach and Walker cite relatively strong differences between Detroit and Newark in political alienation levels of young black males. Thus, comparative studies of alienation in cities with different types of political environment provide one way of including structure as an independent variable. Since differences in structure occuring at the *national* level tend to be much more dramatic, however, and may therefore lead to even greater differences in levels of political alienation, cross-national studies are of great importance. In this type of research, the countries are taken as indicators of certain types of political cultures and structures and political attitudes of people living in the different countries are compared. An outstanding example of this type of research is the study by Almond and Verba (1963) of political attitudes in five countries.

One difficulty that arises when city or country is used as a variable is the gross nature of these measures. It is frequently difficult to specify precisely what aspects of the cultures and structures of the political systems are responsible for observed attitudinal differences in their citizens. A similar problem occurs when population size of city or town of residence is used as an independent variable. Here too, size of city is usually a surrogate for a measure of political structure which the researcher would prefer to have but doesn't. And since size of city may be more or less related to so many structural characteristics, it is often unclear what the influencing mechanisms really are. Is population size a valid indicator of political access, for example, or are there significant differences in political access in cities of the same population size? Thus, research designs become increasingly complex as comparisons are made among cities or countries that are considered to be equal or equivalent on a large number of possibly confounding variables and to differ only on one or a few variables whose effects we wish to isolate.

In spite of the difficulties involved in investigating alienation from large political units, research in this area has made important advances along a number of fronts in recent years. Progress has been made in clarification of the concept of political alienation and in assessment of the individual-level correlates and behavioral consequences of this attitude. One of the major questions which requires more intensive investigation is the effect of the political structure itself on political alienation.

DIMENSIONS OF POLITICAL ALIENATION

Ada W. Finifter

In recent years there has emerged in this country a radical questioning and rejection of established political institutions unparalleled since the Civil War in its intensity and scope. One objective indicator of this trend since World War II is the marked rise in voluntary renunciation of American citizenship, an act which represents the formal and final estrangement of the individual from his former political ties.[1] Available evidence suggests that estrangement from the polity is also widespread in countries throughout the world as fundamental questions are being raised about the legitimacy of political institutions and political leadership.

Attitudes toward the political system have long been a concern of political scientists. Major orienting theories of the political system suggest that citizen support plays a crucial role in determining the structure and processes of political

SOURCE: Reprinted in slightly abridged form from *The American Political Science Review*, LXIV, 2 (June 1970), 389–410, by permission of the author and publisher. Tables and footnotes renumbered.

[1] While the motivations involved are unknown, renunciation of nationality appears to have strong content validity as a "hard" indicator of political estrangement. Formally recorded renunciations of nationality have increased consistently over the last two decades, from 149 in 1950 to 679 in 1968. (See *Annual Reports,* Immigration and Naturalization Service, United States Department of Justice.) This represents almost a quadrupling of the rate, from .15 per 100,000 voting age population in 1950 to .57 per 100,000 voting age population in 1968.

systems. Almond and Verba, for example, use the concept "civic culture" to refer to a complex mix of attitudes and behaviors considered to be conducive to democratic government.[2] Easton underscores the fundamental importance of attitudes for system stability, focusing especially on "diffuse support" as a prerequisite for the integration of political systems. He suggests that "(w)here the input of support falls below [a certain] minimum, the persistence of any kind of system will be endangered. A system will finally succumb unless it adopts measures to cope with the stress."[3]

The conversion of these general theoretical ideas into systematic empirical theory requires further rigorous and comprehensive analyses of types of citizen support and the development of empirical indicators for this domain.[4] The concept of alienation, which may be conceived as one end of a continuum whose opposite extreme is defined by the concepts of support or integration, offers a useful

[2] Gabriel Almond and Sidney Verba, *The Civic Culture* (Princeton: Princeton University Press, 1963).

[3] David Easton, *A Systems Analysis of Political Life* (New York: John Wiley, 1965), p. 220.

[4] For an example of Easton's own concern with the operationalization of "support," see David Easton and Jack Dennis, "The Child's Acquisition of Regime Norms: Political Efficacy," *American Political Science Review,* LXI (March, 1967), 25–38. References to other empirical studies of support and alienation will be found in the footnotes to the present article; an extensive list of earlier studies is found in f. 4 of Easton and Dennis, *op. cit.*

vantage point from which to pursue this goal. The long history of intellectual concern with alienation has resulted in a literature rich in concepts and suggestive hypotheses which may provide a valuable perspective from which to develop an empirical theory relating citizen attitudes to the structures and processes of the political system.

I. Dimensionalizing Political Alienation

There have been a number of recent theoretical and empirical efforts to explicate and clarify the concept of alienation.[5] The most fruitful of these involve attempts to specify particular *modes* of alienation by identifying the essential meanings of this attitudinal orientation.[6] This approach seeks to decompose a global concept into its component parts and thus may be referred to as one of

[5] See, for example, Melvin Seeman, "On the Meaning of Alienation," *American Sociological Review,* 24 (December, 1959), 783–791; Dwight Dean, "Alienation: Its Meaning and Measurement," *American Sociological Review,* 26 (1961), 753–758; Lewis S. Feuer, "What Is Alienation: The Career of a Concept," *New Politics,* 1 (Spring, 1962), 116–134; Arthur G. Neal and Salomon Rettig, "Dimensions of Alienation among Manual and Non-Manual Workers," *American Sociological Review,* 28 (August, 1963), 599–608; Kenneth Keniston, *The Uncommitted* (New York: Dell, 1965), esp. pp. 449–476; and Charles J. Browning, *et al.,* "On the Meaning of Alienation," *American Sociological Review,* 26 (1961), 780–781.

[6] See, especially, Seeman, *op. cit.,* and Neal and Rettig, *op. cit.* In his stimulating discussion, Keniston uses the term "mode" to express whether alienation is manifest as an attempt to change society (alloplastic) or is, rather, directed inwardly toward change in the individual himself (autoplastic). Keniston, *op. cit.* Although the behavioral expression of alienation is of obvious relevance to a theory of political alienation, it seems to me that it does not need to be made part of the definition of the concept itself but might be treated as a separate variable whose relation to the *attitude* of alienation is conditioned by other variables such as the opportunities for social change present in the system, or certain psychological characteristics of the individual.

dimensionalization of the concept. The research reported here utilizes this approach in developing concepts and measures of *political* alienation. In this respect it differs from most past efforts in that its focus is on attitudes which refer specifically to the institutions of government and the political process. Even when concerned with the specification of the mode of alienation, much previous research has been non-specific regarding the particular social institutions toward which such attitudes are directed. Since it has not been established, however, that alienation is normally an attitude which is either generalized over several modes *or* over a number of different social institutions, it would seem most useful to specify both the *mode* of alienation and the particular institutional *referent* in the operationalization of the concept. In this way, the actual extent of generalization, both as to mode and referent, can be determined by empirical investigation. In a sense, the present research "holds constant" the institutional referent of alienation by dealing only with attitudes toward aspects of the political system; the goal is to specify major modes of alienation directed toward this particular institutional sector.

It is useful to distinguish at least four different ways in which alienation toward the polity may be expressed.[7]

1. "Political powerlessness" may be defined as an individual's feeling that he cannot affect the actions of the government, that the "authoritative allocation of

[7] The concepts of "powerlessness," "meaninglessness," and "isolation," used here are based on Seeman's discussion of their generic types; the present discussion specifies how these modes of alienation relate to *political* institutions. The concept of "normlessness" developed here departs from the meaning attached to this term by Seeman. In addition to these four types, Seeman also discusses a type of alienation identified as "self-estrangement." The sense in which this type of alienation can be said to have an institutional referent is unclear.

values for the society," which is at the heart of the political process, is not subject to his influence. Political decisions, which determine to a great extent the conditions under which the individual lives, may appear to he *happening to* individuals who feel powerless, independent of or in spite of their own judgment or wishes. This mode of alienation is closely related (inversely) to the concept of "political efficacy," which has achieved such prominence in studies of voting behavior.[8]

2. "Political meaninglessness" may be said to exist to the extent that political decisions are perceived as being unpredictable. A perceived random pattern of decision making would, of course, prevent an understanding of the political system. This mode of alienation is distinguished from the first in that in the case of powerlessness decisions may be clear and predictable, but are simply not subject to the influence of the individual; in the case of meaninglessness, however, the individual perceives no discernible pattern. This feeling is illustrated by an individual's inability to distinguish any meaningful political choices, and the sense that political choices are themselves meaningless, because one cannot predict their probable outcomes nor, consequently, use them to change social conditions.

3. Following Durkheim's use of "anomie," which denotes a devitalization of social norms regulating individual behavior, "perceived political normlessness" is defined as the individual's perception that the norms or rules intended to govern political relations have broken down, and that departures from prescribed behavior are common. A belief that officials violate legal procedures in dealing with the public

or in arriving at policy decisions exemplifies this mode of alienation.

4. "Political isolation" refers to a rejection of political norms and goals that are widely held and shared by other members of a society. It differs from perceived normlessness in which there is implicit *acceptance* of some set of norms from which *others* are perceived to be deviating. Political isolation can be illustrated by a belief that voting or other socially defined political obligations are merely conformist formalities, or, indeed, that public participation is inappropriate in the formulation of public policy. This type of alienation is consistent with Lane's description of alienated individuals as feeling that "the rules of the game are unfair, loaded, illegitimate; the Constitution is, in some sense, fraudulent."[9] To the extent that social norms are dynamic, however, a state of isolation at one point in time may entail a different attitude set than isolation at another time. Similarly, to the extent that social norms differ from culture to culture, alienation in this mode can only be understood with reference to the prevailing normative patterns of particular societies.

Conceptual dimensionalization of an attitudinal domain implies a set of hypotheses about the relationships among empirical measures of the various dimensions. Although some previous work on alienation has demonstrated separate dimensions empirically,[10] studies using measures with direct *political* relevance frequently *assume* the existence of separate attitudinal dimensions without actually providing evidence to substantiate

---

[8] See especially the work emanating from the University of Michigan studies, most notably Angus Campbell, Philip E. Converse, Warren E. Miller and Donald E. Stokes, *The American Voter* (New York: John Wiley, 1960).

[9] Robert E. Lane, *Political Ideology* (New York: The Free Press, 1962), p. 162.

[10] See Neal and Rettig, *op. cit.;* the same authors' "On the Multidimensionality of Alienation," *American Sociological Review,* 32 (February, 1967), 54–64; and Elmer L. Struening and Arthur H. Richardson, "A Factor Analytic Exploration of the Alienation, Anomie and Authoritarianism Domain," *American Sociological Review,* 30 (1965), 768–776.

this assumption.[11] The present study pursues this line of inquiry further by exploring the dimensionality of attitudes toward the political system. If the hypothesis that distinct modes of political alienation exist can be substantiated, then it would seem imperative that future discussions of attitudinal support for political systems specify the sense in which "support" or "alienation" is being used, and consider the likelihood that different modes of support or alienation may be differentially related to other theoretically important variables.

II. Construction of Measures

The data used in this study are derived from interviews collected from a nationwide probability sample in the United States in early 1960. A description of sampling procedures has been published elsewhere.[12] Twenty-six questions, whose manifest content was judged related to

the political alienation domain, were examined to determine their dimensionality. These items, arranged according to their final allocation to two scales of political alienation, are presented in Table 1. . . .

The scales used in this research resulted from an interplay between factor and item analysis techniques which are described here in summary fashion.* The matrix of correlation coefficients among alienation measures was analyzed by the principal components method.[13] Eight components with eigenvalues above 1.0 were extracted. . . . The first three components extracted were retained for rotation by the Varimax criterion. The initial three-component solution was judged to be unacceptable for its poor approximation to simple structure.[14] The pattern of loadings suggested that rotation to two components might yield a clearer solution. This was indeed the case. These results, combined with the item analysis data, isolated five items which were of questionable relation to these dominant

[11] See for example, Robert E. Agger, Marshall N. Goldstein, and Stanley A. Pearl, "Political Cynicism: Measurement and Meaning," *Journal of Politics,* 23 (August, 1961), and Kenneth Janda, "A Comparative Study of Political Alienation and Voting Behavior in Three Suburban Communities," in *Studies in History and the Social Sciences* (Normal: Illinois State University, 1965), pp. 53–68. However, in a recent publication, Aberbach reports that factor analysis confirmed the dimensionality of several different measures of alienation, including two measures of political alienation. He does not report the factor loadings, although he describes them as "strong." His data support the utility of considering specific types of political alienation separately. See Joel Aberbach, "Alienation and Political Behavior," *American Political Science Review,* LXIII (March, 1969), 86–99. Two recent articles dealing with support for particular political institutions also use factor analytic techniques to dimensionalize attitudes. See Jack Dennis, "Support for the Party System by the Mass Public," *American Political Science Review,* LX (September, 1966), 600–615 and G. R. Boynton, S. C. Patterson and R. D. Hedlund, "The Structure of Public Support for Legislative Institutions," *Midwest Journal of Political Science,* XII (May, 1968), 163–180.

[12] See Almond and Verba, *op. cit.,* pp. 519–523. The data were made available by the Inter-

University Consortium for Political Research. Neither Professors Almond nor Verba nor the Consortium bear any responsibility for the analyses or interpretations presented here.

* Editor's Note: Factor analysis is a statistical procedure used to indicate whether, and in what manner, many questions about related concepts or topics actually measure a smaller number of underlying dimensions or "factors." Essentially, the procedure involves analysis of the relationships between all of the original items in order to discover these factors, which account for the relationships. A "loading" is calculated to represent the degree to which each item is related to each factor. Based on the size of these loadings, we can differentiate among the items as to the strength of their relationships to each of the underlying dimensions and can then interpret the dimensions according to the content or nature of the variables which have high loadings.

[13] For a comparison of the components and factor models see Harry H. Harman, *Modern Factor Analysis* (Chicago: The University of Chicago Press, 1967), Chapter 8.

[14] See L. L. Thurstone, *Multiple Factor Analysis* (Chicago: University of Chicago Press, 1947), p. 335, and J. P. Guilford, *Psychometric Methods* (2nd ed.; New York: McGraw-Hill, 1954), p. 508.

*Table 1. Questions Used as Measures of Political Alienation**

COMPONENT I: "POLITICAL POWERLESSNESS"

13a. If you wanted to discuss political and governmental affairs, are there some people you definitely wouldn't turn to—that is, people with whom you feel it is better not to discuss such topics? About how many people would you say there are with whom you would avoid discussing politics? (*discuss with no one*)

14. Some people say that politics and government are so complicated that the average man cannot really understand what is going on. In general, do you *agree* or disagree with that?

15. How do you feel about this? Thinking of the important national and international issues facing the country, how well do you think you can understand these issues? (*not at all*)

16. How about local issues in this town or part of the country? How well do you understand them? (*not at all*)

23. If you made an effort to change this regulation, how likely is it that you would succeed? (hypothetical local regulation considered to be "very unjust or harmful") (*not at all likely*)

24. If such a case arose, how likely is it that you would actually try to do something about it? (local regulation) (*not at all likely*)

27. If you made an effort to change this law, how likely is it that you would succeed? (hypothetical national law considered to be "very unjust or harmful") (*not at all likely*)

28. If such a case arose, how likely is it you would actually try to do something about it? (national law) (*not at all likely*)

31a. Thinking now about the national government in Washington, about how much effect do you think its activities, the laws passed and so on, have on your day-to-day life? Do they have a great effect, some effect, or *none*?

32a. Now take the local government: about how much effect do you think its activities have on your day-to-day life? Do they have a great effect, some effect, or *none*?

72f. People like me don't have any say about what the government does. (*Agree*—Disagree)

COMPONENT II: "PERCEIVED POLITICAL NORMLESSNESS"

18a. One sometimes hears that some people or groups have so much influence over the way the government is run that the interests of the majority are ignored. Do you *agree* or disagree that there are such groups?

31b. On the whole, do the activities of the national government tend to improve conditions in this country, or would we be *better off without them?*

32b. On the whole, do the activities of the local government tend to improve conditions in this area, or would we be *better off without them?*

34. Suppose there were some question that you had to take to a government

* Question numbers refer to the original interview schedule as reported in Gabriel Almond and Sidney Verba, *The Civic Culture* (Princeton: Princeton University Press, 1963), Appendix B. Code categories were arranged to represent assumed ascending degrees of political alienation, the highest point of which is *underlined* for each question.

office—for example, a tax question or housing regulation. Do you think you would be given equal treatment? I mean, would you be treated as well as anyone else? (*No*)

35. If you explained your point of view to the officials, what effect do you think it would have? Would they give your point of view serious consideration, would they pay only a little attention, or would they *ignore* what you had to say?

37a. If you had some trouble with the police—a traffic violation, maybe, or being accused of a minor offense—do you think you would be given equal treatment? That is, would you be treated as well as anyone else? (*No*)

37b. If you explained your point of view to the police, what effect do you think it would have? Would they give your point of view serious consideration, would they pay only a little attention, or would they *ignore* what you had to say?

51. The Republican party now controls the administration in Washington. Do you think that its policies and activities would ever seriously endanger the country's welfare? Do you think that this *probably would happen,* that it might happen, or that it probably wouldn't happen?

52. If the Democratic party were to take control of the government, how likely is it that it would seriously endanger the country's welfare? Do you think that this *would probably happen,* that it might happen, or that it probably wouldn't happen?

72d. All candidates sound good in their speeches, but you can never tell what they will do after they are elected. (*Agree*—Disagree)

ITEMS OMITTED

45. Some people feel that campaigning is needed so the public can judge candidates and issues. Others say that it causes so much bitterness and is so unreliable that we'd be better off without it. What do you think? Is it needed or would we be *better off without it?*

46. Do you ever get angry at some of the things that go on in election campaigns? Do you *often* get angry, do you sometimes get angry, or do you never get angry?

47. Do you ever find election campaigns to be pleasant and enjoyable? Do you often, do you sometimes, or do you *never* find them pleasant and enjoyable?

48. Do you ever find election campaigns silly or ridiculous? Do you *often,* sometimes, or never find them silly or ridiculous?

72a. The way people vote is the main thing that decides how things are run in this country. (Agree—*Disagree*)

---

components, and they were eliminated.[15] A second principal-components analysis was performed on the remaining twenty-one items. Seven components with eigenvalues above 1.0 were found; the first two were clearly dominant (4.3 and 2.0) while the remaining values dropped rapidly (1.4, 1.3, 1.2, and 1.0). Because

[15] Specifically, the results of the two-component, twenty-six item solution demonstrated that (a) Qs. 45 and 72a had weak loadings on *both* components, and (b) Q. 46 loaded *negatively* on its dominant component. To investigate further the structure of the items, Qs. 46 and 72a were eliminated, and two scales were formed using a cluster scoring procedure. Item analyses (based on response choice-total scale biserial correlations) indicated that Qs. 46, 47, and 48 were only weakly related to the dominant content of their scales. Since all three of these questions concerned attitudes toward election campaigns (as did Q. 45, which was eliminated because of its weak loadings), it seemed reasonable to conclude that the domain tapped by these questions was essentially different from that of the other items and all were eliminated.

of their clarity and strength, the first two components were retained for rotation, resulting in the pattern displayed in Table 2. This solution was accepted as a satisfactory approximation to simple structure. All of the items are clearly associated with one of the two major components.

The manifest content of the eleven items constituting the first component strongly suggests the "powerlessness" dimension of alienation described above. As stipulated in the *a priori* description of this dimension, the defining items (15, 23, 24, 27, and 28) refer to the individual's ability to understand important national and international issues facing the country, his propensity to do something about either a local regulation or a national law that he thinks unjust, and his subjective assessment of the efficacy of such efforts. Other items (14, 16, and 72f) share similar content, relating to the individual's ability to understand and affect the political process. Two of the items (31a and 32a) tap the respondent's understanding of the multifarious effects of government on the lives of citizens. Question 13a measures a fear or shunning of political discussion, which indicates a

Table 2. Rotated Component Structure of Twenty-One Alienation Items

QUES-TION	CONTENT	COMPO-NENT I	COMPO-NENT II
28	Likelihood of action to change unjust national law	.69	.06
15	Understanding of national and international issues	.68	.13
24	Likelihood of action to change unjust local regulation	.66	.08
27	Perceived efficacy of efforts to change national law	.62	.11
23	Perceived efficacy of efforts to change local regulation	.60	.16
31a	Effect of national government on daily life	.56	—.07
16	Understanding of local issues	.54	.11
32a	Effect of local government on daily life	.49	—.09
72f	People like me have no say about government activities	.47	.34
14	Politics and government are too complicated for average man	.35	.24
13a	Extent of avoidance of political discussions	.34	.08
37b	Consideration to point of view by police	.14	.62
37a	Treatment by police	.03	.59
34	Treatment in government office	.05	.59
35	Consideration of point of view by officials	.18	.57
51	Prudence of Republican party policies	.02	.49
52	Prudence of Democratic party policies	—.01	.42
31b	Benefits deriving from national government activities	.22	.40
18a	Elite vs. majority rule	—.16	.39
32b	Benefit deriving from local government activities	.24	.38
72d	Reliability of candidates for public office	.19	.31

feeling of low ability to cope with the political environment. These interpretations support the identification of the first component as "political powerlessness."

The defining items of the second component are 34, 35, 37a, and 37b. These questions refer to the treatment expected by the individual from two different governmental agencies. These questions appear to assume a norm of equal and considerate treatment of citizens by government officials, and may be considered to refer ultimately to the legal norm represented by the constitutional guarantee of equal protection.[16] Lack of congruence between this norm and actual behavior may be considered as an indication of deterioration in the normative structure. Accordingly, the *subjective* assessment of the existence of this state can be interpreted as a condition of "perceived normlessness." That is, the individual who thinks that he would receive unequal treatment is making this judgment with reference to a state of affairs that thinks *should* exist because it is affirmed by the political culture.

Another pair of questions (51 and 52) that load highly on this second compon-

[16] Consistent with this interpretation, Almond and Verba report that these questions were intended to measure the "qualities our respondents imputed to the executive side of government." *Op. cit.,* p. 106. At a different point in their analysis, however (see especially Chapter 8), they use these questions as measures of "administrative competence," which might be construed as a sub-type of *powerlessness.* There is clearly some conceptual overlap here. Although a sense of departure from community norms is being used in the present study to define "perceived normlessness," it is obvious that, when the particular norm in question refers to the role the individual should play in his interactions with political decision-makers, assessments of norm deviations may also reflect feelings of powerlessness. That items 34, 35, 37a, and 37b have quite low loadings on the factor that is here called "powerlessness" increases confidence that their interpretation in terms of role expectations and norm deviations is more adequate than an interpretation using the powerlessness concept.

ent ask for the respondent's judgment as to the likelihood that the policies of either of the major political parties would endanger the country's welfare when that party is in control of the government. These questions refer to a set of norms about the role of political parties. This role includes the expectation that the parties will act with a degree of patriotism, judgment, and knowledge that will ensure the country's security and wellbeing. Failure to comply with these expectations would likely be perceived as a normative violation of great magnitude. Similar reasoning may be applied to items 31b and 32b. If the effects of governmental actions are such that the public would be better off without them, norms specifying that such activity be in the national welfare will be perceived as having been violated. The remaining two items of the second component (18a and 72d), which concern the influence of people and groups on government actions and the reliability and trustworthiness of elected officials, can also be taken as measures of cynical feelings regarding compliance with certain widely held ideals and norms of the political culture.

Although we do not have a direct measure of the extent to which the norms referred to here are in fact shared, some measure of their importance is indicated by Almond and Verba's finding that, when respondents were asked to mention the "things about this country that you are most proud of," 85% of Americans mentioned aspects of the political system such as the Constitution, political freedom, or democracy. These sources of pride are all strongly associated with the norms of equality, responsibility, and responsiveness which have been suggested here as providing the point of reference for answers to the questions constituting this component. In no other country studied did even as many as half of the respondents mention political characteristics as a source of pride.[17] Because the main theme shared by these questions appears to be the extent to which political leaders and government officials observe important norms of the political culture, the second component is called "perceived political normlessness." The stipulation of normlessness as "perceived" is meant to indicate that the respondent *himself* does not necessarily feel anomic, but rather that he believes that frequent deviations from accepted norms occur *in the political process.* In this sense, this concept is related to the concept of "political cynicism," since the questions used to measure cynicism all appear to have either a legal or an informal norm as an implied referent against which respondents are asked to judge the behavior of politicians.[18] It may be a more fruitful concept in that whereas "cynicism" has no apparent theoretical roots, "perceived normlessness" has theoretical ties in the alienation framework and in the Durkheim-Merton-inspired theories of anomie, in which the term is used to signify a devitalization of social norms.[19]

Each respondent was assigned a score on each of the two dimensions of alienation on the basis of his responses to the questions discussed above. A cluster scoring procedure, in which each item is assigned uniquely to the scale on which it has its highest loading, was used. The internal consistency reliability coefficients of the powerlessness and perceived normlessness scales were .77 and .62 respectively.[20] Both measures were approximately normally distributed, with a slight positive skew in the perceived normlessness scale. In the interests of greater reliability, a modification in the original sample was made consisting in the elimination of 102 cases for which there were serious data gaps. All analyses which follow are based on the refined sample of 868 cases.

The examination of the meanings of each of the questions in the two scales suggests that the scales have content validity as measures of the concepts of political powerlessness and perceived political normlessness. The establishment of these two distinct measures of alienation should aid in future theoretical clarification of the concept and in the development of more specific hypotheses relating alienation to various personal characteristics and social conditions. As a step toward this goal, the relationships between these two scales of alienation and a variety of other variables are explored below. Since the two scales are only weakly related ($r = .26$, indicating only 7% shared variance), we can reasonably expect that the two dimensions of alienation will be *differentially* related to other variables. If the strength or the direction of the relationships between the measures of alienation and various social and psychological variables are significantly different, then the utility of the dimensional approach will be further substantiated.

---

[17] Almond and Verba, *op. cit.,* p. 102.

[18] See Agger, *et al., op. cit.,* p. 479, for a list of the questions used.

[19] See especially Robert K. Merton, *Social Theory and Social Structure* (rev. ed.; New York: The Free Press, 1957), pp. 131–194. Another related concept inspired by Durkheim's analysis of anomie has recently been discussed by Inkeles, who develops the concept of "political anomie" along lines which are strikingly similar to those defining "perceived political normlessness." Inkeles defines political anomie as the individual's *feeling* that others are not complying with the rules of society, and operationalizes it as "the individual's *perception* of the extent to which politicians and government officials pay attention to the common man, serve the public rather than their own careers, and keep their campaign promises after the election." Alex Inkeles, "Participant Citizenship in Six Developing Countries," *American Political Science Review,* LXIII (December, 1969), p. 1125. Emphasis in original. The content of the first and third of Inkeles' defining questions is essentially the same as Qs. 18a and 72d of the perceived political normlessness scale.

[20] The Hoyt method was used. See Cyril J. Hoyt and Clayton L. Stunkard, "Estimation of Test Reliability for Unrestricted Item Scoring Methods," *Educational and Psychological Measurement,* 12 (1952), 756–758.

III. Correlates of Two Dimensions of Political Alienation

The analyses reported below are directed to the question of the sources of political alienation. In previous studies many different variables have been shown to be associated with one or another type of alienation. Most studies, however, have considered only a limited number of variables and thus the literature is replete with demonstrations of bivariate relationships between measures of alienation and various personal characteristics. In the present study an attempt is made to consider a wide variety of variables simultaneously, and to evaluate their relative importance in multivariate models. In this way the development of parsimonious theory may be advanced.

Zero-order Pearson correlations between the two dimensions of alienation and all predictor variables are presented in Table 3.[21] For conceptual clarity, the independent variables are arranged in three groups, corresponding to the general concepts of (1) social status, which includes religion, nativity, race, sex, age, education, occupation, and income; (2) social cohesion, which includes marital status, number of children, years of residence in the community where the individual lives, frequency of church attendance, number of organizations to which the respondent belongs, whether the re-

[21] Bivariate plots between each predictor variable and each alienation scale showed no significant departures from linearity. The relationship between age and powerlessness was the only one which was very slightly curvilinear, with the youngest age group (18–25) having as high a mean powerlessness score as the 41–50 age group, but not nearly as high as that of the oldest group. This result confirms neither previous findings of a linear relationship between these variables, reported by several investigators, nor those findings indicating extreme curvilinearity, with the youngest being more alienated than any other age group. See W. E. Thompson and J. E. Horton, "Political Alienation as a Force in Political Action," *Social Forces,* 38 (March, 1960), 190–195.

Table 3. Correlations Between Dimensions of Alienation and Predictor Variables

	Power-lessness	Norm-lessness
Jewish	—09	—02
Catholic	01	—03
Protestant	02	03
Nativity	—07	10
Race	14	22
Sex	12	—08
Age	12	01
Education	—44	—16
Occupation	—32	—12
Income	—31	—18
Marital Status	—08	—03
Number of Children	07	04
Years Residence	03	—01
Church Attendance	—17	—11
Organizations	—38	—13
Officership	—31	—13
Pol. Participation	—64	—10
Party ID	—07	—06
ID Strength	—10	—07
Faith in People	—37	—37
Community Size	—01	05
Northeast	—09	—06
South	09	08

Decimals are omitted. N = 868. Correlations of .06 are significant at the .05 level; correlations of .08 are significant at the .01 level. Codes for all independent variables are given in the Appendix.

spondent was ever an officer in any of these organizations, an index of political participation, party identification, strength of party identification, and an index of faith in people; and (3) geo-cultural environment, including size of community and region of residence. Codes for all variables are presented in the Appendix.

The zero-order relationships between powerlessness and social status reported here are consistent with the findings of several previous studies which used different indicators of alienation.[22] In addition, the Survey Research Center studies have found consistently that the political efficacy scale (the inverse of powerlessness) is positively related to being male, and to education, income, and occupation.[23] Within the cluster of status measures used in the present study, education is by far the single most important predictor of powerlessness, accounting for 19% of the total variance. Because of the important effects of education on job and income opportunities, it is likely that education also has important indirect effects through its influence on occupation and income, each of which is also fairly strongly related to powerlessness. However, since income level of the parental home is an important determinant of the level of education achieved by the respondent, it is difficult to reject the economic determinism hypothesis without more information on socio-economic background than is available in this study. These data do

demonstrate, however, that in a contemporaneous prediction of powerlessness, education is a far more important variable than income. Nevertheless, income and occupation each independently explain about 9% of the variance in powerlessness scores. In contrast, income accounts for only about 3% and occupation for about 1% of the variance in normlessness.

Race is another measure of general social status found to be related to indicators of alienation in previous studies.[24] In each case, Negroes are more highly alienated than whites. In the present study, although race seems to be of some slight importance in predicting powerlessness ($r = .14$, $r^2 = .02$), its relationship to this form of alienation is essentially a function of education: when educational attainment is controlled, the strength of the relationship between race and powerlessness drops to less than one-fourth of its initial potency ($r = .067$, $r^2 = .004$). Given similar educational achievement, Negroes apparently feel hardly any more powerless concerning the political process than do whites. Moreover, considering that Negroes as a group are less well-educated than whites, that they generally hold lower prestige occupational positions, and that they earn less income, the zero-order correlation between race and powerlessness is perhaps smaller than one would expect.

The low correlation between powerlessness and race contrasts with the stronger effects of race in the case of normlessness. Even when income and education (the two next most powerful status predictors of normlessness) are *both* held constant, race maintains most of its original explanatory power, with the second order partial reduced only to .175. In contrast, the corresponding second order partial for race and powerlessness is an insignificant .035. This difference means that, given similar achieved status, ascrip-

[22] For example, see Agger, *et al., op. cit.,* 484–487; Russell Middleton, "Alienation, Race, and Education," *American Sociological Review,* 28 (December, 1963), 973–977; John Haer, "Social Stratification in Relation to Attitudes Toward Sources of Power," *Social Forces,* 35 (December, 1956), 137–142; and Richard Quinney, "Political Conservatism, Alienation, and Fatalism," *Sociometry,* 27 (September, 1964), 372–381. My review of previous studies intentionally omits those using Srole's anomia scale as a measure of alienation. The heavy emphasis on personal life situations in the Srole scale suggests that it may largely measure personal disorganization or maladjustment rather than attitudes toward aspects of social structure. The two may be related, but this is an empirical rather than definitional question, and the indiscriminate use of the Srole scale as a *de facto* measure of "alienation" serves mainly to confuse these concepts. Furthermore, there is some empirical evidence that anomia and some measures of alienation are independent dimensions. See the articles cited in note 10.

[23] Angus Campbell, Gerald Gurin, and Warren E. Miller, *The Voter Decides* (Evanston: Row, Peterson and Company, 1954), pp. 190–192; Campbell, *et al., The American Voter, op. cit.,* pp. 516–520.

[24] See, for example, Middleton, *op. cit.* and Campbell, Gurin, and Miller, *op. cit.*

tive racial status is not important as a cause of political powerlessness, but it does remain an important cause of perceived normlessness. However, since it is obviously more difficult for Negroes to attain that same achieved status, this type of statistical controlling procedure is in danger of being misleading except as it points out possible effects of social change. That is, the implication of these findings is that if opportunities for educational and material advancement were equal, it is likely that Negroes would feel no more powerless than whites. In contrast, race *would* remain the most powerful status variable in determining the perception that public officials commonly violate community norms. Indeed, of all the independent variables considered, race is second in power only to the measure of faith in people for explaining normlessness, and even with this measure of interpersonal trust controlled, race still has a significant effect on normlessness (r = .16).

Another ascribed characteristic correlated with perceived normlessness is sex: men perceive norm violations somewhat more frequently than do women. This is the more interesting in view of the fact that women feel more powerless than men. The differential relationship between sex and the two dimensions of alienation indicates the contemporary persistence of the political role traditionally assigned to women. The present findings indicate that many women feel they have little capacity to affect the political system, yet they are less critical of it than are men. This is an important aspect of what has been called the "subject" political orientation.[25]

Nativity, another ascribed characteristic, also has divergent effects on the two types of alienation. Whereas foreign-born respondents are likely to feel somewhat more powerless than the native-born (and the Southern Europeen feels even more powerless than the northern European),

we find that the opposite is true for perceived normlessness. That American birth is associated with lower levels of powerlessness is explicable by the higher educational attainment of native-born citizens, since education decreases feelings of powerlessness. Why then should American birth be associated with *increased* perceptions of normlessness? It will be noted that the nativity ranking orders native-born Americans highest, those born in Northern or Western Europe second, and those born in Southern Europe, or in other areas of the world, lowest.[26] This ranking clearly corresponds also to one of similarity of the political system of the country of origin and that of the United States. Similarity of these political systems is likely to be related to greater knowledge of the American system. The reason for the correlation between nativity and perceived normlessness may then lie in the fact that those with greater knowledge of and familiarity with the American political system would be more apt to perceive the norm deviations which do, in fact, occur, than would those to whom the political structure is less familiar.[27] Another possible explanation for this finding may lie in the bases from which these judgments are made. The native-born American probably has the highest expectations regarding the behavior of public officials, rooted in an idealized orientation toward government and authority common in public schooling. Violations of this textbook image may thus evoke more negative responses (as in a frustration-aggression reaction). The political culture of the Southern European, to take the other extreme, tends to

[25] Almond and Verba, *op. cit.*, esp. Chapters 1 and 8.

[26] The ranking of ethnic prestige follows Gerhard Lenski, "Status Crystallization: A Non-Vertical Dimension of Social Status," *American Sociological Review*, 19 (1954), p. 407.

[27] Litt found that familiarity with Boston politics (as measured by length of residency in that city) increases political cynicism. Edgar Litt, "Political Cynicism and Political Futility," *Journal of Politics*, 25 (May 1963), 312–323.

stress a more realistic and a more cynical image of the workings of government.[28] Given their lower expectations, persons socialized in this type of political culture might therefore be more tolerant of what they may perceive to be the far less frequent occurrence of norm violations in their adopted country.[29]

In summary, then, the relationships between the social status characteristics and each of the two dimensions of political alienation differ in several important respects. In particular, Negroes tend to have higher scores on the measure of perceived normlessness than do whites, while the difference between the races on the measure of powerlessness is of much less importance. Both nativity and sex have opposite effects on the two types of alienation. Women tend to feel more powerless than men but less often perceive norm violations. The native-born, in general, feel less powerless than the foreign-born, but the foreign-born are less critical of the operations of the political system.

It is clear that important differences exist also in the effects of various aspects of social cohesion on the two kinds of political alienation. Political participation has a very high negative correlation with feelings of political powerlessness ($r = -.64$), alone accounting for 41% of its variance. The "faith in people" scale, de-signed to measure a person's "global attitude toward human nature,"[30] also has a strong inverse correlation with feelings of powerlessness ($r = -.37$). Since the faith in people scale is a measure of interpersonal trust in social relations it is understandable that it should be related to the way in which politics, a process involving considerable emphasis on interpersonal activity, is viewed. A further indicator of social cohesion which has a strong negative relation to powerlessness is the number of organizational memberships the individual reports ($r = -.38$), which is slightly more strongly related to powerlessness than is the experience of having been an officer in these organizations ($r = -.31$). Finally, frequency of church attendance is also negatively related to feelings of powerlessness ($r = -.17$). Considering the relationships *among* this set of variables, the highest correlations exist among organizational memberships, political participation, and faith in people, with church attendance somewhat less strongly related to this cluster. It is perhaps reasonable to postulate the existence of an underlying "community solidarity" factor which operates to reduce feelings of powerlessness. While these activities and attitudes tend to cluster, faith in people, political participation and church attendance have strong independent effects on this type of alienation. However, membership in general voluntary organizations alone, without participation in the political process itself, does not substantially reduce feelings of political powerlessness. The partial correlation between organizational memberships and powerlessness when political participation is controlled reduces to only $-.08$ while the corresponding partial for faith in people is $-.26$ and for church attendance, $-.15$. These results suggest important relationships be-

[28] For descriptions of attitudes toward authority in different political systems see Almond and Verba, *op. cit.*, esp. Chapters 4 and 14; Lawrence Wylie, *Village in the Vaucluse* (New York: Harper and Row, 1964), Chapter 10; and David Easton and Robert D. Hess, "The Child's Political World," *Midwest Journal of Political Science,* 6 (1962), 229–246. Easton and Hess comment particularly on the idealization of authority encouraged in American socialization practices.

[29] Then, too, it is possible that the foreign-born may be more hesitant to make statements critical of American government to an American interviewer. Since the items in the normlessness scale tend to focus on government officials they may be more threatening in this respect than the items in the powerlessness scale, which may be perceived more in terms of the respondent's own shortcomings.

[30] Morris Rosenberg, "Misanthropy and Political Ideology," *American Sociological Review,* 21 (December, 1956), p. 690. The reliability of this scale in the current project was .58.

tween political attitudes and the broader context of social interaction.

The participation measures are much less strongly related to perceived normlessness than to powerlessness. For example, neither organizational memberships, nor being an officer, nor political participation (each of which explains between 10% and 41% of the variance in powerlessness) can explain as much as 2% of the variance in the perceived normlessness scores. Thus, the pattern of community participation, which tends to decrease feelings of powerlessness with respect to the political process, has practically no effect on whether or not one perceives norm-violating behavior by government officials. Frequent participators appear almost as likely to perceive such behavior as apathetics. Faith in people, however, *is* equally powerful in predicting both types of political alienation. This variable is, in fact, the most powerful of all independent variables in predicting perceived normlessness, accounting for 15% of the variance.

The "social cohesion" variables present certain problems of conceptual status. They are related to each other in complex ways that must eventually be explicated if adequate causal models are to be developed. In addition, they are related to the measures of alienation more complexly than the simple independent-dependent variable model of regression analysis used here suggests. For example, participation variables have been treated in the literature as both independent and dependent with respect to political attitudes. Campbell and his associates consider political efficacy as an independent variable in predicting levels of political participation,[31] and Horton and Thompson,[32] Janda,[33] and Aberbach[34] consider the effects of political alienation on vot-

ing behavior. Agger and associates have shown that their political cynicism measure is related to frequency of political discussion,[35] a finding similar to one by Douvan relating "political effectiveness" to political discussion.[36] On the other hand, analyses by Rose and Almond and Verba are distinguished by their emphasis on organizational affiliations as *preceding* feelings of competence,[37] while competence itself is viewed as a *product* of the diffusion of group values to the members. It has also been suggested that feelings of efficacy and actual participation probably reinforce each other. Some sense of subjective competence may precede participation, but the skills and familiarity with the political process that result from participation are likely, in turn, to increase the subjective sense of ability to influence the system.[38] It seems clear that a complex feedback process exists among these variables. Development of an adequate theory of alienation will depend on the success with which these types of variables are incorporated in their dual role as both cause and effect of attitudes. Newly developing techniques for analyzing reciprocal causal models hold promise for reaching this goal.[39]

492; and W. E. Thompson and J. E. Horton, "Political Alienation as a Force in Political Action," *Social Forces*, 38 (March, 1960), 190–195.

[33] Janda, *op. cit.*

[34] Aberbach, *op. cit.*

[35] Agger, *et al.*, *op. cit.*, pp. 495–497.

[36] Elizabeth Douvan, "The Sense of Effectiveness and Response to Public Issues," *Journal of Social Psychology*, 47 (1958), 111–126.

[37] Arnold M. Rose, "Attitudinal Correlates of Social Participation," *Social Forces*, 37 (1959), 202–206; by the same author, "Alienation and Participation: A Comparison of Group Leaders and the 'Mass'," *American Sociological Review*, 27 (December, 1962), 834–838; and Almond and Verba, *op. cit.*, pp. 307–322.

[38] Robert A. Dahl, *Who Governs?* (New Haven: Yale University Press, 1961), Chapter 26.

[39] For a pioneering application of methods of analyzing reciprocal causation, see Otis Dudley Duncan, Archibald O. Haller, and Alejandro Portes, "Peer Influences on Aspirations: A Reinterpretation," *American Journal of Sociology*, 74 (September, 1968), 119–137.

[31] Campbell, *et al.*, *The American Voter*, *op. cit.*, pp. 479–481.

[32] John E. Horton and Wayne E. Thompson, "Powerlessness and Political Negativism: A Study of Defeated Local Referendums," *American Journal of Sociology*, 67 (1962), pp. 491–

This discussion has proceeded with a separate consideration of variables on different levels of analysis. Status variables may be considered as relatively stable (indeed, some are immutable) characteristics of the individual. Community cohesion variables, on the other hand, are dynamic characteristics of the individual as he relates to others in his environment. We may also consider the effect of certain characteristics of the environment itself. Being from either the Northeastern or the Southern region of the country is related to one's level of both powerlessness and perceived normlessness, but the regional characteristics have opposite effects. As compared to Southerners, Northeasterners appear to feel more confident of their ability to understand and influence government decisions and of the normative compliance of political leaders. The correlations between community size and the two types of alienation indicate that this lesser alienation in the Northeast is not due to the higher urbanization in this area. Indeed, as will be discussed below, the correlations between community size and both forms of alienation increase positively when controlled for certain relevant variables. The relationship between region and alienation may be viewed as a reflection of the generally lower socioeconomic status of persons living in the South. When either education or income is controlled, the relationships between being from the South and both of the alienation variables are reduced. However (as in the case of the relationship between race and alienation), one may question the validity of controlling for such variables, since this procedure tends to obscure the historical factors which have made the South a distinctive region.

IV. Multivariate Models

A large number of variables have been considered, and an attempt has been made to identify those whose effects are most important. Obviously, however, there is an extremely large number of ways in which these variables could be combined to form prediction equations. From the enormous number of possible equations it is desirable to be able to select one model on which substantive explanations could be focused. The problem of choosing an explanatory model may be interpreted as one of striking a balance between maximizing explanatory power and minimizing the number of variables included so as to achieve theoretical parsimony. In order to find such an optimal equation, a stepwise correlation program was used. The criterion adopted for termination of the equation was that the increase in R^2 resulting from the addition of a variable be statistically significant at the .05 level. This criterion increases confidence that an increment in explanatory power of a given size is unlikely to have happened because of sampling or other random error (within the usual confidence limits), and that the variable in question makes a genuine contribution to explanation.

Table 4 presents the regression coefficients for the two equations that meet this criterion. First, it should be noted that the full twenty-three variable equation increases explained variance in powerlessness from 50.7% to only 51.5% and in normlessness from 17.9% to only 18.9%. Thus, it seems clear that, in each case, the stepwise regression procedure has permitted the selection of a relatively small subset of variables (less than one-third of those originally available), whose power is such as to explain 98% and 95%, respectively, of the variance controlled by the full set of variables. In both cases, also, explanation of variance increases only marginally over and above the explanation possible with the one most powerful predictor alone. In the case of powerlessness, explained variance increases from 41% to 51% with the addition of six variables to political participation and for normlessness from 13% to 18% with the addition of six variables

Table 4. Regression Coefficients for Final Equations*

VARIABLE	POLITICAL POWERLESSNESS	PERCEIVED POLITICAL NORMLESSNESS
Political Participation	—.55	——
Education	—.14	——
Age	.13	——
Jewish	—.05	——
Faith in People	—.14	—.30
Church Attendance	—.10	—.07
Community Size	.07	.07
Sex	——	—.07
Income	——	—.08
Nativity	——	.10
Race	——	.13
	R = .712	R = .423
	R^2 = .507	R^2 = .179

*Standardized coefficients are presented. Dashes indicate that the variable concerned did not have enough independent predictive power for this dependent variable to be included.

to faith in people. While beginning with different initial variables in each case would result in slight changes in these figures, the important point, *normally obscured by successive bivariate analyses,* is that the variables with which we typically work are often sufficiently inter-related so that we do not actually increase explanatory power greatly by continually increasing the number of predictor variables.[40] Thus, determination of the most powerful explanatory variables appears to be a rational and useful research strategy.

Considering the powerlessness model first, a comparison of the standardized re-

gression coefficients indicates that political participation is by far the most important predictor. The appearance of community size may seem strange in that, of all variables, this one had the lowest zero-order correlation with the dependent variable. An examination of the stepwise calculations reveals that the major impetus to the rise in the partial correlation between population size and powerlessness was the inclusion of education. With education controlled, this correlation increases (partial $r = .06$), indicating that within educational levels, there is a weak but significant positive relationship between community size and feelings of political powerlessness. Large urban concentrations apparently do contribute to a sense of estrangement between the citizen and his government. This relationship is suppressed at the zero-order level because of the tendency of highly educated individuals to locate in larger cities and the negative relationship between education and powerlessness. The alienating effects of the urban environment do not appear

[40] On the other hand, this very inter-relatedness may lead to difficulties in obtaining stable estimates of regression coefficients. As Farrar and Glauber suggest, the problem of multicollinearity is most usefully viewed as one of degree of severity rather than as one of categorical existence. The size of the correlation coefficients among the independent variables in the present study does not appear to constitute a serious problem. See Donald E. Farrar and Robert R. Glauber, "Multicollinearity in Regression Analysis: The Problem Revisited," *Review of Economics and Statistics,* 49 (1967), 92–107.

to result from differential social cohesion in rural and urban areas. There are few important correlations between community size and the measures of social cohesion used in the present study and the direction of those which do exist is not consistent with the hypothesis that the reason for higher alienation in larger cities lies in lower social cohesion. If no distinct urban behavior patterns can be implicated in the positive relationship between community size and powerlessness, it is possible that type of political structure may be a useful concept in future investigations of this phenomenon.

The inclusion of age in the final regression equation also merits examination. Significant events accompanying the aging process, such as loss of spouse and enforced retirement from gainful employment, probably increase personal frustration. It may be that these feelings of frustration or helplessness are generalized to the political realm, thereby increasing the sense of political powerlessness. But such a higher level of alienation among the aged is partly obscured at the zero-order level by the *positive* correlation between age and political participation ($r = .11$). The multivariate model points up the importance of higher political participation in keeping political powerlessness among the aged at a lower level than it would otherwise reach. Indeed, as the effects of other integrating variables are held constant, the effect of age becomes increasingly strong and clear. For example, with political participation, education, and faith in people controlled, age is a more powerful predictor of powerlessness than it was at the zero-order level (partial $r = .14$).

Considering now the final equation for predicting perceived *normlessness,* there are several interesting comparisons between the set of predictor variables included here and those included in the equation for powerlessness. Most noteworthy is the absence in this equation of the single most important variable in the powerlessness equation, political participation. Cynicism about the behavior of public officials is evidently sufficiently persistent that participation, even in the political process itself, does not serve to reduce it substantially. Education, age, and being Jewish, all of which influence the degree of powerlessness, are also absent from the perceived normlessness model. Conversely, three ascribed status characteristics (sex, race, and nativity) which had less important effects on levels of powerlessness and were not included in the final equation for that variable, are relatively important among the predictors of perceived normlessness. Men are more likely to be critical of the political system, as are Negroes and those born in this country. Two separate but related explanations seem necessary to account for these findings. Men, being more attentive to politics than women, may be more aware of norm violations that occur in the political process. This is essentially the argument that was offered above to explain the positive relationship between prestige of birthplace and normlessness. However, Negroes may score higher than whites on this type of alienation precisely because they are the *objects* of the unfair treatment which is an important part of the definition of normlessness.

In contrast to the absence of measures of secular participation in the model for normlessness, religious participation (church attendance) appears in both equations. Population of place of residence is another variable which shows a small but persistent influence on both modes of alienation.

The most important variable in predicting perceived normlessness is faith in people. Since interpersonal confidence was also important for explaining powerlessness, this finding might be read to imply that political alienation is merely a derivative expression of a general personality characteristic that could be expected to have similar manifestations in other spheres. However, studies demonstrating inchoate attitudes toward politics in young children[41] suggest that the development of these attitudes does not wait on a well-formed structure of attitudes toward social relations in general, but may occur at the same time as more generalized attitudes are formed.[42] The pattern of inter-correlations among faith in people, the alienation scales, and several of the status variables suggests that fundamental attitudes of trust or cynicism with respect to the motives of other people, as well as attitudes toward particular social institutions, may be transmitted as part of class sub-cultures. The correlation between income and normlessness, for example, is higher than would be expected on the basis of a developmental sequence leading from income to faith in people to perceived normlessness (the predicted r is —.11; the observed r is —.18). On the other hand, the relationship between faith in people and perceived normlessness is far too high to be a spurious product of the correlations between income and faith in people and income and normlessness (the predicted r is —.05; the observed r is —.37). It seems likely, therefore, that attitudes toward specific social institutions and generalized attitudes toward human nature develop concurrently and in interaction with each other.

V. Summary of Findings

In recent discussions of alienation a variety of meanings have been distin-guished, such as powerlessness, normlessness, meaninglessness, and isolation. The present analysis began by considering the ways in which these modes of alienation may be useful in exploring attitudes toward the political system. Empirical measures of two of these types of political alienation were developed. The high level of prediction achieved using the powerlessness scale as a dependent variable suggests that its use in future research would be worthwhile. An important further step would be to continue the establishment of the predictive validity of the measure by studying the types of political behavior that tend to be associated with varying degrees of powerlessness. For example, some research has demonstrated that it is useful to dimensionalize political participation itself;[43] we may therefore find that varying levels of powerlessness tend to be associated with different *types* of participation, rather than merely with different *degrees* of participation considered as a global behavior. We will return to this question below. In comparison with the powerlessness results, explanation of variance in the perceived normlessness scale, while still substantial, is much lower. One reason for this may be the lower reliability of this scale which imposes a lower ceiling on predictability. Increasing the reliability of the scale, perhaps by adding more items, for example, may improve prediction.

An important consideration in improving our understanding of both types of alienation is the need for variables that simply are not measured in the present study. If alienation is at least partially a function of social experience, it is ob-

[41] See, for example, David Easton and Jack Dennis, "The Child's Image of Government," *The Annals of the American Academy of Political and Social Science,* 361 (September, 1965), 40–57; Fred I. Greenstein, *Children and Politics* (New Haven: Yale University Press, 1965); and Robert D. Hess and Judith V. Torney, *The Development of Political Attitudes in Children* (Chicago: Aldine Publishing Company, 1967).

[42] Verba suggests that attitudes toward specific political issues may develop *before* more coherent or inclusive ideologies. See Sidney Verba, *Small Groups and Political Behavior* (Princeton: Princeton University Press, 1961), pp. 41–42.

[43] See W. S. Robinson, "The Motivational Structure of Political Participation," *American Sociological Review,* 19 (1952), 151–156 and Bernard M. Finifter, "Styles of Participation in Political Life: Differential Multivariate Prediction with and without Allowance for Interaction Effects," paper presented to the Midwest Society of Multivariate Experimental Psychology, Chicago, May, 1968.

viously imperative to consider the kinds of experiences people have with the political system and the responses they have received to their own or their peers' efforts to participate. The addition of contextual variables, such as characteristics of local political structures, to the predictive models would also be necessary in order to examine the relationship between political reality and individual attitudes. Of tremendous utility also would be the incorporation of significant political events as natural experimental variables in research programs that permit repeated measurements on the same or related study populations. In these ways an assessment of the effects of political conditions on the development of attitudes of alienation could be approached.

An important finding of this study is that there are some significant differences in the variables that are associated with each type of alienation. Individuals with high powerlessness scores are unlikely to participate in community activities, whether secular or sacred. They are likely to be older, to have less education, and to have low faith in people. Conversely, living in smaller communities or being Jewish are characteristics that tend to reduce this type of alienation. High scores on the perceived normlessness scale are most likely for individuals with low faith in people, who are native-born, Negro, male, have low income, live in large cities, or attend church infrequently. Since education and income are related, the fact that education appears in the powerlessness equation and income in the normlessness equation should not be stressed greatly unless additional research confirms this difference. Nevertheless, the difference is theoretically interesting. The sense of injustice of the poor, reflected in their higher scores on perceived normlessness, may be partially mitigated by the fact that it is not the poor *per se* who feel most powerless, but rather the poorly educated. That education and income are not

completely overlapping stratification variables (i.e., that the class system is not a caste system) prevents the intensification of the sense of alienation that might otherwise exist in the lower social classes.

There is a group of characteristics, however, which tend to be associated with *both* types of alienation. These are low faith in people, infrequent church attendance, and large city size. This cluster of variables may be an appropriate indicator of the impersonality of contemporary life which so many analysts have indicted as a major source of all types of alienation. The significant *differences* in predictors of the two types of alienation involve political participation, age, sex, nativity, and race. Results obtained in this study leave little doubt that participation in the political process is far more important in reducing powerlessness than in its effect on normlessness. In fact, there is some suggestion that participation may tend to increase perceptions of normlessness. Although participation and perceived normlessness are negatively related at the zero-order level, the regression coefficient for participation in the complete twenty-three variable equation for normlessness *is* positive (and tracing this value during the stepwise procedure indicates that it is consistently positive after faith in people is controlled at the second step). This finding is suggestive only, since political participation does not contribute at a statistically significant level to the explanation of perceived normlessness. However, the fact that men and native-born citizens (both of which characteristics are significantly associated with participation) have higher normlessness scores than do women and the foreign-born (who participate less) strengthens the implication that high scores on normlessness are partially a function of knowledge and experience with the political system.[44]

[44] Results of an analysis of interaction effects provide some further support for the suggestion that political participation may increase per-

VI. Alienation and the Political System

Because the dimensional approach to political alienation clarifies and specifies attitudes toward the political system, it may be a useful basis for the development of more specific hypotheses regarding the effects of attitudes on political behavior. The concluding section of this paper is devoted to a brief and admittedly speculative exploration of some types of political engagement which may be associated with different combinations and levels of the dimensions of political alienation. My purpose in this discussion is to illustrate how this approach to developing concepts and measures can be useful in suggesting research hypotheses that address themselves to the larger theoretical problems of change and stability in political systems.

Alienation is commonly regarded as a threat to the survival of the political system. If we examine the relationships between alienation, political behavior, and the states of political systems more closely, however, it is reasonable to suggest that not all types of alienation need be viewed as necessarily "dysfunctional." To the extent that alienated individuals are non-participants, for example, Berelson has suggested that they serve to soften and blur crippling divisions in the body politic that may result from extreme political conflict.[45] This suggests the hypothesis of a positive relationship between political participation and debilitating system cleavages, at least above a certain critical level of participation. Thus, in Berelson's view, the contribution of apathy to a political system is to permit the maintenance of its usual decision-making

patterns. However, the persistence of a political system, in the sense of a shared normative structure, is not necessarily dependent on the perpetuation of a particular set of existing political institutions. Indeed, conflicts often exist between basic normative patterns and particular political institutions. When such conflicts are recognized, political institutions may be deliberately changed to conform to the basic normative patterns. The recognition of such conflicts between basic norms and particular political institutions is an important source of political change. As Geertz points out, it is in the incongruities between cultural patterns and social organization that "we shall find some of the primary driving forces in change."[46]

Applying this culture-structure differentiation to the results of the present research, I have suggested that to those scoring high on perceived normlessness, important aspects of the political culture (such as equality of citizens and responsibility of office holders) appear to be violated by the political structure, that is, by actual behavior of office holders or aspects of the political process itself. Systemic stresses that may be created by the behavior of persons who so perceive the political system (such as protest marches, strikes, etc.) are frequently directed toward reducing the inconsistency between the political culture and the structures by which it is implemented. It is difficult to classify such behavior using the customary language of functionalism. Protest behavior patently does not appear to be "functional." However, insofar as protest can act as a catalyst for needed social change, it is similarly awkward to classify it as "dysfunctional." It is precisely this opposition of "functional" and "dysfunctional" which has contributed to the criticism that the functional mode of analysis

[*footnote 44 continued*
ceived normlessness. The analysis identified a small but theoretically interesting sub-group (N =56) of white, mobile, college-educated people with high faith in people among whom higher political participation is associated with higher alienation.
[45] Bernard Berelson, Paul F. Lazarsfeld, and William N. McPhee, *Voting* (Chicago: University of Chicago Press, 1954), p. 316.

[46] Clifford Geertz, "Ritual and Social Change," in N. J. Demerath, III and Richard A. Peterson (eds.), *System, Change, and Conflict* (New York: The Free Press, 1967), p. 233.

has overemphasized the *status quo* and failed to provide any substantial theoretical basis for dealing with social change.[47] As a partial response to this need, it may be useful to introduce a new typological concept to describe conditions involving system disturbances that may culminate in higher levels of integration in social systems (as, for example, by narrowing gaps between cultural patterns and social organization). The concept "orthofunctional"[48] is suggested to describe such conditions. Thus, this concept might be useful to describe systemic stresses that, while initially disruptive, generate increasing system integration by the modification of conditions that violate widely-shared norms or otherwise inhibit intra-system cohesion.

Feelings of powerlessness may be considered "functional" in permitting the orderly maintenance of the *status quo;* perceptions of normlessness may be considered "orthofunctional" insofar as they may lead to demands for greater compliance with legal or cultural norms. If this interpretation of normlessness is plausible, it follows that people may perceive a condition of political normlessness precisely because of their *allegiance* to a set of ideals to which the community formally adheres, but which are commonly violated. The civil rights revolution, and the student and Vietnam war protests are based in large part on perceptions of violations of culturally accepted norms and demands on the political system for compliance and rectification. Such demands may be temporarily disruptive, but can be viewed as orthofunctional in that they may lead to adjustment and correction of system deviations from cultural norms.

The possibility that various types of alienation may have different consequences for political systems is a major reason for separately investigating their correlates, but it is also a compelling reason for studying their interrelationships. The findings of the present research indicate a substantial amount of independence between the alienation dimensions of powerlessness and perceived normlessness. This relatively weak relationship suggests a classification combining different levels of these two dimensions. Insofar as political behavior depends on modes and levels of political alienation, a provisional typology combining alienation and types of political engagement can be proposed (see Figure 1). This paradigm is highly tentative, and is intended to suggest some directions and hypotheses for future research on the relationship between alienation and political activation rather than to report on or synthesize research already accomplished.

Of the four cells, the types of political action associated with relatively low levels of perceived normlessness (i.e., the lower two quadrants) have been most extensively explored. The heavy reliance on random sampling of the general public in political behavior research has perhaps made this inevitable. These styles of participation are of the conventional "middle class" conformative type, including activities such as voting and attending to the mass media.[49] These kinds of activities tend to support existing political institutions.

---

[47] See, for example, Lewis Coser, *The Functions of Social Conflict* (New York: The Free Press, 1956), pp. 15–31; and Wayne Hield, "The Study of Change in Social Science," *British Journal of Sociology* (March, 1964), 1–11.

[48] From the Greek "orthos," to straighten, correct, or make right, as in orthopsychiatry, orthopedics, etc. As an analytic concept, "orthofunctional" is not intended to increase the *explanatory* power of a functional analysis. See A. James Gregor, "Political Science and the Uses of Functional Analysis," *American Political Science Review,* LXII (June, 1968), 425–439.

[49] See David Riesman and Nathan Glazer, "Criteria for Political Apathy," in A. W. Gouldner (ed.), *Studies in Leadership* (New York: Harper and Brothers, 1950), pp. 505–559, for this characterization of most activities used by social scientists as measures of political participation. The current "participation revolution" makes this characterization even more telling today than it was in 1950.

| | | Political Powerlessness | |
		High	Low
Perceived Political Normlessness	High	*Extreme Disengagement* Separatist and revolutionary movements Complete withdrawal	*Reform Orientation* Protest groups working within institutional framework
	Low	*Apathy* Very low level of political involvement	*Political Integration* Conformative participation

Figure 1. Types of Political Behavior Associated With Combinations of Two Types of Political Alienation (Hypothetical)

Moving to the upper two quadrants, the probability that normlessness will be orthofunctional is likely to be at its highest when perceptions of norm violations are combined with a low sense of political powerlessness. Many reform-oriented protest group activities, such as those of CORE or the Southern Christian Leadership Conference, and many domestic agrarian movements, such as the National Farmer's Organization, would fall in this category. The goals of these groups are directed at correcting specific social conditions that impede the integration of certain sub-groups into the system as a whole. In this sense their activities can be thought of as orthofunctional even though they may create serious temporary disturbances in system equilibrium. Individuals who participate in these types of groups feel that the system is at least potentially responsive to their efforts. Those engaging in activities suggested in the upper left quadrant, on the other hand, have probably given up hope that the political system will ever be responsive to their demands. The combination of high perceived normlessness and high levels of political powerlessness seems likely to lead to fundamental, radical rejection of established methods of accomplishing political goals.[50] Whether this rejection is mani-

fested in total withdrawal from political activities or in revolutionary activity will likely depend on opportunities for political activation or on certain personal characteristics. For example, previous research has demonstrated a moderately strong relationship between ego strength and sense of political efficacy.[51] Since we would expect low ego strength to conduce to withdrawal rather than to revolutionary activity, the revolutionaries of the upper left quadrant may come from that small minority of individuals who feel highly powerless politically but yet maintain a strong sense of *personal* efficacy. Opportunities for political activity may further limit the behavior of those in this group. Similarly, other variables will affect the behavior suggested for other combinations of alienation, but the activities suggested may be significant trends.

The kinds of political movements suggested as possible consequences of high

[50] Some substantiating evidence for this hypoth- esis lies in Ransford's finding that among Negroes in the Watts area, infrequent contact with whites was related to willingness to use violence under the two conditions of a high sense of powerlessness and a high dissatisfaction with treatment received as Negroes. See H. Edward Ransford, "Isolation, Powerlessness, and Violence: A Study of Attitudes and Participation in the Watts Riot," *American Journal of Sociology,* 73 (March, 1968), 581–591.

[51] Campbell, *et al., The American Voter,* pp. 516–518.

perceived normlessness are similar to the "value-oriented" (revolutionary) and "norm-oriented" (protest) movements distinguished by Smelser.[52] Value-oriented movements are concerned with basic changes in the nature of man and society while norm-oriented movements are based on less ambitious desires for the restoration or modification of particular social norms. Thus value-oriented movements are comprehensive in their goals while norm-oriented movements seek to make incremental or adjustive changes only. The typology posited above suggests that value-oriented movements are more likely when individuals not only perceive gross violations of political norms but also feel highly powerless to affect the political system. Where feelings of powerlessness are not so strong, it is hypothesized that norm-oriented movements will dominate attempts at political change.

That the correlation between these two dimensions of alienation is fairly low means that the coincidence of extremely high levels on both is likely to be relatively infrequent. Thus, we would expect that the type of threat to orderly system change represented by revolutionary movements will be correspondingly rare, *unless large numbers of people are drawn from the lower left and upper right quad-*

rants into the upper left. While the research reported here has investigated some sources of powerlessness and perceived normlessness, the conditions under which these attitudinal orientations *change* remain to be illuminated.[53] Although it appears likely that recruits to the high powerlessness, high perceived normlessness quadrant come mainly from those already highly alienated on one dimension, there may be certain conditions which draw even those normally not alienated in either way to this state of extreme disengagement. The nature of the general population sample used in this research precludes adequate representation of the type of political posture associated with the joint occurrence of high powerlessness and high perceived normlessness. Nevertheless, systematic knowledge about this type of political activity and its associated attitudinal structure is vitally needed. Although it was possible in the present study to operationalize only two of the four proposed modes of political alienation (and further research may uncover additional types as well), the great popular unrest evident throughout the world today indicates that intensive exploration of the entire alienation domain constitutes a challenge of the highest priority for empirical political theory.

---

[52] See Neil J. Smelser, *Theory of Collective Behavior* (New York: The Free Press of Glencoe, 1963).

[53] For some interesting ideas on the subject of change in basic political attitudes, see William A. Gamson, *Power and Discontent* (Homewood, Illinois: The Dorsey Press, 1968), esp. pp. 172–183.

Appendix

CODES FOR INDEPENDENT VARIABLES

Variable	*Coding*
3. Jewish (Q. 84a)	1 = Jewish; 0 = Non-Jewish
4. Catholic (Q. 84a)	1 = Catholic; 0 = Non-Catholic
5. Protestant (Q. 84a)	1 = Protestant; 0 = Non-Protestant
6. Nativity (Q. 1a)	1 = S. Europe; 2 = N. Europe; 3 = United States
7. Race (Q. 91)	1 = Negro; 0 = White
8. Sex (Q. 90)	1 = Female; 0 = Male
9. Age (Q. 85)	Ascending Order, 1 to 7
10. Education (Q. 61)	Ascending Order, 1 to 8
11. Occupation (Q. 74)	Ascending Order of Prestige, 1 to 9
12. Income (Q. 86)	Ascending Order, 1 to 8
13. Marital Status (Q. 4a)	1 = Single, Divorced, Widowed, Separated; 2 = Married
14. Number of Children (Q. 4b)	Ascending Order, 1 to 6
15. Years Residence in Community (Q. 2)	Ascending Order, 1 to 6
16. Frequency of Church Attendance (Q. 84b)	Ascending Order, 1 to 5
17. Number of Organizations (Q. 83)	Ascending Order, 1 to 5
18. Officership (Q. 83c)	1 = Has been an officer; 0 = Has never been an officer
20. Party Identification (Q. 38)	1 = Democrat; 2 = Independent; 3 = Republican
21. Strength of Party Identification	1 = Independent; 2 = Weak; 3 = Strong
23. Population of Community (Q. 88)	Ascending Order, 1 to 6
24. Northeast (Q. 89)	1 = New England or Middle Atlantic States; 0 = Other States
25. South (Q. 89)	1 = South Atlantic and East South Central States; 0 = Other States

19. Political Participation Index*

   11a. Do you follow the accounts of political and governmental affairs?
   12. What about talking about public affairs to other people?
   25. Have you ever done anything to try to influence a local decision?
   29. Have you ever done anything to try to influence an act of Congress?
   38d. Have you ever been active in a political campaign? That is, have you ever worked for a candidate or party, contributed money, or done any other active work?
   44. What about the campaigning that goes on at the time of a national election: Do you pay much attention to what goes on, just a little, or none at all?
   83d. Are any of the organizations you belong to in any way concerned with governmental, political, or public affairs? For instance, do they take stands on or discuss public issues or try to influence government actions?

22. Faith in People Index*

   7. Some people say that most people can be trusted. Others say you can't be too careful in your dealings with people. How do you feel about it?
   21. Speaking generally, would you say that most people are more inclined to help others, or more inclined to look out for themselves?
   72b. If you don't watch yourself, people will take advantage of you. (Agree-Disagree)
   72e. Human nature is fundamentally cooperative. (Agree-Disagree)
   72h. No one is going to care much what happens to you, when you get right down to it. (Agree-Disagree).

*Codes for individual questions were arranged in ascending order of the concept being measured and were summed for the total score. The Political Participation Index ranged from 0 to 13; the Faith in People Index ranged from 0 to 10.

PERCEPTIONS AND EXPECTATIONS OF THE LEGISLATURE AND SUPPORT FOR IT[1]

Samuel C. Patterson, G.R. Boynton, and Ronald D. Hedlund

This report is a detailed analysis of images of political authority structures which emerge from theoretical concerns of Talcott Parsons and David Easton. Neither of them, however, directly suggested the particular hypothesis our analysis tests. While we have generally followed Easton's nomenclature in establishing the theoretical context of our investigation, sociologists will find that our analysis can as easily be couched in Parsonian terms. In brief, this investigation can be located in Parsons's paradigm of the societal interchange system within the interchange between the goal-attainment subsystem and the integrative subsystem. More specifically, we are dealing with interchanges between legislative collectivities and the public. Our analysis focuses explicitly upon what Parsons has called "generalized support" (1960, pp. 170-98; 1966, pp. 71-112; 1967, pp. 223-63).

SOURCE: Reprinted from *The American Journal of Sociology*, 75, 1 (July 1969), 62–76, by permission of the authors and The University of Chicago Press. Copyright 1969 by The University of Chicago.

[1] This research was supported by grants and other research assistance from the National Science Foundation, the Social Science Research Council, the Research Department of the *Des Moines Register and Tribune*, the University of Iowa Graduate College and Computer Center, and the Laboratory for Political Research, Department of Political Science, University of Iowa. We are especially indebted to Glenn Roberts, Director of the Research Department and the Iowa Poll of the *Des Moines Register and Tribune* and his staff, for indispensable help in conducting our survey, and to Ted Hebert of the Laboratory for Political Research for his management of the coding of the survey data.

If we conceive of a legislative institution as a part of a legislative system, in Easton's (1963, pp. 153-340) terms, we can see that most of the available analyses of interactions between legislative systems and their environments have been in terms of *demands*. Thus, a great deal of the work on legislative politics has focused on constituency or party pressures, interest-group demands, or executive control. Very little research has focused upon citizen *support* of the legislature as a political institution (Jewell and Patterson 1966, pp. 339-57).

Our analysis of citizens' legislative support is based on a number of assumptions. First, we assume that the persistence and maintenance of legislative systems is heavily dependent on some adequate level of public support. We have found very little encouragement in research findings for imputations of high levels of citizen knowledge, concern, choice capability, or party issue awareness from "demand-input models" of mass public-legislature relations (Wahlke 1967). Thus we are inclined to think that it is now appropriate to think of legislative representation from the perspective of support as well as of demands.

rector of the Research Department and the Iowa Poll of the *Des Moines Register and Tribune* and his staff, for indispensable help in conducting our survey, and to Ted Hebert of the Laboratory for Political Research for his management of the coding of the survey data.

Second, we assume that meaningful support for a legislature is not likely to flow in the general population from specific policy output. Rather it comes from diffuse predispositions in the mass public to *(a)* commitment to the legislature as a representative institution and *(b)* to compliance with its enactments. As a result, our research has focused on public attitudes toward the legislature as such, and not upon popular support for particular policy alternatives or specific legislation.

Finally, we have assumed that *(a)* generalized predispositions in the mass public to support the legislature as an institution can be measured by using standard attitude assessment techniques, and that *(b)* citizens will differ in their relative legislative support.[2] The field research which sought to operationalize citizens' legislative support and a host of other variables thought to be related to support was conducted in Iowa in November 1966. A household probability sample of 1,001 adults, representing the population of the state, was interviewed by professional staff under the auspices of the Iowa Laboratory for Political Research. Seven attitudinal statements about the legislature were used to measure support (to be discussed in detail later), and, by combining these items, respondents were scored in terms of their relative support for the legislature.

The basic hypothesis to be dealt with in this paper is that *legislative support in the mass public is a function of congruencies between perceptions of the legislature and expectations about it.* We expect high levels of legislative support from citizens whose feelings about what the legislature is like come close to their expectations of it. And, low levels of legislative support should be exhibited by those for whom there are wide gaps be-

tween their perceptions of the legislature and what they expect of it. Theoretically, a severe crisis of support should occur for legislative systems in which there is a very wide gap between what the citizens expect it to be like and how they actually perceive it to be operating. Wide gaps in civic perception-expectation differentials of this sort for substantial proportions of the population presumably contribute heavily to political reforms or, ultimately, to revolution.[3] These relationships are summarized in figure 1. The curve in the figure plots a measure of aggregated differentials between citizen perceptions and expectations about the legislature. The curve is S-shaped and skewed to the upper right because we would expect sharper correlations between perception-expectation differentials and support in the middle ranges of the former. And we would expect, in the American case, a higher incidence of positive support than of low support. We expect our Iowa data to fall somewhere within the box in the center of the diagram because citizens' legislative support levels are generally high, and great gaps between expectations and perceptions do not appear to occur.

Figure 2 adds time to the hypothesis, and presents the case in which the perception of the legislature falls somewhat (but tolerably) below the expectation of the legislature for a period of time. But hypothetically, an increasing disparity between the two produces a crisis of support which might ultimately result in sufficient stress on the system to lead to revolutionary change. Though time is an obvious factor in our theoretical scheme, our data are cross-sectional so we can deal only with one point in time.

These comments may clarify our analytical tasks. We need to compare measurements of civic perception-expectation differentials and measurements of legis-

---

[2] For a report from this project which identifies the degrees of legislative support in different social and political strata, see G. R. Boynton, Samuel C. Patterson, and Ronald D. Hedlund (1968).

[3] See, for instance, James C. Davies (1962) and Raymond Tanter and Manus Midlarsky (1967).

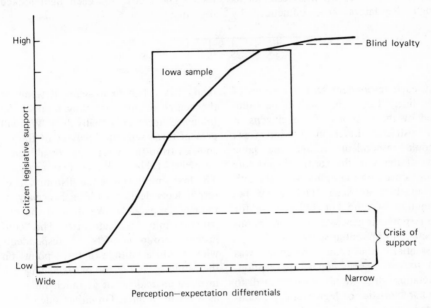

Figure 1.

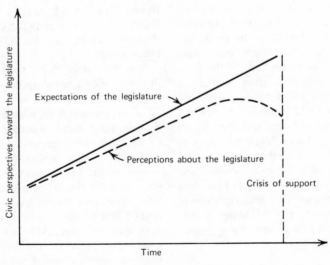

Figure 2.

lative support. How can what we have been calling civic perception-expectation differentials be measured? We have sought to do this with two sets of data from the Iowa survey. One set of data was devel-oped from a series of interview questions asking respondents to scale on a one-ten metric a series of actors or agencies by whom legislators should be influenced, and in the same way to scale the same agencies in terms of whether respondents thought legislators were influenced by them. The metric for each item looked like this:

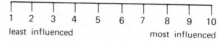

First, each respondent scored a series of items like, "Legislators should be influenced by the opinions of the citizens of their districts." Later in the interview, schedule respondents scored the same kinds of items in the form, "Legislators are influenced by the opinions of the citizens in their districts." Differences between the "is" and "ought" scoring for each respondent generated his perception-expectation differential score.

Essentially the same procedure was used to assess respondents' perception-expectation differentials with regard to the characteristics of legislators. We confronted respondents with a set of characteristics which legislators might exhibit, and we asked them to tell us to what extent legislators ought to have the attribute in question, and to what extent members of the legislature had these characteristics.

Thus, we have not sought to measure expectations and perceptions of the legislature as a vague abstraction. Rather, respondents were asked to deal with two concrete aspects of legislative representation: influence agencies and the characteristics of legislators. Since responses to our questions about these two matters have considerable intrinsic interest, and we need to explicate the shape of our data regarding them so that our use of them in analyzing support can be better understood, we shall now present the aggregate results from the Iowa sample.

Public Attitudes Toward Legislative Influence

Our respondents rated the thirteen agencies of legislative influence listed in Table 1. First, they indicated on a ten-point scale the ones which they thought ought to be influential in the legislature;

then, they rated them again in terms of the degree of influence they thought the influence agencies actually had. We will present three separate analyses of the responses from the two ratings of influence agencies. Table 1 shows two analyses. The first simply shows the distribution of respondents dealing with each agency of influence separately. We divided the distribution into three categories. The "congruent" group consists of respondents who, within a latitude of three points on the rating scale, felt the particular agency in question had about as much influence as it ought to have. On either side of this congruent group we show the proportions of the sample who felt the particular agency had more or less influence than it should. The second analysis in Table 1 shows the sample means for each rating, the rank orders, and the differences between means.

It is plain from Table 1 that there are discontinuities among agencies of influence with the legislature in terms of public perceptions and expectations. Of the agencies rated, constituents are thought to be the most underrepresented in terms of influence in the legislature. Forty-four percent of the Iowa sample felt that constituents have less influence in the legislature than they should have, while they ranked first as the agency that ought to have such influence. Although ratings of constituent influence produced a large negative mean difference between expectations and perceptions of influence, constituents were also rated by respondents as the agency which has the most influence in the legislature. In general, the order of expected and perceived influence follows that of (1) constituents and polls reflecting public opinion, (2) experts,

Table 1. Differences between Influence in the Iowa Legislature Agencies
Ought to Have and Influence They Do Have (N = 1,001)

Legislative Influence Agencies	Say Agency Has Less Influence Than It Should (%)	Are Con-gruent (%)	Say Agency Has More Influence Than It Should (%)	Influence Agency Ought to Have		Influence Agency Does Have		Mean Dif-fer-ence
				Mean	Rank	Mean	Rank	
Constituents	43.7	48.2	8.2	8.20	1	6.84	1	−1.36
Statewide opinion polls ..	34.2	50.3	15.6	6.72	2	6.13	3	− .59
Experts in legislature	29.3	52.2	18.6	6.64	3	6.24	2	− .40
Experts in state gov't	25.1	53.9	16.0	6.42	4	6.19	5	− .23
Governor	13.8	47.9	38.4	4.92	5	5.99	6	+1.07
Labor	18.0	43.6	31.2	4.58	6	5.64	7	+1.06
Party leaders in the legislature ..	8.6	36.3	40.3	4.51	7	6.13	3	+1.62
Chamber of Commerce	20.2	57.6	22.3	4.17	8	4.39	10	+ .22
Farm Bureau	15.8	44.2	34.7	4.12	9	4.99	9	+ .87
Chairmen of state parties	9.4	45.0	45.7	3.80	10	5.58	8	+1.78
National Farmers Organization ..	14.6	56.7	27.7	3.59	11	4.15	12	+ .56
Banks	10.9	40.0	29.3	3.19	12	4.22	11	+1.03
Insurance companies	7.9	53.6	38.6	2.58	13	4.11	13	+1.53

(3) party leaders, and (4) interest groups. For constituents, polls, and experts, respondents tended to feel that agencies have *less* influence than they should in greater proportions than the view that they have *more* influence than they should. For all of the other agencies of influence, a higher proportion of respondents felt they had more influence than they should rather than less. The rank order correlation between perceived and expected influence agencies is very high ($r_s = .91$).

The largest gaps in differences in mean rankings are for legislative and extra-legislative party leaders. Legislative party leaders fall at the median rank in expected influence, but are ranked third by respond-ents in the aggregate in perceived actual influence (tied with statewide public opinion polls). But a relatively high proportion of the respondents felt party leaders have more influence in the legislature than they should. Again, note that 46 percent of the Iowa sample indicated that state party chairmen have more influence than they should. The difference of score means here is very high and positive (they score higher in perceived than in expected influence).

Interest groups generally fall at the bottom of the rank orders of perceived and expected influence. Unlike constituents and experts, who show a negative difference between expected and perceived influence, but like party leaders (including the governor), interest groups are thought to have more influence than they should. Labor, banks, and insurance companies show the highest differences in means, while farm organizations and the chamber of commerce show the least differences between expected and perceived influence.

Table 2 shows the results of a factor analysis of the "ought" responses from this analysis.* Four factors were extracted and rotated by the Kaiser varimax method. The factorial structure of responses rating the influence agencies ought to have is very clear-cut and conforms exactly to our intuitive groupings. The same factor analysis was run for responses to the ratings of perceived actual influence, and this analysis produced virtually the same factorial structure, so we have not shown it. The factor analysis reinforces with con-

*Editor's note: For a brief explanation of factor analysis, see the editor's note on p. 192.

crete evidence our tendency to talk about perspectives on the Iowa influence structure in terms of four major groups of agencies rather than thirteen separate agencies.

From the standpoint of our analytical objectives, it is comforting to find some variance in perceptions and expectations of influence. From the point of view of the stability of the Iowa political system, it can be suggested that there does appear to be a relatively high degree of congruity between expected and perceived influence. Not only do Iowans tend to feel that influence lies about where it ought to, but they tend to regard the system as structured such that citizens have the most influence on the legislature and interest groups the least influence, with experts and party leaders occupying the middle ground. Both the perceived and expected influence structures and the congruency between them undoubtedly indicate satisfaction with the system and should mean generally high levels of legislative support in this population.

Table 2. Factor Analysis of Agencies Which Ought to Be Influential in the Legislature

LEGISLATIVE INFLUENCE AGENCIES	FACTORS			
	I	II	III	IV
1. Farm Bureau	.793	.018	—.177	.011
2. National Farmers Organization	.776	—.038	—.133	.182
3. Insurance companies	.631	.188	.244	.265
4. Labor	.616	.158	—.083	.266
5. Banks	.569	.177	.245	.459
6. Chamber of Commerce	.522	.305	.023	.390
7. Legislative experts	.085	.857	—.067	.131
8. Experts in state government	.160	.794	—.111	.187
9. Statewide public opinion polls	.095	—.031	—.822	.190
10. Constituents	.011	.365	—.612	—.100
11. Party leaders in legislature	.082	.151	—.031	.838
12. Chairmen of state parties	.291	.123	.022	.762
13. Governor	.272	.054	—.205	.527
Cumulative total variance (%)	33.6	45.1	54.1	61.6
Cumulative explained variance (%)	54.6	73.3	87.9	100.0

Note.—Items *1-6*, interest groups; *7, 8*, experts; *9, 10*, constituents and polls reflecting public opinion; *11-13*, party leaders.

Civic Perspectives on Legislator Attributes

What kind of a person *should* a legislator be in the minds of his constituents? and, What do constituents think legislators *are* like? If citizens' images of legislators depart severely from their conceptions of the kinds of people who should represent them, then support for the legislature is likely to be low. We asked respondents in the Iowa sample to evaluate a set of twenty attributes which have variously been suggested as characteristics legislators have, or ought to have. These attributes are listed in Table 3. First, respondents were asked to indicate to what extent they thought legislators ought to have each attribute, ranking each on this scale:

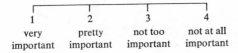

1	2	3	4
very important	pretty important	not too important	not at all important

Then, respondents were asked to make judgments about roughly what proportion of the members of the legislature actually had each attribute, gauging them on this scale:

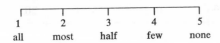

1	2	3	4	5
all	most	half	few	none

The entries of mean scores in Table 3 were generated by assigning one–four points for responses to the first set of rankings, and scoring respondents from one to five on the second set.

As a group, the respondents in the Iowa sample ranked attributes of good character, knowledge and ability, and social status highest, and they ranked attributes of personal gain or manipulation lowest. When the rank orders for attributes legislators have are compared to ranks for characteristics they should have, some rather dramatic shifts occur, especially at the top of the ranks. While being completely honest ranks first as a trait legislators should have, it drops to the median rank of attributes legislators are

perceived to possess. The highest ranking for perceived attributes is for political party loyalty. On the other hand, citizens tend to regard legislators as more friendly, influential in their districts, and prestigious than they should be, in terms of ranked importance. At the same time, the two ranked orderings are highly correlated ($r_s = .64$).

It is apparent that the items listed in Table 3 could be grouped into several sets, and doing so helps to reduce the complexity of dealing with twenty categories. More importantly, we were interested in a clear analysis of what we were measuring in assessing differences between expected and perceived legislative attributes. Thus, we factor analyzed both the ratings of characteristics respondents felt it was important for legislators to have and those attributes respondents felt actually characterized the legislature.[4] The factor analysis of legislator attributes is displayed in Table 4; the factorial structure for actual perceived characteristics is so similar that we have not shown it. Six factors accounted for more than half of the variance in scores, and the factorial structure is quite unambiguous. We have added to the factor analysis presented in Table 4 the mean of the means of items from Table 3 included in each factor, and the rank order of factors based upon these means.

The highest ranking factor in terms of mean scores, Factor II, included items having to do with the purposive activity of legislators and is among the top two factors in accounting for variance explained. The second ranking factor, Factor IV, including honesty, knowledge of and influence in the legislative district, and community prestige, can be given the summary label the "community status" factor. The factor ranking third, Factor

---

[4] Because two of the items in table 3 did not produce unambiguous factor loadings ("friendly toward others" and "just an average citizen"), they were omitted from further analysis.

Table 3. Means and Ranks of Scores for Characteristics of Legislators (N = 1,001)

CHARACTERISTICS OF LEGISLATORS	IMPORTANT FOR LEGISLATORS TO HAVE THE CHARACTERISTIC		EXTENT TO WHICH LEGISLATORS ACTUALLY HAVE CHARACTERISTIC	
	MEAN	RANK	MEAN	RANK
Completely honest	1.08	1	2.50	10
Study problems thoroughly	1.18	2	2.36	8
Know will of people of district	1.27	3	2.31	7
Hard working	1.30	4	2.30	6
Interested in serving others	1.32	5	2.26	5
Special knowledge about state government	1.46	6	2.40	9
Friendly toward others	1.51	7	2.14	2
High prestige in community	1.64	8	2.17	4
Influential in own district	1.64	9	2.16	3
Concerned with small details	1.97	10	3.01	17
Trained in legal work	2.01	11	2.84	15
Just an average citizen	2.09	12	2.51	11
Loyal to his political party	2.14	13	2.06	1
College graduate	2.46	14	2.66	12
Change things slowly if at all	2.51	15	3.10	18
Held previous office	2.55	16	2.69	14
Between ages 45-55	2.78	17	2.68	13
Political beliefs that do not change .	2.92	18	2.85	16
Only interested in reelection	3.58	19	3.35	19
Seek personal gain or profit	3.64	20	3.54	20

V, can be called the "slow and deliberate change" factor from the manifest character of the two items highly loaded on it. The fourth ranking factor in terms of means, Factor I, accounts for nearly one-third of the explained variance and deals with the experience or preparation of legislators. The party loyalty factor, Factor VI, ranks fifth in mean scores, followed by self-motivation, Factor III. The factor analysis and mean scores for the twenty legislator attributes rated by respondents suggest, therefore, the following hierarchy of expectations about the characteristics of legislators: (1) purposive activity, (2) community status, (3) slow and deliberate change, (4) experience, (5) party loyalty, and (6) self-motivation. A similar analysis was carried out for respondents' ratings of the twenty basic attributes in terms of whether legislators actually exhibited them. The rankings of similar factors for perceived actual attributes were: (1) community status, (2) purposive activity, (3) party loyalty, (4) experience, (5) slow and deliberate change, and (6) self-motivation. This shift in the rankings of factors suggests the nature of differences between Iowans' expectations and perceptions of legislator attributes. The community status and purposive activity factors reverse positions; party loyalty exchanges places with slow and deliberate change; experience remains fourth in rank, and self-motivation is at the bottom of both rankings.

Table 4. Factor Analysis of Characteristics Legislators Ought to Have

CHARACTERISTICS OF LEGISLATORS	FACTORS						MEANS OF ITEMS INCLUDED IN FACTOR	RANK OF IMPORTANCE OF FACTORS
	I	II	III	IV	V	VI		
1. Held previous office	.719	—.007	.091	—.043	—.047	.105	2.45	4
2. Trained in legal work	.686	.141	.000	—.036	.247	—.007		
3. College graduate	.583	.074	—.029	—.047	—.036	.336		
4. Between ages 45-55	.471	—.062	.341	—.040	.114	.142		
5. Interested in serving others	—.009	.804	—.043	—.084	.059	—.010	1.32	1
6. Study problems thoroughly	—.082	.737	.007	—.174	.062	.047		
7. Special knowledge of state gov't	.345	.713	—.007	—.004	—.012	—.085		
8. Hard working	.057	.436	—.193	—.340	—.052	.289		
9. Seek personal gain or profit	.018	—.067	.813	—.001	.058	.018	3.61	6
10. Only interested in reelection	.109	.004	.755	.027	.010	.130		
11. Influential in own district	.333	—.069	.133	—.653	.055	—.131	1.45	2
12. Know will of people in district	—.143	.323	.039	—.637	—.152	—.169		
13. Completely honest	—.169	.101	—.105	—.552	.144	.226		
14. High prestige in community	.250	.147	—.037	—.513	.088	.166		
15. Concerned with details	.054	.078	—.063	—.138	.804	—.121	2.24	3
16. Change things slowly	.112	—.006	.206	.043	.655	.256		
17. Political beliefs that don't change	.091	—.023	.275	.073	.052	.703	2.53	5
18. Loyal to political party	.287	.020	—.009	—.167	.040	.691		
Cumulative total variance (%)	16.8	30.1	36.9	43.2	49.3	55.0	....	....
Cumulative explained variance (%)	30.6	54.6	67.0	78.5	89.6	100.0	....	....

Note.—Items 1-4, experience factor; 5-8, purposive activity; 9, 10, self-motivation; 11-14, community status; 15, 16, slow and deliberate change; 17, 18, party loyalty.

Measurement of Legislative Support

We measured our dependent variable —public support for the legislature—with seven Likert-type items, which are given in Table 5. These items measure the degree of citizens' commitment to the legislature as an institution and their predispositions to compliance with its enactments. In the table we have simply shown responses trichotomized as high, medium, or low support. We have factor analyzed these items, and two distinct factors develop. One is a compliance factor and the other is an institutional commitment factor. Since raw scores from these separate factors are highly correlated ($r = .66$), our measurement of the dependent variable will proceed from the data for all seven items together.

Although the data in Table 5 make it

Table 5. Attitudes of Support Toward the Iowa Legislature (%)

LEGISLATIVE SUPPORT ITEMS	DIRECTION OF SUPPORT	LEGISLATIVE SUPPORT				
		HIGH	MEDIUM	LOW	DON'T KNOW	TOTAL
There are times when it almost seems better for the citizens of the state to take the law into their own hands rather than wait for the state legislature to act	Disagree	28.0	51.7	14.4	5.9	100.0
If you don't particularly agree with a state law, it is all right to break it if you are careful not to get caught	Disagree	42.1	52.6	2.1	3.2	100.0
There are times when it would almost seem better for the governor to take the law into his own hands rather than to wait for the state legislature to act	Disagree	11.8	54.0	25.8	8.4	100.0
Even though one might strongly disagree with a state law, after it has been passed by the state legislature one ought to obey it	Agree	21.6	71.7	2.9	3.8	100.0
One should be willing to do everything that he could to make sure that any proposal to abolish the state legislature were defeated	Agree	9.8	62.6	13.9	13.7	100.0

Table 5 continued

LEGISLATIVE SUPPORT ITEMS	DIRECTION OF SUPPORT	LEGISLATIVE SUPPORT				
		HIGH	MEDIUM	LOW	DON'T KNOW	TOTAL
If the Iowa legislature continually passed laws that the people disagreed with, it might be better to do away with the legislature altogether	Disagree	16.4	62.1	12.4	9.1	100.0
It would not make much difference if the constitution of Iowa were rewritten so as to reduce the powers of the state legislature	Disagree	6.9	59.2	12.1	21.8	100.0

Note.—$N = 1,000$ male adults.

clear that large proportions of the Iowa respondents expressed attitudes of compliance with the laws passed by the legislature, preference for legislative lawmaking, and commitment to the existence of the legislature as an institution, some notable variations are evident. The least support of the legislature was evinced by the question of the governor taking the law into his own hands rather than waiting for the legislature to act. More than one-fourth of the sample agreed that there were times when the governor should do this and only 12 percent strongly disagreed. Nearly one-sixth agreed that sometimes citizens should take the law into their own hands without waiting for the legislature to take action, although more than one-half disagreed and more than one-fourth disagreed strongly.

In contrast, very marked support for the legislature was indicated by the high proportion in the sample of those whose responses showed that they felt citizens ought to comply with laws passed by the legislature whether they agreed with them or not. Less than 3 percent were willing to agree that it was all right to disobey the law. These data suggest that, for some people, extraordinary action by the governor or by citizens can sometimes be acceptable substitutes for the legislative process. But outright failure to comply when the legislative authority has been exercised is rarely acceptable.

There was a higher incidence of no response to the question on the items involving retention of the legislature and reduction of its powers, but the pattern for the three items is quite similar for those who did respond. Across these items, about 12 percent were willing to consider abolishing the legislature or reducing its constitutional powers. More than two-thirds did not wish to reduce legislative power; 72 percent agreed that proposals to abolish the legislature should be defeated, and more than 78 percent disagreed that the legislature should be abolished if it persistently passed disagreeable laws.

Perception-Expectation Differentials and Support

Although the general level of public support for the Iowa legislature seems very high, it is variable enough for analytical purposes. We can proceed now to test our basic hypothesis, which we shall do by testing two subhypotheses:

(a) If there is a wide differential between the legislative influence citizens perceive is wielded by interest groups, constituents, experts, and party leaders, and the influence citizens expect they ought to have, then legislative support will tend to be low. If perceived and expected influence are roughly congruent, legislative support will tend to be high.

(b) If there is a wide differential between the attributes which citizens perceive as actually characterizing legislators and their expectations about what a legislator ought to be like, then legislative support will tend to be low. If perceived and expected attributes are roughly congruent, legislative support will tend to be high.

We are now in a position to present the analysis of these hypotheses.

The conditions in the Iowa data obviously are not ideal for the support of these hypotheses. The sample is very homogeneous in that support for the legislature is very high and not extraordinarily variable, and there are not great gaps between expectations about the legislature and perceptions of it in the terms in which we have measured these things. If there is any substantial support in the data for our hypotheses, we would consider the test a strong one, since they have been tested in an unlikely place for dramatic support of them.

We have tested our two subhypotheses in the following manner: for each set of factors (shown in Tables 2 and 4) for expectations and perceptions we selected the most congruent and the most incongruent respondents on the basis of two criteria: consistency of responses and level of expectations. The application of these criteria led to the selection of respondents which would juxtapose the most congruent and the most incongruent perception-expectation responses for each factor. Respondents were also factor scored from the principal component analysis of the legislative support items, so

that differences between congruent and incongruent respondents could be assessed in terms of mean factor scores for legislative support. The tests for mean differences in support between congruent and incongruent groups with respect to both subhypotheses are arrayed in Table 6. As a whole, this array displays means which do not show great absolute differences. However, for half the factors, differences between extreme congruent and incongruent groups in support for the legislature were statistically significant. Insofar as so-called influence agency factors were concerned, significant differences did occur between congrunt and incongruent respondents with respect to general public and interest group influence. In both cases, mean differences were significant at the .05 level. With respect to legislator attribute factors, significant differences were extant for half of the factors. Mean legislative support scores of congruent and incongruent groups were different at the .01 level for the community status and self-motivation factors, and different at the .05 level for the experience factor. Furthermore, in the cases of the other factors, mean legislative support in the congruent group was somewhat higher than in the incongruent group, although the differences were not statistically significant.

Conclusion

The basic hypothesis tested in this paper is that congruence between perceptions and expectations about the legislature leads to high support for the legislature, and incongruence between perceptions and expectations leads to low support for the legislature. The Iowa sample provides tentative confirmation of this hypothesis. There is a quite remarkable congruence between perceptions and expectations in Iowa. The very high correlation between the rankings of perceptions and expectations is a clear indication of this congruence. Support for the legislative insti-

Table 6. Mean Legislative Support Scores for Congruent and Incongruent Perception-Expectation Groups

| | PERCEPTION-EXPECTATION DIFFERENTIALS | | | | |
| | CONGRUENT | | INCONGRUENT | | SIGNIFICANT DIFFERENCES |
FACTORS	MEAN	N	MEAN	N	(t-test)
Influence agency factors:					
Public	2.39	61	2.16	178	$p < .05$
Experts	2.34	175	2.20	65	N.S.
Interest groups	2.31	179	2.09	35	$p < .05$
Party leaders	2.29	90	2.18	162	N.S.
Legislator attribute factors:					
Purposive activity ...	2.22	125	2.19	93	N.S.
Community status ...	2.51	150	2.10	81	$p < .01$
Slow and deliberate change	2.35	116	2.27	95	N.S.
Experience	2.34	157	2.19	78	$p < .05$
Party loyalty	2.25	134	2.17	88	N.S.
Self-motivation	2.46	144	2.25	91	$p < .01$

tution in Iowa is also quite high. This is indicated in Table 5, where the answers to the seven items dealing with support are presented. Another indication of this high level of support can be given. When the answers to the seven support items are combined, a scale of support can be developed with a range from a low score of four to a high score of twenty-eight. The mean for the total sample is 22.3, which is highly skewed in the supportive direction. Thus, as they are measured for the Iowa sample, congruence between perceptions and expectations is high and support for the legislature is high, suggesting the validity of the basic hypothesis.

Congruent and incongruent groups on each of ten factors were compared on their levels of legislative support. For each factor, the congruent group had a higher mean support score than did the incongruent group; however, in only five cases was this difference statistically significant. While each of these groups constitutes only a small subset of the total sample, the analysis of their support scores adds confirmation to the general hypothesis we have explored.

We already have shown that support for the legislative system is sensitive to differences in social and political structure (Boynton, Patterson, and Hedlund 1968). Legislative support increases as one looks from the bottom to the top of the structure of socioeconomic status, and is greater at high than at low levels of political awareness and participation. One of the next steps in our analysis will be to investigate the nexus between perception-expectation differentials and differences in social and political structure as joint determinants of variations in support for the legislature.

REFERENCES

1. Boynton, G. R., Samuel C. Patterson, and Ronald D. Hedlund. 1968. "The Structure of Public Support for Legislative Institutions." *Midwest Journal of Political Science* 12 (May): 163–80.

2. Davies, James C. 1962. "Toward a Theory of Revolution." *American Sociological Review* 27 (February): 5–19.

3. Easton, David. 1963. *A Systems Analysis of Political Life.* New York: Wiley.

4. Jewell, Malcolm E., and Samuel C. Patterson. 1966. *The Legislative Process in the United States.* New York: Random House.

5. Parsons, Talcott. 1960. *Structure and Process in Modern Societies.* New York: Free Press.

6. ———. 1966. "The Political Aspect of Social Structure and Process." In *Varieties of Poli-*

tical Theory, edited by David Easton. Englewood Cliffs, N.J.: Prentice-Hall.

7. ———. 1967. *Sociological Theory and Modern Society.* New York: Free Press.

8. Tanter, Raymond, and Manus Midlarsky. 1967. "A Theory of Revolution." *Journal of Conflict Resolution* 11 (September): 264–80.

9. Wahlke, John C. 1967. "Public Policy and Representative Government: The Role of the Represented." Paper presented at the Seventh World Congress of the International Political Science Association, Brussels, September.

POLITICAL TRUST AND RACIAL IDEOLOGY*

Joel D. Aberbach and Jack L. Walker

I. Introduction

No government yet established has had the loyalty and trust of all its citizens. Regardless of the popularity of its leaders or how careful they are in soliciting opinions and encouraging participation in the process of policy-making, there are always those who see inequalities and injustices in the society and harbor suspicions of the government's motives and intentions. Resentment and distrust are elements of disaffection and the first step toward resistance. Therefore, even the most dictatorial governments have usually striven to increase their credibility and popularity. For democratic governments, however, the problem of combating distrust and en-

SOURCE: Reprinted from *The American Political Science Review,* LXIV, 4 (December, 1970), 1199–1219, by permission of the authors and publisher.

* The principal grant which supported this study came from the National Institute of Mental Health. Additional support also came from the Horace H. Rackham Faculty Research Fund and the Institute of Public Policy Studies, The University of Michigan. Thanks are due to Steven L. Coombs and William A. Gamson who read and criticized an earlier version of this paper and to James D. Chesney and Douglas B. Neal who assisted in the data analysis.

couraging voluntary acceptance of its institutions and decisions is a paramount concern. One of democratic theory's distinctive characteristics is its strong emphasis on voluntary consent, both as a basis of political obligation and as a central attribute of citizenship. The concern expressed by democratic thinkers about the elements of due process and the protection of opportunities for widespread participation is directed toward the creation of citizens who voluntarily accept the society's goals; "the demand for consent is the demand that the government must be more than self-appointed and must, in some significant way, be the chosen instrument through which the body politic and community acts. . . ."[1]

Democracy's guiding ideal is the substitution of mutual understanding and agreement for coerciveness and arbitrary authority in all phases of social and political life. The existence of distrustful citizens who are convinced that the government serves the interests of a few rather than the interests of all is a barrier to the realization of the democratic ideal. In

[1] Joseph Tussman, *Obligation and the Body Politic* (New York: Oxford University Press, 1960), p. 23.

Sabine's words: "full understanding cannot be reached except on the basis of mutual respect and with a mutual acknowledgment of good faith and the acceptance of the principle that the purpose of understanding is to protect all valid interests."[2] Leaders in a representative democracy cannot be successful until they have gained the trust of the citizens; this is even more important in American society where racial and ethnic minorities are actively searching for a new, more dignified role as political equals.

Besides its important normative implications, the level of trust in government also is an important determinant of political change. The rise and fall in the number of distrustful citizens over time is a sensitive barometer of social conflicts and tensions. When any sizable group becomes distrustful and begins to make demands, the government is prompted to reallocate its resources or change its institutions to accommodate these new pressures. If the political system is flexible and adaptive enough, needed adjustments can be made without any consequent outbreak of violence, but if distrustful groups are denied access to decision-makers, or if institutions are too rigid to change, destructive conflict and a breakdown in the social order are possible. Under the right political conditions, distrustful groups, which exist in all societies, may produce the kind of creative tensions needed to prompt social change, but under other conditions, these same tensions either may lead to violent disruption or indiscriminate and cruel repression. A society's leaders may either strive to meet the demands of the distrustful group, or instead, they may endeavor to isolate and attack the group, making it a scapegoat for the resentment and hostility of the majority. Rising distrust is often a stimulant to social change, but its consequences depend on the re-

sponse it provokes from leaders and other elements of the society.

The level of trust in government strongly influences the kind of policies and strategies available to political leaders. As Gamson has argued, when the level of trust is high, "the authorities are able to make new commitments on the basis of it and, if successful, increase such support even more. When it is low and declining, authorities may find it difficult to meet existing commitments and to govern effectively."[3] Levels of trust and allegiance differ greatly among countries and these differences determine both the number of options open to the government and the relative danger of political fragmentation.[4] The distribution of trust among different social groups in the society also may have an important effect on the relative success of different governmental policies, and a sensitive awareness of its importance should allow a political leader to adopt more successful strategies of persuasion.

Widespread trust in government is recognized by students of both normative and empirical questions as the foundation for democratic order. This paper presents a comparative analysis of political trust in the black and white communities of Detroit, Michigan—a city which has a history of racial conflict and experienced major civil disturbances in 1943 and 1967. We discuss: (1) the concept of political trust; (2) the levels of trust in both racial communities; (3) the principal social and political sources of trustful and distrustful attitudes; (4) the contrast between the correlates and nature of political distrust in the black and white communities; (5) the behavioral consequences of distrust; and (6) the racial ideologies linked to political trust in both communities.

[3] William A. Gamson, *Power and Discontent* (Homewood, Ill.: Dorsey, 1968), pp. 45–46.

[4] Gabriel A. Almond and Sidney Verba, *The Civic Culture: Political Attitudes and Democracy in Five Nations* (Princeton: Princeton University Press, 1963), p. 490.

[2] George Sabine, "The Two Democratic Traditions," *The Philosophical Review*, 61 (1952), p. 471.

II. A Review of the Literature

Given the widely acknowledged importance of political trust in maintaining political stability or promoting change[5] it is surprising that empirical research on the origins and consequences of trust is so scarce. In addition, the small body of literature which does exist raises more questions than it answers. Studies contradict each other as conceptual and measurement problems abound. Sometimes political trust is clearly related to social status[6] and sometimes not.[7] Often it is correlated with feelings of political efficacy,[8] but not always.[9] In most instances it is strongly related to measures of trust in other people,[10] but again, not always.[11]

At least some of this confusion is due to the fact that the reported research has taken place in different settings. We know that levels of trust vary according to what Litt has called the "political milieu" in

[5] Gamson's work, *op. cit.*, builds on the concerns of Parsons and Easton. See, especially, Talcott Parsons, "Some Reflections on the Place of Force in Social Process" in Harry Eckstein (ed.), *Internal War* (New York: Free Press, 1964), pp. 33–70, and David Easton, *A Systems Analysis of Political Life* (New York: Wiley, 1965).

[6] Robert E. Agger, Marshall N. Goldstein and Stanley A. Pearl, "Political Cynicism: Measurement and Meaning," *The Journal of Politics,* 23 (1961), 477–506 and Herbert McClosky, "Consensus and Ideology in American Politics," *American Political Science Review* (1964), 361–383.

[7] Donald E. Stokes, "Popular Evaluations of Government: An Empirical Assessment," in Harlan Cleveland and Harold D. Lasswell (eds.), *Ethics and Bigness: Scientific, Academic, Religious, Political and Military* (New York: Harper, 1962), pp. 61–73; and Joel D. Aberbach, *Alienation and Race* (unpublished Ph.D. Dissertation, Yale University, 1967), especially pp. 102–126 and 206–208.

[8] Stokes, *op. cit.*, p. 68; Agger, *op. cit.*, p. 494; and Edgar Litt, "Political Cynicism and Political Futility," *The Journal of Politics,* 23 (1963), p. 321, Table 5.

[9] Litt, *op. cit.*, p. 320, Table 2.

[10] See Morris Rosenberg, "Misanthropy and Political Ideology," *American Sociological Review,* 21 (1956), 690–695.

[11] Litt, *op. cit.*, p. 320, Table 1.

which distrust "may be acquired as a *community norm,* a part of the political acculturation process in the city's daily routine."[12] Not only can the political milieu influence the level of trust, but the relationships between variables are not always the same in each setting. For example, in Litt's comparative study of a middle class neighborhood in Boston and a comparable area in adjoining Brookline there is no relationship between feelings of political trust and political efficacy in Boston and yet there is a strong relationship in Brookline. The explanation offered is that in Boston, a city noted for blatant corruption in its political life, "community-wide suspicions of 'base practices' may go hand in hand with a belief that the professional practitioner of politics will still turn an attentive ear to the plaints of his constituents,"[13] while in Brookline, a community with a history of clean government, those who are distrustful are fully convinced that political leaders will not be responsive to their requests. In Brookline the citizens' distrust can be traced to personality variables, while in Boston the political milieu is the dominant factor.[14]

A study of distrust at the federal level raised similar issues. Stokes, using data from the Survey Research Center's 1958 national election study, found a correlation between feelings of political efficacy and political trust. He hypothesized that under certain conditions one could find subjective powerlessness linked with a positive attitude toward government, but "in the context of democratic values, feelings of powerlessness toward public authority tend to create feelings of hostility toward the authority."[15] While Stokes re-

[12] *Ibid.,* p. 319.

[13] *Ibid.,* p. 320.

[14] *Ibid.,* p. 317. Litt finds that the "degree of personal trust, unrelated to political cynicism in Boston, is directly related to the expression of cynical comments about politicians in the suburban community."

[15] Stokes, *op. cit.*, p. 67.

ported a relationship between political trust and efficacy similar to that found among Litt's Brookline residents, his national sample resembled Litt's Boston respondents in that social status variables were at best weakly correlated with trust.

The setting of the research apparently is important in determining both the level of distrust and the relationship between it and other variables. If we are to explain successfully the origins and consequences of distrust, therefore, we must systematically introduce into our measures factors associated with the political settings of the population. To do so we must deal with conceptual problems which are intimately tied to problems of measurement. The concept of political distrust is defined by Stokes as a "basic evaluative orientation toward the . . . government."[16] However, items in many of the scales designed to measure political distrust often involve simple clichés about the quality of politics and politicians with little or no indication as to the governments or figures involved. McClosky, who employs such items in his measure, is quite concerned about their validity and therefore about the interpretation of his results. "It is," he says, "impossible in the present context to determine the extent to which scores contained in these tables signify genuine frustration and political disillusionment and the extent to which they represent familiar and largely ritualistic responses."[17] This is not to deny that some element of disaffection may be tapped by questions of this kind, but one can only guess at how much. We cannot tell which politicians the subject is reminded of, or the relative importance of most of the images conjured up by the statements. The goal of scholars in the field is to get below this surface veneer to tap deeper hostility.

To do this it would seem vitally important that the subject be stimulated to think about some more focused symbol than "politicians"[18] and that the items not be phrased in simple agree-disagree form. This will not completely avoid the problem of imperfect measurement due to ritualistic responses, but it should mitigate it somewhat by making the statement of disaffection more meaningful to the subject.

Stokes' scale is a model of what we seek here. Before the items are presented to the respondent he is told:"Now I'd like to talk about some of the different ideas people have about the government in Washington and see how you feel about them. These opinions don't refer to any single branch of government in general."[19] A series of items (see below for examples) follows which are not in agree-disagree form and which are reversed so that the positive alternative is not presented first in each case. These questions measure whether the respondent believes that the government generally does the right things, and whether it serves the public interest. The format is designed to cut down response-set problems and, in this case, focus the respondents' attention on the collective workings of an identifiable set of political arrangements and institutions.

As Gamson says, "it is possible for individuals simultaneously to feel high confidence in political institutions and alienation towards those who man them."[20] In fact, according to Gamson, it is important to find out whether political trust is gen-

[18] See Aberbach, *op. cit.*, pp. 25–42 for a detailed discussion of the importance of specifying the focus in measuring disaffection and pp. 46–56 for a critique of the political trust literature using this perspective. A briefer discussion can be found in Joel D. Aberbach, "Alienation and Political Behavior," *American Political Science Review*, 63 (1969), pp. 86–99. See, also, Kenneth Keniston, *The Uncommitted: Alienated Youth in American Society* (New York: Harcourt, Brace & World, 1965), pp. 453–455.

[19] Inter-University Consortium for Political Research (ICPR), *1966 Election Study* (Ann Arbor, 1968), p. 129.

[20] Gamson, *op. cit.*, p. 19.

[16] *Ibid.*, p. 64.

[17] McClosky, *op. cit.*, p. 370.

eralized—that is, in the simplest case, whether people dissatisfied with a given decision or set of decisions first begin to distrust the authorities, then perhaps the institutions and procedures of the regime, and finally become so disenchanted with the political community itself that they wish to separate themselves from the community. Where trust is high a negative decision may be bearable because of a belief in the integrity of the authorities and the legitimacy of the procedures employed. Where trust is low, negative outputs may be unbearable and lead to an intensification of distrust or separatist feelings. If several sets of authorities prove unsatisfactory, citizens are likely to "conclude that the institutions themselves may be the source of bias, and 'throwing the rascals out' will have little effect if indeed it is even possible."[21] The existence of high levels of trust allows authorities to make commitments which build more trust and weather situations in which citizens are unhappy about governmental outputs. A distrustful citizenry, however, is suspicious of every perceived governmental move, impatient for results and prone to deeper and more extreme levels of distrust. Ultimately, this process may lead to acts which undermine the political system.   ·

III. The Origins and Consequences of Political Trust

There are two general approaches to explaining political trust employed in the existing literature. Gamson, for example, emphasizes political factors. The content of decisions and the reactions they provoke are seen as the basic sources of po-

litical trust and distrust. Other scholars stress personality factors which are basically independent of political considerations as explanatory variables. They believe that: "If one cannot trust other people generally, one can certainly not trust those under the temptation of and with the powers which come with public office. Trust in elected officials is seen to be only a more specific instance of trust in mankind."[22]

Litt has introduced the idea that both political and personality variables are potentially important as explanatory factors. The relative importance of each class of variables, however, depends on the political environment or "milieu" prevailing in the community being examined. Stokes draws attention to the importance of generalized political expectations born of widely held democratic values as influences on political trust. Individuals may be influenced in their thinking by a local government's reputation for political corruption, and this seems to affect the relative influence of personality factors in explaining the existing degree of political trust. Trustful attitudes are also determined, however, by general public expectations about the nature of democratic governments, and a government's general record of performance in certain policy areas.

We do not suppose that levels of political trust are immutable. We conceive, instead, of a process in which this basic orientation toward the system[23] slowly changes as individuals are subjected to outside influences. In Gamson's model, for example, the individual's level of distrust is based on his judgement of the content of political outputs important to him and the procedures used to reach

---

[21] *Ibid.,* p. 51. Gamson suggests a series of conditions which discourage the generalization of political distrust. Among them are the disaggregation of large issues into smaller ones, an emphasis on the ad hoc nature of decisions (so that citizens do not see in negative decisions the application of general rules or principles), and a structural situation in which memberships of groups with varying goals and experiences overlap.

[22] Robert E. Lane, *Political Life* (Glencoe: Free Press, 1959), p. 164.

[23] M. Kent Jennings and Richard G. Niemi discuss political trust in these terms on p. 177 of their article on "The Transmission of Political Values from Parent to Child," *Americal Political Science Review,* 62 (1968), 169–184.

decisions. These judgements cumulate through time and are affected by cues from his experiences with government and his group allegiances. For a person with a high level of trust, a bad decision may be seen as an understandable, if unfortunate, mistake which does not call the political system's legitimacy into serious question. For a person with a moderate level of trust, however, the same bad decision is more likely to serve as proof of fundamental faults in the political system and may precipitate a rapid decrease in political trust. For the already distrustful person, the bad decision is merely further proof that the system is evil and may move him to some extreme, perhaps violent, protest.

There are numerous feedback loops in the complex process which generates or maintains trust. For example, satisfactory outputs stimulate trust, but trust itself predisposes a person to view outputs positively. The same process operates when we view trust or distrust as an element leading to radical ideologies or behavior. A distrustful person, for example, should be more disposed to take part in violent activities or to endorse radical interpretations of social ills than a trusting one, but his behavior or endorsement reinforces his distrust or tends to lower his previous level of trust.

We will need extensive time-series data to study this developmental process in detail and to determine precisely the levels of trust and the structural conditions which are sufficient to maintain a stable system or to inhibit the generalization of distrust. We are currently gathering data which we hope will carry us in this direction.[24] Many important questions, however, can be answered simply using data collected at one point in time, although this limits us to inferences about feedback loops and to primary reliance on summary measures (overall assessments gauged at one point in time) of people's satisfaction with their status in life and their political achievements.

IV. The Data

Our data come from a survey of the residents of Detroit, Michigan, completed in the fall of 1967. A total of 855 respondents were interviewed (394 whites and 461 blacks). In all cases whites were interviewed by whites, and blacks by blacks. The total N came from a community random sample of 539 (344 whites and 195 blacks) and a special random supplement of 316 (50 whites and 266 blacks) drawn from the areas where rioting took place in July 1967.[25] When we discuss the attitude patterns in the communities we will use the random sample data. However, since there are few meaningful differences between the distributions and relationships in the random and riot-supplement samples, we have employed the total N in the analysis so that a larger number of cases are available when controls are instituted.

V. Levels of Political Trust: A Racial Comparison

We defined political trust, following Stokes' lead, as a basic evaluative orientation toward government. Our measure of trust is a revised version of his. The following questions were asked at various points in the questionnaire:[26]

[24] This paper is based on data gathered in 1967 in Detroit. In 1968 we re-interviewed a random subsample of the original sample (N=295) and we will interview a larger number of respondents in 1970, many of them for the third time. Our study will also include interviews done in 1967 and 1970 with administrators in the Detroit city government and with business, civic and labor leaders who are members of the New Detroit Committee.

[25] Riot areas were defined by a location map of fires considered riot-related by the Detroit Fire Department.

[26] The wording of these questions is drawn from Survey Research Center questionnaires. Preliminary statements of the kind cited above were included. See ICPR, *op. cit.*, pp. 129–132.

1. How much do you think you can trust the government in Washington to do what is right: just about always, most of the time, some of the time, or almost never?

2. Would you say that the government in Washington is pretty much run for the benefit of a few big interests or that it is run for the benefit of all the people?

3. How much do you feel that having elections makes the government in Washington pay attention to what the people think: a good deal, some, or not very much?

4. How much do you think we can trust the government in Detroit to do what is right: just about always, most of the time, some of the time, or almost never?

5. How much do you feel having elections makes the government in Detroit pay attention to what the people think: a good deal, some, or not very much?

In the minds of Detroit residents there is a generalized sense of trust in the federal and local governments.[27] While trust in the Washington government on the in-

dividual items is always higher than trust in the Detroit government, the differences are slight. Detroit city government is relatively well run, nonpartisan, and generally not in such ill repute as the governments of cities like Boston or Newark.[28] This is apparent in Table 1 where we compare the levels of political trust exhibited by blacks in Newark and Detroit. It is clear that Litt is correct and the particular political setting is an important determinant of the level of trust. Since this is so, in the Detroit case we are fortunate to have an adequate distribution of responses to the attitude items so that we can examine the relationship between political trust and a general personality variable like trust in people which many scholars believe is the foundation of political trust under ordinary circumstances.

[27] A single political trust index was constructed. The items formed a clear dimension when data from the study were factor-analyzed. The factor

analyses (varimax rotation) were performed on the whole data-set and separately for blacks and whites. Questions on Detroit and Washington are equally weighted so that the index runs from 0 to 4.

[28] For confirmation of this view see: Edward C. Banfield, *Big City Politics* (New York: Random House, 1965), pp. 51–65; and David Greenstone, *Report on the Politics of Detroit* (Joint Center for Urban Studies of the Massachusetts Institute of Technology and Harvard University, 1961), Chapter 2.

Table 1. Trust in Detroit and Newark Governments for Riot Area Black Males: 15–35 *

Item: HOW MUCH DO YOU THINK YOU CAN TRUST THE GOVERNMENT IN (NEWARK/DETROIT) TO DO WHAT IS RIGHT: JUST ABOUT ALWAYS, MOST OF THE TIME, SOME OF THE TIME, OR NONE OF THE TIME?

TRUST CITY GOVERNMENT

	JUST ABOUT ALWAYS	MOST OF THE TIME	SOME OF THE TIME	NONE OF THE TIME	%
Newark (N=232)	2%	9	50	38	=100%
Detroit (N=71)	10%	21	51	18	=100%

* The figures for Newark are recomputed from the table in the *Report of the National Advisory Commission on Civil Disorders* (New York: Bantam Books, 1968), p. 178. This survey, conducted for the Commission by Nathan Caplan of The University of Michigan, covered only males 15 to 35 living in the riot zone and we drew comparable respondents from our sample to facilitate comparison.

When we compare the political trust of blacks and whites (Table 2) we find that the blacks are less trusting. This holds for all of the individual items as well as the index as a whole. This actually represents a change in the usual pattern, as blacks have always had at least the same distribution as whites on answers to these political trust questions.[29] No survey data exist concerning levels of trust which prevailed at earlier times, but through the years the federal government and local governments in much of the North, for all their shortcomings, have been the black man's friend in an otherwise hostile environment. The federal government, especially, won him his freedom, gave him the best treatment he received in his bleakest days in the South, provided relief in the Depression and in the difficult periods which have followed, and has done the most to secure him his rights and protect him during his struggle for equality.[30] In addition, the government in Washington has been the symbol of

the American Negro's intense identification with and "faith in the American Dream."[31] Now, at least in cities like Detroit, this sense of trust is being undermined as many black people are beginning to reject their traditional ties with paternalistic friends and allies, and are striking out at the more subtle forms of discrimination and deprivation found in the North. These expressions of distrust, as we shall see in more detail below, are accompanied by a militant racial ideology and an expressed willingness to resort to almost any means necessary to achieve their goals.

VI. *Explaining Political Trust*

A. AS A FUNCTION OF TRUST IN PEOPLE

As we have mentioned, one commonly held hypothesis about the origins of political trust is that it is "only a more specific instance of trust in mankind"[32]—which is a personality factor basically independent of political considerations. Our survey

[29] See Stokes, *op. cit.,* pp. 61–73 and Aberbach (1967), *op. cit.,* pp. 119–126.

[30] For example, see William Brink and Louis Harris, *The Negro Revolution in America* (New York: Simon and Schuster, 1964), pp. 131 and 232–233 on Negro attitudes towards various political institutions and figures.

[31] Louis E. Lomax, *The Negro Revolt* (New York: Harper and Row, 1962), p. 250; and also see Gunnar Myrdal, *An American Dilemma* (New York: Harper and Row, 1944), pp. 3–5, 880 and 1007 on the Negro as an "exaggerated American."

[32] Lane, *op. cit.,* p. 164.

Table 2. Political Trust in the Detroit Black and White Communities

	POLITICAL TRUST INDEX			
	LOW 0-1	2	HIGH 3-4	
Black Random Sample (N=186) $\bar{x}=1.66*$	52	13	35	=100%
White Random Sample (N=327) $\bar{x}=2.13*$	33	24	43	=100%

* The mean in the Black Riot Area Sample (N=341) is 1.67 and 1.66 in the Total Black Sample (N=461).

The mean in the White Riot Area Sample (N=75) is 2.12 and 2.11 in the Total White Sample (N=394).

contained a standard version of the Rosenberg Trust-in-People measure[33] which should provide an excellent means of testing the relationship between interpersonal trust and political trust. Given the similarities in the concepts *and* the measures, in fact, anything short of a strong relationship would raise serious questions about the hypothesis and one would expect "personality" variables other than trust in people to show even weaker direct effects on political trust.

The relationship between the indicators of trust in people and political trust is positive but weak. Rank-order correlation coefficients (Gamma) between the two are .17 for blacks and .16 for whites.[34] Clearly, political trust is more than a mere specific instance of trust in mankind. A strong relationship between interpersonal trust and political trust would hold ominous implications for American race relations given the low level of trust in people which most studies have discovered among blacks. In our data, for example, over 50 per cent of the whites but less than 30 per cent of the blacks have high scores on our trust-in-people scale. The pattern of these differences hold with education controlled and was the same in the Michigan Survey Research Center's 1964 national survey where similar questions were asked.[35]

B. AS A FUNCTION OF SOCIAL BACKGROUND FACTORS

A simple and plausible explanation of variation in political trust is that the so-cially advantaged are more trusting than the disadvantaged because they possess the status and the skills which bring them societal rewards and honors, while the disadvantaged achieve relatively little, and as a result, have little faith either in their fellow men or their government.[36] Our data forces us to reject this simple explanation. There is virtually no relationship between indicators of social advantages, such as education, occupation and income, and political trust.[37] If such factors have an effect, it is indirect.

There are other background factors, however, which have a greater influence on political trust. Individuals who were born in the South are somewhat more trustful than those born in the North[38] and people who have active affiliations with churches (i.e., are members of churches or church-related groups) are more trusting than those who are inactive.[39] These relationships are not strong, but reflect important acculturation patterns; persons born in the North more readily adopt a "worldly" cynicism about government, and individuals who have broken away from the traditional moorings of the church are also less likely to believe that government represents a benevolent authority. Our measures of this acculturation process are crude and indirect at best. In future studies we intend to create more explicit measures of this form of modernization which will enable

---

[33] See Rosenberg, *op. cit.* The version we used consists of two of the three questions regularly asked by SRC in their surveys. They are:

1. Generally speaking, would you say that most people can be trusted or that you can't be too careful in dealing with people?

2. Do you think that most people would try to take advantage of you if they got a chance or would they try to be fair?

[34] See Aberbach, *op cit.* (1969), pp. 92–93 for somewhat similar findings for whites using 1964 SRC national sample data.

[35] Aberbach, *op. cit.* (1967), pp. 104–114.

[36] The notion of a "theory of social disadvantages" as a general explanation for attitudes of estrangement is developed at length by Marvin E. Olsen, "Political Assimilation, Social Opportunities, and Political Alienation" (unpublished Ph.D. Dissertation, The University of Michigan, 1965).

[37] For example, the correlation (Gamma) between education and political trust is .08 for blacks and .03 for whites.

[38] The correlation (Gamma) between regional birthplace and political trust is .14 for blacks and .13 for whites.

[39] The correlation (Gamma) between active affiliation with a church and political trust is .24 for blacks and .15 for whites.

us to ascertain more exactly the strength of its impact on political trust.

C. AS A FUNCTION OF POLITICAL EXPECTATIONS

Since political trust does not seem to be merely a reflection of basic personality traits, or a simple product of social background, we turn to political factors in search of a more satisfactory explanation. As a person gains experience in the political realm, he slowly builds an assessment of himself as a political actor and develops his ideas about the fairness of the political process and the utility of its outputs. These evaluations are summaries both of his actual experiences and his expectations. They are answers to a series of questions:

(1) Am I, or can I be, influential?

(2) Do governmental outputs make a difference in my life—are they beneficial?

(3) Do I, or will I, receive equal treatment if I have a grievance about governmental decisions?

Each answer is an element in the political equation suggested by Gamson where political trust is a function of an individual's cumulative assessment of the procedures and outputs of the political process.[40] Also, if Stokes is correct, in a system infused with the democratic ethos, perceived influence is as important as the quality and justice of the outputs themselves in determining political trust.[41]

Obviously, political expectations are a complex function both of factors in an individual's personality and his assessment of a political situation. We cannot hope to sort out these elements in the attitudes we use as predictors, but we assume that political evaluations have strong foundations in the cumulative political experiences of an individual or group. In the process model we are developing, political experiences and expectations have a more immediate effect on political trust than personality factors, and are themselves conditioned by a respondent's level of trust. Because of these feedback relationships, we would expect individuals' political experiences and expectations and their feelings of political trust to be strongly associated. We do not assume that all governmental decisions will affect political trust, but we are struck by Gamson's idea that "disaffection begins to be generalized when an undesirable outcome is seen as a member of a class of decisions with similar results."[42]

In order to investigate these relationships we have utilized measures of our respondents' sense of political competence, their beliefs about the importance of the actions taken by government, and their expectations concerning the kind of reception they would receive at a government office. (The questions employed and the methods used in constructing indices are listed in the footnotes to Table 3.) A look at Table 3 will show that each of the political indicators is much more strongly related to political trust than was our measure of trust in people. These are substantial relationships, indicating the power of a political explanation. Controlling for education does not change the basic picture in two of the three cases, even though a variable like political competence is strongly related to education. However, the effect of education on the gamma between trust and expectations of equal treatment is worth further discussion.

First of all, a feeling that one would receive worse treatment than other peo-

---

[40] Gamson, *op. cit.,* p. 51.

[41] Stokes, *op. cit.,* p. 67: "When the individual's sense of political efficacy is compared with his positive or negative attitude toward government, it is apparent that a sense of ineffectiveness is coupled with feelings of hostility. This relation is more than a tautology. In other cultures or other historical eras a sense of ineffectiveness might well be associated with a positive feeling. In the context of democratic values, feelings of powerlessness toward public authority tend to create feelings of hostility toward that authority."

[42] Gamson, *op. cit.,* p. 51.

Table 3. Correlations (Gamma) Between Political Expectations and Political Trust, by Race and Education

Political Experience and Expectations	Blacks			Whites		
	Zero-Order	Low* Edu-cation	High* Edu-cation	Zero-Order	Low* Edu-cation	High* Edu-cation
Political Competence**	.40	.37	.45	.32	.30	.44
Impact of Governmental Actions***	.40	.42	.43	.32	.34	.21
Expectations of Equal Treatment****	.26	.32	.13	.42	.51	.33
N =	(461)	(322)	(122)	(394)	(254)	(124)

* Respondents in the low education group include all individuals who have completed high school, while those in the high education group have, at minimum, gone beyond high school to either special training or college. These definitions of low and high education are retained throughout the paper. The N's for each group are also the same. We chose education as a status indicator and dichotomized the sample in order to preserve the maximum number of cases for the analysis.

** The following items were used in the political competence index:

1. How much political power do you think people like you have? A great deal, some, not very much, or none?

2. Suppose a law were being considered by the Congress in Washington that you considered very unjust or harmful. What do you think you could do about it?

2a. If you made an effort to change this law, how likely is it that you would suceed: very likely, somewhat likely, or not very likely?

3. Suppose a law were being considered by the common council that you considered very unjust or harmful. What do you think you could do about it?

3a. If you made an effort to change this law, how likely is it that you would succeed: very likely, somewhat likely, or not very likely?

*** How much difference do you think it makes to people like yourself what the government in Washington does? A good deal, some, or not very much?

**** Suppose that there was some question that you had to take to a government office—for example, a tax question, a welfare allotment, or a housing regulation. Do you think that most likely you would be given a harder time than other people, would be treated about the same as anyone else, or would be treated a little better than most people.

All variables are coded so that positive experiences and expectations receive high scores.

ple in attempting to solve a problem at a government office is more strongly related to political trust for whites than for blacks. Naturally, there are more blacks who expect unequal treatment (35 percent versus 12 percent of the whites), but if we correctly gauge the intensity of emotion re-flected in answers to this question in our survey, white respondents who believe they would receive a harder time at a government office are even angrier than blacks with similar expectations. Many of the whites are evidently convinced that blacks receive special treatment and are given favors without deserving them. One typical white respondent said he would be given unequal treatment

because the white people are discriminated [against]. If you have a home and are working and you have pride, they just don't come to your assistance. One who has no will power or pride, they'll give you assistance.[43]

For the minority of whites with such extreme views (especially those in the lower education group), the emerging assertiveness of blacks is clearly a factor of the utmost importance in determining their level of political trust.

Expectations of treatment in a government office is of less direct importance for blacks, especially the upper educated group. This is not because all upper status blacks expect equal treatment (25 percent do not), but results from the fact that there is a relatively flat distribution of political trust scores across categories of our expectations-of-equal-treatment measure. One possible explanation, which is supported by data we will now present, is that distrust among upper status blacks does not arise so much from actual or expected discrimination as from empathy for others in the black community who experience these insults in worse form. The stronger relationship for lower education blacks indicates a more direct effect of expected discrimination on trust for this group, but even here the effect is weaker than for whites. Something more

than blatant personal mistreatment underlies black political distrust.

D. AS A FUNCTION OF FEELINGS OF DEPRIVATION

There is a large literature concerning the relationship between psychological deprivation and political unrest (defined as violence or propensity to engage in violent behavior)[44] and a developing literature, using aggregate data, which speculates about the relationship between deprivation and feelings that the government is not legitimate.[45] One of the best psychological measures of deprivation now available is the Cantril Self-Anchoring Scale which indicates the discrepancy between an individual's definition of the "best possible life" for him and his past, present, or future situations.[46] After each respondent gives a definition of the life "he would most like to lead" in his own words, he is shown a picture of a ladder

[43] This quote is from one of the respondents included in our 1968 panel. The 1967 questionnaire did not probe answers to the close-ended question on equal treatment in a government office. After examining the 1967 interview protocols, we believed that whites who felt they would receive unequal treatment often ascribed this to reverse discrimination and we used the 1968 interviews to confirm this hypothesis.

A poll by the Gallup organization reported in *Newsweek* (October 6, 1969) gives evidence of somewhat similar feelings among "a substantial minority of whites" that "the black man already has the advantage." (p. 45).

[44] For examples of analyses employing aggregate data see Ivo K. Feierabend, Rosalind L. Feierabend, and Betty A. Nesvold, "Social Change and Political Violence: Cross-National Patterns" and James C. Davies, "The J-Curve of Rising and Declining Satisfactions as a Cause of Some Great Revolutions and a Contained Rebellion," pp. 632–688 and 690–731 respectively in Hugh D. Graham and Ted. R. Gurr (eds.), *The History of Violence in America* (New York: Bantam, 1969). An example of the use of psychological data is Don R. Bowen, Elinor Bowen, Sheldon Gawiser and Louis H. Masotti, "Deprivation, Mobility and Orientation Toward Protest of the Urban Poor," pp. 174–187 in Louis H. Masotti and Don R. Bowen (eds.), *Riots and Rebellion: Civil Violence in the Urban Community* (Beverly Hills: Sage Publications, 1968).

[45] A particularly interesting analysis of this type which is used to speculate about urban unrest in the United States is found in Ted Gurr, "Urban Disorder: Perspective from the Comparative Study of Civil Strife," pp. 51–69 in Masotti and Bowen, *op cit*. More details on the measures used in Gurr's study can be found in Ted Gurr, "A Casual Model of Civil Strife: A Comparative Analysis," *American Political Science Review*, 62 (1968), 1104–1125.

[46] See Hadley C. Cantril, *The Pattern of Human Concerns* (New Brunswick: Rutgers University Press, 1965). Our respondents were given the following set of questions:

with ten rungs and asked to imagine that the top rung represents the best possible life which he has just described. He is then asked to rank, in comparison with his ideal, his present life, his life five years ago, and what he expects his life to be like five years in the future. A person's position on these scales is a function of his own definition of the best possible state of affairs. His standards may be determined by class or race models, or expectations created by the mass media, but no simple objective indicator of achievement like income or occupation will be an adequate substitute for this psychological measure.[47]

We use these measures of deprivation as indicators, based on standards meaningful to each individual, of a deep-rooted dissatisfaction or expectation of dissatisfaction which may be blamed on government. They are conceptually and empirically independent of the *political*-expectations indices employed in the previous section since a person may be deeply dissatisfied with the general course of his

life, but feel politically powerful, believe he receives equal treatment from government and feel that governmental outputs have a beneficial impact. In other words, the two sets of indicators are related, but do not have the same psychological significance for the individual, and each has an independent effect on political trust.[48]

We employed two sets of self-anchoring scales in our surveys: One was the standard "best possible life" question explained in note 46 and a second sought the respondents' definitions of the "best possible race relations" as a base for selecting rungs on a ladder running from 0 to 10.[49] Both whites and blacks gave a wide variety of definitions of the "best possible life" in response to that question, with almost none of them directly involving race relations. While whites were much more satisfied with their past and present lives, both racial groups are strongly optimistic about the future.[50] When we turn to race relations we find very substantial differences in the patterns of answers. Blacks talk almost exclusively in terms of

[*footnote 46 continued*
Now could you briefly tell me what would be the best possible life for you? In other words, how would you describe the life you would most like to lead, the most perfect life as you see it? (Show R card with a Ladder.)
Now suppose that the top of the ladder represents the best possible life for you, the one you just described, and the bottom represents the worst possible life for you.

"Present Life" A. Where on the ladder do you feel you personally stand at the present time?
"Past Life"   B. Where on the ladder would you say you stood five years ago?
"Future Life"   C. Where on the ladder do you think you will be five years from now?

[47] In our study, for example, income is correlated (Gamma) .29 for whites and .23 for blacks with position on the "present life" ladder. Income is thus a meaningful predictor, but these are far short of simple one-to-one relationships.

[48] This proposition was tested for each racial group by a multiple regression analysis in which the measures of trust in people, the background factors, political experiences and expectations, and the ladders were used as predictors of political trust. The political variables and the relevant ladders each had an independent effect on trust with all of the other variables controlled. Multiple R's were .52 for the blacks and .49 for the whites.
[49] See footnote 46 above for the wording on the "best possible life" questions. The "best possible race relations" items were in the same form with the following sentences as the initial stimulus:

Here in Detroit, as in many places, different races of people are living together in the same communities. Now I would like for you to think about the very best way that Negroes and white people could live in the same place together. In other words, what would be the very best kind of race relations, the most perfect you could imagine?

This item was adapted from that used by Donald R. Matthews and James W. Prothro, *Negroes and the New Southern Politics* (New York: Harcourt, Brace and World, 1966), pp. 285–294, 513–514.

total integration, better personal relationships with whites, the disappearance of color consciousness, and respect and dignity for all, while more than 30% of the whites spontaneously endorse segregation or separation of some kind. In addition, many more whites than blacks are pessimistic about the future in this area[51] with the correlation between expressed separationist feelings and whites scores on the future ladder at (Gamma) .40.[52] The white community, not the black, is divided over the desirability of integration and whites are more depressed than

blacks about the prospects for future race relations in Detroit.

This fact is reflected in Table 4 which indicates how much more potent a predictor of political trust the present and especially the future race relations ladders[53] are for whites than for blacks. The situation is reversed when we look at the "best possible life" ladders. Here the correlations are higher for the black sample. In addition, for whites, controlling for education has only mild effects on the relationship between the ladders and trust (the high education group is somewhat more homogenous on the ladders than the low education group), but it substantially increases the correlations in the low education black group. The signs are actually reversed in four of six cases for the high education black group where those who are dissatisfied are actually more trusting than those who are satisfied.

If we look back at the discussion of the correlation in Table 3 between expectations of equal treatment and political trust we recognize certain similarities to the relationships we are now describing; in both cases a racial question is a better

[50] Income and job advancement were desired by 28% of the blacks and 16% of the whites, good health or family life by 22% of the blacks and 20% of the whites and personal property (homes, cars, etc.) by 15% of the blacks and 11% of the whites. The major difference was that 13% of the whites (as opposed to 3% of the blacks) said the life they were now living was the best possible and 23% of the whites, compared with 9% of the blacks, mentioned peace and tranquility.

% Scoring High (7–10) on "Best Possible Life" Ladders, by Race

	Past Life	Present Life	Future Life
Blacks	13%	23%	64%
Whites	49%	47%	66%

We will present more complete descriptions and analysis of the answers to the "best possible life" question in Joel D. Aberbach and Jack L. Walker, *Race and the Urban Community* (Boston: Little Brown, forthcoming).

[51] Our "Best Possible Race Relations" ladders yielded the following results:

% Scoring High (7–10) on "Best Possible Race Relations" Ladders, by Race

	Past Race Relations	Present Race Relations	Future Race Relations
Blacks	10%	22%	61%
Whites	39%	23%	40%

[52] The correlation (Gamma) is .09 for blacks because there is virtual unanimity in the black

community on integration. See Joel D. Aberbach and Jack L. Walker, "The Meanings of Black Power: A Comparison of White and Black Interpretations of a Political Slogan," *American Political Science Review,* 64 (1970), p. 883.

[53] Ted Gurr stresses the importance of "anticipated interference with human goals" in his analysis of discontent. He says that,

analysis of the sources of relative deprivation should take account of both actual and anticipated interference with human goals, as well as of interference with value positions both sought and achieved. Formulations of frustration in terms of the "want:get ratio," which refers only to a discrepancy between sought values and actual attainment, are too simplistic. Man lives mentally in the near future as much as in the present. Actual or anticipated interference with what he has, and with the act of striving itself, are all volatile sources of discontent.

See p. 254 of Ted Gurr, "Psychological Factors in Civil Violence," *World Politics,* 20 (1968), 245-278.

Table 4. Correlations (Gamma) between Ladder Positions on Self-Anchoring Scales and Political Trust, by Race and Education

	Blacks			Whites		
Scales*	Zero-Order	Low Edu-cation	High Edu-cation	Zero-Order	Low Edu-cation	High Edu-cation
"Best Possible Life" Ladders						
Past Life	.18	.27	—.12	.02	.06	.03
Present Life	.31	.39	.05	.20	.23	.20
Future Life	.30	.38	—.11	.15	.14	.13
"Best Possible Race Relations" Ladders						
Past Race Relations	.16	.22	.04	—.04	—.07	.00
Present Race Relations	.13	.23	—.17	.26	.29	.17
Future Race Relations	.10	.17	—.11	.37	.40	.29

* The ladders were trichotomized as follows: 1–3 = 0; 4–6 = 1; 7–10 = 2. (This is the division used by Cantril, *op. cit.,* p. 257). Therefore, a positive coefficient indicates that the higher a person's score on the various ladders, the higher his trust in government.

predictor of trust in the white community, and in both cases the upper education black group is quite different from the lower education black group. In summary:

1. Blacks are less likely than whites to lose faith in the government when they expect discriminatory treatment in a government office or when they see failures in achieving the pattern of race relations they favor. For high education blacks there are even cases when the relationship between the race relations ladders and political trust is negative.

2. Lower status blacks tend to be very bitter about government when they fail to achieve their personal goals in life while higher status blacks do not.

3. While higher status black people are somewhat more satisfied and less discriminated against than lower status blacks, this is not enough to account for the differences in relationships found here since there is a fairly uniform level of trust no matter how poorly the higher status person expects to be treated or how deprived he feels. In fact, the deprived high education black person is likely to be a little

more trusting than those in the same group who are relatively satisfied.

The data for the white community are relatively easy to interpret: racial issues, especially those involving integration and governmental treatment of blacks become so important that they have superseded considerations of personal achievement, especially for the lower status group. Some of this may be due to the fact that our survey was conducted soon after a major disturbance, but large numbers of whites are clearly upset about the future of race relations and some actually feel discriminated against because of their race.[54] Government officials are faced with an increasingly angry, bitter and frightened group of white people who feel persecuted and unrepresented.[55] These feelings are undermining their basic trust in government and making them much more sympathetic to political candidates

[54] We have already seen above that there are some whites who believe that they would receive unequal treatment at a government office because of their race. Even more astounding, however, is the fact that in our 1968 survey of a random sub-sample of the original (1967) sample 46% of the

who call for repression of the blacks in the name of law and order.

A more complex process is at work in the black community. In Table 5 we see that the indicators of reported discrimination are differentially related to political trust for the lower and upper education segments of the black sample. Experiences of discrimination in obtaining housing or on the job are associated with distrust for the lower education group, but not the upper education group. Even police mistreatment, the most volatile issue in Detroit's black community, is much more strongly related to political distrust in the lower education segment of the population. (This is not because only lower status blacks experience mistreatment, since about 15 percent of each group report some form of bad experience.) However, when the issue is simply whether a community problem is recognized as important or not, the relationship between recognition and distrust is stronger in the upper education group. Their distrust, unlike that of the lower education respondents, may not be rooted so much in concerns about *personal* ex-

whites believed that if they were black they would be either making advances toward their goals in life or advancing more rapidly toward their goals. This compares to 57% giving similar answers in the black community. Unfortunately, this question was not on our 1967 questionnaire.

[55] More than half of the white respondents in our sample could not name any national or local leader who represented their views on race rela-

tions and whites actually scored lower than blacks on our measure of subjective political competence. See our discussion of these points in Joel D. Aberbach and Jack L. Walker, "The Meanings of Black Power: A Comparison of White and Black Interpretations of a Political Slogan," a discussion paper issued by the Institute of Public Policy Studies, The University of Michigan, 1968, pp. 27—34.

Table 5. Correlations (Gamma) between (A) Personal Experiences of Discrimination and (B) Recognition of Serious Community Problems and Political Trust for Blacks, by Education

	ZERO-ORDER	LOW EDUCATION	HIGH EDUCATION
(A) *Personal Experiences*			
Personal Experiences of Discrimination Index (Police Excepted)*	—.15	—.18	.00
Personal Experiences of Police Mistreatment**	—.43	—.57	—.21
(B) *Recognition of Serious Community Problems*			
Crowded Conditions	.02	.05	—.22
Poor Education	—.01	.00	—.21
The Way the Police Act	—.21	—.21	—.24

* This is a simple additive index of personal experiences of discrimination in Detroit in obtaining housing, in the schools, from a landlord, or in obtaining, holding or advancing on a job.

** This is an index of reports of police mistreatment experienced by the person himself.

A negative coefficient indicates that the more a person has been discriminated against, mistreated, or recognizes a community problem as serious, the lower his trust in government.

periences of expectations, nor even in considerations of larger and more abstract feelings about the conditions of race relations in Detroit, but in *empathy*—a feeling of identification with the black political and social community which includes persons from all social classes. This is part of a group identification gaining momentum in the middle class which identifies the fortunes of the black community, rather than prospects of the individual, as the key in evaluating decisions and institutions.[56] This could be the reason that our ladder measures of personal achievement are so successful as predictors for the lower education group and yet so unsuccessful for the upper education group. If some upper status blacks are identifying with others in the community who are persecuted, we would expect segments of both the lower and upper status groups to share a racial ideology of protest which is related to feelings of political trust. We will test this proposition in the next section.

VII. Political Trust and Racial Ideology

Our data give clear evidence of a developing racial ideology in Detroit's black community.[57] The elements of this belief system include a favorable interpretation of black power, the choice of militant

black leaders as representatives of one's own point of view on race relations and a revolutionary interpretation of the meaning or significance of the 1967 disturbances. Scholars studying other cities have reached similar conclusions.[58] This ideology is not a manifestation of growing sentiments for separation,[59] but of a militantly expressed ideology of protest which demands quick and effective action to better conditions for *all* black people. Unfortunately, it is opposed by an equally militant ideology held by a large segment of the white community which demands racial separation and the curtailment of programs designed to aid disadvantaged blacks. These are the kinds of emotional issues which destroy trust in government and undermine the normal constraints on intemperate or even violent political behavior.

We will now examine the relationship between elements of these belief systems and political trust. Here, even more than in the previous section on explanations of political trust, we are dealing with a process in which a set of beliefs influences the level of trust which in turn influences or deepens the beliefs; the man who sees the 1967 riot as a justified reaction to social

[56] Lupsha has discussed the same basic phenomenon: "Anger can occur without one's being frustrated or deprived. One can learn that certain events, or violations of one's rights and values, should be responded to with hostility. One can be angry and aggressive because one's values or sense of justice (a learned phenomenon) have been affronted, without any blocking of the individual's goal-directed activity, or awareness of any personal "want-get ratio" deprivation, or any personal feelings of "anticipated frustration." One can be angry and aggressive simply because one believes the behaviors of the situation are wrong or illegitimate." See p. 288 of Peter A. Lupsha, "On Theories of Urban Violence," *Urban Affairs Quarterly* (1969), 273–296.

[57] Aberbach and Walker, *op. cit.* (1970), pp. 379–386.

[58] See, for example, T. M. Tomlinson, "The Development of a Riot Ideology among Urban Negroes," *American Behavioral Scientist* (1968), 27–31.

[59] Less than 2 percent of our black sample endorsed the idea of the separation of the races. This is not surprising in light of the history of the concept integration as a symbol of equality in the black community. We used the word separation in our questions in order to overcome the obvious connotations of segregation, but few of our respondents were attracted by the term and almost none used it spontaneously in their definitions of the "best possible race relations." Even among intellectuals, most of the debate about race relations revolves around various forms of social pluralism as opposed to assimilation. One of the major goals of our panel study is to examine the ways in which people modify their ideals about desirable forms of race relations and community goals through time. See Aberbach and Walker, *op. cit.* (1970), p. 383, especially footnote 49.

injustice is more likely to develop or sustain distrust of the government, but, in a cumulative spiral, this distrust strengthens his belief in the justification of the riot as a reaction to oppression. Since we are measuring these phenomena at a single point in time we cannot give our process model an adequate empirical test. Before progress can be made in verifying and refining our model, data on the same individuals must be collected on several different occasions.

Bearing in mind the restrictions placed on our efforts by the nature of our data, we turn first to our black respondents (Table 6) and see that each of the elements we have measured in the developing racial ideology is related to political trust. Blacks who label the 1967 disturbances as a revolutionary protest against mistreatment, favorably interpret the black power slogan, or select a militant as the leader best representing their views on relations between the races, are also like-

ly to distrust the government. These sentiments are not a function of social status and, as we can see, the relationships are as strong or stronger for the upper educated black group as for blacks with lower levels of educational achievement. We should emphasize that these relationships are quite strong when we take into account the fact that the elements in the black ideology are all measured with open-ended survey questions. It is possible, therefore, to speak as we did before of a *black political community,* crossing social class lines, marked by a developing racial ideology focused on militancy and pride and connected with a strong distrust of government. This growing solidarity is a political phenomenon of the utmost importance for a minority community which needs to mobilize the skills of its growing middle class.

Turning now to the white community, we again find that racial variables are of great importance as predictors of trust,

Table 6. Correlations (Gamma) between Militant Ideology and Political Trust for Blacks, by Education

	ZERO-ORDER	LOW EDUCATION	HIGH EDUCATION
Favorable Interpretation of "Black Power"*	—.39	—.39	—.37
Favorable Explanation of the July, 1967, Disturbance**	—.22	—.20	—.25
Leader Best Representing the Respondents Views on Relations Between the Races***	—.23	—.19	—.32

* Favorable interpretations of black power (given a high score on this index) consist almost exclusively of notions about a "fair share" for blacks or "racial unity" in the black community as a tactic in bettering conditions. See Aberbach and Walker, *op. cit.,* for an extensive discussion of this.

** This is an index in which a high score indicates a revolutionary label for the disturbance and a belief that those who took part did so not because they were riffraff or criminals, but because they had been mistreated by society.

*** Respondents selected, without any cues from the interviewer, the leader who "best represented" their views on relations between the races. The selections were then scored from militant black leaders (high) through to conservative white leaders. See Aberbach and Walker, *op. cit.,* p. 385, for distributions.

Table 7. Correlations (Gamma) between Attitudes on Integration, Public Expenditures and Political Trust for Whites, by Education

	ZERO-ORDER	LOW EDUCATION	HIGH EDUCATION
Integration*	.28	.29	.28
More Money for Improvements**	.35	.31	.39

* This is a summary index of responses to items calling for the endorsement or rejection of a general policy of integration or separation, school integration and the description of the "best possible race relations" coded according to the degree of integration or separation endorsed. We used the word separation in preference to segregation to insure that black respondents could comfortably endorse this alternative; only 2% did so.

** The following close-ended question was asked in the middle of our section on the riot and conditions in the black community: "Do you feel that more money or less money should be spent on trying to improve conditions?"

only here views on integration versus separation and spending public money to improve conditions in the ghetto are key factors in determining the level of trust. Whites are almost evenly divided on these issues (about 50 per cent of our white sample favor integration and approximately the same percentage endorse spending more money).[60] Such an overwhelming majority of blacks (over 90 per cent) favor both, however, that analysis of the correlates on these questions is not very fruitful.

The racial issue and the means of dealing with it inspire great emotion in the white community and threaten to undermine trust in the government for a substantial segment of the population. As Table 7 demonstrates, separationists and those opposed to spending more money to improve ghetto conditions are decidedly more distrustful of government than

integrationists and those willing to spend more money. The relationships hold for those with high levels of educational achievement as well as those with lower levels of education. In addition, attitudes on integration and scores on the race relations ladders have independent effects on the level of trust,[61] so that, for example, integrationists who are dissatisfied with the current or emerging course of race relations are more distrustful of the government than those who are satisfied, and they are also more distrustful than satisfied or optimistic segregationists. It is easy to envision situations in which events or governmental policies and pronouncements embitter both segregationists and integrationists, thereby dealing a double blow to the level of political trust in the white community.

VIII. Political Distrust and Political Behavior

Distrust of the government creates a tension in the polity which can build for some time, but ultimately seeks release.

[60] The correlation (Gamma) between the two is .49 for whites. The exact distributions by race on spending public money are as follows:

Spend More Money to Improve Conditions

	More	Same	Less	DK, NA	
Blacks	94%	4	1	1	=100%
Whites	50%	28	19	3	=100%

[61] For example, the correlation (Gamma) between political trust and scores on the future race relations ladder is .36 for segregationists and .27 for integrationists. It is .37 for the entire white sample.

Table 8. Political Distrust and Potential Political Behavior for Blacks and Whites

Political Trust	Blacks — Can you imagine a situation in which you would riot?*			Whites — If the election for mayor of Detroit were held tomorrow and the candidates were Jerome Cavanaugh and Mary Beck, who would you vote for?		
	Yes or Maybe	*No*	(N)	*Beck*	*Cavanaugh*	(N)
Low 0	54	46	(129)	74	25	(42)
1	35	65	(86)	42	58	(36)
2	35	65	(94)	52	48	(60)
3	21	79	(75)	39	61	(46)
High 4	17	83	(59)	26	74	(69)
	Gamma = .40			Gamma = .35		

(Percentages are across.)

* The word "riot" was not actually used. Respondents were asked early in the interviews to give their own label to the events of July, 1967, and this term was used throughout by the interviewer.

Among other things, people can revolt, engage in limited displays of violence like riots, demonstrate, or support candidates for elective office who give voice to their fears and frustrations. The mode of expression depends on the depth of the discontent, traditions of violence in the society, loyal coercive forces available to the government, and the availability of free electoral processes.[62] At this point many distrustful blacks have taken to the streets and distrustful whites troop to the polls to vote for so-called "law and order" candidates.

We asked respondents whether they could "imagine any situation" in which they would take part in a disturbance like the one Detroit had in July of 1967 and we also conducted a mock mayoral election in which the choice lay between the incumbent mayor (Jerome Cavanaugh) and a very vocal member of the Detroit Common Council (Mary Beck) who had

[62] Gurr, "Urban Disorder: Perspectives from the Comparative Study of Civil Strife," *op. cit.* See Aberbach, *op. cit.* (1969) for an extended discussion of political distrust and political behavior.

been courting backlash support. Since very few whites could envisage taking part in a disturbance, of the 1967 variety at least, and few blacks would ever vote for Miss Beck, we could only employ each indicator for one racial group. This is simply a matter of convenience. We certainly do not wish to imply that blacks would never vote for extremist candidates or that whites would never engage in violence.

As Table 8 indicates, distrustful whites are indeed strongly in favor of Miss Beck and distrustful blacks are better able to imagine situations in which they would riot. Distrust clearly stimulates a willingness to engage in violence or favorably predisposes people toward voting for extremist candidates. Moreover, high levels of trust serve to dampen the behavioral impact of adverse experiences while low levels of trust lead to volatile situations in which each insult increases the probability of extreme behavior. In statistical terms, political distrust and adverse experiences interact.

A classic example of this interaction can be seen in the Detroit black community where political distrust and reported experiences of discrimination interact to inspire willingness to engage in a civil disturbance (See Table 9). When trust is low, experiences of discrimination have a very powerful effect on a person's ability to imagine a situation in which he could take part in a civil disturbance, but high trust seems to serve as a dike which blunts somewhat the political effects of these experiences. Persons who are low in trust seem to interpret each experience of discrimination as further proof that the political system is evil and must be dealt with by any means, while those who are trusting have a less severe reaction to these experiences. High levels of trust are resources which governments can use to gain time in order to correct wrongs in the society. When trust is low injustices have a stronger and more immediate impact since the reservoir of good will has been destroyed.

IX. Political Trust and Racial Ideology: An Overview

We conceive of political trust as a central element in a dynamic process. Earlier research has shown that the most important variables which influence trust differ somewhat according to the political environment in which the research takes place, and our own analysis demonstrates that determinants of trust differ from group to group. Since our study is based on data collected from only one city we cannot claim universal applicability for our findings, but we believe that data collected in Detroit have characteristics which make them eminently suitable for studies of political trust. Data from our Detroit sample, unlike those gathered in cities like Boston or Newark which have reputations for corruption and inefficiency, are distributed in such a way that legitimate examinations of the relationships between political trust and several of its possible determinants can be conducted successfully.

Our analysis shows that political trust is not merely a reflection of our respondents' basic personality traits, or a simple function of general social background factors. Our most important explanatory variables are those which arise from the workings of the social or political system, such as the citizen's expectations about the treatment he will receive from government officials, general feelings of deprivation and well-being, and beliefs about

Table 9. Experiences of Discrimination and Willingness to Take Part in a Civil Disturbance by Level of Political Trust for Blacks*

TRUST	LOW (0–1)			HIGH (2–4)		
Reported Experiences of Discrimination	Can you imagine a situation in which you would riot?					
	Yes or Maybe	*No*	*(N)*	*Yes or Maybe*	*No*	*(N)*
Few (0–1)	30	70	(122)	22	78	(139)
Medium (2)	60	40	(31)	30	70	(37)
Many (3–4)	71	29	(61)	36	64	(44)
	Gamma = —.65			Gamma = —.26		
			(Percentages are across.)			

* This is a simple additive index of reports of personal experiences of discrimination in Detroit in obtaining housing, in the schools, from a landlord, or in obtaining, holding, or advancing on a job.

the status or acceptability of one's group in society. Levels of trust are determined by these factors and, in turn, are influenced by them in a chain of interactions which continues as the political system operates. Repeated setbacks or disappointments are necessary to dissipate trust when it is high, and when trust is low, numerous successes are needed to increase it. Gamson argues that when a group has become extremely disaffected it is especially difficult to regain their trust because they may see any concessions made to them merely as proof that a corrupt system responds only to threats.[63] Our analysis lends support to many of Gamson's propositions, but his explanation of changes in levels of political trust cannot be given a conclusive empirical test until data are collected at several points in time from the same respondents. We are now collecting such data from our Detroit sample and will report our results in later work.

The determinants of trust are not the same for every social grouping within our sample. Among lower status blacks, high political distrust is related to expectations of discriminatory treatment in contacts with government officials, low feelings of political competence, experiences of racial discrimination, complaints about arbitrary or unjust behavior by the police, and low evaluations either of one's present situation in life or one's personal future prospects. Those lower status blacks who believe themselves to be suffering from some form of deprivation tend to become distrustful of the political system.

For upper status blacks, on the other hand, adverse experiences and dissatisfaction with their current achievements do not necessarily lead to political distrust. In fact, the small number who are dissatisfied with their present lives are slightly more trusting than those who are satisfied. Political distrust is highest among those middle class blacks who have a strong sense of identification and empathy with the problems of the black community. The accommodating, apolitical "black bourgeoisie" described by E. Franklin Frazier[64] is fast disappearing. The emerging concern with the nature of black identity or the meaning of the black heritage are reflections of the desire of blacks to find places of dignity and respect in the American social system. No matter how satisfied or dissatisfied they may be with the courses of their own private lives, many middle class blacks increasingly feel bound up with the black community and its problems. They are anxious to obtain assurances that the society will recognize the legitimacy and value of their culture and life style. They look to the government's policies and to the society's ceremonial or ritual acts for evidence that their status and importance is being recognized.

Political distrust among whites is rooted in their resentment and dissatisfaction with the course of American race relations and in a sense of political powerlessness. Our interview protocols are filled with bitter, angry outbursts, especially from the lower status whites, who believe they are victims of a cynical government which is willing to grant any black demand in exchange for votes and popularity. Most of the concessions being made, especially the symbolic gestures, seem to come at their expense. They feel leaderless and powerless in this new, confusing environment. In the past, their self respect and social orientation have been founded on myths of racial superiority which are being destroyed in the social revolution now taking place. Behind their anger we detect a sense of profound bewilderment and fear. White anxieties may be expressed in support of political leaders who seem to recognize their dignity and promise a return to "law and order,"

---

[63] Gamson, *op cit.*, pp. 172–178.

[64] E. Franklin Frazier, *Black Bourgeoisie* (Glencoe: Free Press, 1957).

but they are as much victims as oppressors. Whatever our view of them, however, these restless whites are a potentially powerful political element which must be taken into account when public policies are being developed.

X. Policy Implications

Emerging from our analysis are the outlines of an ominous confrontation between the races. The growing sense of solidarity and racial identification among blacks is being matched by rising, increasingly bitter resentment among elements of the white community. More often than in past decades, the anger and resentment of both sides is being translated from generalized racial hostility into focused political demands for specific programs or policies from agencies of both local and national government. These developing tensions may precipitate the kinds of social changes being called for by blacks, but they could lead to an altogether different result. If both black and white citizens lose sufficient confidence in the essential trustworthiness of the government, the society may reach its political "tipping-point," constraints on intemperate or even violent protest may completely disappear, and the stage will be set either for large-scale anti-democratic efforts at change by blacks and/or massive attempts at reaction and repression by whites.

The government's success in avoiding a complete break-down in race relations depends, to a significant degree, on its success in building political trust. Declining trust can be a stimulant to social change. The direction or nature of the changes, however, will be determined by the reactions of the government or the rest of society to the demands of distrustful groups. If public officials are able to build or maintain high levels of trust, a broader range of policy options are opened for consideration and governments can more easily risk short term opposition from some groups in the hope of achieving an important long term result. When trust is low, however, groups are unlikely to give the government the benefit of the doubt and may begin to call for immediate fulfillment of their demands. A dangerous process of competitive mobilization may begin. In Gamson's words: "The presentation of demands by one group stimulates their presentation by others. Thus, it is possible for the loss of trust to encourage a 'deflationary' spiral akin to a run on the bank."[65] The level of trust, in other words, determines the amount of patience or forebearance citizens can be expected to exercise. Since the problems of finding an equitable and peaceful new basis for racial harmony cannot be quickly solved, governments must have time to deal with them successfully. By building trust, governments may buy the time they need.

The level of political trust existing at any time is the result of a complex process involving interactions with many variables. It is a changing reflection of a society's politically relevant conflicts and tensions. When trust is high, officials are in a better position to make commitments or adopt controversial policies aimed at the solution of difficult problems. Since high levels of trust are an important resource which cushions the impact of programs some groups find intensely objectionable, whenever substantial segments of the population begin to grow distrustful, it is important for the government to act before the level of trust drops to the point where the resources to solve societal problems and rebuild trust cannot be mustered. When distrust is growing leaders are faced with the delicate problem of making policies which reach the sources of dissatisfaction at a time when any action is likely to make some group angry —often even some of those among their traditional political constituencies. This is a high political price which leaders seek to avoid, thereby making the problem

[65] Gamson, *op. cit.*, p. 45.

worse for themselves and often much worse for their successors. It is difficult to devise policies which can solve social problems, and still more difficult to build coalitions which can enact these policies and support their enforcement. The problem is doubly difficult when political trust is low.

In this section on the implications of our analysis for public policy we emphasize racial problems because they are the major concerns of our study and a fundamental problem faced by the nation, but we recognize that the legitimacy of our political system currently is being undermined by controversies over many other social problems. It is not possible to separate cleanly the racial crisis from the problems of poverty, the Vietnam War, the development of huge private and public bureaucracies, and the student rebellions. The government's response to all of them has contributed to political distrust. A thorough treatment of the problems of political disaffection would range far beyond the racial crisis, but our discussion is necessarily confined to these difficult issues by the limits of the data we have collected and the space available to us.

Effective public policies, which have the important side benefits of encouraging a growth in political trust, must be designed to meet the needs of the people they are meant to serve. As our analysis demonstrates, the factors influencing political trust among Detroit's population are not easily categorized. The causes of the suspicions and hatreds which have created the racial tensions we describe are deeply rooted in our history. No single, simple governmental program can be expected to eliminate the dangers we face or usher in a period of mutual compromise and understanding among blacks and whites. No matter what may be done, we are moving through an extremely difficult period of transition in race relations which almost inevitably will be accompanied by hurt feelings and racial con-

flict. The level of turmoil we experience, however, and the impact it has on the shape of American institutions, will depend in large part on the decisions made and the programs instituted by public officials. Even though the situation contains many intractable elements, if disaster is to be averted, the government must intervene whenever possible with effective efforts to build a truly inter-racial society.

Racial harmony cannot be achieved unless the damage done by the innumerable insults and racial slurs exchanged between whites and blacks during the last two centuries can be at least partially repaired. The desires of blacks for symbolic assurances of good faith, however, are becoming increasingly difficult to grant because of mounting white resentment. Any policy which seems to grant benefits to blacks is interpreted by segments of the white community as unfair, preferential treatment. Many of the whites in our sample believe that blacks are getting "something for nothing" simply because they are "trouble makers." During the last two decades many highly significant symbolic gestures have been made which were designed to signify that blacks were being included as full partners in American society. These gestures have fueled the fires of white resentment, helped to stimulate a major realignment in Southern politics, and prompted the rise of political candidates like George Wallace. Black aspirations have also risen during this period, so that gestures which once were appropriate or satisfactory are now denounced as "tokenism." This emotion-laden struggle over symbolic assurances threatens to destroy the government's credit within both racial communities at once, and it constitutes the central dilemma of domestic policy making in contemporary American politics.

We do not believe this dilemma can be avoided through a policy of prudent immobility. Although there is no easy way to reach a new state of racial accommodation, governments must make an effort to encourage that development. There are many ways in which governments may seek to halt the erosion of political trust caused by heightened racial tensions, but there is no policy, including inaction, which may be implemented without costs or dangers. Every governmental action will stimulate an intense reaction from some element within one of the two racial communities. Our analysis indicates, however, that if there is to be any hope of a resurgence of trust in the integrity of American governmental institutions, the promise that all public forms of racial discrimination will be eliminated must be fulfilled. As our findings demonstrate, personal experiences of racial discrimination are an important determinant of political distrust among lower status blacks. The persistence of discrimination against members of the black community is also one of the most important factors encouraging despair among upper status blacks. The constitution requires that racial discrimination be eliminated, and repeated declarations that it would be stopped have been made during the last two decades by public officials. Reducing efforts to fight discrimination at this time would only encourage disaffection and cynicism in both racial communities. It would lead citizens to view their government, rightly, as an unprincipled entity willing to retract its pledges of justice in response to threats. If our hypotheses about political trust are valid, this would lead even those who successfully made the threats to distrust government more than before.

Many courses of action are open to those wishing to attack the problems growing out of the contemporary racial crisis, but none will have a reasonable chance of success unless it involves a genuine effort at broad social reform. The developing sense of community among blacks in Detroit, to which we have referred so often, is founded on a common outrage about the material and social status of

their group. Fundamental social changes have transformed the black community since World War Two and led to the widespread protests which marked the past decade. As a result of this controversy over the status and welfare of black Americans, an impressive new awareness of politics and public leaders has developed within the black community which is stimulating both higher expectations and greater impatience with the slow pace of change. The efforts of government to respond to black demands, no matter how small their scope or limited their success, have led to the creation of groups and the generation of similar demands for change and improvement within the white community. Many formerly quiescent ethnic and racial minorities and a significantly large segment of the white middle class have become critical of economic and social inequalities which were accepted as inevitable or simply ignored in the recent past. By responding to protest in the black community, the government has opened itself to similar demands from many other groups. It has also stimulated even higher expectations about its performance among all its citizens. Under these circumstances, once a process of competitive mobilization has begun, vigorous action to meet demands is necessary if the government hopes to maintain its integrity and the trust of its citizens.

Broad social reform does not come cheaply. Our analysis leads us to conclude that significant changes in the quality of public services and recognizable improvements in the level of well-being among large segments of the population are necessary if the society's problems are to be solved. In short, unless some means are found to raise large amounts of money for domestic programs, far beyond that now being used for these purposes, the problems arising from the racial crisis are almost certainly going to get worse.

When both the competence and good faith of the government are being called into question, action to deal with widely perceived social problems is urgently needed. The policies called for, however, must be designed to meet several important political criteria. Vitally needed money alone, even in unprecedentedly large amounts, will not necessarily insure the government's creditability. Democratic governments which wish to build trust must also convince the public that policies are the result of consultation and citizen participation, that the opinions of average people matter, and that individuals will receive a fair hearing from public officials. Plans for establishing neighborhood city halls, instituting a system of ombudsmen to aid citizens in making complaints against public officials, creating citizen review boards, electing advisory committees, and decentralizing large public agencies all come in response to the demand that rigid and insensitive public bureaucracies be eliminated. These proposals differ somewhat, but they all share the aim of improving the responsiveness of government to the complaints and desires of its citizens.

Plans for creating more responsive bureaucracies through various forms of administrative reorganization will have little chance of success unless they are accompanied by significant improvement in the benefits offered by government. The need for increased public expenditures and the need for a heightened sense of governmental responsiveness are closely linked. Programs which are designed merely to give the citizens a new assurance of the government's concern for their well-being without seeing that outputs are actually improved may produce better relations between citizens and officials in the short run, but in the long run they are likely to create even greater cynicism and disaffection.

Our analysis indicates that policies which do not result in increased benefits or better governmental services will be inadequate either to build political trust or to deal with the racial crisis. Our data also suggest that the agencies of government must become more responsive and sensitive to the needs and fears of both blacks and whites, and that individual citizens must be given more opportunity to influence bureaucracies whose actions affect their lives in fundamental ways. There are several policies now being proposed which might meet these criteria. One such option, which has recently received considerable publicity, is the decentralization of large city school districts into smaller units based essentially on established racial and ethnic communities. Advocates of this reform argue that it combines meaningful social change, through increased funds and improved services, with heightened administrative responsiveness, through a locally elected school board and increased consultation by teachers with members of the community. The plan is also meant to promote a new awareness and pride in cultural identity among blacks which will eventually lead to greater motivation for learning, an improved educational climate, and higher scholastic achievement. Plans for community control over important city services call for recognition of the fact that little progress has been made toward racial integration and that society has long tolerated the existence of many ethnic and racial enclaves within the cities. Decentralization is designed to capitalize on these social trends rather than combat them in order to promote racial pride and, ultimately, better education.

Decentralization of the administration of city services along racial lines may be initially satisfying to certain militant elements in the black community, and to many hostile, segregationist whites. By officially separating these antagonists and concentrating on enrichment of the existing communities decentralization plans are supposed to lay the foundation for a new racial harmony based on an even greater degree of cultural and racial pluralism than now exists. We believe, however, that there are serious dangers in any policy which grants legal recognition to the racial divisions within our society and employs them as official administrative categories.

The problems of resource allocation will likely be exacerbated once districts are clearly separated on racial and ethnic grounds. The temptation to deny a fair share of essential resources to minority groups will receive legitimation as each district of the newly decentralized system is inevitably called upon to provide the major sources of funds for its operations. This will only tend to encourage debilitating conflicts along racial and ethnic lines and likely cut down the funding available to the districts which need it most. The result will be programs which do not live up to heightened expectations and decreased political trust. The prospects will be increased for competitive mobilization of racial and ethnic groups and uncontrollable conflicts in the future.

We do not mean to discourage or belittle the importance of efforts to encourage a heightened sense of awareness and pride among blacks in their cultural identity. We do not believe, however, that the government should play a large role in this effort. Political leaders should concentrate, instead, on turning the society's attention away from an exclusive concern with racial conflict to a new broader concentration on problems of economic equality, the provision of medical care, housing, education and job training, the control of industrial planning and development, and the problems of environmental pollution. As coalitions of support are built on each side of these new controversies, racial conflicts might be displaced or reduced in importance. Schattschneider has observed that political "conflicts divide people and unite them at the same time, and the process of consolidation is as integral to conflict as the proc-

ess of division."[66] Struggles over fundamental social issues, rather than pitting whites and blacks against each other on primarily racial grounds, might unite the two racial communities in pursuit of shared goals.

In other words, the best hope of obtaining an enduring racial peace and building political trust at the same time is through a massive, general attack on the outstanding social problems of the society which affect both whites and blacks. If these efforts at social reform are large and extensive enough, they would less likely be seen as special benefits designed solely for black people. Although there appears to be significant white opposition to spending more money to improve conditions in the ghetto and great ambivalence about the pace of change in the status of blacks, there is a sense that something must be done and a large reservoir of support probably exists among working and middle class whites for extensive new expenditures on such things as housing, health and education which are aimed at improving the environment for all.

The value of truly large scale efforts to rebuild the cities, provide employment and job training, improve health care and meet other social problems is that through their magnitude and impressiveness alone, even if no special effort is made to emphasize their utility for black people, they might convince the black community that the government cares for their welfare and intends to provide them with the same benefits being provided for whites. Programs of this kind would provide material benefits greatly desired both by working class blacks and whites, and at the same time, might supply the symbolic assurances needed by the middle class blacks, without unduly antagonizing the whites. Edelman assures us that policies which distribute tangible rewards may also have significant symbolic overtones:

[66] E. E. Schattschneider, *The Semi-Sovereign People* (New York: Holt, Rinehart and Winston, 1960), p. 64.

"Because the requisite conditions are always present in some degree, every instance of policy formulation involves a 'mix' of symbolic effect and rational reflection of interests in resources, though one or the other may be dominant in any particular case."[67]

The public policies we advocate would not achieve racial harmony and widespread political trust in the short run— no policy can achieve that. The reforms we envisage would call for a large scale reallocation of resources which would certainly set off monumental political struggles, leading possibly to governmental stalemate. It may be impossible, given the rhetorical legacy of the past twenty years, to convince discontented whites that programs of general social reform are not merely further cynical efforts to pay off the black community. The time may have passed when broadly based interracial coalitions of support for social reform can be created. It also may be impossible to create responsive, efficient and flexible governmental agencies of the

[67] Murray Edelman, *The Symbolic Uses of Politics* (Urbana: University of Illinois Press, 1964), pp. 41–42.

size needed to carry out the large national programs we have in mind.

There are no easy solutions to the current American racial crisis, especially in view of the questions being raised in so many quarters about the legitimacy of established governmental institutions and their ability to successfully meet the many demands being placed upon them. Our data reveal considerable political disaffection among blacks, but there is little desire as yet for separation from the political community as a whole. Blacks overwhelmingly support integration and even those who find violence acceptable still display a willingness to participate vigorously in conventional politics. Events and policies of the next few years may cause political distrust to be generalized to the point where people wish to separate themselves completely from the American political community, but this is not an inevitable development. A workable, interracial society will not evolve without positive, calculated efforts to create it, but if genuine programs of social change are aggressively pursued, citizens may slowly gain new trust in the government, a process which might spiral upward with repeated successes.

THE MALEVOLENT LEADER: POLITICAL SOCIALIZATION IN AN AMERICAN SUB-CULTURE*

Dean Jaros, Herbert Hirsch, Frederic J. Fleron, Jr.

Perhaps the most dramatic finding of recent research on the political socialization of children is that youngsters appear to be overwhelmingly favorably disposed toward political objects which cross their vision. Officers and institutions of govern-

SOURCE: Reprinted from *The American Political Science Review,* LXII, 2 (June 1968), 564–575, by permission of the authors and the publisher.

ment are regarded as benevolent, worthy, competent, serving and powerful.[1] The implications of such findings are striking

* The data on which this paper is based were collected under Contract #693 between the University of Kentucky Research Foundation and the Office of Economic Opportunity.

[1] Robert D. Hess and David Easton, "The Child's Changing Image of the President," *Public Opinion Quarterly,* 14 (Winter, 1960), 632–642;

indeed. Childhood political dispositions may represent the roots of later patriotism; we may be observing the building of basic regime-level supportive values at a very young age.[2]

These findings are by no means new; in fact, they might be classified as part of the conventional wisdom of the discipline. Moreover, they are extremely well documented, and the study of childhood political socialization has advanced to consider far more than basic regime-level norms. Despite all this, however, there are still many empirical questions to be asked about such norms. Perhaps the recent assertion that the political scientist's model of socialization is "static and homogeneous"[3] is particularly apropos here. Consider two closely related characteristics of the appropriate literature: (1) the "positive image" which children have about politics and political figures has been synthesized from data gathered largely in the United States and to some extent in urban, industrialized communities within the United States;[4] and (2) empirical explanation of the favorable disposition which children manifest has not prog-

ressed very far. Though there may be hypotheses about how children get this way, there has been little systematic testing of the relationships between variables.

There is some danger that the major findings may be essentially "culture bound." There are few data on the political values of children in other countries or even in rural, racial, or ethnic subcultures within the United States. Moreover, what evidence there is hints at important cross-cultural variations in political learning;[5] less positive images may characterize other cultures. Political socialization is the process by which the child learns about the political culture in which he lives.[6] The content of what is socialized may well differ from culture to culture or from sub-culture to sub-culture.

The failure to explain children's positive orientations toward politics may be a function of the cultural problem. If the great majority of children in one culture manifest a glowing image, variance in disposition is not prominent, and empirical explanation in terms of accounting for variance may not suggest itself as a crucial task; also it may be quite difficult. In order to explain children's political images, one has to have a distribution of affect; there have to be some relatively negative images to come by. Research into children's political views in other cultures or sub-cultures may provide us with such negative images. But even if it does not generate the necessary data to conduct explanatory analysis, it would lessen the culture bound nature of findings in political socialization.[7]

[*footnote 1 continued*
Fred I. Greenstein, *Children and Politics* (New Haven: Yale University Press, 1965), pp. 27–54; Robert D. Hess and Judith V. Torney, "The Development of Basic Attitudes Toward Government and Citizenship During the Elementary School Years: Part I," (Cooperative Research Project No. 1078; University of Chicago, 1965), pp. 102–105; Dean Jaros, "Children's Orientations Toward the President: Some Additional Theoretical Considerations and Data," *Journal of Politics,* 29 (May, 1967), 368–387.

[2] David Easton and Robert D. Hess, "The Child's Political World," *Midwest Journal of Political Science,* 6 (August, 1962), 243; Greenstein, *op. cit.,* 53.

[3] Roberta S. Sigel, "Political Socialization: Some Reactions on Current Approaches and Conceptualizations," (Paper presented at the 1966 Annual Meeting of the American Political Science Association, New York, Sept. 6–10, 1966), p. 14.

[4] The Chicago area, New Haven, and Detroit provided the research environments for some of the studies cited in Note 1.

[5] Robert D. Hess, "The Socialization of Attitudes Toward Political Authority: Some Cross-National Comparisons," *International Social Science Journal,* 14 (No. 4, 1963), 542–559.

[6] Gabriel A. Almond and G. Bingham Powell, Jr., *Comparative Politics: A Developmental Approach* (Boston: Little, Brown, and Co., 1966), pp. 23–24.

[7] Michael Argyle and Peter Delin, "Non-Universal Laws of Socialization," *Human Relations,* 18 (February, 1965), 77–86.

This paper attempts to realize these desiderata through a study of childhood socialization in the Appalachian region of eastern Kentucky. Appalachia may be classified as a sub-culture within the United States for at least two reasons. First, the poverty and isolation of the region impose characteristics that differentiate it from most other areas in the country. Secondly and relatedly, many cultural norms of Appalachia differ radically from those considered to be standard middle-class imperatives.[8]

I. Two Explanations of Children's Political Authority Orientations

There are several relatively untested hypotheses about the sources of the positive notions children are observed to hold toward the political. Many of them prominently involve the family as a socializing agent. Because of the intriguing nature of family-related variables in Appalachia, the region provides an excellent context in which to investigate these assertions.

Among these explanations is the view that the family directly transmits positive values about government and politics to the child while shielding him from stimuli which have negative connotations, such as stories of political corruption, expedient bargaining, etc.[9] In short, the family directly indoctrinates the child as to the benevolent nature of political authority, to view the political world in essentially the same terms as characterize the parents' generally supportive outlook on the political regime.[10] In Appalachia,

in contrast to most of the rest of the United States, there is a great deal of overt, anti-government sentiment in the adult population. Rejection of and hostility toward political authority, especially federal authority, has long characterized the region.[11] It is very difficult to believe that here parents could transmit positive images of regime symbols to their children. In fact, ". . . the civic instruction which goes on incidental to normal activities in the family,"[12] suggested as a likely cause of children's favorable affect, would in Appalachia be a source of political cynicism.

Secondly, we might take the thesis that the family is an important socializing agent because the child's experiences with his immediate authority figures (parents) are somehow projected to include more remote agencies, including the political. The father, perceived as providing and benevolent, supposedly becomes the prototypical authority figure.[13] For the child, the regime becomes "the family writ large,"[14] especially sacred as its image benefits from the emotional kind of bond that exists between parent and child. In Appalachia, there is a high degree of family disruption. The father may well

[8] Several analyses contributory to this assertion are: Virgil C. Jones, *The Hatfields and the McCoys* (Chapel Hill: University of North Carolina Press, 1948); Jack E. Weller, *Yesterday's People* (Lexington: University of Kentucky Press, 1965); Harry M. Caudill, *Night Comes to the Cumberlands* (Boston: Little, Brown and Co., 1963).

[9] Greenstein, *op. cit.*, pp. 45–46; Easton and Hess, *Midwest Journal of Political Science*, 6 (November, 1962), 229–235.

[10] Herbert Hyman, *Political Socialization* (Glencoe, Ill.: Free Press, 1959), Chapter 4;

Leonard W. Doob, *Patriotism and Nationalism* (New Haven: Yale University Press, 1964), pp. 119–126.

[11] Weller, pp. 33–56, 163; Also Thomas R. Ford (ed). *The Southern Appalachian Region: A Survey* (Lexington: University of Kentucky Press, 1960), pp. 12–15. These may characterize the entire American South. Indeed, some basic socialization data from the South could be most interestingly compared with that gathered elsewhere. But apart from South-wide considerations, there are historical reasons why one would expect such values to be especially strong in Appalachia.

[12] Greenstein, *op cit.*, p. 44.

[13] Harold D. Lasswell, *Power and Personality* (New York: Viking Press, 1962), pp. 156–159; Sebastian DeGrazia, *The Political Community* (Chicago: University of Chicago Press, 1948), pp. 11–21; James C. Davies, "The Family's Role in Political Socialization," *Annals*, 361 (September, 1965), 10–19.

[14] Easton and Hess, *Midwest Journal of Political Science*, 6 (November, 1962), 242–243.

not live at home. Far from providing a glowing prototype of authority, he may be a pitifully inadequate figure, unemployed or absent, not providing for his family, deserving of (and receiving) scorn.[15] If the Appalachian child generalizes the father figure or the family authority structure to the political, he is not very likely to be generalizing a positive configuration.[16]

II. Method

Data were gathered from a nearly complete enumeration (N = 2,432) of rural public school children in grades 5–12 in Knox County, Kentucky during March,

1967. Paper-and-pencil questionnaires were administered in classrooms in connection with an evaluation of a Community Action Program of the Office of Economic Opportunity. This paper is based on the responses of a random sample of 305 of these subjects.[17]

Affect toward political authority was measured in two ways: through reports of images of the President,[18] and through "political cynicism" scale scores.[19] Images of the President were used because this figure apparently occupies a key position in the development of both cognitions of and affect toward the regime.[20] The Presi-

---

[15] The effects of widespread unemployment in the coal industry and other economic malaises are well known. Because they are unable to provide, men reportedly invent physical disabilities or contrive "abandonments" of their dependents in order to qualify their families for public assistance. Such men become ciphers: Weller, *op. cit.,* pp. 76–78; Ford, *op. cit.,* pp. 245–256. In addition to anecdotal accounts of such situations, there are some hard data which are consistent with these assertions. The great proportion of Appalachian men who are not in the labor force (23% in Knox County, site of the present study, as opposed to 11% in the U.S. as a whole) plus a high unemployment rate (11% in Knox County) suggests a large number of non-providing fathers (Source: U.S. Census of Population, 1960). A high incidence of incomplete families can also be confirmed. Fully 22% of the Appalachian children sampled for the present study reported father-absence, while only 12% of the Survey Research Center's national sample of high-school seniors are from fatherless homes. The authors wish to thank Richard Niemi for the last datum.

[16] At this point, it should be noted that these two general hypotheses do not exhaust the list of suggested socialization processes. In fact, some observers stress the efficacy of altogether different agencies, for example the public school: Hess and Torney, *op cit.,* pp. 193–200. But even with this emphasis, such observers believe that some political values are implanted in youth by their parents, namely, those which "insure the stability of basic institutions" (p. 191). This is a reference to what we have called "regime level" values, which are the sole topic of this paper. At least for socialization to this kind of political affect, testing of family-related hypotheses is of undoubted importance. See M. Kent Jennings and Richard

Niemi, "Family Structure and the Transmission of Political Values," (Paper presented at the 1966 annual meeting of the American Political Science Association, New York, Sept. 6–10, 1966).

[17] A few schools, not accessible by road, did not participate in the study. The cost of including them would have been very high and the returns realized very small. These schools had a total enrollment of less than fifty and a somewhat smaller number than this in grades five through eight. The questionnaire was administered by regular classroom teachers who had been instructed in its use. Every attempt was made, however, to convince the subjects that despite the context, they were not being tested. Teachers were asked explicitly to communicate this notion. This mode of administration probably produced fewer invalid responses than exposing the subjects to a non-indigenous investigator who would have aroused suspicion.

Knox County was chosen as the site for this study because it to some extent typifies Appalachia. That is, it is isolated, rural, and poor. No air or rail passenger transportation is available and only one U.S. highway crosses the county. Knox County has an annual per capita income of $501 as compared with $2223 for the U.S. as a whole. It is 84% rural while the nation is only 30%. (Source: U.S. Census of Population, 1960).

[18] For commentary on images of the President, see Fred I. Greenstein, "More on Children's Images of the President," *Public Opinion Quarterly,* 25 (Winter, 1961), 648–654.

[19] For remarks on political cynicism, see Robert E. Agger, Marshall N. Goldstein, and Stanley A. Pearl, "Political Cynicism: Measurement and Meaning," *Journal of Politics,* 23 (August, 1961), 477–506.

[20] Fred I. Greenstein, "The Benevolent Leader: Children's Images of Political Authority," *Amer-*

dency provides an introduction; notions first held toward this role are probably subsequently generalized to other political institutions and to the entity of government itself.[21] The specific instrumentation is that developed by Hess and Easton.[22]

By contrast, political cynicism, "rather than referring to specific political issues and actors . . . is a basic orientation toward political actors and activity. It presumably pervades all encounters with political objects."[23] In short, political cynicism relates to a basic, general evaluative posture toward politics. Though perhaps a developmental descendant of images of the President, this variable represents far less specifically focussed regime-level affect. The specific instrumentation is the political cynicism scale developed by Jennings and Niemi.[24]

In addition to desiring variables important in the introduction of children to politics and ones which seem to encapsu-

late a more generalized and developed kind of regime-level affect, we chose these measures because of the fact that they have generated reliable data. We wished to take advantage of direct replicative possibilities.

Unfortunately, no direct information about the political values of the parents of our sample is presently available.[25] Though the aggregate view of political institutions and personalities held by Appalachian adults is reportedly less positive than those of other Americans, the only personal level data available are child-reported. Our indicators of parental affect toward political authority consist of two family-related items from Easton and Dennis' scale of political efficacy.[26] Two problems arise in using these items as indicators of parental values. First, the index in question was designed to measure a variable in children, not adults. However, the items "inquire about the relationship between government and the child's family. . . ." The index is not regarded as a direct reflector of children's efficacy *per se*. In fact, it shows how a child has come to "view expected relationships between adult members of the system and the authorities" as well as tapping a "nascent attitude" of the child himself.[27] Youngsters tend to evaluate political objects in child-related terms.[28] Clearly this index does not measure that kind of dynamic. The items can be interpreted as a report on family (adult) orientations to political authorities. Indeed, such a report, involving the perception of

ican Political Science Review, 54 (December, 1960), 936; Easton and Hess, *Midwest Journal of Political Science,* 6, 241.

[21] Greenstein, *Children and Politics,* p. 54.

[22] Hess and Easton, *Public Opinion Quarterly,* 14, 639.

[23] Jennings and Niemi, *op. cit.,* p. 13.

[24] *Ibid.,* footnote 30.

[Editor's note: The following items were used:

1. Do you think that quite a few of the people running the government are a little crooked, not very many are, or do you think hardly any of them are?

2. Do you think that people in the government waste a lot of the money we pay in taxes, waste some of it, or don't waste very much of it?

3. How much of the time do you think you can trust the government in Washington to do what is right—just about always, most of the time, or only some of the time?

4. Do you feel that almost all of the people running the government are smart people who usually know what they are doing, or do you think that quite a few of them don't seem to know what they are doing?

5. Would you say that the government is pretty much run by a few big interests looking out for themselves or that it is run for the benefit of all the people?]

[25] The evaluation of the Community Action Program in Knox County involved the solicitation of data from a sample of adults. These data can be arranged with those on youngsters to form parent-child pairs. These data are being exploited by Herbert Hirsch.

[26] David Easton and Jack Dennis, "The Child's Acquisition of Regime Norms: Political Efficacy," *American Political Science Review,* 61 (March, 1967), 25–38.

[27] *Ibid.,* p. 32.

[28] Greenstein, *American Political Science Review,* 54, 938–939.

children, may be a more significant independent variable than the actual values of the parents. A person's values, of course, can have no direct impact on the behavior of another individual. Any effect must be mediated through the influencee's cognitive and evaluative processes.

Secondly, given this, can items which tap efficacy be said to reveal anything about "positive" or supportive regime-level attitudes among adults? Though it is easy to imagine people highly enthusiastic about their political authority without possessing "citizen competence,"[29] it is probable that in democratic societies sense of efficacy is in fact related to general affect toward political authority. Inefficacious feelings are related to alienation and what has been called "political negativism."[30] These are the very antithesis of supportive dispositions. Moreover, recent scholarship has specifically considered efficacy to be a crucial variable in regime-level supports.[31]

The nature of the family authority structure is measured by 1) "father image" items analogous to Hess and Easton's Presidential image items[32] and 2) noting whether the father in fact lives at home.[33]

III. The Appalachian Child's Affect Toward the Political

Our subjects' evaluations of political authority have a very prominent feature: they are dramatically less positive than those rendered by children in previously reported research.

Table 1 describes the affective responses of the Appalachian children to the President and directly compares them to Hess and Easton's findings on Chicago-area children. Though our sample includes children from fifth through twelfth grades and Hess and Easton's from second through eighth, it is possible to make comparisons using only the fifth through eighth grade portions of both. It is clear that for all five President-evaluation items, the distribution of responses of the Knox County youngsters is significantly less favorable than that of the Hess and Easton sample. In fact, when compared against "most men," the President does not do particularly well. In aggregate, he is not a paramount figure, and there are a fair number of youngsters (about a fourth) that express overtly unfavorable reactions to him.

Hess and Easton, it will be recalled, note that age greatly affects the nature of their sample's responses. Generally, they showed that the very favorable view that the very young have of the President's personal qualities (Items 2, 3, and 5) declines with increasing age, while high regard for his performance capabilities is maintained or even increased as the child grows older.[34] The diminution of "personal" portions of the image is not interpreted as a disillusionment with authority, but as increasing realism. The maintenance of the role-filling portions is regarded as most relevant to future adult behavior, translating into respect for political institutions.[35] In short, the changes of children's images of the President with age present a very fortunate configuration considered from the standpoint of loyalty and support for the regime. The Knox County data, bleak to begin with, show

[29] Gabriel A. Almond and Sidney Verba, *The Civic Culture* (Princeton: Princeton University Press, 1963), Chapter 6.

[30] John E. Horton and Wayne Thompson, "Powerlessness and Political Negativism," *American Journal of Sociology*, 67 (March, 1962), 435–493.

[31] Easton and Dennis, *op. cit.*

[32] Hess and Easton, *Public Opinion Quarterly*, 14, 635–642.

[33] On father-absence see: David B. Lynn and William L. Sawrey, "The Effects of Father-Absence on Norwegian Boys and Girls," *Journal of Abnormal and Social Psychology*, 59 (September, 1959), 258–262; George R. Bach, "Father-Fantasies and Father-Typing in Father-Separated Children," *Child Development*, 17 (March, 1946), 63–80.

[34] Hess and Easton, *Public Opinion Quarterly*, 14, 635–642.

[35] *Ibid.*

Table 1. Fifth-Eighth Grade Children's Evaluations of the Persident

Response	Knox County data[a]	Chicago area data[b]	Smirnov two-sample test
1. View of how hard the President works compared with most men.			
harder	35%	77%	
as hard	24	21	
less hard	41	3	$D = .42, p < .001$
Total	100% ($N = 128$)	101% ($N = 214$)	
2. View of the honesty of the President compared with most men.			
more honest	23%	57%	
as honest	50	42	
less honest	27	1	$D = .34, p < .001$
Total	100% ($N = 133$)	100% ($N = 214$)	
3. View of the President's liking for people as compared with most men.			
like most everybody	50%	61%	
likes as many as most	28	37	$D = .20, p < .01$
doesn't like as many	22	2	
Total	100% ($N = 125$)	100% ($N = 214$)	
4. View of the President's knowledge compared with most men.			
knows more	45%	82%	
knows about the same	33	16	$D = .37, p < .001$
knows less	22	2	
Total	100% ($N = 124$)	100% ($N = 212$)	

[a] The Knox County subjects were provided with a "don't know" option apparently not available to their Chicago-area counterparts. This was done to avoid forcing the subjects, who are relatively undeveloped intellectually, to choose among possibly meaningless options. As expected, choice of the don't know alternative was very frequent. For each of the five items above, approximately 30% responded that they did not know. In the interest of comparability, the data do not include these responses. Reported non-responses (about 1%) to items 4 and 5 are likewise excluded from the Chicago-area data.

[b] These data are compiled from those reported in Hess and Easton, *op. cit.*, pp. 636–637.

Table 1 continued

Response	Knox County data[a]	Chicago area data[b]	Smirnov two-sample test
5. View of the President as a person.	best in world	6%	11%	
	a good person	68	82	
	not a good person	26	8	$D = .19, p < .01$
	Total	100% ($N = 139$)	101% ($N = 211$)	

few such encouraging tendencies when controls are imposed for age. Even extending the analysis to the older portions of the sample does little to effect change. To be sure, the personal portions of the image appear slightly less positive than those of younger children. Only 31% of the high-school seniors think the President likes almost everybody, while 31% think he likes fewer people than most men; no twelfth graders think the President is the best person in the world, while 31% think he is not a good person. But overall, the picture is static. *Tau* correlations between age and positive responses to the three personal image items range between .02 and .04 and are not significant.

In those portions of the image supposedly more crucial to adult regime-level behavior, there is no increase in favorable response to the President. However, a decline in the proportion of overtly unfavorable reactions does produce a significant relationship between age and positiveness on the item dealing with how hard the President works ($\tau_c = .14$, $p < .05$) and a perceptible though not significant relationship between age and positiveness on the item dealing with the President's knowledge ($\tau_c = .09$, $p > .05$). At best, these are modest trends. There is relatively little ground for saying, "The President is increasingly seen as a person whose abilities are appropriate to the demands of his office. . . ."[36]

Furthermore, the very high incidence of "don't knows" does not decline significantly with age (see note to Table 1). Such a high rate was to be expected of a deprived, unsophisticated population. But the fact that it remains high even among high-school seniors (mean non-response rate is 27%) provides further evidence that, politically speaking, nothing is happening to these Appalachian youth as they mature. They certainly do not appear to be developing into adults devoted to symbols of extant political authority.

Finally, the stark contrast of these data to those on other American children is heightened when the consideration of social class is introduced. It has often been observed that lower class children have a greater propensity to idealize political figures.[37] This may well be due to the fact that such children are less politicized than their middle-class counterparts. Being less developed and less knowledgeable, they have developed fewer critical faculties and continue to exhibit the "immature" response of excessive deference. It is impossible to determine whether the same class phenomenon operates within Appa-

[36] *Ibid.,* p. 639.
[37] See for example, Greenstein, *Children and Politics,* Chapter 5.

lachia, for the sample as a whole is overwhelmingly lower class.[38] But because of their lower class position relative to the rest of the country, Knox County youngsters generally should be highly idealizing. The data, of course, reveal the diametric opposite. It is clear that Appalachia constitutes a distinct sub-culture, one in which there are operative variables sufficiently powerful to prevent the occurrence of what is by now expected as a matter of course.

Table 2 describes the more generalized affect manifested in political cynicism. The scores of the Knox County youngsters are compared to those of the Survey Research Center's nation-wide sample of high school seniors.[39]

The greater cynicism of the sub-culture sample is evident. Since the Survey Research Center deals only with high school students, perhaps comparisons should be made only with the high school portion (grades 10–12) of the Knox County sample. Though this portion is significantly more cynical, the small number of subjects in it perhaps recommends use of the entire sample. One might think that the introduction of younger respondents would depress cynicism scores (age and cynicism are reportedly positively related in children),[40] but this does not happen to any great degree. In any event, even the entire 5–12 grade Knox County sample is significantly more cynical than the SRC twelfth graders. The implication of

this, of course, is that in Appalachia, unlike the rest of the United States, there is relatively little change in cynicism with maturation. That this is the case is revealed by the nonsignificant $\tau_c = -.02$ between school grade and political cynicism score. Early in life these children appear to become relatively cynical and they stay that way.

Thus, though at this point it remains unexplained, there is no doubt that Appalachian children manifest far less favorable political affect than do their counterparts elsewhere in the United States. Regardless of the index in question, the responses of our sample stand in sharp contrast to other research. Just as supportive dispositions in citizens have been asserted to have early roots, so may the Appalachians' often-noted rejection of political authority germinate during early years. Moreover, also in some contrast to findings of other research, the affective orientations of these subjects does not change greatly with increasing age. These negative images are relatively static. This nonvariant affect suggests the operation of a pervasive socialization agent early in the lives of these children.[41] This in turn suggests the desirability of examining the causal efficacy of variables related to an early agent frequently assumed to be an important socializer: the family. It is to this task that we now turn.

---

[38] No reliable information on social class could be secured from the children themselves. Information on occupation or estimated family income simply was not given by these youngsters. Assigning class on the basis of the neighborhood in which individuals live, as Greenstein did, requires that virtually every subject be placed in the lowest social stratum. These rural residents are universally poor. Only 9% of the county's families have incomes over $6,000, and these are almost entirely to be found in the "urban" county seat, which was not sampled. (Source: U.S. Census of Population 1960).

[39] Jennings and Niemi, *op. cit.*, p. 15.

[40] Greenstein, *Children and Politics*, pp. 39–40.

[41] This non-variance, a preliminary look at our data suggests, may be due to the homogeneity and isolation of the area. Family, peer groups, schools and other possible agents of socialization indigenous to the region probably manifest substantially the same configuration of values. Thus if families transmit an initial set of political notions to children, subsequent exposure to school, peers, etc., is likely to reinforce rather than change values. The remote location of the county probably insulates it from electronic or printed media and other external stimuli. Any value implications at variance with indigenous norms which such sources might transmit are thus prevented from having a widespread effect on maturing children.

Table 2. Political Cynicism Scores*

	Knox County data (whole sample)	Knox County data (high school only)	SRC national sample	Smirnov two sample test
most cynical 6	8%	26%	5%	Knox County data (whole sample)
5	11	22	3	and SRC national sample, $D=.16$,
4	19	11	13	$p<.001$
3	19	20	37	Knox County data (High school
2	23	15	25	only) and SRC national sample,
least cynical 1	21	6	17	$D=.40$, $p<.001$
Total	101% N=305	100% N=54	100% N=1869	

* It has been assumed that the Political Cynicism Scale generated Guttman scalar patterns in the Knox County Data as it did in the SRC National Sample. To compensate for the possible invalidity of this assumption, the items were conservatively dichotomized and conservatively scored. Only choice of the most cynical available alternative was considered a cynical response. Failure of a respondent to choose the most cynical alternative *for whatever reason,* including non-response, resulted in the recording of a non-cynical item score.

IV. The Family as Transmitter of Specific Political Values

What kinds of general explanatory propositions about the socialization process are consistent with these data? If parents typically transmit the substantive content of their values about government to their children, then the very negative political affect observed among Appalachian youngsters should be related to similar assessments on the part of their mothers and fathers.[42] Evidence on this

[42] In the absence of additional data, it is difficult to show empirically that the parents of this sample have negative dispositions toward political authority. However, responses to the family political value items, when the distribution is dichotomized, reveal about equal number of agreements (negative dispositions) and disagreements (positive dispositions). Following each item is the percentage of respondents expressing agreement:

"I don't think people in the government care much about what people like my family think," 58%;
"My family doesn't have any say about what the government does," 43%.

The authors are fully aware of the precarious nature of the family value measures. Their proxy nature makes them somewhat suspect. The

can be gained by examining the nature of the relationship between our family political orientation items and childrens' political affect (Table 3).

Since responses to family political orientation items were recorded in terms of degree of agreement (from disagree very much to agree very much), they constitute ordinal variables as do the presidential image and cynicism measures. The evidence on the amount of impact they have on these child political affect variables, however, is mixed. Some fairly substantial *taus* are accompanied by others approaching zero. But it is interesting to note where the significant relationships occur. Primarily, they involve Presidential competence items and the cynicism scale. These may be the most important dependent variables. Several scholars have observed that childhood evaluations of the personal qualities of the President,

data they generate are displayed, however, because they are suggestive and because they indicate the kind of research which, in the authors' opinions, should be performed more often. In subsequent publications based on the Appalachian data, direct information on parental values and children's perceptions thereof will be available (See note 25).

Table 3. Relationship between Family Political Orientation and Child's Political Affect

Family political orientation item	Child's political affect measure	τ_c	Significance
"I don't think people in the government care much what people like my family think"*	view of how hard President works	.23	$p < .001$
	view of the honesty of the President	.06	$p > .05$
	view of the President's liking for people	.18	$p < .001$
	view of the President's knowledge	.01	$p > .05$
	view of the President as a person	.05	$p > .05$
	political cynicism scale	—.20	$p < .001$
"My family doesn't have any say about what the government does."*	view of how hard President works	.10	$p > .05$
	view of the honesty of the President	.06	$p > .05$
	view of the President's liking for people	.07	$p > .05$
	view of the President's knowledge	.13	$p < .01$
	view of the President as a person	.06	$p > .05$
	political cynicism scale	—.13	$p < .01$

*Disagreement scored as positive value.

which here do not relate to family political orientation, are "less functionally relevant" to future adult behavior than are assessments of role-filling capabilities. As stated above, these observers express no alarm at the decline with age of evaluations of Presidential benevolence. Similarly, the fact that parental values do not seem to influence them may not be great evidence about the inefficacy of familial values in conditioning important childhood orientations.

If political cynicism represents a more developed kind of evaluation, it is significant that it appears to depend upon these parental variables. Regarded as an important encapsulator of youthful political affect, this construct may be a crucial indicator whose antecedents should be known.

Family political values, then, appear to have some effect on children's political affect. Especially given the fact that the affective variables in question appear to be among the most significant, the direct transmission hypothesis takes on some credibility. This suggests the desirability of more detailed investigations of the content of intra-familial political communication.

V. The Family as Prototypical Authority Structure

A totally different kind of dynamic is implied in the notion of relations with the family as a model for political affect. It is not, however, incompatible with the notion that the family transmits specific value content to the young. It is entirely possible that both processes operate simultaneously. Moreover, since the relationships are relatively small, our data on value transmission fairly demand that additional explanatory tacks be taken. Table 4 demonstrates the effects of father-image and integrity of the family on Appalachian children's political orientations. Again, evidence is somewhat mixed. Three father image items[43] are placed

[43] The father image items are analogous to the Presidential image items used by Hess and Easton. Though there are five Presidential image items,

Table 4. Relationship between Family Authority Characteristics and Child's Political Affect

Family authority characteristics	Child's political affect	τ_c	Significance
View of father's liking for people	view of President's liking for people	.05	$p > .05$
	political cynicism	—.07	$p > .05$
View of father's knowledge	view of President's knowledge	.02	$p > .05$
	political cynicism	.02	$p > .05$
View of father as a person	view of President as a person	.05	$p > .05$
	political cynicism	—.03	$p > .05$
Father living with family[a]	view of how hard President works	—.08	$p < .05$
	view of President's honesty	—.09	$p < .05$
	view of President's liking for people	—.12	$p < .05$
	view of President's knowledge	—.23	$p < .001$
	view of President as a person	.00	$p > .05$
	political cynicism	.05	$p > .05$

[a] This is a dichotomous variable—either the father lives at home or he does not. However, since father's living at home constitutes a less disrupted family authority structure, we continue to apply ordinal statistics.

against their Presidential-image parallels and against cynicism. There is almost a complete lack of relationship. Not only does the "great overlap of the images of father and President"[44] fail to appear among these children, but the more generalized political affect measured by cynicism does not depend on how they see their fathers. In short, there is no evidence at all to support the hypothesis that evaluations of family authority figures are directly projected to remote, political ones.

If the father image hypothesis thus suffers, another dynamic by which the family might serve as a model for regime affect fares even worse. The presence or absence of the father might be thought to have political consequences for children. A fatherless home is disrupted and generally thought to have negative implications. Children might project their negative evaluations of such homes onto the political authority.[45] If this were the case, children from fatherless homes should have less positive views. Table 4 reveals exactly the opposite. There are generally low to moderate, but significant, negative relationships between having a father at home and evaluating the President in a favorable light. Fatherless children are more positive toward the political. How can this remarkable result be interpreted? One could argue that there is a cathartic process at work; that there is some sort of psychic necessity (possibly anxiety-related) to regard authority as benign. Perhaps unfortunate home life heightens this need which is then manifested in positive evaluations of the political.[46] This does not seem likely, for as we have just seen, specific negative evaluations of their fathers are not related to childrens' positive political orientations.

only three father image analogues are used because of objection to asking respondents to evaluate their fathers' honesty or diligence at work.
[44] Hess and Easton, *Public Opinion Quarterly,* 14, 640.
[45] Davies, *op. cit.,* 13–15.
[46] Judith V. Torney, *The Child's Idealization*

Rather than resulting in negative authority orientations, father-absence could interfere with the transfer of specific political value content from family to child. A major agent in the transfer process may be absent. Though mixed, there is some evidence in previous research of "male political dominance" in the family. Fathers may be particularly important communicators of political values.[47] Children from fatherless homes become more dependent upon their mothers. But mothers are not typically strong political cue-givers. Hence, the typical adult political values of Appalachia will not be so effectively transmitted in the fatherless home. These adult values supposedly involve relatively unfavorable assessments of political authority. The fatherless child escapes close contacts with these values and emerges more positively disposed toward political authority. When this agent is absent, perhaps the media, or other agents bearing more favorable cues, assume a more prominent role in the socialization process.

This interpretation, which of course returns us to the transmission-of-specific-values hypothesis, is strongly supported by additional analysis of the data. First, it is clear that there is no unknown process operating to produce more positive adult political values in fatherless families. Fatherless and two-parent families are identical in this regard (*tau's* between father at home and family political value items are —.03 and .00). Though the starting point is the same, it is also clear that the

of Authority (unpublished M.A. thesis, University of Chicago, 1962).
[47] Greenstein, *Children and Politics,* p. 119; Kenneth P. Langton, *The Political Socialization Process: The Case of Secondary School Students in Jamaica,* (Unpublished Ph.D. dissertation, University of Oregon, 1965), p. 119. On the other hand, male dominance in the political learning of the young fails to appear in some research: Hyman, *Political Socialization,* pp. 83–89; Eleanor E. Maccoby, Richard E. Matthews, and Anton S. Morton, "Youth and Political Change," *Public Opinion Quarterly,* 18 (Spring, 1954), 23–39.

transmission process is greatly attenuated in fatherless homes. This can be seen by imposing a control for father-presence on the relationship between family political orientation and child's political affect (Table 5). The data for father-present children are very similar to the collapsed data shown in Table 3, except that the relationship between family value and child affect is generally somewhat stronger. But for father-absent children, the relationship generally declines and in several cases is actually reversed. Not only can the fatherless family not promulgate its political values, but it seems to leave its children very vulnerable to the socialization of other agents, agents with rather different (more positive) values. To be sure, child political cynicism, which is related to family political values, does not appear to be governed by these considerations. Other family-related roots may affect this variable—perhaps those which relate to generalized cynicism.

Table 5. Relationship between Family Political Orientation and Child's Political Affect, with Father-Presence Controlled

Family political orientation item	Child's political affect measure	Father-present children τ_c	Father-absent children τ_c	Significance of the difference
I don't think people in the government care much what people like my family think*	view of how hard the President works	.25	.12	$p < .001$
	view of honesty of the President	.12	—.10	$p < .001$
	view of President's liking for people	.23	.04	$p < .001$
	view of President's knowledge	.00	.06	$p < .01$†
	view of President as a person	.10	—.11	$p < .001$
	political cynicism scale	—.18	—.26	$p < .01$†
My family doesn't have any say about what the government does*	view of how hard the President works	.17	—.15	$p < .001$
	view of honesty of the President	.10	—.06	$p < .001$
	view of President's liking for people	.17	—.23	$p < .001$
	view of President's knowledge	.17	.03	$p < .001$
	view of President as a person	—.06	.08	$p < .001$†
	political cynicism	—.13	—.16	$p < .05$†

* Disagreement scored as positive value.
† Relationship not in predicted direction.

VI. Conclusion

Children in the relatively poor, rural Appalachian region of the United States are dramatically less favorably inclined toward political objects than are their counterparts in other portions of the nation. Moreover, the image which these children have does not appear to develop with age in the fashion observed for others; there is no indication that a process conducive to the development of political support is operative in Appalachia. Here, children's views appear to be relatively static. These findings have two implications. First, they point to the possibility that the often-emphasized highly positive character of children's views of politics may be a culturally bound phenomenon. One should exercise much caution in accepting such views as a universal norm. Secondly, the occurrence of such divergent findings underscores the desirability of *explaining* children's political orientations.

Since, at the sub-cultural level, these atypical findings are paralleled by (1) atypical adult (parent) political values, and (2) atypical family structure, two broad hypotheses involving the effect of family-related variables on children's political affect were tested. Examination of the hypothesis that parents directly transmit the content of their political values to their children produced some confirming evidence. Reported parental values showed moderate relationship to certain aspects of children's political affect. This was especially true of the competence items in Presidential images (supposedly the most important for subsequent behavior) and of political cynicism, a more generalized kind of system affect.

The thesis which posits the family as prototypical authority structure fares less well, however. There is no support at all for the notion that affect toward the father is extended to remote, political authority. Relationships between specific aspects of children's father images and parallel components of Presidential im-

ages are not significant. Nor is there evidence that disrupted family structure, measured by father-absence, contributes to negative political evaluations. In fact, father-absence is associated with more favorable political valuations in Appalachian children! This remarkable result is interpreted as supporting the first hypothesis regarding the direct transfer of value-content from family to child. Where the father is absent, an agent communicating the predominantly negative adult political values to youngsters is lost. This notion seems the more plausible when it is observed that there is a marked relationship between family political values and child political affect among father-present families, but no such relationship —if anything a slight negative gradient— among father-absent families.

Thus, of the two broad hypotheses posited at the outset, our data support the notion of direct value transfer, while leading us to doubt that the family is an effective authority prototype. Though these findings are offered as significant in and of themselves—they certainly suggest the importance of closer examination of parent-child political communication processes in the understanding of regime-level values—there are other implications. The explanatory relationships presented here are of relatively modest magnitudes. The small amount of variance in children's political affect which is explained here by the family suggests that we should search for other agents of socialization, or for other dynamics which may operate within the family. A preliminary view of other of the Knox County data suggests that there may be conditions under which other, less personal agents assume a great role. Fortunately, the move toward cross-cultural and explanatory analysis of childhood socialization will proceed and these and related questions will be joined.[48]

[48] The forthcoming doctoral dissertation by Herbert Hirsch explores other socialization agents at greater length.

PART VI

ALIENATION AND THE SOCIAL SYSTEM: STABILITY AND CHANGE

Introduction

Studying social change is problematic. Not only is it inherently difficult to study systems in motion, but in a changing universe it is difficult to know which of a multitude of interrelated potential causes may have been most important in bringing about particular changes. The problems are compounded by the fact that some changes of great significance, such as revolutions, occur relatively infrequently, and cannot be studied experimentally to test particular hypotheses.

To investigate the role of alienation in social change is therefore a very complex problem. The difficulties also are increased because appropriate attitudinal data are generally not readily obtainable. Instead of being able to rely on relatively available aggregate indicators of the state of a social system, such as gross national product, population trends and so on, the researcher interested in alienation must have access to valid and reliable survey data based on adequate sampling procedures. Moreover, once particular stages of social change have occurred, it may be impossible to ascertain reliably the attitudes which existed before the change. Unless this problem can be solved, it is exceedingly difficult to assess the role and importance of attitudes in social change.

In the absence of systematically collected attitudinal data on alienation, however, it is sometimes possible to substitute other types of measures. Forms of human expression such as letters, musical lyrics, novels and autobiographies occasionally serve as source material for studies of alienation. Social scientists may also use nonattitudinal measures that appear to be valid indicators of alienation. For example, emigration from a political system in the absence of economic hardship, truancy from a school, and the incidence of industrial sabotage might be used as indicators of alienation from the political, academic, and economic systems.

Investigators particularly interested in the effects of attitudes on events already past may also collect a form of substitute "before the fact" data by

269

asking respondents retrospective questions to ascertain their feelings at a prior point in time. This approach is used by Maurice Zeitlin in his study of the effect of work alienation on support for the Cuban revolution. Zeitlin's study examines a hypothesis Marx and others subscribed to, that the worker's alienation from work would be generalized to the *political* system, and the consequent political alienation eventually would result in the overthrow of that system. As Zeitlin points out, the major hazard in using retrospective data in a study of this type is that *present* attitudes may cause the respondent selectively to recall and color his *past* attitudes so as to increase consistency between the two attitude sets. In the case of the particular variables analyzed by Zeitlin, this difficulty is compounded by the special salience of work attitudes in the ideology of the Cuban revolution. Nevertheless, while recognizing that the attitudes measured after the fact are not necessarily precisely the same as those actually held before, Zeitlin argues that recall bias is not a significant invalidating factor in his analysis and that both theory and empirical evidence support his interpretation that alienation from work indeed led to support for the revolution.

The Zeitlin study is unique in providing attitudinal data on work and politics in a revolutionary situation. We do not have available the additional studies that are necessary to specify further the conditions under which transference of attitudes toward work to the political system results in support for revolutionary movements. One necessary condition might be the extent to which work organization is a salient aspect of the ideology of either the extant political system or its preferred alternative. In situations where conflict and ideologies center largely around political rather than economic issues, transference may be much less likely. In the contemporary United States, for example, revolutionary ideologies focus largely on access to the political decision-making process and on the distribution of effective political participation. These emphases may partially explain why the American radical left has had relatively little success in mobilizing the working class to a position of political opposition. Although this lack of success may be due in part to a lack of alienation from work (necessary as a trigger mechanism for a transference effect), it seems more likely that work alienation exists but is not generalized to the political realm because work relationships are not focal aspects of the revolutionary ideology. In the absence of such ideological emphasis, the relevance of political change for work organization may be unclear. This relevance is obvious in the classical ideologies of socialism, however, and was clearly present in the ideology of revolutionary Cuba.

More generally, transference of attitudes from any one social sector to another may thus depend on the inclusiveness of the ideologies current in each sector. If the ideology of a particular social sector is sufficiently broad or abstract to suggest behavior patterns in *other* social sectors, attitudinal transference will be facilitated. Imagine the example of an academic institution: if the values of the *political* system seem to imply particular forms of social control in high schools and colleges, then alienation from school may be generalized to the political system. This is much less likely to be the case where the form of social control in a school is viewed as an idiosyncratic expression of a particular school official's personality. To engage attitudes developed within one social sector, the ideology of another must be relevant for change in the first as well.

This analysis is consistent with a specification Zeitlin makes of the relationship between work attitudes and revolutionary support. Zeitlin finds that among workers who have favorable work attitudes after the revolution and who discuss their prerevolutionary work alienation in terms of *exploitation* by the capitalist system, *all* are favorable to the revolution. On the other hand, among workers who feel favorable afterwards but who give as reasons for prerevolutionary work alienation factors *other than exploitation* (emphasizing, for example, economic insecurity, maltreatment at work, and other nonexploitative discontents), only three-quarters are supportive of the revolution. Zeitlin argues that the reason for this difference lies in the *inherently political nature* of the first type of work alienation, which could be eliminated only by revolutionary change in the political and economic structure, whereas the incremental changes in the work situation demanded by the second type of alienation could have been made by the old political and economic systems as well. Thus, the particular type of discontent or alienation from work also affects the transference phenomenon. When the changes implied by the alienation are thought to be possible only if prior political change occurs *and* when work organization is a salient aspect of the revolutionary political ideology, then generalization of work alienation to the political system is very likely.

Another research strategy for studying the relationship of alienation to social change is illustrated in Eric Allardt's study of alienation and economic development. Allardt uses Communist voting strength in the communes of Finland as an indicator of the degree of alienation from the Finnish economic and political systems. By reporting the relationships found in previous survey work between Communist vote and several attitude measures of alienation, he argues for the validity of this indicator.

The major question which Allardt addresses is how levels and types of alienation change *as a function of social and industrial development*. Alienation is therefore the dependent variable in Allardt's analysis, and division of labor and pressure toward social uniformity are the major independent variables. His research strategy involves comparing the sources of Communist voting strength in the developed industrial areas of Finland with the sources of its strength in the less developed, primarily rural areas. The conditions correlated with Communist voting in these two areas are very dissimilar. It is theoretically very interesting, moreover, that the different conditions closely parallel the differences between alienation and anomie which were discussed in the first section of this book.

Allardt points out that in industrial areas, the factors associated with

Communist voting strength all represent *stable* social patterns where individuals feel great pressure toward uniformity. Little room is available for expression of individual needs and views. This condition, a convergence of strong pressure toward uniformity and a high degree of industrialization, seems very similar to the conditions analyzed in Marx's essay on "Alienated Labour." The individual is repressed by the society and his yearning for freedom leads to alienation and protest. Compare these conditions with the factors Allardt shows to be related to Communist voting in the less developed "backwoods" areas. Here the factors all represent *instability and uncertainty* or a weak pressure toward uniformity. Social and economic change prevails and social norms are rapidly breaking down. These factors all exemplify Durkheim's anomie. Allardt goes even further in distinguishing between these two states. He subsumes four different types of alienation under the rubric of "uprootedness" in the backwoods areas, while "powerlessness" alone is taken to define the Marxian type of alienation in the industrial areas. Thus, a major distinction is drawn between powerlessness and the other forms of alienation. Yet both of these types of alienation lead to the same social protest manifestation—a high proportion of Communist voting strength. As Allardt discusses, however, the motivational bases of the Communist vote in these two areas vary significantly. Allardt concludes his analysis by looking at the other side of his original question to suggest the different forms of social change and protest likely to *follow* from the different types of alienation.

The last two selections are also concerned with theoretical explorations of how alienation affects social change. One approach to this problem is offered by William Gamson, who is interested in both the political causes and effects of alienation from political authorities. Gamson presents an analysis of the dynamic relations between government and "solidary" groups—those organized partisan groups that attempt to achieve social change by influencing public policy. He is basically concerned with three interrelated questions: (1) Why do solidary groups differ in the means by which they attempt to influence political authorities and thereby induce social change? (2) How do the attempts of political authorities to control such groups differ as a function of the means of influence used by the groups and the degree to which the groups are perceived by authorities to be politically alienated? (3) What happens to a group's level of political alienation as a result of the way the political authorities react to its influence attempts?

In their attempts to affect the decisions of authorities, solidary groups utilize three basic means of influence–persuasion, inducements, and constraints. These means vary in the extent to which they disadvantage political authorities. *Persuasion* offers no advantages or disadvantages; rather it is an attempt to change the orientation of political authorities by providing information and arguments supporting the policy or action favored by the group. *Inducements* offer the possibility of new advantages, such as campaign assistance or financial contributions, or the withholding of a *dis*advantage, such as campaign opposition, *in exchange for* a favorable decision. The use of *constraints* as a means of influence involves the addition of new disadvantages to the situation of the authorities. The threat of physical violence to achieve political goals is an obvious example of the use of constraints but so also are activities such as strikes, demonstrations, and threats to withdraw past support unless the desired action is effected.

Gamson argues that the particular means of influence chosen by a solidary group is largely a function of the level of political trust of the group. His definition of political trust is an interesting and significant variant of the powerlessness dimension of alienation. Rather than referring to the individual's or group's perception of its *ability* to influence political decisions, political trust is defined in terms of the group's perception of the *necessity* for it to attempt to influence decisions. A group's "political trust can be defined as the probability, P_b, that the political system (or some part of it) will produce preferred outcomes even if left untended" (Gamson, 1968, p. 54). If the group perceives that, whether it acts or not, the political authorities will produce decisions which are favorable to it, then it does not need to attempt to influence the authorities, and can be defined as a "confident" group. "Confidence is the belief that for any given decision, $P_b = 1.0$" (p. 54). Alternatively, a group may feel neutral with respect to the likelihood that the government will make a decision favorable to it. For example, it may perceive the authorities to be indifferent or uninformed as to the group's interest, and therefore its P_b would hover around .5. Finally, for "alienated" groups, $P_b = 0$. In this case, the group is fairly certain that the authorities will act *against* its interests.

Just as solidary groups have various means of influence at their disposal, so authorities may attempt to control the activities of these groups in different ways. They may try to *persuade* groups of the wisdom of the particular course of action followed, they may use *sanctions* to reward or punish supportive or recalcitrant groups, and finally they may attempt to *insulate* groups by denying access to resources and authorities. Gamson argues that the means of control authorities use with any given group have important effects on changes in the level of political trust of the group. In this way, a feedback cycle is set up.

While it is difficult to break into a feedback cycle at any one point and talk about that point as the beginning of the chain of relationships, Gamson does begin his analysis with group attempts to effect social change by influencing political decisions. Political alienation is a key variable in this process in that it determines what types of influence attempts will be made. In turn, political alienation is itself affected by the success or failure of these influence attempts. An unexpected conclusion that Gamson reaches is that alienation is *reinforced or increased* when groups *successfully* apply constraints in their attempts to influence government policy. This hypothesis, if valid, has considerable significance for government policy in cases where strikes, violent demonstrations, and other tactics involving constraints are used to influence public policy. Empirical research to explore this hypothesis is clearly needed.

David Easton presents a broad discussion of the importance of supportive attitudes for political systems, and the ways in which political authorities respond to problems created by political alienation. Easton's analysis centers around the concept of "political support." From his discussion, it is clear that "support" defines one end of a continuum whose opposite pole is a generalized form of political alienation. Low political support is therefore another way of referring to high political alienation. Easton argues that if support levels are too low (or conversely, alienation too high), the very existence of a political system may be seriously threatened. Certainly, Zeitlin's research lends credence to this hypothesis. Clearly, however, revolution is not the only possible result of political alienation. Political systems may take creative steps to stem the tide of revolution by encouraging political support. Easton analyzes a variety of ways in which political systems may do this. Some of the steps which may be taken are largely symbolic, but many involve significant social and political changes that make the system more responsive to the needs and wants of its members.

In many ways, therefore, Easton's discussion can be regarded as a more inclusive framework for the problem Gamson addressed under the rubric of "social control mechanisms." Easton is concerned mainly with the longer range policies used by political authorities and other members of a political system in responding to political alienation. These policies, however, involve change and adaptation as well as control. Easton and Gamson both agree that the political process is more than a game of strategy in which control is exercised so as to contain efficiently alienated political groups. Rather, the major function of political authorities is to design substantive policies responding to the needs of the members of the political system. For Easton, for example, the failure of the authorities to provide adequate and appropriate "outputs" is an important factor in loss of support. Effective and responsive policy decisions are ultimately very powerful means for decreasing political alienation. Easton also considers changes in political structure as an adaptive response to widespread loss of support. Thus, while many of the studies in this book focus on the ways in which structural variables affect alienation, the selections in this concluding section emphasize the role of alienation itself in bringing about social change.

ALIENATION AND REVOLUTION

Maurice Zeitlin

"Every age has its key ethical concept around which it can best formulate the cluster of its basic problems," and to many of our thinkers that concept is alienation.[1] The frequent use in social science today of some variant of the concept testifies "to the central place occupied by the hypothesis of alienation."[2] Much of the concept's value in sociological analysis, however, is diminished because in the very process of trying to "remove the critical, polemic element in the idea of alienation,"[3] the concept itself has become alienated from its classical meaning as a radical attack on the existing social structure. In fact, in most sociological writing it is "no longer clear what alienated men are alienated from."[4]

The concept, in one of its most important classical meanings was an attack on the exploitation of the worker in industrial capitalist society. Thinkers as diverse as John Stuart Mill, Tocqueville, Karl Marx, and Friedrich Engels independently arrived at a similar critique of the worker's alienation from his work through their observations of developing capitalism.

Mill, for example, thought that the workers' alienation from their work would lead them to become discontent with the existing social order:

> I cannot think it probable that they will be permanently contented with the condition of laboring for wages as their ultimate state. To work *at the bidding* and for the *profit of another, without any interest in the work* . . . is, *not even when wages are high,* a satisfactory state to human beings of educated intelligence who have ceased to think themselves naturally inferior to those whom they serve.[5]

Mill, therefore, proposed a reorganization of industry which would allow the workers to share in both the management and profit of industry, as means of "healing the widening and embittering feud be-

SOURCE: Reprinted from *Social Forces*, 45, 2 (December 1966), 224–236, by permission of the author and publisher. This selection also appears as Chapter 8 of Maurice Zeitlin, *Revolutionary Politics and the Cuban Working Class* (Princeton University Press, 1967; Harper Torchbook, 1970).

[1] Lewis Feuer, "What is Alienation? The Career of a Concept," *Sociology on Trial,* Maurice Stein and Arthur Vidich, eds. (Englewood Cliffs, New Jersey: Prentice-Hall, 1963), p. 127.

[2] Robert Nisbet, *The Quest for Community* (New York: Oxford University Press, 1953), p. 15.

[3] Melvin Seeman, "On the Meaning of Alienation," *American Sociological Review,* 24 (December 1959), p. 784.

[4] John Horton, "The Dehumanization of Anomie and Alienation: A Problem in the Ideology of Sociology," *British Journal of Sociology* (December 1964), p. 284. A major study appeared recently, however, which is an excellent excep-

tion to this criticism, namely, Robert Blauner, *Alienation and Freedom* (Chicago: University of Chicago Press, 1964), which attempts to locate the differential conditions of work under which industrial workers are likely to feel estranged from their work.

[5] John Stuart Mill, *Principles of Political Economy,* II (Boston: Little, Brown & Co., 1848), p. 327. (Italics added)

tween the class of laborers and the class of capitalists . . ." He could not be persuaded

that the majority of the community will forever, or even for much longer, consent to hew wood and draw water all their lives in the service and *for the benefit of others; or* . . . that they will [not] be less and less willing to cooperate as subordinate agents in any work, when *they have no interest in the result* . . .[6]

These words from Mill adumbrated the theory of the alienation of labor and its political consequences developed in the works of Marx and Engels. They all emphasized what they believed were the generally destructive psychological consequences of the worker's position in industrial production.

In particular, however, Marx focused on two levels of the organization of capitalist production in which alienation is inherent:

1. The locus of control over the organization of production within the plant itself. Marx argued that the worker is deprived of his individual rationality to the extent to which the process of production is made rational from the standpoint of the organizer of production, namely, the capitalist. Because control, planning, and organization of production are the prerogative of the capitalist, the worker is degraded to the level of a mere productive force, separated or alienated from his own knowledge, judgment, and will, which are now required only for the plant as a whole.[7]

2. The locus of control over the means of production and the products of production within the capitalist system as a whole. Neither the tools that the worker works with, nor the products he produces are his property. Therefore, in the very process of production, the worker becomes alienated from his work because it is not in his own interest but that of the capitalist. The more the worker produces, and the more he expends himself in his work, the more not he, but the owner of his labor power benefits. Thus, at work, the worker himself is the property of the capitalist, and is alienated not only from his work and the products of his work, but from himself.[8]

As a result of the process of alienation of both the worker's rationality and his product, "every remnant of charm in his work" is destroyed and it becomes transformed into "hated toil."[9] Usurped of their individual rationality and their collective product, the workers, Marx believed, would not only find their work degrading and suffer psychological deprivation, but also would become discontent with the capitalist system as a whole. This discontent, in turn, would be a major revolutionary motivating force. Marx assumed, in other words, that the *objective* relationship of the alienation (i.e., separation) of the workers from control of the social organization of production and the products of their work, would result in their *subjective* estrangement from the capitalist system. This process of estrangement—along with the problematic development of class consciousness—would lead eventually to the proletarian revolu-

---

[6] *Ibid.,* p. 338.

[7] Karl Marx, *Capital* (New York: Modern Library), pp. 396–397, 708–709. It might be worth noting the evident kinship between Marx's concept of individual rationality and rational organization, and Karl Mannheim's concept of "substantial rationality" as opposed to "functional rationality." Cf., *Man and Society in an Age of Reconstruction* (New York: Harcourt, Brace & World, 1954), pp. 52-60, 216.

[8] Karl Marx, *Economic and Philosophic Manuscripts.* This aspect of alienation, the objective separation of the worker from the products of his work, was the conceptual germ of Marx's later concept of exploitation in which the value created by the worker over and above the value he is repaid in wages is appropriated by the capitalist.

[9] Marx, *Capital,* p. 708.

tion and the "emancipation of the working class." As Marx put it:

> The proletarian class . . . feels itself crushed by this self-alienation, sees in it its own impotence and the reality of an inhuman situation. It is . . . a revolt to which it is forced by the contradiction between its humanity and its situation, which is an open, clear and absolute negation of its humanity.[10]

Since Marx, there has been a tradition in political analysis of relating work and its discontents to the development of radical working class politics. In the sociological literature on working class politics, the connection between work dissatisfaction, social resentment, and political radicalism often has been noted. There is also a literature on the working class that Hodges has aptly termed the "sociology of cynicism," in which more often implicitly but occasionally explicitly, attitudes of general hostility toward and resentment of society are linked to alienation from work.[11]

[10] *Die Heilige Familie, Marx-Engels Gesamtausgabe,* Vol. 3, Part 1, pp. 205–206, cited in *Karl Marx: Selected Writings in Sociology and Social Philosophy,* T. B. Bottomore and M. Rubel, eds. (London: Watts & Co., 1956), pp. 231–233.
[11] Seymour Martin Lipset, Paul F. Lazarsfeld, Allen Barton, and Juan Linz, "The Psychology of Voting: An Analysis of Political Behavior," in *Handbook of Social Psychology,* Vol. 2, Gardner Lindzey, ed. (Cambridge, Massachusetts: Addison-Wesley Publishing Co., 1954), pp. 1124–1170; Donald Clark Hodges, "Cynicism in the Labor Movement," *American Journal of Economics and Sociology,* 21 (January 1962), pp. 29–36; Ely Chinoy, *Automobile Workers and the American Dream* (New York: Doubleday & Co., 1955); Paul Goodman, *Growing Up Absurd* (New York: Random House, 1960); George Friedmann, *Anatomy of Work* (New York: The Free Press of Glencoe, 1961); C. Wright Mills, *The New Men of Power* (New York: Oxford University Press, 1948); Hadley Cantril, *The Politics of Despair* (New York: Basic Books, 1958); Karl Bednarik, *The Young Worker of Today: A New Type,* (ed.) J. P. Mayer, (tr.) R. Tupholm (Glencoe, Illinois: The Free Press, 1955).

Ironically, for instance, Ely Chinoy's interviews with auto workers in Detroit apparently convinced him that the workers' alienation explained the widespread interest among them in small business and, to an extent, in farming, "and their responsiveness to the values of the small-business tradition." He concluded, therefore, that

> Paradoxically, the very process of alienation which Marx thought would transform workers into class conscious proletarians has instead stimulated their interest in small business and in small-scale private farming, institutions which Marx asserted were doomed to extinction.[12]

Chinoy did not try to measure the political attitudes of the workers he interviewed, however, nor examine the extent to which their longing to get out of the factory represented hostility toward a society that exploited them and their work. The fact is that despite the theoretical orientations and the numerous suggestions for research on the subject, in few studies has there been analysis of the relationship between work attitudes and political attitudes,[13] nor especially of the political meaning of alienation from work.

Alienation and Revolution

The Cuban revolution gave new public esteem and respect to manual labor, nationalized industry, and abolished the private appropriation of the workers' products.[14] In-plant relationships were also

[12] Chinoy, *op. cit.,* p. 86.
[13] See Richard Centers, *The Psychology of Social Classes* (Princeton: Princeton University Press, 1949), pp. 160, 170–172, 203; Richard Hamilton, *Affluence and the French Worker: The Fourth Republic Experience* (Princeton: Princeton University Press, forthcoming), chap. 12; and Juan Linz, "The Social Bases of West German Politics," unpublished Ph.D. dissertation, Columbia University, 1959, pp. 215ff.
[14] Wyatt MacGaffey and Clifford Barnett, *Twentieth Century Cuba* (New York: Anchor Books, 1965), p. 168.

altered radically in an egalitarian direction by the revolution. Here, then, was an exceptional opportunity to study the political meaning to the workers of fundamental changes in their work situation—in their role in the organization and control of production and of the products of their work.

Whatever the nature of the actual changes in the workers' roles in the organization of production (changes about which we could not be certain from our limited observations),[15] we could analyze how the workers themselves perceived these changes and their new existential situation, and how these attitudes related to their view of the revolution.

Methods

Our data are from our interviews with industrial workers in Cuba in the summer of 1962. What is significant about this period as far as this particular study is concerned is that the Revolutionary Government had by now clearly consolidated its power (the Bay of Pigs invasion being a year in the past); the original relatively undifferentiated popular euphoria already had been replaced by relatively clear lines of social cleavage generated in response to actions taken by the Revolutionary Government; *it was now two years since the nationalization of industry, and more than a year since Fidel Castro had declared the revolution to be "socialist";* and, therefore, a study of the relationship between alienation and revolution could now be meaningful and valuable.

Our interviews were carried out with a randomly selected sample of 202 industrial workers employed in 21 plants widely scattered throughout the island's six provinces. I chose the plans from a list of all those functioning under the direction of the Ministry of Industries.

The plants were selected by means of a

self-weighting random sample in which the probability that a plant would be chosen was directly proportional to the number of workers employed in it. This sampling method tended to exclude the smaller industrial establishments (known in Cuba as "chinchales") which abounded there. In each plant, ten workers were selected by a method designed to obtain a simple random sample. My wife and I interviewed the workers, each of us separately interviewing five workers per plant. All of our interviewing was done in complete privacy, in a location provided within the work-center, such as a storage room or office or classroom. We told each worker interviewed (as well as anyone else concerned) that the writer was a correspondent for *The Nation;* that we had permission from the Minister of Industries, Ernesto "Che" Guevara, the plant administration, and the union delegate to interview workers in the plant; that the worker was chosen to be interviewed by a scientific method of randomization; we did not care to identify him personally in any way and his answers would be entirely anonymous; we simply wanted to know his opinions about some things at work and in Cuba in general, so as to be able to write an objective report about the condition of the Cuban working class.

It might be objected, of course, that such survey research could not obtain meaningful results since Cuba was already a police state in the summer of 1962. This is obviously a pertinent question, but one which I cannot take the space to discuss at length here. The reader will, for now, have to be content with the elliptical assertion that I think that this objection is without foundation, and that it was our observation that Cubans could and did inquire and speak freely about whatever they wished—at this time. There were no formal safeguards of freedom of speech and association, and the potentialities for totalitarian rule were great during the period of our interviews, but that potential had yet to become a reality. We were

---

[15] See my article "Labor in Cuba," *The Nation* (October 20, 1962), pp. 238–241, for a more detailed discussion of my observations of the workers during the period of my research in Cuba.

able to carry out our interviewing without disturbance or interference of any kind and to obtain, I believe, data quite as valid as those obtained in any competent survey research.

The interview schedule was organized in such a way as to begin the interview with questions which were, on the surface, far removed from political questions of any kind. These were questions pertaining to length of residence in a particular place, or length of time working in the workplace, and so on. Questions of more or less obvious political content came somewhere in the middle of the interview, and from these I selected five that, I think, taken in concert adequately indicate how the workers view the revolution, and combined these into an "index of attitude toward the revolution." Of these five questions, two were open-ended questions to which the variety of responses possible were limited only by the worker's imagination, and three were forced-choice questions.

The open-ended questions were:

A. Speaking generally, what are the things about this country that you are most proud of as a Cuban?

B: What sort ["clase"] of people govern this country now?

One hundred and fifteen of the workers in our sample gave answers to question "A" which were clearly favorable to the revolution. We counted responses as "favorable" to the revolution only if they could be regarded as clearly indicating support, or if they explicitly stated support, of the revolution.

One hundred and twenty-five workers replied to question "B" in terms clearly favorable to the revolution.

Given the double meaning in Spanish of the word "clase," which can mean "type," "sort," or "kind," as well as "class," the workers could, of course, choose to interpret the question's meaning in a number of ways. As with the preceding question, we counted as favorable re-

plies only those which could be clearly regarded as such.

The workers were also asked the following two questions with fixed alternatives:

C. Do you believe that the country ought to have elections soon?

D. Do you think that the workers now have more, the same, or less influence on ["en"] the government than they had before the revolution?

In addition, we included this question as an "action criterion":

E. Do you belong to the militia?

The index of attitude toward the revolution was constructed of the five questions taken together by coding all favorable responses (militia membership included) as $+1$, and all others as 0 (zero):

Index[16]

Points	Definition	(N)
3-5	Favorable	142
	(4-5, very favorable, N = 100; 3, moderately favorable, N = 42)	
2	Indecisive	24
0 and 1	Hostile	36
	Total:	202

[16] Answers to questions "C," "D," and "E," were distributed as follows: (C) No—136; Yes —44; No opinion—22. (D) More influence— 170; the same—17; less—8; No opinion—7. (E) Member—110; non-member—92.

Item analysis of the workers' answers to the five questions indicates that the latter form an acceptable Guttman scale, 88 percent of the workers giving answers exactly (67%) or consistently (21%) in conformity with a Guttman model. The coefficient of reproducibility equals 0.95.

A more detailed methodological discussion than the present one appears in my forthcoming *Revolutionary Politics and the Cuban Working Class* (Princeton: Princeton University Press); in "Economic Insecurity and the Political Attitudes of Cuban Workers," *American Sociological Review*, 31 (February 1966), pp. 35–51; and in "Political Generations in the Cuban Working Class," *American Journal of Sociology*, 71 (March 1966), pp. 493–508.

FINDINGS

We asked the workers what they thought of the way the administrators of their plant were doing their jobs, and 23 percent thought their plant administration was doing either a poor (7%) or merely acceptable (16%) job. In some instances, the workers indicated they had little to do with the administration of the plant, as, for example, was true of an electrical worker in Santiago who told us:

> I really do not know the administrative part of the plant, and I have no information about the way the administrators are working.

Most workers, though (56%), thought their administrator was doing his job well despite the fact, as a worker at the Uruguay Central put it:

> he was a worker in another *central* before the nationalization. He's doing well, but he's not as well prepared or trained as he should be.

Other workers, like an old anarchist in the Manacas brewery, were proud that the administrator was a former worker:

> I think all agree that our administrator is one of us, nothing more. He attends to everything well. He gives us his ideas and takes ours. He is one of the workers here. He worked as a mechanic in another *central* before the revolution, and the government selected him from there.

A minority of workers (20%) were even enthusiastic about the new administrators.

> Oh, he's a fine compañero. He was a worker and he understands the workers' lives,

said a worker at the nationalized Shell and Esso refineries in Regla (which were now under unified management),

> and this is the reason we selected him for the administration.

A nickel worker emphasized that the new administration

> shares with the workers. He does not have privileges like they had before, and like the office workers had.

An electrical worker in the Matanzas plant said the administrator was distinguished from the workers only by

> his technical knowledge, but he works for the same interests as the workers.

While to an old West Indian worker in Vibora's agricultural equipment plant the change was simple and fundamental. As he told me in his special brand of English:

> In everythin' we work pretty contented. Work is not like in time gone past by when you got to run and kill yourself. With this government who rule now I work more contented. The other government abused the workin' people. This one try to help 'em.

These different perspectives on the way their plants were now run, of course, were reflected in the position the workers took on the revolution. As Table 1 indicates, there is a direct relationship between their judgment of the caliber of their plant administrators, and their attitudes toward the revolution.

If the structure of formal and informal relations between administrative personnel and production workers, as the worker perceives them, has an important impact on his general perspective toward his society, so too, has his conception of the opportunity structure in the plant. A worker who sees a huge gap between himself and his peers, on the one hand, and the management on the other, is not likely to believe he has much of a chance of advancing in the plant (even if it is no longer under capitalist ownership and management).[17]

[17] Cf., Blauner, *op. cit.,* p. 178.

Table 1. Opinion of Plant Administration and Attitude toward the Revolution (in percent)

Plant Administrators are Doing their Jobs*	Favorable	Indecisive	Hostile	(N)
Poorly or Acceptably	51	11	38	(47)
Well	70	17	13	(114)
Very Well	90	0	10	(21)
Excellently	90	0	10	(20)

* The question was: "Do you think the administrators of your plant are doing their jobs poorly, acceptably, well, very well, or excellently?"

When we asked the workers what they thought the chances for promotion or for wage raises were in their plant, two thirds of them thought the chances good, another 13 percent fair, and the remaining fifth poor. Their remarks emphasized the structural changes wrought by the revolution and their new collective—rather than individual and individualistic—opportunities. Many workers pointed out that they themselves knew workers who were now technicians or plant administrators. Others, as did a brewery worker, for example, emphasized the expectations they had for the economic development of the country, and the expanding educational opportunities:

Well, the industries are growing. Almost all of us are studying and many will become administrators and engineers. Before, we could not have done such a thing.

An electrical worker in Santiago said:

Our opportunities for promotion are excellent because the capacity of our plant is being raised, as is its production. Besides, there is a project afoot for an electric turbine plant of seventy thousand kilowatt hours, and another one in Gibara nearby, that will raise our generation capacity—as well as our need for workers.

Elimination of the need to have "pull" or to bribe someone to get ahead, and the application of universalistic standards of judgment were among the more frequent reasons the workers gave for believing their chances for improvement were now good. A Havana brewery worker said:

You get ahead now according to your capacity, and by strict examination, as well as in accordance with the years you have been working in the plant, and if the one in line can't do it, then the next one gets the chance. The costs of production are all posted and the wage costs are made public and we know exactly what everyone earns, and this is much different. Today one doesn't come in off the street, and pay off someone, no. Now he has to stand in line with the rest and earn it in accordance with his ability.

Others, of course, were not quite so sanguine about their opportunities: An oil worker at the former Texaco plant in Santiago said:

Before, at least the unions tried to raise wages. Now you work, and you work, and you work again, and still the wages are frozen.

A cement worker said (unintentionally emphasizing the new equalitarianism):

There aren't any [opportunities] not for now anyway. You work at the same wage you got before, no matter what place you are working, so what's the point? For example, the chief of personnel here gets the same he got when he worked here as an electrician.

Thus, these different perceptions of the opportunity structure are also related to the workers' views of the revolution, as Table 2 indicates. The better he thinks his chances for promotion or higher wages are, the more likely the worker is to support the revolution.

I think that the excerpts from our interviews with the workers indicate that many of the workers believe that the revolution , *and the nationalization of industries in particular,* has had a significant impact on their work attitudes. Many made spontaneous allusions to the consequences of nationalization for their attitudes toward their work. But our questions asked about their *present* attitudes, without reference to the past. The important point, however, is what *changes* have actually occurred in how they view their work since the nationalization of industries. What did they think of their work before, and what since? To answer this question, as posed, obviously is impossible, since we have no prerevolutionary survey data on our workers' attitudes toward their work. It *is* possible, though, for us to see *how the workers themselves think the nationalization of industries* affected their views of their work. What do they say when asked a simple open-ended question as to why they hold their present attitudes toward work? We asked the workers the following questions: What do you think of your particular work? Would you say you like it a lot, more or less, or a little? What are your reasons for

thinking this way about your work. Did you think differently before the industries were nationalized? If so, how?

These questions made it possible for us to

1. separate the workers who said they had changed their attitudes toward work since nationalization from those who reported no change; and

2. construct a typology of the four possible types of attitude change that could have occurred since nationalization among the workers who were workers before the revolution.

Taking the present work attitudes of the workers who said they liked their work "a lot," and defining them as "positive," and the remaining workers' attitudes as "negative," and classifying their prenationalization attitudes by inference, also as positive or negative, we get the four types in Table 3.[18]

[18] Unfortunately, I did not think of asking the workers a forced-choice question about their prenationalization attitudes toward their work paralleling the question about their present attitudes. Had I done so, constructing the typology would have been a simple task, and the typology would have been more precise. As it is, I was compelled to infer, by analyzing the workers' replies to the open-ended question about the changes in their work attitudes since nationalization, what their prenationalization attitudes were—that is, infer at least to the extent of classifying those prenationalization attitudes as "positive" or "negative." In practice, fortunately, this was not particularly difficult to do, and there was little or no guesswork involved—since the question obviously

Table 2. Perception of Opportunity for Promotion or Higher Wages in Plant and Attitude toward the Revolution (in percent)

The Chances for Promotion or Higher Wages in This Plant are*	Favorable	Indecisive	Hostile	(N)
Good	81	12	7	(131)
Fair	65	11	23	(26)
Poor, or "don't know"	42	11	47	(45)

* The question was: "What do you think the chances are for promotion or higher wages for a worker in this plant?"

Table 3. Change in Work Attitude since the Nationalization of Industries and Attitude toward the Revolution (in percent)[1]

Type of Change in Work Attitude	Favorable	Indecisive	Hostile	(N)
Negative Positive	84	9	7	(64)[2]
Negative Negative	72	8	20	(25)
Positive Positive	62	15	23	(53)
Positive Negative	20	0	80	(5)

[1] This and the following tables exclude the workers in our sample who were not workers before the revolution.

The type of change in the work attitudes of five workers was not clear, and they are not included here, or in Tables 4 or 5.

$$ [2]\ x^2 = \sum_{i=1}^{r} \sum_{j=1}^{k} \frac{(0-E)^2}{E} = 9.20, \text{ significant above the .01 level.} $$

For computation of x^2, this table was dichotomized into positive change in work attitude and all others, and favorable to the revolution and all others.

The typology is meant, quite simply, to indicate how the workers themselves see the relationship between their present work attitudes and those they held before nationalization. Does the worker think his attitude has changed, and if so how?— in what direction? It is then quite valid to compare the differential support for the revolution among these different types of workers, as long as we remain clear that we are not assuming these were ontologically real changes.

Clearly, as Table 3 indicates, the workers whose attitudes toward work were positively transformed since nationalization, are more likely than others to support the revolution. Moreover, the contrast is sharper when only the workers who are very favorable to the revolution in each type are compared. Then we find that 70 percent of the workers whose work attitudes became positive since nationalization are very favorable to the revolution, compared to 44 percent, 32 percent, and none, respectively, of the other three types shown in Table 3.

We have assumed, to this point, in accordance with most prior theory, that the

tapped feelings the workers wanted to discuss at length. The answers of some workers did pose classificatory difficulties, though, not only because they were insufficiently specific about the past, but also because not all changes were qualitative changes. Some were simply changes of degree. Some workers, in other words, liked their work less, but still liked it sufficiently well to say they liked it a lot; others liked their work more, but were still generally negative about their work. As a result of these two kinds of difficulties, we found it best to exclude five workers from our typology of work attitude changes, since the change that had occurred in their attitudes since nationalization was not clear.

Another and more subtle methodological problem is that we interviewed the workers, after all, some two years after the nationalization of industries. By then, of course, the connection between the causes and consequences of their work situation and work attitudes may have become transparent. Some workers—we have no way of knowing how many—may have realized that they had been discontent with their work before the industries were nationalized, although they had not known this consciously before. The workers' retrospective reports of their work attitudes are, therefore, not necessarily the same as the actual attitudes they had toward their work before nationalization. It was the very transformation of their work situation which made them aware of their past discontent—a discontent which they may have felt only vaguely or not at all in the past. What this means, quite simply, is that had we really interviewed the workers before the industries were nationalized, their work attitudes might have been quite different from the ones they now recall having.

work attitude is the intervening variable in the psychological process that leads to the development of the worker's political outlook. That is, the objective structure of work relations creates an attitude toward work that may be a starting point for the worker's developing attitude toward the existing social structure in general. It is probable, of course, that in that complex world outlook which each worker develops, the attitudes he has toward his work and toward society as a whole are inseparable, and reciprocally interact with and affect each other. The process might even be that the worker's *political outlook* is the *source* of his attitude toward his work. Radical workers, for example, who believe that whatever the specific conditions of their work they are necessarily exploited in a capitalist system, may be more likely to consider their work degrading. George Friedmann has made a similar point:

> . . . There is no doubt that a job takes on a sense of greater value in the worker's mind when he feels himself in sympathy with the aims of the community as a whole. . . . Therefore, when a considerable proportion of the working population of a capitalist country contract out of it because of their conviction that they are being exploited, any attempt to overcome the harmful effects of specialization is rendered vain in advance.[19]

We might want, then, to look at the relationship in Table 3 differently, name-

[19] Friedmann, *op. cit.,* p. 90.

ly, at how the work attitudes of workers who view the revolution differently have changed since nationalization. As Table 4 indicates clearly, the relationship, when looked at in this way, is also strongly in the predicted direction; the revolutionary workers are far more likely to report positively transformed work attitudes since nationalization than the indecisive or hostile workers. However, while the reader is entitled to look at the relationship this way, since the time order cannot be *definitively* established, I think that on theoretical and historical grounds there is reason to believe that the order of attitude development was from work to revolution. My basic assumption, supported by my own research as well as the research of other political sociologists, is that the pressures arising from the work situation are among the major ones impinging on the worker, and are decisive in the development of his political attitudes. Prior theory and research tell us this, but we know it also on simple logical grounds of time order. The nationalization of industries took place in the late summer of 1960, and was a decisive event in the revolution's radicalization, in fact, in defining the nature of the revolution itself. It was this event, perhaps more than any other, which politically divided the Cuban population, essentially along class lines, and which was certainly *the* event of most significance in the working lives of the workers. Thus, it seems more than likely that the changes at work and in the situation of their fellow workers and themselves in the society that came with the

Table 4. Attitude toward the Revolution and Change in work Attitude since the Nationalization of Industries (in percent)

| Attitude Toward the Revolution | Type of Change in Work Attitude | | | | |
	Negative Positive	Negative Negative	Positive Positive	Positive Negative	(N)
Favorable	53	18	32	1	(106)
Indecisive	37	12	50	0	(16)
Hostile	16	20	48	16	(25)

nationalization of industries, and consequently the change in their work attitudes, was a major variable in the development of their attitudes toward the revolution, rather than the reverse. Of course, once set in motion, it is obvious that the two attitudes (toward work and the revolution) probably have interacted with and reinforced each other.

A major determinant of the workers' attitudes toward the revolution, as I have shown elsewhere, was their prerevolutionary experience with unemployment and underemployment. The fewer the months worked before the revolution, the more likely a worker was to support the revolution.[20] How important, therefore, their changed work attitudes are in the workers' conceptions of the revolution, can be seen from the fact that even when we control for their prerevolutionary employment status, the workers whose work attitudes have been positively transformed since nationalization are still more likely than others to support the revolution (Table 5). Among workers with each type of change in work attitude, it should also be noted, the prerevolutionary unemployed are more likely than the employed to support the revolution.

It bears emphasizing that while unemployment apparently tends to eliminate political differences flowing from work

[20] These findings are analyzed in my "Economic Insecurity and the Political Attitudes of Cuban Workers," *op. cit.*.

attitudes, it precisely among those workers who were regularly employed and least insecure economically that the impact of their work attitudes on their political attitudes was greatest.

Estrangement

In our discussion so far we have equated "estrangement" and work dissatisfaction. To a great extent this is a valid equation, since the general theoretical question posed is the interconnection between work discontent and general social discontent. Marx, however, was not attempting to analyze the general sources of work dissatisfaction—although he gave us many insights in that direction. In his analysis, he focused on the historically specific form of work dissatisfaction which he thought to be inherent in the structure of capitalist production relations. That is, estrangement *(Entfremdung)* was specifically the result of workers' alienation *(Entaüsserung)* from ownership of the means of production, and control of the organization and products of production. It was this objective structure that would lead, Marx believed, to the workers' estrangement, first from their work, and then from capitalism as a whole. Work and politics—estrangement and class consciousness—would meet: the workers would become aware that to abolish the conditions which led to their estrangement from work, they would have to destroy the conditions of existence of

Table 5. Change in Work Attitude Since the Nationalization of Industries, Prerevolutionary Employment Status, and Attitude toward the Revolution

Type of Change in Work Attitude	Percentage Favorable Months Worked Per Year Before the Revolution	
	9 or less	10 plus
Negative Positive	92 (36)	75 (28)
Negative Negative	82 (11)	64 (14)
Positive Positive	80 (15)	55 (38)
Positive Negative	— (0)	20 (5)

their class and, thereby, the capitalist system.

Thus, presumably implicit in Marx's theory of alienation would be the following hypothesis: The workers whose source of work discontent, as they see it, is their objective alienation from control over the organization and products of production, would be more likely to become politically radical not only than other workers, but also *than other workers who are also discontent with their work.* To test this hypothesis it would be necessary, then, to distinguish subtypes of work discontent among which would be "estrangement" in the Marxian sense, and relate workers having these subtypes to those having given types of political attitudes and behavior. In practice, however, it would be difficult to distinguish such types for analysis.

In Chinoy's study of automobile workers' attitudes, there is a clue to one analytically important way of operationally distinguishing such subtypes. Thus, a machine operator told Chinoy:

> *The main thing is to be independent and give your own orders and not have to take them from anybody else.* That's the reason the fellows in the shop all want to start their own business. Then the profits are all for yourself. When you put a screw or a head on a motor, *there's nothing for yourself in it.* So you just do what you have to do in order to get along. *A fellow would rather do it for himself. If you expend the energy, it's for your own benefit then.*[21]

This machine operator was emphasizing, I think, exactly what Marx called the alienation of the workers from the products of their work, and indirectly alluding also to the workers' loss of control over the organization of production. For this machine operator, alienation apparently was the source of his discontent

with his job and of his desire to get out of the plant and run and own a small business if possible.

This suggests that it might be of value to distinguish (a) the workers whose discontent with their work derives *(as they themselves subjectively perceive it)* from their lack of control over the organization and/or the products of their work, from (b) the workers whose source of work discontent lies elsewhere. The former workers would presumably fit the specific Marxian category of estrangement. In short, on the basis of their spontaneous answers to open-ended interview questions, we could categorize workers as "estranged" or not, and then see if the "estranged" workers were more likely to be politically radical than other workers, and in particular, than other workers who were also discontent with their work.

This question, of course, is not directly relevant to our study, although a similar question is:

Do the workers who believe that it was the *abolition* of their alienation from control over the organization and products of production that led to their present positive attitudes toward their work, differ in their attitudes toward the revolution from other workers? In particular, are these workers who were, by their own account, estranged from their work before nationalization, more likely to support the revolution than other workers whose work attitudes became positive only since nationalization?

In our interviews, as already noted, we asked the workers what their reasons were for their present work attitudes, and whether or not and in what way they thought differently about their work before the nationalization of industry. We can, therefore, categorize the workers in accordance with the themes of their answers to this question. I have categorized as estranged before nationalization those workers whose answers expressed the

---

[21] Chinoy, *op. cit.,* p. 86. (Italics added)

conviction that their work attitudes became positive since nationalization because, in contrast to their situation before nationalization:

A. the workers and the administration of the plant or factory in which they worked were now one and the same;

B. the products of their work were now their own, and/or they were now working in the interest and for the benefit of themselves and their fellow workers.

There was, for example, a beer and malt worker who said:

The boss paid us a miserable salary. The revolution put the workers to work, and paid more. The profits of the industries are now used for schools and for highways that we ourselves go to build . . . We don't have a boss now. We ourselves run the brewery. There are no overseers, but rather *responsables* [persons encharged with responsibility for a particular task]—because we need technical advisers. . . . Before I didn't want to work. Now, I work of my own will, at whatever is necessary. . . .

A sugar refinery worker also emphasized the common effort of the workers for their common benefit:

Everything is now done in accordance with the needs of the workers. We now have decent human beings who work with us, as we work with them. Before, we didn't know with whom or for whom we were working. When I work now, I work of my own free will [mi propia fuerza], not like before when I worked only out of need. Now, the chief helps us resolve any problems. Say something breaks, he doesn't say: 'Fix it!' but 'C'mon, let's see what *we* can do'—and we do it. It's a job we do because we want to.

A copper miner was brief and to the point:

Before, a raise in production benefited *the bosses*. Not now.

In contrast to these workers, the majority of workers whose attitudes toward their work had become positive since nationalization, focused in their replies essentially on the overall improvement in their personal well-being, dignity, and economic security, rather than on the abolition of alienation. Typical of these workers was the maintenance man at a sugar central who said:

I never knew when I was going to [have] work before; how could I like that?

In different words, workers in the paper mill, tobacco factories, oil refineries, nickel processing plant, and so on, emphasized the elimination of maltreatment at work and of the fear of lay-offs and unemployment:

The bosses pushed us around before. Now they don't expect enough of us! Now, if I want to talk to a fellow, I don't have to look over my shoulder.
Now I have secure work. I don't worry about getting sacked or laid-off.
Before I always worked—61 years old, and I worked since I was a kid. There was no other way to live. But I couldn't even work most of the year. I left for home at the end of the *zafra* [sugar harvest]. Now I work the whole year.

To what extent, then, do these latter workers differ in their support of the revolution, from those workers who were "estranged" from their work before the industries were nationalized? The difference is clear. *Every one* of the 25 workers to whom the abolition of alienation was the crucial reason for the positive change in their work attitudes, favors the revolution (Table 6). It should also be noted that 84 percent of the prenationalization estranged are very favorable to the revolution compared to 61 percent of the others whose work attitudes became positive since nationalization. Thus, not only were the workers whose attitudes toward work were positively transformed by the nationalization of industry more likely than other workers to support the revolution, but *especially distinct, given their unanimous support of the revolution, are the workers who attribute their changed work attitudes to the abolition of alienation.*

This, it might be plausibly argued, should have been "obvious." For, looked at differently, those workers whom we have termed "estranged" before nationalization, quite clearly were expressing the conviction that they had been exploited in the past under capitalism. Here, in fact, is the conceptual and actual connection between *alienation* and *exploitation,* wherein *estrangement* is a *sense of exploitation.* It is, therefore, inherently a *political* attitude. For once the worker develops the conviction that he is not working in his own interest but in the interest of the owners and managers, he has developed the conviction that he is being exploited. He has, indeed, developed something akin to a radical political outlook.

In contrast, the argument might continue, the workers whose primary concern was their general economic security and working conditions, were on a level of consciousness that is not necessarily political in its implications. Their outlook is akin to "bread and butter unionism." Their demands, moreover, conceivably could be solved under capitalism. But for the workers to whom their alienation

from control of their work and the products of their work is crucial, only a socialist revolution could suffice to eliminate their estrangement.

I think there is much of substance in this argument. It is, in essence, the hypothesis suggested earlier, except that it is phrased as an assertion that estrangement and radical politics *must* go together, that indeed, they are one and the same. That, however, is precisely the question, since whether or not the workers sense that they are being used for the profit of others necessarily leads to hostility to the system as a whole that translates itself into a leftist political outlook is an *empirical question.* How they respond politically probably depends on the alternatives perceived and presented in their experience. As we have seen, for instance, Chinoy's research on American auto workers suggested to him that estrangement may express itself in the urge to establish an independent small business—perhaps, even to move into the position of exploiting others—rather than in the political demand for the abolition of capitalism.

Our data have suggested, in contrast, that estrangement is more likely than other types of work dissatisfaction to lead to a revolutionary political outlook. The caveat must be added, of course, that we dealt here with the workers' retrospective views of their situation under Cuban capitalism—rather than with their actual views, which may have differed considerably. The big question, then, is whether

Table 6. Type of Prenationalization Work Discontent and Attitude toward the Revolution, among Workers Whose Work Attitudes Became Positive Since Nationalization Only (in percent)

Type of Prenationalization Work Discontent	Favorable	Indecisive	Hostile	(N)
Estrangement	100	0	0	(25)
Other Discontent	74	15	10	(39)

or not the same relationship between estrangement and support for left-wing politics exists among workers in capitalist countries. If this is so, the implication is clear that no matter how high their wages might become, nor how comfortable their nonworking lives might seem, a core of workers will continue to exist under capitalism who will be estranged from the system itself, and who cannot and will not be at one with themselves until that system is abolished.

TYPES OF PROTESTS AND ALIENATION

Erik Allardt

A Basic Paradigm

Two basic characteristics of any collectivity, society or group, are (1) that there is some degree of pressure toward uniformity, and (2) that there is some division of labor in the collectivity. Throughout the history of sociology a core theoretical problem has been to analyze how these two variables explain solidarity and conflict. It has, however, been pointed out that there are considerable difficulties in combining theories about pressure toward uniformity with theories about division of labor.[1] The same has been said about solidarity and conflict. It has been contended that there are difficulties in developing theories that would render good explanations of both solidarity and conflict.[2] A major point of departure here is that this position is too pessimistic.

There is, to be sure, also conflicting empirical evidence regarding in particular the relationship between pressure toward uniformity and solidarity and conflict. Notably within the field of small group research it has often been shown how group solidarity and pressure toward uniformity are positively related. On the other hand, political sociologists dealing with large-scale and highly industrialized societies have been apt to stress an almost contrary result: they have emphasized crisscrossing cleavages and the variety of interests as conditions for solidarity.[3]

The results stressing the positive relationship between pressure toward uniformity and solidarity have been summarized and formalized in Festinger's theory on social comparison processes. In small group research the term solidarity is usually replaced by the term cohesion, and cohesion is usually defined in terms of the attraction of members to the group. The wish to stay or leave the group is often used as a good indicator of this attraction. In any case, Festinger's central notion is that the individual strives to compare himself with others as regards his abilities and opinions; therefore, situations in which comparisons are possible are attractive. The more uniform the individuals are in their opinions and abilities, the greater the possibility of comparisons.

SOURCE: Reprinted with permission of The Macmillan Company from MASS POLITICS edited by Erik Allardt and Stein Rokkan. Copyright © 1970 by The Free Press, a Division of The Macmillan Company.

[1] See, e.g., James S. Davis, "Structural Balance, Mechanical Solidarity and Interpersonal Relations," *The American Journal of Sociology,* LXVII (1963), pp. 444–462.

[2] See S. M. Lipset, "Political Sociology," in R. K. Merton, L. Broom, and L. S. Cottrell, Jr., *Sociology Today* (New York: Basic Books, 1959), p. 112.

[3] S. M. Lipset, "Party Systems and the Representation of Social Groups," *The European Journal of Sociology* I (1960), pp. 1–38.

Consequently, the more uniformity in the group, the more attractive it is, and, accordingly, when cohesion is defined through attraction, the more uniformity, the more cohesion in a social group.[4]

An examination of the empirical evidence Festinger cites for his theory indicates that he almost always refers to groups which are very undifferentiated. His theory is not verified in groups requiring a high degree of differentiation such as work groups with a clearcut division of labor. On the contrary, dissimilarity seems to increase cohesion.[5] This is even more evident when studying total and differentiated societies; in them strong pressures toward uniformity seems to make for a decrease in solidarity.

Of course, cohesion in small groups and solidarity in large-scale societies have to be defined somewhat differently. The wish to stay or leave the group, used as an indicator for attraction is hardly useful in the study of solidarity in total society. A citizen cannot withdraw from his society in the same way as he can withdraw from a small group or from an association. Solidarity with a society may be defined through the concept of legitimacy. Solidarity prevails as long as people believe that the sociopolitical system of their society is legitimate, or do not act in order to change the system through noninstitutionalized means. If solidarity is defined in this fashion then, of course, legitimacy conflicts are simply the obverse of solidarity. The relation between solidarity and conflicts other than those related to legitimacy has to be studied empirically, and such conflicts may very well increase solidarity.

In any case, it seems that Festinger has derived his propositions by excluding one important form of social processes, namely the phenomenon Homans labels *human exchange*. The activities or goods exchanged can, of course, be of many kinds. One can exchange love, respect, protection, as well as material goods. Of crucial importance here are such exchange relations in which the goods or items exchanged are of many different kinds. There are certainly many situations in which individuals explicitly or implicitly compare themselves with dissimilar persons. In such a situation the question phrased by Homans is apt to arise: does a person's reward for the exchange correspond to his costs and investments? Two persons may help each other precisely because they have strongly dissimilar skills. In such a situation the comparison may focus on the question of whether the Other is able to give as much in exchange as Person gives, but the point is that their behavior may be far from similar or uniform.[6] It is only as regards the result, the ability to match the other in rewards given, that they have to be similar. The exchange of dissimilar items is what we usually call a situation of division of labor. In fact, it seems as if Festinger's main proposition can be applied only to situations where there is no or very little exchange or differentiation within the group. We may, therefore, reformulate Festinger's proposition: when there is a small amount of exchange or division of labor, then the more the uniformity, the stronger the cohesion (or solidarity).

When exchange relations dominate and rewards are principally obtained through exchange of dissimilar activities and goods, the situation is entirely different. Apparently what really counts in an exchange relation is the outcome, the fact that the rewards exchanged between two persons roughly correspond to each other. The question is, what other kinds of be-

[4] L. Festinger, "A Theory of Social Comparison Processes," *Human Relations* 7 (1954), pp. 117–140.

[5] See Herman Turk, "Social Cohesion Through Variant Values: Evidence from Medical Role Relations," *The American Sociological Review* 29 (1963), pp. 28–37.

[6] G. C. Homans, *Social Behavior: Its Elementary Forms* (New York: Harcourt, Brace & World, 1961).

havior are likely to be educed from groups in which there is a great amount of exchange. Since the outcome is what counts, and this can be obtained through an exchange of dissimilar things and goods, some tolerance towards dissimilarity has to be developed. Exchange relations can hardly persist unless people are willing to grant each other great personal freedom. Tolerance toward deviance has to be developed. Therefore, pressures toward uniformity are likely to result in a decrease in the attraction to a situation or a group. We may conclude: the greater the amount of exchange in a group and the less the uniformity, the stronger the cohesion (or solidarity).

The distinction between solidarity through uniformity and solidarity through variety leads to Emile Durkheim's theory on the division of labor.[7] Durkheim's basic idea is that mechanical solidarity rests on what he calls likeness, whereas organic solidarity is due to the division of labor. A society with mechanical solidarity is held together mainly through normative coercion; deviants are severely punished, and penal, repressive law is important. With increasing division of labor, restitutive law regulating relations of exchange comes into the foreground. The necessity to punish deviants diminishes, and as a consequence, men are willing to grant each other more freedom and equality.

Durkheim's analysis can be seen as resting on the association between three major variables: the degree of solidarity, the degree of pressure towards uniformity and the degree of division of labor. A slight reformulation of Durkheim is, of course, needed. Instead of saying, as Durkheim does, that mechanical solidarity is based on similarity and organic solidarity is based on the division of labor, we can assume that they are two separate variables that can be used together to explain both types of solidarity. Durkheim speaks of uniformity or similarity, but the crucial variable seems to be pressure towards uniformity, as is also indicated by his stress on penal law and punishments. The two independent variables, pressure toward uniformity and division of labor, are theoretical terms and need, of course, a specification when used in empirical studies. As a preliminary and theoretical definition, we may state that division of labor is defined in terms of the number of dissimilar items for exchange: the higher the number of items for exchange, the greater the division of labor. Strong pressure towards uniformity may be defined as having two necessary conditions: *(a)* existing social norms are specific and related to strong sanctions that are applied with great consistency, and *(b)* there are no or very few conflicts between norms.

Durkheim not only speaks of the conditions that increase solidarity, but he also mentions situations in which solidarity is weak or lacking. It is perhaps significant for Durkheim that he deals with exceptions as if they were mainly exceptions to organic solidarity. As long as one treats pressure toward uniformity and division of labor as separate variables, it is logical to think of two types of low or weak solidarity, as indicated in the typology of Fig. 1.

Since solidarity is defined as the obverse of legitimacy conflicts, we may reformulate the contents of the table in the following propositions:

1. The less developed the division of labor and the stronger the pressure toward uniformity, the less the likelihood of legitimacy conflicts.
2. The less developed the division of labor and the weaker the pressure toward uniformity, the greater the likelihood of legitimacy conflicts.
3. The more developed the division of labor and the stronger the pressure

[7] E. Durkheim, *The Division of Labor in Society,* translated by George Simpson (New York: The Free Press, 1960).

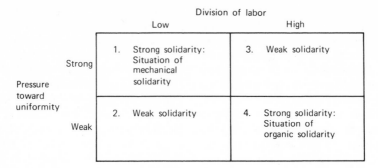

Figure 1.

toward uniformity, the greater the likelihood of legitimacy conflicts.

4. The more developed the division of labor and the weaker the pressure toward uniformity, the less the likelihood of legitimacy conflicts.

By presenting this crude typology it is by no means maintained that the degree of solidarity is influenced only by our independent variables. The expansion of the typology can be pursued in two major ways. One alternative is to introduce new variables into the typology, whereby the number of major types would greatly increase. Another way is to show that a number of specific situations are really special cases of the major types. Partly due to the empirical data available, the latter alternative is here judged to be more fruitful.

The two independent variables are of course not very easy to operationalize. In studies of total societies the degree of division of labor can be measured in a number of ways. For gross comparisons between societies and communities, the degree of industrialization or indices of economic development may be taken as sufficiently precise indicators.

Pressure toward uniformity is a more difficult concept to operationalize, and it seems also difficult to find an overall indicator useful in different social systems.[8]

It is, however, possible to indicate types of societies and communities in which the pressure toward uniformity may be regarded as particularly strong:

1. Tribal societies. Many, if not all, tribal societies can be characterized as having strictly enforced and severe social norms. There are nonspecialized and diffuse pressures directed toward large, rather vaguely defined categories of ascriptive statuses.[9]

2. Brutal dictatorships.

3. Societies strongly stratified according to social class or social rank. In such societies lower-class individuals are hindered by class barriers to indulge in social exchange. Inequalities of an economic nature, thus, are subsumed under factors which make for a strong pressure toward uniformity. Economic factors relate to our model in two ways. The overall economic output is one aspect of the division of labor whereas the distributive process accounts for the pressure toward uniformity.

4. Societies in which constraints are

---

[8] It has been indicated by Veronica Stolte Heiskanen, *Social Structure, Family Patterns and*

Interpersonal Influence (Helsinki: Transactions of the Westermarck Society, XIV, 1967), p. 17, that pressure toward uniformity always has to be specified according to the substantive system under investigation.

[9] Ulf Himmelstrand, "Conflict, Conflict Resolution and Nation-Building in the Transition from Tribal 'Mechanical' Solidarities to the 'Organic' Solidarity of Modern (or Future) Multi-Tribal Societies," Paper presented at the Sixth World Congress of Sociology, Evian, 1966.

particularly imposed on groups that earlier have had a good social position. There may be, for instance, middle-class groups that are loosing in status and rank because other groups have become more powerful. They are likely to experience constraints imposed on them, and they will tend to develop aggressive political attitudes. As in case 3, however, the pressure toward uniformity is strong only for a part of the population.

An Empirical Illustration: Industrial and Backwoods Radicalism

Finnish political life, and particularly the strength of the Communist movement in Finland, provides a good case for testing the propositions derived from the basic paradigm. The Finnish Communist movement has had a rather heavy mass support. During the period after World War II, the Communists have received between 20.0 and 23.5 per cent of the total vote in national elections. Furthermore the Finnish working-class vote has been almost equally divided between the Communists and the Social Democrats.

Although caution is necessary, it is reasonable to say that the Communist vote during the 1950's more strongly indicated a protest against the system than the votes for other parties. It is, however, hardly so that the Finnish Communist voters regard the whole Finnish sociopolitical system as illegitimate.[10] Rather they are apt to accept the political system, whereas some aspects of the economic system as well as certain administrative bodies are foci of protest and discontent. Survey studies indicate that a much greater proportion of the Communists than, for instance, the Social Democrats express discontent of an economic nature. Likewise, a greater proportion of the Commu-

nists than of the Social Democratic voters also express discontent with the administrative leadership in Finnish society, with the courts, with the Armed Forces, and so forth. This is particularly true for the 1950's, the period covered by the findings used in this paper.[11] In any case, the Communist vote reflects a certain type of protest, which may be formulated so that the Communist voters more often than others are questioning the legitimacy of the Finnish sociopolitical system. When studying conditions of societal solidarity it is therefore fruitful to study the social sources of Communist support and to compare it with the support of other parties having a large lower-class vote.

In popular Finnish political terminology, Communist support is often described in terms that are clearly related to one of our independent variables, namely to division of labor. The communism in the southern and western parts of Finland is often labeled *Industrial Communism* whereas the communism in the north and the east is known as *Backwoods Communism*. As the names suggest, Industrial Communism exists in regions which are industrialized and developed whereas Backwoods Communism is concentrated in less developed, rural regions. The problem here is to specify under what conditions Industrial and Backwoods Communism are strong. Their background is, of course, different as regards the degree of industrialization in the communities in which these two forms of communism exist but the question is whether there are also other differences.

The social background of these two kinds of radicalism have been studied both through survey studies and ecological research. The data units in the ecological analyses have been the 550 com-

[10] Very perceptive views on the nature of the Communist protest in the Finnish society have been presented by Ulf Torgerson, "Samfunnsstruktur og politiska e legitimitetskriser," *Tidskrift for samfunnsforskning* 8 (1967), pp. 65–77.

[11] The data referred to in this paper are presented in E. Allardt, "Patterns of Class Conflict and Working Class Consciousness in Finland," in E. Allardt and Y. Littunen, eds., *Cleavages, Ideologies and Party Systems* (Helsinki: The Westermarck Society, 1964), pp. 97–131.

munes in the country. The communes, both the rural and urban ones, are the smallest administrative units in Finland, and they have a certain amount of self-government. Primarily because of the long historical tradition of local self-government, the communes form natural areas in the sense that the communes are important for people's identification of themselves. The communes are also the territorial units for which statistical data are easiest to obtain. In the analyses a file of seventy quantitative ecological variables referring to conditions in communes in the 1950's were used as a starting point.[12]

In analyzing the data, factor analysis was used primarily, although the correlation matrices reveal from the start many consistent patterns. Because a single factor analysis is not always interesting—it gives just a structure or a conceptual framework—the communes were divided into five groups. For each of the five groups of communes (called communities) in what follows, separate correlational and factor analyses were done. Of the five groups, three represented the more developed regions in southern and western Finland, and two the more backward regions in northern and eastern Finland:

Groups of developed communities
1. Cities and towns
2. Rural communities with a Swedish speaking population along the Southern and Western Coast of Finland.
3. Rural communities in Southern and Western Finland

Groups of less developed communities
4. Rural communes in Eastern Finland
5. Rural communes in Northern Finland

The intention of making separate analyses for the five different regions was to in-

quire whether Communist voting strength is explained by different or similar background factors in different regions.[13]

The comparisons of the findings for the five regions reveal some quite consistent patterns. The background factors of Communist strength in the three developed regions are very similar, and so are the background factors in the two less developed regions. However, the background factors in Communist strength in the developed regions, on the one hand, and in the backward regions, on the other, seem to be very different.

In the developed regions the Communists are strong in communities in which

1. *political traditions* are strong. This is indicated mainly by the fact that the Communists tend to get a heavy vote in those communities in which there are stable voting patterns.

2. *economic change* is comparatively slow. This is mainly indicated by the fact that communities with a strong Communist support have had a rather slow rise in per capita income during the 1950's. These communities were modernized and industrialized in an earlier period.

3. *social security* is comparatively high. The communities with a heavy Communist vote are those in which there is no or very little unemployment and those in which the standard of housing is high.

4. *migration both into and out of the communities is small.* The communities with a heavy Communist vote have a very stable population.

The foregoing are the conditions prevailing in those developed communities in which the Communists get a heavy vote. When focusing on the background factors of Communist strength in the less developed and more backward communities, a very different pattern is revealed. In the more backward communities the Communist vote is heavy when:

---

[12] Erik Allardt and Olavi Riihinen, "Files for Aggregate Data by Territorial Units in Finland," in S. Rokkan, ed., *Data Archives for Social Sciences* (Paris: Mouton, 1966).

[13] The data are presented in E. Allardt, *op. cit.,* pp. 97–131.

1. *traditional values* such as the religious ones, have recently declined in importance.

2. *economic change is rapid.* In the backward regions the Communists are strong in those communities which have had a considerable rise in the per capita income during the 1950's and weak in those communities in which the income rise has been small.

3. *social insecurity prevails.* Communities with Communist strength are those in which unemployment has been common. It may be said that unemployment in Finland is mainly a question of agrarian underemployment. Unemployment strikes those who are both small farmers and lumberjacks.

4. *migration is heavy.* There is a heavy migration both into and out of the communities.

While Communist strength in the developed regions, the so-called Industrial Communism, seems to be associated with background factors reflecting stability, almost the contrary is true for Backwoods Communism. It is strong under conditions of instability and change.

Observations of particular strongholds in the developed and in the backward communities strongly support the results of the statistical analysis. The strongest Communist centers in the developed regions are towns that industrialized comparatively early. They are often towns in which one or a few shops completely dominate the community. Some of the communities voting most heavily Communist in rural Finland are located in Finland's northernmost province of Lapland. These communities are usually those in which there are many indications of a rapid modernization process.

In order to correctly assess the social background of Industrial and Backwoods Communism, it is important to observe also the background factors of the voting strength of the main competitors of the Communists. The Social Democrats are the competitors for the working-class vote in the more developed regions in southern and western Finland. In the backwoods of the north and the east, however, the Agrarians are the ones who compete with the Communists for the lower class vote. The data and the findings clearly indicate that the Social Democrats in the south and in the west, on the one hand, and that the Agrarians in the north and the east, are strong in clearly different communities than the Communists. In the developed regions the Social Democrats are strong in towns and industrial centers undergoing rapid change and having a high amount of migration. In fact, workers who move from the countryside to the cities much more often vote Social Democratic than Communist. As has been shown, the Communists have their strength in communities with little migration. In the backward regions the Agrarians are strong in the most stable, the most traditional and the most backward communities. There are strong indications that a Communist vote in the more backward regions is a symptom of modernization. A switch of the vote from the Agrarians to the Communists is also a switch from traditional, particularistic loyalties to a more universalistic form of political thinking. In northern and eastern Finland the breakdown of regional barriers and loyalties is clearly associated with a tendency to vote Communist.

The results can be summarized in terms of our simple theoretical model. The conditions associated with Communist support in the developed regions reflect hindrances of movement, strong group ties and strong social pressures. Most of the crucial conditions related to Industrial Communism reflect, directly or indirectly, some kind of hindrances to people in using their resources and abilities. Strong political traditions, slow economic change, and a small amount of migration can all be taken as indicators for strong pressures toward uniformity. In the backward regions the contrary is true. Radicalism is strong in those communities in which the social constraints are weak. The decline in traditional values, rapid economic change, social insecurity and a high amount of migration can all be interpreted as indicators of a low pressure toward uniformity. Accordingly, the findings fit very well into the fourfold table earlier presented (see Fig. 2).

Protests and Reference Groups: Institutionalized and Diffuse Deprivation

The theoretical model presented can be used for further explorations of the different kinds of protest displayed by Industrial and Backwoods Communism. According to the model, cells 2 and 3 describe situations in which people are apt to feel discontent and deprivation. There is also a likelihood for legitimacy conflicts in these situations. The political effects of the discontent will presumably depend very much on who the discontented compare themselves with. This leads to a consideration of the concept of reference group–a tricky concept because as we know, it has many denotations. Of these denotations, however, two seem to be crucial. On the one hand, a person's reference group is the group with which he identifies himself and from which he obtains his social norms and standards for social perception: this is his *normative reference group*. On the other hand, the term also refers to a group with which a

person compares himself when he evaluates his status and his rewards: this is his *comparison reference group*. These two kinds of reference groups cannot always be empirically separated because the group for identification and the group for comparison often seem to be the same. In Festinger's theory of social comparisons it is assumed, for instance, that the two kinds of reference groups usually coincide because a person tries to be similar to those to whom he is comparing himself. It is obvious, however, that these two kinds of reference groups do not always coincide, and that we need a specification of the conditions under which the group for identification and the group for comparison are the same, different or altogether absent.

It goes without saying that there are many kinds of groups that may function as foci for identification and comparison. The groups relevant here are those related to a person's social status and the evaluation of his rewards. In modern industrialized societies social classes or strata are presumably most often used when a person either tries to justify the rewards he gets or tries to evaluate whether his rewards are just or unjust. In any case, when speaking here of normative and comparison reference groups they denote groups identifiable in a total society, such as classes or strata.

It will be argued that the two major

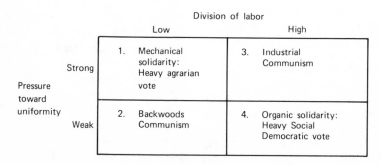

Figure 2.

kinds of reference groups tend to coincide in situations of mechanical and organic solidarity, whereas this is not the case in the two situations of weak solidarity.

In a society of mechanical solidarity the satisfaction of individuals and their ability to predict the behavior of others is mainly produced through similarity and strong attachment to specific social norms. Outgroups and, accordingly also, alternative comparison groups are simply not available. As a result the group for identification and for comparison tend to be the same. We may summarize:

5. The less developed the division of labor and the stronger the pressure toward uniformity (mechanical solidarity), the more the normative and the comparison reference groups tend to be the same.

In a society of organic solidarity, individual satisfaction and also ability to predict how other people behave is obtained mainly through intensive social exchange of items of many different kinds. People will be satisfied if they are hindered as little as possible in exchanging rewards. They compare their rewards and inputs with those with whom they are in exchange, and they tend to regard their exchange partners as norm-senders. In a summary form:

6. The more developed the division of labor and the weaker the pressure toward uniformity (organic solidarity), the more the normative and the comparison reference groups tend to be the same.

In a situation of high division of labor and strong pressure toward uniformity, there exists a rather high amount of social exchange but it is inhibited in many ways. The potentialities for a free exchange are hindered for instance by class and race barriers. Usually there will exist a very clear demarcation line between the rulers and the ruled. This is also the situation, described by Marx, in which the proletariat develops class-consciousness and clearly realizes its special position. Intraclass communication becomes strong, whereas interclass communication declines. In more general terms, people will tend to feel closely tied to their own group, whereas they compare themselves to members from other groups in evaluating their rewards. In summary form:

7. The more developed the division of labor and the stronger the pressure toward uniformity, the more people will tend to have distinct normative and comparison reference groups, and the more the normative and comparison reference groups will tend to be different.

If the situation described by proposition 7 prevails for a longer period of time, the deprivation felt because the rewards received are experienced as unjust will become institutionalized. Groups with a history of being deprived will tend to socialize their younger members to experience relative deprivation. The result can be labeled *institutionalized relative deprivation.*

The situation of low division of labor and weak pressure toward uniformity (cell 2) also leads to deprivation but of an entirely different kind. The division of labor is undifferentiated, and the individuals have few opportunities for the social exchange of rewards of different kinds. At the same time the social constraints are weak, and the individuals will experience difficulties in predicting the behavior of others. They have, so to speak, neither social norms nor the wishes of exchange-partners to rely on. The result is that groups both for identification and comparison tend to be lacking. In this situation the individual feels deprived because he cannot find relevant reference groups. The result can be labeled *diffuse deprivation.* As a summary:

8. The less developed the division of labor and the weaker the pressure toward uniformity, the less the likelihood that people have relevant normative and comparison reference groups.

Some specific behavior patterns are likely to be found in situations of institutionalized relative deprivation as well as in situations of diffuse deprivation. In situations of institutionalized relative deprivation, one can expect a high amount of social participation and organizational activities. The individuals are strongly tied to their communities and social classes but are isolated from the total national community. Social participation tends to be planned and instrumental.

In situations of diffuse deprivation, one may expect a low level of organizational activity. Political participation, if high, can be expected to be expressive and momentary. The individuals are isolated not only from the national community but also as individuals.

Backwoods and Industrial Radicalism as Illustrations of Diffuse and Institutionalized Deprivation

The relationship between the two forms of radicalism and the two types of deprivation can be substantiated by at least three independent observations of the Finnish Communist movement:

1. The Communists in the developed communities in the southern and western parts of the country have an efficient organizational network. According to the studies of some particular cities in the more developed parts of Finland, it appears that there is a network of Communist organizations that corresponds to the national network of all associations and voluntary organizations. The Communist network performs for its members the same social functions as the national network for citizens in general. There are women's clubs, sports associations, chil-

dren's clubs, and so on. The situation is on this count very different in the north and the east. It is true that the population in the northern and eastern parts of the country has become politically alerted since World War II. This increase in the political consciousness is mainly displayed only during elections. It has not displayed itself as a general increase in social and intellectual participation. The Communist support in the north and the east is concentrated in groups in which the opportunities for social and intellectual participation is slight. A nation-wide study of youth activities shows that the young Communist voters in the north and the east belong to the most passive in the country as far as general social participation is concerned.[14]

2. Many observations of the Communist centers in the developed regions of the South and the West show how the Communist alternative in the elections is the conventional and respectable one. The Communist voters in these communities are well integrated in their communities and stable in their jobs. The population, and notably the Communist voters, in backward regions in the northern and eastern parts of Finland are in an entirely different position. This is already clear from the settlement patterns in the north and the east compared to the south and the west. Whereas life in the latter region has been always much more village-centered, the houses and farms in the north and the east have always been more isolated. Many of the Communist voters are small farmers who have to work as forestry workers in the winter. Unemployment in Finland has mainly the character of agrarian underemployment and this seasonal unemployment is particularly strong in those northern and eastern communities in which the Com-

[14] Yrjö Littunen, "Aktiivisuus ja radikalismi," with an English Summary: "Activity and Radicalism," *Politiikka,* A Quarterly Published by the Finnish Political Science Association, 2 (1960) 4, pp. 182–183.

munists receive a heavy support. Today work for the unemployed is provided by the Government but it means that the unemployed have to leave their homes and communities for longer periods. In any case, whereas the Communist voters in the developed regions are strongly tied to their communities, the Communist supporters in the north and the east are much more migratory. This observation is also supported by the results from factor analysis in which a great amount of migration was characteristic for communities with a heavy Communist vote.

3. According to survey findings, the Communist voters in the more developed regions are the first to decide how to vote during election campaigns. Among the Communist voters in the north and the east, however, there is a very high proportion of voters who make their decision at the last minute. According to a national survey in 1958, as many as 82 per cent of the Communist voters in the south and the west have made their voting decisions at least two months before the elections while only 56 per cent of the Communist voters in the north and the east made their decision at that early moment. The latter was the lowest percentage in all groups established on the basis of party and geographical area.

The difference between Backwoods and Industrial Radicalism can be now summarized.

Backwoods Radicalism

Exists in communities of low division of labor and weak pressure toward uniformity

Diffuse deprivation

Low organizational and social participation

High expressive political participation

Loosely integrated into their communities

Isolated as individuals from groups

Industrial Radicalism

Exists in communities of high division of labor and strong pressure toward uniformity

Institutionalized deprivation

High organizational and social participation

High instrumental political participation

Strongly integrated into their local communities

Strongly tied to their social class but isolated from the total national community

Descriptions of the social background of radical movements on the Left resemble closely those given here as related to Backwoods Radicalism. In particular, this seems to be true for those findings and propositions usually subsumed under the label of the theory of mass society. According to this theory, the supporters of radical movements are usually described as uprooted and without ties to secondary groups which in turn would bind the individuals to the community or society at large.[15] This description goes for Backwoods Radicalism, but it does not offer an explanation of Industrial Radicalism. Traditional Marxist theory, on the other hand, seems to render a good explanation of Industrial Radicalism. As stated before, Industrial Radicalism is characteristic for situations in which the proletariat already has developed a clear class-consciousness and in which intraclass communication is high but interclass communication low. The communities in which Industrial Radicalism is strong have polarized class conflicts, and very much of a two-class situation, as is assumed in traditional Marxist theory.[16]

[15] See especially William Kornhauser, *The Politics of Mass Society* (New York: The Free Press, 1959).

[16] See, e.g., T. B. Bottomore and M. Rubel, eds., *Karl Marx: Selected Writings in Sociology and Social Philosophy* (London: Watts, 1956), pp. 178–202.

Attitudes to Modernization and Social Change: Observations in the Australian New Guinea

In testing the model here presented it is worthwhile to look also at other data than those related to Finnish communism. The model should give some help in explaining protests in different settings. Of particular interest are developing societies. In them, however, it does not seem to be relevant to study legitimacy conflicts in the same manner as in studying already established societies. What can be done, however, is to inquire whether reactions to social and political change in developing societies can be described in terms of our structural variables, division of labor and pressure toward uniformity. The observations presented here are chosen from Australian New Guinea. The choice of New Guinea has, it has to be admitted, personal reasons.[17] The author knows New Guinea better than other developing societies. It is, however, not difficult to present a rationale why examples from New Guinea are particularly fruitful here. New Guinea, and particularly the Australian territories, provide today an example of a society in which there is both a nonindigenous administration and an extremely rapid modernization process. Few areas provide such a wide range of both individuals and behavior patterns on the dimension of modernization.

We have discussed societies as social systems without paying much attention to the multitude of subsystems within a society. A more important problem, however, is that developing societies often contain several almost independent political and social systems that do not constitute subsystems of each other. In colonial and developing societies we may thus talk about *the traditional, the colonial* and *the*

future system. As such, these systems are, of course, abstract types. Some individuals may be committed to and even try to define their identity in terms of all the systems. The crucial point, however, is that division into the three systems provides a qualitative variable by which differences between individuals can be described. A discussion about solidarity and attraction to the society and its political system is hardly possible without distinguishing between these three types. In developing societies the main question is perhaps not the degree of solidarity but rather to which system attraction is directed.

The question is: how will our structural variables determine the attachment to these different systems? A tentative answer, based on observations in New Guinea, is given in the typology of Fig. 3.

A short description of these types and their commitments is called for. In Australian New Guinea, as probably elsewhere, the most distinctive representatives of the various types are found among leaders and individuals with some kind of influence. The types refer mainly to such individuals.

1. Local Traditionals have few items for exchange, and their behavior is strongly regulated by traditional norms and values. The most outstanding representatives of this type are to be found among leaders of tribes and villages that have remained largely untouched by the modernization process. Their main reaction to change consists of explicit resistance.

2. Acculturated Deferentials have few items for exchange and are rather free from norms and values of the traditional village or tribal society. They have to observe rules in their interaction with whites and administration officials; but when no superiors are in sight they tend to lack rules for behavior altogether. They perceive themselves as having a small number of items for exchange, particularly

---

[17] The observations are more fully reported in E. Allardt, "Reactions to Social and Political Change in a Developing Society," in K. Ishwaran, ed., *Politics and Social Change* (Leiden: Brill, 1966), pp. 1–10.

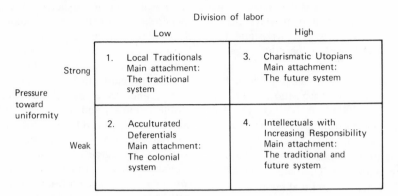

Figure 3.

when compared with Charismatic Utopians. Representatives of this type are particularly found among indigenous individuals who have served the colonial administration for a long time. They may possess a deep-seated aggression toward whites, but it is unlikely that this would be expressed in overt behavior. Their main attitude is that of deference and anxiety about showing enough loyalty to the administration. They may be characterized as definitely uninterested in social change.

3. Charismatic Utopians feel that they have many items for exchange but the exchange process is hindered by rules, inequality, color bars, and so forth. The most outstanding representatives are leaders of local politico-economic movements. Some of these leaders, such as Paliau, who operated in Southern Manus,[18] and Tommy Kabu in the Purari Delta,[19] have been described in anthropological literature. As leaders they rely on their charismatic qualities, but in their action programs they stress the technical, the rational and the economic. They want to get rid of the Australians and the Euro-peans but at the same time they try to copy the methods and techniques of the Australians and the Europeans. In today's New Guinea they are the only ones who are really concerned about technical advancement and instrumental adaptation to modernization, but they also tend to overstress it. They are overtly hostile to everything traditional. They are, accordingly, strongly commited to social change and their world is the new society.

4. The Intellectuals with Increasing Responsibility are today mainly found among young teachers, doctors, journalists, government clerks, and so on. In New Guinea, they are still few in number. Individuals who have spent a part of their life in European and international centers of learning and culture, as in the case with intellectuals in the new Asian and African countries, are still lacking. What is crucial, however, is that the type of intellectual who has strongly dominated the political scene in new states is clearly coming into prominence in New Guinea also.

In fact, the Intellectuals with Increasing Responsibility are much more attached to the traditional pattern of life than both the Acculturated Deferentials and the Charismatic Utopians. Even in Australian New Guinea it seems to be quite clear that these usually young edu-

[18] P. Worsley, *The Trumpet Shall Sound* (London: MacGibbon & Kee, 1957), pp. 183–192.
[19] R. F. Maher, *New Men of Papua: A Study in Culture Change* (Madison, Wis.: University of Wisconsin Press, 1960).

cated individuals, who represent the intellectual in developing states, have greater interest in the traditional ways of life than the older deferent clerks and low-status officials within the administration. The young intellectuals also seem to be much more respected among the indigenous population than those who are strictly committed to serving the Australian administration. The intellectuals have a two-fold attachment. They consider both the traditional and the new society legitimate. They are interested in social change but feel that cultural revival ought to be combined with it.

On the basis of the discussion the following hypotheses can be formulated:

9. Individuals living under conditions of low division of labor and strong pressure toward uniformity are apt to resist and to be hostile to social change.

10. Individuals living under conditions of low division of labor and weak pressure toward uniformity are apt to be indifferent to social change. If hostile reactions occur, they will take the character of wish-fulfillment beliefs.

11. Individuals living under conditions of high division of labor and strong pressure toward uniformity are apt to have favorable attitudes toward social change and hostile attitudes to those who are conceived of as resisting social change.

12. Individuals living under conditions of high division of labor and weak pressure toward uniformity are apt to have favorable attitudes toward both social change and the existing social system.

These hypotheses deal with individual attitudes toward change under different structural conditions. Our point of departure was the degree and kind of legitimacy conflicts in different societies of different social structures. It is apparent that what is called organic solidarity and organically solidary societies presuppose social change. In the case of colonial or developing societies this is also obvious. With increasing division of labor, change initiated to eliminate inequalities tends to increase solidarity to the new developing system and decrease the likelihood for hostile outbursts and movements. This is certainly true for differentiated and industrialized societies also. In societies with a high degree of division of labor, exchange relations will easily become institutionalized in such a fashion that some individuals will be excluded from exchange unless social change is often initiated. Social change is an extremely general concept, and change can take many directions. We cannot simply say that social change is a prerequisite for organic solidarity. We may, however, say that in societies with high division of labor, social changes that decrease existing inequalities tend to increase solidarity. This may be seen as a continuous process, as the institutionalization of exchange relations easily leads to the establishment of obstacles in exchange.

Types of Alienation

Both the findings about Finnish communism and the observations on the attitudes among the indigenous elite toward modernization in the Australian New Guinea suggest two distinctive types of alienation. In the situation of relatively high division of labor and strong pressure toward uniformity, the ones hindered from obtaining rewards from social change will experience *powerlessness.* Powerlessness is a state in which the individual feels that he does not have any control over the rewards he receives. If we want to apply Marxist terminology, we may say that powerlessness is a state of feeling separated from the means of production. If powerlessness leads to political reactions, it will result in fairly systematic and instrumental activities.

This is true for both Industrial Radicalism and for some of the strongly organized New Guinean movements led by such men as Paliau. The individuals will feel that they lack power and influence, and when they react politically they aim at changing the whole power structure.

In the situation of low division of labor and weak pressure toward uniformity, the kind of alienation displayed is best described by the term *uprootedness* or simply *uncertainty*. Uprootedness is a feeling state in which the individual does not clearly know what to believe, what rules to follow, what his position or motives are, how the situation is structured. Uprooted people, too, can easily become mobilized, but it is apparent that political activities of uprooted people are strongly expressive and unsystematic. The political reactions consist less of systematic attempts to change the power structure than of a search for normative and comparison reference groups.

Alienation is, of course, a term that varies in meaning, but the structural model here applied can at least be used for suggesting how some of the different meanings of alienation relate to each other. In an often-quoted paper, Melvin Seeman distinguishes between five major forms of feelings of alienation: powerlessness, meaninglessness, normlessness, self-estrangement, and isolation.[20] As Seeman does, it is assumed here that alienation is a kind of feeling state. The conditions for the emergence of alienation have to be clearly separated from alienation itself. Among such conditions one could list factual isolation, factual separation from the means of production, and so forth. Seeman's five forms are obtained through an analysis of the literature, but Seeman does not offer a systematic typology in which the types are logically related to each other. One distinction is

already mentioned here, and it seems also in Seeman's list reasonable to distinguish powerlessness from the rest. Powerlessness belongs in our typology in cell 3, whereas all the other forms can be subsumed under the concept of uprootedness or uncertainty and belong in cell 2, characterized by diffuse deprivation.

By elaborating the concept of pressure toward uniformity, it seems possible to suggest a certain relationship between the different forms of uprootedness and uncertainty. Pressure toward uniformity can manifest itself in a number of ways. We may say that social values, social norms, role-expectations can educe and contain demands for uniform behavior. All of them can restrict social exchange. In addition to values, norms and role-expectations, lack of situational facilities may constitute hindrances for exchange. In his work on collective behavior, Neil Smelser assumes that these four factors form a hierarchical and cumulative order in such a fashion that values determine norms, roles and situational facilities, whereas, for instance, norms do not determine values but strongly influence both role-expectations and situational facilities. Lowest in the hierarchy we have the situational facilities. Smelser's typology of collective movements follows the same pattern. Value-oriented movements that are focusing on the change or restoration of social values influence not only the values in society but also the norms, roles and situational facilities. Collective movements focusing on situational facilities such as the panic and the craze, on the other hand, do not influence values, norms and roles.[21] In the same fashion it seems possible to arrange the forms of alienation in a cumulative pattern. Uncertainty concerning values (or goals, purposes, and so forth) may be labeled as

[20] Melvin Seeman, "On the Meaning of Alienation," *American Sociological Review,* 24 (1959), pp. 783–791.

[21] Neil J. Smelser, *Theory of Collective Behavior* (New York: The Free Press, 1963), pp. 23–34.

meaninglessness, uncertainty regarding norms (or institutionalized means) as anomic alienation, uncertainty regarding roles (or motives, and so forth) as self-alienation, and uncertainty regarding situational facilities as situational alienation. Their relationships can be described by the following cumulative pattern:

Table 1

Forms of Alienation	UNCERTAINTY REGARDING			
	Values	Norms	Roles	Situations
Meaninglessness	+	+	+	+
Anomic alienation	−	+	+	+
Self-alienation	−	−	+	+
Situational alienation	−	−	−	+
No alienation	−	−	−	−

All these forms may educe political reactions which very much will follow the pattern described by Smelser. If mobilized, the alienated who feel meaninglessness will be apt to join value-oriented movements. Anomic people will be particularly easy to mobilize into norm-oriented collective' movements, whereas self-alienated people are easy to mobilize into sudden collective outbursts of hostility. People who feel themselves lost in a situation will easily panic or join a craze. There are no possibilities to test the hypotheses of the cumulative nature of alienation here because the political phenomena analyzed either have to be classified as powerlessness or meaninglessness. It seems reasonable, however, to state that many movements of the Radical Right are norm-oriented movements. They occur in particular when new forms and rules have been introduced, and when it is felt that traditional political rules have been violated. Such norm-oriented movements do not aim at changing the values of society; they aim at restoring traditional rules and forms of behavior. Many supporters of the Radical Right definitely aim at the upholding of prevailing values although they strongly detest, for instance, the behavior of the present politicians.

One objection against the assumption of the cumulative pattern of alienation is that it is possible to point out cases in which individuals seem to be alien to some prevailing values although they almost slavishly stick to the norms or to their roles. They may be called ritualists, in accordance with Merton's famous paradigm of modes of adaptation.[22] They are not included among the alienated here as it seems reasonable to assume that they cannot be described as uprooted or torn by feelings of uncertainty. As long as feeling states and not the consequences for the system is used as the criterion for alienation, it seems difficult to classify the ritualists among the alienated. They are usually strongly committed to the system to which they belong in spite of the fact that their behavior may have dysfunctional consequences for the system they are serving. Ritualists are presumably not easily mobilized, and in this sense ritualism does not result in political reactions.

In terms of the structural variables in the model, the discussion of the types of alienation can now be summarized in the four-fold scheme of Fig. 4.

The distinction between powerlessness and uprootedness is fairly well substantiated by the empirical evidence presented. The assumption of the cumulative nature of the forms of uprootedness is a hypothesis advanced on purely conceptual grounds.

[22] Robert K. Merton, *Social Theory and Social Structure* (New York: The Free Press, 1957), p. 140.

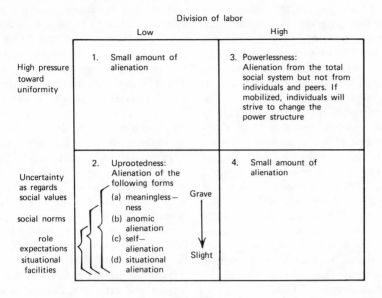

Figure 4.

MEANS OF INFLUENCE, POLITICAL TRUST, AND SOCIAL CONTROL

William A. Gamson

Impact of Trust on Means of Influence

The propositions in this chapter have a strong parallel to those suggested by Etzioni (1961) in discussing compliance relations in organizations and we will draw heavily from Etzioni's arguments in justifying them. Etzioni distinguishes three types of social control by the officers of an organization over the organization's lower participants. The three types are only slightly different from the means of influence suggested here. Etzioni argues that the extent to which an organization

SOURCE: Reprinted from *Power and Discontent* (Homewood, Illinois: The Dorsey Press, 1968), 163–183; 190–193, by permission of William A. Gamson.

will rely on one rather than another differs from organization to organization. Furthermore, "most organizations tend to emphasize only one means of [social control], relying less on the other two . . . The major reason for . . . specialization seems to be that when two kinds of [social control] are emphasized at the same time over the same subject group, they tend to neutralize each other" (Etzioni, 1961, p. 7).

The use of constraints, for example, affects the attitudes of authorities in such a way that persuasion is rendered more difficult. The resources required for persuasion are jeopardized or destroyed by threatening the authorities. The classic example of one means affecting another, Etzioni points out, is the difficulty of rehabilitation programs in prisons which emphasize the use of threats to maintain order and of therapy programs in mental hospitals where custodial problems are emphasized by the nonprofessional staff.

For similar reasons, the means of influence directed by a partisan group against a particular set of authorities will tend to emphasize a dominant means. What this means will be is determined by two factors: (1) whether the conditions currently exist for the most efficient and least costly use of this means of influence, and (2) whether the use of a particular means will affect the relationship with authorities in such a way that future costs of influence will be affected. Let us examine how this applies to the three states of political trust.

CONFIDENT GROUPS

A confident solidary group will tend to rely on persuasion as a means of influence. For a confident group, the conditions for successful persuasion are maximized. The authorities, the group believes, are committed to the same goals and are viewed as its agents. On many issues, no influence at all should be required to bring about desired outcomes. However, because of the ambiguity of consequences of some decisions or because of a particularly strong personal concern, a solidary group may not be willing to accept even a favorable probability of a desired outcome without trying to improve on it further. They may fear, for example, that the blandishments of competing groups have obscured the nature of the particular issue leaving open the possibility of "error" on the part of well-intentioned authorities. But whatever the reason for influence, a confident group believes in the goodwill of authorities toward its interests and welfare. It is merely a question of implementing this goodwill in a particular case. This can be

achieved through presenting information and arguments, drawing on the friendship and loyalty of the authorities, and activating their commitment to whatever collectivities and values the authorities and the solidary group share.[1] As Lane (1962, p. 144) describes the attitudes of his high-trust respondents toward influence, "The best way to use power is by persuasion; people shouldn't be forced to do things they don't want to do."

Persuasion may still have considerable costs even in such favorable circumstances. Political campaigns have long been recognized as occasions whose primary function is to activate the party faithful rather than to convert rival party members. To this extent, such campaigns may be viewed as an effort in persuasion by a partisan group (in this case the party leaders and activists), directed toward a set of authorities in whom they feel confidence (the party rank and file in the electorate). Such campaigns, of course, can be very costly in energy, money, and other resources despite their nature as efforts at persuasion. But whatever these costs of persuasion may be, they are likely to be less when aimed at a sympathetic group of authorities who are simply being asked to act in ways congruent with their own interests and values than when aimed at a group with different or conflicting interests.

Other means of influence, on the other hand, are likely to have adverse effects on the relationship between confident solidary groups and authorities. This is most obviously true in the case of constraints. To add disadvantages to the situation of the authorities or to threaten to do so may produce resistance. This resistance means that the general predisposition of authorities is changed so that it is less favorable to the interests of the solidary

---

[1] I am speaking here of the group's perceptions of the authorities. In fact, such confidence may be misplaced and subject to change through subsequent experience with authorities.

group on future decisions than it was in the past. In other words, constraints may result in a lowering of P_b for future decisions.[2]

It is possible to reduce this resistance by concealing the agency of the constraints, for example, by making the authorities feel someone else is responsible for the new disadvantages. Or resistance can be mitigated if the partisan is able to convince the authority that he has no personal discretion in his actions but is being compelled by outside forces or people and cannot, therefore, be held responsible. Schelling (1960) makes a similar point in emphasizing the use of commitment as a bargaining strategy. If one can convince the target that it is the *situation* which forces one's disagreeable actions, the resistance generated by constraints will be mitigated.

But even with mitigation, the repeated use of such a means of influence creates a poor atmosphere for efforts at persuasion. Constraints can undermine the persuasion resources which a group possesses. Such resources as reputation and personal attraction may be diminished or destroyed since they depend on the attitudes of the target of influence toward the group. Thus, some academic critics of American foreign policy with friends in the State Department are reluctant to engage in any public opposition to American policy. Efforts to discredit a policy and influence the public against it are a form of constraint. Those who feel that they have persuasion resources are reluctant to place them in jeopardy by actions which might alienate the officials whom they wish to influence. To the extent that such officials cultivate and encourage such beliefs without responding to influence, they are using a social control device which effectively contains influence attempts. Whether

influence or social control dominates the mix is problematic and undoubtedly varies from case to case but it is useful to view the relationship from both sides. From the potential partisan perspective, confident groups will hesitate to use constraints on authorities because of the danger that such influence attempts will make future influence both more necessary and less easy.

The argument against using inducements is not as strong but is similar. While inducements are not as likely to cause resistance, they may if they are offered too crudely and openly so that they are defined as a "bribe." But even when they do not create resistance, they may lead to subtle changes in the relationship which have undesirable consequences for the future influence attempts of a group. This point is clearest perhaps if we think of the partisan and the authority as close friends. There is an important difference between the diffuse reciprocal obligations of a friendship and the tacit bargains and contracts of associates. An action carried out for the sake of friendship does not imply any specific *quid pro quo;* it is simply one of the demands that both parties to a relationship must accept to maintain it. But it is also part of the expectations of the relationship that neither party will exploit the friendship by making such demands excessive. One is sometimes reluctant to ask a friend for a favor precisely because he is not free to refuse as he would be in a more contractual, arm's length relationship. The diffuseness of the obligation places a corresponding demand for self-restraint on the parties if the relationship is to be maintained.

To offer a specific inducement to a friend is to violate the norms of friendship. If one offers a *quid pro quo* for a favor, it implies that one also expects a *quid pro quo* when he performs a similar favor. In general, it implies a different relationship in which each act of influence becomes a separate transaction creating

[2] P_b is the probability that the political system will produce preferred outcomes without the group doing anything to bring them about. This may be thought of as the probability before or without influence.

credits or debts for the parties involved. If the partisan wants a favorable outcome he must not expect to get it for nothing. If his credit is good, immediate payment may not be required but at some time in the future he may expect to be called upon to reciprocate. Such a shift in relationship involves a change in the initial predisposition of the authority who must now be regarded as neutral in the absence of influence instead of favorably predisposed as before. Thus, as with constraints, by the use of inducements future influence will become both more necessary and less easy.

The situation is not basically changed if the basis of confidence in the authorities is not friendship but joint membership in the same collectivity. Again, to offer an inducement is an implicit contradiction of the existence of this joint membership. If one is being asked to act in his own interest, which he incidentally happens to share with the partisan making the influence attempt, then why should he require an inducement for acting? The offer suggests, instead, the separate and independent interests of buyer and seller. The seller has decision outcomes which do not directly affect him and the buyer has resources, the control of which the seller desires. In contrast, a confident trust relationship suggests a set of commitments which are not fully activated or a lack of information, but the offer of an inducement implies the absence of such conditions. In doing so, it moves the relationship from confidence toward neutrality and again increases both the necessity and difficulty of influence.

NEUTRAL GROUPS

A neutral solidary group will tend to rely on inducements as a means of influence. The proper conditions for persuasion do not clearly exist for such groups. The authorities do not share the goals of the group but rather have their own set of goals which do not necessarily

conflict with or complement those of the solidary group. There is no a priori reason for believing that the authorities will either favor or oppose the outcome desired. There is no reason to feel that if the authorities were fully informed about the consequences of their prospective actions they would favor the alternative desired by the group. For them to recognize that a particular choice will greatly satisfy such a group is no argument, in itself, for making this choice.

If a group of authorities has control of something (a binding choice) that is unimportant to them and important to a solidary group and the latter has something (inducement resources) that is important to authorities, then the conditions for a successful transaction exist. While any given solidary group may or may not have such resources, the first of these conditions is implied in part by the neutral trust orientation. Such neutrality means that there is no reason to think that a decision which is important to the solidary group will be regarded as such by authorities; thus, it is available for appropriate inducements, felicitously offered.

With a neutral trust relationship, then, the proper conditions for inducements do exist but the proper conditions for persuasion do not. Constraints are again likely to have adverse effects for reasons identical to the ones given above. By creating hostility, they run the risk of changing the initial predispositions of authorities from neutral to unfavorable. The probability of favorable outcomes without influence may then become very low making future influence both very necessary and very difficult.

ALIENATED GROUPS

An alienated solidary group will tend to rely on constraints as a means of influence. Such a group, unlike the others, has little to lose by constraints. Since the probability of favorable outcomes is already very low in the absence of influence, it is hardly necessary to worry about resentment. Such resentment does not materially increase either the necessity or the difficulty of influence. The attitude that "the only thing they understand is force" is a perfect manifestation of this trust orientation.

An appeal to an alienated group that it is "hurting its cause" by acts of constraint falls on deaf ears. Thus, to point out to poor Negroes in urban ghettoes that riots are resented is a rather irrelevant communication to a group which feels there is little likelihood of obtaining favorable actions from authorities in the absence of such riots. Civil rights leaders may deplore such actions because of their disapproval of violence per se and their concern about the direct injury to people and property which the riots produce. Furthermore, less-alienated groups within the Negro community may feel the loss of the ability to activate the commitments of authorities to shared norms against injustice and poverty. But the belief in such shared norms implies a confidence which the rioters presumably lack. For the extremely alienated, not only is there little to lose through generating resistance, but they can hardly be unaware that their major resources are constraints—the capacity to create trouble if their needs are not met.

The conditions for the successful use of other forms of influence are generally absent for alienated groups. It makes little sense to talk of persuading authorities who are viewed as systematically biased against one's interests. Such bias need not reflect hostility or even awareness of the solidary group's concerns; rather, it may simply stem from the fact that the authorities systematically favor a conflicting set of interests while maintaining a sense that they are acting fairly. But whether they are actively hostile or hold interests antagonistic to the alienated group, they are not likely to be persuaded by fuller in-

formation on the consequences of their choices. In fact, such information should persuade them to choose alternatives which are worse for the alienated group; confusion and lack of information is more desirable for it increases the chances of a favorable "error." Nor can the commitment of authorities to shared collectivities and values be appealed to because the alienated orientation assumes the lack of these.

The conditions for the use of inducements are not as obviously absent but are still lacking. Since the transactions referred to here are rarely if ever made the subject of explicit written agreements, they are built in large part on good faith. "You can't do business with Hitler," it used to be said, suggesting that even an exchange requires some degree of trust. This trust should not be confused with the more diffuse kind associated with friendship. It might be called, following Lieberman (1963), interest-trust or *i*-trust. This does not involve any belief in altruism or generosity on the part of the other party, only the belief that there is sufficient common interest for him to place the maintenance of a continuing exchange relationship over the specific advantage he might get by defaulting on any given transaction. But even such an *i*-trust is lacking for alienated groups who believe that the basis for such a neutral relationship is absent.

SOME PARTIAL EVIDENCE

The hypotheses suggested above can be tested. I have tried to make them persuasive by argument and by illustration, but the examples do no more than establish a certain plausibility. There is one piece of more systematic evidence which, while it is far from definitive, does support the connection between the use of constraints and alienation. Almond and Verba (1965, p. 62) report the percentage of citizens in five countries who are alienated in their expectations about government outputs. These percentages run from 12 percent in the United States to 71 percent in Mexico with Great Britain, Germany, and Italy falling in between.

Rummel (1963) and Tanter (1965) have measured the level of internal violence in different countries. If we take this as a measure of the tendency of partisan groups to use constraints, then we ought to find that internal violence is positively correlated with the degree of alienation as measured by Almond and Verba. Tanter (1965) reports a factor analysis of nine measures of conflict behavior within nations: assassinations, general strikes, guerrilla war, major government crises, purges, riots, revolutions, demonstrations, and deaths by intergroup violence. He identified two factors which he labeled "turmoil" and "internal war." The turmoil factor offers a better measure of the frequency of constraints since it loads most highly on demonstrations, riots, assassinations, and general strikes.

Table 1 presents the factor scores for the five countries on which we have an alienation score. The two measures have

a correlation coefficient of 0.69. Given the small number of countries involved and the very gross approximations of the variables of alienation and constraints, caution is clearly in order in interpreting this correlation. But at least it suggests that some more systematic support can be found for the hypotheses offered.

Change in the Trust Orientation

In the discussion above, we have taken trust as the independent variable and have tried to use it to explain the choice of a means of influence. We now treat the trust orientation as itself subject to change and examine the impact of particular means of influence on such changes.

SUCCESSFUL INFLUENCE

The hypothesized combinations of political trust and means of influence may be called *congruent* ones, i.e., alienation-constraints, neutrality-inducements, and confidence-persuasion. *Use of a congruent means of influence increases the strength and stability of the existing trust orientation if it is perceived as successful.* The connection between trust and

Table 1. Degree of Alienation and Frequency of Constraints for Five Countries

COUNTRY	PERCENTAGE ALIENATED*	CONSTRAINT SCORES**
United States	12	414
Great Britain	26	327
West Germany	26	60
Italy	42	604
Mexico	71	701

r = 0.69

*These figures are from Almond and Verba (1965, Table II.10). They are contaminated somewhat for our purposes by the inclusion in them of "parochials" (individuals who are unaware of the impact of the government on their lives) in addition to "alienates" (individuals who have negative expectations about the impact of government).

**These figures are from Tanter (1965). They are the scores on "turmoil," a general factor with high loadings on demonstrations, riots, general strikes, and assassinations.

choice of means is confirmed for a solidary group by successful use of congruent means. A confident group has its confidence reinforced by being able to persuade authorities. A neutral group has its neutral contractual orientation reinforced by concluding a successful transaction in which authorities have accepted some inducement. An alienated group is reinforced in its belief that only force is understood by the successful use of constraints. Note that this hypothesis contradicts a possible alternative one that successful influence increases confidence. Instead, it will be argued that successful influence may sometimes reinforce alienation rather than lessen it and that the effect of successful influence on political trust depends on the *means* of influence used.

Suppose that a noncongruent means of influence is chosen. It is such situations that produce shifts in political trust and these shifts can be in either direction. Chart 1 helps to make the direction clear. The use of a means of influence below the diagonal will increase confidence while the use of a means of influence above the diagonal will decrease it.

Use of a means below the diagonal involves the selection of a means which implies greater confidence than exists. If such influence is successful in spite of expectations to the contrary, it suggests that the original trust orientation was insufficiently confident. First take the case of a neutral group which success-fully uses persuasion. It suggests that the common interest with authorities may be greater than had been allowed. They required no *quid pro quo* to take the desired action but were willing to do it without any special inducement or personal gain. They must, therefore, have had a predisposition to act in that direction which the influence attempt activated. But if the predisposition toward favorable action existed in this case, perhaps it exists more generally and one can expect favorable outcomes even without influence. Thus, the thrust of such an event is toward greater confidence.

An alienated group which successfully uses persuasion should be in for an even more abrupt shock. That the target of influence was willing to act favorably without being constrained to do so is difficult to explain. Perhaps the conflict of interests is not as total as had been believed and there is some coincidence of interests as well. Again a favorable predisposition is implied which contradicts the general belief that the initial predisposition is unfavorable. Of course, any particular instance can be simply treated as an exception but if such exceptions occur with any frequency or if they occur on issues regarded as critical, then they should create a push toward greater confidence.

Even an alienated group that used successful inducements should be pushed in this direction. If authorities whom one cannot do business with turn out ready

Chart 1. Effect of Successful Use of Given Means of Influence on Political Trust

| | MEANS OF INFLUENCE | | |
TRUST ORIENTATION	PERSUASION	INDUCEMENTS	CONSTRAINTS
Confidence	R	−	−
Neutrality	+	R	−
Alienation	+	+	R

Key: R = reinforces existing trust orientation.
  + = changes it in direction of increased confidence.
  − = changes it in direction of decreased confidence.

to do business, then the initial belief is weakened. It is not that they are against us, a group might reason as a result, but only that they are for themselves. They are not malicious but only indifferent. They are not our friends but at least they may be our venders. Again there is a shift away from alienation.

The successful use of a means of influence above the diagonal implies greater alienation than initially existed; it suggests that the original trust orientation was overly confident. All of these cases are interesting examples of situations in which successful influence may increase alienation. If a confident group must offer an inducement to gain a favorable outcome, something is amiss. The authorities should require no inducement to do what is in the mutual interest of partisan and authority. That they ask or accept such an inducement implies that such mutuality of interest is lacking. Can a favorable predisposition be said to exist if one must offer an inducement to activate it? At the very least, it must be a weak one and the greater the inducement necessary to produce a favorable outcome, the weaker the initial predisposition must be.

If a confident group uses constraints to gain a favorable outcome, the implication of overconfidence is even stronger. Presumably the authorities would act against one's interest if they were unconstrained but a confident trust orientation implies the opposite. Why constrain somebody to do something that he wants to do anyway? Presumably, because the authorities did *not* seem to want to do it and if unconstrained would have acted against one's interest. But this suggests that the initial confidence was unrealistic and pushes toward decreased confidence in the future.

A neutral group which makes successful use of constraints is also acting in a way contradicted by their trust orientation although the overall argument is least clear at this point. In a neutral re-

lationship, influence involves reciprocity. Inducements are given and favorable decisions are received. But such reciprocity is absent in constraints. The authorities still give favorable outcomes but they receive nothing in exchange. For partisans to act in such a fashion is unfair dealing on their part unless they are dealing with hostile or biased authorities who deserve no better treatment. In other words, for a group to make such absence of reciprocity justifiable to themselves, they must feel that a *quid pro quo* was not warranted and deserved. This makes sense if the authorities are regarded as themselves unfair and negatively biased. Thus, the successful use of constraints by a neutral group pushes it toward an alienated orientation.

UNSUCCESSFUL INFLUENCE

It is not clear, given our arguments for the congruence of certain combinations of means of influence and trust, why noncongruent cases should ever occur. They do, of course, and this requires some explanation. First of all, we do not expect any group to make exclusive use of a single means of influence. We have argued only that one element in the mix will tend to be dominant and the particular element and its strength will be determined by trust orientation. A confident group should have a high probability of using persuasion, a lesser probability of using inducements, and a still smaller probability of using constraints.

Implicit in the occurrence of a successful noncongruent influence attempt is the occurrence of a previously unsuccessful congruent attempt. The unsuccessful attempt may be viewed as weakening the stability of the trust orientation without changing its direction. It then becomes a question of whether one moves to the right or left as one leaves the diagonal in Chart 1. Clearly this is only a question for neutral groups; confident groups can only move above the diagonal to inducements or constraints that will lessen confidence and alienated groups can only move below the diagonal to inducements or persuasion that will increase confidence.

Which direction will neutral groups move in following an unsuccessful use of inducements? The answer seems to rest on the nature of the failure. We can imagine two situations: (1) the authorities reject the inducements because they suggest that bargaining is improper, or (2) they reject the inducements because the suggest that they are insufficient. In the first case, unsuccessful inducements should be followed by persuasion attempts while in the second case they are followed by attempts at constraint. If the required inducements are exorbitant, it hardly suggests that an effort at persuasion will be successful. On the contrary, it implies the unlikelihood of favorable action if no advantage is added to the situation of the authorities. There is no such implication for the rejection of the bargaining process. While it does not imply that persuasion will be successful, it does suggest that the choice will be based on the orientation of the authorities and that it is appropriate to aim one's influence here rather than at their situation.

We have dealt with both successful and unsuccessful congruent attempts and with successful noncongruent attempts. This leaves us with unsuccessful noncongruent attempts. We may assume as

before that instances off the diagonal imply unsuccessful previous congruent attempts. Unsuccessful noncongruent attempts, as Chart 2 indicates, have the predicted effect of reinforcing the existing trust orientation. The general argument for this set of hypotheses is that trust orientation creates an expectation that such means of influence are inappropriate and an unsuccessful use of this means confirms this expectation. This argument, however, is more convincing for the cases below the diagonal than for those above.

Below the diagonal of Chart 2 we have groups using a means of influence which implies a greater trust than they enjoy. It is not surprising to an alienated group that they are unable to persuade or induce the authorities. This is what they have been led to expect and they simply find their original attitude confirmed. Similarly, a neutral group does not expect to get something for nothing; it should do nothing more than confirm this belief when they find they are unable to persuade. If we assume that a noncongruent attempt has been preceded by an unsuccessful congruent one, then the two unsuccessful experiences are offsetting. Trust orientation is weakened by the first but reinforced by the second and will remain unaltered by the influence experience.

It might be argued that unsuccessful influence attempts will decrease confidence but I am explicitly not arguing that here. Trust orientation is affected

Chart 2. *Effects of Unsuccessful Use of Given Means of Influence on Political Trust*

| TRUST ORIENTATION | MEANS OF INFLUENCE | | |
	PERSUASION	INDUCEMENTS	CONSTRAINTS
Confidence	W	R	R
Neutrality	R	W	R
Alienation	R	R	W

Key: R = reinforced existing trust orientation.
  W = weakened existing trust orientation.

by the nature of the decisions made and the satisfaction or dissatisfaction with them. To the extent that unsuccessful influence attempts imply unfavorable outcomes, we would expect them to be associated with a decrease in confidence but this decrease comes from the bad outcomes rather than the experience of unsuccessful influence. The effect would be no different if influence had not been attempted at all and the same outcomes had resulted. However, political trust is affected not only by decision outcomes but also by influence experience and it is these hypothesized effects that are summarized in Charts 1 and 2.

Social Control and Trust

The trust orientation of solidary groups is not only related to the means of influence chosen but to the social control response as well. Trust is relevant to authorities for two reasons: (1) It affects the means of influence a partisan group is likely to use. While all influence puts limitations on the freedom of authorities, constraints are particularly unpleasant because they add or threaten to add new disadvantages. (2) It affects the capacity of authorities to achieve collective goals. To the extent that they must make commitments without the prior consent of those who will ultimately be called on to supply the resources, they require high general trust.

Both of these reasons argue for the advantage to authorities of high confidence on the part of potential partisans. Furthermore, some systems require such confidence even more than others. Etzioni argues

> Organizations that serve culture goals have to rely on normative [control, i.e., persuasion] because the realization of their goals requires positive and intense commitments of lower participants to the organization . . . and such commitments cannot be effectively attained by other [types of control] . . . . The attainment of culture

goals such as the creation, application, or transmission of values requires the development of identification with the organizational representatives (Etzioni, 1961, p. 82).

When an organization must bring about some change in the orientation of the members, persuasion is the most appropriate technique. A heavy reliance on sanctions leads to a "calculative" involvement of members. "Manipulation of pay, fines, and bonuses does not lead to internalization of values," Etzioni writes (1961, p. 84). Insulation in such situations may lead to the containment of influence but interferes with or makes impossible high confidence.

Colleges and universities are recognizing increasingly that their means of control of students interacts heavily with the achievement of their educational objectives. One may contrast, for example, a small liberal arts college such as Antioch with a large, state university in their respective mechanisms of control. A university is a more complex organization and its control structure reflects the greater diversity of its goals. Heavy reliance on grades (i.e., sanctions) and the exclusion of students from major influence on educational policies (i.e., insulation) may effectively contain influence over large areas of decision but they do not seem as effective in producing high confidence in the university administration on the part of students. In contrast, Antioch College has included high participation by students in the affairs of the college for many years and justified it explicitly as part of its educational program. The higher trust generated by such participation may make *persuasive* controls more potent but it is probably less effective overall in containing the influence of students. However, the loss in controlling influence is compensated by the gain in trust; this trust, in turn, increases the ability of the college to give the students major responsibility for their own education.

The above example illustrates a central point: the "power" of a system to achieve collective goals is affected by the means of control employed. With an appropriate means of control, the system not only contains influence but increases its total resources; with an inappropriate means of control, it may contain influence but so consume its resources in doing so that it diminishes its effectiveness in achieving collective goals.

The desire to increase confidence, then, is one determinant of the type of control sought and this will vary with the requirements of the system for high member commitment. The existing trust orientation toward authorities is a second determinant because it affects the means of influence a group will use. These two factors are considered together as we examine the social control relationship toward groups with different trust orientations.

CONFIDENT GROUPS

Authorities will tend to rely on persuasion as a means of control over confident solidary groups. The arguments here are a variant of the earlier discussion on means of influence. Persuasion is the means of control most consonant with building and maintaining a positive trust orientation. When initial trust is high, a basis for persuasion exists. Confidence implies that the solidary group is already persuaded of its common interest with authorities. Persuasion only requires convincing the group that the authorities have things well in hand and that it will be well served without pestering the authorities unduly on specific decisions.

Other means of control tend to reduce the confidence of solidary groups. Insulation removes opportunities for the development and maintenance of confidence. Constraints as a means of control create resentment toward authorities, reduce trust, and encourage the use of constraints by solidary groups as a means of influence. Inducements, as argued above, encourage a calculative and neutral trust orientation toward authorities. In short, all means of control other than persuasion hinder the maintenance and development of high confidence, a doubly undesirable consequence. The resultant loss of credit leaves the authorities less able to achieve collective goals while at the same time it increases the probability that constraints will be used against them as a means of influence.

NEUTRAL GROUPS

Authorities will tend to rely on sanctions and particularly on inducements as a means of control over neutral solidary groups. While persuasion still is valuable to the extent that it can be used successfully, it is more difficult to use with a neutral group. Authorities are cast more in the role of broker or referee among competing groups. Inducements have a distinct advantage over constraints because they are less likely to alienate the solidary group and, hence, less likely to produce constraints as a means of influence. As Pareto argued in accounting for the shifts in control from "lions" to "foxes," force is used to better advantage *against* authorities in the process of attaining power than against one's subjects in the process of maintaining discipline when in power. Insulation provides fewer protections against the development of alienation by a solidary group than does participation of the group in a system of exchange.

ALIENATED GROUPS

Authorities will tend to rely on insulation as a means of control over alienated solidary groups. Insulation offers protection against the use of constraints by alienated groups. By preventing their access to resources and their ability to apply them, authorities can control the capacity of groups to use constraints without altering their inclination to use them.

Other means of control offer difficulties of one sort or another. Sanctions involve some access. Constraints used against alienated groups have fewer disadvantages than when used against neutral or confident groups because there is less trust to be destroyed. Still, it is necessary for a group to have something to lose before it can be subjected to effective constraints. Giving it something to lose can hardly be done without at the same time giving it some access.

Inducements are likely to be very costly with alienated groups. Such groups do not operate in a spirit of compromise; half a loaf does not appear better than none. As a consequence, authorities will find such groups unreasonable to bargain with and insatiable with respect to inducements. "Give them an inch and they take a mile," is the classic expression of such attitudes toward alienated solidary groups. Finally, persuasion is difficult since it will tend to be regarded as lying and manipulation. In short, insulation offers authorities the most satisfactory protection from alienated solidary groups.

INFLUENCE AND SOCIAL CHANGE

Influence which leads to a rapid and major reorganization of society is most likely to come from an alienated group or collection of groups which constitute a social movement. The success of such a movement in bringing about social change must be regarded, from the standpoint of the authorities, as a failure of social control. If successful social control had been operating, then influence would have been contained and, at the least, change would have occurred more slowly. "Effective conflict regulation,' Dahrendorf suggests (1959, p. 234), "serves to reduce the suddenness of change. Well-regulated conflict is likely to lead to very gradual change. . . ."

Major changes through the influence of social movements can occur for two reasons: bad decisions or social control errors. Authorities may make decisions which adversely affect such a large and influential group that even the most skillful efforts at social control are in-

sufficient to contain influence. Or, the techniques of social control used may be so clumsy and ineffective that they stimulate rather than contain influence

Partisan groups may try to increase their resources by deliberately trying to create an "error" in social control (that is, the use of an inappropriate control device which increases potential influence). Such errors may be quite important in accelerating the pace of change: it may lead a social movement to new allies and stronger commitment of its supporters, it may lead to the withdrawal of legitimacy and trust from existing authorities and thus weaken their ability to enforce decisions and make new commitments, and it may create such serious instability that many who were not convinced of the need for change will now find the status quo intolerable. In this situation, the natural advantage which accrues to those supporting the status quo switches to those who support change. A sense of this reversal has on occasion led revolutionaries to welcome a worsening of social conditions. They reason that the resultant crisis will weaken existing arrangements and thereby enhance the possibilities of social change. Unfortunately, many different kinds of changes may follow and the relative probability of changes that are deplored may be enhanced even more than the probability of desired changes.

While social control errors may accelerate the pace of change, a group which deliberately tries to create them is playing with fire. Political professionals, as Dahl (1961, p. 320) points out, "have access to extensive political resources which they employ at a high rate with superior efficiency. Consequently, a challenge to the existing norms is bound to be costly to the challenger, for legitimist professionals can quickly shift their skills and resources into the urgent task of doing in the dissenter."

Still, the application of social control is a delicate business, requiring great self-control and intelligence on the part of authorities if it is to dampen influence more than stimulate it. The shattered remains of many administrations and regimes testify to the fact that errors are made. It is worth examining some of these more specifically. Removal of partisan leaders by exile, imprisonment, or execution can backfire. It offers a movement with strong secondary leadership an opportunity to mobilize its supporters to the fullest and to draw in sympathetic bystanders, particularly if the pretext for repression is a weak one. But repression may be successful if the solidary group is sufficiently weak and the regime is sufficiently strong, making repression an extremely dangerous control device for a solidary group to invite.

A complementary and less risky error is the admission of a partisan group to access through an exaggerated estimate of their strength. In general, an error of repression is most likely when the authorities underestimate the strength and support of a solidary group; an error in granting access is most likely when the authorities overestimate the strength and support. It also follows that the less accurate the estimate of a solidary group's strength, the more likely it is to benefit by an access error. Or, put in other words, the more accurate the authorities are in their perception of a solidary group's strength, the less likely they are to make a social control error of this sort.

Similar considerations apply to social control errors in the use of constraints. Attempts to degrade and slander partisans can arouse sympathy and support for them among a wider group. If there is latent support, constraints may bring it into the open and thus strengthen the group. It may also succeed in scaring off some supporters, perhaps at the same time it helps the group grow. Attacks can do both simultaneously by polarizing the attitudes of potential followers.

A good illustration of the interplay between social control errors and the ebb and flow in the strength of a social movement is provided by an incident in the protest movement against American military actions in Vietnam. In October, 1965, a group of students staged a sit-in at a local Selective Service Board in Ann Arbor, Michigan, as part of a national protest against the war in Vietnam. This action and the generally strident tone of the protest helped to lend sustenance to administration charges that the protesters were an isolated fringe group without substantial wider sympathy in the community and nation. This impact was offset, however, by an error on the part of Selective Service officials. Several of the students were reclassified and this action rallied widespread support for the students on civil liberty grounds and brought the Selective Service System under a barrage of criticism. While the Selective Service System was only a subsidiary target for the protest movement, it was viewed as an instrument of the Vietnam policy and its self-created vulnerability proved a convenience to the protesters.

SOCIAL CONTROL AND
CHANGES IN TRUST

The above hypotheses relating trust to means of social control suggest congruent combinations. Use of a congruent means of social control, like use of a congruent means of influence, maintains the existing trust orientation. The use of a noncongruent means tends to produce changes in trust.

A confident group can be moved toward neutrality or alienation by heavy reliance on sanctions and insulation. A neutral group can be made more confident by involving its members in relationships that increase identification with authorities and encourage potential partisans to internalize the authorities' goals. A neutral group can be made more alienated by heavy reliance on constraints and by insulating it from relationships that increase identification and internalization. An alienated group can be made more confident by involving it in a system of exchange with authorities and a series of relationships which encourage identification and internalization.

However, social control is only one of two responses available to authorities. They may also alter the policies they pursue. To the extent that the alienation of a solidary group is based on a realistic appraisal of the decisions produced by authorities, altering outcomes is a much more direct means of raising confidence. To remove insulation from an alienated group will surely make the control problems of authorities more acute if such groups continue to be systematically neglected in the decisions of such authorities. The best long-run strategy for authorities in building confidence concentrates on equity in allocating resources and effectiveness in generating them and makes social control a secondary consideration and by-product.

REFERENCES

1. Almond, Gabriel A. and Verba, Sidney. *The Civic Culture.* Boston: Little, Brown & Co., 1965.

2. Dahl, Robert A. *Who Governs?* New Haven, Conn.: Yale University Press, 1961.

3. Dahrendorf, Ralf. *Class and Class Conflict in Industrial Society.* Stanford, Calif.: Stanford University Press, 1959.

4. Etzioni, Amitai. *A Comparative Analysis of Complex Organizations.* New York: The Free Press, 1961.

5. Lane, Robert E. *Political Ideology.* New York: The Free Press, 1962.

6. Lieberman, Bernhardt. "i-Trust," Research Memorandum, S.P. 105. New York: Department of Psychology, State University at Stony Brook, 1963.

7. Rummel, Rudolph J. "The Dimensions of Conflict Behavior within and between Nations," *General Systems Yearbook,* Vol. 8 (1963), pp. 1–50.

8. Schelling, Thomas C. *The Strategy of Conflict.* Cambridge, Mass.: Harvard University Press, 1960.

9. Tanter, Raymond. "Dimensions of Conflict Behavior within Nations, 1955-60: Turmoil and Internal War," *Papers,* Vol. III, Peace Research Society, Philadelphia: University of Pennsylvania, Department of Regional Science, 1965.

RESPONSES OF POLITICAL SYSTEMS TO STRESS ON SUPPORT

David Easton

Support as an Input of Systems

A political system may be described in any one of a number of ways depending upon the particular kind of emphasis we wish to give to it. At the most general level it is highly useful to depict a political system as a set of interactions through which valued things are authoritatively allocated for a society. But in addition to this formulation, a political system may be viewed as a means for resolving differences or as a set of interactions through which demands are processed into outputs. From another perspective, it is a means through which the resources and energies of society are mobilized and oriented to the pursuit of goals. In the last sense, the description is particularly helpful in highlighting the need for marshaling the support of the members if the system is to be able to act at all.

Fluctuations in support may stress a system in one or all of three different ways. First, without support for some of the authorities, at least, demands could not be processed into outputs. Only the smallest, least differentiated system could handle its demands if each time a decision had to be made, a new set of rulers arose and if each output requir-

SOURCE: Reprinted from David Easton, *A Systems Analysis of Political Life* (New York: John Wiley & Sons, Inc., 1965), by permission of the author and publisher. Reprinted section is condensed from pp. 153–467.

ing implementation gave rise to a different set of administrators. Most systems require some relatively stable set of *authorities*.

Second, without support it would be impossible to assure some kind of stability in the rules and structures through the use of which demands are converted into outputs, an aspect that will be designated as the *regime*. And third, support is vital in order to maintain minimal cohesion within a membership, an aspect of a system that I shall identify later as its *political community*. These three systemic consequences of the input of support will provide us with a framework for its analysis. Our inquiry into support will be directed toward the way in which solidarity around these three foci or *political objects*—the authorities, regime and political community—may be stressed and buttressed. These constitute the domain of support.

As measures of overt support, a variety of activities are typically taken into account: the numbers belonging to organizations; the regularity with which citizens or subjects perform their obligations; manifestations of open hostility such as breaches of the law, riots, or revolutions; and expressions of preferences for other systems through emigration or separatist activities. Hence the ratio of deviance to conformity as measured by violations of laws, the prevalence of violence, the size of dissident movements, or the amount of money spent for security, would provide individual indices of support. Although critical measurement problems would exist with regard to the construction of a single overall index or to a decision favoring the division of indicators into a variety of independent measures, the illustration of possible types does help to provide a concrete image of the kinds of overt activities from which the level of support might be inferred.

Most of these measures refer to past or current supportive activities of members. But to determine the probable future behavior, it becomes important to be able to make inferences, from observable actions or otherwise, about the state of mind of the members toward basic political objects.

Like all attitudes, covert support might be measured on an ordinal scale ranging from low to high. At the high end of the continuum we would place members who are so intensively supportive in their attitudes that they virtually obliterate themselves as independently acting persons. They would substitute the needs, ideals, and standards of the supported object for their own. Here we might locate members motivated by blind faith, unquestioning loyalty, or uncritical patriotism. At the low end of the continuum we would find those whose support is extremely negative, those who feel the deepest hostility to a system and are most decisively disengaged.

If we call the high end of the continuum positive support, those on the other end could be said to display negative support, as indicated in Diagram 1. Somewhere at the midpoint in the range

between these two ends of the scale, we would expect to find members who are indifferent to the political system. Here the input of positive support declines but has not been quite transformed into negative support (the actual withdrawal of all support or the presence of incipient feelings of hostility). The members are neither prepared to accept nor reject a system. Although terminological rigor would call upon us always to add to the idea of support, the qualifying adjectives positive or negative, this might be forcing ordinary usage too hard. Accordingly, unless the context indicates otherwise, the concept "support" will be used in a positive sense only and such synonyms as opposition, hostility, or decline of support will be used to indicate negative support.

Objects of Support: The Political Community

A member of a system will be said to extend support to his political community insofar as he stands ready to act on behalf of maintaining some structure through which he and others may play their part in the making of binding decisions or is favorably oriented towards its perpetuation, whatever form it may take from time to time and however insignificant the role of the average member may be in the division. A group of people who come together to draw up some kind of constitution to regulate their political relationship—as in the case of the thirteen colonies in America— thereby indicate their intention to share a division of political labor. The particular structure of the relationship may change, the members of the system may

High or positive support	Passive acceptance, acquiescence, or indifference	Low or negative support

←——→

Increasing support   Decreasing support

Diagram 1 Support Scale

be ranked, subdivided and rearranged politically so that the structural patterns are fundamentally altered. But as long as the members continue to evince an attachment to the overall group in which the changing interrelationships prevail and through which demands in a system are processed, they will be supporting the existence of the same and continuing community.

Not all changes in a political system need affect the political community. This is why there will always be residual ambiguity if we describe a political system as having changed and yet fail to specify the basic objects with regard to which the change has occurred. Authorities typically come and go, regimes or constitutional orders may change. In both cases the community may remain quite stable. If we take metropolitan France alone as an example, in its community aspects it has experienced little change since the French Revolution aside from minor fluctuations at its geographic boundaries. But this is not equally the case for France's regimes which have undergone innumerable drastic transformations. Governmental changes, if not at the administrative, at least at the leadership level, have been too numerous to count easily.

But political communities are capable of changing. This occurs at moments when the membership undergoes some internal subdivision indicating that whole groups have withdrawn their support from the pre-existing division of political labor. The American Civil War, like any political fission, illustrates concretely what occurs with the cessation of the input of support. The war itself offered evidence that the members of the American political system could or would no longer contribute together to the prior division of political labor through which binding decisions had been made for the society. Their attachment to the most inclusive group in and through which the tasks necessary for the processing

of demands to authoritative outputs were performed, was destroyed.

It was no longer a question in the United States of whether the South would support one or another alternative government, or whether it could envision its demands being satisfied through the normal procedures of the regime. The issue turned on whether the members could conceive of themselves continuing as a group that was part of and subject to the same set of processes for arriving at political decisions and taking political action. Support for such a group, which shared a division of political labor, had temporarily crumbled.

In principle, in addition to the kind of subdivision sparked by civil strife, a political community may lose its support, and thereby be destroyed, in several typical ways. Through emigration, if permitted, individuals may withdraw from a political community. If the trend is sufficiently pronounced as in the case of an informal but large-scale separatist movement, it could well affect the size, composition, and structure of the political community. The longing of some 60,000 members of the Ras Tafari sect in Jamaica to return to Nigeria or Ethiopia indicates the consequences of disillusionment with the benefits to be gained from continued participation in the Jamaican political community. In effect the poorest and most alienated blacks are saying not only that they dislike the authorities and regime of the whites and browns, but that they no longer have any feeling left for contributing by their presence to a common political structure with the whites and browns. They are choosing to share their labors, in resolving political differences, with the Nigerians or Ethiopians, the regime and governmental forms being left open-ended.

Perhaps the most decisive indicator of the withdrawal of support from a political community consists of group separation. By collective action a subgroup may hive off to join some pre-existing political community, in this way transferring support from one shared division of political labor to another, or to found an entirely new political system.

Objects of Support: The Regime

In referring to the persistence or change of a political system we may have in mind something quite different from the political community. The German political community had remained relatively intact after the first World War and in 1933. Yet no one could doubt that in both periods the system underwent fundamental changes when it shifted from the monarchy to the Weimar Republic in the first case, and from this Republic to the Nazi order in the second.

The political community that is Great Britain has experienced some limited modifications in the last century and a half, if we set aside the colonial empire and its vicissitudes. But in that period, Britain witnessed the introduction of the party system, many new rights for individuals and groups, popular suffrage, and a host of other clear constitutional changes of a kind that on any grounds may be considered fundamental in character.

If the members of a system consistently failed to support some kind of regime, this lack of support would drive the essential variables beyond their critical range and would thereby prevent a system from operating. It is this potential outcome associated with the regime that compels us to characterize it as a second fundamental component of a system.

The need for a regime stems from an elemental fact about human organization, however uncomplex it may be. Even if members of a group displayed the strongest feelings of mutual identification in a political community, they would still be left with the task of establishing some regularized method for or-

dering their political relationships. Ultimately, for the outputs to be accepted as binding, the members would need to accept some basic procedures and rules relating to the means through which controversy over demands was to be regulated and work out some ends that would at least broadly and generally guide the search for such settlements.

The regime as sets of constraints on political interaction in all systems may be broken down into three components: values (goals and principles), norms, and structure of authority. The values serve as broad limits with regard to what can be taken for granted in the guidance of day-to-day policy without violating deep feelings of important segments of the community. The norms specify the kinds of procedures that are expected and ' acceptable in the processing and implementation of demands. The structures of authority designate the formal and informal patterns in which power is distributed and organized with regard to the authoritative making and implementing of decisions—the roles and their relationships through which authority is distributed and exercised. The goals, norms, and structure of authority both limit and validate political actions and in this way provide what tends to become a context for political interactions.

Persistence of a system as a means for converting wants to binding decisions will depend in part, therefore, upon the capacity of the system to stimulate enough support so as to maintain some kind of viable regime. Without values, norms and structures of authority as broad and relatively stable limits (at least of a kind that can be activated and vitalized in moments of need or crisis) it is doubtful whether sufficient minimal order would prevail so as to enable the members to devote their time and energies to the tasks involved in processing demands through to outputs. If the politically relevant members are to be able to rally and commit human and other resources to the attainment of the specific ends involved in political outputs, they must be prepared to share an understanding of the range of matters that are subject to political action. They must also be willing to support rules through which differences may be negotiated and settled as well as structures through which the initiative and responsibilities may be taken. These are what we have identified as the regime of a political system.

Objects of Support: The Authorities

The occupants of the authority roles need to be clearly distinguished from the roles themselves. The presidency, prime ministership, or legislator are offices or highly formal roles that may endure for generations, even centuries, whereas the incumbents patently will change periodically. If we use the concept "authorities" to identify these occupants, generically it can be said to include members of a system who conform to the following criteria. They must engage in the daily affairs of a political system; they must be recognized by most members of the system as having the responsibility for these matters; and their actions must be accepted as binding most of the time by most of the members as long as they act within the limits of their roles.

If a system is to be able to deal with its daily affairs of converting demands into binding outputs, it is not enough for the members to support the political community and the regime. It is true, support for the structure of authority or for a given system of government as we often phrase it—as for a democracy or for the authority of a royal clan in a dominant lineage—would assure the perpetuation of the basic rules and structures through which demands might be processed. But it would not provide for any members of the system to conduct this business. Support for a pattern of relationships that we call a system of

government or regime is quite different from support for a given set of occupants for the roles of which the regime is composed.

The vital part played by support for the actual incumbents is brought out more prominently if we look at the negative condition. If the members lose confidence in the ability of any authorities at all to cope with the problems of the day, the effect on support to other levels of the system may be very serious, at least for the persistence of that kind of system. But if no authorities are seen as being equal to the tasks of managing the affairs of state and confidence in any set of authorities or any government is completely undermined—historically a most unusual but possible condition—the result is that no set of persons will be able to mobilize enough support behind them to make and put into effect the necessary day-to-day decisions. Clearly, the system would become paralyzed; it would lose its capacity to act as a collectivity.

STRESS THROUGH THE EROSION OF SUPPORT

Decline in support will stress a system but the decline alone need not lead to its fall. Even though the flow of support for an object were to slow to a mere trickle, this need not automatically bring about the abandonment of that object in favor of another.

It is true, at times in history, the withdrawal of support has been so sudden or widespread that a system has been left in utter chaos; or, as in the case of some developing systems today in Africa, insufficient support has been forthcoming during a transition period so that it is extremely difficult to keep a government in power, a constitution alive, and a community together. But where preexisting systems of some stability are threatened with loss of support, unless a counter-elite or organized groups are available and ready to give direction and impulse to the disaffected, the *status quo* can survive for long periods. Apathy, inertia or inadequate leadership have accounted for the persistence of political objects in many systems when the level of support is astonishingly low. Presumably this would be an indication that the politically relevant groups have not moved beyond the point of indifference on our support continuum. If they have shifted to outright antagonism—negative support—it would suggest that their morale, commitment, or resources may be such as to vitiate any will to act or to undermine their capacity to do so. But in the normal course of events, manifest antagonism would be the prelude to positive action of some kind.

Regardless of how we might specifically account for the existence of low support input, on the one hand and reluctance or inability to shift attachment to a new political object on the other, the main point is that erosion of support needs to be viewed only as a threat to the system. When support begins to slip away visibly, this is a danger signal to those who remain attached to the political objects and will typically trigger responses to prevent the support from falling too low.

OUTPUT FAILURE

Its Meaning. Since the failure of the authorities to produce adequate outputs is postulated as a major possible determinant of a decline in the input of support, our first task is to clarify the meaning to be attributed to this idea. Output failure will be said to occur under any one of the following circumstances. First, it arises when the authorities fail to take any action to meet the demands of the relevant members of a system. This will result in an imbalance between demands and outputs; that is, between what members have indicated they would like to see done and what the authorities are in fact able or willing to do.

Second, even if members have put in no specific demands about a matter, output failure may still occur. This is the case when the authorities fail to take action that anticipates conditions which may later arise and to which relevant members of the system might then object. It becomes output failure if the members blame the authorities for not having had the foresight or wisdom to have prepared for such an eventuality. Whether or not such an accusation is justified is immaterial. The effect on support is in considerable part not a matter of who, in fact, is to blame but whom the members of the system perceive as culpable. The fact that Hoover was not primarily responsible for the Great Depression is of importance; but from the point of view of the input of support it was more significant that a large proportion of the American membership saw him as the person to blame.

Third, the authorities may take action of an important nature that they interpret as a response to demands. But the outputs may in fact be considered by the affected members as quite inappropriate for the conditions or incompatible with their demands. In that event the failure has not been in the quantity but in the quality of the outputs. The probability is that the outputs would encounter more hostility than support and in that way add to any shortage of support.

Clearly, output will always be relative in character: relative to the number and kinds of demands as well as to the number of members in the system voicing these demands. At what point in the failure to meet demands, support will decline, constitutes an empirical matter. But theoretically, we need to recognize that at some point this will occur.

Its Effects. A further basic assumption here will be that if a system is unable to meet a minimal number of demands of most of the relevant members with some minimal frequency, it will be impossible to prevent these members from developing feelings of deep discontent. Initially, the discontent might be directed toward the authorities. But if, where possible, these are changed and especially if this happens again and again, and still little improvement in outputs occur, it will be impossible to prevent the dissatisfaction from shifting toward the regime and even the political community.

History amply testifies to the plausibility of this kind of progression of the effects of output failure. Many pacific and certainly most revolutionary transformations in regime or political community have occurred in this manner. They are preceded by repeated if not exhaustive efforts to eliminate present discontents by first appealing to the existing authorities for remedial action. Especially is this true where authorities occupy their positions ascriptively or by coercion and, accordingly, cannot easily be removed or changed. But frequently, even where the authorities have undergone periodic changes, as each set in turn proves unable to stem the tide of discontent, at some point, the relevant members will feel they have reached the end of the road as far as waiting and compromise are concerned. Unable to obtain their objectives by influencing the authorities, they are likely to feel the need to turn to more drastic measures in the form of efforts to modify the regime fundamentally or even to break up the community.

Most socio-political revolutions fit into this pattern as do even less traumatic and dramatic efforts to modify constitutional arrangements. They reflect persistent and recalcitrant output failure, at least as so perceived by the relevant members in the system. However, whether the loss of support resulting from output failure leads to the destruction of a system or its transformation will depend on a number of other contingencies as well. It is a necessary but not always sufficient condition.

The importance of outputs as one major variable contributing to the decline of support is demonstrated further, if such additional evidence is required, that to the extent that outputs are perceived or felt to meet demands, present or anticipated, they will thereby go a long way toward relieving any stress due to other conditions. Outputs themselves may frequently represent a vital kind of positive response to stress arising out of the erosion of support due to other causes and I shall treat them in just this way later, under the category of specific support.

Its Causes. What conduces to the outcome that I have described as output failure? The causes are varied and numerous; the task will be to devise a conceptually economical way of handling this multiplicity.

Output failure may be a product of the qualities of the authorities themselves—their human fallibility, their lack of wisdom, of skill in governing or of responsiveness to the members—or to the shortage of the necessary resources.

Major tendencies to output failure will be set in motion as a result of the degree of internal dissension and conflict to be found among the members of the system. Cleavages may so divide the relevant members that they find themselves unable to cooperate, negotiate, or compromise their differences even to the minimal extent necessary so as to discover some kind of acceptable output resolution. And cleavages give rise to other difficulties that compound these effects on support. Since cleavage will be interpreted as a central condition in inducing output failure and undermining support in other ways, it is to the basic consequences of cleavage that we must turn if we are to understand those conditions to which a system must be able to respond if it is to avoid or cope with stress in some way.

Cleavage as a Source of Stress

Cleavages may be defined either as differences in attitudes, opinions and ways of life or as conflict among groups. We may distinguish these as social diversity, or attitude cleavage, and political cleavage respectively. Unless the context indicates otherwise, I shall adopt a unified meaning so that the single word "cleavage" will henceforth embrace both types of divisions. What is clear is that potential stress on support for the political objects will derive both from the predispositions toward conflict implicit in the presence of social diversity because it breeds different attitudes, opinions and, therefore, demands; and from the more easily identifiable stress due to actively expressed conflicts among support groups.

THE CONSEQUENCES OF CLEAVAGES

Although I am emphasizing the stressful tendencies of cleavage in this unified meaning, I would not want this understood as implying that diversity and active conflict among groups must work in one direction only. Neither social diversity nor political cleavage is a synonym for disunity. They represent conditions that may also help to integrate a system. We need, therefore, to distinguish clearly and to bear constantly in mind the way in which diversity and cleavage may also promote support for a system.

Positive Supportive Consequences. The opportunity provided members to express conflicting points of view or to align themselves in contending support groups so as to influence the processing of demands may contribute to the unity and persistence of a system. Where the regime norms permit the free expression of diverse views, it is plausible to assume that, aside from any other consideration, it has a cathartic effect for the relationships of the members. In enabling them to vent their grievances and hostilities, it frees the air for the task of negotiating and compromising differences.

Evidence from research on small subsystems, such as trade unions, indicates that the presence of a legitimate internal opposition favors greater loyalty than the imposition of dictatorial rule.[1] If what is true for the smaller group may be extended to the broader political system, we would assume that it is valid to say that social diversity and political cleavage, under conditions of freedom of discussion and organization, contribute to the persistence of the political objects and under conditions of suppression work in the opposite direction.

Furthermore, many kinds of differences as well as cleavages may be complementary, compatible, or at least neutral with respect to each other. If different groups expressing conflicting demands have something to offer each other in the way of a trade for mutual support, any centrifugal forces set up by group cleavages may be avoided or mitigated. This suggests that differences alone need not mean stressful conflict if they are not competitive or mutually exclusive.[2]

Complementary but diverse attitudes or demands may even draw members together in support of all aspects of a system. At the legislative level, logrolling is a well-known manifestation of the way in which groups may go even further than the achievement of a mere accommodation of objectives. They are able to combine forces to their mutual advantage. To the extent that such co-

[1] S. M. Lipset, M. Trow, and J. S. Coleman, *Union Democracy* (Glencoe, Illinois: Free Press, 1956). For additional discussion of positive effects see L. A. Coser, *The Functions of Social Conflict* (Glencoe, Illinois: Free Press, 1956), especially chapters 4 and 7, and M. Gluckman, *Custom and Conflict in Africa* (Glencoe, Illinois: Free Press, 1955).

[2] K. W. Deutsch, S. A. Burrell, et al., *The Political Community and the North Atlantic Area* (Princeton: Princeton University Press, 1957), p. 90.

operation is possible, cleavage need not create dissatisfaction with a system and undermine support for its objects.

Hence, tendencies arising out of diversity and cleavage will contribute to the input of support for a system and need to be balanced against the opposite effects that they also induce. But even though cleavage may have such positive consequences, this is not to suggest that any system could maintain a sufficient input of support without creating conditions that lead to some degree of consensus. A system that was rent by cleavages and in which the members could agree on little else than to disagree, would seem to have little likelihood of surviving.

In the first place, by definition, cleavage spells diversity in points of view. It means as well that competing groups of members, organized or not, are to be found aligned behind one or another of these points of view. Regardless of the positive effects, even under conditions of free discussion and organization, the mere fact of such differences in outlooks and in organization must interfere with the extent to which the members of a political system are able to achieve compromises and to cooperate with regard to any objectives. Except under some very special conditions of complementarity in aims, each group or aggregate that differs with the other is competing for a share of the limited values in any system. Any increase in the degree of cleavage can be expected to aggravate the difficulties in the way of obtaining a settlement over outputs.

But, in the second place, not only do cleavages hamper the negotiation of coalitions based on possible resolutions of disagreements among groups. In addition, the hostilities engendered among the various groups may leave such scars over time that finally the participating members, profoundly dissatisfied with their total situation, may find themselves unable to accept a common regime

or political community. Their expectations about the future may be so colored by past frustrations that they may find it impossible to agree on any set of occupants for the authority roles, or on the ground rules for continuing to discuss differences. They may even become disinclined to continue to share the same division of labor as a single political community.

Finally, cleavages add to the centrifugal forces in a system by virtue of the fact that the groups involved, through their very presence, offer points of emotional attachment that seriously compete with the basic political objects for the loyalty of members. The particularistic orientations that group loyalties encourage offer an alternative that siphons support away from the system itself. This assumes that bitterness and discontent have already been aroused by output failures or by the recurrent trials and tribulations in seeking to work out what are at best unhappy compromises. In thus taking shelter within the plural groups to seek their basic satisfactions there, members will tend to aggravate an already divisive situation. Communal groupings and encapsulated minorities demonstrate just this kind of pull on the support of members in a system.[3]

[3] Cf. with the comments of Myron Weiner, *The Politics of Scarcity: Public Pressure and Political Response in India* (Chicago: The University of Chicago Press, 1962), p. 231, about India: "The problem of governmental responsiveness as opposed to governmental authoritarianism leads us appropriately to an exploration of the actual threats to the political system that are posed by community associations. Intense identification with one's community to the exclusion of a sense of national identification and a concern for the national interest could be an inhibiting factor in India's modernization. The adoption of the regional language through the school system and the colleges could decrease mobility of both individuals and ideas. Pressures for the employment of members of particular castes or linguistic groups, or for the exclusion of those who come from other states, could decrease efficiency in administration, in the colleges,

Structural Regulation of Support

Some erosion of support is inevitable in all systems; cleavage among collectivities and accompanying output failure could not be entirely avoided. In all systems, sharp conflict in competition for scarce social and economic values represent a normal aspect of political interaction. If we accept this assumption, we may infer that without some provision to compensate for the dissatisfaction with outputs or to regulate the relationships among actually or potentially conflicting groups, a system would be open to the constant and ultimate danger of disorder or chaos. How is this avoided? What varied means or responses typically prevent such forces from coming to a head?

Basic Types of Responses. The processes through which systems seek to maintain a minimal level of support for the political objects do not vary randomly among all systems. It is possible to identify typical kinds of responses to stress on support. In part, I shall show, they are geared to the direct reduction in cleavages through what will be called *structural changes,* especially in the regime. In part, they are designed to build up a reservoir of support upon which a system may draw credit in times when things are going badly from the point of view of providing satisfactions for the members of the system. This I shall examine under the heading of *diffuse support.* In further part, the responses may offer passing rewards for the support of some set of authorities without necessarily intending to add to the contentment with the regime or community. But support for the latter two objects may emerge as an added dividend. This kind of response, I shall describe as outputs; they will breed *specific support.*

HOMOGENIZATION

One of the major ways in which a system may respond to stress from the kind of cleavage brought about by intense social diversity is through efforts to encourage homogenization of the membership—the reduction or elimination of religious, linguistic, or other cultural differences among groups. To do this, the response may be of a sort that seeks to modify the regime rules (norms) in a number of ways. Where a system is able to provide, compatible with other rules of its regime, for a gradual program of fusing cultures, although this may not be expected to lead to utter hómogeneity, it can bring about some shrinkage in the gap among divergent groups.

But history has shown that such efforts at blending groups have normally proved unsuccessful as a source of marshaling support for the objects of a system. They tend to generate the opposite effect, leading to a secondary response on the part of the system in the form of coercion so as to bolster support. Extended periods of time alone, involving complicated and diffuse processes of assimilation, probably feasible only under conditions of loose political ties as in the case of early Britain or France, may bring about some measure of cultural uniformity and integration.

EXPRESSIVE STRUCTURES

Even if we leave this as a moot point, the fact is that a general kind of response adopted to maintain an adequate input of support for the community and regime itself, under conditions of multiple, rivalrous cultural units, has consisted of so structuring the regime that each group or grouping obtains institutional recognition in the political sphere and self-expression as a unit. Cooperation is encouraged by the creation of mutual

[*footnote 3 continued*
and in private employment. And the pressure of a number of ethnic minorities for the creation of separate states could, and does, continue to inject conflict, violence, and political instability into a number of states."

benefits to be derived by each of the participants to such an arrangement.

Although policies in the direction of homogenization may also be continued, the major hope of avoiding stress may lie in attempting to incorporate and manage rather than to eliminate the diversity of cultures. Typically, to this end the general structural response in a regime has been the introduction of some form of federal or confederal system. Through it, relatively self-contained cultural-linguistic-religious units retain a degree of control over their own continued identity.

REPRESENTATIVE STRUCTURES AS A RESPONSE

The differences among diverse groups may be shielded from aggravation by building into the system additional expressive structural means that give the groups an opportunity to attempt to resolve their differences, if at all possible, under acceptable ground rules. A major device for this purpose is to be found in all kinds of representative structures, including those typical of but not exclusively confined to democratic regimes. It is a response that seeks less to mute the differences or blend groups than to provide avenues for negotiation and reconciliation.

As a possible response to cleavages, representative structures in their many forms operate so as to enable groups to obtain access to the centers of authority in the system. Either the recruitment processes permit elites from the groups to occupy some of the authority roles; or the members of the group obtain some kind of sanctions, such as the popular vote, over those who do occupy these roles. The rise of middle class groups in the feudal and absolutist political systems of Europe led to just these kinds of adaptation in the existing regimes. These are vital and obvious functions of representative structures.

But representation does more than modify the elite recruitment patterns or means of control. It provides those who are affiliated with groups an opportunity to meet each other in a common forum so as to undertake negotiations to discover the exact nature of their differences, the degree of flexibility of each other's positions, and the extent to which reconciliation of points of view and demands is feasible. This lies at the heart of political interaction as demands move to conversion into outputs. It is a process no less typical of dictatorial than of democratic systems, of non-literate or traditional than of modern ones.

If we are to attribute a cleavage-reducing quality to representation, we must be prepared to interpret representation in a very broad sense. To confine it exclusively to popular representation in legislatures, as we find it in systems using popular electoral processes, would be to restrict this kind of cleavage response to simply one manifestation of representative structures.

Even in systems that provide representation based on general popular suffrage, competition and conflict among groups lead to the search for every possible avenue for bringing demands to bear upon the formulation and execution of decisions. The selection of administrative personnel to reflect the political points of view of groupings—say, of a particular ethnic or religious composition —or of specific occupational groups is a well-recognized way of coping with the general competition and cleavage over influence on outputs.

THE INTERSECTION OF POLITICAL STRUCTURES

A further structural mechanism for coping with cleavage stress is to be found in positive action that invites the overlapping of groups and groupings.[4]

[4] For the consequences of overlapping membership toward muting cleavages, see D. B. Truman, *The Governmental Process* (New York: Knopf, 1951), p. 510 ff; G. Simmel, *The Web*

For example, in systems where the regime permits party competition for the control of political office, the structure of the parties may develop in such a way as to encourage maximum inclusiveness. In recent decades the literature of political science has dealt extensively with the cleavage-reducing potential of the coalition as compared to the single-interest party so frequently found in multi-party political systems. Where each party restricts its appeal to only a limited class of members, cleavage is reinforced; where the parties seek to embrace the widest mixture of groups and individuals, as in two or three party systems, the political divisions are softened. In such instances the parties are able to draw together a variety of groups and thereby bring about some prior reconciliation of points of view.

Research has also suggested that electoral rules are responses available, at least for such competitive parties, for reinforcing the divisive or integrative consequences of party formations. The single member constituency, we suspect, encourages more inclusive points of view among representatives, whereas proportional representation and its variants offer incentives for the promotion of single and therefore divisive interests.

In the USSR, the Party is itself composite in character, drawing its membership from broad strata of the population. It also follows a calculated policy of seeding strategic social groups with party members. Multiple or overlapping membership of a limited sort is deliberately attempted by interlocking party members with membership in other groups. In this way, an effort is made to avert the growth of significantly diverging points of view among organizations and groups.

MODIFICATIONS IN REGIME NORMS

In addition to responses that affect the basic structure of a regime, various kinds of responses involving the manipulation or changes of other aspects of the regime contribute to the alleviation of the effects of cleavage on the input of support.

The Depoliticizing Norms. Since I intend only to illustrate the function of norms as responses muting cleavages, the part that they play may best be illuminated by considering that subclass of norms that helps to depoliticize political issues. Empirically, no system seems to forego the opportunity to use this mechanism and without it, probably no system could begin to handle the strains occasioned by cleavages due to issue conflict.

If each political controversy terminated completely upon the adoption of some output in relation to it and no residue of hostility were left behind among the participants, the effects of issue conflict in cleavages would be much less than they are. If no decision, once made, were ever challenged, resisted or raised again for new consideration, the issue would be completely deprived of further importance for cleavage. Each participant would start from the beginning, as it were, with regard to each new issue. Issues would simply smolder, flare up, and finally die away into a cold ash.

But this represents a limiting case that never occurs in reality. The fact is that the controversy surrounding an issue may leave a deposit of bitter hostility among the participants. If we now consider what would happen if parties and other groups managed to keep all issues alive, regardless of the steps taken

[footnote 4 continued
of Group-Affiliations, trans. R. Bendix (Glencoe, Illinois: Free Press, 1955); T. Parsons, " 'Voting' and the Equilibrium of the American Political System" in E. Burdick and A. J. Brodbeck (eds.), *American Voting Behavior* (Glencoe, Illinois: Free Press, 1959), pp. 80–120; R. E. Lane, *Political Life: Why People Get Involved in Politics* (Glencoe, Illinois: Free Press, 1959), chapter 14; and E. E. Schattschneider, *Party Government* (New York: Rinehart, 1942)

o resolve them, we can appreciate the need for all systems to make provision for taking some issues out of the arena of controversy.

If no issue could be withdrawn, the overflow effect could lead to a combining of issues of such an explosive character that the resulting cleavages could not help but destroy a system. This possible outcome would not stem only from the presence of an excessive number and variety of issues. It would also arise from the alignment of antagonistic support groups implicit in the notion of cleavage. In this speculative case of issue immortality, the stress of excessive numbers and variety of issues would link up with the stress from the increasing hostility among support groups.[5]

Types of Depoliticizing Responses. It appears that if a system is to take some steps to prevent issues from perpetuating themselves indefinitely and agglutinating around support groups, some means must be adopted for depriving issues of political value. Systems have developed a number of different kinds of responses.

In the first place, it has been suggested that sometimes there is a tacit agreement among the politically relevant strata to withdraw from the arena of political importance any disputed matter that might remain after some major conflict.[6] Normally this response might

be expected to occur only after considerable conflict has already been generated about an issue and the strains so occasioned have been recognized as highly dangerous to the regime or community. Alternatively, in anticipation, a struggle of this sort might be aborted before it even starts, by agreeing to consider it outside of politics.

Such withdrawal from political contention assumes that the politically relevant members are able to adopt or accept as a norm the idea that it is inappropriate or politically unacceptable to throw the relevant issues into the arena for dispute. But where, in advance, these members have been able to establish some constraints on the introduction of issues, they may be able to incorporate norms explicitly into the formal or informal constitution of the regime. The norms thereby acquire the status not of an implicit understanding but of a political settlement and indicate in advance a serious intent to exclude the particular area from political dispute. This is a second kind of response leading toward the withdrawal of issues from political life.

Constitutions that forbid governments from trespassing on certain areas such as religion or freedom of speech, that establish official languages, or provide for the procedures in selecting and rejecting political authorities, thereby help to depoliticize these matters. Not that

---

[5] Of course, I make the further assumption that each issue would not call up a new and unique combination of forces behind it. Rather there would be a tendency, as there is at least in those systems with political parties or factions within single parties, for positions on issues to correspond to existing group divisions. This assumption is entirely reasonable since existing groups will seek to take advantage of each old and each new issue, as a means of extending the base of its support among the members of the system.

[6] ". . . the gradual depoliticization of the continuing difference between Protestant and Catholic religious values in the course of the eighteenth century furnished an essential precondition for the successful amalgamation of Germany and Switzerland, respectively, in the course of the following century. Examples of a partial

depoliticization of conflicting values include the partial depoliticization of the slavery issue in the United States between 1775 and 1819, and of the race problem after 1876. Similarly, Germany saw a reduction in the political relevance of the liberal-conservative cleavage after 1866 with the emergence of the National Liberal Party. A similar reduction of political relevance occurred in regard to the conflict of Scottish Presbyterianism with the Episcopal Church in England and Scotland after 1690, and in the further abatement of the Protestant-Catholic issue in Switzerland after the mid-eighteenth century, and further after 1848." K. W. Deutsch, S. A. Burrell, *et al.,* *op. cit.,* pp. 46–47.

any agreed-upon constitutional restraints on the use of power are forever locked in some drawer labeled "not for political use." But being in that drawer, either they are in fact less accessible or it is evidence that the members of the system prefer to put them outside the realm of day-to-day controversy.

The two kinds of responses I have been talking about —tacit agreements and incorporation into constitutional restraints—act in a way so as to prevent, if possible, the sparking of a cleavage-inducing issue. There is a third kind of response that takes an existing controversy, removes it from the open political arena, and siphons it through special channels in a system so that the effects of the cleavage are controlled. This consists of the processes of adjudication. In modern society, what we call legal settlements may be viewed as a universal response to the stress inherent in political cleavages. It has long been recognized as a means, not for eliminating conflict but for regulating it so that it is less likely to create unnecessary stress on the political system.

Adjudicative processes provide presumed or known and accepted rules under which differences can be adjusted and, thereby, they may whittle conflict down to a minimum. Even though adjudication may require the formal alignment of members on different sides, and, in fact, it has often been compared to a stylized but pacific jousting match, the degree of cleavage is confined to the actual partipants. In many judicial systems those who may feel affected by the ultimate outcome tend to be excluded, unless they can demonstrate a very special interest. Hence this procedure helps to confine a dispute, to prevent it from spreading and infecting other members. It thereby helps to reduce the degree of cleavage that might otherwise be generated if either violence or legislative methods had been adopted as a mode for seeking settlement.

Furthermore, adoption of judicial processes implies the antecedent acceptance of the idea that an established rule does or must exist for the settlement of the issue, that it has some degree of commonly recognized equity and justice about it, that it has the sanction of the community behind it, and that it ought to be obeyed. Without such assumptions a process of judicial settlement could not prevail. The submission of disputes to judicial settlement predisposes the disputants to accept the settlement and therefore, to limit the duration of the cleavage. Not that appeals may not be made from the judicial processes to the field of legislation or violence, a mark of the failure of judicial processes in reducing cleavage. By regularizing the process of adjusting difference, expectations with regard to the outcome are stabilized, and if, in addition, sentiments of justice and equity are associated with the rules applied, the degree of discontent attached to a judicial resolution of a conflict is minimized.[7]

The Generation of Diffuse Support

No system could rely exclusively on direct measures, such as those of modifying the structure and norms of the regime, as devices to alleviate cleavage or to compensate for output failure. However careful, facilitative, and powerful the authorities of a regime were,

[7] Judicial decisions of the Supreme Court in the United States might seem to dispute this interpretation since they have regularly served as the focal point for the alignment of hostile groups. In some cases, as recently with respect to racial integration, they have even sparked new manifestations of old cleavages. But we have only to think of the severity of conflicts that might have arisen, if the resolution of racial cleavages were left entirely in the hands of the normal legislative or other political processes, to realize the ultimate tendency, even in this case, of judicial processes to moderate the cleavages. Nor does this interpretation mean that judicial processes need never aggravate differences. We can speak only of average tendencies, not of all possible outcomes in individual instances.

however successful efforts might be in regulating cleavage, there could be little expectation of ever coming close to erasing all conflicting differences. Some dissensus and political cleavage must always prevail.[8]

Fortunately whether or not, through structural changes of the kind dealt with, efforts to compensate for the dangers inherent in political cleavages could alone ever prove adequate to permit the persistence of any system is a theoretical point we do not have to consider further. Empirically, we can point to no system that relies exclusively on such mechanisms. In every system two other general categories of responses are constantly available to maintain a minimal level of support for the various political objects. I shall identify these as specific and diffuse support.

OUTPUTS AND SPECIFIC SUPPORT

Implicit in what I have already said about outputs is the idea that, in part, support for any of the political objects will, in the long run, depend upon the members being persuaded that outputs are in fact meeting their demands or that they can be expected to do so within some reasonable time. Output failure can be said to occur when members feel that outputs are not likely to do so.

But what is of importance here is that, at times, the input of support may flow as a consequence from some specific satisfactions obtained from the system with respect to a demand that the members make, can be expected to make, or that is made on their behalf. Where support is in this way a *quid pro quo* for the fulfillment of demands, I shall call it specific support.

For example, a trade union seeks a higher minimum wage and persuades

the legislature to approve of it. Elderly members and those responsible for them seek publicly controlled programs of medical care. Farmers appeal for a more generous underpinning of the prices for their produce and obtain laws to that effect. A manufacturer argues for and wins a higher tariff for his goods. Here the gratifications can all be related specifically to the outputs. Even in the case of what the economists call indivisible benefits—such as the satisfactions obtained from knowing that the country is well defended, that the authorities are working toward a peaceful world, that the various public services are well attended to, or that the monetary and other resources are being frugally spent—the linkage between the outputs or actions of the authorities on the one side, and the response of the members on the other is, in principle at least, sufficiently close so as to be able to trace out the effects of the one on the other. In the eyes of the members, there is some connection between their wants or demands and the activities of the authorities.

THE INSUFFICIENCY OF
SPECIFIC SUPPORT

Against the stimulation of specific support as a response related to the persistence of a system, we know from history that members of a system have proved able to tolerate long periods of frustration in the satisfaction of their wants without support falling below the minimal level and passing over the threshold into stress. Indeed, no regime or community could gain general acceptance and no set of authorities could expect to hold power if they had to depend exclusively or even largely on outputs to generate support as a return for specific and identifiable benefits. Other means of adaptation to stress are necessary.

Postponement of Benefits. If a system were forced back on specific support alone, responses to encourage its growth

[8] L. A. Coser, *op. cit.*; R. Dahrendorf, *Class and Class Conflict in Industrial Society* (Stanford: Stanford University Press, 1959); and M. Gluckman, *Custom and Conflict in Africa* (Glencoe, Illinois: Free Press, 1955).

might often prove futile. It is not always feasible to balance outputs against demands so that the wants of most politically relevant members are met most of the time. All systems require of individual members, groups and often of whole generations that they sacrifice present goods for future rewards. Frequently it is transparent to all that present actions can benefit only future generations. In effect, a system asks its members to subordinate present known wants to future uncertain rewards for unknown descendants.

If it were not that, as members of political systems, we are all so accustomed to accepting the validity of such "sacrifices," we might well consider it an extremely doubtful matter as to whether we could expect people to postpone their present demands for tenuous future gains for remote others. Yet in the face of the apparent impracticality of such an imposition, whole ideologies of sacrifice, implicit in Marxism and in the varied less structured belief systems of developing countries, are able to thrive on the prospect they hold out of delaying material gains to the future generations.

DIFFUSE SUPPORT

This analysis enables us to identify diffuse or unconditional attachment as a second type of support. As we have seen, specific support flows from the favorable attitudes and predisposition stimulated by outputs that are perceived by members to meet their demands as they arise or in anticipation. The specific rewards help to compensate for any dissatisfactions at failing to have all demands met. But simultaneously, members are capable of directing *diffuse* support toward the objects of a system. This forms a reservoir of favorable attitudes or good will that helps members to accept or tolerate outputs to which they are opposed or the effect of which they see as damaging to their wants.

At its highest level of input, although from the point of view of an ethic of rationality, not necessarily in its most admirable form, the reservoir of diffuse support might be fed by a feeling of blind loyalty to the authorities, regime or community. Such unquestioning loyalty reflects a kind of attachment for which specific benefits are not expected except for the psychic satisfactions of identification with or subordination to a higher cause or object. If we assume that most kinds of patriotism reflect some degree of deep attachment, such attitudes enable a system to violate the expectations of its members with considerable impunity. If excessive and noisy patriotism is a poor symbol of true support, at least the notion of *la patrie,* in its finest sense, identifies the presence of powerful ties to the political community for itself alone rather than for what the individual expects to derive from it, ties that only persistent failure in outputs would be likely to sever.

But regardless of the many names we have for the sentiments that define diffuse support, its one major characteristic is that since it is an attachment to a political object for its own sake, it constitutes a store of political good will. As such, it taps deep political sentiments and is not easily depleted through disappointment with outputs.

Diffuse Support for Authorities and Regime: The Belief in Legitimacy

The inculcation of a sense of legitimacy is probably the single most effective device for regulating the flow of diffuse support in favor both of the authorities and of the regime. A member may be willing to obey the authorities and conform to the requirements of the regime for many different reasons. But the most stable support will derive from the conviction on the part of the member that it is right and proper for him to accept and obey the authorities and to abide by the requirements of the regime. It reflects the fact that in some vague or explicit way he sees these objects as conforming to his own moral principles, his own sense of what is right and proper in the political sphere.

The strength of support implicit in this attitude derives from the fact that it is not contingent on specific inducements or rewards of any kind, except in the very long run. On a day-to-day basis, if there is a strong inner conviction of the moral validity of the authorities or regime, support may persist even in the face of repeated deprivations attributed to the outputs of the authorities or their failure to act.

Systems give the appearance of behaving on the assumption either that feelings of legitimacy cannot be readily stored or, if so, any reserve can be quickly dissipated. Special measures appear to be necessary to assure its continuing input. It may be that the pressures from cleavages and output failures, ineluctable as they are in all systems, are intuitively felt to be gnawing constantly at the bases of support. At the least, the behavior of all systems suggests that there is the fear that without constant efforts to inspire a conviction about the rightness of the regime and its authorities, members might quickly lose the feeling that there is a special "oughtness" about the outputs. Special measures are everywhere taken to insure its input—everywhere, that is to say, where legitimacy is the source of support for the objects of a system.

Broad legitimating principles and values are reinforced by subsidiary, derivative, and related norms through which the principles are implemented. In addition, constant efforts are made to associate the day-to-day authorities with the structural legitimacy of the regime itself. Just as through their personal qualities, leaders may be successful in spreading the aura of legitimacy over a regime, the appeal of an existing regime

as legitimate is used to validate the actions of the particular incumbents of the authority roles.

Every system seeks to strengthen ties of legitimacy through the propagation of appropriate ideologies. Such symbolic responses are intensified through concrete expression in rituals, ceremonies and physical representations of the regime.[9] Together, on the varied and numerous occasions when they are brought into play, they serve to bolster an aura of sanctity, respect, and reverence for the existing political institutions and to reassert the legitimacy of the incumbent authorities. Accession and installation ceremonies, display of the physical symbols of authority such as coats of arms, wands, or seals of state, favored ceremonial treatment for individuals representative of the special character of the regime, special penalties for offenses against such representative persons, displays on patriotic holidays and events, all stand as specific and variable responses that nurture diffuse support. By focusing on the major political values of the system, on the exemplary character of the incumbents of authority roles, or on their conformity to the regime, such procedures are able to contribute to the reinforcement of sentiments of legitimacy.

Diffuse Support for Authorities and Regime: The Belief in a Common Interest

In many although not all systems, as an additional source of diffuse support, we usually find a belief that has quite different consequences from those I have referred to as legitimating ideologies. This is the conviction that there is something called the interest of the realm, the public, common, or national interest, the general good and public welfare, or

---

[9] For a discussion of the means used, C. E. Merriam, *Political Power* (New York: McGraw-Hill, 1934).

the good of the tribe, of "our people." The authorities through the regime are represented as the major spokesmen for this interest. This common interest is viewed as taking priority over local, ethnic, class, or other component interests within a society.

Regardless of the particular words used to express this notion, in part it is closely affiliated with the conception of legitimacy. In systems where the idea of a general interest is a test of policy cherished by most members, any perceived, serious, and persistent deviation from it by the authorities would certainly help to undermine belief in their legitimacy. If the feeling were to prevail that the regime itself militated against the public interest, in time continued acceptance of the regime as right and proper could not be taken for granted. But separate and apart from any possible effect on beliefs in legitimacy, the conviction that there is a general good, that it can be determined or defined, that it makes intuitive sense to use it as a guide for political action, and that the authorities through the regime ought to pursue and promote this general good, have important consequences for the solidarity of the members behind a regime and its related authorities.

Wherever the conception of a general interest actively operates, it helps to regulate or limit the disposition toward divisive behavior on the part of the politically relevant members in general. It accomplishes this basically through the fact that such a belief pushes in the direction of establishing common standards for evaluating outputs. Not that all members of a system will interpret the consequences of outputs in identical terms. But however they may perceive the results of policies or administrative acts, for example, if members assume they are all using a similar standard for judging their desirability—a shared idea of a common good—this will reduce one of the major sources of differences.

This does not mean that the adoption of a political vocabulary that speaks of a general interest or common good will necessarily invest the phrase with the same content; it may conceal inextinguishable valuational differences that do in fact exist among members in conflict over policy. Nor need the adoption of a common test for evaluating policy eliminate strife; members may still use the same test but because of conflicting judgments in applying it, they may stand diametrically opposed. Nevertheless, as we shall see, this vocabulary does have possible beneficial aspects from the point of view of the input of diffuse support.

We can perhaps better appreciate this tendency if we envisioned a political system in which the members assumed just the opposite, that is, that there was not and could not be a general interest, however it is described. Presumably debate would be formulated exclusively in terms of what would be best for each of the participants. This does not signify that the disputants would necessarily be unable to reach agreement on outputs; self-interest might dictate a strategy of mutual accommodation. But what would be lacking is a prior conviction that a policy could be found that would transcend the demands of any particular group and yet be acceptable to all on the basis of some criterion other than particularistic wants. To the extent that this conviction is absent, it could not help but aggravate the differences. To the extent that such a belief is present, at the very least it backstops any failure of expediency and, at its level of most effective operation, it offers a positive base for compromise.

In practice, it is undoubtedly true that outputs promoted on the grounds that they serve a broader and higher interest may reflect or be designed primarily to meet the wants and demands of a narrow or limited combination of political groups. Nevertheless, regardless for the moment of this concealed effect, the ideology of a common interest does serve as a social sanction or norm to impel members to substitute for their own private or particular wants, a new or different one, that of a higher entity or ideal called the common good. It helps to orient the members of the system to the wants of others in the system and to the necessity of outputs that transcend particular demands. Insofar as members can be induced to accept an output as satisfying the common good, the failure of outputs to accord with particular demands can be more readily or willingly accepted. It can be justified and interpreted as a necessary subordination of private wants to the general good.

In thereby tempering the degree of discontent that might otherwise be stimulated by dissatisfaction with the authorities or the regime, or by the lack of a *quid pro quo* for support, the idea of a common interest helps to maintain the input of a broader, diffuse kind of support for the authorities and regime.

Diffuse Support for the Political Community

Whatever other measures that may be taken, most systems typically anticipate possible stress, due to a decline in support, by striving to arouse and nurture among its members what I have earlier called a sense of political community or of mutual political identification.

STIMULATION OF A SENSE OF POLITICAL COMMUNITY: PARAMETERS AS RESPONSES

The Impact of the Division of Political Labor. What means have typically arisen to help create and encourage feelings of mutual political identifications? In part it appears as an automatic product of existing sets of interlocking roles, groups and institutions. The complex web of communications and political relationships forms social and political ties that help to reinforce their own

maintenance once they have come into existence, whatever the initial cause.

Although any division of political labor will set in motion many cleavages and other centrifugal political forces, the facts of sharing political processes, participating in interdependent political roles, and partaking in the same communication network will in themselves contribute to perpetuating the need to do so. The growth of an administrative staff, of an orientation to the same sets of leadership cadres even if they are in partisan conflict over day-to-day policy, the assimilation of similar kinds of political techniques, styles and general know-how within the context of a given group of people, and sensitivity to each other's cultural cues in various roles, help to predispose members of a system to seek to continue the group within which these interactions have taken place and continue to be possible. The resulting learned patterns of political interaction and habits of communication within a group are not easily or lightly abandoned. Not that these tendencies are necessarily decisive. Pressures of output failure, severe cleavages, or feelings of oppression and exclusion may quickly override them.

But, it may be argued, interdependence created by a political division of labor just constitutes a set of consequences that accompany political existence. They can scarcely be considered responses to potential stress even in a general sense.

It cannot be denied that there is some merit to this position. But it need not discourage us entirely from viewing the political consequences of a division of labor as responses. Members of a system or a potential political community are not ignorant of the fact that participation in some form of political interaction is relevant to strengthening the feelings of common political bonds. This is very much the source of arguments in favor of the formation of international functional organizations, for universal participation in the United Nations and, in all cases, for seeking to bring disputing and contending groups together in some kind of organization for purposes of meeting and talking together regularly. Part of the motivation for suggestions along these lines may lie in the desire to promote the ethical position that pacific settlement of differences is superior to the use of violence. But, in addition, these proposals involve the premise that the interactions themselves offer an opportunity for some sense of mutual identification to take root and grow. Whether, in fact, this does occur is not the question here. All that we need conclude is that any steps that members of a political system take to encourage such continuing interaction or to promote any conditions of political cooperation represent the use of means to regulate the level of mutual identification.

Responses through Modification of Parameters. In fact, we may go further and say that many of the variable conditions in the environment of a political system are available to the members for regulating feelings of mutual political identification. This puts a somewhat different light on recent research in international relations and new nations, for example, as it affects the parameters of political integration. In effect we may now conceive that such studies illuminate the range of alternative responses through which a sense of political community may be created or developed.

For example, the conclusions from such research on the conditions that contribute to increasing the social homogeneity of a society, may now be interpreted as possible response mechanisms for infusing the members of the political system with a deeper sense of mutual identification. Until recently the emphasis of this research has been on mechanisms that have sought to reduce diversity in society. It has been based on the premise that the more complex and differentiated the society, the wider the geographic dispersion of the members, and the broader the heterogeneity of customs, language, or religion, the greater the need for communications of all sorts to increase the positive feelings and orientation of the members toward each other.

Empirically, the validity of the premise seemed borne out by the great emphasis in new nations on the adoption of restricted common languages for official purposes, on centralized control over educational institutions and curricula, and on careful regulation of mass media. Implicit is the assumption that by manipulating these social parameters so as to increase the literacy level, improve the media of communication, encourage the compatibility of religions and the goals of the members and the uniformity of language, a broad consistency of values and general culture might be attained. Thereby identification as members of a common political unity might have the opportunity of emerging.

From more recent inquiry, however, we would be led to conclude that even though modifications of such social parameters may be helpful and necessary, they would remain quite insufficient to bring about a high sense of political community. To do so, it may be necessary to link to them other kinds of measures that increase the "mutual responsiveness" of the members and their expectations of strong future rewards as participants in a system. In addition, efforts would be required that create the perception of an equitable balance of rewards among the component units in the system, buttressed with a relatively high degree of mutual predictability of behavior.[10]

It is true that the deliberate creation of conditions such as these has been

[10] K. W. Deutsch and S. A. Burrell, *et al., op. cit.,* chapter 4 has a complete list and detailed discussion of them.

suggested because of their particular relevance to the developing integration of whole social entities such as societies. Yet for political systems, in our conceptualization they do constitute independent, external variables. Their manipulation in the appropriate direction through political action could be expected to generate or strengthen any sense of political community. This sentiment in turn would add to the store of diffuse support for the political community.

STIMULATION OF A SENSE OF POLITICAL COMMUNITY: POLITICAL VARIABLES AS RESPONSES

Political Responses in General. The literature on nationality and nationalism has dealt exhaustively with the varied devices for stimulating a sense of cohesion. Concrete responses for the expression and reinforcement of a sense of community appear in patriotic ceremonies, the physical symbols of group identity such as totems, flags, songs, canonized heroes and, in literate societies, even in such trivial manifestations as the coloring of territorial maps. As in the case of the authorities and the regime, the processes of political socialization operate on maturing members of a system and contribute to the internalization of supportive attitudes toward the political community. Where such socialization is effective, it leaves the conviction that the perpetuation of the given division of political labor is a good in and of itself.

Ideology as a Special Response. The sense of political community may be described as a we-feeling among a group of people, not that they are just a group but that they are a political entity that works together and will likely share a common political fate and destiny. Ideology plays an important role in promoting this belief and sentiment.

To some extent, a feeling such as this will emerge as a by-product of a common history and of related shared traditions and expectations—the past experiences that the group has already undergone and which have been transmitted to each succeeding generation. To some extent it will be based upon what happens to the contemporary generation regardless of past experience. But in both instances, whether we are referring to the shared history of the members of a system or to the current collective experiences, if these factors are to have any impact on the community feelings of the members of the system and especially upon upcoming generations, they must be interpreted and codified in a form that makes them readily visible, accessible, and transmissible over the generations. Ideology performs this function for the political community.

Thus, the common ties of membership in a political system have been expressed in the form of kinship bonds traced back through common ancestors as revealed in a patronym or other group symbol, as attachment to the soil of a common geographically defined region, or in the assertion of a common nationality. The nation may be held out as the ideological symbol in terms of which the members of a system interpret their common political bonds as against the particularistic identification with tribe, village, region or class. Its potency for raising the level of otherwise uncommitted diffuse support is well enough established in the modern period to require no further elaboration. In their belief structure, members may see themselves as a "people" with a common past, destiny, and fate—a sentiment latent in the idea that "we" are French or American and that "they" are alien and outsiders. These belief systems need to be contrasted with the ideas held by members in other political systems that their primary bond stems from the fact that each has a personal obligation to a ruler or chief. Only in him, rather than in some collectivity, is the unity of the group to be expressed and maintained. Even the word community itself, used in its practical or lay meaning rather than its theoretical sense, stands as an ideological mechanism for summoning up support for the political community.

The Nature of Outputs

Where the stress on a system threatens to reduce the level of support for one or another of the political objects, we have considered the various kinds of responses that typically emerge to enable it to cope with the stress through stimulating the input of diffuse support. Not that the system need survive or persist in its original form. Change, adaptation, self-maintenance, or redirection of efforts and goals are all equally means of coping with stress. But the important thing is that through the encouragement of diffuse support, it is possible for a society to perpetuate attachment to some set of authorities, to some regime, and to some kind of political community.

We have now come to the point where we can consider the second major kind of response by which a system, through the actions of its authorities, may seek to cope with the erosion of support. This response consists of a flow of outputs which, through their consequences, feed back into the system and may thereby add to (or subtract from) the level of support available to the political objects. Because of its direct relationship to the outputs, I have previously labeled it specific support.

Through various responses, the authorities may succeed in generating, not the diffuse attachment associated with legitimacy, dedication to a common interest, or identification with a political community, but the favorable attitudes that stem from offering the members of a system some felt or perceived returns and that accordingly appeal to their sense of self-interest. It is a form of

what might be called political pump priming.[11]

The link between outputs and the input of support is much more direct and discernible than in the case of diffuse support. Yet each kind of support will spill over to the other and influence it. Empirically, that is to say, the prolonged encouragement emerging from specific support, as I have noted before, will be likely to lead to deep attachment to the various political objects in general. If a person feels favorably disposed toward an object for specific reasons and with sufficient frequency, he may develop an attachment to the object for its own sake alone.

AUTHORITATIVE OUTPUTS

Authoritative Statements. When they appear as statements, authoritative allocations take the form of verbal indications of the binding rules that are to guide the performance of tasks. They are decisions on the part of the authorities that certain actions should be or will be taken. In a legal system, they appear as laws, decrees, formal legislation, regulations, or administrative and judicial decisions. In non-legal systems, they may simply be the opinion of a council of elders or of a paramount chief, about what ought to be done under the circumstances. But whatever the specific form, they stand as authoritative outputs since they indicate that the authorities intend that activities will be undertaken to maintain or modify the distribution of some of the valued things in the given society.

Although it is true that such statements are usually prolegomena to action to be taken under their authorization or justification, nevertheless, aside from these performances, the statements themselves may act independently so as to

[11] A term suggested to me by Professor Lawrence Senesh, Department of Economics, Purdue University.

contribute to or ameliorate stress on a system due to output failure. For example, the promised or indicated output may never occur; it may prove impossible to implement the decision, or the authorities concerned may never have seriously intended to do so. Yet the verbal output may in itself affect the attitude of the members and to obtain the input of their support, this may be sufficient.

The importance of all statements derives from the fact that persons obtain some satisfaction from symbols, as we shall see in greater detail shortly. Verbal symbols, such as those embodied in ideologies, are able to stimulate or relieve inner tensions and articulated demands. In many cases, the statement that a given situation exists, or that sometime in the distant future action will be taken, or that action is already under way may be enough, regardless of the actualities, to provide members with the gratifications they seek in the political processes or with the release from frustrations they would like to avoid. A law protecting civil liberties, even if it is not regularly or vigorously invoked and enforced, may nevertheless constitute an output capable of purchasing considerable support for the authorities or hostility (negative support) on the part of those opposing it. How far verbal expression can go in either direction is another matter. Man does not live by words alone; but they can substitute for real nourishment over considerable intervals of time.

Authoritative Performances. By implication, I have already suggested the general nature of authoritative performances. Binding decisions concerning what will or ought to be done may not be enough. Members also seek the actual goods and services implied; or the authorities expect that the goods and services required by the authoritative decisions will be forthcoming. Performances may take the form of compelling others to do something, such as to pay taxes or serve in the armed forces. Performances may involve doing things for others such as extinguishing a fire, arresting a violator of the peace, transmitting funds or food in the execution of foreign aid.

In cases such as these, the allocation of values is a direct implementation of a verbal statement of the intention to perform the actions, if the circumstances arise. Performance consists of the actions actually taken in the light of the circumstances that exist when an effort is made to implement the formal decision. The performance represents the effective as against the formal allocation of values.

But a statement of intention is not intrinsic to performance outputs and need not precede the action. The authorities may just act without forewarning or any foreshadowing of their inclinations. Whether or not there are verbal outputs that precede or accompany the performance outputs is a matter of indifference here. What we are concerned with is the effort to isolate the possible independent effect, not of what the authorities say or promise, but of what they do or have done, on the generation of specific support.

Performance outputs will assume two forms. In one, some tangible objects or facilities will be provided; in the other, some intangible services.[12] Tangibles are the stock in trade of authorities as sources for stimulating support. Money may be distributed as through the payment of unemployment insurance or public relief. Physical facilities, visible and usable, may be provided in the form of

[12] Here I am indebted to an original and stimulating discussion of outputs in a forthcoming work by Bertram Gross entitled *The Managing of Organizations: The Administrative Struggle*, 2 vols. (New York, Free Press of Glencoe, 1964), especially chapters 21–23. In it, Gross distinguishes between tangible and intangible outputs of organizations. He compellingly demonstrates the considerable possibilities for measuring outputs of both kinds, a task which passes beyond our scope.

highways, power plants, dams, military hardware. In socialized societies, the authorities undertake to provide most of the major goods and facilities and accordingly have at their disposal vast means for influencing the level of support in a negative as well as a positive direction.

But in all systems the authorities also engage in allocating intangible services such as law and order, defense, transportation, education, or medical attention. Performances such as these may be related to tangible things, their possession or use, as in the case of dams, highways, railways, or hospitals. But the ultimate satisfaction comes from the services provided through these facilities.

Intangible outputs often embrace various kinds of psychic rewards which may be distributed by the authorities and which may be even more capable of fostering support than material goods. Through outputs it has been possible to contribute to a group's sense of dignity or worth, as in cases where discrimination on the grounds of race, creed, or color has been prohibited, or where ethnic groups may be carefully included in positions of esteem among the authorities. Where outputs enable deprived groups to share in the basic values of a society, even though such groups may not be materially better off and even though improved social services may not be put at their disposal, the opportunity to participate in these values may arouse deep and enduring supportive sentiments. Although status, prestige, recognition, and social equality are states of mind that cannot be legislated into existence, outputs that help to allocate these values in a system, intangible as they are, cannot be neglected in our consideration of sources of support.

ASSOCIATED OUTPUTS

Associated outputs are those statements and performances that are connected in some way with the authoritative outputs and which could not have the consequences they do unless they were so associated. In and of themselves either these statements and performances would prove ineffective or they would have little chance of occurring.

Associated Statements. The associated statements that I am calling outputs, we meet in the guise, sometimes, of ideological convictions or rationales and at others, as simple articulations of policy. In each case they derive their effectiveness for fostering or eroding support from the fact that they accompany and help to interpret or explain authoritative statements or actions. The full implications and meaning of a binding decision or set of actions may not be apparent to the members of a system or the allocations involved may not be appreciated in the way considered desirable by the authorities. Whatever capacity such authoritative outputs may have to increase or discourage support may be reinforced or counteracted as the case may be, by associated statements that succeed in interpreting, explaining, or elaborating the implications of the outputs.

For example, in developing systems, decrees restricting freedom of speech and organization may be made more palatable when the authorities link them to the need to cope with conditions permitting rapid economic growth and retaining national independence. The ideologies of nationalism and of the significance of material growth induce members to tolerate or accept such outputs more readily. The ideological statements accompany the outputs but unlike the laws limiting freedom, these statements do not represent binding allocations. Yet the ideological statements, as associated outputs, may have an enormous influence upon the way in which the authoritative outputs are received. They may make the difference between acceptance and total rejection.

Associated statements may also appear in the form of policies. We are accustomed to thinking of policies in two senses.[13] In the one, we refer to the decision rules adopted by authorities as a guide to behavior. This is the meaning of the term when we talk about those policies that are in fact adopted by authorities as the binding operating rules. This is what we may mean when we question the wisdom of the policy of a government as incorporated into its laws on a subject. In this sense, policies would just be a term for a kind of authoritative verbal output.

But the term is also used in a second and broader sense to describe the more general intentions of the authorities of which any specific binding output might be a partial expression. As such, the statements of policies are not binding for the members. But by revealing the intentions of the authorities, they do help to interpret the meaning and direction of authoritative outputs and to this extent may encourage or discourage their acceptance by the membership.

Associated Performances. The satisfactions coming from a political system are also intimately connected with performances which assume the form of tangible goods and intangible services associated with authoritative action and yet which do not themselves acquire any binding quality. In many instances, the growth of specific support owes as much to these associated performances as to those that are manifestly authoritative in character.

Incidental to the position that a person in authority holds, he will be able to take action that possesses a binding quality and accordingly falls into our category of authoritative outputs. But in addition, the position of authority will improve his opportunity to grant benefits, advantages, favors and facilities that stem from the range of discretion, power, special knowledge, and skills linked with his position. Through control over money, position, prestige and power itself, a person in authority may be able to regulate informally the allocation of these values so as to influence the level of specific support, both positively from those who benefit and negatively from those who may suffer.

Various motivations may lurk behind associated performances of this kind. To begin with, they need not all be self-centered or incompatible with the dominant ethics of the system. In many instances, it is true, such action may be designed to build up a following of one's own, as in the case of a legislator with his eye on the next election, or an administrator who seeks to strengthen his relationship with his clients. Typically, persons in positions of authority in all legal systems quickly become accustomed to fortifying support for themselves, with incidental consequences for the political objects, through performing numerous small and large services for individual or groups of members, services that are over and beyond the production of authoritative outputs.

For example, in representative systems, the legislator's proximity to the formulation and execution of binding decisions puts him in a strategically effective position for adding informal benefits as a bonus to his constituents in the way of outputs. Indeed, with respect to the French political system and its characteristic *immobilisme* during the Third and Fourth Republics and the virtual formal ineffectiveness of French legislators today, it is said that a major factor that has kept the system operating at even a modest level of effectiveness, has been the capacity and willingness of the legislators to perform such extra-legal services through the permanent bureaucracy. An examination of the sources of specific support for the political objects in the French system cannot neglect the role of such associated performance outputs.

But the motivation behind such outputs may also reflect a desire to do a job well, in accordance with the criteria

[13] See N. D. Feld, "Political Policy and Persuasion" 2 *Conflict Resolution* (1958) 78–89, for a distinction between policies and decisions.

of the occupation, out of a sense of duty under the spur of one's craft, or in dedication to the purposes of a profession. Without thought of personal advantage, the fulfillment of a task may seem to an administrator to require special favors for or help to his clients, over and above what might be formally required or even expected. Persons in positions of authority quickly become accustomed to utilizing their discretion, knowledge, and power to gain advantages otherwise not obtainable for their clients and yet which do not pass beyond law or recognized ethics.

Finally, the motivation for outputs of this kind may lie in anticipation of favors or some special reward contrary to the recognized and accepted rules of the system. Bribery and corruption are classic illustrations of this kind of associated performance outputs. But even though practices may be demonstrably illegal or merely reprehensible according to the prevailing ethical code, as long as they contribute to the services performed for members of society, we would have to include them within the category under discussion. Extended reliance on this kind of outputs as a source of specific support for political objects may well prove more effective in stressing than in maintaining a system. This would seem to be demonstrated by the extensive corruption that has accompanied the decline of numerous systems, such as the Roman Republic. But the data compel us to face up to the fact that although systems will vary enormously in the degree to which members obtain part of their gratifications through the operation of corruption, it is doubtful whether any system has been able entirely to escape such sources of specific support.[14]

[14] Compare with what M. Weiner has to say in explaining some of the consequences in India today. "(Party) machines played an important part in integrating immigrants into American life. They sponsored Americanization programs, facilitated contact between communities, and opened

FEEDBACK AND THE POLITICAL SYSTEM

It is apparent that to attain any objectives related to the level of support in a political system, possession of a capacity to produce outputs would not be enough. The system must provide some means for bringing to the attention of its decision centers, the authorities, information about the state of the system and its environment and the results of any actions already taken. In this way, this information may be compared with what had been anticipated and it may be taken into account in any follow-up future action. Through such feedback, the authorities are aided in determining the extent to which their outputs are contributing to the alleviation of stress from loss of support and the extent to which they have succeeded in adding to the store of positive support.

channels between the citizen and his government. Most important, the new, potentially revolutionary citizens were given the feeling that government was not intractable, unlike many of the European governments from which they had fled. Admittedly, much was done through a patronage system that often overlooked merit, and there was considerable corruption. But looking back to the late nineteenth centuries, it is apparent that this may have been a small price to pay for acculturating immigrants into a democratic society." *op. cit.,* p. 71.

Indirectly, R. E. Lane in *Political Ideology* (New York: Free Press, 1962) makes somewhat the same point. There he reports that "the laissez-faire morality of Eastport, and America in general in the twentieth century, has a special application to the matter of corruption. As we have seen, most people believe it is there, and not on a petty scale either, although mostly confined to the local and subordinate ranges of politics. But most of the men also believe that the use of governmental power to give your friends jobs, or to get contracts for firms you're interested in, is simply another method of payment, like a medical-fee system or a church tithing system. They do not see how it affects the quality or service in any serious way. And, since they think the level of temptation very high, they do not believe the degree of wickedness implied is very great. It does not affect their confidence in a responsible government; it is not, indeed, a source of great concern for them." p. 327.

The feedback may be completely ignored, of course. In that event, the effectiveness of the authorities in achieving their objectives would very probably be seriously impaired by their failure to find out what was in fact happening to the supportive frame of mind of the politically relevant members in the system. This would be particularly true where the authorities sought not just to maintain a minimal level of support for a given state of the system but decided to branch out in the search for new bases of support or to construct a fundamentally different kind of regime or community.[15] In political life as in other social systems, feedback can be shown to be fundamental both for error-regulation, that is, to keep a system pointed in an established direction—preservation of the *status quo*—or for purposive redirection, that is, to move off in search of new goals to conquer.

Support for the basic political objects, we have seen, may be diffuse in character. Specific mechanisms of regulation, as in the stimulation of legitimacy, a sense of common interest, or a bond of political community, arise that may permit a system to maintain an adequate inflow. But where these break down or operate ineffectively, or where, as is typically the case, they are by themselves inadequate, additional means are available to all systems through the production of outputs. Whether or not the outputs lead to an increase or decline in support will depend, however, on more than the extent to which they satisfy demands or create conditions that alleviate future demand provoking conditions. If stress from inadequate support is to be averted, the nature of the distribution of satisfactions in the system, their effect upon the members who are politically powerful, and the patterns of satisfaction over time are all of equal importance. The inflow of support for the various political objects is a product of a rather complex equation.

[15] The conditions under which support is freed from an ascribed basis and made available to those who can win it (achieved support) form a main theme of S. N. Eisenstadt's volume, *The Political Systems of Empires* (New York: Free Press of Glencoe, 1963).

SELECTED BIBLIOGRAPHY

Abcarian, Gilbert, "Radical Right and New Left: Commitment and Estrangement in American Society," in William J. Crotty, ed., *Public Opinion and Politics: A Reader.* New York: Holt, Rinehart, and Winston, 1970, 168–183.

Abcarian, Gilbert and Sherman M. Stanage, "Alienation and the Radical Right," *Journal of Politics,* 27, 4(November 1965), 776–796.

Aberbach, Joel D., "Alienation and Political Behavior," *American Political Science Review,* LXIII, 1(March 1969), 86–99.

Aberbach, Joel D. and Jack Walker, Political Trust and Racial Ideology," *American Political Science Review,* LXIV, 4(December 1970), 1199–1219.

Abramson, Paul R. and Ronald Inglehart, "The Development of Systemic Support in Four Western Democracies," *Comparative Political Studies,* 2, 4(January 1970), 419–442.

Agger, Robert E., Marshall N. Goldstein and Stanley A. Pearl, "Political Cynicism: Measurement and Meaning," *Journal of Politics,* 23(August 1961), 477–506.

Aiken, Michael, Louis A. Ferman and Harold L. Sheppard, *Economic Failure, Alienation, and Extremism.* Ann Arbor: University of Michigan Press, 1968.

Aiken, Michael and Jerald Hage, "Organizational Alienation: A Comparative Analysis," *American Sociological Review,* 31, 4(August 1966), 497–507.

Allardt, Erik, "Types of Protests, and Alienation," in Erik Allardt and Stein Rokkan, eds., *Mass Politics: Studies in Political Sociology.* New York: The Free Press, 1970, 45–63.

Almond, Gabriel A. and Sidney Verba, *The Civic Culture: Political Attitudes and Democracy in Five Nations.* Princeton: Princeton University Press, 1963.

Angell, Robert C., "The Moral Integration of American Cities," *American Journal of Sociology,* 57, 1(July 1951), Part 2.

Aptheker, Herbert, ed., *Marxism and Alienation.* New York: Humanities Press, 1965.

Avineri, Shlomo, *The Social and Political Thought of Karl Marx.* Cambridge: Cambridge University Press, 1968.

Baker, Kendall L., "Political Alienation and the German Youth," *Comparative Political Studies,* 3, 1(April 1970), 117–130.

Bell, Daniel, "The 'Rediscovery' of Alienation," *Journal of Philosophy,* LVI, (November 1959), 933–952.

Bell, Daniel, "Work and Its Discontents," in his *The End of Ideology,* revised edition. New York: The Free Press, 1960, 227–272.

Bell, Wendell, "Anomie, Social Isolation, and the Class Structure," *Sociometry,* 20, 2(1957), 105–116.

Blauner, Robert, *Alienation and Freedom.* Chicago: University of Chicago Press, 1964.

Blood, M. R. and C. L. Hulin, "Alienation, Environmental Characteristics, and Worker Responses," *Journal of Applied Psychology,* 51 (1967), 284–290.

Bonjean, Charles M. and Michael D. Grimes, "Bureaucracy and Alienation: A Dimensional Approach," *Social Forces,* 48, 3(March 1970), 365–373.

Bottomore, T. B., *Karl Marx: Early Writings.* New York: McGraw Hill, 1964.

Boynton, G. R., Samuel C. Patterson, and Ronald D. Hedlund, "The Structure of Public Support for Legislative Institutions," *Midwest Journal of Political Science,* XII, 2(May 1968), 163–180.

Braybrooke, D., "Diagnosis and Remedy in Marx's Doctrine of Alienation," *Social Research,* 25, 3(Autumn 1958), 325–345.

Brookes, R. H., "The Anatomy of Anomie—Part I," *Political Science,* 3, 2(September 1951), 44–51.

Brookes, R. H., "The Anatomy of Anomie —Part II," *Political Science,* 4, 1(March 1952), 38–49.

Browning, Charles J., *et al.,* "On the Meaning of Alienation," *American Sociological Review,* 26, 5(1961), 780–781.

Bullough, Bonnie, "Alienation in the Ghetto," *American Journal of Sociology,* 72, 5(March 1967), 469–478.

Burrows, David and Frederick R. Lapides, *Alienation: A Casebook.* New York: Thomas Y. Crowell Company, 1969.

Campbell, Angus, Philip Converse, Warren E. Miller, and Donald E. Stokes, *The American Voter.* New York: John Wiley & Sons, Inc., 1960.

Campbell, Angus, Gerald Gurin, and Warren E. Miller, *The Voter Decides.* Evanston: Row, Peterson & Company, 1954.

Chinoy, Ely, *Automobile Workers and the American Dream.* Garden City: Doubleday and Company, Inc., 1955.

Clark, John P., "Measuring Alienation Within a Social System," *American Sociological Review,* 24(December 1959), 849–852.

Clinard, Marshall B., ed., *Anomie and Deviant Behavior.* New York: The Free Press, 1964.

Crozier, Michel, *The Bureaucratic Phenomenon.* Chicago: The University of Chicago Press, 1964.

Davol, Stephen H. and Gunars Reimans, "The Role of Anomie as a Psychological Concept," *Journal of Individual Psychology,* 15 (1959), 215–225.

Dean, Dwight G., "Alienation and Political Apathy," *Social Forces,* 38, 3(March 1960), 185–189.

Dean, Dwight G., "Alienation: Its Meaning and Measurement," *American Sociological Review,* 26, 5(October 1961), 753–758.

De Grazia, Sebastian, *The Political Community: A Study of Anomie.* Chicago: University of Chicago Press, 1948.

Dennis, Jack, "Support for the Party System by the Mass Public," *American Political Science Review,* 60, 3(September 1966), 600–615.

Douvan, Elizabeth, "The Sense of Effectiveness and Response to Public Issues," *Journal of Social Psychology,* 47 (1958), 111–126.

Dowdy, Edwin H. R., "Alienation and Legitimacy," *Australian and New Zealand Journal of Sociology,* 2, 1(1966), 38–44.

Durkheim, Emile, *Suicide,* (1897), trans. by John A. Spaulding and George Simpson. New York: The Free Press, 1951.

Easton, David, *A Systems Analysis of Political Life*. New York: John Wiley and Sons, Inc., 1965.

Easton, David and Jack Dennis, "The Child's Acquisition of Regime Norms: Political Efficacy," *American Political Science Review*, 61 (March 1967), 25–38.

Epperson, David C., "Some Interpersonal and Performance Correlates of Classroom Alienation," *School Review*, 71 (Autumn 1963), 360–376.

Erbe, William, "Social Involvement and Political Activity: A Replication and Elaboration," *American Sociological Review*, 29, 2(1964), 198–215.

Faia, Michael A., "Alienation, Structural Strain, and Political Deviancy: A Test of Merton's Hypothesis," *Social Problems*, 14, 4(Spring 1967), 389–413.

Farris, Charles D., "Selected Attitudes on Foreign Affairs as Correlates of Authoritarianism and Political Anomie," *Journal of Politics*, 22 (February 1960), 50–67.

Feuer, Lewis S., "What Is Alienation: the Career of a Concept," *New Politics*, 1, 3(Spring 1962), 116–134.

Finifter, Ada W., "Dimensions of Political Alienation," *American Political Science Review*, LXIV, 2(June 1970), 389–410.

Forward, John R. and Jay R. Williams, "Internal-External Control and Black Militancy," *Journal of Social Issues*, 26, 1(Winter 1970), 75–92.

Fraser, John, "The Mistrustful-Efficacious Hypothesis and Political Participation," *The Journal of Politics*, 32, 2(May 1970), 444–449.

Fromm, Erich, *Escape from Freedom*. New York: Rinehart & Company, 1946.

Fromm, Erich, *Marx's Concept of Man*. New York: Ungar, 1961.

Fromm, Erich, ed., *Socialist Humanism*. New York: Doubleday & Co., Inc., 1965.

Fromm, Erich, *The Sane Society*. New York: Rinehart & Company, 1955.

Gamson, William A., *Power and Discontent*. Homewood: The Dorsey Press, 1968.

Gamson, William A., "The Fluoridation Dialogue: Is it an Ideological Conflict?" *Public Opinion Quarterly*, 25, 2(Winter 1961), 526–537.

Gerth, H. H. and C. Wright Mills, *From Max Weber: Essays in Sociology*. New York: Oxford University Press, 1946.

Goffman, Erving, "Alienation From Interaction," *Human Relations*, 10 (February 1957), 47–59.

Gold, Martin, "Juvenile Delinquency as a Symptom of Alienation," *Journal of Social Issues*, XXV, 2(1969), 121–135.

Goldthorpe, John H., "Attitudes and Behavior of Car Assembly Workers: A Deviant Case and A Theoretical Critique," *British Journal of Sociology*, 17, 3(1966), 227–244.

Gottesfeld, Harry and Gerterlyn Dozier, "Changes in Feelings of Powerlessness in a Community Action Program," *Psychological Reports*, 10, 3(1966), 978.

Gould, Laurence J., "Conformity and Marginality: The Two Faces of Alienation," *Journal of Social Issues*, XXV, 2(1969), 39-63.

Greenberg, Edward, "Children and Government: A Comparison Across Racial Lines," *Midwest Journal of Political Science*, XIV, 2(May 1970), 249–275.

Greenstein, Fred I., "The Benevolent Leader: Children's Images of Political Authority," *American Political Science Review*, LIV, 4(December 1960), 934–943.

Grimes, C. E. and Charles E. P. Simmons, "A Reassessment of Alienation in Karl Marx," *The Western Political Quarterly*, XXIII, 2(June 1970), 266–275.

Gross, Edward, "Some Functional Consequences of Primary Controls in Formal Work Organizations," *American Sociological Review*, 18 (August 1953), 368–373.

Hajda, Jan, "Alienation and Integration of Student Intellectuals," *American Sociological Review*, 26 (October 1961), 758–777.

Hobart, Charles W., "Types of Alienation: Etiology and Interrelationships," *Canadian Review of Sociology and Anthropology*, 2, 2(1965), 92–107.

Hochreich, Dorothy J. and Julian B. Rotter, "Have College Students Become Less Trusting?", *Journal of Personality and Social Psychology*, 15, 3(1970), 211–214.

Hofstetter, C. Richard, "Political Disengagement and the Death of Martin Luther King," *Public Opinion Quarterly*, XXXIII, 2(Summer 1969), 174–179.

Horowitz, Irving, "On Alienation and the Social Order," *Philosophy and Phenomenological Research*, 27, 2(December 1966), 230–237.

Horton, John E., "The Dehumanization of Anomie and Alienation: A Problem in the Ideology of Sociology," *British Journal of Sociology*, 15 (December 1964), 283–300.

Horton, John E. and Wayne E. Thompson, "Powerlessness and Political Negativism: A Study of Defeated Local Referendums," *American Journal of Sociology*, 67, 5(1962), 485–493.

Hughes, Alan, "Authoritarian Orientation, Alienation, and Political Attitudes in a Sample of Melbourne Voters," *Australian and New Zealand Journal of Sociology*, 3, 2(October 1967), 134–150.

Hulin, Charles L. and Milton R. Blood, "Job Enlargement, Individual Differences, and Worker Responses," *Psychological Bulletin*, 69, 1(January 1968), 41-55.

Inkeles, Alex, "Participant Citizenship in Six Developing Countries," *American Political Science Review*, LXIII, 4(December 1969), 1120-1141.

Inkeles, Alex and R. Bauer, *The Soviet Citizen*. Cambridge: Harvard University Press, 1961.

Israel, Joachim, *Alienation: From Marx to Modern Sociology*. Boston: Allyn and Bacon, Inc., 1971.

Janda, Kenneth, "A Comparative Study of Political Alienation and Voting Behavior in Three Suburban Communities," in *Studies in History and the Social Sciences: Studies in Honor of John A. Kinneman*. Normal, Illinois: Illinois State University, 1965, 53–68.

Jaros, Dean, Herbert Hirsch and Frederic Fleron, Jr., "The Malevolent Leader: Political Socialization in an American Sub-Culture," *American Political Science Review*, LXII, 2(June 1968), 564–575.

Johnson, Kenneth F., "Ideological Correlates of Right Wing Political Alienation in Mexico," *American Political Science Review*, 59, 3(September 1965), 656–664.

Josephson, Eric and Mary, eds., *Man Alone: Alienation in Modern Society*. New York: Dell Publishing Company, 1962.

Keniston, Kenneth, "The Psychology of Alienated Students," in Chad Gordon and Kenneth Gergen, *The Self in Social Interaction*, Vol. I. New York: John Wiley, 1968, 405–413.

Keniston, Kenneth, "The Sources of Student Dissent," *Journal of Social Issues*, XXIII, 3(1967), 108–137.

Keniston, Kenneth, *The Uncommitted: Alienated Youth in American Society*.

New York: Harcourt, Brace and World, 1965.

Killian, Lewis M. and Charles M. Grigg, "Urbanism, Race and Anomie," *American Journal of Sociology,* 67 (May 1962), 661–665.

Kon, Igor S., "The Concept of Alienation in Modern Sociology," *Social Research,* 34, 3(Autumn 1967), 507–528.

Kornhauser, Arthur, Harold L. Sheppard and Albert J. Mayer, *When Labor Votes.* New York: University Books, 1956.

Lane, Robert E., *Political Ideology.* New York: The Free Press, 1962.

Lefcourt, Herbert M., "Internal Versus External Control of Reinforcement," *Psychological Bulletin,* 65, 4(1966), 206–220.

Lenski, Gerhard E. and John C. Leggett, "Caste, Class, and Deference in the Research Interview," *American Journal of Sociology,* 65 (March 1960), 463–467.

Levin, Murray B., *The Alienated Voter.* New York: Holt, Rinehart and Winston, 1960.

Levin, Murray B. and Murray Eden, "Political Strategy for the Alienated Voter," *Public Opinion Quarterly,* 26 (1962), 47–63.

Levinson, Perry, "Chronic Dependency: A Conceptual Analysis," *Social Service Review,* 38, 4(December 1964), 371–381.

Lipsitz, Lewis, "Work Life and Political Attitudes: A Study of Manual Workers," *American Political Science Review,* 58, 4(December 1964), 951–962.

Litt, Edgar, "Political Cynicism and Political Futility," *Journal of Politics,* 25, 2(May 1963), 312–323.

Lukes, Steven, "Alienation and Anomie," in Peter Laslett and W. Runciman, eds., *Philosophy, Politics and Society,*

3rd Series. Oxford: Blackwell, 1967, 134–156.

Lutterman, Kenneth G. and Russell Middleton, "Authoritarianism, Anomia, and Prejudice," *Social Forces,* 48, 4(June 1970), 485–492.

Lyons, Schley R., "The Political Socialization of Ghetto Children: Efficacy and Cynicism," *The Journal of Politics,* 32, 2(May 1970), 288–304.

Lystad, Mary H., *Social Aspects of Alienation: An Annotated Bibliography.* Chevy Chase, Maryland: National Institute of Mental Health, 1969.

McClosky, Herbert and John H. Schaar, "Psychological Dimensions of Anomy," *American Sociological Review,* 30, 1(February 1965), 14–40.

McDill, Edward L., "Anomie, Authoritarianism, Prejudice and SES: An Attempt at Clarification," *Social Forces,* 39 (1961), 239–245.

McDill, Edward L. and Jeanne Clare Ridley, "Status, Anomie, Political Alienation, and Political Participation," *American Journal of Sociology,* 68, 2(September 1962), 205–213.

Marcson, Simon, ed., *Automation, Alienation and Anomie.* New York: Harper and Row, 1970.

Marcuse, Herbert, *One-Dimensional Man.* Boston: Beacon Press, 1964.

Marsh, C. Paul, Robert J. Dolan and William L. Riddick, "Anomie and Communication Behavior: The Relationship Between Anomia and Utilization of Three Public Bureaucracies," *Rural Sociology,* 32, 4 (December 1967), 435–445.

Mason, Gene L. and Dean Jaros, "Alienation and Support for Demagogues," *Polity,* I, 4(Summer 1969), 479–500.

Meier, Dorothy and Wendell Bell, "Anomia and Differential Access to the Achievement of Life Goals,"

American Sociological Review, 24 (April 1959), 189–202.

Merton, Robert K., *Social Theory and Social Structure*, revised edition. New York: The Free Press, 1957.

Middleton, Russell, "Alienation, Race, and Education," *American Sociological Review*, 28, 6(December 1963), 973–977.

Miller, Curtis R. and Edgar W. Butler, "Anomia and Eunomia: A Methodological Evaluation of Srole's Anomia Scale," *American Sociological Review*, 31 (June 1966), 400–406.

Miller, George A., "Professionals in Bureaucracy: Alienation Among Industrial Scientists and Engineers," *American Sociological Review*, 32, 5(October 1967), 755–768.

Mills, C. Wright, *The Power Elite*. New York: Oxford University Press, 1956.

Mills, C. Wright, *The Sociological Imagination*. New York: Oxford University Press, 1959.

Mizruchi, Ephraim H., "Aspiration and Poverty: A Neglected Aspect of Merton's Anomie," *Sociological Quarterly*, 8, 4(Autumn, 1967), 439–446.

Mizruchi, Ephraim H., *Success and Opportunity*. New York: The Free Press, 1964.

Mouledous, Joseph and Elizabeth, "Criticisms of the Concept of Alienation," *American Journal of Sociology*, LXX, 1(July 1964), 78–82.

Muller, Edward N., "Cross-National Dimensions of Political Competence," *American Political Science Review*, LXIV, 3(September 1970), 792–809.

Neal, Arthur G. and Salomon Rettig, "Dimensions of Alienation Among Manual and Non-Manual Workers," *American Sociological Review*, 28 (August 1963), 599–608.

Neal, Arthur G. and Salomon Rettig, "On the Multidimensionality of Alienation," *American Sociological Review*, 32, 1(February 1967), 54–64.

Neal, Arthur G. and Melvin Seeman, "Organizations and Powerlessness: A Test of the Mediation Hypothesis," *American Sociological Review*, 29 (April, 1964), 216–226.

Nettler, Gwynn, "A Measure of Alienation," *American Sociological Review*, 22 (December 1957), 670–677.

Nisbet, Robert A., *The Quest for Community*. New York: Oxford, 1953.

Nisbet, Robert A., *The Sociological Tradition*. New York: Basic Books, Inc., 1966.

Olsen, Marvin E., "Alienation and Political Opinions," *Public Opinion Quarterly*, 29, 2(1965), 200–212.

Olsen, Marvin E., "Two Categories of Political Alienation," *Social Forces*, 47, 3(March 1969), 288–298.

Oppenheimer, Martin, "The Student Movement as a Response to Alienation," *Journal of Human Relations*, 16, 1(1968), 1–16.

Patterson, Samuel C., G. R. Boynton, and Ronald D. Hedlund, "Perceptions and Expectations of the Legislature and Support for It," *American Journal of Sociology*, 75, 1(July 1969), 62–76.

Pearlin, Leonard I., "Alienation from Work: A Study of Nursing Personnel," *American Sociological Review*, 27 (1962), 314–326.

Pinard, Maurice, "Structural Attachments and Political Support in Urban Politics: The Case of Fluoridation Referendums," *American Journal of Sociology*, 61 (1963), 513–516.

Pinner, Frank, "Parental Overprotection and Political Distrust," *Annals of the American Academy of Political and Social Science*, 361 (September 1965), 59-70.

Polk, Kenneth, "Class, Strain and Rebellion Among Adolescents," *Social Problems*, 17, 2(Fall 1969), 214–224.

Ransford, H. Edward, "Isolation, Powerlessness, and Violence: A Study of

Attitudes and Participation in the Watts Riot," *American Journal of Sociology*, 73, 5(March 1968), 581–591.

Rhea, Buford, "Institutional Paternalism in High School," *The Urban Review*, 2(February 1968), 13–15, 34.

Rhea, Buford, *Measures of Child Involvement and Alienation from the School Program*. Washington: Office of Education (1966), ERIC #ED-010405.

Rhodes, Albert L., "Anomia, Aspiration, and Status," *Social Forces*, 42 (May 1964), 434–440.

Roberts, Allan and Milton Rokeach, "Anomie, Authoritarianism and Prejudice: A Replication," *American Journal of Sociology*, 62 (January 1956), 355–358.

Robinson, John P. and Phillip R. Shaver, *Measures of Social Psychological Attitudes*. Ann Arbor: Survey Research Center, University of Michigan, 1969.

Rose, Arnold M., "Alienation and Participation: A Comparison of Group Leaders and the 'Mass'," *American Sociological Review*, 27 (December 1962), 834–838.

Rose, Arnold M., "Prejudice, Anomie, and the Authoritarian Personality," *Sociology and Social Research*, 50, 2(January 1966), 141–147.

Rosenberg, Morris, "Misanthropy and Political Ideology," *American Sociological Review*, 21 (December 1956), 690–695.

Rosenberg, Morris, *Occupations and Values*. New York: The Free Press, 1957.

Rotter, Julian B., "Generalized Expectancies for Internal vs. External Control of Reinforcements," *Psychological Monographs*, LXXX, 1, Whole No. 609 (1966), 1–28.

Rotter, Julian B., Melvin Seeman, and Shephard Liverant, "Internal vs. External Control of Reinforcements: A Major Variable in Behavior Theory," in Norman F. Washburne, ed., *Decisions, Values, and Groups*, Vol. 2. London: Pergamon Press, 1962, 473–516.

Sapolsky, Harvey M., "The Fluoridation Controversy: An Alternative Explanation," *Public Opinion Quarterly*, XXXIII, 1(Summer 1969), 240–248.

Schaar, John, *Escape from Authority*. New York: Harper & Row, 1961.

Schulman, Jay, "Ghetto-Area Residence, Political Alienation, and Riot Orientation," in Louis H. Masotti and Don R. Bowen, eds., *Riots and Rebellion: Civil Violence in the Urban Community*. Beverly Hills: Sage Publications, 1968, 261–284.

Schwartz, David C., "Psychological Correlates of Urban Political Alienation: An Extension of Simulation Results Via Sample Interview Survey," *Western Political Quarterly*, XXIII, 3(September 1970), 600–610.

Scott, Marvin B., "The Social Sources of Alienation," in Irving Louis Horowitz, ed., *The New Sociology*. New York: Oxford University Press, 1965, 239–252.

Sears, David O., "Black Attitudes Toward the Political System in the Aftermath of the Watts Insurrection," *Midwest Journal of Political Science*, 13,4(November 1969), 515–544.

Seeman, Melvin, "Alienation and Social Learning in a Reformatory," *American Journal of Sociology*, 69, 3(1963), 270–284.

Seeman, Melvin, "Alienation, Membership, and Political Knowledge: A Comparative Study," *Public Opinion Quarterly*, 30, 3(Fall 1966), 353–367.

Seeman, Melvin, "On the Meaning of Alienation," *American Sociological Review*, 24, 6(December 1959), 783–791.

Seeman, Melvin, "On the Personal Consequences of Alienation in Work," *American Sociological Review*, 32, 2(April 1967), 273–285.

Seeman, Melvin, "Powerlessness and Knowledge: A Comparative Study of Alienation and Learning," *Sociometry*, 30, 2(June 1967), 105–123.

Seeman, Melvin and John W. Evans, "Alienation and Learning in a Hospital Setting," *American Sociological Review*, 27 (December 1962), 772–782.

Simmons, J. L., "Liberalism, Alienation, and Personal Disturbance," *Sociology and Social Research*, 49, 4(1965), 456–464.

Simmons, J. L., "Some Intercorrelations Among 'Alienation' Measures," *Social Forces*, 38 (March 1966), 370–372.

Smith, Duane E., "Alienation and the American Dream," in William P. Gerberding and Duane E. Smith, eds., *The Radical Left: The Abuse of Discontent*. Boston: Houghton-Mifflin Company, 1970, 345–362.

Srole, Leo, "Anomie, Authoritarianism, and Prejudice," *American Journal of Sociology*, 62 (July 1956), 63–67.

Srole, Leo, "Social Integration and Certain Corollaries: An Exploratory Study," *American Sociological Review*, 21, 6(1956), 709–716.

Stinchcombe, Arthur L., *Rebellion in a High School*. Chicago: Quadrangle Books, 1964.

Stokes, Donald E., "Popular Evaluations of Government: An Empirical Assessment," in Harlan Cleveland and Harold D. Lasswell, eds., *Ethics and Bigness*. New York: Harper & Brothers, 1962, 61–72.

Stone, Clarence N., "Local Referendums: An Alternative to the Alienated-Voter Model," *Public Opinion Quarterly*, XXIX, 2(Summer 1965), 213–221.

Struening, Elmer L., and Arthur H. Richardson, "A Factor Analytic Exploration of the Alienation, Anomie and Authoritarianism Domain," *American Sociological Review*, 30, 5(1965), 768–776.

Swados, Harvey, "The Myth of the Happy Worker," in Maurice R. Stein, Arthur J. Vidich, and David M. White, eds., *Identity and Anxiety*. New York: The Free Press, 1960, 198–204.

Taviss, Irene, "Changes in the Form of Alienation: The 1900's vs. the 1950's," *American Sociological Review*, 34, 1(February 1969), 46–57.

Tefft, Stanton K., "Anomy, Values and Culture Change Among Teen-Age Indians: An Exploratory Study," *Sociology of Education*, 40, 2(Spring 1967), 145–157.

Templeton, Fredric, "Alienation and Political Participation: Some Research Findings," *Public Opinion Quarterly*, XXX, 2(Summer 1966), 249–261.

Thompson, Wayne E. and John Horton, "Political Alienation as a Force in Political Action," *Social Forces*, 38, 3(March 1960), 190–195.

Tinder, Glenn, *The Crisis of Political Imagination*. New York: Charles Scribner's Sons, 1964.

U.S. Department of Health, Education, and Welfare, *Toward A Social Report*. Washington: Government Printing Office, 1969.

Waisanen, Fred B., "Stability, Alienation, and Change," *Sociological Quarterly*, 4, 1(Winter 1963), 18–31.

Watts, William A. and David Whittaker, "Profile of a Noncomformist Youth Culture: A Study of the Berkeley Non-Students," *Sociology of Education*, 41, 2(Spring 1968), 178–200.

Wilensky, Harold L., "Varieties of Work Experience," in Henry Borow, ed., *Man in a World at Work*. Boston: Houghton-Mifflin, 1964, 125–154.

Wittes, Simon, *People and Power: A Study of Crisis in Secondary Schools.* Ann Arbor: Institute for Social Research, 1970.

Zeitlin, Maurice, "Alienation and Revolution," *Social Forces,* 45, 2(December 1966), 224–236.

Zeitlin, Maurice, *Revolutionary Politics and the Cuban Working Class.* New York: Harper & Row (Harper Torchbooks), 1970.

Zurcher, Louis A., Jr., Arnold Meadow and Susan Lee Zurcher, "Value Orientation, Role Conflict and Alienation from Work: A Cross-Cultural Study," *American Sociological Review,* XXX (1965), 539-548.

Index

Abcarian, Gilbert, 8
Aberbach, Joel D., 182-184, 187, 192n, 202,
    226, 228n, 229n, 233n, 234n, 239n, 241,
    242n, 243n, 245n
Acquiescence Response Set, 56, 58
Activism, *see* Participation
Adolescence, 100-101
Adorno, Theodore W., 45n, 48, 49, 64n, 83n
Africa, 323
Age, 36, 205, 207, 258, 260, 261
Agger, Robert E., 182, 192n, 197n, 199n, 202,
    228n, 256n
Agrarians (Finnish), 295
Aiken, Michael, 106, 169n, 170n
Alienated labor, 3-6, 12-18, 103, 106; *see also*
    Alienation from work
Alienation, and anomie, 3-4, 24-32
  among blacks, 66-75, 198-201, 204-205,
    226-253
  and blocked social advancement, 146-148
  causes of, 28-29, 38, 59, 104-107, 125, 181-
    184; *see also* specific types of alienation
    and causal variables
  changes in level of, 5, 10, 18, 30-31, 137,
    310-318
  consequences of, 7, 33-34, 39-45; *see also*
    specific consequences
  definitions of, 8, 38, 46-54; *see also* specific
    types of alienation
  and division of labor, 24, 26
  diffuse, 6, 55-83
  dimensions of, 1, 4, 8-9, 29, 103, 123, 181,
    189-211; *see also* specific types of aliena-
    tion
  discrepancy theme in, 8-11, 47, 87, 123-124,

    182-183, 213-225, 237-242
  expectancy bases of, 6-11, 46-54, 68, 106,
    230, 235-237, 246
  generality of, 48
  and human nature, 4-5, 9, 24-32, 58
  indicators of, 6, 269, 271
  intensity of, 7, 9, 38
  meaning, 1, 3-10, 24-54, 302-304; *see also*
    specific types of alienation
  measurement of, 56-58, 61, 72, 106, 185-
    188, 206, 319-321
  measures of, 63-64, 67-69, 76, 90, 139, 157,
    169, 192-197, 215-225, 229, 231-232,
    256-257
  objective vs. subjective, 5-6, 10, 24, 46-47,
    107, 109
  and personality, 2, 43, 48, 56, 105, 141,
    153-164, 205, 228, 230-231
  philosophical vs. empirical analyses, 6
  political, 181-267
  and political participation, 59, 183-185, 208-
    210, 242-246, 304
  for political system, 304, 319
  referent of, 1, 6-7, 9, 33-34, 39, 53, 56, 138,
    151-152, 182, 184-185, 190, 229-230, 232
  and revolution, 210-211, 270-271, 275-289
  from school, 85-102
  social, 117-118
  at work, 130-137
  structural causes of, 139, 157, 164-179
  types of, 9, 34-37, 86-87, 302-304
  typologies of, 7, 8, 38-45, 303-304
  see also Alienation from work; Anomia; Es-
    trangement; Isolation; Meaninglessness;
    Normlessness; Political alienation;

357

and Powerlessness
generality of, 48
Alienation from work, 3-6, 12-18, 29, 34, 103-
    179
  in bureaucracies, 130-179
  changes in, 125-137, 282-289
  compared with political alienation, 185-188
  and cultural group, 153-164
  and job satisfaction, 108, 147-149, 159, 286
  and organizational stucture, 166-179
  as powerlessness, 9, 46
  and professional incentives, 172-179
  and revolution, 270-271, 275-289
  work group and, 149-151
  work shift and, 149-151
Allardt, Eric, 271, 272, 289, 293n, 294n, 300n
Almond, Gabriel A., 59, 188, 189, 192n, 193n,
    196n, 197n, 200n, 201n, 202, 227n,
    254n, 258n, 309, 310n, 318
Andrews, Frank M., 166
Angell, Robert C., 6
Anomia, 60-65
  and anomie, 6, 55, 60-62
  causes of, 62, 71-72
  and delinquency, 57
  meaning, 60-64
  measures of, 63-64, 69
  and powerlessness, 70
  and prejudice, 64
  and residential patterns among Negroes, 67-
    75
  and socioeconomic status, 59, 64-65
  as type of alienation, 8, 56
  see also Normlessness
Anomie, 18-32
  and anomia, 6, 55, 60-62, 271-272
  causes of, 28-29
  and deviance, 10, 57
  distinguished from alienation, 3-5, 24-32,
    271-272
  and division of labor, 25
  and human nature, 4-5, 8, 9, 24-32
  meaning of, 24-32
  and normlessness, 49-50, 52, 117, 191
  objective vs. subjective, 10, 24, 56
  and suicide, 18-23
  see also Normative integration; Normative
    regulation; Normlessness; and Norms
Apathy, political, 59, 208, 210; see also Par-
    ticipation
Appalachia, 185, 187, 253-267
Archibald, Katherine, 122n
Arendt, Hannah, 119n, 131n
Argyle, Michael, 254n
Argyris, Chris, 110n, 153n, 170

Aspirations, and anomie, 18-23, 27-28
  disappointment of, and alienation, 9-10, 86,
    104-105, 146
  effect of education on, 121, 165-167, 172-
    176
  and social order, 31
  see also Expectations
Assassinations, 310
Assembly-line technology, 114, 117, 126-131,
    133, 136
Attitudes, political, 57-58, 76-83
Authoritarianism, 56, 65, 83
  and anomia, 64
Authorities, political, 305-319, 322-323
Authority, 88-90, 92, 96, 102, 105
Automation, 104, 117, 126-129, 130, 134-135,
    137
Autonomy, 90, 93, 106
Avineri, Shlomo, 24n

Bach, George R., 258n
Bakke, E. Wight, 31n, 153n
Baldwin, James, 67n
Banfield, Edward C., 232n
Barnett, Clifford, 277n
Barrett, Donald N., 153n
Barth, Ernest A. T., 66n
Baumgartel, Howard, 170
Becker, Howard S., 165, 169n
Bednarik, Karl, 277n
Belknap, Ivan, 62n
Bell, Daniel, 4, 54n, 104
Bell, Wendell, 71n
Bendix, Reinhard, 330n
Berelson, Bernard, 208
Berlin, I., 24n
Blacks, 181, 184, 226-253, 321; see also Ne-
    groes; Race
Black militancy, 184, 242-243
Blau, Peter M., 164, 165n
Blauner, Robert, 8, 29, 103, 104, 110, 121n,
    122n, 155, 275n, 280n
Blood, Milton R., 109
Blue-Collar work, 125-127
Blum, Fred, 112n, 117n, 120
Bogue, Donald, 66n, 70
Bonjean, Charles M., 106
Boston, 187, 228, 246
Bottomore, T. B., 12n, 277n, 299n
Bowen, Don R., 237n
Bowen, Elinor, 237n
Boynton, G. R., 182, 192n, 213, 214n, 225
Bright, James, 127n, 130n
Brink, William, 233n

Brodbeck, A. J., 330n
Bronson, Louise, 162
Brookline, 228
Broom, L., 289n
Brown, Paula, 166
Browning, Charles J., 8, 190n
Buber, Martin, 154
Bullough, Bonnie, 8, 57, 66
Burdick, E., 330n
Bureaucracy, 29, 105-106, 115-116, 118, 130-178, 249
  effect on personality, 163
  professional workers in, 164-179
  supervisory relationships, 140-146, 170-179
Burgess, Ernest, 66n
Burrell, S. A., 326n, 331n, 338n
Business, *see* Industries
Butler, Edgar W., 57

Campbell, Angus, 182, 191n, 199n, 202, 210n
Cantril, Hadley, 48, 237, 240n, 277n
Capitalism, and work alienation, 12-18, 24, 28, 37-38, 103, 106-107, 112-113, 185, 271, 275-276, 285, 288
Caplan, Nathan, 232
Carper, James, 165
Caudill, Harry M., 255n
Cayton, H. R., 66n
Centers, Richard, 277n
Change, *see* Political change; Social change
Chesney, James D., 226n
Chicago, 187
Children, 185
  attitudes toward political leaders, 253-267
Chinoy, Ely, 112, 120n, 277, 286, 288
Church attendance, 201, 207, 234; *see also* Religion
Civil rights, 209, 309
  . movement, 43
Civil War, 189, 321
Clark, John P., 6, 138, 139, 157
Class, 206, 238, 296-299
  consciousness, 37, 297, 299
  see also Socioeconomic status
Cleavage, 326-329
  reduction in, 328-332
Clegg, Hugh, 112n
Cleveland, Harlan, 228n
Clinard, Marshall B., 57
Cohen, Albert K., 88n, 89
Cohen, Yehudi A., 154, 155n
Cohesion, 289-291
Coleman, James S., 67n, 326n
College, 10, 85, 314; *see also* School
Communism, 33, 271-272, 293-295, 298-299

Comparative studies, *see* Cross-cultural studies
Comparison processes, 289-290, 296-298
Competition, 154
Conflict, 289-305
Conformity, among high school students, 92, 94, 96
  and anomia, 65
  and anomie, 50
  and deviance, 89-90
  as opposite of alienation, 38-39, 41, 44
  organizational pressures for, 163
  political, 209-210, 319
  see also Uniformity
Control, 111, 123
  internal vs. external, 47, 50, 57
Converse, Phillip E., 191n
Coombs, Steven L., 226n
Corruption, 228, 230, 246, 255, 344
Coser, Lewis, 209n, 326n, 333n
Cottrell, L. S., 289n
Cressey, D. R., 90n
Cross-cultural studies, 153-164, 187-188, 254, 267, 300, 310
Crozier, Michel, 106
Cuba, 270, 275-289
Cultural background, 105, 153-164
Cultural integration, 328-329, 338
Curriculum, 85, 87, 96-100

Dahl, Robert A., 202n, 316, 318
Dahrendorf, Ralf, 113, 316, 318, 333n
Dalton, Melville, 171n
Davies, James C., 214n, 226n, 237n, 255n, 265n
Davis, James A., 170n, 289n
Dean, Dwight G., 8, 52n, 138n, 190n
Dean, Lois, 136n
DeGrazia, Sebastian, 4, 255n
Delin, Peter, 254n
Delinquency, 41, 44-45, 57, 88, 94, 96
DeMan, Henri, 123
Demerath, N. J. III, 208n
Demonstrations, 273-274, 310; *see also* Participation, political
Dennis, Jack, 189n, 192n, 206n, 257, 258n
Deprivation, 237, 297-299, 303
Detroit, 183, 187, 226-253
Deutsch, K. W., 326n, 331n, 338n
Deviance, 10, 41, 50, 65, 89, 319
  suppression of, 79-81
Dickson, William J., 31n, 153n
Dietricke, David C., 88n
Diffuse support, 328, 334-339
Discrimination, 64, 183-184, 187, 241, 246, 250; *see also* Prejudice

Distrust, political, 226-253
Division of labor, and alienation, 271, 289-305
   from work, 24-26, 28, 115-116, 125
  and automation, 137
  and craft production, 129-130
Dohrenwend, B. F., 26n
Doob, Leonard W., 255n
Douvan, Elizabeth, 202
Dowdy, Edwin H. R., 8
Dozier, Edward P., 155n
Drake, St. Clair, 66n
Drug addiction, 65
Duncan, Otis Dudley, 202n
Dunlop, John, 114n
Durkheim, Emile, 4, 5, 8-10, 18, 24-28, 30-32, 45, 49, 55, 57, 60-63, 65, 117, 191, 197, 272, 291

Easton, David, 189, 201n, 206n, 213, 226n, 228n, 253n, 254n, 255n, 257, 258, 259n, 264n, 265n, 274, 319
Eckstein, Harry, 228n
Economic and Philosophical Manuscripts, 3
Economic conditions, 136
Economic development, 271-272, 292, 294-296, 300
Economic security, 113
Edelman, Murray, 252, 253n
Education, and political alienation, 199-200, 203-205, 207
  and political trust, 236-237, 239, 241-242
  and work aspirations, 121
  see also Socioeconomic status
Edwards, Allen L., 169n
Ego strength, 210
Eisenstadt, S. N., 345n
Emigration, 33, 181, 319, 321
Employment, conditions of, 111, 113
Engels, Frederick, 26n, 30, 275, 276, 277n
Engineers, 164-179
Epperson, David C., 87
Erikson, Erik, 121n
Estrangement, 3, 45, 86, 285-289
Ethiopia, 321
Ethnic group, 105
Etzioni, Amitai, 164, 166, 168n, 170n, 305, 306, 314, 318
Eunomia, 61
Evans, John W., 59, 74n, 138n
Exchange, 290-291, 297, 300, 302, 303
Exile, 33
Expatriation, 181, 189
Expectations, 6-11, 46-54, 68, 106
  of political institutions, 213-225, 230, 235-237, 246, 250, 309
Exploitation, 271, 275, 288

Expressive alienation, 86, 88, 90-91, 96

Factory, 103, 106-107, 114, 116-117, 120, 125
  size of, 133-134, 137
Faith in people, 58-59, 76-83, 200-202, 205-207, 233-234
  measures of, 76, 212, 234
False consciousness, 6
Family, 29, 155
  as a socializing agent, 255, 256, 262-267
Farrar, Donald E., 204n
Fayerweather, John, 156
Feierabend, Ivo K., 237n
Feierabend, Rosalind L., 237n
Feld, N. D., 343n
Festinger, Leon, 289, 290, 296
Feuer, Lewis, S., 190n, 275n
Finifter, Ada W., 8, 56, 58, 181-183, 189
Finifter, Bernard M., 206n
Finland, 271, 289-305
Fleron, Frederic J., Jr., 185, 253
Fluoridation, 183
Ford, Thomas R., 255n, 256n
Foreman, 132
Forward, John R., 184
Frazier, E. Franklin, 66n, 70, 73n, 247
Freedom, 26, 106, 111, 123, 272
  of speech, 78-79
Freidson, Eliot, 170n
Frenkel-Brunswik, E., 64n
Friedmann, Eugene, 121n, 123n
Friedman, Georges, 30, 120n, 277n, 284
Friedsam, Hiram J., 62n
Friendship, 154
Fromm, Erich, 4, 33, 34, 37, 45n, 52, 53, 65, 107, 110n, 112, 154
Functionalism, 208
Functional rationality, 48, 116
Futility, 182

Galenson, Walter, 114n, 121n, 122n
Gamson, William A., 183, 211n, 226n, 227, 228n, 229, 230, 235, 247, 248, 272-274, 305
Gawiser, Sheldon, 237n
Geertz, Clifford, 208
Gerth, Hans H., 46, 107, 111n, 155n, 169n
Ghetto Life, 66-75, 309
Glauber, Robert R., 204n
Glazer, Nathan, 48n, 53, 54, 209n
Gluckman, M., 326n, 333n
Goals, 10-11, 18-23, 50, 57, 104, 165; *see also* Expectations
Goffman, Erving, 51, 52n
Goldner, Fred H., 166

Goldsen, Rose K., 76n
Goldstein, Marshall N., 182, 192n, 228n, 256n
Goldthorpe, John H., 108
Goodman, Paul, 277n
Gore, Pearl Mayo, 67n
Gouldner, Alvin W., 46, 114n, 155n, 209n
Governmental policies, *see* Public policy
Graham, Hugh D., 237n
Greenberg, Edward, 185
Greenstein, Fred I., 185, 206n, 254n-257n, 260n, 261n, 265n
Greenstone, David, 232n
Greenwood, Ernest, 170n
Gregor, A. James, 209n
Grimes, Michael D., 106
Gross, Bertram, 341
Guerrilla war, 310
Guilford, J. P., 192n
Gurin, Gerald, 199n
Gurr, Ted R., 237n, 239n, 245n
Gusel, Paul, 67n

Haer, John, 199n
Hage, Jerald, 106, 169n, 170n
Hajda, Jan, 86, 138n
Haller, Archibald O., 202n
Hamilton, Richard, 277n
Harding, John, 63n
Harmon, Harry H., 192n
Harris, Joan, 67n, 69n
Harris, Louis, 233n
Havighurst, Robert, 121n, 123n
Hedlund, Ronald D., 182, 192n, 213, 214n, 225
Heiskanen, Veronica Stolte, 292n
Herzberg, F., 113n, 121n
Hess, Robert D., 201n, 206n, 253n-256n, 257, 258, 259n, 264n, 265n
Hield, Wayne, 209n
High school, 9-10, 85-102
Himmelstrand, Ulf, 292n
Hirsch, Herbert, 185, 253, 257n, 267n
Hochreich, Dorothy J., 59
Hodges, Donald Clark, 277
Hoffer, Eric, 48, 53
Hollingshead, A. B., 95n
Homans, G. C., 290
Hopelessness, 57
Horney, Karen, 33, 37
Horowitz, Irving L., 24n
Horton, John E., 6, 24n, 184, 198n, 202n, 258n, 275n
Hoyt, Cyril J., 197n
Hughes, Everett C., 170n
Hughes, Helen MacGill, 66n

Hulin, Charles L., 109
Human nature, and alienation, 4-5, 9, 24-32, 58
  attitudes toward, 76-83
Hyman, Herbert, 255n, 265n

Ideology, political, 334, 339, 341, 342
  and faith in people, 58, 76-83
  racial, 183, 226-253
  and revolutionary support, 270-271
Income, 198-199, 203-204, 207; *see also* Socioeconomic status
Industrial community, 117-118
Industrial decentralization, 134
Industrial democracy, 112
Industrialism, 103-137, 271-272
Industrialization, 24-32, 37, 117, 124, 292-293
Industrial sabotage, 117
Industries, aero-space, 164-179
  automobile, 128, 133-136, 286, 288
  banks, 157-164
  blue-collar, 125-128
  chemical, 135-137
  continuous process, 117, 134-137
  craft, 129, 130, 132
  nationalization of, 282-289
  textile, 128, 132-133, 135
  see also Technology
Influence, 272-273, 305-318
Inkeles, Alex, 125n, 197n
Integration, 5, 299
  cultural, 328-329, 338
  moral, 6
  normative, 55, 117-118
    individual vs. social, 55, 61
  racial, 57, 66-75, 239-240, 244, 251, 253, 332
  social, 60
    at work, 132
Intellectuals, 51-52, 72, 86
Interaction, social, 51
Interest groups, 217-218, 272
Interest-trust, 309
Interpersonal relationships, 82, 155, 163
Iowa, 182, 213-225
Ishwaran, K., 300n
Isolation, meaning of, 51-52, 63, 72, 123
  political, 191
  social, 65, 154, 184, 255, 298-299
  among students, 86
  as type of alienation, 3, 7-9, 11, 67, 181, 303
  at work, 117
Israel, Joachim, 107

Jamaica, 321
James, W. H., 47n

Janda, Kenneth, 192n, 202
Jaques, Elliot, 112n, 126n
Jaros, Dean, 185, 187, 253, 254n
Jennings, M. Kent, 230n, 256, 257, 261n
Jewell, Malcolm E., 213, 226n
Job satisfaction, 108, 121, 163, 170
  and alienation, 147-149, 159, 286
Job size, 109, 116
Jobs, 86, 100
  status of, 122
Jones, M. R., 54n
Jones, Virgil C., 255n
Judicial processes, 332

Kahler, Erich, 34, 37, 45
Kaiser, Henry, 218
Kaplan, Normen, 165n
Keniston, Kenneth, 6, 7, 9, 32, 87, 190n, 229n
Kentucky, 255
Kerr, Clark, 125n
Kibbutz, 30
Kitsuse, John I., 88n
Kluckhohn, Clyde, 153n
Knowledge, 207, 213
Koch, S., 54n
Kornhauser, William, 164n, 165, 167n, 171n,
  299n

Labor, objectification of, 12-13, 16-17; *see also*
  Work
Lane, Robert E., 182, 191, 230n, 233n, 306,
  318, 330n, 344n
Langton, Kenneth P., 265n
Lapland, 295
LaPorte, Todd, 171n
Laslett, Peter, 24n
Lasswell, Harold D., 62, 63n, 154n, 228n,
  255n
Lazarsfeld, Paul F., 277n
Leaders, political, childrens' attitudes toward,
  253-267
  recruitment of, 329
Learning, 74
Learning theory, 47, 68
Leggett, John C., 57
Legislatures, 213-225, 329, 332
Legitimacy, 290-293, 296, 300, 302, 334-336
Lenski, Gerhard E., 57, 200n
Lerner, Daniel, 154n
Lesieur, Frederick, 113n
Levinson, Daniel J., 64n, 153n
Lewis, Oscar, 155
Lieberman, Bernhardt, 309, 318
Linz, Juan, 277n
Lindzey, Gardner, 277n

Lipset, Seymour Martin, 114n, 121n, 122n,
  277n, 289n, 326n
Litt, Edgar, 187, 200n, 228n, 229, 232
Littunen, Yrjö, 293n, 298n
Liverant, Shepard, 45n, 57, 68n
Lomax, Louis E., 233n
Lukes, Steven, 4, 5, 24
Lupsha, Peter A., 242n
Lutterman, Kenneth G., 56
Lynn, David B., 258n
Lyons, Schley R., 185

Maccoby, Eleanor E., 265n
McClelland, David C., 49n, 155, 156n
McClosky, Herbert, 57, 228n, 229
McCone, John A., 67n
McDill, Edward L., 57
MacGaffey, Wyatt, 277n
MacIver, Robert M., 62, 63n
McPhee, William N., 208n
Maher, R. F., 301n
Mannheim, Karl, 48, 49, 116, 276n
Manual Labor, 100, 130, 277
Marcson, Simon, 164n
Marriage, 96, 98-99
Martin, Norman H., 125n
Marx, Karl, 3-6, 8, 9, 12, 24-28, 30-33, 37, 45-
  47, 53, 103, 106-108, 110n, 111n, 112,
  117, 119, 120n, 122, 124, 135, 270, 272,
  275-277, 285, 286, 297, 299, 302, 334
Masotti, Louis H., 237n
Mass society, 124, 133, 138, 299
Matthews, Donald R., 238n
Matthews, Richard E., 265n
Mayer, J. P., 277n
Mayo, E., 31n, 118, 153
Meadow, Arnold, 105, 153, 155n, 162
Meaninglessness, and anomia, 56
  and anomie, 63
  meaning of, 48-49, 51, 123
  political, 191
  of school, 101
  as type of alienation, 3, 8-9, 181, 303-304
  of work, 28, 115-117, 129-130, 136
Meeker, Marchia, 67n, 69n
Meier, Dorothy L., 71n
Meltzer, Leo, 171
Menzel, Herbert, 169n
Merriam, C. E., 335n
Merton, Robert K., 10, 11, 41, 45, 49, 50, 51n,
  52, 57, 62n, 65, 89n, 146n, 155, 163,
  197, 289n, 304
Mexicans, 105, 153-164
Middleton, Russell, 8, 56, 67n, 199n
Midlarsky, Manus, 214n, 226n

Migration, 162, 294-296, 299
Mill, John Stuart, 275, 276
Miller, Curtis R., 57
Miller, George A., 105, 106, 164
Miller, Warren E., 191n, 199n
Mills, C. Wright, 46, 49n, 53, 107, 111n, 155, 169, 277n
Minority groups, 57, 185; *see also* Blacks; Mexicans; Negroes; and Race
Misanthropy, 55, 58-59, 76-83; *see also* Faith in people
Mizruchi, Ephraim H., 24n
Mobility, 154
Modernization, 295, 300-301
Money, 12, 108
Monotony, 120
Morale, 63
Moral integration, 6
Morse, Mary, 29
Morse, Nancy C., 114n, 121n, 123n, 169
Morton, Anton S., 265n
Myrdal, Gunnar, 233n

Nationalization of industries, 282-289
Nativity, 198, 200, 204-205, 207
Neal, Arthur G., 8, 56, 59, 70n, 190n, 191n
Neal, Douglas B., 226n
Negroes, 66-75, 227-253, 309
   effect of religion on powerlessness and residential patterns, 73-74
   political alienation among, 198-201, 204, 207, 210
   see also Blacks; Race
Nesvold, Betty A., 237n
Nettler, Gwynn, 7, 48n, 51, 52, 138n
New Guinea, 300-303
Newark, 187, 232, 246
Niemi, Richard G., 230n, 256n, 257, 261n
Nigeria, 321
Nisbet, Robert A., 45, 52n, 138n, 275n
Normative integration, 55, 117-118
   individual vs. social, 55, 61
Normative regulation, 4-5, 18-23, 26-27, 182
   breakdown of, 9, 62, 303
   see also Normative integration; Normlessness; and Norms
Normlessness, and anomia, 56, 67
   and anomie, 117
   meaning, 8-9, 49-51
   political, 181-182, 189-211
   as type of alienation, 303
Norms, and alienation, 10, 89, 309
   and anomie, 29, 55, 63
   breakdown of, 29, 49, 55, 63, 272; *see also* Normative regulation, breakdown of

class differences in, 255
discrepancy with social policy, 87
distinguished from values, 39, 322
in industrial community, 118
modification of, 328
political, 191, 196-197, 209-210, 304, 330-332
and pressure toward uniformity, 291, 303
and reference groups, 296-297
and work experience, 105
North, 198, 203, 233-234
Northwood, L. D., 66n
Nursing personnel, 130-152

Obedience, 89; *see also* Conformity
Occupation, 198-199; *see also* Socioeconomic status
Occupational differentiation, 133-134
Officer, James E., 162n
Olsen, Marvin E., 57, 182, 234n
Organizations, 298, 305, 314
   control, 170-171, 172-179
   influences of values on workers, 162
   membership in, 198, 201-202, 319
   structure, 164-179
Orth, Charles D., 165
Orzack, L. H., 168
Ownership, of work tools, 111-112
Output failure, 324-325, 333, 341
Outputs, 340-344

Palmer, Gladys, 114n
Pappenheim, Fritz, 37
Parsons, Talcott, 41, 124n, 154, 155n, 160, 163, 213, 226n, 228n, 330n
Participation, 298-299, 337-338
   political, and alienation, 87, 304
   and anomia, 57
   and deprivation, 298-299
   and legislative support, 225
   measures of, 212
   and personal control, 184
   and political alienation, 182, 201-210
   and revolutionary ideology, 270
   see also Demonstrations
Participatory democracy, 59
Particularism, 154-164
   and cultural group, 158
   and job satisfaction, 159
Patriotism, 320, 334
Patterson, Samuel C., 9, 182, 185, 192n, 213, 214n, 225, 226n
Pearl, Stanley A., 182, 192n, 228n, 256n
Pearlin, Leonard I., 104-106, 138, 141n, 157, 158, 160, 183, 186

Pelz, Donald, 166
Perception – expectation differentials, 213-225; *see also* Expectations
Perlman, Selig, 113
Personality, 43, 48, 56, 105, 141, 153-164, 205, 228, 230-231
Peterson, Richard A., 208n
Plamenatz, J. P., 24n
Podheretz, Norman, 47n
Political alienation, 181-267
  causes, 181, 188, 198-207, 230-242, 246-248
  changes in, 211, 230-231, 247, 272-274, 323
  compared with alienation from work, 185-188
  consequences of, 208-210, 242-246
  and deprivation, 237-242
  dimensions of, 181, 189-211
  governmental response to, 248-253, 274, 319-345
  measures of, 185-188, 192-197, 206, 215-225, 229, 231-232, 256-257
  and personality, 205, 228, 230-231
  and political expectations, 235-237
  political factors as causes of, 230-231
  problems in studying, 185-188
  referent of, 185
  and size of city, 188, 198, 203-205, 207
  structural causes of, 186-188
  see also Political trust
Political campaigns, 194, 306
Political change, 208, 227, 269-345
Political community, 319-322, 337
Political competence, 235-237; *see also* Political efficacy
Political corruption, 228, 230, 246, 255, 344
Political culture, 196-197, 200, 208
Political cynicism, 187, 197, 255-267
Political efficacy, 183, 199, 202, 210, 228, 257-258
Political institutions, 9, 182
  perceptions of, 213-225
Political leadership, recruitment of, 329
Political movements, 43
Political parties, 330
  leaders, 217-218
Political regime, 319, 322-323
Political socialization, *see* Socialization
Political structures, 182, 186-188, 205, 225
  change in, 208, 227, 328-332
Political support, 213-225, 319-345
Political system, 9
  effect of alienation on, 227, 230, 248-253
  feedback, 344
  need for citizen support, 189

response to alienation, 274, 319-345
Political trust, 183, 226-253, 273, 305-318
  change in, 310-318
Polls, 216-218
Portes, Alejandro, 202n
Poverty, 23, 59, 85, 185, 249, 255, 309
Powell, G. Bingham, 254n
Powerlessness, and anomia, 56, 70
  and capitalism, 28
  definition of, 7-8, 46
  and expectations, 9, 50-51, 182
  industrial, 111-115, 124
  meaning of, 7-8, 46-48, 123, 182-184, 272-273, 302-304
  measures of, 68, 139, 192-197
  personal, 184
  political, 189-211, 228, 247
  political consequences of, 208-211, 302-304
  and poverty, 59
  and residential patterns among Negroes, 67-75
  as type of alienation, 3, 55, 57
  at work, 111-115, 124, 127, 129-152
Prejudice, 45, 55-57, 60-65; *see also* Discrimination
President, images of, 256-267
Private property, 12, 17-18, 28
Professional incentives, 171-179
Professional training, 105, 165-166, 172-179
Proportional representation, 330
Protest, among Communist voters, 293
  as manifestation of political alienation, 181, 184, 209-211
  as racial ideology, 242
  among students, 86, 317
  types of, 289-305
  see also Demonstrations
Prothro, James W., 238n
Public policy, and discrepancy with traditional values, 10, 87
  to deal, with alienation, 273-274
    with racial hostility, 248-253
  effect on confidence levels, 314, 317-318
  failure to produce adequate outputs, 324-325
  outputs to increase support, 340-344
  and the public interest, 336
  strategies in influencing, 307
Purcell, Theodore, 114n, 125n, 136n

Quinney, Richard, 199n

Race, and access to political structure, 186-187
  and political alienation, 183, 198-200, 205, 207
  and political ideology, 226-253
  and social exchange, 297, 301

see also Blacks; Negroes
Race relations, effect of on willingness to use
   violence, 184
   and political trust, 234, 239, 247
   and public policy, 248-253
Radicalism, 277, 286, 288, 293, 298-299
Radical left, 270
Radical right, 304
Ransford, H. Edward, 184, 210n
Rebellion, 52
   high school, 88-102
   see also Protest
Redfield, Robert, 155
Redl, Fritz, 88n, 90
Reference groups, 296-298, 303
Reform, social and political, 210-211, 214, 250
Religion, 14, 23, 33, 36
   effect, on political alienation, 198, 205
      on powerlessness and residential patterns
         among Negroes, 73-74
   and work motivation, 119
   see also Church attendance
Representation, 329
Residential patterns, 66-75
   and anomia, 70-73
   and powerlessness, 70-73
Rettig, Salomon, 8, 56, 70n, 190n, 191n
Revolution, characteristics of leaders, 184
   and civic perception - expectations differen-
      tials, 214
   as manifestation of alienation, 38, 41
   as outgrowth of political alienation, 210-211,
      310
   and output failure, 325
   and political support, 319
   and work alienation, 270-271, 275-289
   workers' attitudes toward, 279-289
   see also War
Reynolds, Lloyd, 114n
Rhea, Buford, 87, 170n
Richardson, Arthur H., 8, 191n
Ridley, Jeanne Clare, 57
Riegal, John W., 171n
Riesman, David, 53, 154, 209n
Riihinen, Olavi, 294n
Riots, 181, 183-184, 245, 309-310, 319
Ritti, R. R., 166
Ritualists, 304
Robinson, John P., 57
Robinson, W. S., 206n
Roethlisberger, Fritz J., 31n, 153n
Rokkan, Stein, 289n, 294n
Roles, 303
Roper survey of workers, 121-122
Rose, Arnold M., 57, 202

Rosenberg, Morris, 58, 59, 76, 141n, 201n,
   228n, 234
Rotter, Julian B., 45n, 46n, 47, 57, 59, 67n,
   68
Roy, Donald, 115n
Rubel, M., 277n, 299n
Rummel, Rudolph J., 310, 318
Runciman, W., 24n
Rundquist, Edward A., 63n

Sabine, George, 227
Sanford, R. Nevitt, 64n
Sawrey, William L., 258n
Scanlon plan, 113n
Schaar, John, 57
Schattschneider, E. E., 252, 330n
Schelling, Thomas C., 307, 318
School, 9, 29, 85-102, 270-271
   curriculum, 85, 87, 96-100
   grades, 314
   universities, 10, 85, 314
School bond proposals, 184
Scientists, 164-179
Scott, Marvin B., 8
Scott, W. Richard, 164, 165n
Seeman, Melvin, 7-9, 11, 26n, 45, 56, 58, 59,
   66n, 67, 68n, 70n, 72n, 74n, 103, 106,
   110n, 111n, 116n, 138, 169, 181, 190n,
   275n, 303
Segregation, *see* Integration, racial
Selective Service System, 317
Self-actualization, at work, 131
Self-estrangement, in Horney and Marx, 37
   meaning, 38, 52-54
   as type of alienation, 3, 8, 303
   at work, 106, 118-124, 130, 136, 169
Selznick, Phillip, 31, 113n
Sex, effect of on political alienation, 199-200,
   204-205, 207
Shaver, Phillip R., 57
Shepherd, Clovis, 165, 166
Shils, Edward A., 154, 155n, 163
Shister, Joseph, 114n
Siegal, Sidney, 158n
Sigel, Roberta S., 254n
Silberman, Charles, 67n
Simmel, Georg, 141n, 329n
Simpson, George, 25n, 291n
Size of City, effect on political alienation, 188,
   198, 203-205, 207
Sletto, Raymond F., 63n
Smelser, Neil, 211, 303, 304
Social change, 269-345
   and alienation, 36
   and anomie, 28, 31

difficulties in studying, 269-274
effect on Communist vote, 294-296
and protest, 300-302
in school reform, 251
Social class, *see* Socioeconomic status
Social control, 132, 271, 274, 305-318
"errors," 316-317
Social Democrats (Finnish), 293, 295
Social indicators, 6
Social integration, 4, 9, 25, 65
at work, 134-137
Socialism, 106-107, 185
Socialization, 62, 106, 184-185, 201, 253-267,
297, 339
of workers, 6
Social movements, 4, 89, 303, 316-317
Social norms, *see* Norms
Social policy, *see* Public policy
Social structure, 90, 104
Socioeconomic status, and anomia, 64
and deviance, 57
and diffuse alienation, 59
future, 90, 96-97, 99
and idealization of political figures, 260
and isolation, 154
and legislative support, 225
and political alienation, 198-201, 203-205
and political trust, 228-229, 234
and prejudice, 65
and pressures toward uniformity, 292-293
and reference groups, 296
see also Class; Education; Income; and Oc-
cupation
Solidarity, 25, 289-305
mechanical, 291, 297
organic, 291, 297, 302
see also Integration
Solidary groups, 272-273, 306-318
South, 198, 203-204, 233-234, 321
Species-being, 14-16
Species-life, 5, 15-16
Srole, Leo, 51n, 55-58, 60, 67, 69, 71, 199n
Stagner, Ross, 136n
Status obeisance, 141-144
Stein, Maurice R., 275n
Stinchcombe, Arthur L., 9, 55, 85-88, 164n
Stokes, Donald E., 191n, 228-231, 233n, 235
Stouffer, Samuel A., 76n, 156, 158
Strikes, 273-274, 310
Strodtbeck, F. L., 49n
Struening, Elmer L., 8, 191n
Students, 85-102, 314
cultural alienation among, 35, 38, 42
high school, 88-102, 261-262
political activity of, 43, 85, 209, 249, 317

role of, 10
see also School
Stunkard, Clayton L., 197n
Subject political orientation, 200
Substantive rationality, 129
Success, 97
Suchman, Edward A., 76n
Suicide, 4
Suicide, 4, 18-23
Supervision, at work, 132, 140-146, 170-179
Support, 319-345
changes in, 323
diffuse, 328, 334-339
effect on political system, 319
measures of, 319-321
specific, 328, 333, 340-344
Surace, Samuel J., 164n
Sutherland, Edwin H., 90

Tanter, Raymond, 214n, 226n, 310, 318
Teachers, 90, 92-93, 99, 101
Technology, 114-116, 118, 124-125, 127, 130,
136, 154
assembly-line, 114, 117, 126-131, 133, 136
changes in, 127-137
continuous process, 117, 126-128, 131, 134-
137
craft, 127-128, 129, 130-132
Teenagers, 29
Templeton, Fredric, 57
TenHouten, Warren D., 164n
Thompson, Wayne E., 184, 198n, 202, 258n
Thurstone, L. L., 192n
Tilgher, Adriano, 119
Toby, Jackson, 156, 158
Toennies, Ferdinand, 124n
Tomlinson, T. M., 242n
Torgerson, Ulf, 293n
Torney, Judith V., 206n, 254n, 256n, 265n
Touraine, Alain, 127n
Trow, M., 326n
Truman, D. B., 329n
Trust, 200-201, 206, 233-234
political, 226-253
Tumin, Melvin M., 54n
Tupholm R., 277n
Turk, Herman, 290n
Turner, Ralph H., 164n
Tussman, Joseph, 226n

Uncertainty, 303
Unemployment, 285, 287, 294-295, 298
Uniformity, pressure toward, 289-305; *see also*
Conformity
Unions, 85, 113, 132-133, 136

United States, 187, 192, 255, 270
Universalism, 105, 154-164, 295
Universities, 10, 85, 314; *see also* School
Uprootedness, 303
Urbanization, 117, 119
USSR, 330

Values, and alienation, 8-11, 41, 54, 87, 104-
    106, 153, 163, 230
  effect on question interpretation, 161
  and norms, 39, 304, 322
  role of in research on alienation, 32
  value-oriented movements, 303
Veblen, Thorstein, 49n
Verba, Sidney, 59, 188, 189, 192n, 193n, 196n,
    197n, 200n, 201n, 202, 206n, 227n,
    258n, 309, 310, 318
Vidich, Arthur J., 275n
Vietnam War, 85, 209, 249, 317
Violence, 245, 273, 310, 319, 332
Vocational training, 100
Vollmer, Howard, 113n
Voting, 183-184, 245, 271, 293, 298-299
Voting studies, 182

Wager, L. Wesley, 164n
Wages, 18, 108, 289
Wahlke, John C., 213, 226n
Walker, Jack L., 184, 187, 226, 239n, 241,
    242n, 243n
War Civil, 189, 321
  guerrilla, 310
  Vietnam, 85, 209, 249, 317
  see also Revolution
Warner, William L., 125n
Washington, Joeseph R., Jr., 73n
Watts, Lewis G., 66n
Watts, William A., 87
Weber, Max, 45, 46, 89, 107, 111n, 119, 154,
    168, 169n, 179
Weiner, Myron, 327n, 344n
Weinstein, Eugene, 67n
Weiss, Robert S., 114n, 121n, 123n
Weller, Jack E., 255n, 256

Whittaker, David, 87
Whyte, William H., 155
Wilensky, Harold L., 104, 119n, 166, 169n
Williams, Jay R., 184
Williams, Robin M., Jr., 62n, 63n, 76n
Wineman, David, 88n, 90
Wittes, Simon, 87
Wolin, S. S., 31n
Women's Liberation, 9
Work, freedom to structure job, 171
  intrinsic and extrinsic involvement, 53-54,
    108-109, 130-131, 168-169
  meaninglessness, 101
  monotony, 120
  pace of, 114
  psychological need for, 119-120, 123
  responsibility, 126, 129, 134
  self-estranged, 118-123
  and self-expression, 9
  supervision, 128, 132, 140-146
  wages, 18, 289
  worker's relationship to, 116
  see also Alienation from work; Industries;
    Job satisfaction; and Workers
Workers, attitudes of, toward authority, 133
  and automation, 31
  and careers, 100
  as commodities, 12-18, 37, 113, 135
  and division of labor, 26
  effect of sex on work role, 132
  loss of control over work, 37, 110-137
  orientation of toward time, 130-131
  relation of to industrial society, 33
  as slaves, 13, 18
  social position of, 21
Work groups, 118, 134-135, 148-151
Workmanship, 115
Worsley, P., 301n
Wylie, Lawrence, 201n

Zeitlin, Maurice, 106, 270, 271, 275
Zurcher, Louis A., Jr., 105, 106, 153, 155
Zurcher, Susan Lee, 105, 153